# TEXT MESSAGING

# TEXT MESSAGING

READING AND WRITING ABOUT POPULAR CULTURE

## John Alberti
*Northern Kentucky University*

**HOUGHTON MIFFLIN HARCOURT PUBLISHING COMPANY**

Boston     New York

Executive Publisher: Patricia Coryell
Editor in Chief: Carrie Brandon
Senior Sponsoring Editor: Lisa Kimball
Senior Marketing Manager: Tom Ziolkowski
Discipline Product Manager: Pina Daniel
Senior Development Editor: Judith Fifer
Senior Project Editor: Samantha Ross
Senior Media Producer: Philip Lanza
Content Manager: Janet Edmonds
Art and Design Manager: Jill Haber
Cover Design Manager: Anne S. Katzeff
Senior Photo Editor: Jennifer Meyer Dare
Senior Composition Buyer: Chuck Dutton
New Title Project Manager: James Lonergan
Editorial Associate: Sarah Truax
Marketing Assistant: Bettina Chiu
Editorial Assistant, Editorial Production: Anne Finley

Cover image: © Rodolfo Clix

Credits begin on page 539, which constitutes an extension of the copyright page.

Printed in the U.S.A.

Library of Congress Control Number: 2007932138

Instructor's examination copy
  ISBN-10: 0-618-83294-7
  ISBN-13: 978-0-618-83294-1
For orders, use student text ISBNs
  ISBN-10: 0-618-72223-8
  ISBN-13: 978-0-618-72223-5

1 2 3 4 5 6 7 8 9-DOC-12 11 10 09 08

# CONTENTS

## 6 CHAPTER SIX
## Pop Goes the News: Whom Do You Trust? 319

# PREFACE

*Text Messaging: Reading and Writing About Popular Culture* uses popular culture in the composition classroom as both an accessible subject for students to think and write about and a source of new, real-world locations for student writing. Students not only consume popular culture, they live and participate in it on a daily basis. *Text Messaging* builds on the interactive dimension of popular culture, helping students transition to college-level writing while also bringing the discourses and rhetorical forms of popular culture—from blogs to websites to instant messaging—into the classroom as sites of critical thinking and social action.

*Text Messaging* asks students to think and write about the world in which they live; students see the immediate relevance of the subjects they are reading and writing about while they develop critical thinking skills. *Text Messaging* builds on the ways students already actively and critically participate in popular culture by recognizing that students have returned to writing as a means of everyday communication in forms such as social networking and instant messaging. Several key premises underlie the interactive approach of *Text Messaging.*

## FOCUS ON BRIDGES AND CONNECTIONS

*Text Messaging* combines traditional instruction in essay and research writing with the new writing genres familiar to many of today's students, such as instant messages, email, and blogs, in order to create connections between traditional and new sites of writing. The text builds on the tradition of the college composition course as a bridge into academic discourse, but also covers computer-based writing, collaborative websites like Wikipedia and wiki-writing, and visual rhetoric. Features include:

- Introductory chapters grounded in considerations of the rhetorical triangle (audience, purpose, subject) that provide a firm foundation for reading and writing, even as students are encouraged to expand their critical thinking, reading, writing, and viewing skills into new cultural forms.
- Engaging, analytical readings that encourage students to think and write critically about the forms, content, and impact of pop culture in their lives, in their communities, and around the world.

- Thoughtful use of new writing genres (such as email, wikis, blogs, instant messages, and social networking sites) as part of invention activities and assignments. Many students are already using these genres; teaching students to think rhetorically about them will help improve their writing in both new and traditional academic genres.
- Coverage of both traditional and new media as research tools, such as using email and wiki sources to find information in conjunction with Web searches and library work.
- Engaging and challenging visuals that encourage critical viewing and writing about visual "texts," increasingly important skills in popular culture.

## FOCUS ON INTERACTIVITY

*Text Messaging* draws on the interactive and participatory aspects of popular culture to strengthen the idea of writing as a way of changing as well as commenting on the world around us. Similarly, readings and activities in *Text Messaging* ask students to think of popular culture as an arena of social action, a rhetorical space where various subjects, institutions, and agencies try to influence and shape our beliefs, perceptions, and behaviors. Popular culture is uniquely suited as a dynamic and rhetorically rich field for the composition classroom. Popular culture is becoming more interactive, and this book encourages students to think of themselves not just as consumers of pop culture but as active agents who help shape and produce it. Features include:

- A rhetorically based focus on popular culture as social activity, highlighting a collection of multimedia writing practices that people use to communicate with and change the world around them.
- Assignments that allow students to write thoughtful, analytical academic essays based on the readings as well as on personal experiences with pop culture.
- Assignments based on the interactive nature of popular culture that invite students to explore how their writing can function within popular culture through Web- and computer-based textual production, including webpages, blogs, and social networking sites. This focus on interactivity also allows students to experience the dynamic and evolving nature of pop culture and pop culture discourse communities, and encourages students to think of themselves as active participants in the shaping and creation of popular culture.

## GLOBAL PERSPECTIVE

*Text Messaging* also builds on the realization that as popular culture has grown increasingly interconnected and interactive, it has become increasingly global, too. As the immediate availability of the Internet allows instantaneous communication among cultures and nations around the world with the click of a keyboard, writers and users need to negotiate barriers of language and culture by developing new hybrid forms of writing within the global information network. From examining and writing about the cross-pollination of movie genres between Asia, the United States, and Europe, to looking at how rap music has become a part of the conflicts in the Middle East, to the ways that online writing challenges ideas about identity, race, and gender, *Text Messaging* not only works on developing student awareness but also provides opportunities for students to interact in global cultural systems.

## READINGS AND VISUALS

*Text Messaging* features more than 45 readings drawn from a variety of sources and which demonstrate a variety of traditional and emerging rhetorical traditions. Readings range from print journalism and academic writing, to graphic novels, to examples of cybertexts such as blogs, instant messages, and YouTube videos. Readings are drawn from mainstream print newspapers and magazines, online magazines such as *Salon* and *Wired,* blogs such as film.com, and accessible academic texts such as S. Craig Watkins's *Hip Hop Matters.*

Since texts in contemporary popular culture combine what used to be thought of as the "visual" and the "verbal," *Text Messaging* includes a number of visual texts, including advertisements, film stills, artwork, photographs, and websites. *Text Messaging* draws on the growing field of visual rhetoric and emphasizes the visual and design aspects of texts in order to help students deepen their understanding of the process of writing and designing their own works.

## PEDAGOGY

The pedagogy of *Text Messaging* helps students question, analyze, and engage with the world of pop culture that surrounds them every day. The text builds upon the standard model of composition readers by incorporating newer, computer-based and popular culture–based rhetorical practices throughout the book. In addition to traditional formal academic writing assignments, *Text Messaging* invites students to create Internet-based texts such as websites and blogs.

Each readings chapter (Chapters 3–8) includes three sections:

- **Reading Culture** provides a collection of written primary texts ranging from traditional essays and academic writing to graphic novels and blog entries. Each reading includes an introduction, a set of "Before You Read" questions that can be used to jumpstart discussion of the reading or as writing assignments, and "Working with the Text" questions that help students comprehend the selection and analyze how they and others participate in pop culture.

- **Viewing Culture** presents a variety of visual and written texts related to the chapter's theme. Activities in these sections ask students to analyze visual texts as forms of composition.
- **Creating Culture** focuses on a hybrid form of popular culture related to the chapter's topic and asks students to use writing as a means of participating in the interactive dimension of contemporary popular culture. Examples range from constructing mash-ups to developing a visual autobiography to exploring and creating an entry on Wikipedia. The Creating Culture sections encourage students to actively shape and create popular culture, rather than to just passively watch or consume.

Not only will this expanded set of discursive practices in *Text Messaging* enable students to transition from more familiar to less familiar kinds of writing, the incorporation of popular forms of writing allows the instructor to approach issues of style, grammar, and syntax from a comparative perspective as students are asked to reflect on, analyze, and write about the different formal conventions found in different kinds of writing. This comparative approach allows students to develop a critical understanding of mechanics and style while also developing a critical eye for popular culture.

## SUPPLEMENTS

### For Instructors

For instructors, the author has prepared a complete Instructor's Resource Manual, which can be found on the password-protected instructors' website, accessed at **college.hmco.com/pic/alberti1e.** The IRM includes teaching suggestions for the course as a whole and specific suggestions for each chapter, a synopsis and comments on each reading, suggestions for assigning and responding to in-text exercises, and additional exercises and website references.

### For Students

The student website, which can also be accessed at **college.hmco.com/pic/alberti1e,** includes specific suggestions for each chapter, including additional readings, Web links, suggested research topics, and links to visuals. Students will also find notes and suggestions on each "Creating Culture" project.

### MySpace Page

In addition, the author has created a MySpace page, located at **myspace.com/albertiauthor,** where instructors or students can informally "meet and greet" the author, get a guided tour of the book, and find weekly updates with links to articles and websites about popular culture.

# ACKNOWLEDGMENTS

I would like to express my gratitude to the reviewers who read the book at various stages of development and whose suggestions helped in the creation of the first edition of *Text Messaging*:

Katie Andraski, Northern Illinois University
Steve Beatty, Arizona State University
Samantha Blackmon, Purdue University
Alex Blazer, University of Louisville
Amy Braziller, Red Rocks Community College
Rodney Dick, Mount Union College
Clark Draney, College of Southern Idaho
Robert Dunne, Central Connecticut State University
Africa Fine, Palm Beach Community College
Jay Gordon, Youngstown State University
Mark M. Hall, Central Carolina Community College
Brenda Hammack, Fayetteville State University
Melissa Heidari, Columbia College
Brooke Hughes, California State University, Bakersfield
Lauren Ingraham, University of Tennessee at Chattanooga
Mark Allen Jackson, West Virginia University
Richard Lee, SUNY Oneonta
Julie Lumpkins, Columbia State Community College
Gloria H. Markett, Bethune-Cookman College
Juan Martinez, University of Central Florida
Tracy McLoone, George Mason University
Michael Posey, Franklin University
Caroline J. Smith, George Washington University
Jennifer Sutter, Pikes Peak Community College
Leslie Kreiner Wilson, Pepperdine University
Jeremy Zitter, Orange Coast College

Even though my name is on the cover of this book, the creation of a book like this is really a group effort, as any textbook writer will attest, and I am immensely grateful for the opportunity to work with the supportive, creative, energetic, professional, and, most of all, understanding team at Houghton Mifflin. This project started as a series of informal conversations and an invitation to submit a proposal from Michael Gillespie, when he was Senior Sponsoring Editor for English. Suzanne Phelps Weir, the Editor in Chief for English, shared Michael's enthusiasm for the project, and that enthusiasm has translated into all the support and encouragement an author could ask for.

Since then, it has been my privilege and pleasure to work closely with both Lisa Kimball, the current Senior Sponsoring Editor, and Senior Development Editor Judith Fifer. Their belief in the project has kept me inspired, and their experience and skill have improved the book far beyond anything I could have hoped for. I feel lucky to have had the chance to work with them.

Freelance Development Editor Laura Olson likewise shared enthusiasm and commitment to the project, making many crucial and helpful suggestions and providing superlative research skills. Senior Project Editor Samantha Ross shepherded the project through the copyediting and production process with efficiency, grace, and tact, helping keep me on task and moving toward our publication deadline while maintaining the highest standards. She has made the editing and proofreading process a pleasure. Finally, Kate Cebik proved to be an amazingly resourceful and imaginative photo researcher, locating terrific visuals and coming up with quick solutions that always improved the book.

As always, I am grateful for the support of my colleagues at Northern Kentucky University, where the students in my classes continue to motivate and inspire me, nowhere more so than in writing a textbook that addresses the experiences of the digital generation. Most of all, I rely on the love and encouragement of my partner, Kristin Dietsche, the most innovative writing teacher I know, and our daughter Martha Dietsche-Alberti, my most valuable guide to the world of digital culture, who helped show me the creative possibilities of the online writing world.

John Alberti

# Reading and Writing About Popular Culture

# WHAT IS POPULAR CULTURE?

If you Google the word *culture,* you may be directed, among other places, to the website of the WordNet 2 language project[1] at Princeton University, where you will find some of the following definitions:

- Civilization.
- All the knowledge and values shared by a society.
- The tastes in art and manners that are favored by a social group.
- The attitudes and behaviors that are characteristic of a particular social group or organization.

As you can see, these definitions range from the very general ("All the knowledge and values shared by a society") to the specific ("The attitudes and behavior that are characteristic of a particular social group or organization"). But even the more specific definition uses general, abstract language ("attitudes," "behaviors") that lacks the solidity of everyday experience. To get at this more concrete, real sense of culture, let's start by looking at what might be a typical day for a modern college student:

Your portable music player wakes you up with a song randomly selected from the hundreds you have stored on it. Flipping on cable TV while you munch a power bar, you click from weather to twenty-four-hour news to a classic episode from the original *Star Trek.* You could start your computer to check the *New York Times* homepage for current headlines, go to an entertainment news site to see which movie won the weekend box office competition, or scan scores at a sports website.

Opening your closet (or maybe digging through a pile on your floor), you select your wardrobe for the day. You might go for clothes associated with a particular designer or clothing store (the name of which might be emblazoned on the clothing itself), or you may be into thrift-store chic, wearing funky fashions you purchased for a few dollars at the local Goodwill or for considerably more at a boutique store that specializes in clothes that look like they are from a thrift store. Maybe your look is hip hop, neo-punk, Goth, preppy, or nerdy. Your shoes might be cheap sneakers from a discount store or a popular name brand that cost over $100.

Meanwhile, friends have been sending you text messages written in instant-messaging shorthand ("How R U?" "Gr8!") on your cell phone all morning. You make plans to meet before class or have lunch, or you simply chat for the fun of it. As you ride to work or school, listening to your favorite song on your MP3 player, you share the road with cars and trucks in a dizzying array of shapes and sizes, from mini-autos that seem like toy cars to behemoths modeled on army transports.

[1] WordNet is a language database developed by the Cognitive Science Laboratory at Princeton University. Rather than listing words alphabetically, as in a standard dictionary, WordNet groups them into sets of synonyms, or words that represent a common idea. WordNet is designed to be used by researchers in linguistics and by cognitive scientists interested in how the mind creates and understands language.

Many of the vehicles are adorned with an array of stickers and magnets that offer a joke, announce political and social opinions and beliefs, reveal school and sports loyalties, or advertise various products.

And speaking of advertising, almost everywhere you look and everywhere you go today, you see and hear advertising messages of all kinds, on billboards, the sides of buses, clothing, the walls of your classroom, and maybe even on the people you meet in the form of tattoos and corporate logos shaved into haircuts.

After hours, you might catch a movie with friends, possibly a major studio release at a local multiplex, an independent film at an art house, a DVD mailed to you by Netflix, or maybe you stay home and watch a movie on a cable channel. You end your day with an elaborate espresso drink purchased at a coffee outlet or even at a bookstore.

O N E

EXERCISE

## Your Personal Cultural Inventory

The description of a typical day you have just read is by necessity a generic one, not based on any one person in particular. To help focus your attention on your own connections to the cultural world around you and to begin to make the idea of popular culture more concrete for you, choose a day and compile your own personal cultural inventory. Keep a notebook or laptop with you, and at various times during the day, stop and inventory the connections with the cultural world that you have made, from what you decided to wear to what you decided to buy. Write your inventory in the style of the description of a typical day above. Finish with a discussion of what you learned or realized about your daily interaction with culture. Compare your lists with others in your class. What patterns can you see? What do you have in common with your classmates, and where are the points of difference?

Everything listed in this brief profile, from what you wear on your body to what you put into it, from the kinds of music you like to the ways you access that music, from the language you use to interact with others and express your identity to the technology you use to send those messages, are all part of culture. More specifically, they are often part of what is called **popular culture.** What is popular culture? It might be easier to ask, What *isn't* popular culture? The scholars at the Department of Popular Culture at Bowling State University describe their work this way:

> Popular culture studies is the scholarly investigation of expressive forms widely disseminated in society. These materials include but are not restricted to products of mass media such as television, film, print, and recording. Thus, popular culture studies may focus on media genres such as situation comedies, film noir, bestselling novels, or rap music. Other, nonmediated aspects of popular culture would include such things as clothing styles, fads, holidays and celebrations, amusement parks, both amateur and professional sports, and so forth.

As you can see, any topic that ranges from television shows to holidays to theme parks is pretty broad. Historically, popular culture has often been defined in relation to what is sometimes called high or serious culture. People who use these latter terms usually mean things like classical music, literary writing, fine art, opera, or the theater. Basically, if you study it in school or experience it in a museum or concert hall, it's high culture; if it's simply part of your everyday world, it's popular culture.

But even this comparison ultimately raises more questions than it answers. Who determines, for example, what makes some kinds of writing literary or serious? One irony of the attempt to define popular culture in terms of high culture is that just about every work of high culture—Mozart's operas, Shakespeare's plays—began their existence as part of popular culture: as text, performances, or art work meant for popular consumption. Today, popular culture is a growing area of study in universities around the world.

So why do we study popular culture? Studying the artifacts of popular culture—whether songs, plays, TV shows, commercials, or tattoos—certainly tells us a lot about the individuals and groups that produce and consume them. It is important, however, to see popular culture not just as a collection of things but also as an activity, a series of activities really, that constitute the ways we live our lives in contemporary society. Popular culture is like the air we breathe: it's all around us, yet its operations and influences are often invisible to us. But just as we take in air and convert it into our physical selves, so we take in popular culture and use it to create our lives and lifestyles, often in ways we aren't completely conscious of. And language plays a central role in creating culture, allowing us to reimagine, explore, communicate with, and transform the world around us.

## HOW DO WE THINK ABOUT CULTURE?

The phrases *critical thinking* and *critical analysis* (as well as *research writing*, as we shall examine in Chapter 2), can seem like purely academic activities that go on only within the walls of a classroom, but they are also part of our everyday experience of popular culture. Take, for example, going out to the movies. Typically, the premier of a new movie, especially but not only big-budget Hollywood movies, will be preceded by news stories on television, in newspapers and magazines, and on the Internet discussing and creating anticipation for the new film. Stars of the movie will appear on talk shows and other television programs to add to the hype.

Once members of the general public are able to see the movie, people begin writing critical evaluations of it. When we think of these critical evaluations, we often think of movie reviews, whether in newspapers, on TV or radio, or posted online at websites. How-

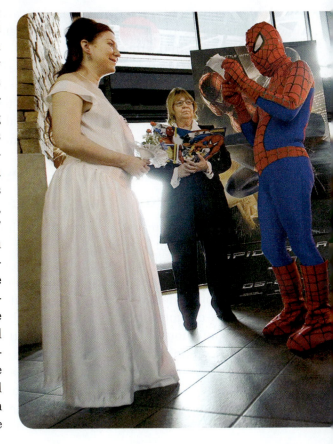

ever, the evaluation and appraisal of any movie really starts much earlier and much more informally among the audience members themselves, beginning with their spontaneous reactions during the viewing experience, such as laughing, gasping, or even uttering the occasional "cool!" When the movie ends and the lights come up, the buzzing starts: "So, what did you think?" "I liked it!" "It was okay, I guess." "Did you get who the bad guy was supposed to be?" Post-performance audience conversations and instant reviews are as old as the performing arts, and artists and others in show business have always been eager to hear from the public. A movie director will sometimes lurk in the back of a theater, listening to what the audience is saying. Movie studios will run special previews where viewers are asked to fill out questionnaires or participate in a focus-group discussion. And, of course, box-office receipts provide perhaps the most crucial reviews of all, at least from a business perspective.

What all of these reactions suggest, from formal reviews written by professional critics to our informal post-movie chatter on the way out of the theater, is that critical reading and analysis is as natural a part of everyday life as watching a TV show or reading a magazine. We may not necessarily think of ourselves as cultural critics, but any act of reading, viewing, or listening summons the same core skills and activities that are used in the college classroom and in college writing.

If this seems a strange or new idea to you, it may be partly a matter of terminology. If you turned to a friend after a movie and asked, "What is your critical reading of this popular culture text?" you might get an odd look in response. In a fundamental way, though, a simple, "What do you think?" really asks for the same kind of response as the more academic-sounding first version of the question. The difference between your theater lobby discussion and one in a classroom is more a matter of style than kind. In the classroom, where the goals are to practice and strengthen our analytical and critical reading skills, the discussion and exercises ask for a more deliberate, structured, and self-reflective approach than in the theater.

So just what are these critical reading skills? In the section that follows and throughout *Text Messaging,* we will explore examples of critical responses and interactions with pop culture texts as part of the process of becoming more aware of and practiced in the critical reading, analysis, and evaluation skills that already form part of how we relate and respond to the world of popular culture.

## Critical Reading and Writing: An Example from *The Simpsons*

We have been looking at some examples of how critical reading and writing are natural parts of our everyday interactions with the culture around us, not a special way of thinking that we do only in classrooms. Clearly, though, there are differences between our informal conversations about popular culture and the kinds of academic writing that students and their instructors practice in college. We can more usefully understand these differences, however, as points along a continuous line of development rather than as better or worse ways of critically examining our social experiences.

Most of our informal chatting or texting about the world around us is transitory, lasting only as long as the walk to the parking lot or an evening's Web surfing. Some of these conversations, however, might spark an idea that sticks with us, one we continue to puzzle over, discuss further, and perhaps eventually turn into a structured, deliberate critical reading and writing project. Let's take a quick look at three examples of critical reading and writing, from the casual conversation to a published essay about *The Simpsons*.

- As part of a first-year college writing course, the instructor plays an episode of *The Simpsons* entitled "Lisa the Iconoclast," where the spiky-haired second grader has to decide whether to go public with information she has dug up as part of a school research project that reveals Jedediah Springfield, the supposedly heroic pioneer founder of Springfield, as a liar and a fraud. After class is over, two students share their appreciation for the show as they walk out of the room:

Student A: "Don't you love *The Simpsons*?"
Student B: "Yeah, they're like a TV show that makes fun of being a TV show."
Student A: "I like how they never play it straight and always take things back. Like at the end when you think Lisa is doing the right thing by not telling what she knows because people need heroes to believe in, and then they show the sniper that has her in his sights, like maybe it's as much fear as doing the right thing."
Student B: "Yeah, they never end with some fake 'moral' to make everything come out alright."

Notice how the students use the back-and-forth of causal conversation to move from a general statement about the show ("Don't you love *The Simpsons*?") to trying to pin down more exactly the particular qualities they appreciate about the program ("Yeah, they never end with some fake 'moral' to make everything come out alright.").

- Next, the teacher asks the students to write down their responses to specific questions about the show, including whether the students agreed with Lisa's decision not to expose the truth about Jedediah Springfield. Here are some sample answers:

"I liked the ending because it fit the adult humor. I hope kids don't take it too seriously, though."

"I guess I didn't exactly dislike the ending. Things don't always turn out the way we wish they did."

Lisa "should have said the truth. . . . [I]t was kind of nice she didn't say anything to disappoint the people."

(*Note:* These are actual responses from college writing students quoted in an academic essay by Vincent Brooks, "Myth or Consequences: Ideological Fault Lines in *The Simpsons*.")

Here the writing situation is a bit more formal: the students aren't working on a completed essay, but they are responding in writing to a specific question. Notice not only how they start their responses with attempts at formulating thesis statements but also how they are still wrestling with their conflicting reactions to the episode.

- Now let's look at a passage from a published academic essay about *The Simpsons*: "Countercultural Literacy: Learning Irony with *The Simpsons*." The writer, J. Kevin Dettmar, is an English professor who has spent time thinking and writing about how *The Simpsons* often presents its viewers with story lines that don't settle on single, neat conclusions. Drawing on his own ideas and those of others, he presents his final argument about why he thinks *The Simpsons* is a valuable television program:

*The Simpsons* does not resolve the large structural problems of American culture in twenty-three minutes, as *The Cosby Show,* for example, typically did; instead, the show suggests that the culture's flaws are too deep and longstanding to admit of simple answers, but that one can remain happy and sane living at a somewhat oblique angle to that culture. Thus, *The Simpsons* doesn't always eschew the traditional sitcom "happy ending," but that happy ending is likely to be the commitment to continue living on the margins of the American Dream rather than being magically reconciled to it.

In one sense, we could say that this paragraph is just a more detailed way of saying, "Yeah, they never end with some fake 'moral' to make everything come out alright," but those details are exactly the point. We can look at Dettmar's version not as a replacement for that original, informal observation, but as the development of that idea, one that provides more specific counterexamples (for example, *The Cosby Show*) and that argues for a new way of understanding the mixed reactions we found in the second group of responses. Along the way, we as writers not only learn how to make our ideas clearer to our readers but to ourselves as well.

## Critical Reading Questions

Did you ever watch a movie, listen to a piece of music, or read a story in school that confused you? This confusion can lead to frustration and often even a sense of anger directed at the person or people who produced the text you are struggling with. "What are they trying to say?" you might ask, and "Why did they tell their story or make their point in this way rather than another?" "Do they want to make me mad?" "Don't they know who their audience is?" "Who are they trying to impress?"

These kinds of questions all form a part of the act of **critical reading.** These additional questions can help us understand the situation of the people who produced the texts we read, watch, and listen to:

1. What do you think motivated the creators or writers to produce this text? What motivates you to read, listen to, or view it? Perhaps finding out more about the creator's motives can help you achieve a clearer or richer understanding of the choices made in producing the text.

2. What did the creators or writers want to accomplish with their text? As with the writing process, you can always assume multiple purposes. Which of these purposes do you think of as most important?

3. Who did the creators imagine their audiences to be? Just by examining the text, what evidence can you find that helps you begin answering this question? What additional kinds of information might you need to build on your own initial analysis?

4. How similar or different are the social contexts in which the text was produced and those in which you encountered the text? How do these differences explain your reactions to the text? This question is especially but not only important for historical texts written in a different time and place. It is equally important in the increasingly globalized context of contemporary popular culture. You need to examine what cultural assumptions you do and do not share with the producers of the texts you consume to turn confusion and frustration into greater understanding and enjoyment.

## HOW DO WE "VIEW" CULTURE? UNDERSTANDING VISUAL TEXTS

You may have heard or read that we live in a visual age in which people are more comfortable and familiar dealing with pictures and images than with words and language. In part, this observation does reflect real historical developments. Never before have we been able to make such a huge variety of human-constructed images in such a variety of media (print, videos, movies, the Internet, etc.) and distribute them around the world so widely and so cheaply. Just take a look around the room in which you are reading these words. Whether it is a library, a classroom, your bedroom, a local coffee house, or outside in a park or on the beach, chances are you can easily spot a variety of pictures and other images as parts of signs or advertisements, or even inscribed on the skin of others around you.

Sometimes a visual text can be just as confusing as a written one.

On the other hand, we shouldn't be surprised that humans have put so much effort into developing so many different ways to create and disseminate images. We have always been visual beings, and our keen ability to see so many kinds of colors as well as our stereo-optic vision (two eyes facing forward, giving us a highly developed sense of depth perception) make sight a key sense for humans the way smell is for dogs or hearing for aquatic mammals. In fact, as you may have already thought by now, no human technology reflects the importance of vision and visual information to humans more than writing and reading.

Before we begin exploring the differences between communicating in print and communicating in images, between written rhetoric and visual rhetoric, let's begin by emphasizing some important similarities:

- Written language is made of images.
- Visual design has always been an intrinsic part of written texts.
- Much of what we think of as purely writing concerns—format, punctuation, even spelling—can also be understood as visual concerns.

## Written Language Is Made of Images

It may be one of those facts so obvious it's easy to forget, but the basic building blocks of writing—the letters of the alphabet, the combinations of those letters we call written words—are pictures. After all, what is a letter *S* but a drawing of a curved line? We may take the pictorial nature of letters and words for granted now, but we certainly didn't when we were children just learning written language. Look at alphabet books designed for small children, or an alphabet poster you might find on the wall of a preschool or kindergarten classroom. The creators of those collections of letters deliberately emphasize their intensely visual qualities to help very new letter writers with the complex task of hand-eye coordination necessary to draw them. Not only will letters be associated with pictures of things that start with those letters, but the letters themselves may be drawn in bold colors and in exaggerated ways that emphasize the dominant visual characteristics of each letter: the two prominent rounded half-circles of the *B*, the perpendicular crossing lines of the *T*.

## Visual Design Has Always Been an Intrinsic Part of Written Texts

Given the fundamentally visual nature of writing and reading, we shouldn't be surprised that visual design has always been part of the history of writing. In fact, in many ways our new visual culture is really a case of back to the future. The earliest books, with pages made from paper or animal skins, featured extensive calligraphy and illustrations, the most famous examples being the illuminated texts of medieval Europe and Arabia.

An example of an illuminated manuscript from the thirteenth century. These texts were made by hand. The gold on the page is real gold.

## WRITING CONCERNS ARE ALSO VISUAL

Even on a more basic level, visual design is an intrinsic part of even the simplest kinds of writing. Consider spaces between words, for example. They seem common sense now, and certainly writing without spacing looks bizarre to modern eyes:

youprobablyfindyourselfstrugglingtoreadthisphrasewithoutthespaces.

Yet many early manuscripts had no such spacing. After all, we don't speak with spaces between each word we pronounce, and you can fit more writing onto each page without spaces (especially important when paper was expensive and hard to produce). In fact, all punctuation can be thought of as aspects of visual design—periods, commas, semicolons, quotation marks. And what are paragraphs but means of representing organizational units in a visual way by breaking up long running text?

In the age of word processing, of course, visual elements of writing that used to be available only to professional printers can be manipulated easily by any writer: font types, sizes, and colors; the insertion of pictures in the middle

C was a Captain,
all covered with lace.

Children's ABC books emphasize the visual dimension of writing.

of text; left, right, and center justification. Webpages may be the ultimate expression of this renewed attention to the visual dimensions of writing and rhetoric. Perhaps we should think of them as electronic illuminated manuscripts—now with hyperlinks that in a sense can take writing and composition into three dimensions.

## The Difference of the Visual

Now that we have reminded ourselves that both pictures and written words are images, we can now take a step back and consider what different kinds of images they are. Consider the following instantly recognizable combination of visual design and writing:

Again, this is the kind of image we decode so easily we may not even think of it as reading. But let's change one aspect of the sign:

Does the sign mean the same thing as before? If you were driving down the street, would the second sign confuse you at all? Clearly, the word STOP is the same, as is the octagonal shape. But the color green sends a new message, one you may even find in conflict with the word.

Now try reading the following list of colors out loud:

RED
GREEN
YELLOW
ORANGE
BLUE

Have any trouble? What caused the interference? Let's go back to the word *stop* again. In groups, discuss the different impressions made by these different versions:

STOP
STOP
STOP
STOP
**STOP**

Which version seems the most serious? Which the most playful? Most important, how do these different fonts create these different impressions?

One way of understanding what is going on here is to think of letters, colors, and words as all belonging to different symbol systems that we mix together in a text to create meanings and that readers also mix together when they decode those texts that we create. While some aspects of a symbol system seem pretty consistent across a culture (*red* means "stop," *green* means "go" in the United States), most are more ambiguous (Is blue a calming color or a sad color? Does green suggest money or nature?). And as we can see from the example of the fonts, any visual aspect of a written text can be changed, and any change can make its own contribution to the meaning of a text.

## Precision Versus Richness of Meaning

Any change to the visual aspect of a written text is one reason why different writing situations will be governed by different styles and writing conventions. Most school and university-based writing, as you have discovered, often comes with specific guidelines about presentation: a narrow range of font choices and sizes, double-spacing, one-inch margins, etc. The point is not simply to make more rules. The reason is that academic writing places a high value on trying to be as precise and unambiguous in meaning as possible, whether the writing is a lab report or an analysis of a poem. Newspapers share many of the same values, and they also have very specific guidelines for their visual designs.

In another writing situation, however, you may value richness of meaning as a higher priority. In putting together a literary magazine, for example, you may want to experiment with the font design of the title of the publication, so that instead of trying to limit possible interpretations, you invite readers to use their imaginations in coming up with different associations and meanings. Neither value, precision nor richness is better or worse than the other, and they are not even really opposites (many poets will tell you that they choose words with precision in order to enhance the richness of their meaning), but in general they provide a useful set of qualities to use in assessing different texts.

## The Language of Images

Letters and words are types of images, and the pictures, drawings, and other visual representations that most people commonly think of as images also have their own syntax and rhetoric. Look at any poster or flyer on the walls of your campus announcing an upcoming event, advertising a class, or inviting you to join a campus club. Chances are the sign will feature a combination of words and images. In fact, the image will often be the first thing you notice about a poster and the reason you read further. Of course, if the image is too big, you may not even notice the poster as informational; you may regard it simply as a random work of art. Too small, and you won't notice the image at all. Just as important, the image needs to relate to the intended message of the sign in an understandable way. Like the title of a book or the opening of an essay, the image needs to introduce you and interest you in the subject of the flyer.

The fact is, even though pictures and images seem self-evident, we "read" and interpret them just as much as we do letters and words. One clear way to think about how pictures and images work like a language is to consider those images that take the place of words. Take the following image, one you've probably seen your whole life:

This kind of image is so familiar to us, we may think that its meaning is obvious and unambiguous. Yet such images are the result of careful planning, design, and testing. A sign like this, after all, needs to be understood by people regardless of the language they speak, and even English speakers need help. The term *restroom* is an American euphemism. In other English-speaking countries, the more direct *toilet* is common. That means choosing images to represent gender that will have meaning across lines of culture, in remote rural areas and in the middle of big cities.

Even though a restroom sign seems pretty ordinary and unexciting, coming up with visual answers to these challenges can involve sensitive issues of representation and stereotyping. The outline of the dress, for example, not only suggests the idea of *women* but also implies that women are distinguished by wearing certain kinds of clothing that men never wear, almost a uniform. As gender roles and identities change and develop, the association of *women* with *dresses* can come to seem less natural and more like a value judgment. The issue of sensitivity in representation was equally an issue in the development of signs indicating access for people with disabilities. While the schematic wheelchair design has become as familiar as the signs for men and women, it likewise continues to pose questions related to how people with disabilities are represented and treated in society.

Now think about creating an image that will be meaningful not only for people around the world today, but for thousands of years into the future. That's the challenge faced by the U.S. government as it tries to develop warning signs for nuclear waste repositories. Such signs can't rely on language alone. Will English as we know it, or any other modern language, still exist in the year 3000? In 4000? How can we come up with an image that will convey an extremely complex message—Danger! Do not disturb! Extremely dangerous materials!—across the vast cultural changes that will occur over the next millennia? Just think about what the world was like in the first century AD, or in 1000 BC. Scholars still struggle to understand the visual materials produced by ancient societies. How well will we communicate when we've become the ancient society?

The more complex the message, the more complex the grammar of images. Take, for example, the airline safety cards found in commercial airliners. Like restroom signs, these cards need to convey information through imagery to people who speak various languages. However, this information is much more complicated, dealing with the airplane's safety rules and the procedures to follow in the event of a crash landing. Airline safety cards from the Australian airline Qantas from the late 1940s and early 1950s even included attempts at humor; although air travel was just beginning to gain popular acceptance as a routine form of transportation, many people were still apprehensive about flying.

Even in the relatively brief history of commercial airline travel (still less than 100 years old), the language of imagery has changed as society has changed. Precautions that might have seemed important at an earlier time (for example, warning men to loosen neckties in the event of an emergency) can strike us as quaint or even nonsensical today. And just as the inherent ambiguity of language is a rich source of comedy, whether in the form of jokes, puns, or slips of the tongue, the cartoonlike images in contemporary airline safety cards have also inspired comical revisions of the original meanings:

In the event of an airline evacuation, style points will be given based on form and artistic impression.

If you stare at the emergency exits long enough, they might open on their own. But that is unlikely.

Throughout *Text Messaging,* we will also consider the language of images in popular culture along with the idea of language as images.

# HOW DO WE WRITE ABOUT CULTURE?

One of the most surprising aspects of the emergence of digital technologies, home computers, the Internet, and even cell phones is what we might call the return to writing. For over a century, since the invention of telephones and radio in the nineteenth century and television in the twentieth, the development of new technologies for communication usually meant people could rely less on reading and writing as essential ways to share information, ideas, and feelings. Even as literacy rates continued to rise, once commonplace social activities such as letter writing and keeping a journal became increasingly rare, more like hobbies than necessary parts of everyday life. After all, sending a letter to a distant friend or family member meant waiting days, even weeks for a reply, when a phone call was instant and immediate.

As digital technology has made popular culture increasingly interactive, however, writing—a communications technology thousands of years old—has made a comeback. Thousands of people maintain blogs and webpages at sites such as MySpace and Facebook, typing daily entries of their thoughts and opinions, updating lists of favorites activities and pop culture texts, and responding to emails. Discussion boards and listservs produce long exchanges, debates, and dialogues, all carried out in writing. Perhaps most ironically, cell phones—the latest technological incarnation of the invention long blamed for the disappearance of writing from everyday life—now function as portable typewriters, and expert users around the world have developed their abilities to quickly key in written messages without even looking.

Even the mundane act of typing, which used to be seen as a discrete job skill useful mainly for people going into office work or higher education, has reemerged as a fundamental activity in modern life. More and more, actual typing and keyboarding classes are becoming obsolete, as children teach themselves to type on personal computers at younger and younger ages. Judged only in terms of the amount of written text produced, young people are writing more and more often than at any time in the recent past.

## Product and Process

Of course, many people don't consider themselves to be writing when they are IMing, sending email, or texting friends on their cell phones, at least not writing in what they think of as the traditional sense, and many writing professionals—teachers, published authors, and editors—might agree with them. In fact, the title of this textbook suggests how popular culture has created a space between older ideas of writing and newer, digital forms of printed communication by coming up with a new term: *text messaging.* Somehow this phrase sounds more contemporary, more scientific and techno-savvy than merely *writing.* Perhaps best of all, the term rarely shows up in school assignments or in the titles of courses.

If we take the term as more than just a faddish euphemism or bit of cyberjargon, however, we can also see how it asks us both to think of writing in new ways and to consider the connections between the old and new, between writing and messaging, connections that can be useful in the classroom as you make your transition to the world of academic writing. The two parts of the term—*text* and *messaging*—point to the two key components of the activity described by the single word *writing*: **product** and **process.** It can be especially useful to separate these two aspects of writing because many of the difficulties writers sometimes face, including writer's block and procrastination, result in part from confusing these very different aspects of writing.

**Product,** the "text" part of *text messaging,* refers to the final arrangement of words on a page or pixels on a screen. The product is often seen as the end point of writing, but in many ways it is just the beginning: of a conversation, a listserv discussion, a scholarly debate. As we will explore, the phrase *final arrangement* also reminds us that all written texts are visual products, that what the words say *and* how they look *and* how they can be combined with other images are all parts of how texts communicate meaning and information.

**Process,** the "messaging" part of *text messaging,* refers to the how of writing, the activities of brainstorming, drafting, *and* revising that produce texts. A focus on process also includes the fundamentally social aspect of writing, including the reasons why a writer begins to write, the various goals and purposes the writer hopes to achieve, and the social context of the writing process, such as audience and the conventions of different writing situations.

Now let's look at both aspects of writing more closely.

# A   STUDENT   EXAMPLE

Heather has just started her first semester in college, and she's decided to do something pretty brave. Although she's not a theater major, she always enjoyed acting in high school and wants to continue in college. She's decided to try out for the fall musical, only there's a catch. In addition to asking students to sing and act at an audition, the director is requiring everyone to write a brief, one-page essay about why they want to be in the play. She's already nervous about auditioning. Now she needs to write an essay to a person she doesn't even know in response to a question that seems obvious. Why would the director ask her to do such a thing?

# Getting Started as a Writer

To many writing students and instructors, it might seem strange to associate everyday kinds of writing such as text messaging, email, and blogs with academic writing. Punching out a message to a friend on a cell phone between classes feels very different from sitting down to write a five-page essay. In the first case, you create messages almost without thinking about it, and the messages are pretty short. Spelling and grammar are casual concerns, and the subject matter is probably trivial to anyone but the specific sender and receiver. In the second case, the writer might sit staring at a blank sheet of paper or screen for minute after minute, waiting for inspiration to strike, because the essay needs to say something significant. The care you take with proofreading and editing can mean the difference between a good grade and a poor one, and the stakes in general seem so much higher.

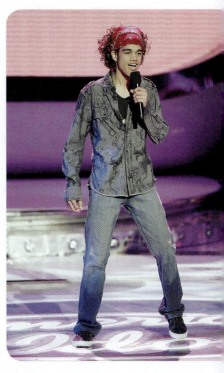

Fans don't just want to watch pop culture, they want to participate in it.

These differences are very real, of course, but they may also cause us to overlook some fundamental similarities in the writing process that span technologies and writing situations. An instant message or a note left for a roommate are certainly less formal than an essay assigned in class, but they are all still governed by sets of conventions that regulate how the communication should take place. We can think of these conventions as the rules of different writing situations, and that comparison is useful as long as we keep in mind that these rules are not set in stone. They're more like the rules of a game that can be adjusted to meet different needs, just as you might simplify the rules of Monopoly to allow a younger player to participate, or the way most video games allow you to pick a challenge level and turn different rules on and off. The key is that all the players in the game agree to the adjustments.

The conventions of formal school writing are easy to see, but if you look closely at even very informal styles of writing, you can still find the underlying rules. The need for brevity as well as creativity, for example, has created a whole set of new spellings and acronyms for use in instant and text messaging, from substituting numbers 4 words to shorthand phrases like LOL and IMHO.[2] In fact, much as slang has always done, these forms of writing help point out who

2 LOL = laugh out loud; IMHO = in my humble opinion.

is in and out of different social groups (there's often no quicker way, for example, to spot a parent lurking online than his or her misguided attempts to imitate IM speak or the use of overly correct sentences). Beyond spelling, online listservs and IM buddies observe all sorts of rituals, forms of politeness, and style conventions. There are unspoken rules about when teasing becomes flaming, for example, and conventions about what can or can't be talked about online.

## Determining Purpose and Audience

One fundamental part of the writing process shared by all forms of writing is motivation. Writing is a way of doing things in the world, of trying to achieve certain purposes and to meet certain goals, whether setting up a lunch date or trying to convince members of a community to vote a certain way in an upcoming election. Sometimes these motives are so obvious that we don't even notice them, as when a bored student types out "anyone there?" in a chat room. Other times, especially with writing for school, the motives can become confused or complex: a paper topic may suggest that your motive as a writer should be to defend your interpretation of a short story, but the desire to get a good grade or complete another assignment may be more powerful incentives.

To determine your purpose for writing and the audience for your work, ask yourself the following questions:

1. **Why am I being asked to write?** Sometimes we initiate a writing task ourselves, but just as often, in fact more often in terms of writing for class, we initiate writing in response to a request or even demand, whether a message from a friend or an assignment in school. Begin answering this question by stating what the assignment is, but continue by speculating about the reasons and motives behind the invitation to write. What does the person asking you to write really want to know from you? Do you see this as different from what the person seems to be asking you? In terms of writing for school, what are the educational goals your instructor wants you to achieve? What do you think he or she wants you to learn from this assignment?

2. **What do I want to accomplish with my writing?** Sometimes the answer to this question is easy: if you're writing an email home to borrow money, the purpose seems obvious. However, even the simplest writing tasks might really be trying to accomplish multiple purposes (for example, I want to borrow money, but I'm also trying to impress on my reader how continually strapped for cash I am, making him or her feel sorry for me rather than seeing me as complaining). For school writing, it's important to think past just getting a grade (unless the assignment is to argue why you should receive a certain grade). Find a purpose in the assignment that is meaningful to you, that will hold your attention and interest.

3. **Who are my readers, and what might they want to get out of reading what I write?** First, describe your core audience in terms of basic demographics and their relationship to you. (Are they peers? Older than you? Younger than you? Do you see them as having higher, lower, or the same status as you?) Then think about what their purposes and motives are in reading what you have to write. How does this process change when your audience is an instructor?

4. **What is the social context? How formal is the writing situation? How well do I know my readers?** Is this a private communication, or might multiple readers you don't know about have the chance to read what you write? (For example, a letter to the editor of the school newspaper may be intended primarily for other students, but faculty and staff members will also be able to read it.)

Whether these questions strike you as unusual or not, they are really just bringing out into the open parts of the writing process that go on whether we realize it or not every time we write. When we send an email to a friend, part of our comfort in doing so comes from feeling confident about the answers to these questions. We are so familiar with some types of writing that we begin to

# A STUDENT EXAMPLE

Remember Heather's question from before: "Why would the director ask her to do such a thing?" Actually, that's a great question; it's a big part of determining purpose and audience. After fortifying herself with a frosty frappuccino, Heather decides to take her question seriously. She tries to put herself in the shoes of the play's director. Why *does* she want her to write this essay? What would the director hope to learn from Heather's essay that would help her decide whom to cast? Heather guesses that saying she really wants to be in the play isn't enough—everyone will say that. Instead, maybe the director is also concerned with picking people who are responsible and committed, who will show up and get right to work. Or maybe the director wants to know who has done their homework about the musical itself and can write about what he or she likes about the story, the characters, or the themes. Heather knows what she wants her writing to do: help her land a part. So she decides to ask other students trying out what they think about the question, and she works up her courage to go to the director's office to see if she can give her any insight.

take the answers for granted. All we have to do, though, is introduce one variable into the equation—an argument that makes you reluctant to write and your reader to read, a family tragedy that creates emotional turmoil, even a long absence from writing to each other—to make us more self-conscious about the writing situation. Suddenly, we become aware of details—such as exactly how casual our opening greeting should be, whether we should use conversational or formal sentence structures, judging if slang is appropriate—that we usually think come naturally.

## Invention Strategies

The process of getting started, of coming up with something to write on that blank piece of paper or on the screen in front of us, is called invention. For some writers, this is their favorite part of the process. They love the freedom of the blank page, the endless possibilities that exist when they're just beginning. For others, that same freedom and those same limitless options are what make invention so difficult. When you can go anywhere with your writing, how do you choose which direction to go, and how do you know it's the right one?

Whether writers find the invention process exhilarating or stressful, most experienced writers develop a set of strategies for approaching invention. In fact, all writers have strategies, whether they are aware of them or not. Some can be helpful, some not so much. Even procrastination can be thought of as a strategy à la "I'll think better in the morning when I'm rested." There's a grain of truth in that idea, unless it's used over and over to put off a project. Writing down a list of ideas, talking to a friend, even going on a long walk—all can work as part of the invention process.

As with other stages of the writing process, the key to the invention stage is to remember that writing is not something that happens all at once out of nowhere. Consider how most electronic exchanges or day-to-day conversations grow. Someone offers an observation or opinion; another person agrees or disagrees, often adding his or her own spin on the idea. The first person then considers that response and comes up with another version of the first opinion, either defending a position, elaborating or better defining an idea, or producing a specific example. Back and forth the process goes, growing in depth and complexity. Each participant realizes that they are not just adding their preexisting ideas and opinions to the mix, but that they are in fact discovering new concepts and points of view they didn't have before. Sometimes, a person changes his or her mind completely.

This step-by-step process of give and take, of offering ideas, getting feedback, and revising and responding, is what we mean by the writing process. Rather than the single, one-time production of a long, complete text, writers

Invention and revision are part of every writer's process. This example comes from the notebook of the late Kurt Cobain.

build up their work piece by piece, making changes, shifting and adding ideas, trying out new strategies and angles. Writers, whether in school or in cyberspace, who have spent a long time and gotten a lot of experience taking part in this back-and-forth process about a particular topic develop the ability to anticipate various reader responses because of this experience. This is one definition of what it means to develop expertise. But even the experts are still carrying on a process of give and take, even if it's mainly in their heads.

When writing for school, we can lose sight of this necessary process, the "messaging" part of *text messaging,* because we often find ourselves working on our papers all alone, often late at night, sometimes right before a deadline. The growing experience we have with electronic forms of writing, whether email or text messaging, can remind us that writing is always a two-way street, that writing about something always means writing *to* someone, and what we write depends on the responses and reactions we get from readers. Following are some common invention strategies for beginning the writing process.

**FREEWRITING:** Sometimes the least helpful feedback we get is from that little voice inside our head that tells us what we are writing isn't good enough or that it won't work. Freewriting is a way to loosen up your imagination and creativity and prevent self-censoring from starting the editing process too soon. Simply set yourself a manageable time limit—five to ten minutes is good—and during that time, the only rule is that you have to keep writing with no stopping. If no ideas are coming to mind, just write "I can't think of anything to write." Keep at it; more quickly than you might think, you will find yourself exploring ideas and testing out concepts and strategies.

**LISTING AND CLUSTERING:** Many people find text messaging easy to do because they don't think of it as actual "writing," and the invention strategies of listing and clustering similarly let you get started with your writing project by focusing on ideas rather than the final structure of your argument. Listing means just what it says. Whatever your topic or assignment, start by listing everything you think you know about the subject and any opinions you have. Continue by listing questions you have and other points of view that you are aware of. When you've worked on the list a bit, draw lines between items that seem related, or circle items that seem especially interesting. You can then start a new list based on the circled items.

Clustering is similar to listing, but it can be especially appealing if you are primarily a visual learner. Start with the topic or idea on which you are working. Then surround that idea with others that seem related to it or with examples that seem relevant. Draw lines to indicate which ideas are most related to other ideas. For each new idea, surround it with additional ideas and examples:

I was Sandy in *Grease*.

I was in *Seussical* and *Music Man*.

I was in the chorus in two and had a part in one.

I was in three plays in high school.

Why you can depend on me as an actor

I had a job and was in plays.

I never missed a rehearsal.

I worked at Pizza Hut.

# A  STUDENT  EXAMPLE

After talking with the director, Heather decided that she was right with her first guess: the director wants to gauge the seriousness of the students who are trying out. She decides to use clustering to brainstorm ideas she can use in her essay. She starts with her main idea: "why you can depend on me as an actor." She continues with something easy: listing her acting experience. She was in three plays in high school, and in one she had a leading role. She lists the specific plays, and then adds details about her experiences: when she was in the chorus, she came down with the flu in the middle of the run, but she still managed to perform every night. When she was the lead, she also made costumes. She missed a family weekend trip because she had to work on the play. She also had a part-time job while she was acting. Her manager wasn't always understanding of her time. Once, she even risked getting fired when she had to change work schedules at the last minute.

*continued*

She keeps adding to her cluster over the course of a day. She draws lines between ideas and examples that seem similar, but she still hasn't figured out exactly where to put everything. She's not even sure that she will include everything in her essay. Almost getting fired from her job, for example, might show how dedicated she is to the show, but it might also suggest that she couldn't balance her time demands as well as she thought, or that she was irresponsible toward her employer. These are all decisions she will make and revise during the drafting process.

**TALKING AND TEXT MESSAGING:** Believe it or not, talking with a friend about a paper you need to write is actually part of writing the paper (even though it might feel like procrastinating). As we've seen, the activity of give and take, of floating ideas, getting feedback, and revising and recasting, is central to the writing process. The various forms of text messaging, whether in a chat room, via an email, or in an instant message, can allow you to carry on these preliminary discussions and come away with a written record that you can use in drafting.

## DRAFTING AND REVISING

One of the key points to make about the writing process is that there isn't any one specific time that writing begins. When you walk out of class after receiving a new assignment and you think about what you might have to say about the topic as you walk to your next class, you've begun writing. When you think about what you might say to your friend about a movie you just saw as your computer boots up, you have begun writing. Drafting—producing the first versions of what will eventually be your final text—might seem like the point when writing officially begins, but it's just as accurate to think of drafting as an evolving part of the invention process. Drafting can mean filling in the spaces between different ideas produced during brainstorming, or taking bits and pieces from a freewriting activity and expanding and arranging them. The main idea is that the same social activity of give and take is just as important to the drafting process as it is to invention.

As you begin to flesh out your paper, take advantage of opportunities to share your work. Electronic forms of communication can facilitate this exchange by allowing it to occur over distance and at various times during the day. However you do it, frequent feedback—from peers, instructors, tutors in a writing center—is crucial to drafting. Plus, the social aspect of feedback can make writing a less lonely activity and provide opportunity for constructive criticism as well as positive feedback.

The need for constant feedback is the reason drafting and revising are included together. Many writing classes have deadlines for first or rough drafts of an assignment, with time set aside for you and your classmates to offer advice about each other's work, advice that can be used to reshape, revise, and rewrite the original draft. That is not to say, however, that feedback and revision should or needs to happen only once in the writing process. Instead, the classroom activity is meant to focus attention on something that should be occurring as often as possible during the entire writing process (in fact, the words you are now reading were produced as the result of a continuous process of invention and revision involving the author, editors, and writing teachers).

## FOCUSING YOUR DRAFT AND FINDING A THESIS

Most student writers can come up with a definition for a thesis: it's the main point of a paper; it's the central topic; a thesis is the argument you want to make. And most student writers also learn that the thesis should come in the first paragraph, usually in the form of a thesis statement. None of these definitions or the guideline about putting the thesis in the first paragraph is wrong. In fact, they describe a great deal of nonfiction writing, especially academic writing by students. They just don't tell the whole story, and when they turn into rigid rules instead of useful strategies, they can even become counterproductive.

Remember that in writing, as in all forms of communication and expression, what matters most is not whether a given text follows the rules; what counts is what works. The study of rhetoric going back to the time of the ancient Greeks has been nothing if not pragmatic. When the earliest scholars of rhetoric like Aristotle began writing guidebooks for orators, they didn't base their advice on what they thought the rules should be, but on what they observed were the most effective strategies used by successful communicators. Their empirical approach continues to be the strongest influence on writers and artists today: taking notice of what successful creators do (that is, the writers and artists you most admire), and trying to imitate them, adding your own variations along the way.

Clearly, the idea of putting your main idea at the start of your writing makes logical sense: it can spark your reader's interest and clue her in to what to expect in the essay. In the drafting and revising process, however, the pressure to start your paper with your thesis can lead to writer's block. As we have seen, the writing process is a process of discovery. As you begin your draft writing, you may not know yet exactly what your thesis or main point is. Your brainstorming activities have given you some ideas about the general topic you are pursuing and the directions you might take, but until you start trying out your ideas in the drafting process, you may not know exactly what your specific focus is going to be.

# Writing into Your Thesis

Here's a common response many writing instructors make when they are grading a paper: "Your paper has a lot of good ideas, and you clearly are thinking hard about the topic. The essay lacks focus at the beginning, but by the end, you seem to be finding a thesis and focus for the paper." This lack of focus at the beginning might seem like a writing mistake, but it really shows us how the writing process works. When the writer started the draft, he was still floating several possible directions for the paper in his head. Because he didn't know exactly where to go yet, he kept his statements pretty general. As he continued to write, however, he saw different connections emerging, and he began to discover the point he really wanted to make by the final paragraph.

This is called writing into your thesis. Most experienced writers are familiar with the phenomenon and will often write several exploratory drafts to see what ideas emerge. Once a focus begins to develop, they go back and revise, focusing the essay from the start on this central idea. Sometimes this first revision does the trick; more often, the writing process is a series of stops and starts, new beginnings and rewrites. The time pressures of school deadlines sometimes lead students into turning in these exploratory drafts as their final version; that's why the focus doesn't start to emerge until the end. Here's a tip: when you finish a draft (and *finish* can simply mean when you get tired of working on it), put it aside and complete the following sentence: "The main point of my essay is _____." Now show it to a friend or classmate and ask him or her to fill in the same sentence. Compare the results you get. The closer you get to agreement, the more focused your essay is becoming.

# A STUDENT EXAMPLE

Brainstorming had given Heather lots of specific examples of what a responsible student actor she was. When she started writing her draft, however, she wasn't sure where to begin. She knew what the overall main point of her essay was—"why you can depend on me as an actor"—but she still didn't know which of her examples she should make her strongest one, or exactly in what order to list them.

So she decided to just start with the example she had the most information and details about: having a starring role in *Grease* while also working a part-time job in high school. To get going, she put off writing her introduction and plunged into describing her experiences in the play in chronological order. She discovered as she wrote that certain events during her involvement in *Grease* made her think of other examples from her high school drama career. For example, a conflict between her work schedule and rehearsal times when she had a starring role reminded her of her first experience in a high school production, when the flu made her miss a cast meeting. She learned an important lesson from that earlier experience, one that allowed her to handle the later conflict more successfully. She decides to write that connection down before she forgets it, even though she is still in the middle of her *Grease* narrative.

By the time she runs out of ideas working on this first draft, she discovers that she has made several such connections, and she realizes that a more focused thesis is emerging from her essay: her experiences as a high school actor not only demonstrate how responsible she is, they also show how she learned to become a responsible actor. Instead of trying to convince her reader that she is simply an exceptional person who never makes mistakes (something her reader is unlikely to believe), she wants to argue that the challenges she has faced as a student actor have both tested her commitment to performing and also taught her how to deal with problems that inevitably come up. Now she has the opening for her essay!

## PROOFREADING AND EDITING

Proofreading and editing are crucial parts of the writing process. Imagine waking up in the morning, getting dressed, and rushing out the door without ever once looking in a mirror. It's possible to do, of course (although some in the class may not be able to imagine it), but you know you would be taking a risk. And the stakes become higher depending on what you are rushing off to: a lazy afternoon playing video games with a friend (low stakes)? A job interview (higher stakes)? A first date (maybe the highest stakes)?

There's an analogy here to your writing, and it's also at this stage that process and product begin to overlap. To use another metaphor, you can think of proofreading and editing as the polishing stages of the process. The metaphor is especially useful because it indicates that issues like spellchecking, correcting common syntactical errors like subject/verb agreement or fused sentences, and fine-tuning punctuation are last-stage concerns, when we can devote full attention to these tasks and when they won't distract from invention or drafting challenges.

The getting-dressed analogy also reminds us how carefully we polish and revise depends on the formality of the situation and the stakes involved. It might seem to some, for example, that we skip the proofreading and editing part in very informal kinds of writing, such as dashing off a quick note or sending an email reminder. But even informal writing involves some form of checking and polishing. As we have already observed, various conventions, rituals, and rules govern all forms of writing and text messaging. We may not always be aware of the final checking we do, just as we might glance in our passing reflection and fix our hair without realizing it, but we do it nonetheless.

## USING THIS BOOK: READING, VIEWING, AND RESPONDING TO CULTURE

In *Text Messaging,* we will be using writing to investigate how we interact with popular culture. Some specific questions we will ask include: Who makes popular culture? Where does it come from? How is it transmitted and disseminated? What does it mean? How does popular culture transmit and transform our values, beliefs, attitudes, ideas, even our most basic sense of ourselves as individuals? In so doing, you will come to a deeper understanding of popular culture and develop your skills, habits, and self-awareness as a writer using language as a means of interacting with and creating culture. In short, you will come to see, experience, and explore language and writing as popular culture activities.

Chapters 3 to 8 each contain four parts:

- The introductory section in each chapter gives an overview of the issues related to a particular area of pop culture.
- **Reading Culture** presents a series of readings drawn from various media, from print publications to the Internet, that explore these issues in more detail and invite you to use writing to participate in the discussion.
- **Viewing Culture** will explore "reading" and "writing" images as part of interacting with the topic of the chapter.
- **Creating Culture** will cap off your exploration of the chapter's theme by inviting you to actively participate in the increasingly interactive nature of popular culture.

The following Reading Culture and Viewing Culture exercises are typical of the sort of activities you will find in *Text Messaging.* Practice using the critical reading and writing skills introduced in this chapter in response to the essay and visual images in the next few pages.

# READING CULTURE

## POPULAR CULTURE IN THE TWENTY-FIRST CENTURY

### "Cultural Renaissance or Cultural Divide?"

#### Bill Ivey and Steven J. Tepper

*Bill Ivey and Steven J. Tepper are director and associate director, respectively, of the Curb Center for Art, Enterprise, and Public Policy at Vanderbilt University in Nashville, Tennessee. Bill Ivey has also been involved in the country music business for many years and is a former director of the National Endowment for the Arts.*

*In their essay "Cultural Renaissance or Cultural Divide?" Ivey and Tepper describe what they and many other commentators see as a radical new shift in terms of how we relate to popular culture in the twenty-first century, a shift as dramatic as that caused by the invention of the phonograph, motion picture, and radio at the turn of the twentieth century. They argue that this trend toward greater participation by more people in the creation of art and culture holds great promise for enriching our lives and for making a more democratic culture. They also caution, however, that other economic forces may create a divide between cultural haves and have-nots, between those who use new developments in technology and mass media to lead more creative, imaginative lives and those whose connection to popular culture will rely mainly on a narrow selection of preprocessed, corporate-produced music, literature, movies, and television.*

### Before You Read

1. Take a creativity inventory of your friends, classmates, and people around school to get a sense of how much people listen to, read, and watch popular culture *and* create it as well. Ask people if they play a musical instrument or sing, write poems or stories, create visual art, write screenplays, etc. Then do a similar inventory of people one or two generations older, such as people your parents' age or your grandparents' age. How much did they participate in creative activities when they were younger? How many are still active? What comparisons can you make in terms of cultural participation over the last several decades?

2. How important is being creative to you, and how would you define creativity? When you look ahead to your life after college, what role would you like creativity to play?

3. How familiar are you and your classmates with the newer technologies changing the nature of popular culture? Ask yourself and your peers whether you own, are familiar with, or participate in:

- instant messaging.
- text messaging via cell phone.
- an iPod or other MP3 player.
- podcasting.
- blogging.
- social networking on the Web.

Interacting with popular culture, then and now.

America is on the threshold of a significant transformation in cultural life. There have been many cultural shifts in recorded history: Gutenberg's invention of the printing press and the rise of the reading public, the growth of a mercantile class and the birth of private art markets independent of the church and the king, the invention of gas streetlights and the beginning of urban nighttime entertainment. The most recent cultural transformation, still with us today, was set in motion on the threshold of the twentieth century.

To fully grasp this change, consider the substance of cultural life in the late nineteenth century. Imagine that you live in Amherst, Mass.; Brooklyn, N.Y.; or Durham, N.C. You wake up every day and read your local newspaper—typically one connected to your local political party. Your values are shaped primarily by local experiences. Your opinion of Italian immigrants is formed by buying meat from a vendor at the farmer's market. You head to Main Street to enjoy live concerts, plays, or vaudeville shows put on by local artists and, occasionally, traveling actors and musicians. If you want to hear that Sousa march again, however, you'll have to bring the orchestra back. Much of the rest of your entertainment happens at home, reading novels that bring you the outside world, but just as often sitting around the piano in the parlor or playing the guitar on the porch. Accompanying all your activity is a constant refrain of storytelling. In your world, stories are told—by you, your family, your neighbors, local elites. The content of the stories is familiar. Your everyday experiences are reflected in most forms of culture that you consume and enjoy.

Beginning in the early twentieth century, with advancements in recorded sound and broadcasting, the growth of the moving-picture industry, and the rise of national record companies, our local and vernacular world was transformed. As it became possible to mass-produce culture, national corporations and then big media conglomerates emerged to package it and distribute it widely. Families hovered around their new music boxes and listened to emerging national stars—professionals like John McCormack, the Irish tenor, and Nora Bayes, the vaudeville singer turned celebrity. Indeed, professionals were becoming responsible for making our culture, entertaining us, and telling us our stories: stories produced by people we had never met, about people we had never met. Our knowledge of poor people, rich people, white people, black people, urban life, rural life, art, and culture was increasingly colored by what we heard on the radio, saw in newsreels and movies, and encountered through other forms of national news and entertainment media.

The professionalization and nationalization of culture in the United States was reinforced by the flowering of the nonprofit arts, first in major cities and later in smaller ones. The Metropolitan Opera and the Museum of Fine Arts, Boston, had been founded by the late nineteenth century, and similar institutions became increasingly popular as the twentieth century wore on. In the second half of that century, investments by the Ford Foundation, the Rockefeller Foundation, and the National Endowment for the Arts created an explosion of nonprofit, professional arts organizations that brought, for the most part, elite European art forms to citizens in every corner of the country. In the early 1960s, there were only a few thousand nonprofit arts organizations; today, there are close to 50,000, and virtually every small to midsize city can boast a symphony orchestra, a museum, several professional theaters, and a professional dance company. By the end of the twentieth century, the arts in America had become highly institutionalized and professionalized. Much of the support for the growing nonprofit sector was directed toward organizations that employed skilled professional artists, reinforcing the emphasis on well-established institutions and stars. Training, repertoires, and artistic styles were heavily influenced by national standards; while venues remained local, the art was decidedly not.

Thus three interrelated trends underlay the last big transformation in American culture. First, technology allowed previously fleeting art and entertainment to be "captured" and thereby produced and distributed on a mass scale. Second, local and vernacular art and entertainment were eclipsed by a culture that was increasingly defined by the tastes of a national elite at Columbia Records, or Universal Studios, or nonprofit arts organizations. Third, the amateurs at home were overshadowed by the new class of creative "professionals," and audiences were increasingly socialized to be passive consumers, awaiting their favorite radio broadcasts or sitting in darkened theaters and concert halls, applauding on cue.

What is the next great cultural transformation? And how does it compare with that earlier transformation? The twenty-first century represents what Henry Jenkins, a media scholar at the Massachusetts Institute of Technology, calls "a revitalization of folk culture...." The new art and art making are participatory: much of the art can be produced and consumed in the home, many people contribute and learn from each other (without necessarily considering themselves professional artists), and much of what is made is considered community property. Jenkins argues that the twentieth century's effort to industrialize and professionalize artistic production, which today we view as normal, may, in fact, represent a strange chapter in the history of creativity—an aberration. What sets the new participatory culture aside from the older local participatory culture of the nineteenth century is that amateur art making is taking place in the shadow of giant media. Moreover, there is now an explosion of cultural choice made possible by new technologies and a renewed mingling of high and popular art.

## WHAT ARE THE DRIVERS OF THIS NEW CULTURAL TRANSFORMATION?

First, there is evidence of a rise in amateur art making. Charles Leadbeater, a well-known British social critic, has argued that the twenty-first century will be shaped by the "Pro-Am Revolution": professional amateurs. From rap musicians who got their start by making homemade tape recordings, to thousands of amateur astronomers whose careful observations that employ relatively cheap but high-powered telescopes contribute to scientific breakthroughs, to the hundreds and thousands of bloggers emerging as a shadow news-media corps, citizens are increasingly spending significant amounts of their leisure time engaged in serious, creative pursuits. Those pro-ams are people who have acquired high-level skills at particular crafts, hobbies, sports, or art forms; they are not professionals but are often good enough to present their work publicly or to contribute seriously to a community of like-minded artists or creators. Pro-ams typically make their livings in other work but are sufficiently committed to their creative pursuits to view them as a possible second career later in life. The International Music Products Association refers to such amateurs as "weekend warriors"—people who play music seriously in their free time as part of bands, chamber groups, ensembles, etc. The association estimates that, fueled by the pro-am revolution, the sale of guitars in the last ten years has increased threefold.

In part, amateur art making is on the rise because technology has both reduced the high costs of artistic production and met the challenges of finding an audience. Amateur filmmakers can purchase sophisticated cameras and editing software for a few thousand dollars and distribute their films online, sometimes to a broad public, but often just to other filmmakers seeking a community where they can share work in progress, offer and receive advice, and develop networks to help them with future film projects. Many of those films are now showing up on Al Gore's television station, Current, where about a third of the programming is contributed by viewers. The same trend can be seen in recorded music, with the rise of do-it-yourself independent music, the growth of pro-am record labels, and the advent of affordable home studios. What is happening in today's world of music production makes the 1970s garage-band phenomenon look like a prequake tremor. The same trends are evident in publishing, home design, gardening, and other cultural pursuits.

With the exception of manufacturers of musical instruments and production gear, no one has bothered tracking the exact dimensions of pro-am activity, but it is fair to say that serious and talented amateurs, many of them producing high-quality innovative work, dwarf the number of professional artists in this country. It is not just music and movies—knitting clubs are becoming hip, open-source software attracts thousands of programmers and millions of users, kids are redesigning video games with the support of the gaming companies. Even new religious movements—like the "emergent church" movement—are largely run by committed amateurs who provide ministry; lead prayer groups; and teach about religious subjects on a part-time, volunteer basis.

In tandem with the democratization of cultural production and the establishment of a pervasive do-it-yourself creative ethos, we are witnessing the emergence of the "curatorial me." Handed the capacity to reorganize cultural offerings at will through new devices like the iPod or TiVo, citizens are increasingly capable of curating their own cultural experiences—exploring new types of culture, choosing when and how they want to experience art and entertainment, searching out communities of like-minded fans with whom to dig deeper into the substance of what they see and hear. The "curatorial me" is another emerging form of active engagement with art and culture. Although not producing art themselves, citizens have developed the skills and expertise to be connoisseurs and mavens—seeking out new experiences, learning about them, and sharing that knowledge with friends.

The invention of a "curatorial me" is made possible by an explosion of cultural choice. A new work of fiction is published in the United States every thirty seconds. Most cable packages offer more than 100 television stations, and satellite provides hundreds of radio stations as well. Through online music services like Rhapsody or iTunes, we have access to millions of songs. We can read newspapers from around the world online while drinking our morning coffee; we can browse paintings and drawings from world-renowned museums without leaving our computer. Such cultural offerings have little need for the mass audiences demanded by global media, flourishing instead by linking up with small groups of committed fans.

For today, as Chris Anderson, *Wired*'s editor in chief, has written in the magazine, more and more consumers and audiences will travel down the right side of the distribution curve, finding art and culture that is off the beaten track. Industry analysts predict that record labels will increasingly earn revenues not only from megahits but from songs and artists that are deep in their catalogs—songs and artists that would likely not find their way onto a shelf at Wal-Mart but that, nonetheless, might find a small fan base scattered across the world. The combination of the rise of serious amateur art making, the explosion of choice, and the sophistication of Internet-savvy consumers will create new micromarkets, challenging the dominance of twentieth-century mass markets.

Feeding that trend is a deep change in the way we connect culture with status. In the late nineteenth century, refined art began to separate from popular art—claiming for itself a higher ground. Highbrow snobbery was often explicitly promoted as the antidote to lowbrow tastes. Listening to classical music, for example, carried a badge of social and intellectual distinction. According to an article in the *American Sociological Review* by Richard A. Peterson, an emeritus professor of sociology at Vanderbilt University, hierarchical markers of taste have eroded. Today people define their status by consuming as omnivores rather than as snobs. A new kind of cosmopolitanism underlies the mixing and matching of different cultural forms.

As an illustration, imagine an encounter between two people on the street: a classical-music lover and a lover of rock music. If you are asked to predict which of them is likely to listen to Latin music, ethnic music, jazz, and blues, who would it be? It turns out that the classical-music fan is much more likely to enjoy those nonelite art forms, according to data from the National Endowment for the Arts' national survey of public participation in the arts. If fact, when you analyze the NEA statistics, the classical-music fan is more likely to listen to just about every genre of music. Today's cosmopolitan consumer culture is not bound by old hierarchies.

The rise of what Richard Florida, best-selling author and public-policy analyst at George Mason University, calls the "creative class" is part of the twenty-first century's emerging patterns of cultural consumption and participation. Florida identifies a new generation of students and workers who define themselves in terms of a creative ethos: they want to be creative in their lives, both at work and in their leisure time. "Creatives" want to make things, to work at jobs where they can solve puzzles and use their expressive and creative skills, to forge and convey their identity through their cultural consumption—their music, books, and clothing. Further, they want to live in interesting cities filled with street-level culture. Florida argues that the creative ethos dovetails with the new economy—an economy largely based on intellectual property rather than traditional raw materials. No doubt Florida exaggerates the extent to which creativity defines our age: after all, most of his creative-class workers eventually grow up and move to the suburbs and start families. But he is onto something, and it meshes with the idea of a pro-am revolution.

A creative energy is animating a new generation of young people. In a survey of incoming college freshmen, significantly more students today than a decade ago report a life's ambition of producing an original piece of art or becoming accomplished in a performing art or writing. Granted unprecedented access to the means of making art, today's youth want, in the words of Lynne Conner, who teaches theater arts at the University of Pittsburgh, to "co-author" meaning. As she writes..., "they don't want the arts; they want the arts experience."

Inexpensive digital technology, Internet communication, and a new enthusiasm for hands-on art making hold out the promise of a rich, postconsumerist expressive life. But some pundits and scholars see a more ominous trend. Rather than a democratization of culture, they track a growing monopolization of culture brought about by the convergence and consolidation of media and entertainment industries. Since 1996 local radio stations have been bought up by major conglomerates like Clear Channel; media giants like Viacom, Disney, and Time Warner control more than 75 percent of all cable and broadcast viewing; local newspapers have been bought up by Gannett, Knight Ridder, and the Tribune Company. Google increases its share of the search-engine market and Internet use every day. Consolidated ownership, centralized control of content, and bottom-line pressures in public companies, critics argue, are leading us toward less diversity, less risk, and fewer opportunities for new or emerging artists or art forms to find audiences. Such trends are crowding out local and independent voices. Citizens are increasingly confronting a homogenized culture that does not speak to their unique expressive needs. Thus critics see a growing cultural deficit, not cultural democracy, in the United States.

Bolstering their concerns, strong anecdotal evidence in many art forms suggests that the gates are too narrow—many artists and works of art find it difficult to connect with potential audiences. For example, most contemporary radio stations program only a few recordings, generally playing no more than two dozen titles in a given week, half of what they played ten years ago. Of those cuts, only twelve are "recurrents"—hits that are still moving up the charts; the remainder of the playlist is made up of older, established favorites. For a record industry that places more than 30,000 compact discs in distribution each year and that is dependent on radio to present new work to audiences, tight playlists keep far too many recording artists out of the system and limit consumer choice. Constraints are just as pronounced in retail. Old-style record stores carried copies of many titles; today most of the recordings sold are sold by three big-box outlets, Target, Best Buy, and Wal-Mart. Those chains stock only a few thousand titles, primarily featuring the very CDs that provided hit songs featured on the radio. Given the narrow gates of radio and retail, few recordings find their way through the system to achieve success. And the Internet doesn't yet provide a way around established media: digital-music downloads, for example, account for only 4 percent of music sales. Consolidation has produced similar constraints in book publishing and film.

Simultaneously, many critics contend, nonprofit museums and performing-arts organizations have also narrowed the gates, attempting to maximize attendance and contributions by advancing conservative, repetitious programming choices. And small and medium-size organizations are facing competitive pressures from the growing number of big performing-arts centers—cathedrals of cultural consumption that might bolster a city's image, but that bring with them some of the same constraints endemic in the consolidated media industries....

Who is right? The cultural optimists (a thousand flowers are blooming, we are drowning in a sea of possibility, and we are surrounded by a new creative ethos) or the cultural pessimists (the market is too restricted, people are suffering from a dearth of cultural opportunities, and demands of the new service economy are leaving many workers with little time or energy to engage with art and culture)?

Both sides are right; each sees a separate side of the cultural coin. They are both right because America is facing a growing cultural divide, a divide separating an expressive life that exudes promise and opportunity from one manifesting limited choice and constraint. It is not a gap marked by the common signposts—red versus blue states, conservatives versus liberals, secularists versus orthodox. And it is more embedded than the digital divide that separates citizens from technology. It is a divide based on how and where citizens get information and culture.

Increasingly, those who have the education, skills, financial resources, and time required to navigate the sea of cultural choice will gain access to new cultural opportunities. They will be the ones who can invest in their creative hobbies, writing songs, knitting, acting, singing in a choir, gardening. They will be the pro-ams who network with other serious amateurs and find audiences for their work. They will discover new forms of cultural expression that engage their passions and help them forge their own identities, and will be the curators of their own expressive lives and the mavens who enrich the lives of others; they will be among Florida's creative class.

At the same time, those citizens who have fewer resources—less time, less money, and less knowledge about how to navigate the cultural system—will increasingly rely on the cultural fare offered to them by consolidated media and entertainment conglomerates. They will engage with arts and culture through large portals like Wal-Mart or Clear Channel radio. They will consume hit films, television reality shows, and blockbuster novels, their cultural choices directed to limited options through the narrow gates defined by the synergistic marketing that is the hallmark of cross-owned media and entertainment. Finding it increasingly difficult to take advantage of the pro-am revolution, such citizens will be trapped on the wrong side of the cultural divide.

So technology and economic change are conspiring to create a new cultural elite—and a new cultural underclass. It is not yet clear what such a cultural divide portends: what its consequences will be for democracy, civility, community, and quality of life. But the emerging picture is deeply troubling. Can America prosper if its citizens experience such different and unequal cultural lives?

Thomas Bender, a historian at New York University, has tracked "the thinning of American political culture" in a book of that title. Bender argues that, in the nineteenth century, there was a "thick" interdependence between social life and politics. People participated in political parties, they engaged in political debate with neighbors, and they attended rallies and campaign gatherings. In short, political culture had a "thick texture"—politics was embedded in social life and helped form and narrate everyday experience. Today, by contrast, the rise of national media, public polling, consumerism, celebrity politicians, expensive media-driven political campaigns, and weak political parties have created a thin political culture; citizens have become passive political consumers. The exact same trend can be detected in our artistic and cultural lives.

In the twentieth century, as new media industries emerged, the United States moved away from thick cultural engagement. As art and art making were integrated less into everyday life, we experienced a type of thin participation, defined more by national celebrities, professionals, experts, spectacle, big media, and passive participation. In the twenty-first century, we can observe encouraging signs of renewed thickening—but not for everyone. Our challenge today—as educators, artists, and arts leaders—is to figure out a way to thicken our cultural life for all Americans.

---

## Working with the Text

1. In describing the transformation in popular culture at the turn of the twentieth century resulting from the invention of new mass media technologies such as the phonograph and movies, Ivey and Tepper refer to the "professionalization and nationalization of culture in the United States." How would you define what they mean to someone who hasn't read the article? Come up with a list of specific examples of "professional" or "national" culture that would be familiar to your readers.

2. The authors quote British writer Charles Leadbeater, who argues that the popular culture of the twenty-first century will feature a "Pro-Am Revolution." Define what you think Leadbeater means by his use of the term "Pro-Am." Which aspects of contemporary culture in the information age is he referring to with each half of the term "Pro-Am"? Can you find specific examples of people you know or are familiar with who seem to exemplify what he means by the "Pro-Am Revolution"?

3. The writer Richard Florida says that young people today "define themselves in terms of a creative ethos: they want to be creative in their lives, both at work and in their leisure time." Similarly, Ivey and Tepper quote Lynne Conner, who claims that contemporary youth "don't want the arts; they want the arts experience." If you are a traditional-age college student, how would you respond to these generalizations about your generation? If you are an older student, do you see any developing differences between the importance you attach to the value of creativity and that of other students in the class or other younger people you are familiar with? Instead of initially agreeing or disagreeing, list aspects of your experience that both do and don't fit Florida's and Conner's arguments. Then use these examples to write a personal response to either or both Florida and Conner. Think of your response as constructive criticism: make suggestions about how they might revise or better define their observations.

4. As a counterweight to their mainly positive view of the impact of information age technology, Ivey and Tepper also refer to writers who

warn of a potential cultural divide between people who use new technology to increase their creative participation with culture and those who are faced instead with a shrinking number of cultural choices. Can you find examples of both sides of this cultural divide in your own experience? Refer to the inventories of your relationship to popular culture that you may have done at the beginning of this chapter and in the Before You Read section for evidence of either side of the cultural divide.

5. The phenomenon of reality television suggests both aspects of the new developments in popular culture that Ivey and Tepper discuss. On the one hand, the cast members of reality television are not (necessarily) professional actors or entertainers, audience members are invited to participate in the show through voting and posting to online message boards, and many of the shows suggest that anyone can be a star. On the other hand, almost all of these shows are produced by giant entertainment corporations, and in spite of the open-ended element suggested by the phrase *reality TV,* most such shows are also highly scripted, edited, and organized. Choose a specific example of reality television with which you are familiar, such as *American Idol, Survivor,* or *America's Next Top Model,* and analyze it in terms of the argument made by Ivey and Tepper. In what ways does this program represent the "Pro-Am Revolution"? In what ways does this show signal a more homogenized, less diverse culture?

# VIEWING CULTURE

## MOVIE POSTERS THEN AND NOW

Let's explore some of the ways the visual and verbal aspects of rhetoric and communication work together by looking at two posters from the early and later days of the *Die Hard* franchise. The first is a poster for the original movie that has become an immediately recognizable cultural icon. The second, from the fourth film in the series, *Live Free or Die Hard,* shares some of the same design features as the first but was created almost twenty years later. Examine them and then try to answer the questions that follow.

### Before You Read

1. Before you look at the posters, write about what you usually notice about movie posters. Ask friends and family members outside class what they usually see first in movie posters. What information are they most interested in? What makes a poster memorable? Can you or they think of examples of posters that made you want to see movies you wouldn't have seen otherwise?

2. Based on your experiences as a moviegoer, what are the different styles of movie poster? What are some common patterns for poster design and layout? For example, what are some different ways that the actors' names are listed? When do they seem to be more or less prominent?

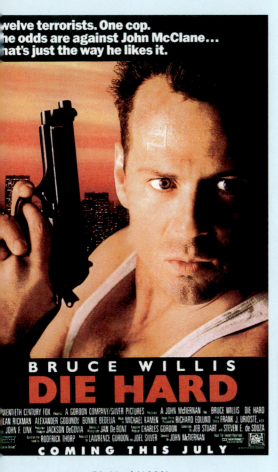

Die Hard (1988)

Live Free or Die Hard (2007)

## Working with the Text

1. Movie posters are advertising, and the basic motives behind their
   production seem clear: to entice viewers into seeing the film. Each
   poster tries to attract an audience by creating specific impressions
   about the movie. In the 1988 poster, what impressions or attitudes do
   you see the poster as creating? What specific details, both words and
   images, lead you to think this way? How successful is the strategy in
   terms of your own reactions? In the later poster, the impressions created
   also connect the new movie to previous *Die Hard* films. How do the
   poster designers draw on or alter those original impressions? Do you
   see any changes in approach between the two posters? Does anything
   surprise you about the original poster?

2. Based on what you see in each poster, who seem to be the target audiences? Do these audiences seem to change from the earlier poster to the more recent one? Again, does anything surprise you about these changes?

3. Now consider other examples of posters then and now, this time featuring movies of the 1970s that have been remade in the 2000s. In addition to the ways in which these posters reflect the visual styles of their times, consider as well how the newer poster wants us to think about the remake in relation to the original.

*The Poseidon Adventure (1972)*

*Poseidon (2006)*

*Willy Wonka and the Chocolate Factory* (1971)

*Charlie and the Chocolate Factory* (2005)

# CREATING CULTURE

## YOUTUBE AND VIRAL VIDEOS

When the first eight-millimeter home movie cameras appeared shortly after World War II, moviemaking became an activity even nonprofessionals could participate in, and families began making motion picture records of vacations, holidays, birthdays, and all sorts of everyday events. Still, there was no mistaking the difference between home movies and what you would see in a movie theater or on your television screen, and they were almost exclusively shared among family and friends.

With the advent of camcorders in the late seventies, sound was added to the mix, and many cameras included some special effects, such as fade-outs or the ability to put background music on the tape. The relative ease of using a camcorder led to an explosion in the number of events being recorded, and gradually some of these homemade videos began showing up in the mass media. Some of these videos captured newsworthy events, and, in the case of the videotaped beating of Rodney King by members of the Los Angeles police department, the video itself was a newsworthy event suggesting the media power of amateur video. Other television programs began featuring home videos sent in for entertainment purposes, and slowly attitudes toward amateur moviemaking began to change because people began thinking of the possibility that their videos might attract wider attention.

As home computers and the Internet have brought digital technology and the World Wide Web to millions more people every year, a new phenomenon has emerged that is creating its own new form of mass media: the viral video. Taking its name from the contemporary media critic Douglass Rushkoff's idea of the media virus, a viral video is any video that begins to reach a wide audience through the electronic version of word of mouth: websites, emails, and instant messages. Bypassing the traditional media gatekeepers of television networks and movie studios, these videos are posted on websites like YouTube and are available to anyone and everyone.

The types of videos found on these sites vary tremendously, from people recording their everyday activities to music lessons, to cute kittens, to minimovies and videos taken off the air and cable TV. Viral video has become a new form of instant commentary as news events now quickly appear on viral video websites in the form of doctored news feeds and parodies. Thousands of these videos are posted each day, and the competition for viewership is fierce. The vast majority escape the notice of most website visitors and are seen, à la home movies, only by family and friends, but at any time a given video can become an instant hit, seen by millions around the world, and just as quickly disappearing again.

---

## Working with the Text

1. Check out a popular video website such as YouTube or Google Video. How are the videos organized? Who may post a video on the site? What are the rules, if any, regarding content? Look at some of the most popular videos. What patterns do you see in the viewing habits of site visitors? If you were to define qualities that would most likely make for a successful viral video, what would they be?

2. In 2005, an aspiring moviemaker named David Lehre focused attention on the viral video phenomenon through the popularity of his short video, "MySpace the Movie," a satirical look at the social network website MySpace. The success of his viral video even led to his being contacted by major movie studios. In what ways does Lehre's example suggest an opening up of media culture to people and voices that otherwise wouldn't be able to access mass media, and in what ways might it suggest that viral videos will mainly imitate mainstream media?

# TWO

CHAPTER

on at first. A

popular cultu

included ever

cake recipes

yone does!" (

hing.) A defi

nd values sha

rship seem pe

ulture as som

ticular posse

ion at first.

popular cult

included ever

cake recipes

yone does!" (

hing.) A defi

nd values sha

rship seem pe

ulture as som

ticular posse

ion at first.

popular cult

included ever

# Who Owns What?
# Ideas and Authority in
# the Information Age

This might sound like a s

question at first. After all,

the expansive definitions of p

culture we found in Chapt

definitions that included ever

from pop songs to jump-rope

to cake recipes, the obvious

might very well be "Everyone

(Or "No one does!"—which a

# WHO OWNS POPULAR CULTURE?

This might sound like a strange question at first. After all, given the expansive definitions of popular culture we found in Chapter 1, definitions that included everything from pop songs to jump-rope chants to cake recipes, the obvious answer might very well be "Everyone does!" (Or "No one does!"—which amounts to the same thing.) A definition of culture such as "All the knowledge and values shared by a society" makes the question of ownership seem peculiar indeed; the definition itself describes culture as something we share, not something in anyone's particular possession.

While it may be true that no one owns popular culture in general, we can certainly own artifacts and examples of popular culture: a DVD, a pair of shoes, a poster hanging on a bedroom wall, an iPod. In fact, many people automatically associate popular culture with the consumer products made by the commercial entertainment industries: music recordings, movies, books, television shows, theme park rides, advertising, etc. Some critics even distinguish between high culture and popular culture on the basis of whether the artifact involved, especially a work of artistic creativity, was made primarily for commercial purposes or "purely" as a means of self-expression (although this distinction has proven notoriously unstable. Many forms of high culture, like a symphony orchestra and concert hall, rely on the maintenance of an expensive infrastructure, while many forms of popular culture need only a guitar, a stool, and an open mic night at a local coffee house). In any case, popular culture and commerce obviously have a close relationship with each other. But even in the case of commercial culture, who can we say "owns" popular culture?

# THE DIGITAL DILEMMA IN POPULAR CULTURE: WHO OWNS AN IDEA?

Questions of ownership in relation to popular culture have never been more complex and more important than they are today, especially as the Internet and digital technology make participation in popular culture available to more and more people. The questions of "Who owns popular culture?" and "Who can own an idea?" involve issues that affect both the global economy as well as your day-to-day life as a creator and consumer of popular culture, and more specifically as a writer entering the culture of college.

Take, for example, the question of whether you can own an idea. This question has been a source of debate and discussion at least since the emergence of market-based economies in the late Renaissance. With every new technological development and change in the way cultural products are created and disseminated, bought and sold, the argument over owning ideas starts up again, and the digital age is no different.

It's easy to see why the question of owning ideas is a tricky one. Unlike material objects that have an obvious physical presence—a car, a cell phone, even a dog or cat—ideas don't have height, weight, color, or mass. Even asking for a definition of the word *idea* can lead into subtle and complex philosophical discussions. Just try it in class. Have everyone write down a definition of *idea,* share these definitions with each other, then write down what you came up with on the board or an overhead. How much agreement do you have? Even more important, how specific are you able to get?

Because ideas themselves are impossible to get a hold of in a physical sense, we sometimes associate owning ideas with owning the physical products created by ideas or that embody ideas, such as a song, a work of art, or (especially relevant to writers) the specific words put down on a page or glowing on a computer screen. The question of who owns or who should get credit for an idea is a matter of practical concern for every writer, especially writers in school who are incorporating research—and therefore other people's ideas—in their own writing. You might learn, for example, that when you put the exact same words from a source into your writing, you need to put those words in quotation marks and indicate where they came from. But most style guides say you must also acknowledge using the ideas of other writers, even if you paraphrase them or put them into your own words. Determining when an idea is specific enough to require naming your source remains one of the trickiest questions research writers encounter when they are trying to avoid plagiarism.

Since the invention of printing presses and other technologies that have allowed us to make multiple copies of books, pictures, sheet music, records, videotapes, etc., owning an idea has meant, for all practical purposes, controlling what happened to these physical products: who could make copies of your book, the music to your song, your picture. When we were dealing with tangible objects such as paper, film, or paint, we literally had something we could hold onto. Even with these physical versions of ideas, however, people still argued over just what parts of these objects represented the "idea." For example, if you write an essay, a book, or a graphic novel, you don't invent the language you use (although you might coin a few new words here and there). Instead, you are really creating a new pattern or arrangement of preexisting words that represents your idea. And even then, some of these patterns—common phrases, clichés, expressions—appear in many different books.

The digital age has not just compounded these questions, it has fundamentally changed the terms of the debate. *Digital* refers to the computer-based practice of converting all forms of information, whether language, picture, art, or sounds, into binary computer code. The basics of the code are pretty simple: various combinations of 1 and 0 (by comparison, the genetic code of DNA uses combinations of four chemicals to produce all living things on earth). Once a computer program creates a code for a particular kind of information, another computer with the right program can read the code and create the appropriate sound, picture, or text. A DVD, for example, has thousands and thousands of tiny indentations that represent long sequences of 1s and 0s. A DVD player uses a laser to read these indentations, and from this code creates a movie or video.

In fact, from the point of view of the computer, there's no real difference among pictures, words, and sounds; they are all just long strings of 1s and 0s. This fact is important for at least two main reasons:

- Duplication of information has never been easier, as anyone who regularly downloads songs from the Internet knows. Even with magnetic tape, the high-tech reproduction method for most of the second half of the twentieth century, you had to record copies of songs in real time. Now, a song is just a bunch of 1s and 0s, which computers can swap quickly or which can be downloaded literally by the thousands onto a portable MP3 player.[1]

- Because all of the information is 1s and 0s on a computer, you can manipulate words, images, and sounds by directly manipulating the 1s and 0s. In the past, for example, to alter a photograph, you actually had to manipulate the physical materials of film and paper: cutting and pasting, changing developing times and techniques, rephotographing combinations of pictures. It was a process that took a lot of equipment and expertise. Now, however, basic digital photography computer programs allow anyone to dramatically alter any photograph, switching one head for another, changing the colors, and creating all sorts of special effects.

The ease with which digital information can be copied, transmitted, and transformed has had a major impact on questions of who owns ideas and who owns popular culture. On one hand, many mass media companies, artists, and writers worry about how easy it has become to "steal" ideas. The use of quotation marks around the word *steal* points to a related concern: that the simplicity of transferring digital information is transforming social ideas about what constitutes stealing. Someone making multiple copies of the DVD of a popular movie and selling them over the Internet or on the street seems like an obvious case of stealing to most people, but what about a person allowing friends to download songs off a new CD, or making the songs available for free on a website? The exercise below asks you to think about this question of the ethics of copying digital information.

---

[1] MP3 refers to a type of computer file that allows music to be transmitted, shared, and stored electronically, whether online or on portable music players.

# O N E

## File Stealing or File Sharing?

You have probably heard about the controversy surrounding the downloading of digital music files like MP3s. In fact, your college or university may have a specific program in place to discourage the practice using university computers or university Internet access. The practice of file sharing assumes many forms, from emailing a song file to a friend, to websites (such as the original Napster) that allow thousands of users to exchange music. The phrase *file sharing* itself, however, points to one reason why this question has proven so tricky. Where is the line between "sharing" and "stealing"? If you loan a friend a CD of yours for a few days, that clearly seems to be "sharing." But what if you burn a copy of the CD? Many CD owners would still consider that sharing, while most record companies would call that "stealing."

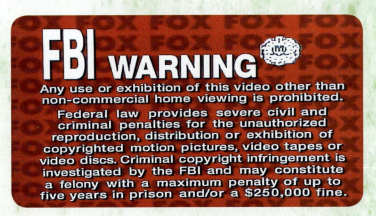

# FBI WARNING

**Any use or exhibition of this video other than non-commercial home viewing is prohibited.**
**Federal law provides severe civil and criminal penalties for the unauthorized reproduction, distribution or exhibition of copyrighted motion pictures, video tapes or video discs. Criminal copyright infringement is investigated by the FBI and may constitute a felony with a maximum penalty of up to five years in prison and/or a $250,000 fine.**

How do people in the class feel about this issue? When you buy a CD, what are you buying? Do the sound files become your property? Or is the record company selling you and you alone permission to access files that still belong to the copyright holder? These questions are being discussed and debated in legislatures and courtrooms around the country, and they can involve technical legal issues, but let's start with our everyday sense of and reaction to these issues. What are the practical rules, whether spoken or unspoken, people use in their day-to-day lives to deal with these questions? How are people reacting to the idea that file sharing is seen as file stealing by many people?

Write about your own reactions, and then expand your research by talking with friends and others on and off campus. Compare and contrast your reactions as a class, and then work on producing a document expressing your findings about what attitudes and opinions seem to be guiding the daily practice of the people you have spoken to.

If digital technology has raised new concerns about ownership and authority, many people also see the digital revolution as dramatically expanding the creative possibilities of popular culture. Just as important, the ease with which text, sound, and images can be copied, transformed, rearranged, and distributed allows for greater participation in the production of popular culture. Desktop publishing, podcasts,[2] websites, blogs: now almost anyone with access to a personal computer can make the jump from being consumers to being producers of popular culture.

Hip hop culture, for example, although it predates the digital revolution, has embraced the possibilities afforded by computer technology to create songs, videos, images, fashions, etc., that take the form of the collage: mixing, recombining, and transforming bits and pieces from every corner of popular culture. Like cultural recyclers, hip hop artists create new ideas out of old ideas in ways that blur the lines between the old and new.

# RESEARCH AND ARGUMENT IN THE INFORMATION AGE

While many see the digital revolution as a dramatic new development in how we relate to popular culture, many of these changes are really variations on familiar aspects of the writing process. Writing is all about creating new combinations from previously existing materials. Writers take the everyday material of language—words, phrases, clichés, syntax, slang, etc.—and rearrange them in unique new ways. Each of these new combinations—essays, notes, novels, poems, lyrics, speeches, etc.—go on to become the raw materials for other writers to use. In this way, every new piece of writing, whether an award-winning biography or an email you send to a friend, is both made from and remakes the common language we all use. An older term for this process might be *research.*

For many students, the terms *research paper* and *research writing* suggest a strange and difficult kind of writing project found only in schools. The word *research* itself can sound intimidating, carrying with it an association with laboratories full of test tubes, Petri dishes, and complex machinery, or dusty libraries full of dull, heavy books. In reality, *research* simply refers to a more careful, organized version of an activity we do every day: asking questions. Whether you are checking a movie start time or deciding if you need to take a coat with you when you leave for the theater, you engage in various, everyday forms of research, from looking out the window to checking a weather website,

2 The word *podcast* refers to any kind of audio or video program that can be downloaded onto home computers or portable music players from the Internet. Podcasts take their name from the iPod, the most popular MP3 player.

to calling for show times. The more complex the question you are trying to answer or problem you are trying to solve, the more deliberate and structured your research will be. Planning a weekend trip to another city, for example, involves getting and comparing information about hotels, investigating events and things to do, and figuring out the best route to take to get there. All of this is research.

# T W O

EXERCISE

## Everyday Research

Explore how common research is in your day-to-day life by making an inventory of the most typical kinds of research you do each day. Start by breaking your day into component parts: for example, Getting Up and Getting Ready, Driving to Work, or Social Hour. Then, focus on each segment of the day and list the kinds of question-asking/research activities you perform. Include both simple and more complex kinds of tasks, from checking to see what's in the fridge for breakfast to checking MapQuest for directions. In fact, you might divide your activities into Simple and Complex, or some other division that indicates the level of care and time that goes into each kind of research. When you finish, compare your findings for your day with those of your classmates. Try to come up with an estimate of how much research per day you typically do.

The more you think about it, the more you might ask, "What isn't research?" That's an excellent question. As we have seen in this chapter, one important fact about creativity in general and writing in particular in the information age is that every new cultural text, whether a book or a movie, a song or a website, is really made out of materials from earlier texts. What we call originality refers to a unique way of taking apart and putting together preexisting ideas, images, sounds, words, and symbols. The concept of recycling captures this useful way of thinking about creativity, a concept endorsed over the centuries by artists and scientists, philosophers and poets, inventors and political leaders, who again and again emphasize that their own achievements were built out of the work of others who had come before them.

What does all this have to do with research writing? Just this: using research in your writing doesn't mean adding something extra to "normal" writing. It may be more helpful to say that *all* writing is research writing because all of our ideas, however original or new they might seem, derive from and have connections to other ideas we have heard of and thought about, whether we are aware of it or not. When teachers and scholars refer specifically to doing research or assigning a research paper, they are not really talking about some new or radically different kind of writing. Instead, they are asking us to include as part of our writing process a careful, organized consideration of where our ideas have come from, of the component parts we have recycled and recombined into our new text.

# T H R E E

## Where Do Your Ideas Come From?

Continue your investigation into everyday research by examining and tracing where ideas have come from in an informal piece of writing you have done. Choose a sample of your previous writing (whether an essay for school, an entry on a blog,[3] or part of a chat or journal entry) where you express an idea, attitude, or opinion. Specifically, choose writing that you did not consciously think of as research writing.

Choose an idea or opinion you express and ask yourself what previous reading, listening activity, or discussion might have influenced you in thinking this way (this activity works well with two people interviewing each other as well). For example, if you wrote about what you like to see in a movie, where did these preferences come from? A first answer might be, "This is just what I like," but our taste in movies derives from very specific sources and experiences. None of us has seen every movie ever made; our preferences often come from our experience of individual scenes in particular movies. So a statement such as "I like fast-moving action scenes" can become "I like fast-moving action scenes that combine many different elements, such as

*continued*

EXERCISE

---

[3] Short for "web log," a blog is simply a kind of online journal, a website where someone shares his or her thoughts and ideas on any subject at all. Bloggers range from professional writers, scholars, and experts to anyone who has opinions that he or she would like to share.

the battles in the *Lord of the Rings* movies. For example, in *The Return of the King*, the final battle features not only armed soldiers on foot and on the backs of different animals but also flying dragons, elephantlike creatures, and even ghosts." Already you have found one possible source for your love of action-adventure movies.

Perhaps a political opinion was influenced by something a teacher said in class, an observation by a parent, or something you saw on a television program: all of these can function as sources for ideas and attitudes.

## THE RESEARCH PROCESS

To sum up, research writing does not refer so much to a different kind of writing as to a different approach to writing: a careful, organized method for asking questions and detailing how we explore and answer those questions. Along the way, we again encounter the two questions we have explored in this chapter: Who owns an idea? and Who is an authority? Another way of putting these same questions is "Where did this idea come from?" and "How much can I trust it?" First, let's define a basic research strategy:

- Defining questions.
- Locating sources.
- Evaluating sources.
- Using sources.
- Citing sources.

## Defining Questions

In a sense, all communication can be thought of as question-based, from the informal, everyday "How are you?" to school assignments, to the most advanced scientific studies. In organizing a more formal research project, the first step is to identify and clarify the main question driving the research. Coming up with this initial question, though, is just the first stage in this process. To start figuring out how to respond to a question, we usually need to ask other questions to focus our task and indicate some likely places to start.

For example, if I begin with the question, "What makes a television show successful?" I have indicated a general line of investigation, but the question itself is so broad it's hard to know where to begin. If you imagine someone asking you that question as part of an informal conversation, you would almost naturally begin asking additional questions, such as:

- What do we mean by "successful"? What are the different ways of defining success in relation to a television show?

- Is there one definition of success that would apply to every possible kind of television show? Are there particular kinds of television shows (e.g., sitcoms, sports shows, reality programming) that we might want to concentrate on?
- Why do we want to answer this question? Are we trying to offer advice about how to succeed in television? Or are we trying to understand better how people respond to television?

Once we begin asking questions like these, we can begin to focus and narrow our original question in order to make the project more manageable. Here are some examples of more focused questions:

- What elements do highly rated sitcoms share in common?
- What are three main reasons for the rise in the popularity of reality television?
- What are the different ways that television viewers and producers define success in a television program?

Once we have narrowed and focused our initial question, we can come up with a list of additional questions that will constitute our research project. Some of these questions will result from the process of narrowing the initial question. In our example, the definition of success could lead to a question like "What are some different measures of success for a television program?" Perhaps the most important questions in guiding a research project, however, are:

- What do I already know about this question?
- What do I already think the answer might be to this question?
- What do I need to find out to determine whether I'm on the right track or not?

Even a question that doesn't initially seem to call for any further research, such as "What's your favorite kind of music?" can lead to these other questions. You may have an answer right on the tip of your tongue, but if you want to pursue the question in a more detailed and organized way, you can ask yourself, "Why do other people who like this kind of music say they do?" "Do they agree or disagree with me?" "Are there people who don't like this kind of music?" "Why not?"

At the end of this first part of the research process, you should have a list of questions that you can then organize in order of priority and importance, from your main question to a short list of secondary questions.

## Locating Sources

A source is any potential provider of information, from a friend in class to a book in the library, from a newspaper to a website, from a grandparent to a database. We will discuss evaluating sources for reliability and accuracy in the next section, but a general rule of thumb to use in looking for sources is the greater the number and variety of sources, the more comprehensive and sophisticated your understanding of the subject will be. This rule of thumb includes the principle that "there is more than one side to any story" in relation to controversial or contested issues, but the exploration of any subject benefits from widening the range of sources you consult. Just as diversity of life makes for a healthy ecosystem, a diversity of sources makes for a healthier information system in your writing.

A good way to start any new research project is to look for overview sources, information that can help you get a sense as well as a brief history of the general issues involved in your subject. For example, if you're interested in whether playing video games strengthens the learning process or distracts from it, start by trying to get a general sense of the history of video games or a thumbnail sketch of what some of the main arguments have been about video games. Then you can determine which arguments or which aspects of gaming you want to focus on in particular. Here's a similar kind of overview of the main places to look for sources:

- **People:** The most obvious but sometimes the most overlooked source of information, talking to people can be a great way to get that quick overview of a subject (something any professional journalist knows). Many of the exploratory writing questions in *Text Messaging* encourage you to begin thinking about a topic by asking those around you or those most immediately affected by the topic (if you're writing about video games, for example, ask some video gamers about their experiences). Later in this chapter, we'll discuss how to assess the reliability of various human sources, but searching out people recognized as experts in a field is an especially good way to get information and to locate further sources. As a college student, you spend every day on a campus filled with a variety of experts on a diversity of subjects: the faculty. Why not begin a research project by making an appointment to talk to a faculty member who may know something about your topic?
- **The Internet:** You might be surprised that I list the Internet before discussing more traditional print sources of information, but the reality is that, for more and more people, student and nonstudent alike, the Internet is the initial research site of choice. This is not necessarily because the Internet is a better or more reliable source of information than, say, books in a library, but the ability of search engines such as Google and Yahoo! to instantly locate thousands of potential sources from a home computer make the Internet an easy first stop. The advantage of the Internet is clear: it's quick, convenient, and easy to use, and for people who do not have ready access to a well-stocked library, the Internet can level the research playing field.

Speed and convenience come with a price, however: most of the information on the Internet is only loosely organized, and although search engines try to list sources according to relevance and usefulness, the sheer numbers that result from an online search can be overwhelming. It took only 0.17 seconds for Google to respond on the subject of video games, for example, but the search produced 1,250,000,000 potential sites! In this case, too many is almost the same as none at all.

- **Institutionally organized print sources:** These are also known as published books and periodicals (including newspapers and magazines) in the library. I'm emphasizing the concept of *institutionally organized* because that phrase points to what most distinguishes traditional print sources from most Internet-based resources: a formal system of review, collection, organization, and evaluation of information. A library catalog or periodical database allows you to access a smaller but more carefully organized collection of materials on any given subject. These materials themselves are the results of various screening processes, from publishers and editors determining what articles and books are worthy of publication on the basis of commercial, academic, or public interest to librarians selecting materials that are likely to prove useful to scholars and students. For example, when I entered "video games" into the subject line of the catalog for my local university library, I received only twenty-five titles—a far cry from the more than 1 million websites referenced by Google—but these are twenty-five sources that have made the cut for various reasons. As we will see, this selection process does not necessarily guarantee accuracy, relevance, or usefulness, but the greater level of organization found in a library can help ease the search process.

Perhaps most important, libraries feature librarians, allowing you to combine two of these sources. A reference librarian is a great place to start any research process. He or she can not only help guide you through the various library resources but also around the Web as well.

## Evaluating Sources

No skill is more important in the information age than the ability to critically evaluate information. The Internet has exponentially increased the amount and variety of information we can connect to, but it has also raised the stakes in terms of needing to question the reliability of that information. Of course, the importance of evaluating sources is not new, and if anything Internet access and the World Wide Web have helped make all of us even more aware of the need for critical thinking. Whether they believe the Internet has increased the spread of "bad" information or helped students develop their critical thinking abilities, however, all writing instructors would agree that carefully evaluating sources of all kinds is crucial for contemporary college student writers.

In evaluating any source, whether an article in *Newsweek,* a report on CNN, a favorite band's MySpace page, or something you heard in one of your lecture courses, you can start with one basic question: How do they know what they know? This question soon leads to others: Where did this person get his or her information? Why should I trust him or her? Why is he or she giving us this information? What kind of argument is he or she trying to make? In general, we can break down the question of "How do they know what they know?" into two different areas:

- Fact checking.
- Bias.

A consideration of these two aspects of evaluating sources will also help clarify the distinction between what are sometimes called academic sources and popular sources, an important difference in the culture of college research writing.

**FACT CHECKING:** "No two fingerprints are alike." "The Eskimo have a dozen different words for snow." "The divorce rate is increasing." You can probably add to this list of "facts" that everyone knows—or thinks they know. Often, we group these ideas seemingly so self-evident that we never question them into the category of "common sense," facts no one can dispute. Or can they? Let's go back to our basic tool for evaluating sources: how do we know what we know? "No two fingerprints are alike." How do we know? Who told us? How did this person know? If we just think about this fact a little bit, we might realize that to verify this claim, we would have to compare the fingerprints of everyone on earth, something that is practically impossible. In fact, within the world of forensic science (the field of crime detection popularized on *CSI*), there is quite a lively debate about whether fingerprinting is really a valid method of crime detection and criminal conviction.

Fact checking as readers and researchers is not only an important tool in evaluating any research source, it also helps us distinguish between different kinds of publications on the basis of how carefully they check their own facts. Some magazines, for example, have a fact-checking department, researchers who comb through articles about to be published and make sure that all the statements of fact made in them can be verified. Other publications, whether online or on paper, may not be as careful and rely more on common sense as a guide. Academic journals demand that writers carefully detail and cite every source of information in their work, and then they often send the work out to other experts in the field to further check the validity of the arguments made. As a general rule of thumb, the greater the care and detail of the fact checking involved, the more reliable the source, and the more appropriate for use in academic writing. In evaluating any source, ask yourself how much you can find out about the fact-checking procedures used.

**BIAS:** Do you know how tall you are? How old you are? How about your eye color, whether you are right- or left-handed, or how much you weigh? Most people know the answers to these questions about themselves without having to check (whether they will share that information with others is a different story). But how about the length of your index finger? Is your second toe longer or shorter than your big toe? Is your ear lobe creased or uncreased? Chances are the answers to these questions are harder to come by without looking, yet they are all equally facts about you—as much as your height, age, or weight. Clearly, most of us are more familiar with some facts than with others. It seems that not all facts are created equal.

Facts do not exist in a vacuum. All facts depend on the needs and concerns of human beings. We know our eye color in part because our culture attaches importance to this fact, more importance than to the length of our fingers. Another way of putting this idea is that facts are only important in terms of cultural, personal, and social bias. The term *bias* usually carries a negative connotation, especially when we use it to imply being unfair or unjust. But we all bring our own perspectives and values to the consideration of any given situation, and they will inevitably color what facts we think of as important or unimportant. Bias is an inevitable part of research. The real issue has to do with how conscious we are of bias in ourselves and our sources and the allowances we make for it.

The study of popular culture itself provides one example of how bias can affect research. Although television has been a major part of mass media since the late 1940s, it was only in the 1970s that scholars and researchers began taking television seriously as an object of study. Now there are departments of media studies and journals devoted to the scholarly study of television. Even with this greater attention, however, the study of television in particular and popular culture in general still holds an uncertain position in the college curriculum.

The reason for this uncertainty is not a question of facts but a matter of whether various scholars and writers feel that television is worthy of the same serious attention as history, literature, or psychology; that is, whether they have a bias in favor of or against the study of television. Neither point of view is inherently right or wrong, and both are open to debate and discussion, but these different biases influence which facts about television a given writer feels are more or less important. Nor does either bias necessarily reflect a lack of seriousness or open-mindedness. As researchers, we need to be aware of the bias of the writers we consult as well as our own. A general guideline is to look for writers who acknowledge and explain their biases and points of view and who are also able to acknowledge and recognize the validity of alternative perspectives.

**ACADEMIC VERSUS POPULAR SOURCES: PROS AND CONS:** Popular **sources** include any publications, websites, broadcast media, etc., designed for a general audience. Some popular sources have an educational mission, others are geared more toward providing entertainment, and still others are combinations of the two.

- **Strengths:** The biggest strength of most popular sources is their accessibility, especially to readers who may not be familiar with the subjects they are researching. Popular sources can be good for getting a quick overview of a subject or for getting interested in a subject in the first place. Some popular sources, such as newspapers, magazines like *Time* or *The New Yorker,* and websites such as *Wired* or *Salon,* feature careful fact checking and reporting; others, especially entertainment-oriented publications or personal websites, may be considerably less reliable.

- **Weaknesses:** Because most popular sources deal with current events and issues and ongoing news stories, they may not go into a great deal of depth, provide extensive background information, or feature a wide variety of perspectives. While some popular sources are very open in their political orientation and biases, such as the conservative magazine *National Review* or the liberal magazine *The Nation*, or the more conservative *Drudge Report* and more liberal *Daily Kos* political blogs, others may not be as clear in their perspectives or they may even be deliberately misleading. Because the primary purpose of many popular sources is commercial, the need to attract attention by any means possible may overrule the desire for accuracy.

**Academic sources** are publications, websites, and databases that are written by experts in particular fields for other researchers and experts. They are usually associated with colleges, universities, government agencies, and other research institutions.

- **Strengths:** Because these sources are written by experts for other experts, they are the most detailed in providing information about their facts and where the information comes from. Academic sources often produce new information and facts that popular sources draw on. These sources usually go through a lengthy review process and feature more depth and detail than do popular sources.

- **Weaknesses:** Because they are written by experts for experts, academic sources can be less accessible to general readers who might be new to the subject. Some sources may be extremely specialized and specific in their focus. Although academic sources usually offer a careful overview of the existing debate and discussion about a particular issue or subject, they also have their own biases and perspectives, and it may take a practiced researcher to recognize and understand them.

**WIKIPEDIA: A NEW DEVELOPMENT IN RESEARCH:** The Creating Culture section of this chapter focuses on the wiki and open-source movements in digital culture, movements most famously represented by the development of Wikipedia. In some ways a combination of a popular source and an academic source, Wikipedia presents new opportunities and challenges to student researchers. While we will explore these opportunities and challenges in greater depth later, the Wikipedia site itself (http://en.wikipedia.org/wiki/Wikipedia: Researching_with_Wikipedia) provides good advice for student writers in using that source:

- Always be wary of any one single source, or of multiple works that derive from a single source.
- Where articles have references to external sources (whether online or not) read the references and check whether they really do support what the article says.
- In all academic institutions, Wikipedia is unacceptable as a major source for a research paper. Other encyclopedias such as *Britannica* have notable authors working for them and may be cited in most cases.

## Using Sources

As we have discussed, some writers think using research means adding outside sources to one's work, a perspective that views research information and source materials as separate from personal writing. Good research writing, however, combines our personal perspectives with the new ideas, facts, and attitudes we encounter during our writing process. Just as all of our attitudes, opinions, and ideas can be understood as new combinations and interpretations of the attitudes, opinions, and ideas we have encountered in our lives, the goal of research writing is to incorporate your research into your work in an integrated and holistic way, but also in a way that traces and acknowledges how your ideas have developed and grown out of those of others.

The idea of a genealogy is helpful here. Each of us is a unique personality, a combination of genetic information and personal experiences never seen before and never to be duplicated. Yet who we are is also the result of where we come from: our families, regions, and cultures. When a person constructs a family history or genealogy, she is finding out about all the component parts that went into making her who she is. Similarly, your research writing grows out of all the sources you bring to the project, and it should also explore and acknowledge that growth process. Here are some typical ways that our writing shows that growth:

- **Direct quotation:** "What did he say exactly?" We all ask for direct quotation in our everyday communication. We want to judge and interpret for ourselves the words of others, allowing us to compare and contrast our judgments with those of the person providing the quotation.

In writing, this means using the exact language of a source, whether we find that language in a book, in a magazine, on a website, or orally during a lecture. Again, as we know from our experience with everyday research, readers want to see the exact words in their exact order, with ellipses (...) used if any words are left out for space or relevance considerations.

- **Paraphrase and summary:** More often than using direct quotation, we pass along information we have learned from others in our own words: "Basically, he said the new movie was just copying the standard formula for action movies." Those may not have been his exact words, but as speakers and writers we try to do our best to convey the essential meaning. If we agree with the opinions we are paraphrasing or summarizing, we may want to make them our own, but we should still show the genealogy of our ideas: "I agree with his idea that the new movie is just copying a standard formula."

Sometimes, though, we're not sure whom we should credit as the specific source of an idea. In referring to the example above, the same person who offered the opinion about the action movie may also tell us that the movie star is

Keanu Reeves. That may be the first we learned about the casting of the movie, but such information is hardly secret and it isn't an opinion; we can confirm that information from any number of sources. Many times, we can't even remember when we first learned a piece of information. I know that Harrison Ford is in *Star Wars,* for example, but I can't really

Lost in the shuffle, Bob refused to stop and ask for directions.

say when exactly I first learned this. Do we still need to trace the genealogy of sources like these? Two related judgments might guide us:

- **How do we know the information is accurate?** Even if we think we are sure about the star of a movie, there is still a chance that we might be mistaken, or we might be confusing the actor with another, similar actor ("Andy Samberg? I meant Adam Sandler"). And how many people are certain without checking about how to spell a name such as Keanu?
- **If you check your source, acknowledge that checking.** In other words, I can trace not who first told me a piece of information, but when I

verified that information. If I look up a cast list at a reliable source such as a newspaper review or the website Internet Movie Database, I can indicate that to my readers, and in so doing help them to know where they can also check their information.

We'll talk more about using sources in the special section on plagiarism later in this chapter.

## Citing Sources

Just as people doing genealogical research may document what they find in the form of a family tree, writers trace and acknowledge the sources from which they create their work through various formal processes of citation. Again, citation is also a process we use in informal conversation. A phrase as simple as "My mother told me" is a form of citation. Sometimes a listener or reader in such a situation will demand more extensive information: "A teacher told me." "What teacher? In what class? When?" These questions get us closer to the kinds of citation you will use in your writing. As with a skeptical friend, however, the purposes of citation are the same: to acknowledge the genealogy of our ideas; to allow our listeners and readers to judge our sources for themselves; to help others find the information we used; and, last but not least, to give credit where credit is due.

# F O U R

## When Do You Need to Cite an Idea?

The word *ideas* covers a lot of different kinds of concepts. "What goes up must come down" qualifies as an idea, but one so common we don't associate it with any particular thinker or writer (most sayings or proverbs fall into this category). On the other hand, if I write, "The author Malcolm Gladwell uses the word *blink* to describe acts of 'instant cognition,' thinking and decision making that happens in a matter of seconds and that he believes is an underappreciated power of the human mind," the idea seems so specific and original (in fact, most people wouldn't have thought of it if Gladwell hadn't brought it up) that we need to give him credit for an idea that he created and that "belongs" to him. But we can also think of examples of other ideas (maybe most other ideas) that seem to fall in between, ideas that many people have heard of or are aware of but that still might be associated with specific thinkers. Einstein's theory of relativity or Darwin's theory of evolution are two examples; the Preamble to the U.S. Constitution ("We the people") is another. Do we need to give specific credit to the people we associate with these ideas, or are they now a part of

*continued*

the public domain, ideas so many people are familiar with that we no longer need to cite a specific source?

Look at the following list of ideas and discuss as a class whether they would need to be specifically cited if used in an essay you were writing for school. Consult style guides and other reference books, and perhaps ask other instructors in your school's writing program for their opinions:

- The law of gravity.
- The personal is political.
- There is nothing new under the sun.
- Just do it!
- The lyrics to "Happy Birthday."

Continue this process by generating your own list of ideas and concepts you might be unsure about or have had trouble with in the past.

## Plagiarism and Cheating

Maybe you remember hearing this story on the news. Kaavya Viswanathan, a nineteen-year-old college sophomore at Harvard, first attracted national atten-

tion because she was having a novel published by a major publisher, Little, Brown. The novel, *How Opal Mehta Got Kissed, Got Wild, and Got a Life,* was the coming-of-age story of a studious young Indian American teenager who learns how to relax and develop a more well-rounded social life. It was a story that was meant to appeal to young readers and that seemed to reflect in part the experiences of the author.

Then, almost as soon as the publicity campaign for the book began, Viswanathan was accused of plagiarism. Student reporters for *The Harvard Crimson,* the Harvard University newspaper, claimed that Viswanathan had borrowed plot ideas and copied passages from two other young adult novels by the writer Megan McCafferty, *Sloppy Firsts* and *Second Helpings.* Later, a *New York Times* reader found a third source of what seemed to be more copying by Viswanathan in yet another young adult novel.

At first, Viswanathan's publisher said that the novel would be corrected and then republished, but as the controversy continued, the publisher finally decided to cancel publication. Viswanathan eventually admitted that she had plagiarized McCafferty's books, but that the plagiarism was "unconscious and unintentional"; the result, she said, of how much she liked McCafferty's books and was influenced by them. Reaction was split among those following the story as to whether Viswanathan's explanation represented a young writer who made an honest mistake or a cheater trying to make an excuse for bad behavior.

Whatever the truth about Viswanathan's intentions, her case raises questions about plagiarism and copying that relate to both student writers in the classroom and professional writers outside the classroom. Just what exactly is plagiarism? What are its limits? Is unintentional plagiarism possible, and how can we tell intentional from unintentional plagiarism? What is the difference between plagiarizing a source and using a source? Between plagiarizing another writer and being influenced by another writer? As we have been discussing, questions about copying, stealing, borrowing, and plagiarizing are becoming both more important and more complicated in the digital age.

## Defining Plagiarism

Most colleges and universities have established policies regarding plagiarism and academic honesty. Here is an example from the school where I teach, Northern Kentucky University:

A student at Northern Kentucky University shall not:

a. Engage in any conduct involving academic deceit, dishonesty, or misrepresentation.

b. Give, receive, or use unauthorized or prohibited information, resources, or assistance on an examination, assignment, or graduation requirement.

c. Commit plagiarism (e.g., representing another's work, in whole or in part, as one's own) on any examination, assignment, or graduation requirement (including those involving use of the Web, Internet, or other electronic resources).

1. Locate your school's plagiarism policy. Is it a school-wide policy, or is it specific to the English department or writing program? How are students made aware of the policy? Is there a standard statement included on every course syllabus, or do instructors come up with their

own individual policies? What are the penalties or consequences for plagiarism?

2. What are the similarities and differences between your school's policy and the one given above as an example? For example, is plagiarism defined in the same ways? Are there any significant variations?

3. Review your own understanding of the term *plagiarism.* Where do you think you first encountered the word, or is this discussion your first real chance to think about and discuss the idea? What questions have you had about the term?

As you can see, the policy on page 67 provides a quick definition of plagiarism—"representing another's work, in whole or in part, as one's own"— but even this definition raises as many questions as it answers. For example, what is meant by "another's work" exactly? Does that refer mainly to the specific words and sentences written by another author, or might it also include more abstract concepts, such as another writer's ideas or opinions?

Similarly, what could be involved in the action of "representing" another's work? Again, cutting and pasting written passages directly from someone else's text into your own seems like an obvious place to start, but what about other, less hard-and-fast examples of representation? Take the plot of a novel, for example. If I announced that I had just written a novel about an orphan boy being raised by nasty relatives who discovers that he is really a wizard and goes off to have adventures at a magical school for wizards, you would probably immediately suspect I had stolen the idea from J. K. Rowling and the *Harry Potter* series. But what if I said the story was about an orphan who finds out he has a special destiny and goes on a quest to fight for good against evil? That still sounds like *Harry Potter,* but it also sounds like a lot of other stories, from *The Lord of the Rings* to *The Golden Compass* to *Batman.* Or how about a story about star-crossed young lovers whose families disapprove of their romance? A rip-off of *Romeo and Juliet,* or a familiar type of story much older than Shakespeare's play that many writers have used?

A writer begins a story with the words *Once upon a time.* Plagiarism, or following a tried-and-true formula for fairy tales? And when do a series of words become specific enough to say they "belong" to a particular writer? For example, at the Smithsonian Institute's website, they include the following sentence about Jackie Robinson, the first African American to play in the major leagues: "Jackie Robinson broke baseball's color line." That's a very specific sentence, but a quick Google search found fifty-nine other websites that used this exact same phrase, none with quotation marks. And if we expanded our search to books, magazines, and newspapers, we could find hundreds more. Would it be plagiarism to use this sentence as my own in an essay, even after I had read it at the Smithsonian website?

# READING CULTURE

## PLAGIARISM IN THE DIGITAL AGE

### "The Rules of Attribution"

#### Deborah R. Gerhardt

*"Why would a top high school writer—so accomplished that she would eventually attend Harvard—commit professional suicide by publishing text copied from another author's popular novel?" With this question, Deborah R. Gerhardt, an expert in copyright and intellectual property issues, invites us not simply to condemn Kaavya Viswanathan but to try and understand how a bright, ambitious student could become so confused about plagiarism. In looking at the case of* How Opal Mehta Got Kissed, Got Wild, and Got a Life, *Gerhardt points out how tricky it can be for students to understand the concept of plagiarism and encourages instructors to engage students in an ongoing discussion of "the rules of attribution," the guidelines students need to follow to be able to develop successfully as writers while avoiding the kind of disaster that befell Viswanathan.*

### Before You Read

1. What is your understanding of "the rules of attribution"? If you were going to write down guidelines for high school students to follow in avoiding plagiarism, what would you include?
2. Working in groups, come up with textcase scenarios, that is, examples of tricky cases where questions of plagiarism and copying become hard to define. Draw on your own personal experience as well as your imagination to come up with these cases.

Why do smart students commit plagiarism? Why would a top high school writer—so accomplished that she would eventually attend Harvard—commit professional suicide by publishing text copied from another author's popular novel? In reading the gotcha press coverage on Kaavya Viswanathan's novel *How Opal Mehta Got Kissed, Got Wild, and Got a Life,* I can't help wondering how much Ms. Viswanathan knew about copyright infringement and plagiarism while she was writing. We don't send our high-school basketball stars onto the court without teaching them the rules of the game, but I fear that too often we send our high-school writing stars to college and graduate school without teaching them the academic and legal rules that govern their creative work.

Ms. Viswanathan's book was inspired by two novels that resonated with her own experience: Megan McCafferty's *Sloppy Firsts* and *Second Helpings.* She readily admits to having read the novels three or four times. Many passages are so similar that last month the young novelist was accused of plagiarism and copyright infringement, and her public comments about those charges reflect genuine contrition and confusion. She told *The New York Times:* "All I really want to do is apologize to Ms. McCafferty. I don't want her to think I intended to cause her distress, because I admire her so much." This month she was accused of using content from another author's work as well.

In college basketball, the rules are not taught once during a brief orientation and then forgotten. They are repeatedly discussed as the season progresses. As we push young writers into the creative arena, the rules of the writing game should get the same attention. Plagiarism rules are not there just to deter literary thieves. They are codes of honor designed to nurture academic integrity by teaching students to honor the voices of others on the way to finding their own.

Copyright law cannot be understood without thoughtful reflection, because it contains many contradictions. Copyright protection is not supposed to extend to facts, ideas, or general plot lines, yet the copyright laws tell us that the right to create derivative works—for example, a movie from a novel—belongs exclusively to the author. Copyright laws provide broad protection for authors and publishers by assuring that their work will not be copied without compensation, yet they still permit fair use, such as copying excerpts for criticism, comment, or parody. Trying to define the scope of fair use can be a maddening endeavor, but we would serve our students well by at least alerting them to the known ends of the spectrum, to give them some compass to guide them in determining when and how they may use another's content.

We should not expect our students to absorb these complex rules on their own. If we stop to look at our cultural environment through the eyes of Ms. Viswanathan and her peers, we will see that the concepts of plagiarism and copyright are counterintuitive. Copying is essential to learning. When a toddler repeats a word, it is great cause for celebration. That same child will learn to write by copying letters seen in print. In high school and college, students memorize their lecture notes and redeliver this content back to professors on exams, often without the expectation of attribution. The ability to repeat back what they learned (generally without attribution) is richly rewarded.

We encourage our students to recycle objects and ideas they get from others. Discarding paper and plastic in appropriate receptacles has become a routine responsibility in our schools. Students create collages and sculptures from discarded items such as milk jugs and magazines. We assign them to groups to share ideas. We teach them that great writers recycled ideas they found in other great works. A high-school student will learn that Shakespeare brilliantly recast the plot of *Tristan and Isolde* to create *Romeo and Juliet.* She may also learn that Thomas Jefferson could not have drafted the Declaration of Independence without recasting the thoughts of other great philosophers such as John Locke. We would serve our students better if we enriched these lessons with discussions about plagiarism and copyright laws so our students would understand the principles that govern their work in different contexts. They need to learn that they can still work within those principles to create new works inspired by their creative heroes.

When the school day ends, students are inundated with an infinite quantity of recycled content in popular culture. They listen to music that uses famous riffs from other songs. They read books that are turned into movies, and then the characters from those movies appear on an endless array of products, such as breakfast cereals, clothing, toys, and video games. Most students do not know that it takes hours of negotiation and boxes of trademark and copyright licenses to make all this borrowing appear so seamless. The recording industry's lawsuits against students who pirate digital music may have taught our students that copying an entire work can get them in trouble. We must alert our students to the reality that sometimes copyright laws also prohibit copying smaller portions of a work.

It is quite possible—and I believe likely—that Ms. Viswanathan's editors and advisers pushed her to write and publish without first taking the time to explain to her the basic principles of plagiarism and copyright. Much of the alleged copying in her work is not verbatim lifting but the creative recycling of ideas. The rules of what can be borrowed and when attribution must be given are complex and require vigilant attention. She confessed to *The New York Times:* "I feel as confused as anyone about it, because it happened so many times." It is so unfortunate to see a promising young writer taken out of the game because she did not understand the rules. My hope is that this incident will motivate parents and educators to remember that creative work has its rules, and if they want to stay in the game, our students should know them.

## Working with the Text

1. Gerhardt states that copyright law "contains many contradictions." What are some of these contradictions? She goes on to say that instructors should make students aware of "the known ends of the

spectrum" to help them negotiate these contradictions, but she doesn't go into detail as to what these "known ends" are. How would you define some basic guidelines for understanding copyright law?

2. As Gerhardt points out, "Copying is essential to learning," and she provides several examples of how the educational process encourages imitation and copying in students. Add to her examples with some of your own that reinforce her point. Which specific examples do you think make understanding plagiarism and the rules of attribution the most difficult?

3. In her final paragraph, Gerhardt suggests what might be the most difficult distinction facing students who are learning the rules of attribution: the difference between plagiarism and "the creative recycling of ideas." How do you understand this distinction? For you, where are the lines drawn between appropriate and inappropriate uses of sources?

## PLAGIARISM, CHEATING, AND THE ETHICS OF RESEARCH WRITING

The easy ability that computers give us to cut and paste words and images from one source to another makes issues of academic honesty and plagiarism all the more important. On the one hand, computers allow us to quickly and accurately quote material from outside sources with the sweep of a mouse and the click of a button. On the other, digital information can let anyone download an entire essay from one of the many term paper websites (sometimes for free, sometimes for money). The ability to readily manipulate text on the computer has been exciting for teachers of writing when it comes to encouraging students to continuously revise, write multiple drafts, and get frequent feedback from readers. At the same time, however, many instructors have become more concerned that this same ability to transfer large amounts of text has made plagiarism easier and therefore more tempting.

Ironically, while computers and the Internet have made plagiarism easier to do, the same technology, especially the use of search engines like Google and Dogpile, have made detecting plagiarism easier than in the past. Before, an instructor who suspected copying had to search through books in the library in hopes of coming across a purloined passage; now, simply typing a phrase into Yahoo! can instantly provide a source. So what is the bottom line: is plagiarism more or less of a problem in the Internet age?

The rise of new forms of written communication such as email, text messaging, and blogging remind us of the continuing relevance of traditional rhetorical concepts of audience, context, style, and social conventions. So maybe the best way to approach a discussion of plagiarism in the digital age might be to remind ourselves of the basic principles regarding ethics and writing, principles that predate file sharing and downloading:

- **Motive:** Your teacher may have discussed with you the difference between intentional and unintentional plagiarism. Sometimes students plagiarize because they are new to academic writing and they make mistakes, and sometimes students deliberately plagiarize. The distinction is an important one, and it refocuses the question of plagiarism to one of cheating. A question any writer can and should ask is, "Why am I using this material?" If the answer is, "Because I want to learn more about the subject" or "I think it's important to share this with my readers," then you are engaged in a project of creative collaboration with your source materials. If the answer is, "It's quicker than writing it myself," or "It's due in an hour and I need three more pages!" then you should probably think again.

  Of course, intention by itself is not an excuse for plagiarism, nor is ignorance of the rules (you can still get a ticket for speeding even if you honestly don't know what the posted limit is). Still, questions of intention and motive are good places to begin your class discussion of plagiarism.

- **Giving credit where credit is due:** You see it at every awards show. The winner rushes up to the stage, breathless with surprise at receiving the award (or at least pretending to be surprised; many awards shows are for acting, after all). Unfolding a wrinkled piece of paper, the winner begins a long list of thank yous to all the people who helped him or her along the way, from family members to agents and managers and sometimes the Almighty.

  There is a similar ethic at work in citing sources. If another person helped you learn about a subject, aided you in forming your own opinion, or lent evidence to your argument, they deserve to be thanked, and citation is the way to acknowledge that help. The source of that help may never see your particular piece of writing (although if you publish online, he or she very well could), but whoever reads your paper will see it. Such credit recognizes that, in a very deep sense, all writing is collaborative, and that one goal of every piece of writing is to help future writers with their own work. As Deborah Gerhardt points out above, in professional work, contractual agreements and copyright laws require creators to give credit where credit is due when building on the work of others, but the ethical principle is an old one in the world of writing and rhetoric.

- **Providing a resource for other writers:** Following on the idea of giving credit where credit is due, telling readers where you received inspiration and information for your writing will let them take advantage of the same resources. In fact, this is one of the core reasons that many forms of academic writing include works cited pages, bibliographies, or carefully annotated footnotes and endnotes. Each piece of academic writing is not just a source of information in and of itself; it is also a guidepost leading other researchers and writers to the work of others.

In the end, Deborah Gerhardt has a point: there are rules of attribution just as there are rules for basketball. But just as with the rules in basketball, these rules of attribution are a means to an end, not the reason for writing. The object of basketball is not primarily to follow rules; the objective is to have fun through spirited competition played with a sense of cooperation and sportsmanship. The rules can help facilitate this objective, but we all know from experience that simply having referees does not guarantee a good game. In fact, most people who play basketball do so without any formal officiating. The honor system along with a desire to foster friendship and respect are the most powerful factors in motivating people to follow rules.

Similarly, writing—and research writing in particular—is not simply about following rules. It's the spirit of the game that's important, and sometimes nothing ruins that spirit more than arguments over technical definitions of the rules. Understanding the general ethical principles involved, and a close collaboration between students and instructors in the service of developing as writers and entering the communities of academic dialogue, are the foundations for approaching questions of academic honesty and plagiarism. The point is not to see what you can get away with, but how to foster creativity and collaboration.

# CREATING CULTURE

## WIKIPEDIA AND THE WIKI MOVEMENT

The Creating Culture sections in Chapters 3 to 8 will ask you to read about, then actively participate in, making popular culture. The following is an example of the format of one of these sections. Use the research skills you've learned in this chapter to complete this assignment.

## "The Book Stops Here"

### Daniel H. Pink

*Type in almost any request for information using a search engine like Google or Yahoo! and chances are that one of the top responses will be for an entry from the Wikipedia, an online encyclopedia. Unlike more traditional encyclopedias, whether print or online, Wikipedia was not created by a designated group of scholars and experts chosen for their academic credentials, publishing history, or affiliation with major universities and research centers. Instead, Wikipedia is a Web-based "democratic" encyclopedia, with entries written and revised by visitors to the site. Anyone can contribute to Wikipedia.*

*Wikipedia is part of an open-source movement known as wiki (named for a Hawaiian word for "fast"), a movement that stresses a bottom-up approach to cyberculture, where expertise and authority are created through open dialogue, debate, and consensus. At wiki sites, anyone can contribute to the creation of the website. At Wikipedia, this means that anyone can write an entry about any subject or topic of interest to him or her. Rather than being checked for accuracy and thoroughness by experts in the field, entries are revised and updated by other visitors.*

*As many commentators have remarked, this new type of encyclopedia represents a radical break in how information is collected, evaluated, and distributed, and Wikipedia stands as a distinctive popular culture phenomenon of the early twenty-first century. For college students in particular, Wikipedia poses fundamental questions about doing research, citing sources, and academic writing. In "The Book Stops Here," the writer Daniel H. Pink explores how Wikipedia raises questions about the nature of authority and expertise in relation to information, in ways that some find liberating and others disturbing.*

## Before You Read

1. In our everyday lives, both in the classroom and out, we are confronted with a flood of news, ideas, and opinions, and we make decisions, whether consciously or not, about whether to believe what we read, see, or hear. Sometimes we make these decisions carefully, after much thought and consideration; other times we rely on snap judgments or intuition. How do you decide when to trust information you receive? What leads you to believe the expertise of some people but not others? Reflect and write about what makes you more or less likely to believe different sources of information, including information from print, online, and experts.

2. What do you consider yourself an expert in? What would you say you know the most about? Write about what subjects or activities you feel most confident in giving information and advice about. You might also write about a situation or situations where you acted in the role of expert, acting as a teacher, coach, advisor, or guide. What do you see as the limits of your expertise?

**D**ixon, New Mexico, is a rural town with a few hundred residents and no traffic lights. At the end of a dirt road, in the shadow of a small mountain sits a gray trailer. It is the home of Einar Kvaran. To understand the most audacious experiment of the postboom Internet, this is a good place to begin.

Kvaran is a tall and hale fifty-six-year-old with a ruddy face, blue eyes, and blond hair that's turning white. He calls himself an "art historian without portfolio" but has no formal credentials in his area of proclaimed expertise. He's never published a scholarly article or taught a college course. Over three decades, he's been a Peace Corps volunteer, an autoworker, a union steward, a homeschooling mentor, and the drummer in a Michigan band called Kodai Road. Right now, he's unemployed. Which isn't to say he doesn't work. For about six hours each day, Kvaran reads and writes about American sculpture and public art and publishes his articles for an audience of millions around the world.

Hundreds of books on sculptors, regional architecture, and art history are stacked floor to ceiling inside his trailer—along with sixty-eight thick albums containing twenty years of photos he's taken on the American road. The outlet for his knowledge is at the other end of his dialup Internet connection: the daring but controversial website known as Wikipedia.

[In 2001], a wealthy options trader named Jimmy Wales set out to build a massive online encyclopedia ambitious in purpose and unique in design. This encyclopedia would be freely available to anyone. And it would be created not by paid experts and editors, but by whoever wanted to contribute. With software called wiki—which allows anybody with Web access to go to a site and edit, delete, or add to what's there—Wales and his volunteer crew would construct a repository of knowledge to rival the ancient library of Alexandria.

In 2001, the idea seemed preposterous. In 2005, the nonprofit venture [was] the largest encyclopedia on the planet. Wikipedia offers 500,000 articles in English—compared with *Britannica*'s 80,000 and *Encarta*'s 4,500—fashioned by more than 16,000 contributors. Tack on the editions in seventy-five other languages, including Esperanto and Kurdish, and the total Wikipedia article count tops 1.3 million.

Wikipedia's explosive growth is due to the contribution of Kvaran and others like him. Self-taught and self-motivated, Kvaran wrote his first article last summer—a short piece on American sculptor Corrado Parducci. Since then, Kvaran has written or contributed to two dozen other entries on American art, using his library and photographs as sources. He's added words and images to thirty other topics, too—the Lincoln Memorial, baseball player Carl Yastrzemski, photographer Tina Modotti, and Iceland's first prime minister, Hannes Hafstein, who happens to be Kvaran's great-grandfather. "I think of myself as a teacher," Kvaran says over tea at his kitchen table.

To many guardians of the knowledge cathedral—librarians, lexiographers, academics—that's precisely the problem. Who died and made this guy professor? No pedigreed scholars scrutinize his work. No research assistants check his facts. Should we trust an encyclopedia that allows anyone with a pulse and a mousepad to opine about Jackson Pollock's place in postmodernism? What's more, the software that made Wikipedia so easy to build also makes it easy to manipulate and deface. A former editor at the venerable *Encyclopædia Britannica* recently likened the site to a public restroom: you never know who used it last.

So the modest trailer at the end of a dirt road in this pinprick of a town holds some cosmic questions. Is Wikipedia a heartening effort in digital humanitarianism—or a not-so-smart mob unleashing misinformation on the masses? Are well-intentioned amateurs any replacement for professionals? And is charging nothing for knowledge too high a price?

Recovery may take twelve steps, but becoming a junkie requires only four. First comes chance—an unexpected encounter. Chance stirs curiosity. Curiosity leads to experimentation. And experimentation cascades into addiction.

For Danny Wool, chance arrived on a winter afternoon in 2002, after an argument about—of all things—Kryptonite. Googling the term from his Brooklyn home to settle the debate, he came upon the Wikipedia entry. He looked up a few more subjects and noticed that each one contained a mysterious hyperlink that said Edit. Curious but too nervous to do anything, he returned to Wikipedia a few more times. Then one night he corrected an error in an article about Jewish holidays. *You can do that?!* It was his first inhalation of Wiki crack. He became one of Wikipedia's earliest registered users and wrote his first article— on Muckleshoot, a Washington state Indian tribe. Since then, he has made more than 16,000 contributions.

Bryan Derksen wrote the original Kryptonite article that Wool discovered. While surfing from his home in Edmonton, Derksen also stumbled upon Wikipedia and quickly traveled the path to addiction. He read a few entries on Greek mythology and found them inadequate. The Edit link beckoned him like a street pusher. He clicked it and typed in a few changes. *You can do that?!* "I just got hooked," he tells me. He's now made more edits than all but three Wikipedians—some 40,000 additions and revisions.

Number one on the list of contributors is Derek Ramsey, who has automated his addiction. A software engineer in Pennsylvania, Ramsey wrote a Java program called rambot that automatically updates Wikipedia articles on cities and counties. So far, the man and machine combination has contributed more than 100,000 edits.

String enough of these addicts together, add a few thousand casual users, and pretty soon you have a new way to do an old thing. Humankind has long sought to tame the jungle of knowledge and display it in a zoo of friendly facts. But while the urge to create encyclopedias has endured, the production model has evolved. Wikipedia is the latest stage.

In the beginning, encyclopedias relied on the One Smart Guy model. In ancient Greece, Aristotle put pen to papyrus and single-handedly tried to record all the knowledge of his time. Four hundred years later, the Roman nobleman Pliny the Elder cranked out a thirty-seven-volume set of the day's knowledge. The Chinese scholar Tu Yu wrote an encyclopedia in the ninth century. And in the 1700s, Diderot and a few pals (including Voltaire and Rousseau) took twenty-nine years to create the *Encyclopédie, ou Dictionnaire Raisonné des Sciences, des Arts et des Métiers.*

With the Industrial Revolution, the One Smart Guy approach gradually gave way to the One Best Way model, which borrowed the principles of scientific management and the lesson of assembly lines. *Encyclopædia Britannica* pioneered this approach in Scotland and honed it to perfection. Large groups of experts, each performing a task on a detailed work chart under the direction of a manager, produced encyclopedias of enormous breadth. Late in the twentieth century, computers changed encyclopedias—and the Internet changed them more. Today, *Britannica* and *World Book* still sell some 130-pound, $1,100, multivolume sets, but they earn most of their money from Internet subscriptions. Yet while the medium has shifted from atoms to bits, the production model—and therefore the product itself—has remained the same.

Now Wales has brought forth a third model—call it One for All. Instead of one really smart guy, Wikipedia draws on thousands of fairly smart guys and gals—because in the metamathematics of encyclopedias, 500 Kvarans equal one Pliny the Elder. Instead of clearly delineated lines of authority, Wikipedia depends on radical decentralization and self-organization—open source in its purest form. Most encyclopedias start to fossilize the moment they're printed on a page. But add wiki software and some helping hands and you get something self-repairing and almost alive. A different production model creates a product that's fluid, fixable, and free.

The One for All model has delivered solid results in a remarkably short time. Look up any topic you know something about—from the Battle of Fredericksburg to *Madame Bovary* to Planck's law of black body radiation—and you'll probably find that the Wikipedia entry is, if not perfect, not bad. Sure, the Leonard Nimoy entry is longer than the one on Toni Morrison. But the Morrison article covers the basics of her life and literary works about as well as the *World Book* entry. And among the nearly half-million articles are tens of thousands whose quality easily rivals that of *Britannica* or *Encarta.*

What makes the model work is not only the collective knowledge and effort of a far-flung labor force, but also the willingness to abide by two core principles. The first: neutrality. All articles should be written without bias. Wikipedians are directed not to take a stand on controversial subjects like abortion or global warming but to fairly represent all sides. The second principle is good faith. All work should be approached with the assumption that the author is trying to help the project, not harm it.

Wikipedia represents a belief in the supremacy of reason and the goodness of others. In the Wikipedia ideal, people of goodwill sometimes disagree. But from the respectful clash of opposing viewpoints and the combined wisdom of the many, something resembling the truth will emerge. Most of the time.

If you looked up Jimmy Carter on Wikipedia one morning [...], you would have discovered something you couldn't learn from *Britannica.* According to the photo that accompanied Carter's entry, America's thirty-ninth president was a scruffy, random unshaven man with his left index finger shoved firmly up his nose.

Lurking in the underbrush of Wikipedia's idyllic forest of reason and good intentions are contributors less noble in purpose, whose numbers are multiplying. Wiki devotees have names for many of them. First, there are the trolls, minor troublemakers who breach the principle of good faith with inane edits designed to rile serious users. More insidious are vandals, who try to wreck the site—inserting profanity and ethnic slurs, unleashing bots that put ads into entries, and pasting pictures of penises and other junior-high laugh-getters. Considering how easy it is to make changes on Wikipedia, you'd imagine these ne'er-do-wells could potentially overwhelm the site. But they haven't—at least not yet—because defenses against them are built into the structure.

Anybody who is logged in can place an article on a "watch list." Whenever somebody amends the entry, the watch list records the change. So when that anonymous vandal replaced Jimmy Carter's photo with a nose-picker, all the Wikipedians with Jimmy Carter on their watch list knew about it. One of them merely reverted to the original portrait. At the same time, the user who rescued the former president from Boogerville noticed that the vandal had also posted the nose-pick photo on the "Rapping" entry—and he got rid of that image just four minutes after the photo appeared.

On controversial topics, the response can be especially swift. Wikipedia's article on Islam has been a persistent target of vandalism, but Wikipedia's defenders of Islam have always proved nimbler than the vandals. Take one fairly typical instance. At 11:20 one morning [...], an anonymous user replaced the entire Islam entry with a single scatological word. At 11:22, a user named Solitude reverted the entry. At 11:25, the anonymous user struck again, this time replacing the article with the phrase "u stink!" By 11:26, another user, Ahoerstemeir, reverted that change—and the vandal disappeared. When MIT's Fernanda Viégas and IBM's Martin Wattenberg and Kushal Dave studied Wikipedia, they found that cases of mass deletions, a common form of vandalism, were corrected in a median time of 2.8 minutes. When an obscenity accompanied the mass deletion, the median time dropped to 1.7 minutes.

It turns out that Wikipedia has an innate capacity to heal itself. As a result, woefully outnumbered vandals often give up and leave. (To paraphrase Linus Torvalds, given enough eyeballs, all thugs are callow.) What's more, making changes is so simple that who prevails often comes down to who cares more. And hardcore Wikipedians care. A lot.

Wool logs on to Wikipedia at 6 each morning and works two hours before leaving for his day job developing education programs for a museum. When he gets back home around 6:30 pm, he hops back on Wikipedia for a few more hours. Derksen checks his watch list each morning before leaving for work at a small company that sells medical equipment on eBay. When he returns home, he'll spend a few hours just clicking on the Random Page link to see what needs to get done. It's tempting to urge people like Wool and Derksen to get a life. But imagine if they instead spent their free time walking through public parks, picking up garbage. We'd call them good citizens.

Still, even committed citizens sometimes aren't muscular enough to fend off determined bad guys. As Wikipedia has grown, Wales has been forced to impose some more centralized, policelike measures—to guard against "edit warriors," "point-of-view warriors," "revert warriors," and all those who have difficulty playing well with others. "We try to be as open as we can," Wales says, "but some of these people are just impossible." During [the 2004] presidential election, Wikipedia had to lock both the George W. Bush and the John Kerry pages because of incessant vandalism and bickering. The Wikipedia front page, another target of attacks, is also protected.

If that suggests an emerging hierarchy in this bastion of egalitarian knowledge-gathering, so be it. The Wikipedia power pyramid looks like this: at the bottom are anonymous contributors, people who make a few edits and are identified only by their IP addresses. On the next level stand Wikipedia's myriad registered users around the globe, people such as Kvaran in New Mexico, who have chosen a screen name (he's Carptrash) and make edits under that byline. Some of the most dedicated users try to reach the next level—administrator. Wikipedia's 400 administrators, Derksen and Wool among them, can delete articles, protect pages, and block IP addresses. Above this group are bureaucrats, who can crown administrators. The most privileged bureaucrats are stewards. And above stewards are developers, fifty-seven superelites who can made direct changes to the Wikipedia software and database. There's also an arbitration committee that hears disputes and can ban bad users.

At the very top, with powers that range far beyond those of any mere Wikipedian mortal, is Wales, known to everyone in wiki-world as Jimbo. He can do pretty much anything he wants—from locking pages to banning people to getting rid of developers. So vast are his powers that some began calling him "the benevolent dictator." But Wales bristled at that tag. So his minions assigned him a different, though no less imposing, label. "Jimbo," says Wikipedia administrator Mark Pellegrini, "is the God-King."

The God-King drives a Hyundai. On a sunny Florida Monday, Wales is piloting his red Accent from his St. Petersburg home across the bay to downtown Tampa, where on the eleventh floor of a shabby office building a company called Neutelligent manages a vast server farm. In one of the back rows, stacked on two racks, are the guts of Wikipedia—forty-two servers connected by a hairball of orange and blue cables. For the next two hours, Wales scoots to and fro, plugging and unplugging cables while trading messages with a Wikipedia developer on Internet Relay Chat via a nearby keyboard.

Back in St. Pete, Wales oversees his empire from a pair of monitors in Wikipedia's headquarters—two cramped, windowless rooms that look like the offices of a failed tech startup. Computer equipment is strewn everywhere. An open copy of *Teach Yourself PHP, MySQL, and Apache* is splayed on the floor. It may be good to be God-King, but it's not glamorous.

Wales began his journey in Huntsville, Alabama. His father worked in a grocery store. His mother and grandmother operated a tiny private school called the House of Learning, which Wales and his three siblings attended. He graduated from Auburn University in 1989 with a degree in finance and ended up studying options pricing in an economics PhD program at Indiana University. Bored with academic life, he left school in 1994 and went to Chicago, where he took to betting on interest rate and foreign-currency fluctuations. In six years, he earned enough to support himself and his wife for the rest of their lives.

They moved to San Diego in 1998. The times being what they were, Wales started an Internet company called Bomis, a search engine and Web dictionary. He began hearing about the fledgling open source movement and wondered whether volunteers could create something besides software. So he recruited Larry Sanger, then an Ohio State University doctoral student in philosophy, whom he'd encountered on some listservs. He put Sanger on the Bomis payroll, and together they launched a free online encyclopedia called Nupedia. Why an encyclopedia? Wales says he simply wanted to see if it could be done.

With Sanger as editor in chief, Nupedia essentially replicated the One Best Way model. He assembled a roster of academics to write articles. (Participants even had to fax in their degrees as proof of their expertise.) And he established a seven-stage process of editing, fact-checking, and peer review. "After eighteen months and $250,000," Wales says, "we had twelve articles."

Then an employee told Wales about wiki software. On January 15, 2001, they launched a wiki-fied version and within a month, they had 200 articles. In a year, they had 18,000. And on September 20, 2004, when the Hebrew edition added an article on Kazakhstan's flag, Wikipedia had its 1 millionth article. Total investment: about $500,000, most of it from Wales himself.

Sanger left the project in 2002. "In the Nupedia model, there was room for an editor in chief," Wales says. "The wiki model is too distributed for that."

Sanger, a scholar at heart, returned to academic life. His cofounder, meanwhile, became a minor geek rock star. Wales has been asked to advise the BBC, Nokia, and other large enterprises curious about wikis. Technology conferences in the United States and Europe clamor for him. And while he's committed to keeping his creation a "charitable project," as he constantly calls it (wikipedia.com became wikipedia.org almost three years ago), the temptations are mounting.

Late [in 2004], Wales and Angela Beesley, an astonishingly dedicated Wikipedian, launched a for-profit venture called WikiCities. The company will provide free hosting for "community-based" sites—RVers, poodle owners, genealogy buffs, and so on. The sites will operate on the same software that powers Wikipedia, and the content will be available under a free license. But WikiCities intends to make money by selling advertising. After all, if several thousand people can create an encyclopedia, a few hundred Usher devotees should be able to put together the ultimate fan site. And if legions of Usher fans are hanging out in one place, some advertiser will pay to try to sell them concert tickets or music downloads.

It may feel like we've been down this road before—remember GeoCities and theglobe.com? But Wales says this is different because those earlier sites lacked any mechanism for true community. "It was just free homepages," he says. WikiCities, he believes, will let people who share a passion also share a project. They'll be able to design and build projects together. So the founder of the Web's grand experiment in the democratic dissemination of information is also trying to resurrect GeoCities. While some may find the notion silly, many others just want a piece of Jimbo magic.

During our conversation over lunch, Wales' cell phone rings. It's a partner at Accel, the venture capital firm, calling to talk about WikiCities and any other wiki-related investment ideas Wales might have. Wales says he's busy and asks the caller to phone back later. Then he smiles at me. "I'll let him cool his heels awhile."

Wikipedia's articles on the British peerage system—clearheaded explanations of dukes, viscounts, and other titles of nobility—are largely the work of a user known as Lord Emsworth. A few of Emsworth's pieces on kings and queens of England have been honored as Wikipedia's Featured Article of the Day. It turns out that Lord Emsworth claims to be a sixteen-year-old living in South Brunswick, New Jersey. On Wikipedia, nobody has to know you're a sophomore.

And that has some distressed. Larry Sanger gave voice to these criticisms in a recent essay posted on kuro5hin.org titled "Why Wikipedia Must Jettison Its Anti-Elitism." Although he acknowledges that "Wikipedia is very cool," he argues that the site's production model suffers from two big problems.

The first is that "regardless of whether Wikipedia actually is more or less reliable than the average encyclopedia," librarians, teachers, and academics don't perceive it as credible, because it has no formal review process. The second problem, according to Sanger, is that the site in general and Wales in particular are too "anti-elitist." Established scholars might be willing to contribute to Wikipedia—but not if they have to deal with trolls and especially not if they're considered no different from any schmo with an iMac.

Speaking from his home in Columbus, Ohio, where he teaches at Ohio State, Sanger stresses that Wikipedia is a fine and worthy endeavor. But he says that academics don't take it seriously. "A lot of articles look like they're written by undergraduates." He believes that "people who make knowing things their life's work should be accorded a special place in the project." But since Wikipedia's resolute anti-elitism makes that unlikely, Sanger argues, something else will happen: Wikipedia will fork—that is, a group of academics will take Wikipedia's content, which is available under a free license, and produce their own peer-reviewed reference work. "I wanted to send a wake-up call to the Wikipedia community to tell them that this fork is probably going to happen."

Wales' response essentially boils down to this: Fork you. "You want to organize that?" he sniffs. "Here are the servers." Yet Wales acknowledges that in the next year, partly in response to these concerns, Wikipedia will likely offer a stable—that is, unchangeable—version alongside its One for All edition.

But both Sanger's critique and Wales' reaction miss a larger point: You can't evaluate Wikipedia by traditional encyclopedia standards. A forked Wikipedia run by academics would be Nupedia 2.0. It would use the One Best Way production model, which inevitably would produce a One Best Way product. That's not a better or worse Wikipedia any more than Instapundit.com is a better or worse *Washington Post.* They are different animals.

Encyclopedias aspire to be infallible. But Wikipedia requires that the perfect never be the enemy of the good. Citizen editors don't need to make an entry flawless. They just need to make it better. As a result, even many Wikipedians believe the site is not as good as traditional encyclopedias. "On a scale of 1 to 10, I'd give Wikipedia a 7.8 in reliability," Kvaran told me in New Mexico. "I'd give *Britannica* an 8.8." But how much does that matter? *Britannica* has been around since before the American Revolution; Wikipedia just celebrated its fifth birthday. More important, *Britannica* costs $70 a year; Wikipedia is free. The better criterion on which to measure Wikipedia is whether this very young, pretty good, ever improving, totally free site serves a need—just as the way to measure *Britannica* is whether the additional surety that comes from its production model is worth the cost.

There's another equally important difference between the two offerings. The One Best Way creates something finished. The One for All model creates something alive. When the Indian Ocean tsunami erupted late [in 2004],

Wikipedians produced several entries on the topic within hours. By contrast, World Book, whose CD-ROM allows owners to download regular updates, hadn't updated its tsunami or Indian Ocean entries a full month after the devastation occurred. That's the likely fate of Wikipedia's proposed stable, or snapshot, version. Fixing its contents in a book or on a CD or DVD is tantamount to embalming a living thing. The body may look great, but it's no longer breathing.

"You can create life in there," says Wikipedian Oliver Brown, a high school teacher in Aptos, California. "If you don't know about something, you can start an article, and other people can come and feed it, nurture it." For example, two years ago, Danny Wool was curious about the American architectural sculptor Lee Lawrie, whose statue of Atlas sits nearby Rockefeller Center. Wool posted a stub—a few sentences on a topic—in the hopes that someone would add to it. That someone turned out to be Kvaran, who owned several books on Lawrie and who'd photographed his work not only at Rockefeller Center but also at the Capitol Building in Lincoln, Nebraska. Today, the Lawrie entry has grown from two sentences to several thorough paragraphs, a dozen photos, and a list of references. Brown himself posted a stub when he was wondering how many people were considered the father or mother of something. [In 2005] Wikipedia lists more than 230 people known as the father or mother of an idea, a movement, or an invention. And that number will likely be higher tomorrow. As the father of this new kind of encyclopedia puts it, "Wikipedia will never be finished."

In 1962, Charles Van Doren—who would go on to become a senior editor of *Britannica* but is more famous for his role in the 1950s quiz show scandal—wrote a think piece for the journal *The American Behavioral Scientist*. His essay, "The Idea of an Encyclopedia," is similar in spirit to the one Sanger wrote late last year: a warning to his community.

Van Doren warned not that encyclopedias of his day lacked credibility, but that they lacked vitality. "The tone of American encyclopedias is often fiercely inhuman," he wrote. "It appears to be the wish of some contributors to write about living institutions as if they were pickled frogs, outstretched upon a dissecting board." An encyclopedia ought to be a "revolutionary document," he argued. And while Van Doren didn't call for a new production model, he did say that "the ideal encyclopedia should be radical. It should stop being safe."

What stood in the way of this new approach was precisely what encyclopedias prided themselves on. "Respectability seems safe," he wrote. "But what will be respectable in thirty years seems avant-garde now. If an encyclopedia hopes to be respectable in 2000, it must appear daring in the year 1963."

Jimbo and his minions—from Einar Kvaran in his New Mexico trailer to Lord Emsworth in his New Jersey bedroom—may seem daring today. But they're about to become respectable.

Issues of ethics are not new to popular culture. Professor Charles Van Doren admitted being given answers ahead of time by the producers of *Twenty-One*.

## Working with the Text

1. At the beginning of his article, Pink says that the creation of Wikipedia raises some "cosmic questions" about how we get information and who we trust as authorities: "Is Wikipedia a heartening effort in digital humanitarianism—or a not-so-smart mob unleashing misinformation on the masses? Are well-intentioned amateurs any replacement for professionals? And is charging nothing for knowledge too high a price?" Before you read the article, how would you have answered these questions? Has your thinking changed after reading the article and trying out Wikipedia? Pink's comment also raises questions about what we mean by *amateur* and *professional.* How do you and your classmates view these terms, especially in relation to what makes someone an expert?

2. Pink describes three models for creating an encyclopedia: the One Smart Guy model, the One Best Way model, and the One for All model. Describe and define what he means by each model. What does he describe as the strengths and weaknesses of each? Can you think of other cultural activities that could be analyzed with these models (for

example, coaching a basketball team or creating music)? How does Pink's classification system help us think about popular culture in new ways?

3. At the conclusion of his article, Pink points out that while people might disagree about how reliable Wikipedia is compared with traditional encyclopedias, the growth and popularity of Wikipedia suggests that many people find it just as, if not more, useful than other encyclopedias. Test Wikipedia for yourself:

   • Have members of the class choose different subjects and look them up in a traditional, One Best Way model encyclopedia, such as the *Encyclopedia Britannica,* and then on Wikipedia. Compare and contrast the results obtained. Do you find yourself trusting one source more than the other? Why? How similar is the information and the way it is presented? Do you find any discrepancies or disagreements between the two sources?

   • Ask various faculty members around campus how they feel about students using Wikipedia as a reference tool. How do they react when a student cites Wikipedia as a source in a research paper? What range of opinion do you find? Are some faculty members more receptive to Wikipedia than others, and if so, why do you think that is?

4. The whole point of the wiki and open-source movements is that they are available to anyone. Explore Wikipedia even further by taking part in the project. Working individually or in groups (or even as a whole class), choose a subject that you would like to contribute to in Wikipedia. Remember, as a comprehensive encyclopedia, all subjects are open for inclusion, not just subjects that seem academic or formal. Choose a topic that has personal meaning for you or to which you have a personal connection. Do your own research and come up with material to submit to Wikipedia. As you do so, consider the following:

   • Who do you envision as your audience? Who do you think might possibly look up your subject on Wikipedia, and for what reasons?

   • Are you updating an existing entry or creating a new one? If you are working with a current entry, what holes are you trying to fill or what aspects of the subject are you trying to explore? If no entry currently exists, think about the most important fact and details to know for a new visitor to the site.

   • Keep in mind that as soon as you upload an entry, it is likely that others in cyberspace also interested in the subject will review, revise, and "correct" your work.

# THREE

CHAPTER

## Pop Identity: You Are What You Write

In 2000, the following advertisement appeared on AskMe.com, a website where people with questions could connect with other people who had (or claimed they had) answers:

> I AM A LAW EXPERT WITH TWO YEARS OF FORMAL TRAINING IN THE LAW. I WILL HELP ANYONE I CAN! I HAVE BEEN INVOLVED IN TRIALS, LEGAL STUDIES AND CERTAIN FORMS OF JURISPRUDENCE. I AM NOT ACCREDITED BY THE STATE BAR ASSOCIATION YET TO PRACTICE LAW. . . . SINCERELY, JUSTIN ANTHONY WYRICK, JR.

The person advertising his services had been a popular source of legal advice and information on the website, and this posting marked the first time he had identified himself. There was just one hitch: "Justin Anthony Wyrick, Jr." was actually a fifteen-year-old boy named Marcus Arnold who lived in the California desert community of Perris. His only "legal training" had come from watching television shows about lawyers and Court TV.

In spite of the new information about this "law expert," many people who had received advice from Arnold remained loyal to him and insisted that they found his counsel more helpful than any they had received from a "real" lawyer. Arnold's case raises important questions about the meaning of expertise and how we evaluate information in the digital age. Just as important, the example of Marcus Arnold/Justin Anthony Wyrick, Jr., also speaks to the nature of identity—both the various roles each of us plays in society and the idea of our "true" selves. As the quotation marks (or "scare quotes" as some call them) around words such as *real* and *true* suggest, the nature of identity has long been a slippery issue; the advent of the Internet age has only made the situation more complicated, in large part because the Web has reinforced more than ever the profound connection between identity and writing.

It's easy to take for granted how much we are made out of language. Consider, for example, how important naming ceremonies are in every human culture. Not only is the choice of a name for a new baby the source of considerable discussion and careful consideration, but it is often accompanied by elaborate formal rituals. And names are, of course, words—words that link us to family histories, ethnic heritages, and particular places in time. In many cultures, an individual name really consists of many names (the practice of assigning a first, middle, and last name, while common among many families in the United States, is actually among the less elaborate forms of naming in the world), and most of us carry multiple versions of our names: our "formal" names, the names we are called by family and friends, the nicknames we acquire and lose along the way. As you can see, naming is all about language, and it is anything but simple. But which of these names is the "real" you?

# O N E

## A Natural History of Your Names

Compile a list of all the words that could be considered one of your names, from those listed on various official and government documents (birth certificates, driver's licenses, school forms, etc.) to family names, pet names, nicknames, even email addresses and instant-messaging names. Write an essay explaining the history of your various names and what each means to you. How do different names cause you to view yourself differently? What happens when members of the "wrong" group use or hear the wrong name (as when friends hear a family member call you by a name from your early childhood)? How do you think your name might change as you get older? How could career and family changes affect how people refer to you and how you refer to yourself?

## LANGUAGE, IDENTITY, AND WRITING

In 1951, the American poet Langston Hughes wrote the following poem about a college writing class.

### Theme for English B

The instructor said,

    Go home and write
    a page tonight.
    And let that page come out of you—
    Then, it will be true.

I wonder if it's that simple?
I am twenty-two, colored, born in Winston-Salem.
I went to school there, then Durham, then here
to this college on the hill above Harlem.
I am the only colored student in my class.
The steps from the hill lead down into Harlem
through a park, then I cross St. Nicholas,
Eighth Avenue, Seventh, and I come to the Y,
the Harlem Branch Y, where I take the elevator
up to my room, sit down, and write this page:

It's not easy to know what is true for you or me
at twenty-two, my age. But I guess I'm what

I feel and see and hear, Harlem, I hear you:
hear you, hear me—we two—you, me, talk on this page.
(I hear New York too.) Me—who?
Well, I like to eat, sleep, drink, and be in love.
I like to work, read, learn, and understand life.
I like a pipe for a Christmas present,
or records—Bessie, bop, or Bach.
I guess being colored doesn't make me NOT like
the same things other folks like who are other races.
So will my page be colored that I write?
Being me, it will not be white.
But it will be
a part of you, instructor.
You are white—
yet a part of me, as I am a part
    of you.
That's American.
Sometimes perhaps you don't want to be
    a part of me.
Nor do I often want to be a part
    of you.
But we are, that's true!
As I learn from you,
I guess you learn from me—
although you're older—and white—
and somewhat more free.

This is my page for English B.

This poem has become one of the most well-known American poems of the twentieth century; in fact, you may have read it before in school. From the very first stanza, the poem raises questions about identity, language, and writing. In response to a teacher's admonition that if you "let that page come out of you/ Then, it will be true," the speaker of the poem considers whether writing is really "that simple," which is the same as asking whether identity is that

Poet Langston Hughes

simple. As the speaker brings up varied aspects of his identity—some conflicting, some complementary—in particular focusing on questions of racial and national identity, he pauses to focus our attention on some basic English pronouns that define the writing relationship:

> I hear you:
> hear you, hear me—we two—you, me, talk on this page.
> (I hear New York too.) Me—who?

These words—*I, you, me, we*—again seem so ordinary that we take them for granted, but Hughes, through his poem, challenges us to think about them more deeply. When we write *I* for example, whom does that word really refer to?

Such questions can lead us into some of the most fascinating and difficult questions in linguistics, philosophy, and psychology, but for our purposes, "Theme for English B" reminds us that when we take a pen in hand or sit down at a keyboard, we are always involved in the act—and the art—of creating identities, both our own as writers (the *I* of our writing), and that of who we think of as our readers—the *you* of writing. The ancient Greeks had a word for the idea of the created self: *persona,* the word for "mask." Literary critics have adopted the word to refer to the identity that writers create for themselves in their writing. In fact, Hughes's poem is a great example of a persona. Many readers, unfamiliar with Hughes's biography, might assume that he was a twenty-two-year-old African American college student from North Carolina studying in Harlem when he wrote this poem. Hughes actually wrote this poem in his forties, and he was originally from Joplin, Missouri. While the poem is infused with his experiences as a black artist, writer, and political activist living in the first half of the twentieth century, the *I* of "Theme for English B" is a persona, a created identity.

Recognizing the use of personas makes sense in a poem or work of fiction, but how about our original example of Marcus Arnold? When Arnold started his legal advice workshop, was he trying to trick the visitors to his site or was he creating a "persona"? What is the relationship between a persona like this and the idea of a "real" self? The return to writing in the digital age has renewed attention to these questions and also brought about new experimentations with identity, writing, and language. The growth of the World Wide Web and digital technology continues to expand the number and kind of situations where writing and persona creation can take place. In writing studies, we call this growth the creation of new discourse communities—distinct areas and arenas for communication, each governed by different sets of rules, both spoken and unspoken, formal and informal.

# T W O

## List Your Writing Discourse Communities

List all the different places where you construct a written identity or persona for yourself. Another way to put it is this: think of all the situations in which you write the word *I*. For example, there can be the papers you write for class, Post-it Note reminders you write to yourself, text messaging, a Facebook page, etc. Create a classification system for organizing and analyzing these different communities, such as formal versus informal, home versus school, or any system that makes sense to you. Define these different categories in terms of what you see as the different "rules and regulations" that influence how you contribute to these different communities. These rules and regulations do not necessarily have to be official or even explicitly stated. They could just be habits, customs, and common ways of behaving. For example, the culture of social network sites like MySpace creates an environment where writers are supposed to be informal and humorous, even when writing about ideas and issues they care deeply about. Discuss how you think writers in these communities learn these rules and the various ways they may be enforced, whether in friendly ways or not. Which communities do you feel most comfortable in? In which do you feel most self-conscious and why?

In this chapter, you will have the opportunity to explore what creating an identity means in the information age. We will consider online environments and games like Second Life and The Sims, websites where members not only interact with other players around the world but also create new identities for themselves. When our identities are constructed completely through writing, how bound are we to the parts of identity most people have assumed they were born with, aspects such as gender, ethnicity, race, and age? This chapter invites you to become part of this ongoing dialogue and debate about identity and the Web.

# READING CULTURE

## CONSTRUCTING IDENTITY IN A DIGITAL AGE

### "Leading a Double Life"

#### Irene Sege

"You are what you write." What's the relationship between the "you" that you create when writing an essay, email, or poem and the "you" that your friends and family meet face to face? Writers have pondered this question since the invention of writing itself, and it has always had a certain mystery and even romance about it. Consider the idea of a pen pal. You may have had a pen pal, or if not you are most likely familiar with how a pen pal works. A person carries on a written correspondence with someone usually living far, far away. This relationship can last for years, but it is carried on exclusively through writing. The invention of photography, the telephone, and later videocassettes and DVDs have all added to the complexity of the pen pal relationship, but there remains something fascinating about the classic scenario of pen pals who have exchanged only written letters finally meeting in person for the first time, even after five, ten, twenty years or more. It's impossible for any of us not to wonder about the dynamics of that first "real" meeting. How will the in-person pen pal match up with the idea of that person created through his or her letters? We shouldn't be surprised that such meetings often attract media attention.

In the digital age, however, relationships that had once seemed so unusual—no face-to-face or even telephone contact, conducted only through the written word—have become commonplace as people use social-networking sites not just to interact with personal friends but to meet new people from across the country and even across the world. The creation of massive multiplayer online role playing games (MMORPGs) such as World of Warcraft and Second Life have radically transformed the idea of the pen pal into virtual online worlds, where users create elaborate identities that exist only in the game. Just what kind of identities are these new online roles, or, as they are called, "avatars"?

In "Leading a Double Life," Boston Globe reporter Irene Sege writes about the phenomenon of Second Life, a rapidly growing MMORPG website that operates less as a game with a specific goal and identifiable winners than a true virtual reality, where users can go to school, start careers, earn money, enter relationships, even commit crimes and run *afoul of the authorities. Sege focuses in particular on two players who exemplify the increasing interconnections between the virtual world and the "real" world, between our in-the-flesh identities and our online selves.*

## Before You Read

1. When you think of virtual reality, what comes to mind? How would you define the term? What experiences have you had with virtual reality? Would you consider, for example, a MySpace page as a form of virtual reality? How do you see the connection between a social-networking identity and your "real" self?

2. The idea of creating different identities or personas for different social situations is nothing new. Many of us, for example, will speak of our "work" selves or our "school" selves, our "at home" selves or our "with friends" selves. Working individually or in groups, brainstorm specific examples of different social selves that you use or are familiar with. Where do you see the relation between these different selves and what you think of as your "real" self? What are the biggest challenges or problems involved in maintaining these different selves?

In real life, Jeff Lipsky is an ordinary-looking white guy—35 years old, 5 feet 8 inches tall, thinning hair, T-shirt and jeans—who creates abstract drawings in his Tyngsborough townhouse. Online, in the lush, three-dimensional, user-created universe called Second Life, he's the cartoon character Filthy Fluno, a bearded, wide-bodied, wild-tressed, fang-toothed, black gallery owner who sells virtual versions of his drawings to other denizens of this virtual world.

In real life, Rebecca Nesson—slight, 30, short hair—is a lawyer working on a doctorate in computer science who teaches at Harvard Extension School. Her Second Life avatar, or cartoon self, is Rebecca Berkman, who looks like Nesson and who, standing in a virtual amphitheater, leads avatars from as far away as Korea and Houston in a discussion section of the Extension School course CyberOne.

Such is the range of Second Life, a simulated world populated by avatars and built by their human alter egos. Last week the number of registered users crossed the 1 million mark, up from 100,000 in early 2006, leaving Second Life poised to become the next big cyber phenomenon.

Launched in 2003 by California-based Linden Lab, Second Life is a website where users create animated cartoon avatars to represent themselves—usually as humans (often buff, busty, beautiful humans), and sometimes as fanciful or furry creatures. Linden sells land in this virtual frontier, and users (a.k.a. "residents") design and make everything from virtual stores for the land to virtual sweaters for the avatars. They buy things and sell things that exist only "in world"—so many that last month $6.6 million in user-user transactions changed hands. They role play, gamble, teach classes, make music, open restaurants, push politics—all as they guide their avatars through the elaborate virtual landscapes and cityscapes that give Second Life its stepping-into-Wonderland quality.

"Second Life is no more a game than the Web is a game. It's a platform," says John Lester, 39, of Somerville, Linden's community and education manager. "This feels exactly like it felt when the Web was first coming out. I remember feeling the hair on the back of my neck standing up."

Unlike such sites as Sims Online, Second Life's content is created almost entirely by users. The result is a varied, free-wheeling world, a virtual society more spontaneous than the similar There.com, a PG-13, 3D social network with 500,000 users that, unlike Second Life, approves items that users create before introducing them.

A Second Life user and his online avatar.

Second Life has shopping centers and support centers for stroke survivors and corporate centers for companies that view hanging a shingle in-world as the cutting-edge move that launching a website once was. It has replicas of the Flintstones' town of Bedrock and a Darfur refugee camp. An American Cancer Society relay in-world raised $40,000, and an avatar of former Virginia governor Mark Warner was interviewed in Second Life. Reuters just opened a virtual news bureau.

The avatars lend what Lester calls an "emotional bandwidth" to every encounter. Avatars "talk" via text message and appear to be typing whenever they talk. Many products that enterprising users create—and, if they wish, sell—are designed to individualize avatars' experience, whether its coiffures and cars or animations that mimic kissing or skydiving or dancing.

Joining Second Life is free, but buying or selling goods and services and land requires an account. Business is conducted in Lindens, convertible at roughly 275 per dollar.

## VIRTUAL INTIMACY

The avatar Tuna Oddfellow, dashing in silver mohawk and windswept cape, has a virtual Gothic mansion, "Collinwood," that a fellow Second Lifer and aficionado of the old *Dark Shadows* television show built for him gratis. Oddfellow—in real life Matthew Fishman, 38-year-old magician and fundraiser from Watertown—also runs a virtual wedding business, complete with invitations, catered food, disc jockey, and premarital counseling, for avatars he's convinced are committed to each other.

"I can't marry you in Second Life," Fishman says in an interview, "unless you realize you have First Life emotions."

In Second Life, Fishman has experienced both heartbreak and friendship. Last October the woman behind an avatar whom Oddfellow was dating died. They'd never met in real life, but, as avatar Oddfellow, he typed words of comfort to her son's avatar and was comforted himself by avatar friends. He conducted her virtual funeral.

"Second Life," Fishman says, "has taught me that we're not really limited to deep friendships you can reach out and touch."

Just as there's sex on the Internet, so, too, in Second Life. Linden permits sex, nudity, and profanity on private land in "mature" areas open to adults only. Linden investigates reports of abuse of this policy, as well as its rules against harassment, vandalism, and other antisocial behavior, and metes out warnings, suspensions, or expulsions.

Second Life has its share of cybersex-for-hire and deviant sexual activity, but for Fishman simulated intimacy revolves around romance. "There's a wining and a dining," he says. "I'm not the kind of person who in Second Life or First Life will fall into bed with somebody without developing a relationship."

Fishman will soon perform his seventh virtual wedding. "If they're doing this correctly," he says, "it should be the biggest day of their Second Life."

## COMPANIES JOIN IN

Rodica Buzescu of Somerville, who graduated from Harvard in June [2006], is a project manager for Millions of Us, a California-based startup that helps companies establish a presence in Second Life.

Millions of Us joins a coterie of companies and individuals making a living developing objects and experiences in Second Life. It's created virtual Toyotas and built the virtual loft where Warner Bros. invited avatars to preview Regina Spektor's latest album a month before its release.

Linden, which is almost profitable, makes money on virtual land sales and the fee it charges to exchange currency. Otherwise, Second Life entrepreneurs pocket whatever they earn.

With Second Life trailing the 6 million users of World of Warcraft and 114 million members of MySpace, firms like Millions bank on the potential of new cyberworlds, not only as marketplaces but also as buzz generators and virtual meeting grounds.

When American Apparel opened a replica retail store in-world, it was less interested in selling virtual T-shirts than in what Web director Raz Schionning calls a "boundary-pushing experiment" in reaching a young, tech-savvy audience. "When we think about Web marketing, it makes sense," he says, "to not just put your money in banner panels."

Second Life's big industry is fashion, be it clothes or hair or accessories. A virtual gown by Second Life designer Dazzle, for instance, runs 350 Linden.

Top Second Life fashionistas earn $50,000 to $75,000 a year, says Wagner James Au, whose New World Notes blog chronicles Second Life. Competition can be intense. A recent dispute about the legitimacy of modifying virtual "skins"—full-body coverings—for an avatar's personal use became so nasty that designer Torrid Midnight left Second Life.

Meanwhile, Buzescu, 24, an aspiring lawyer, envisions future legal needs. "The issues coming up," she says, "will be with companies with real-life interests coming into environments like this."

## ACADEMIC AVATARS

Rebecca Nesson has never taught a class like "CyberOne: Law in the Court of Public Opinion," a joint enterprise with Harvard Law School sponsored by Harvard's Berkman Center for Internet & Society.

Here she is as avatar Rebecca Berkman, standing outside a virtual replica of Harvard's Austin Hall before thirty avatars of Extension School students. A wolf sits in front, teaching fellow Buzescu is an android, and everyone can fly, all of which adds a touch of whimsy to even the most serious Second Life endeavors, in this case giving far-flung students a virtual place to meet and work on class projects. Gone is off-site education as simply posting videos of lectures online and communicating with students via email.

"It's better than anything I've seen in distance learning," Nesson says.

Harvard is among some eighty academic institutions exploring Second Life. Similar experiments occur on There.com. Others see different potential in

Second Life. In a previous job, Lester used Second Life to help people with mild autism practice socializing. Some predict Second Life will engage people around the world in political discourse, but Berkman research fellow Ethan Zuckerman contends it's too technically sophisticated for developing nations with outdated equipment.

"The idea," he says, "that it's going to be a utopia where we have people from very different cultures interacting seems overly optimistic."

## FANTASY AND REALITY

Jeff Lipsky, meanwhile, is finding the balance between fantasy and reality. When he noticed few African Americans in-world, he gave his avatar, Filthy Fluno, dark skin. His dog's crooked tooth inspired Fluno's fangs.

"When I first started playing I felt like I was one of those white rappers who pretend they're black. I wasn't having that much fun. Now it's more my personality," Lipsky says. "I might do some extra swearing."

One night, while Lipsky, who runs a nonprofit arts group, watched TV with his wife, an avatar art guide named Nata Clutterbuck sold a drawing he'd imported to Second Life. At a recent event in Filthy's Warehouse, he sold $275 worth of virtual drawings and a real drawing for $325.

"I'm bringing my real art to the virtual space. Now I'm bringing things from the virtual space into real life and bringing it back to the virtual life," Lipsky says. "It's wild."

---

# Working with the Text

1. Based on Sege's discussions with Jeff Lipsky, Rebecca Nesson, and others, write about what you see as the biggest attractions of Second Life for its users. What keeps them coming back to the site? If you were to explain to others what Second Life is and why you think it has become so popular, what would you say?

2. According to Second Life player Matthew Fishman/Tuna Oddfellow, his experiences in virtual reality have shown him "we're not really limited to deep friendships you can reach out and touch." What are your initial reactions to the marriages that he creates online? How seriously do you think the participants involved take them? How does Fishman/Oddfellow define "deep friendship," and how does this definition challenge our traditional ideas about friendship?

3. Sege describes Rebecca Nesson/Rebecca Berkman preparing to teach an online course where all the students participate as Second Life avatars. What do you see as the advantages and disadvantages of taking a class

in this way? Who might be most attracted to the idea of using your avatar identity as part of a "real" class?

4. As Sege points out, more and more real-world companies, organizations, and other groups are opening branches in Second Life, including presidential campaigns. Working in groups, choose a real-world business, an activist movement, or a politician and devise a campaign strategy for working in the Second Life world. What aspects of business as usual can they continue in virtual reality? What changes will they have to make? What kinds of challenges are created by interacting with avatars who may have demographic characteristics such as race, gender, or class that are different from their real-life counterparts?

## from *Everything Bad Is Good for You: How Today's Pop Culture Is Actually Making Us Smarter*

### Steven Johnson

*When we talk about what is bad and good for us in popular culture, it's easy to list the usual suspects. Television, video games, loud music: we may be attracted to them, but at the same time we often think of them as guilty pleasures. Reading a book, exercising in the fresh air, working on a crafts project: these seem clearly superior to those more supposedly mindless pursuits. Parents who buy their children the latest* Harry Potter *book can feel good about encouraging reading and a love of language in their offspring. Parents who buy an Xbox or Wii may feel a pang of guilt over indulging their children's less wholesome interests.*

*Just how valid are these assumptions? Is reading a book always better than watching a television show? And just what do we mean by "better," anyway? These are questions that young people have pondered for generations. Adults have always tended to cast a critical eye on new and different forms of entertainment, whether video games today; television in the 1950s; radio a generation earlier; even, ironically enough, the novel itself when it first emerged as mass media in the early eighteenth century.*

*In his book, provocatively titled* Everything Bad Is Good for You: How Today's Pop Culture Is Actually Making Us Smarter, *the cultural critic Steven Johnson argues that, far from encouraging mental passivity and intellectual laziness, much of today's popular culture actually makes greater thinking demands of young people than ever before. From video games such as* The Legend of Zelda *that require complex problem-solving skills to television shows like* Lost *that weave complex plots in a fragmented style over multiple episodes, many newer forms of popular culture can be enjoyed only with intense concentration and even participation from fans. By focusing too much on the content of a game such as* Grand Theft Auto, *Johnson says that critics miss how difficult and cognitively challenging the game actually is. This excerpt is from chapter 1 of his book.*

Let it Bii: The Beatles as
Wii avatars

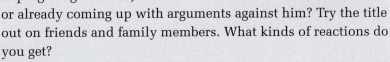

## **Before You Read**

1. Johnson's title,
   *Everything Bad Is Good for
   You: How Today's Pop
   Culture Is Actually Making
   Us Smarter,* clearly wants to
   attract a reader's attention and
   provoke him or her at the
   same time. Write about your
   initial reactions to Johnson's
   title. Do you find yourself
   hoping to agree with Johnson
   or already coming up with arguments against him? Try the title
   out on friends and family members. What kinds of reactions do
   you get?

2. What are your popular culture guilty pleasures: activities and hobbies
   that you enjoy but that you suspect others might see as a waste of time?
   Write about what you like most about these activities, whether it's
   playing a video game, spending time online with friends, or shopping
   at a mall. Come up with your own defense of these activities before
   reading Johnson's essay. In what ways might these activities make
   you smarter?

One of the best ways to grasp the cognitive virtues of game playing is to ask committed players to describe what's going on in their heads halfway through a long virtual adventure like Zelda or Half-Life.[1] It's crucial here not to ask what's happening in the game world, but rather what's happening to the players mentally: what problems they're actively working on, what objectives they're trying to achieve. In my experience, most gamers will be more inclined to show rather than tell the probing they've done; they'll have internalized flaws or patterns in the simulation without being fully aware of what they're doing. Certain strategies just *feel* right.

1 The Legend of Zelda and Half-Life are popular video games.

But if the gamers' probing is semiconscious, their awareness of mid-game *objectives* will be crystal clear. They'll be able to give you an explicit account of what they need to do to reach the goals that the game has laid out for them. Many of these goals will have been obscure in the opening sequences of the game, but by the halfway point, players have usually constructed a kind of to-do list that governs their strategy. If probing is all about depth, exploring the buried logic of the simulation, tracking objectives is a kind of temporal thinking, a looking forward to all the hurdles that separate you from the game's completion.

Tracking objectives seems simple enough. If you stopped playing in the early nineties, or if you only know about games from secondhand accounts, you'd probably assume that the mid-game objectives would sound something like this: Shoot that guy over there! Or: Avoid the blue monsters! Or: Find the magic key!

But interrupt a player in the middle of a Zelda quest, and ask her what her objectives are, and you'll get a much more interesting answer. Interesting for two reasons: first, the sheer number of objectives simultaneously at play; and second, the nested, hierarchical way in which those objectives have to be mentally organized. For comparison's sake, here's what the state of mind of a Pac-Man player would look like mid-game circa 1981:

1. Move the joystick in order to...
  2. Eat all the dots in order to...
    3. Get to the next level in order to...
      4. Reach level 256 (the final one) or a new high score.

Those objectives could be mildly complicated with the addition of one subcategory, which would look like this:

1. Your ultimate goal is to clear all the board of dots.
  2. Your immediate goal is to complete the current maze.
    3. To do this, you must move the joystick through the maze and avoid the monsters.
      3a. You may also clear the board of monsters by eating large dots.
      3b. You may also eat the fruit for bonus points.

A real-world game like checkers would generate a list of comparable simplicity:

1. Your goal is to capture all of your opponent's pieces.
2. To do this, you must move one piece each turn, capturing pieces where possible.
    2a. You may also revive your own captured pieces by reaching the other side of the board.

A map of the objectives in the latest Zelda game, The Wind Walker, looks quite different:

1. Your ultimate goal is to rescue your sister.
2. To do this, you must defeat the villain Ganon.
3. To do this, you need to obtain legendary weapons.
4. To locate the weapons, you need the pearl of Din.
5. To get the pearl of Din, you need to cross the ocean.
6. To cross the ocean, you need to find a sailboat.
7. To do all the above, you need to stay alive and healthy.
8. To do all the above, you need to move the controller.

The eight items can be divided into two groups, each with a slightly different purchase on the immediate present. The last two items (7 and 8) are almost metabolic in nature, the basics of virtual self-preservation: keep your character alive, with maximum power and, where possible, flush with cash. Like many core survival behaviors, some of these objectives take quite a bit of training—learning the navigation interface and mapping it onto the controller, for instance—but once you've mastered them, you don't necessarily have to think about what you're doing. You've internalized or automated the knowledge, just as you did years ago when you learned how to run or climb or talk.

Beyond the horizon of those immediate needs lie the six remaining master objectives. These are forward projections that color the immediate present. They're like constellations guiding your ship through uncertain waters. Lose sight of them and you're adrift.

But those master objectives are rarely the player's central focal point, because most of the game is spent solving smaller problems that stand in the way of achieving one of the primary goals. In this sense, our list of eight nested objectives is a gross simplification of the actual problem solving that goes on in a game like Zelda. Zoom in on just one of these objectives—finding the pearl of Din—and the list of objectives running through the player's mind would look something like this:

To locate the items, you need the pearl of Din from the islanders.
    To get this, you need to help them solve their problem.
    To do this, you need to cheer up the Prince.

To do this, you need to get a letter from the girl.
To do this, you need to find the girl in the village.

With the letter to the Prince, you must now befriend the Prince.
To do this, you need to get to the top of Dragon Roost Mt.
To do this, you must get to the other side of the gorge.
To do this, you must fill up the gorge with water so you can swim across.
To do this, you must use a bomb to blow up the rock blocking the water.
To do this, you must make the bomb plant grow.
To do this, you must collect water in a jar that the girl gave you.

Once on the other side, you must cross lava.
To do this, you must knock down statues on either side of the lava.
To do this, you must throw bombs into holes in the statues.
To do this, you must pull up bombs and aim them.

Once past the lava, you must get into the cavern.
To do this, you must pull statues out of the way.

Once in the cavern, you must get to the next room.
To do this, you need to kill the guards in your way.
To do this, you need to fight with the controller.
To do this, you need to obtain a key to the locked door.
To do this, you must light the two unlit torches in the room.
To do this, you must obtain your own source of fire.
To do this, you must pick up a wooden staff and light it.

I'll spare you the entire sequence for this one objective, which would continue on for another page unabridged. And remember, this is merely a snapshot of an hour or so of play from a title that averages around forty hours to complete. And remember, too, that almost all of these objectives have to be deciphered by the player on his own, assuming he's not consulting a game guide. These local objectives make up the primary texture of the game; they're what you spend most of your time working through. Gamers sometimes talk about the units formed by these steps as a "puzzle." You hit a point in the game where you know you need to do something, but there's some obstruction in your way, and the game conventions signal to you that you've encountered a puzzle. You're not lost, or confused; in fact, you're on precisely the right track—it's just the game designers have artfully deposited a puzzle in the middle of that track.

I call the mental labor of managing all these simultaneous objectives "telescoping" because of the way the objectives nest inside one another like a collapsed telescope. I like the term as well because part of this skill lies in focusing on immediate problems while still maintaining a long-distance view. You can't progress far in a game if you simply deal with the puzzles you stumble across; you have to coordinate them with the ultimate objectives on the horizon. Talented gamers have mastered the ability to keep all these varied objectives alive in their heads simultaneously.

Telescoping should not be confused with multitasking. Holding this nested sequence of interlinked objectives in your mind is not the same as the classic multitasking teenager scenario, where they're listening to their iPod while instant messaging their friends and Googling for research on a term paper. Multitasking is the ability to handle a chaotic stream of unrelated objectives. Telescoping is all about order, not chaos; it's about constructing the proper hierarchy of tasks and moving through the tasks in the correct sequence. It's about perceiving relationships and determining priorities.

If telescoping involves a sequence, by the same token the feeling it conjures in the brain is not, I think, a *narrative* feeling. There are layers to narratives, to be sure, and they inevitably revolve around a mix of the present and future, between what's happening now and the tantalizing question of where it's all headed. But narratives are built out of events, not tasks. They happen *to* you. In the game world you're forced to define and execute the tasks; if your definitions get blurry or are poorly organized, you'll have trouble playing. You can still enjoy a book without explicitly concentrating on where the narrative will take you two chapters out, but in game worlds you need that long-term planning as much as you need present-tense focus. In a sense, the closest analog to the way gamers are thinking is the way programmers think when they write code: a nested series of instructions with multiple layers, some focused on the basic tasks of getting information in and out of memory, some focused on higher-level functions like how to represent the program's activity to the user. A program is a sequence, but not a narrative; playing a video game generates a series of events that retrospectively sketch out a narrative, but the pleasures and challenges of playing don't equate with the pleasures of following a story.

There is something profoundly *lifelike* in the art of probing and telescoping. Most video games take place in worlds that are deliberately fanciful in nature, and even the most realistic games can't compare to the vivid, detailed illusion of the reality that novels or movies concoct for us. But our lives are not stories, at least in the present tense—we don't passively consume a narrative thread. (We turn our lives into stories after the fact, after the decisions have been made, and the events have unfolded.) But we do probe new environments for hidden rules and patterns; we do build telescoping hierarchies of objectives that govern our lives on both micro and macro time frames. Traditional narratives have much to teach us, of course: they can enhance our powers of communication, and our insight into the human psyche. But if you were designing a cultural form explicitly to train the cognitive muscles of the brain, and you had to choose between a device that trains the mind's ability to follow narrative events, and one that enhanced the mind's skills at probing and telescoping—well, let's just say we're fortunate not to have to make that choice.

Still, I suspect that some readers may be cringing at the subject matter of those Zelda objectives. Here again, the problem lies in adopting aesthetic standards designed to evaluate literature or drama in determining whether we should take the video games seriously. Consider this sequence from our telescoping inventory:

> With the letter to the Prince, you must now befriend the Prince.
>> To do this, you need to get to the top of Dragon Roost Mt.
>>> To do this, you must get to the other side of the gorge.
>>>> To do this, you must fill up the gorge with water so you can swim across.
>>>>> To do this, you must use a bomb to blow up the rock blocking the water.
>>>>> To do this, you must make the bomb plant grow.
>>>>>> To do this, you must collect water in a jar that the girl gave you.

If you approach this description with aesthetic expectations borrowed from the world of literature the content seems at face value to be child's play: blowing up bombs to get to Dragon Roost Mountain; watering explosive plants. A high school English teacher would look at this and say: There's no psychological depth here, no moral quandaries, no poetry. And he'd be right! But comparing these games to *The Iliad* or *The Great Gatsby* or *Hamlet* relies on a false premise: that the intelligence of these games lies in their content, in the themes and characters they represent. I would argue that the cognitive challenges of video gaming are much more usefully compared to another educational genre that you will no doubt recall from your school days:

> Simon is conducting a probability experiment. He randomly selects a tag from a set of tags that are numbered from 1 to 100 and then returns the tag to the set. He is trying to draw a tag that matches his favorite number, 21. He has not matched his number after 99 draws.
>
> What are the chances he will match his number on the 100th draw?
>
> A. 1 out of 100
> B. 99 out of 100
> C. 1 out of 1
> D. 1 out of 2

Judged by the standards employed by our English teacher, this passage—taken from the Massachusetts Comprehensive Assessment exam for high school math—would be an utter failure. Who is this Simon? We know nothing about him; he is a cipher to us, a prop. There are no flourishes in the prose, nothing but barren facts, describing a truly useless activity. Why would anyone want to number a hundred tags and then go about trying to randomly select a favorite number? What is Simon's motivation?

Word problems of this sort have little to offer in the way of moral lessons or psychological depth; they won't make students more effective communicators or teach them technical skills. But most of us readily agree that they are good for the mind on some fundamental level: they teach abstract skills in probability, in pattern recognition, in understanding causal relations that can be applied in countless situations, both personal and professional. The problems that confront the gamers of Zelda can be readily translated into this form, and indeed in translating a core property of the experience is revealed:

> You need to cross a gorge to reach a valuable destination. At one end of the gorge a large rock stands in front of a river, blocking the flow of water. Around the edge of the rock a number of small flowers are growing. You have been given a jar by another character. How can you cross the gorge?
>
> A. Jump across it.
> B. Carry small pails of water from the river and pour them in the gorge, and then swim across.
> C. Water the plants, and then use the bombs they grow to blow up the rock, releasing the water, and then swim across.
> D. Go back and see if you've missed some important tool in an earlier scene.

Again, the least interesting thing about this text is the substance of the story. You could perhaps meditate on the dramatic irony inherent in bomb-growing flowers, or analyze the gift economy relationship introduced with a crucial donation of the jar. But those interpretations will go only so far, because what's important here is not the content of the Zelda world, but the way that world has been organized to tax the problem-solving skills of the player. To be sure, the pleasure of gaming goes beyond this kind of problem solving; the objects and textures of the worlds offer rich aesthetic experiences; many networked games offer intriguing social exchanges; increasingly the artificial intelligence embedded in some virtual characters provides amazing interactions. But these are all ultimately diversions. You can't make progress in the game without learning the rules of the environment. On the simplest level, the Zelda player learns how to grow bombs out of flowers. But the collateral learning of the experience offers a far more profound reward: the ability to probe and telescope in difficult and ever-changing situations. It's not *what* the player is thinking about, but the *way* she's thinking.

At first glance, it might be tempting to connect the complexity of video games with the more familiar idea of "information overload" associated with the rise of electronic media. But a crucial difference exists. Information overload is a kind of backhanded compliment you'll often hear about today's culture: there's too much data flowing into our lives, but at least we're getting better at managing that data stream, even if we may be approaching some kind of threshold point where our senses will simply be overwhelmed. This is a quantitative argument, not a qualitative one. It's nice to be able to watch TV, talk on the phone, and read your email all at the same time, but it's a superficial skill, not a deep one. It usually involves skimming the surface of the incoming data, picking out the relevant details, and moving on to the next stream. Multimedia pioneer Linda Stone has coined a valuable term for this kind of processing: continuous partial attention. You're paying attention, but only partially. That lets you cast a wider net, but it also runs the risk of keeping you from really studying the fish.

Probing and telescoping represent another—equally important—tendency in the culture: the emergence of forms that encourage participatory thinking and analysis, forms that challenge the mind to make sense of an environment, not just play catch-up with the acceleration curve. I think for many people who do not have experience with them, games seem like an extension of the rapid-fire visual editing techniques pioneered by MTV twenty years ago: a seismic increase in images-per-second without a corresponding increase in analysis or sense-making. But the reality of MTV visuals is not that the eye learns to interpret all the images as they fly by, perceiving new relationships between them. Instead, the eye learns to tolerate chaos, to experience disorder as an aesthetic experience, the way the ear learned to appreciate distortion in music a generation before. To non-players, games bear a superficial resemblance to music videos: flashy graphics; the layered mix of image, music, and text; the occasional burst of speed, particularly during the pre-rendered opening sequences. But what you actually *do* in playing a game—the way your mind has to work—is radically different. It's not about tolerating or aestheticizing chaos; it's about finding order and meaning in the world, and making decisions that help create that order.[...]

---

## Working with the Text

1. Johnson writes about the importance of asking game players not what is going on in the game while they are playing, but what is going on in their heads: the mental processes they are following to complete the objectives and puzzles they encounter in the game. To make his point about the greater intellectual demands made by today's popular culture, he contrasts some typical contemporary video games with older games,

both electronic and otherwise, such as Pac-Man or checkers. Continue his investigation by examining other forms of games and puzzle-solving activities, whether literal puzzle solving such as a crossword or Sudoku, a sport like basketball, or a game like Monopoly. What kinds of decisions and forms of analysis do players need to do to be successful? Use the outlining format that Johnson employs to describe the thought processes that go on in each game or sport.

2. Define what Johnson means by "telescoping." For example, how does he differentiate telescoping from multitasking, and why does he think this distinction is important? How is telescoping different from the process of following a narrative in a book or movie? What are the different strengths of each, according to Johnson? In what real-world applications would telescoping be useful?

3. Why does Johnson think that comparing the narratives of video games to works of literature is not helpful? What aspects of video games do such comparisons ignore? How does he describe the different virtues of reading literature and playing video games?

4. Use Johnson's ideas to write a proposal for creating a place for video games in schools. You might argue for starting a high school video-game team, or adding gaming as a playtime activity for younger children. At the college level, how could you use Johnson's ideas to argue for more courses in video games or gaming?

## from *Glen to Glenda and Back Again*

### Sherry Turkle

*In the early 1990s, a recurring skit called "It's Pat!" appeared on* Saturday Night Live *featuring a character of indeterminate gender played by the comedian Julia Sweeney. The plot of every segment followed the same pattern: people encountering the title character for the first time became obsessed with trying to figure out Pat's gender. They asked trick questions meant to elicit responses that would fix Pat's identity, and each time he or she answered in an ambiguous way that only frustrated the questioner.*

*The humor of the skit derived from both our social need to know the gender of those we meet even briefly, and the unexpected instability of the cues and clues we look for to make that determination: clothes, hairstyle, vocal mannerisms, names, body shape, and size. As we laughed at the skit, we could also think about why knowing someone's gender seems so important to us as well as how unexamined many of our assumptions about gender identity really are.*

*When it comes to cyberculture, the growing popularity of online communication focuses questions of gender and identity squarely on issues of language use. After all, in a chat room,* on a social-networking site, or playing an online game, what indicators of gender do we have other than language? In the end, all of our evidence for gender comes in the form of writing, of the personal identities created in language by others sitting at their keyboards. The anonymity of the computer quickly led many people to realize they could use the online world to experiment with identity and gender, to create and try out new gender identities for themselves.

The researcher and sociologist Sherry Turkle has been studying and writing about online identity since the 1980s. She has been particularly interested in the phenomenon of multiplayer online role-playing games. In the following article, she discusses her experiences participating in a multiple user domain (MUD) game, where players create their own online identities (MUDs have since evolved into MMORPGs, which are larger and even more complex forms of online role playing). She focuses on her experiments in changing gender online, and she interviews other players who have spent extensive time online enacting another gender.

## Before You Read

Can you tell the gender of a writer? Have students in your class write paragraphs on the topic of "how to tell the gender of a writer" and then duplicate them or post them anonymously. Make guesses about the gender identities of the samples and write and discuss why you made the judgments you did. What cues and clues do you look for in writing that you associate with gender?

A virtual news conference in Second Life attracts investors and Mr. Kool-Aid.

hen I first logged on to a MUD, I named and described a character but forgot to give it a gender. I was struggling with the technical aspects of the MUD universe—the difference between various commands such as "saying" and "emoting," "paging" and "whispering"—and gender was the last thing on my mind. This rapidly changed when a male-presenting character named Jiffy asked me if I were "really an it." I experienced an unpleasurable sense of disorientation that immediately gave way to an unfamiliar sense of freedom.

When Jiffy's question appeared on my screen, I was standing in a room of LambdaMOO—one of the first very popular MUDs—filled with characters engaged in sexual banter, Animal House–style. The innuendoes, double entendres, and leering invitations were scrolling by at a fast clip; I felt awkward, as if I were at a party I'd been invited to by mistake. It reminded me of kissing games in junior high, where it was both awful to be chosen and awful not to be chosen. Now, on the MUD, I had a new option: Playing a male might allow me to feel less out of place. People would expect me to make the first move, and I could choose not to. I could "lurk," stand on the sidelines and observe the action. Boys, after all, were not considered prudes if they were too cool to play kissing games. They were not categorized as wallflowers if they held back and didn't ask girls to dance. They could simply be shy in a manly way, cool, above it all.

Two days later I was back in the MUD. After I typed the command that joined me, in Boston, to the computer in California where the MUD resided, I discovered I'd lost my password. This meant I couldn't play my own character but had to log on as a guest. As such, I was assigned a color: magenta. As "Magenta_guest," I was again without gender. While I struggled with the basic commands, other players were typing messages for all to see: "Magenta_guest gazes hot and enraptured at the approach of Fire_Eater." Again I was tempted to hide from the frat-party atmosphere by passing as a man.

Much later, when I did play a male character, I finally experienced the permission to move freely that I had always imagined to be men's birthright. Not only was I approached less frequently, but I found it easier to respond to unwanted overtures with aplomb, saying something like, "That's flattering, Ribald_Temptress, but I'm otherwise engaged." My sense of freedom didn't involve just a different attitude about sexual advances—which now seemed less threatening. As a woman, I have a hard time deflecting a request for conversation by asserting my own agenda. As a MUD male, doing so (nicely) seemed natural; it never struck me as dismissive or rude. In this way, I was learning about the construction of gender—and learning about myself.

It was easy to see that virtual gender-swapping teaches the first lesson of gender studies: the difference between sex as biology and gender as a social construct. When a man goes online as a woman, he soon finds that maintaining this fiction is difficult. To pass as a woman for any length of time requires understanding just how gender inflects speech, manner, and the interpretation of experience. Women attempting to pass as men face the same kind of challenge. One says: "It is not so easy. You have to think about it, to make up a life, a job, a set of reactions." Pavel Curtis, the founder of LambdaMOO, has observed that when a female-presenting character is called something like FabulousHotBabe, there's usually a real-life man behind the mask. Another experienced MUDder shares this piece of folklore: "If a female-presenting character's description of her beauty goes on for more than two paragraphs, [the player behind the character] is sure to be an ugly woman."

Case, a 34-year-old industrial designer who is happily married to a co-worker, told me that he currently plays on several MUDs as a female character. When I ask whether MUDding ever causes him emotional pain, he says, "Yes, but also the kind of learning that comes from hard times.

"I'm having pain in my playing now," he continues. "The woman I'm playing in MedievalMUSH [her name is Mairead] is having an interesting relationship with a fellow. Mairead is a lawyer. It costs so much to go to law school that it has to be paid for by a corporation or a noble house. A man she met and fell in love with was a nobleman. He paid for her law school. He bought my contract. [Note that Case slips into the first person here.] Now he wants to marry me, although I'm a commoner. I finally said yes. I try to talk to him about the fact that I'm essentially his property. He says, 'Oh no, no, no. We'll pick you up, set you on your feet, the whole world is open to you.'

"But every time I assert myself, I get pushed down. It's an incredibly psychologically damaging thing to do to a person. And the very thing that he liked about her—that she was independent, strong, said what was on her mind—it is all being bled out of her."

Case looks at me with a wry smile and sighs, "A woman's life."

Case has played Mairead for nearly a year, but even a brief experience playing a character of another gender can be evocative. William James said that philosophy is the art of imagining alternatives. Virtual communities can test philosophy about gender issues via action; it's a form of consciousness-raising. For example, on many MUDs, offering technical assistance has become a common way in which male characters "purchase" female attention, analogous to picking up the check at a real-life dinner. In real life, our expectations about sex roles (who offers help, who buys dinner, who brews the coffee) can become so ingrained that we no longer notice them. On MUDs, expectations are expressed in visible textual actions, widely witnessed and openly discussed.

When men playing females are plied with unrequested offers of help on MUDs, they often remark that such chivalries communicate a belief in female incompetence. When women play males on MUDs and realize that they are no longer being offered help, some say those offers of help may well have led them to believe they needed it. As a woman, "First you ask for help because you think it will be expedient," says a college sophomore, "then you realize that you aren't developing the skills to figure things out for yourself."

Shakespeare used the evocative nature of gender-swapping as a plot device for reframing and reconsidering personal and political choices. *As You Like It* is a classic example: The comedy uses gender-swapping to reveal identity and increase the complexity of relationships. In the play, Rosalind, the duke's daughter, is exiled from the court of her uncle Frederick, who has usurped her father's throne. Frederick's daughter, Rosalind's cousin Celia, flees with Rosalind to the magical forest of Arden. When Rosalind remarks that they might be in danger because "beauty provoketh thieves sooner than gold," Celia suggests that they rub dirt on their faces and wear drab clothing, a tactic—becoming unattractive—that often allows women greater social ease. Rosalind takes the idea a step further: They will dress as men.

The disguise is both physical ("A gallant curtle-ax on my thigh, / A boar spear in my hand") and emotional ("and—in my heart, / Lie there what hidden women's fear there will").

Rosalind does not endorse an essential difference between men and women; rather, she suggests that men routinely adopt the same kind of pose she is now choosing. Biological men have to construct male gender just as biological women have to construct female gender. By making themselves unattractive, Rosalind and Celia end up less feminine; they deconstruct their female gender. Both posing as men and deconstructing femininity are games that female MUDders play.

In addition to virtual cross-dressing and creating character descriptions that deconstruct gender, MUDders swap genders as double agents. That is, men play women pretending to be men, and women play men pretending to be women. Shakespeare's characters play these games as well. When Rosalind flees Frederick's court, she is in love with Orlando. In the forest of Arden, disguised as the boy Ganymede, she encounters Orlando, himself lovesick for Rosalind. As Ganymede, Rosalind says she will try to cure Orlando of his love by playing Rosalind, pointing out the flaws of femininity as she does so. In current stagings, Rosalind usually is played by a woman who, at this point in the play, pretends to be a man who pretends to be a woman.

When Rosalind/Ganymede and Orlando meet "man to man," they are able to speak easily, free of the courtly conventions that constrain communications between men and women. In this way, the play suggests that donning a mask—adopting a persona—can be a step toward a deeper truth. This is also how MUDders regard their experiences as virtual selves.

One young woman, Zoe, describes her virtual experience: "I played a man for two years. As a man, I could be firm and people would think I was a great wizard. As a woman, drawing the line and standing firm has always made me feel like a bitch, and, actually, I feel that people saw me as one, too. As a man,

I was liberated from all that. I learned from my mistakes. I got better at being firm but not rigid. I practiced, safe from criticism."

What Zoe's and Case's stories have in common is that a virtual gender swap gave them a greater sense of their emotional range. There was a chance to discover, as Rosalind and Orlando did in the Forest of Arden, that for both sexes, gender is constructed.

Having literally written our gender-swapping online personas into existence, they can be a kind of Rorschach. We can use them to become more aware of what we project into everyday life, and the ways those projections affect others. This means that we can use the virtual to reflect constructively on the real.

Indeed, in my experience, life in cyberspace can provide very serious play. We take it lightly at our risk. And in my research I have found that people who cultivate an awareness of what stands behind the screen personas they craft do best in using virtual experience for personal transformation. Those who make the most of their life on the screen come to it in a spirit of self-reflection.

---

## Working with the Text

1. At the beginning of the article, Turkle discusses her initial experience of having no identifiable gender online and then assuming the identity of a male. What are her impressions about the differences she encounters in assuming a male identity? What were your own reactions to observations such as, "Playing a male might make me feel less out of place"? How do your own thoughts and feelings about gender affect how you respond to Turkle's speculations? Would you have similar ideas and anticipations?

2. In discussing how gender is as much a function of the roles we play as our biological composition, Turkle writes, "In real life, our expectations about sex roles (who offers help, who buys dinner, who brews the coffee) can become so ingrained that we no longer notice them. On MUDs, expectations are expressed in visible textual actions, widely witnessed and openly discussed." In other words, playing with gender in MUDs makes us more aware of just what these expectations are in the "real" world. Working as a class, list what you think some of the social expectations are for sex roles. To generate ideas, you might start by defining a specific situation or scenario.

3. If you were going to write in the persona of a different gender identity, what do you think the biggest challenges would be? Create an alternate identity and try writing in the person of this new identity. To re-create Turkle's experience, you might join a MUD or an MMORPG online and try to "live" in this new identity. If you are already experienced in

online role-playing games, write about these experiences and compare them with Turkle's observations. If you are new to these games, write about what you find most surprising about the experience.

4. In the end, Turkle argues that experimenting with identity online can give users "a greater sense of their emotional range" and that we can use these experiences to "to become more aware of what we project into everyday life, and the ways those projections affect others." After reading Turkle's article, what strikes you as the most important lessons that Turkle and the people she interviewed learned from gender swapping online? If you have participated in the same experiment, do you agree with Turkle's observations? Are there any concerns you have or possible negative consequences you might foresee? What do you think would most attract people and most discourage people from trying new online identities?

## "The Mulatto Millennium: Waking Up in the Age of Racial Ambiguity"

### Danzy Senna

*In the year 2000, the U.S. Census Bureau announced that it would begin reporting a new racial category in its report on the size and demographic makeup of the U.S. population. The term* multiracial *would include all those who checked more than one of the listed racial identities on the census form. The decision was the result of a long discussion and debate over the inclusion of a multiracial category, and the actions by the Census Bureau were met with strong reactions of both approval and dismay. To some, the new category was a step toward recognizing the complexity of racial and ethnic identity in the United States. To others, the change in counting procedures threatened to underreport the numbers of certain historic racial categories in ways that could hurt the continuing battle against racial discrimination.*

*The category of multiracial represents another episode in the long and troubled history of race in the United States. Some claim the category as a way of escape from being pigeonholed into one group or another; others see it as a way to deny the reality of continuing racial oppression. The idea of race has taken on new dimensions in the era of cyberspace, where the creation of online identities raises the prospect of what some call "racial tourism": trying on new racial identities in ways that can be seen as both liberating and demeaning.*

*In her debut novel* Caucasia, *Danzy Senna told a fictional story of two sisters informed by her own experiences growing up as "a black girl with a WASP mother and black-Mexican father," as she describes herself in the essay "The Mulatto Millennium: Waking Up in the Age of Racial Ambiguity." In this piece, which combines a serious discussion of contemporary racial issues in America with a provocative sense of humor, Senna offers her own opinions about the appeal of a multiracial identity in modern-day America.*

## Before You Read

1. What were your earliest memories of encountering the idea of race? What questions and reactions do you remember having? Who did you talk with about this experience? Write a brief essay in which you recall an early experience with the concept of race and discuss what effect you think this experience has had on the development of your own opinions about identity and race in America.

2. What is your personal reaction to the addition of the category of multiracial to the Census Bureau's description of the U.S. population? What do you see as most positive about the decision, and what are the areas of potential concern? As you read Senna's essay, look for ways in which she raises points or provokes ideas about the subject you may not have thought of before.

Strange to wake up and realize you're in style. That's what happened to me just the other morning. It was the first day of the new millennium, and I woke to find that mulattos had taken over. They were everywhere. Playing golf, running the airwaves, opening restaurants, modeling clothes, starring in musicals with names like *Show Me the Miscegenation!* The radio played a steady stream of Lenny Kravitz, Sade, and Mariah Carey. I thought I'd died and gone to Berkeley. But then I realized that, according to the racial zodiac, 2000 is the official Year of the Mulatto. Pure breeds (at least black ones) are out; hybridity is in. America loves us in all of our half-caste glory. The president announced on Friday that beige will be the official color of the millennium.

Before all of this radical ambiguity, I considered myself a black girl. Not your ordinary black girl, if such a thing exists. But rather, a black girl with a WASP mother and black-Mexican father, and a face that harks back to Andalusia, not Africa. I was

A Japanese *ganguro* girl

born in 1970, when *black* described a people bonded not by shared complexion or hair texture but by shared history.

Not only was I black, but I sneered at those by-products of miscegenation who chose to identify as mixed, not black. I thought it wishy-washy, an act of flagrant assimilation, treason-passing, even. I was an enemy of the mulatto people.

My parents made me this way. In Boston circa 1975, mixed wasn't an option. "A fight, a fight, a nigga and a white!" echoed from schoolyards during recess. You were either white or black. No checking "Other." No halvsies. No in between. Black people, the bottom of Boston's social totem pole, were inevitably the most accepting of difference; they were the only race to come in all colors, and so there I found myself. Sure, I got strange reactions from all quarters when I called myself black. But black people usually got over their initial surprise and welcomed me into the ranks. White folks were the most uncomfortable with the dissonance between the face they saw and the race they didn't. Upon learning who I was, they grew paralyzed with fear that they might have "slipped up" in my presence, that is, said something racist, not knowing there was a Negro in their midst. Often, they had.

Let it be clear—my parents' decision to raise us as black wasn't based on any one-drop-of-blood rule from the days of slavery, and it certainly wasn't based on our appearance, that crude reasoning many black-identified mixed people use: If the world sees me as black, I must be black. If it had been based on appearance, my sister would have been black and my brother Mexican, and I Jewish. Instead, my parents' decision arose out of the black power movement, which made identifying as black not a pseudoscientific rule but a conscious choice. Now that we don't have to anymore, we choose to. Because black is beautiful. Because black is not a burden, but a privilege.

Some might say my parents went too far. I remember my father schooling me and my siblings on our racial identity. He would grill us over a greasy linoleum kitchen table, a single bright lightbulb swinging overhead: "Do you have any black friends? How many? Who? And we, his obedient children, his soldiers in the battle for negritude, would rattle off the names of the black kids we called friends.

Something must have sunk in, because my sister and I grew up with disdain for those who identified as mulatto. A very particular breed got under my skin: the kind who answered, meekly, "Everything" to that incessant question, "What are you?" I veered away from groups of them-children, like myself, who had been born of interracial minglings after dark. Instead, I surrounded myself with bodies darker than my own, hoping the color might rub off on me.

One year, while working as an investigative journalist in Hollywood, I made up a list, evidence I've long since burned. Luckily for my career, it was never published. It was an exposé of who is passing in Hollywood, called "And You Thought It Was Just a Tan?" There were three categories:

**Black Folks You May Not Have Known Are Black**
- Mariah Carey
- Jennifer Beals
- Tom Hanks
- Carly Simon
- Slash
- Arnold Schwarzenegger
- Johnny Depp
- Michael Jackson
- Kevin Bacon
- Robin Quivers
- Elizabeth Berkeley
- Paula Abdul

**Black Folks Who May Not Know They Are Black**
- Mariah Carey
- Jennifer Beals
- Tom Hanks
- Carly Simon
- Slash
- Arnold Schwarzenegger
- Johnny Depp
- Michael Jackson
- Kevin Bacon
- Robin Quivers
- Elizabeth Berkeley
- Paula Abdul

**Black Folks You Kinda Wish Weren't Black**
- O. J. Simpson
- Michael Jackson
- Gary Coleman
- Robin Quivers

Needless to say, my list wouldn't have gone over too well with the Mulatto Nation posse (M.N. to those in the know). It was nearly published in a local newsweekly, but the editors balked at the last minute. I bet they're thanking their lucky stars now; in this age of fluidity, it doesn't pay to be blacker than thou.

These days, M.N. folks in Washington have their own census category—multiracial—but the extremist wing of the Mulatto Nation finds it inadequate. They want to take things a step further. I guess they have a point. Why lump us all together? Eskimos have forty different words for snow. In South Africa, during apartheid, they had fourteen different types of coloreds. But we've decided on one word, multiracial, to describe a whole nation of diverse people who have absolutely no relation, cultural or otherwise, to one another. In light of this deficiency, I propose the following coinages:

- **Standard Mulatto:** White mother, black father. Half-nappy hair, skin described as "pasty yellow" in winter but turns caramel tan in summer. Germanic-Afro features. Often raised in isolation from others of its kind. Does not discover "black identity" till college, when there is usually some change in hair, clothing, or speech, so that the parents don't recognize the child who arrives home for Christmas vacation ("Honey, there's a black kid at the door").

- **African American:** The most common form of mulatto in North America, this breed, seldom described as mixed, is a combination of African, European, and Native American. May come in any skin tone, from any cultural background. Often believe themselves to be "pure" due to historical distance from the original mixture, which was most often achieved through rape.

- **Jewlatto:** The second most prevalent form, this breed is made in the commingling of Jews and blacks who met when they were registering voters down South during Freedom Summer or at a CORE meeting. Jewlattos often, though not necessarily, have a white father and black mother (as opposed to the more common black father and white mother). They are likely to be raised in a diverse setting (New York City, Berkeley), around others of their kind. Jewlattos are most easily spotted amid the flora and fauna of Brown University. Famous Jewlattos include Lenny Kravitz and Lisa Bonet (and we can't forget Zoe, their love child).

- **Mestizo:** A more complicated mixture: Either the black or the white parent claims a third race (Native American, Latino) in the parent's background and thus confuses the child more. The mestizo is likely to be mistaken for some other, totally distinct ethnicity (Italian, Arab, Mexican, Jewish, East Indian, Native American, Puerto Rican) and in fact will be touted by strangers as a perfect representative of the totally new race ("Your face brings me right back to Calcutta").

- **Cultural Mulatto:** Any American born after 1967.

- **Blulatto:** A highly rare breed of "blue-blooded" mulattos who can trace their lineage back to the Mayflower. Females are legally entitled to membership in the Daughters of the American Revolution. Blulattos have been spotted in Cambridge and Berkeley but should not be confused with Jewlattos. The blulatto's mother is almost always the white one, and is either a poet or a painter who disdains her WASP heritage. The father is almost always the black one, is highly educated, and disdains his black heritage.

- **Cablinasian:** An exotic breed found mostly in California, the mother of all mixtures: Asian, American Indian, black, and Caucasian. These show mulattos have great performance skills; they will be whoever the crowd wants them to be, and can switch at the drop of a hat. They do not, however, answer to the name black. If you spot a Cablinasian, contact the Benetton promotions bureau.
- **Tomatto:** A mixed or black person who behaves in an Uncle Tom–ish fashion. The Tomatto may be found in positions of power touted as a symbol of diversity in otherwise all-white settings. Even if the Tomatto has two black parents, his skin is light and his features mixed. If we ever see a first black president, he will most likely be a Tomatto.
- **Fauxlatto:** A person impersonating a mulatto. Can be of white, black, or other heritage, but for inexplicable reasons claims to be of mixed heritage. See Jamiroquai.

The categories could go on and on, and perhaps, indeed, they will. Where do I fit? That's the strange thing. I fit into none and all of the above. I have been each of the above, or at least mistaken for them, at different moments in my life. But somehow, none feels right. Maybe that makes me a Postlatto.

I've learned to flaunt my mixedness at dinner parties, where the guests (most of them white) ooh and aaah about my flavorful background. I've found it's not so bad being a fetishized object, an exotic bird soaring above the racial landscape. And when they start talking about black people, pure breeds, in that way that before the millennium used to make me squirm, I let them know that I'm neutral, nothing to be afraid of. Sometimes I feel it, that remnant of my old self (the angry black girl with the big mouth) creeping out, but most of the time I don't feel anything at all. Most of the time, I just serve up the asparagus, chimichangas, and fried chicken with a bright, white smile.

---

## Working with the Text

1. Senna writes that her parents' decision to raise her and her sister as black was not based on any theories of genetic ancestry but as a "conscious choice." What important distinctions do you see Senna making about how her parents reached this decision? What were the main reasons for making this decision? What does Senna seem to admire most about her parents decision-making process?
2. Senna refers to a list she complied as a journalist that she describes as "evidence I've long since burned" and that reveals the "true" racial identities of several Hollywood celebrities circa 1990. How seriously did you initially take her list? What questions does it prompt? Which

celebrities were you most skeptical about? After thinking about and discussing the list, how seriously do you take it now? Then think about the point she is making with the lists. Why do you think she includes these celebrities, and who do you see as the audience for her lists?

3. Senna tries to show what can happen when the process of multiracial specificity goes too far with her second list of "new" racial categories. Which categories did you find most humorous? Which most confusing? Did you find the list effective in getting you to agree with Senna's position? How specifically does this parody of racial categories help enforce her point about why she has always tended to consider herself as black rather than multiracial?

4. In the end, Senna says she has moved from feeling angry about the idea of multiracial identification to being "neutral." What do you think she means by the term *neutral*, especially given how suspicious she has been of attempts to use the idea of the multiracial as a way of avoiding more difficult discussions of race in America? Focus especially on the final sentence in her essay. In what ways does this last sentence summarize the issues she has raised in her essay?

# from *American Born Chinese*

## Gene Luen Yang

*The immigrant's story—the narrative of a stranger in a strange land who struggles to find a place after leaving home for a new world—has been a central part of the American experience since the first encounters between Europeans and the indigenous peoples of the Caribbean in the late fifteenth century. From the story of Cabeza de Vaca, a survivor of a failed Spanish expedition in the sixteenth century who wandered lost until being rescued by native peoples with whom he lived for seven years, the history of the United States has been the story of peoples on the move, both voluntarily and involuntarily, searching for new homes, being forcibly displaced from old ones, creating new identities, and transforming the cultures they find.*

*All these stories, whether comic or tragic, whether focused on the fate of one person or of an entire people, share a similar focus on identity: specifically, the tension between preserving a traditional identity rooted in ethnicity and history, and adapting (or the more contested term,* assimilating*) into a new culture. This tension is never a simple opposition between old and new, between one distinct culture and another. Adaptation and assimilation is as much a process of negotiation and compromise as it is abandoning one way of life for another, and the new identities created in turn change the culture into which the immigrants move. In fact, we can think of American culture less as a stable, unchanging collection of values and beliefs and more like an ever-evolving patchwork quilt, composed of intertwined and intertwining cultural experiences and perspectives.*

The term that some cultural critics use to describe this complex process of cultural and personal transformation is hybrid. This term is taken from the biological fact that while we can categorize living beings according to species, in reality every individual plant or animal represents a unique genetic combination, one never seen before and one that will never be duplicated again, but that carries in its genes the history of every previous unique hybrid. In his graphic novel, American Born Chinese, Gene Luen Yang mixes traditional Chinese folktales and mythology with the experiences of recent Chinese immigrants and their first-generation children (including himself) to tell one such hybrid story of adaptation and assimilation, both on the part of newcomers and on the part of the new culture they encounter.

To tell his story, Yang uses the genre of the graphic novel, a form that developed from the comic book. Both the names graphic novel and comic book point to the hybrid nature of this kind of text, combining the visual and the verbal, the serious and the playful, adulthood and childhood. As we have discussed elsewhere in Text Messaging, however, the hybrid nature of the graphic novel may not separate it so much from "real" novels as remind us that all texts, whether pages between hard covers or pixels on a computer screen, are hybrids: combinations of ideas and inspiration from others that we mix and transform into new and unique forms of expressions.

Gene Luen Yang is a cartoonist and graphic novelist who lives and teaches high school in the San Francisco Bay Area. He began his career as a cartoonist in the fifth grade.

## Before You Read

1. Explore the different reactions and interpretations people have to the terms *graphic novel* and *comic book.* Which term seems more familiar? What associations and assumptions do people make based on these terms? Do some research on the term *graphic novel* to come up with your own explanation of why it was invented and why different writers and artists use (or don't use) it.

2. Write about your own personal history with comic books and graphic novels. If this excerpt is your first experience with either genre, explore your own preconceptions and expectations about what you are going to read. If you are a fan of comic books, how would you introduce the form to someone unfamiliar with it? What misconceptions do you suspect they might have?

3. The title of Yang's book, *American Born Chinese,* can be interpreted several different ways. What are the different ways we might read the title, perhaps by introducing punctuation into the phrase, to express different meanings? In what ways are these different interpretations complementary? In what ways do they contradict each other? Why might a writer create a title like this? How do these multiple meanings for the phrase create expectations for what you are going to read in the excerpt?

MY MOTHER ONCE TOLD ME AN OLD CHINESE PARABLE.

< LONG AGO, A MOTHER AND HER YOUNG SON LIVED NEAR A *MARKETPLACE.* >*

* TRANSLATED FROM MANDARIN CHINESE.

< EVERY DAY WHEN THE SON PLAYED, HE PRETENDED TO BUY AND SELL STICKS HE FOUND ON THE STREET, HAGGLING OVER PRICES WITH HIS FRIENDS. >

< THE MOTHER DECIDED TO MOVE. >

< THEY SETTLED INTO A HOUSE NEXT TO A *CEMETERY.* NOW WHEN THE SON PLAYED HE BURNED INCENSE STICKS AND SANG SONGS TO DEAD ANCESTORS. >

< THE MOTHER DECIDED TO MOVE AGAIN. >

< SHE FOUND A HOME ACROSS THE ROAD FROM A *UNIVERSITY.* THE SON NOW SPENT ALL HIS FREE-TIME READING BOOKS ABOUT MATHEMATICS, SCIENCE, AND HISTORY. >

< THE MOTHER AND HER SON STAYED THERE FOR A LONG, LONG TIME. >

SHE FINISHED THE STORY AS WE PULLED UP TO OUR NEW HOUSE.

MY PARENTS ARRIVED IN **AMERICA** AT THE SAME AIRPORT WITHIN A WEEK OF EACH OTHER.

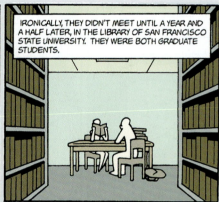

IRONICALLY, THEY DIDN'T MEET UNTIL A YEAR AND A HALF LATER, IN THE LIBRARY OF SAN FRANCISCO STATE UNIVERSITY. THEY WERE BOTH GRADUATE STUDENTS.

FOR TUITION MONEY, MY MOTHER WORKED AT A CANNERY.

MY FATHER SOLD WIGS DOOR-TO-DOOR.

SUAVE!

EVENTUALLY, MY FATHER BECAME AN ENGINEER AND MY MOTHER A LIBRARIAN. JUST BEFORE I WAS BORN, THEY MOVED INTO AN APARTMENT NEAR SAN FRANCISCO **CHINATOWN**. WE STAYED THERE FOR NINE YEARS.

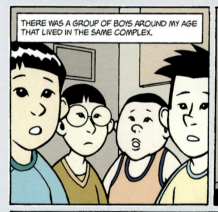

THERE WAS A GROUP OF BOYS AROUND MY AGE THAT LIVED IN THE SAME COMPLEX.

THEY CAME OVER ON SATURDAY MORNINGS TO WATCH CARTOONS. (OUR APARTMENT, BEING ON THE TOP FLOOR, HAD THE BEST RECEPTION.)

<NO, MEGATRON!>

<DON'T DO IT!>

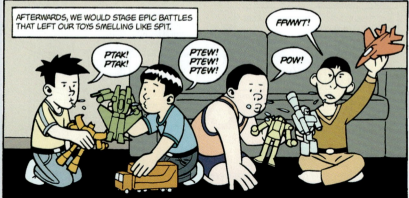

AFTERWARDS, WE WOULD STAGE EPIC BATTLES THAT LEFT OUR TOYS SMELLING LIKE SPIT.

FFWWT!

PTAK! PTAK!

PTEW! PTEW! PTEW!

POW!

EVERY SUNDAY MOTHER USED TO VISIT THE CHINESE HERBALIST JUST AROUND THE CORNER FOR HER ALLERGIES. SHE WOULD ALWAYS TAKE ME ALONG.

CLICK CLACK CLICK

SOMETIMES THE APPOINTMENT LASTED FOR WHAT SEEMED LIKE HOURS. I WOULD SIT IN THE FRONT ROOM, LISTENING TO THE HERBALIST'S WIFE CALCULATE BILLS ON HER ABACUS.

ONE SUNDAY, WHEN BUSINESS WAS ESPECIALLY SLOW AND I WAS ESPECIALLY BORED, THE HERBALIST'S WIFE ASKED,

< SO LITTLE FRIEND, WHAT DO YOU PLAN TO BECOME WHEN YOU GROW UP? >

<...WELL...>

<...I...I WANT TO BE A>

TRANS-FORMER!

..."TRANS- FO- MA?"

< YEAH! > A ROBOT IN DISGUISE! < LIKE THIS ONE! >

< HE CHANGES INTO A TRUCK... >

CLICK CLICK CLACK

<...SEE? > MORE THAN MEETS THE EYE!

< IN THE CARTOON, HE'S ALSO GOT A TRAILER THAT MAGICALLY APPEARS WHENEVER HE TRANS-FORMS, BUT ON THE TOY IT'S A SEPARATE PIECE. >

< SO YOU WANT TO BE A...A...> "TRANS-FO-MA," < HUH? >

< YEAH...BUT MA-MA SAYS THAT'S SILLY. LITTLE BOYS DON'T GROW UP TO BE > TRANSFORMERS.

< OH, I WOULDN'T BE SO SURE ABOUT THAT. I'M GOING TO LET YOU IN ON A **SECRET**, LITTLE FRIEND: >

< IT'S EASY TO BECOME ANYTHING YOU WISH ... >

< ...SO LONG AS YOU'RE WILLING TO FORFEIT YOUR SOUL. >

CLICK CLACK CLICK CLACK

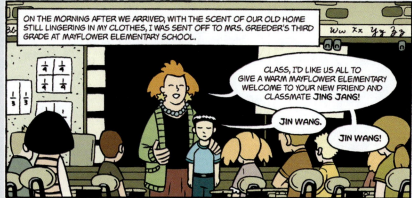

ON THE MORNING AFTER WE ARRIVED, WITH THE SCENT OF OUR OLD HOME STILL LINGERING IN MY CLOTHES, I WAS SENT OFF TO MRS. GREEDER'S THIRD GRADE AT MAYFLOWER ELEMENTARY SCHOOL.

CLASS, I'D LIKE US ALL TO GIVE A WARM MAYFLOWER ELEMENTARY WELCOME TO YOUR NEW FRIEND AND CLASSMATE JING JANG!

JIN WANG.

JIN WANG!

HE AND HIS FAMILY RECENTLY MOVED TO OUR NEIGHBORHOOD ALL THE WAY FROM CHINA!

SAN FRAN-CISCO.

SAN FRAN-CISCO!

YES, TIMMY.

MY MOMMA SAYS CHINESE PEOPLE EAT DOGS.

NOW BE NICE, TIMMY!

I'M SURE JIN DOESN'T DO THAT! IN FACT, JIN'S FAMILY PROBABLY STOPPED THAT SORT OF THING AS SOON AS THEY CAME TO THE UNITED STATES!

THE ONLY OTHER ASIAN IN MY CLASS WAS **SUZY NAKAMURA**.

WHEN THE CLASS FINALLY FIGURED OUT THAT WE WEREN'T RELATED, RUMORS BEGAN TO CIRCULATE THAT SUZY AND I WERE ARRANGED TO BE MARRIED ON HER THIRTEENTH BIRTHDAY.

WE AVOIDED EACH OTHER AS MUCH AS POSSIBLE.

WHAT THE **HELL** IS **THAT**?!

DUMPLINGS.

sniff sniff

HMPH. STAY AWAY FROM MY DOG.

HA!

HEY BE COOL, MAN.

AW, DON'T GET YER **PANTIES** IN A BUNCH, GREG! LITTLE **PANSY-BOY**.

**WHAT DID YOU CALL ME?!**

LITTLE PANSY BOY.

**WHAT?!**

...NOTHIN', NOTHIN'.

COME ON. LET'S LEAVE **BUCKTOOTH** ALONE SO HE CAN ENJOY **LASSIE**.

HA HA! "BUCK-TOOTH!"

ABOUT THREE MONTHS LATER, I MADE MY FIRST FRIEND AT MAYFLOWER ELEMENTARY: **PETER GARBINSKY.** HE WAS A FIFTH GRADER.

EVERYONE CALLED HIM "PETER THE EATER."

HE INTRODUCED HIMSELF TO ME DURING RECESS ONE DAY.

GIMME YER SAND-WICH AND I'LL BE YOUR BEST FRIEND.

OTHERWISE I'LL KICK YOUR BUTT AND MAKE YOU EAT MY BOOGERS.

MY FRIENDSHIP WITH PETER DEVELOPED QUICKLY.

WE HAD A NUMBER OF FAVORITE GAMES-

- "KILL THE PILL" -

- "CRACK THE WHIP" -

- AND "LET'S BE JEWS." HAD TO STEAL AN ITEM OR TWO FROM MRS. GARBINSKY'S DRESSER DRAWER FOR THIS GAME.

HAR! JIN, YOU'RE SUCH A FRIGGIN' RIOT!

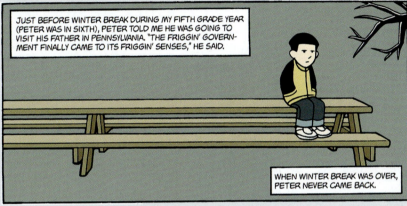

JUST BEFORE WINTER BREAK DURING MY FIFTH GRADE YEAR (PETER WAS IN SIXTH), PETER TOLD ME HE WAS GOING TO VISIT HIS FATHER IN PENNSYLVANIA. "THE FRIGGIN' GOVERN-MENT FINALLY CAME TO ITS FRIGGIN' SENSES," HE SAID.

WHEN WINTER BREAK WAS OVER, PETER NEVER CAME BACK.

TWO MONTHS LATER, WEI-CHEN ARRIVED.

CLASS, I'D LIKE US ALL TO GIVE A BIG MAYFLOWER ELEMENTARY WELCOME TO YOUR NEW FRIEND AND CLASSMATE CHEI-CHEN CHUN!

WEI-CHEN SUN.

WEI-CHEN SUN!

HE AND HIS FAMILY RECENTLY MOVED TO OUR NEIGHBORHOOD ALL THE WAY FROM CHINA!

TAI-WAN.

TAI-WAN!

SOMETHING MADE ME WANT TO BEAT HIM UP.

129

## Working with the Text

1. At the beginning, Jin Wang's mother tells him a story as they move from Chinatown in San Francisco to the suburbs. Why do you think his mother tells him this story? What attitude toward the move is she trying to inspire? From the point of view of the author, what do you think Yang wants you to think about the mother's story? In what ways are we supposed to accept its wisdom, and in what ways do you think Yang wants us to look more critically at the story?

2. Compare the story told by Jin Wang's mother with the subsequent advice he receives from the herbalist's wife: "It's easy to become anything you wish...so long as you're willing to forfeit your soul." What have we seen so far in the story that might represent "forfeiting your soul," at least from the receptionist's perspective? What kinds of advice about "transformation" is Jin Wang receiving?

3. What do the stories of Jin Wang's first two "friendships" suggest about the process of transformation and assimilation he is encountering? How would you characterize his initial friendship with Peter? What does friendship mean in this case? Why is Jin Wang's first instinct to beat up Wei-Chen Sun, the new student from Taiwan? How do you understand the basis for their subsequent friendship?

4. Throughout the story, Yang represents racial and ethnic difference through design elements, such as the use of angle brackets < > to indicate characters speaking in Chinese and the drawing style, including facial features, hairstyle and color, and dress. As a class, discuss the challenges facing a graphic artist in depicting race and ethnicity in a cartoon style. How does Yang deal with the potential problems of stereotyping or caricature, for example? How does he establish trust with his readers? What are the main strategies that he uses?

## PAIRED READINGS: BUFFY VERSUS PRINCESS JASMINE: GIRL POWER OR BACK TO THE FUTURE?

Over two decades ago, a musical performer rose to worldwide popularity and simultaneously began a pop culture debate about the role of women that continues to this day. When Madonna began her string of hit records and music videos in the early 1980s, she seemed to combine contradictory images and messages that won her both admirers and critics. A strong, independent woman artist, Madonna projected a sense of confidence and assertiveness that seemed the embodiment of the women's movement of the sixties and seventies. At the same time, her image also evoked an emphasis on physical attractiveness and references to pin-up models of the past that some saw as a retreat to the woman-as-object role in pop culture. Even her early songs, from "Like A Virgin" to "Material Girl," could be interpreted either as reinforcing stereotypes of women as gold diggers or as mocking them.

Critics of Madonna saw her as a step back into a more sexist past. Admirers of Madonna, including many of her fans, saw her as expressing the new freedom women had gained to express themselves however they liked. In her changing public personas, Madonna represented (and continues to represent) the ability not to be locked into any one idea or image of what it means to be a powerful, successful woman. Now that Madonna has inspired a whole new generation of woman musicians, from Christina Aguilera to Pink to Britney Spears, debate continues about whether images of women in popular culture represent continued progress or a backward slide.

The next two readings in *Text Messaging*—"What's Wrong with Cinderella?" and "Supernatural Girls"—focus on two different recent phenomena in popular culture that each author sees as moving in potentially opposite directions. Read together, these essays can provide a starting point for a discussion of the state of gender roles and stereotypes in contemporary popular culture.

## "What's Wrong with Cinderella?"

### Peggy Orenstein

*The modern women's rights movement has led to dramatic increases in opportunities for girls and women, as well as a radical reorientation in popular beliefs about the proper roles for men and women in American society. In the worlds of business, politics, sports, education, and the arts, barriers have been broken and attitudes have changed. Popular culture has both reflected and in many ways encouraged these changes, nowhere more so than in pop culture directed at children. In the strictly gender-segregated world of the early "Dick and Jane" readers, Dick liked building things and roughhousing, while Jane played only with dolls and wore cute dresses. Contemporary books for children, however, depict girls as adventurous, brave, and resourceful, as interested in playing sports as in playing house.*

*Author and activist Peggy Orenstein asks what to make, then, of princess culture, of the growing popularity among young girls of fantasizing about and dressing up like princesses, particularly those depicted in Disney animated movies such as* Cinderella, Sleeping Beauty, *and* Snow White? *Many champions of women's rights, for instance, have written* about the negative consequences of the Cinderella myth, the belief that a woman's destiny depends on rescue by a handsome young prince. In a world where women can be rock stars, sports heroes, business leaders, and maybe even president of the United States, why is there such a ready market for what seem like outmoded kinds of gender roles? Or is concern over princess culture itself making too much out of harmless children's play?

Orenstein explores all of these questions in "What's Wrong with Cinderella?" and writes from the position of a long-time feminist journalist who is raising a young daughter. Starting with a question posed by her 3-year-old, Orenstein examines the cultural forces and marketing strategies behind princess mania.

## Before You Read

1. Write a word association essay based on your reactions to the word *princess*. What characteristics, attitudes, ideas, and ideals come to mind? Do you or have you had any strong feelings about the word? After completing your essay, share your work with others in the class. What patterns and agreements can you find among students, even across lines of gender? What differences? Do men and women in class react differently to the word *princess?*

2. Orenstein's article deals with the relationship between children's imaginative play and gender roles. Prepare for reading this piece by reflecting on and writing about that particular annual ritual of childhood dressing up known as Halloween. Based on your own experiences or those of another person if you didn't participate in Halloween, construct an inventory of different Halloween costumes. Why did you or your interviewee pick these costumes? How did the costumes reflect different moments in pop culture history? What characters were most popular? Pay special attention to the roles gender played in the choices that people made. Were there any costumes that were off limits to one gender? In what ways did Halloween give permission to try out different roles and costumes that might ordinarily be frowned upon?

I finally came unhinged in the dentist's office—one of those ritzy pediatric practices tricked out with comic books, DVDs, and arcade games—where I'd taken my 3-year-old daughter for her first exam. Until then, I'd held my tongue. I'd smiled politely every time the supermarket-checkout clerk greeted her with "Hi, Princess"; ignored the waitress at our local breakfast joint who called the funny-face pancakes she ordered her "princess meal"; made no comment when the lady at Longs Drugs said, "I bet I know your favorite color" and handed her a pink balloon rather than letting her choose for herself. Maybe it was the dentist's Betty Boop inflection that got to me, but when she pointed to the exam chair and said, "Would you like to sit in my special princess throne so I can sparkle your teeth?" I lost it.

"Oh, for God's sake," I snapped. "Do you have a princess drill, too?"

She stared at me as if I were an evil stepmother.

"Come on!" I continued, my voice rising. "It's 2006, not 1950. This is Berkeley, Calif. Does every little girl really have to be a princess?"

My daughter, who was reaching for a Cinderella sticker, looked back and forth between us. "Why are you so mad, Mama?" she asked. "What's wrong with princesses?"

Diana may be dead and Masako disgraced, but here in America, we are in the midst of a royal moment. To call princesses a "trend" among girls is like calling Harry Potter a book. Sales at Disney Consumer Products, which started the craze six years ago by packaging nine of its female characters under one royal rubric, have shot up to $3 billion, globally, this year, from $300 million in 2001. There are now more than 25,000 Disney Princess items. "Princess," as some Disney execs call it, is not only the fastest-growing brand the company has ever created; they say it is on its way to becoming the largest girls' franchise on the planet.

Meanwhile in 2001, Mattel brought out its own "world of girl" line of princess Barbie dolls, DVDs, toys, clothing, home décor, and myriad other products. At a time when Barbie sales were declining domestically, they became instant bestsellers. Shortly before that, Mary Drolet, a Chicago-area mother and former Claire's and Montgomery Ward executive, opened Club Libby Lu, now a chain of mall stores based largely in the suburbs in which girls ages 4 to 12 can shop for "Princess Phones" covered in faux fur and attend "Princess-Makeover Birthday Parties." Saks bought Club Libby Lu in 2003 for $12 million and has since expanded it to eighty-seven outlets; by 2005, with only scant local advertising, revenues hovered around the $46 million mark, a 53 percent jump from the previous year. Pink, it seems, is the new gold.

Even Dora the Explorer, the intrepid, dirty-kneed adventurer, has ascended to the throne: in 2004, after a two-part episode in which she turns into a "true princess," the Nickelodeon and Viacom consumer-products division released a satin-gowned "Magic Hair Fairytale Dora," with hair that grows or shortens when her crown is touched. Among other phrases the bilingual doll utters: "Vámonos! Let's go to fairy-tale land!" and "Will you brush my hair?"

As a feminist mother—not to mention a nostalgic product of the Grranimals era—I have been taken by surprise by the princess craze and the girlie-girl culture that has risen around it. What happened to William wanting a doll and not dressing your cat in an apron? Whither Marlo Thomas? I watch my fellow mothers, women who once swore they'd never be dependent on a man, smile indulgently at daughters who warble "So This Is Love" or insist on being called Snow White. I wonder if they'd concede so readily to sons who begged for combat fatigues and mock AK-47s.

More to the point, when my own girl makes her daily beeline for the dress-up corner of her preschool classroom—something I'm convinced she does largely to torture me—I worry about what playing Little Mermaid is teaching her. I've spent much of my career writing about experiences that undermine girls' well-being, warning parents that a preoccupation with body and beauty (encouraged by films, TV, magazines, and, yes, toys) is perilous to their daughters' mental and physical health. Am I now supposed to shrug and forget all that? If trafficking in stereotypes doesn't matter at 3, when does it matter? At 6? 8? 13?

On the other hand, maybe I'm still surfing a washed-out second wave of feminism in a third-wave world. Maybe princesses are in fact a sign of progress, an indication that girls can embrace their predilection for pink without compromising strength or ambition; that, at long last, they can "have it all." Or maybe it is even less complex than that: to mangle Freud, maybe a princess is sometimes just a princess. And, as my daughter wants to know, what's wrong with that?

The rise of the Disney princesses reads like a fairy tale itself, with Andy Mooney, a former Nike executive, playing the part of prince, riding into the company on a metaphoric white horse in January 2000 to save a consumer-products division whose sales were dropping by as much as 30 percent a year. Both overstretched and underfocused, the division had triggered price wars by granting multiple licenses for core products (say, Winnie-the-Pooh undies) while ignoring the potential of new media. What's more, Disney films like *A Bug's Life* in 1998 had yielded few merchandising opportunities—what child wants to snuggle up with an ant?

It was about a month after Mooney's arrival that the magic struck. That's when he flew to Phoenix to check out his first "Disney on Ice" show. "Standing in line in the arena, I was surrounded by little girls dressed head to toe as princesses," he told me last summer in his palatial office, then located in Burbank, and speaking in a rolling Scottish burr. "They weren't even Disney products. They were generic princess products they'd appended to a Halloween costume. And the light bulb went off. Clearly there was latent demand here. So the next morning I said to my team, 'O.K., let's establish standards and a color palette and talk to licensees and get as much product out there as we possibly can that allows these girls to do what they're doing anyway: projecting themselves into the characters from the classic movies.'"

Mooney picked a mix of old and new heroines to wear the Pantone pink No. 241 corona: Cinderella, Sleeping Beauty, Snow White, Ariel, Belle, Jasmine,

Mulan, and Pocahontas. It was the first time Disney marketed characters separately from a film's release, let alone lumped together those from different stories. To ensure the sanctity of what Mooney called their individual "mythologies," the princesses never make eye contact when they're grouped: each stares off in a slightly different direction as if unaware of the others' presence.

It is also worth noting that not all of the ladies are of royal extraction. Part of the genius of "Princess" is that its meaning is so broadly constructed that it actually has no meaning. Even Tinker Bell was originally a Princess, though her reign didn't last. "We'd always debate over whether she was really a part of the Princess mythology," Mooney recalled. "She really wasn't." Likewise, Mulan and Pocahontas, arguably the most resourceful of the bunch, are rarely depicted on Princess merchandise, though for a different reason. Their rustic garb has less bling potential than that of old-school heroines like Sleeping Beauty. (When Mulan does appear, she is typically in the kimonolike hanfu, which makes her miserable in the movie, rather than her liberated warrior's gear.)

The first Princess items, released with no marketing plan, no focus groups, no advertising, sold as if blessed by a fairy godmother. To this day, Disney conducts little market research on the Princess line, relying instead on the power of its legacy among mothers as well as the instant-read sales barometer of the theme parks and Disney Stores. "We simply gave girls what they wanted," Mooney said of the line's success, "although I don't think any of us grasped how much they wanted this. I wish I could sit here and take credit for having some grand scheme to develop this, but all we did was envision a little girl's room and think about how she could live out the princess fantasy. The counsel we gave to licensees was: What type of bedding would a princess want to sleep in? What kind of alarm clock would a princess want to wake up to? What type of television would a princess like to see? It's a rare case where you find a girl who has every aspect of her room bedecked in Princess, but if she ends up with three or four of these items, well, then you have a very healthy business."

Every reporter Mooney talks to asks some version of my next question: Aren't the Princesses, who are interested only in clothes, jewelry, and cadging the handsome prince, somewhat retrograde role models?

"Look," he said, "I have friends whose son went through the Power Rangers phase who castigated themselves over what they must've done wrong. Then they talked to other parents whose kids have gone through it. The boy passes through. The girl passes through. I see girls expanding their imagination through visualizing themselves as princesses, and then they pass through that phase and end up becoming lawyers, doctors, mothers, or princesses, whatever the case may be."

Mooney has a point: There are no studies proving that playing princess directly damages girls' self-esteem or dampens other aspirations. On the other hand, there is evidence that young women who hold the most conventionally feminine beliefs—who avoid conflict and think they should be perpetually nice and pretty—are more likely to be depressed than others and less likely to use contraception. What's more, the 23 percent decline in girls' participation in sports and other vigorous activity between middle and high school has been linked to their sense that athletics is unfeminine. And in a survey released last October by Girls Inc., school-age girls overwhelmingly reported a paralyzing pressure to be "perfect": not only to get straight A's and be the student-body president, editor of the newspaper, and captain of the swim team but also to be "kind and caring," "please everyone, be very thin and dress right." Give those girls a pumpkin and a glass slipper and they'd be in business.

At the grocery store one day, my daughter noticed a little girl sporting a Cinderella backpack. "There's that princess you don't like, Mama!" she shouted.

"Um, yeah," I said, trying not to meet the other mother's hostile gaze.

"Don't you like her blue dress, Mama?"

I had to admit, I did.

She thought about this. "Then don't you like her face?"

"Her face is all right," I said, noncommittally, though I'm not thrilled to have my Japanese-Jewish child in thrall to those Aryan features. (And what the heck are those blue things covering her ears?) "It's just, honey, Cinderella doesn't really do anything."

Over the next forty-five minutes, we ran through that conversation, verbatim, approximately 37 million times, as my daughter pointed out Disney Princess Band-Aids, Disney Princess paper cups, Disney Princess lip balm, Disney Princess pens, Disney Princess crayons, and Disney Princess notebooks— all cleverly displayed at the eye level of a 3-year-old trapped in a shopping cart—as well as a bouquet of Disney Princess balloons bobbing over the checkout line. The repetition was excessive, even for a preschooler. What was it about my answers that confounded her? What if, instead of realizing: Aha! Cinderella is a symbol of the patriarchal oppression of all women, another example of corporate mind control and power-to-the-people! my 3-year-old was thinking, Mommy doesn't want me to be a girl?

According to theories of gender constancy, until they're about 6 or 7, children don't realize that the sex they were born with is immutable. They believe that they have a choice: they can grow up to be either a mommy or a daddy. Some psychologists say that until permanency sets in kids embrace whatever stereotypes our culture presents, whether it's piling on the most spangles or attacking one another with light sabers. What better way to assure that they'll always remain themselves? If that's the case, score one for Mooney. By not buying the Princess Pull-Ups, I may be inadvertently communicating that being female (to the extent that my daughter is able to understand it) is a bad thing.

Anyway, you have to give girls some credit. It's true that, according to Mattel, one of the most popular games young girls play is "bride," but Disney found that a groom or prince is incidental to that fantasy, a regrettable necessity at best. Although they keep him around for the climactic kiss, he is otherwise relegated to the bottom of the toy box, which is why you don't see him prominently displayed in the stores.

What's more, just because they wear the tulle doesn't mean they've drunk the Kool-Aid. Plenty of girls stray from the script, say, by playing basketball in their finery, or casting themselves as the powerful evil stepsister bossing around the sniveling Cinderella. I recall a headline-grabbing 2005 British study that revealed that girls enjoy torturing, decapitating, and microwaving their Barbies nearly as much as they like to dress them up for dates. There is spice along with the sugar after all, though why this was news is beyond me: anyone who ever played with the doll knows there's nothing more satisfying than hacking off all her hair and holding her underwater in the bathtub. Princesses can even be a boon to exasperated parents: in our house, for instance, royalty never whines and uses the potty every single time.

"Playing princess is not the issue," argues Lyn Mikel Brown, an author, with Sharon Lamb, of *Packaging Girlhood: Rescuing Our Daughters From Marketers' Schemes.* "The issue is 25,000 Princess products," says Brown, a professor of education and human development at Colby College. "When one thing is so dominant, then it's no longer a choice: it's a mandate, cannibalizing all other forms of play. There's the illusion of more choices out there for girls, but if you look around, you'll see their choices are steadily narrowing."

It's hard to imagine that girls' options could truly be shrinking when they dominate the honor roll and outnumber boys in college. Then again, have you taken a stroll through a children's store lately? A year ago, when we shopped for "big girl" bedding at Pottery Barn Kids, we found the "girls" side awash in flowers, hearts, and hula dancers; not a soccer player or sailboat in sight. Across the no-fly zone, the "boys" territory was all about sports, trains, planes, and automobiles. Meanwhile, Baby GAP's boys' onesies were emblazoned with "Big Man on Campus" and the girls' with "Social Butterfly"; guess whose matching shoes were decorated on the soles with hearts and whose sported a "No. 1" logo? And at Toys "R" Us, aisles of pink baby dolls, kitchens, shopping carts, and princesses unfurl a safe distance from the *Star Wars* figures, GeoTrax, and tool chests. The relentless resegregation of childhood appears to have sneaked up without any further discussion about sex roles, about what it now means to be a boy or to be a girl. Or maybe it has happened in lieu of such discussion because it's easier this way.

Easier, that is, unless you want to buy your daughter something that isn't pink. Girls' obsession with that color may seem like something they're born with, like the ability to breathe or talk on the phone for hours on end. But according to Jo Paoletti, an associate professor of American studies at the University of Maryland, it ain't so. When colors were first introduced to the nursery in the early part of the twentieth century, pink was considered the more masculine hue, a pastel version of red. Blue, with its intimations of the Virgin Mary, constancy, and faithfulness, was thought to be dainty. Why or when that switched is not clear, but as late as the 1930s a significant percentage of adults in one national survey held to that split. Perhaps that's why so many early Disney heroines—Cinderella, Sleeping Beauty, Wendy, Alice-in-Wonderland—are swathed in varying shades of azure. (Purple, incidentally, may be the next color to swap teams: once the realm of kings and N.F.L. players, it is fast becoming the bolder girl's version of pink.)

It wasn't until the mid-1980s, when amplifying age and sex differences became a key strategy of children's marketing (recall the emergence of " 'tween"), that pink became seemingly innate to girls, part of what defined them as female, at least for the first few years. That was also the time that the first of the generation raised during the unisex phase of feminism—ah, hither Marlo!—became parents. "The kids who grew up in the 1970s wanted sharp definitions for their own kids," Paoletti told me. "I can understand that, because the unisex thing denied everything—you couldn't be this, you couldn't be that, you had to be a neutral nothing."

The infatuation with the girlie girl certainly could, at least in part, be a reaction against the so-called second wave of the women's movement of the 1960s and 1970s (the first was the fight for suffrage), which fought for reproductive rights and economic, social, and legal equality. If nothing else, pink and Princess have resuscitated the fantasy of romance that that era of feminism threatened, the privileges that traditional femininity conferred on women despite its costs—doors magically opened, dinner checks picked up, Manolo Blahniks. Frippery. Fun. Why should we give up the perks of our sex until we're sure of what we'll get in exchange? Why should we give them up at all? Or maybe it's deeper than that: the freedoms feminism bestowed came with an undercurrent of fear among women themselves—flowing through *Ally McBeal, Bridget Jones's Diary, Sex and the City*—of losing male love, of never marrying, of not having children, of being deprived of something that felt essentially and exclusively female.

I mulled that over while flipping through *The Paper Bag Princess,* a 1980 picture book hailed as an antidote to Disney. The heroine outwits a dragon who has kidnapped her prince, but not before the beast's fiery breath frizzles her hair and destroys her dress, forcing her to don a paper bag. The ungrateful prince rejects her, telling her to come back when she is "dressed like a real princess." She dumps him and skips off into the sunset, happily ever after, alone.

There you have it, *Thelma and Louise* all over again. Step out of line, and you end up solo or, worse, sailing crazily over a cliff to your doom. Alternatives like those might send you skittering right back to the castle. And I get that: the fact is, though I want my daughter to do and be whatever she wants as an adult, I still hope she'll find her Prince Charming and have babies, just as I have. I don't want her to be a fish without a bicycle; I want her to be a fish with another fish. Preferably, one who loves and respects her and also does the dishes and half the child care.

There had to be a middle ground between compliant and defiant, between petticoats and paper bags. I remembered a video on YouTube, an ad for a Nintendo game called Super Princess Peach. It showed a pack of girls in tiaras, gowns, and elbow-length white gloves sliding down a zip line on parasols, navigating an obstacle course of tires in their stilettos, slithering on their bellies under barbed wire, then using their telekinetic powers to make a climbing wall burst into flames. "If you can stand up to really mean people," an announcer intoned, "maybe you have what it takes to be a princess."

Now here were some girls who had grit as well as grace. I loved Princess Peach even as I recognized that there was no way she could run in those heels, that her peachiness did nothing to upset the apple cart of expectation: she may have been athletic, smart, and strong, but she was also adorable. Maybe she's what those once-unisex, postfeminist parents are shooting for: the melding of old and new standards. And perhaps that's a good thing, the ideal solution. But what to make, then, of the young women in the Girls Inc. survey? It doesn't seem to be "having it all" that's getting to them; it's the pressure to be it all. In telling our girls they can be anything, we have inadvertently demanded that they be everything. To everyone. All the time. No wonder the report was titled "The Supergirl Dilemma."

The princess as superhero is not irrelevant. Some scholars I spoke with say that given its post-9/11 timing, princess mania is a response to a newly dangerous world. "Historically, princess worship has emerged during periods of uncertainty and profound social change," observes Miriam Forman-Brunell, a historian at the University of Missouri—Kansas City. Francis Hodgson Burnett's original *Little Princess* was published at a time of rapid urbanization, immigration, and poverty; Shirley Temple's film version was a hit during the Great Depression. "The original folktales themselves," Forman-Brunell says, "spring from medieval and early modern European culture that faced all kinds of economic and demographic and social upheaval—famine, war, disease, terror of wolves. Girls play savior during times of economic crisis and instability." That's a heavy burden for little shoulders. Perhaps that's why the magic wand has become an essential part of the princess get-up. In the original stories—even the Disney versions of them—it's not the girl herself who's magic; it's the fairy godmother. Now if Forman-Brunell is right, we adults have become the cursed creatures whom girls have the thaumaturgic power to transform.

In the 1990s, third-wave feminists rebelled against their dour big sisters, "reclaiming" sexual objectification as a woman's right—provided, of course, that it was on her own terms, that she was the one choosing to strip or wear a shirt that said "Porn Star" or make out with her best friend at a frat-house bash.

They embraced words like *bitch* and *slut* as terms of affection and empowerment. That is, when used by the right people, with the right dash of playful irony. But how can you assure that? As Madonna gave way to Britney, whatever self-determination that message contained was watered down and commodified until all that was left was a gaggle of 6-year-old girls in belly-baring T-shirts (which I'm guessing they don't wear as cultural critique). It is no wonder that parents, faced with thongs for 8-year-olds and Bratz dolls' "passion for fashion," fill their daughters' closets with pink sateen; the innocence of Princess feels like a reprieve.

"But what does that mean?" asks Sharon Lamb, a psychology professor at Saint Michael's College. "There are other ways to express 'innocence'—girls could play ladybug or caterpillar. What you're really talking about is sexual purity. And there's a trap at the end of the rainbow, because the natural progression from pale, innocent pink is not to other colors. It's to hot, sexy pink—exactly the kind of sexualization parents are trying to avoid."

Lamb suggested that to see for myself how "Someday My Prince Will Come" morphs into "Oops! I Did It Again," I visit Club Libby Lu, the mall shop dedicated to the "Very Important Princess."

Walking into one of the newest links in the store's chain, in Natick, Mass., last summer, I had to tip my tiara to the founder, Mary Drolet: Libby Lu's design was flawless. Unlike Disney, Drolet depended on focus groups to choose the logo (a crown-topped heart) and the colors (pink, pink, purple, and more pink). The displays were scaled to the size of a 10-year-old, though most of the shoppers I saw were several years younger than that. The decals on the walls and dressing rooms—"I Love Your Hair," "Hip Chick," "Spoiled"—were written in "girl-friend language." The young sales clerks at this "special secret club for superfabulous girls" are called "club counselors" and come off like your coolest baby sitter, the one who used to let you brush her hair. The malls themselves are chosen based on a company formula called the G.P.I. or "Girl Power Index," which predicts potential sales revenues. Talk about newspeak: "Girl Power" has gone from a riot grrrl anthem to "I Am Woman, Watch Me Shop."

Inside, the store was divided into several glittery "shopping zones" called "experiences": Libby's Laboratory, now called Sparkle

Spa, where girls concoct their own cosmetics and bath products; Libby's Room; Ear Piercing; Pooch Parlor (where divas in training can pamper stuffed poodles, pugs, and Chihuahuas); and the Style Studio, offering "Libby Du" makeover choices, including 'Tween Idol, Rock Star, Pop Star, and, of course, Priceless Princess. Each look includes hairstyle, makeup, nail polish, and sparkly tattoos.

As I browsed, I noticed a mother standing in the center of the store holding a price list for makeover birthday parties—$22.50 to $35 per child. Her name was Annie McAuliffe; her daughters—Stephanie, 4, and 7-year-old twins Rory and Sarah—were dashing giddily up and down the aisles.

"They've been begging to come to this store for three weeks," McAuliffe said. "I'd never heard of it. So I said they could, but they'd have to spend their own money if they bought anything." She looked around. "Some of this stuff is innocuous," she observed, then leaned toward me, eyes wide and stage-whispered: "But...a lot of it is horrible. It makes them look like little prostitutes. It's crazy. They're babies!"

As we debated the line between frivolous fun and JonBenét, McAuliffe's daughter Rory came dashing up, pigtails haphazard, glasses askew. "They have the best pocketbooks here," she said breathlessly, brandishing a clutch with the words "Girlie Girl" stamped on it. "Please, can I have one? It has sequins!"

"You see that?" McAuliffe asked, gesturing at the bag. "What am I supposed to say?"

On my way out of the mall, I popped into the "'tween" mecca Hot Topic, where a display of Tinker Bell items caught my eye. Tinker Bell, whose image racks up an annual $400 million in retail sales with no particular effort on Disney's part, is poised to wreak vengeance on the Princess line that once expelled her. Last winter, the first chapter book designed to introduce girls to Tink and her Pixie Hollow pals spent eighteen weeks on the *New York Times* children's bestseller list. In a direct-to-DVD now under production, she will speak for the first time, voiced by the actress Brittany Murphy. Next year, Disney Fairies will be rolled out in earnest. Aimed at 6- to 9-year-old girls, the line will catch them just as they outgrow Princess. Their colors will be lavender, green, turquoise—anything but the Princess's soon-to-be-babyish pink.

To appeal to that older child, Disney executives said, the Fairies will have more "attitude" and "sass" than the Princesses. What, I wondered, did that entail? I'd seen some of the Tinker Bell merchandise that Disney sells at its theme parks: T-shirts reading, "Spoiled to Perfection," "Mood Subject to Change Without Notice," and "Tinker Bell: Prettier Than a Princess." At Hot Topic, that edge was even sharper: magnets, clocks, light-switch plates, and panties featured "Dark Tink," described as "the bad girl side of Miss Bell that Walt never saw."

Girl power, indeed.

A few days later, I picked my daughter up from preschool. She came tearing over in a full-skirted frock with a gold bodice, a beaded crown perched sideways on her head. "Look, Mommy, I'm Ariel!" she crowed, referring to Disney's *Little Mermaid*. Then she stopped and furrowed her brow. "Mommy, do you like Ariel?"

I considered her for a moment. Maybe Princess is the first salvo in what will become a lifelong struggle over her body image, a Hundred Years' War of dieting, plucking, painting, and perpetual dissatisfaction with the results. Or maybe it isn't. I'll never really know. In the end, it's not the Princesses that really bother me anyway. They're just a trigger for the bigger question of how, over the years, I can help my daughter with the contradictions she will inevitably face as a girl, the dissonance that is as endemic as ever to growing up female. Maybe the best I can hope for is that her generation will get a little further with the solutions than we did.

For now, I kneeled down on the floor and gave my daughter a hug.

She smiled happily. "But Mommy?" she added. "When I grow up, I'm still going to be a fireman."

---

## Working with the Text

1. What are Orenstein's specific concerns about princess culture? Make a detailed outline of the points she makes and the issues she raises. Rank her concerns in terms of the ones you think she takes the most seriously and the ones she might see as less important.

2. Throughout her essay, Orenstein moves back and forth between personal impressions and anecdotes (such as her experience at the dentist's office with her daughter) and more serious, scholarly research (such as the survey by Girls, Inc. revealing that many school-age girls "reported a paralyzing pressure to be 'perfect'"). Which examples of these different kinds of evidence in Orenstein's essay do you find most compelling and hardest to ignore?

3. Orenstein is writing as an experienced journalist and cultural critic describing what she sees as a significant and potentially disturbing new trend in marketing directed at little girls. She is also writing from the perspective of a concerned parent, wondering how best to negotiate the different cultural and commercial messages she sees aimed at her daughter. What would you do in such a situation? Write a potential letter or email to Orenstein in which you share your views about how you think you might react or, if you are currently raising a daughter, how you respond to these cultural influences. In what ways, if any, do

you think fathers and mothers might take different perspectives or offer different advice?

4. Changes in the predetermined roles for girls in society also involve changes in predetermined roles for boys. Just as many children's books over the last four decades reflect a desire to broaden the future horizons that girls might imagine for themselves, many also offer corresponding messages to boys that they should not be ashamed of being interested in activities and professions traditionally associated with girls. Given Orenstein's focus on this new, potentially old-fashioned emphasis on girliness in princess culture, do some investigating into trends in marketing toward young boys. Are there similar fads aimed at a more macho image for boys? What toys and activities seem most popular for young boys? How gender-specific are they?

## "Supernatural Girls"

### Kathleen Sweeney

*In the mid 1990s, a new television show premiered on what was then the WB Network. It featured an attractive young woman attending a southern California high school. While dealing with the familiar teenage stresses of relationships, homework, and social cliques, she also used her supernatural abilities to battle vampires, demons, and the forces of darkness in general. Although the original movie version of* Buffy the Vampire Slayer *had not been a major success, the television series quickly became a cultural phenomenon. Some viewers initially wondered whether the deliberately stereotypical name Buffy indicated that the program was meant to be taken less than seriously, but dedicated fans saw no contradiction between the action-adventure aspects of the show and its tongue-in-cheek ability to poke fun at itself at the same time.*

*In "Supernatural Girls," multimedia artist and writer Kathleen Sweeney discusses* Buffy *as part of what she sees as the emergence over the last ten to fifteen years of a new pop culture action hero: the powerful adolescent girl. Simultaneously embracing and defying conventional assumptions about gender, these supernatural girls combine emotional sensitivity and physical courage, an interest in beauty and friendship with aggression and assertiveness. In examining the characters of Buffy;* Rogue *from the X-Men movies; Jen Yu from the martial arts classic* Crouching Tiger, Hidden Dragon; *Hermione Granger from the* Harry Potter *series; and Violet from the animated movie* The Incredibles, *Sweeney argues for the importance of these "supernatural girls" as new role models for contemporary girls and young women, pop culture heroes who challenge our assumptions about both male and female social roles.*

## Before You Read

1. When you were growing up, who were your favorite heroes from popular culture? Choose one in particular and write about why you liked this character. What specific attributes, capabilities, or personality features did you most admire? What role did gender play in your attitude toward this character?

2. Look over the list of characters that Sweeney discusses in her essay. Which are you most familiar with and what do you think of them as heroes? Which do you find most interesting and why? Can you anticipate why Sweeney might see them as important new figures in popular culture?

Whether possessing a capacity for magic or the ability to do battle with the undead, there is no question that contemporary teenage heroines have power with a capital P.

—**Debbie Stoller,** *The Bust Guide to the New Girl Order*[1]

In the digital effects era of the past ten years, Supernatural Girls has emerged as the new species of female icon. Bursting out of the "girl" category box, they transcend gender expectations, defend themselves, and vanquish demons. When first introduced, they are often fifteen to nineteen years old. Just like the young starlets who portray them, these characters evolve into young women before our eyes via blockbuster sequels and television syndication. Part of the fascination with Power Girl icons lies in the way they discover their special powers at adolescence. Advances in special effects have combined with a mainstream readiness for "chicks with power" to alter the visual landscape. But just as new technologies like the Internet, DVDs, and iPods have been so seamlessly integrated into daily life in the United States as to obliterate their novelty, a look back at media history as recent as the late 1980s reminds us that Power Girls are a relatively new phenomenon.

Since the mid-1990s, popular culture has expanded its collection of female icons to include teenage girls endowed with special powers like television's *Buffy the Vampire Slayer* (1997–2003) and film characters like Jen Yu of *Crouching Tiger, Hidden Dragon* (2000, by Ang Lee), Hermione Granger of the *Harry Potter* series (2001–2008, by Chris Columbus, Alfonso Cuaró, Mike Newell, and David Yates), Rogue *of X-Men* and *X2* (2000 and 2003, both by Bryan Singer), and Violet of *The Incredibles* (2004 by Brad Bird). Add to these Hayao Miyazaki's animated features *Kiki's Delivery Service* (1989), *Princess Mononoke* (1997), *Spirited Away* (2001), and *Howl's Moving Castle* (2005), and the conflation of girls and the supernatural in the popular imagination expands even further. For a postfeminist discourse seeking balance in gendered images of power, the past decade has witnessed a dynamic shift in representation.

With the recent proliferation of Supernatural Girls, it is easy to forget that teenage girl characters of 1950s, 1960s, 1970s, and 1980s media widely seen by American audiences barely had narratives dedicated to them, let alone the ability to karate-kick evil-doers. Despite the presence of certain enduring teenage girl characters exploring the power of magical, red shoes like Dorothy of *The Wizard of Oz* (1939, by Victor Fleming), teenage girls have historically provided the screaming prelude to a rescue by Super Guys.

Girl characters developed in the 1990s no longer had to dress like men to embody power. Young women in all their blossoming girliness could now defend themselves and rescue those in danger as well. In many ways equally male and female, these supernatural icons are the embodiment of a "beyond gender" merging of the sexes.[2] Biologically female in curviness of form, these characters combine classically masculine attributes of physical strength, fighting skills, and the urge to rescue and protect. Liberated from boy-girl expectations of behavior, snappy dialogue often plays against those stereotypes for humor. These teenage icons have it all: magical and physical powers, good looks, close friends, and resources. They are classic androgynes, approaching the status of Maiden Goddesses.

In Disney's retro animated features *Snow White and the Seven Dwarfs* (1937, by Ted Sears et al.) *Cinderella* (1950, by Clyde Geronimi et al.), and *Sleeping Beauty* (1959, by Clyde Geronimi), the wan protagonists receive supernatural assistance from "magical helpers." Power arrives in the form of rescue and resides ultimately in their "purity and goodness" (read: passivity) and eventual pairing with "The Prince." The post-1990s generation of animated and special effects heroines are often responsible not just for protecting themselves, but also for saving others, and sometimes the entire universe.

Interestingly, this new crop of girl characters includes Disney's *Kim Possible,* shown daily on the Disney Channel since 2002. *Kim Possible* features a teenage Super Girl who is a kung fu expert, top cheerleader, and ace student. The Disney Corporation has been riding the girls-of-power animation bandwagon since producing *Mulan* (1998, by Tony Bancroft and Barry Cook). Girls in power sell. No longer content with characters in the passenger seat, girl viewers are increasingly being acknowledged as a market force intent on a turn behind the wheel.

## *BUFFY THE VAMPIRE SLAYER:* FIGHTING DEMONS IN THE DARK

Five years after the lukewarm reception of the feature film *Buffy the Vampire Slayer* (1992, by Fran Rubel Kuzui), writer Joss Whedon revived the concept as a television series for the nascent WB Network in 1997. With its blond, would-be cheerleader protagonist, *Buffy the Vampire Slayer* provided millennial girl power at maximum ninja speed. Originally marketed to teenagers, *Buffy*

became an audience-crossing critical and cult hit. The show ran for five seasons on the WB Network before transferring to UPN for its final two seasons. Buffy is "The Chosen One," a young woman on a mission to rid the world of demons and vampires. Still in syndication in the U.S. and on BBC Television, *Buffy* combines post-punk goth sensibility with the pre-apocalyptic Y2K fervor of the late 1990s. The show is set in Sunnydale, California, a "center of mystical convergence" that hosts vampires, demons, and other evil creatures in after-hours abundance.

Buffy, if not book learned, has "psychic street smarts." Her nightly patrol in local graveyards to fight and "stake" vampires keeps her multitasking at top speed, offing six or more in a session. With little time for homework, Buffy is constantly in danger of being expelled. The school administrators treat her as a troublemaker, unaware that she is working the late shift for the greater good. Parodying the über achievers of suburbia, she laments, "I have at least three lives to contend with and none of them mesh." In a pinch she turns to Willow, a new, geek girl icon, who not only hacks the city's information systems for needed clues to the demonology puzzles presented to them but tutors Buffy before finals. Unlike the classic brainy girls of Hollywood, Willow has her share of dating intrigue: first with Oz, a coolly brilliant musician who is secretly a werewolf, and then with Tara, a Wiccan lesbian.

Buffy's other best friend, Xander, is the endearingly loyal but insecure guy, constantly trying to prove to Buffy that he is "the man." His courage serves him well in many instances of assisted vampire "dusting," but he turns to Buffy for rescue from industrial strength demons. In many ways Xander represents a masculinity confused by the cross-gendering of a character like Buffy. What is a guy to do when a girl can rescue him?

The most alluring guys on the show are reformed vampires: Angel, a vampire, "cursed" with a soul who helps Buffy conquer evil entities, and later in the series, Spike, a Sex Pistols–inspired Brit wit. But reformed vampires, like reformed addicts, continue to possess a link to the dark side and this is what makes them dangerously attractive to Buffy, whose powers as a Slayer make her no match for a regular teenage boy.

Despite the perennial absence of her divorced biological father, Buffy's "Watcher," the school librarian Giles, functions as a flawed father figure. As partial repentance for a misguided occult past, Giles trains Buffy in slaying techniques, though he himself does not possess her level of power. Instead, he researches techniques for vanquishing the more potent and unusual demons from his ancient leather-bound library.

The term *watcher* implies a theme of voyeurism. As media-gazing consumers, we are all watchers, viewers. Like Peeping Toms, we frame Buffy through windows, down dark alleys, across the schoolyard. The vampire's gaze is legendary. Like us, the vampires and demons are often lurking outside, watching. Watching is a relatively passive activity compared to Buffy's proactive, get-out-and-slay approach. Giles, like Xander, is relatively impotent compared to the blond slayer babe, whose supernatural strength, martial arts skills, and ability to scale fences in a single bound are all part of her "chosen one" package.

As androgyne, Buffy is all action—physical prowess combined with honed instincts. With her sixth sense for demon proximity, she remains one impulse ahead of everyone. Intellectually, she is unthreatening to males (though she pulls a score of 1300 on her SATs). Physically and in terms of sheer bravery and warrior instinct, she is awe-inspiring.

Battling demons becomes a metaphor for the teenage experience, and Buffy is in many ways a response to the concerns outlined by Mary Pipher in her book *Reviving Ophelia: Saving the Selves of Adolescent Girls* (1995). She does not cave in and allow herself to be sucked on by a culture of vampires; she fights back for the good of all.

## ROGUE OF *X-MEN* AND *X2*: A POWER THAT STEALS LIFE FORCE THROUGH TOUCH

In an early scene in *X-Men,* seventeen-year-old Rogue discovers she has a very unusual power—when she touches someone, she takes on their life force. If she holds on too long, she can kill them. This power, like that of all mutants in the films based on the original Marvel comic book series, reveals itself at adolescence. Horrified by her strange power of nefarious touch, Rogue dons gloves and long sleeves and runs away from her Mississippi home.

On the road she meets fellow mutant and future protector, Wolverine, who has retractable metal prongs embedded in his knuckles and can self-heal from any wound. He saves Rogue's life on two occasions by blending his power with hers. Similar to Buffy, the implication is that only one of the mature X-Men can handle her and relate to her. Rogue's power is dangerous; mysterious, and volatile, but dependent upon a connection to others. She is highly conflicted about her "rogue force" identity. Like many teenagers, she has power she cannot control. Rogue of the X-Men comics, however, is far more potent than the scripted character of the Hollywood films, who delivers several chilling "rescue me" screams typical of the classic horror and action genre. Yet Rogue joins a cast of female mentors with impressive powers—Storm, Dr. Jean Grey, and to a certain extent the evil Mystique—an entire set of them.

## JEN YU OF *CROUCHING TIGER, HIDDEN DRAGON*: MYSTICAL MARTIAL ARTS WARRIOR GIRL

With *Crouching Tiger, Hidden Dragon,* Lee introduced a unique teenage girl heroine to the martial arts epic tradition. Jen Yu proves capable of out-maneuvering adult martial artists in sequences choreographed by Yuen Wo Ping, action director of *The Matrix* (1999, by Andy and Larry Wachowski).

Initially, Jen Yu appears as a privileged, aristocratic teenager rebelling against the gendered prison of an arranged marriage. As the narrative unfolds, Jen Yu becomes the star of the film, stealing the 400-year-old Green Destiny sword and marauding through the desert with her free-spirited sparring partner and lover, Lo.

In a film replete with mythological symbols, a flashback sequence reveals how Jen Yu's ivory comb—an ancient symbol of the feminine—was stolen by Lo when her family processional was overtaken in the desert. In the absence of this comb, a stand-in for her female power, Jen Yu seeks a replacement in the form of the Green Destiny sword. The sword, set aside at the beginning of the film by the troubled Li Mu Bai, suggests a masculinity in limbo, which allows for the entry of a maiden female power beyond expectations. Because Jen Yu assumes the sword through thievery, however, she is ultimately deemed unworthy of ownership, despite her mastery of the weapon.

After years of training in womanly decorum, Jen Yu balks at all rules of culture. She refuses an offer by Li Mu Bai to master the Wutan wisdom ways under his tutelage, choosing instead to run wild. Scenes include Jen Yu leap-flying over tile rooftops, vanquishing a host of pompous male warriors in a tea house, running across water, and a final scene, battling with Li Mu Bai in a bamboo forest. Unlike her would-be mentors Yu Shu Lien and Li Mu Bai, Jen Yu has acquired the warrior arts on the sly through a manuscript stolen by her ersatz teacher, the evil Jade Fox. While Jen Yu has superior fighting skills, she never actually defeats Li Mu Bai.

Though she demonstrates remarkable physical skills, Jen Yu misses the moral depth of the warrior code until the end of the film, when it is too late. Her core self-interest and wanton rebelliousness prove her undoing. Aware of her shortcomings following Li Mu Bai's death, she sacrifices herself to the mythic waterfall of Wutan Mountain in a scene of breathtaking cinematic flight.

## HERMIONE GRANGER OF THE *HARRY POTTER* SERIES: A MUGGLE-BORN WITCH STUDIES HER WAY TO MAGICAL POWER

Some critics denounce Hermione Granger's role as secondary to Harry Potter's in the enormously popular series.[3] As the brains of the operation, however, Hermione works collaboratively with Harry to solve the mysteries in their fight against the evil Voldemort. Compared to Hollywood's teen hegemony-in-the-hallways genre, few examples of a non-hostile or non-sexualized friendship such as theirs exist in the lexicon of the school coming-of-age narrative. *Harry Potter* provides a consistent storyline of cross-gendered teamwork that is not trivialized as flirtation. Harry not only encourages Hermione's role in the acquisition of power—he depends on her.

Unique in the popular imagination, Hermione exists concurrently in bestseller print and blockbuster movie form. After reading about Hermione, a massive global audience has been watching her grow up onscreen. Like the other characters in the *Harry Potter* series, she arrives at Hogwarts School at age eleven to begin her training. As a brain-enhancing evolution in advanced magic, her rite of passage into adolescence is far from Lolita-esque.

Unlike Harry, whose lineage is magical, Hermione is a prodigy of mortal parentage. Because of her intelligence and maturity, Hogwarts' senior wizards grant Hermione privileged access to knowledge of time-travel devices, spells, and lore revealed not even to Harry. Without Hermione, it is doubtful this generation of viewers would have catapulted the series to such levels of success. Girl viewers no longer accept male privilege as a given in the realms of power. They want in on the secrets.

## VIOLET OF THE *INCREDIBLES*: INVISIBILITY AS A FORCE FIELD

The animated feature *The Incredibles* depicts an entire family of superheroes whose destiny hinges on teenage girl power. In this narrative, Violet Parr's initial invisibility morphs into a power beyond self-protection.

At the start of the film, the Incredibles have been forced underground by the government due to cost overages and bad publicity. Attempting to live a "normal" suburban life, while suppressing their true powers, the family confronts the limitations of American conformity. Enter the midlife crisis of Bob Parr/Mr. Incredible and the family is finally given an opportunity to utilize their true gifts and return to Super status. What a metaphor for an escape from the middle class!

At the outset, Violet is a certifiable "shrinking violet"—mumbling, shy, and angry. Her secret powers include the ability to disappear at will and to produce a spherical force field around herself and anyone else she chooses to protect. When Violet's father falls in with bad guy Syndrome, her mother, Helen Parr/Elastigirl, pilots a rescue jet on which Violet and her brother, Dash, have hidden as stowaways. When her mother realizes they are on board, she orders Violet to emit a force field against oncoming missiles. Unaccustomed to her power, Violet fails in her initial attempt and the plane explodes. After swimming to safety after the blast, Elastigirl remarks, "Doubt is a luxury we can't afford any more, sweetie. You have more power than you realize.... When the time comes you'll know what to do. It's in your blood."

Playing on viewer knowledge of self-esteem discourse, the mother/daughter dialogue provides a "Eureka" moment. Following this scene, Violet masters her powers and proves effective at protecting her entire family. When caught in Syndrome's force field, Violet's invisibility quotient allows her to disengage from the electric prison to free the entire family, and her force field protects them all from oncoming bullets. Unlike characters with more proactive warrior skills, Violet's powers are comparatively diffusive. This differentiates her from her family members whose powers are also more yang to her yin. What is brilliant about the creation of a character such as Violet, however, is that this seeming "passivity" becomes an ultimate heroic strength.

In a remarkably subtle piece of human-like body language (she is cartoon, after all), Violet emerges from behind her dark hair. No longer a shrinking violet; she becomes an Ultra-Violet, out there and Incredible.

## GIRL POWER ICONS REDUX

With so many mass culture examples, Supernatural Girls have broken through to icon status, changing the parameters of female possibility, even in the realms of fantasy. Due in part to our culture of reruns and serial movies, Buffy, Rogue, Jen Yu, Hermione, and Violet will continue to penetrate our collective narratives, joined no doubt by new characters and concepts in girlhood. While many trends have contributed to mainstream readiness for young female role models of force, power, and beauty, there is no doubt that these breakthrough gender-bending icons have permanently altered accepted definitions of the category "Girl." Lolitas, Ingenues, Tomboys, and Girls-Next-Door[4]—the teenage girl icons of previous generations—have some new little sisters with which to reckon. Perhaps Supernatural Girls will rescue even them from one-dimensional mediocrity.

Kathleen Sweeney, "Supernatural Girls," *Afterimage,* March/April 2006, Vol. 33, Issue 5. Reprinted by permission of the author. Kathleen Sweeney is an award-winning media artist and writer who teaches at The New School and Marymount Manhattan College, New York. "Supernatural Girls" is excerpted from *Maiden USA: Girl Icons Come of Age* (New York: Peter Lang Publishing, 2008). See www.video-text.com for more information about her work.

## Endnotes

1. Marcelle Karp, Debbie Stoller, *The Bust Guide to the New Girl Order* (New York: Penguin Books, 1999), 400.

2. For further discussion of "gender influx," see Judith Butler, *Gender Trouble: Feminism and the Subversion of Identity* (New York and London: Routledge, 1990).

3. See Christine Schoefer, "Harry Potter's Girl Trouble," www.salon.com/books/feature/2000/01/ 13/potter/index.html.

4. For a humorous discussion of these and other icons, see *Guerilla Girls, Bitches, Bimbos and Ballbreakers: The Guerilla Girls' Guide to Female Stereotypes* (New York: Penguin Books, 2003).

## Working with the Text

1. Sweeney argues, "Power Girls are a relatively new phenomenon," a departure from the idea that "teenage girls have historically provided the screaming prelude to a rescue by Super Guys." If Sweeney is right, speculate about why you think this new kind of female teenage hero began to emerge at the beginning of the 1990s. What social, cultural, or other forces might have contributed to the development of the Power Girl? Draw on your own experiences with popular culture in the 1990s to test some of Sweeney's assertions.

2. Any discussion of changing gender assumptions concerning female characters also raises questions about how these changes affect assumptions about male characters. In writing about Buffy and Rogue, for example, Sweeney also talks about the boys and men in their lives, as friends and romantic partners, father figures and mentors, even people to be saved. Extend Sweeney's analysis by examining the topic of changing attitudes about male heroes. If Hermione Granger is more than just a potential victim requiring rescue or a possible love interest in the *Harry Potter* novels and movies, in what ways might Harry represent a new development in the traditional idea of the male hero? What might be most disturbing or most attractive about these new changes?

3. The Power Girls that Sweeney describes all come from action-adventure stories. What other new kinds of girl heroes can you find in pop culture that might be related to the trends outlined in "Supernatural Girls"? What about a character like Lisa Simpson from *The Simpsons,* or the growing number of young women rock musicians? In what ways might they have something in common with a character such as Violet from *The Incredibles,* whose power Sweeney describes as "comparatively diffusive" in comparison with the "more proactive warrior skills" of the rest of her family?

# VIEWING CULTURE

## CREATING AN AVATAR

Avatar creation page from Second Life

Games have always involved role playing. From "let's pretend" and "make-believe" through dressing up for Halloween or putting on costumes in a school play, our playtime activities have featured trying on new identities and imagining ourselves as different than we are in the real world. A big part of the attraction of creating and listening to stories, whether in books, on stage, or on a screen, has been the fantasy of becoming someone or something else, whether it's a student at Hogwarts Academy, Jet Li in a martial arts movie, or even a completely different species such as Black Beauty.

The act of writing has also always involved this process of self-invention and self-transformation. After all, the whole point of written language is that we no longer have to be physically present to communicate with others. Writers have always explored the possibilities of not only conveying ideas but of creating whole new characters and personas for themselves through writing. Fiction writers can pretend to be dozens of different people, and writers have used pseudonyms and pen names to disguise and transform their identities for a variety of reasons, from Mary Ann Evans assuming that nineteenth-century novel readers would take her work more seriously if they thought it was written by a man named George Eliot, to a contemporary writer like Stephen King using the name "Richard Bachman" so readers can experience his work free from the stereotypes they may have about a Stephen King novel.

The digital age and the rise of Web-based writing has only increased the potential—and for many the perils—for creating new identities through writing. As the article by Sherry Turkle earlier in this chapter examined, online writers quickly figured out that they could make whole new identities for themselves in chat rooms and discussion boards. Ethnicity, gender, age, race, nationality, sexual orientation—all aspects of identity were open to experimentation. Most writers use this freedom to explore different perspectives or simply to try something new; some have used disguises for more sinister reasons to deceive and exploit other online users.

While conventional writing takes advantage of the writer's invisibility to open the possibilities for identity transformation, the development of powerful new graphics software has allowed players of video and online games to reintroduce the visual element in creating new identities. Video games have long allowed players to assume already created, onscreen visual identities like Mario the plumber or Sonic the hedgehog while playing the games, but newer games like the Sims and MMORPGs such as Second Life and World of Warcraft allow participants to customize their onscreen physical appearances to smaller and smaller levels of detail, including chin shape and eyebrow length. Magical

Avatar creation page from Yahoo!

powers, wings, fur, and paws: almost any possible option is becoming available for creating an online presence.

Called avatars, these digital identities take their name from the ancient Sanskrit word for a god who assumes a physical form, whether human, animal, or otherwise. As with the Greek concept of persona, or mask, the concept of the avatar recognizes that appearances can be deceptive; that identity, even physical identity, is impermanent and changeable; and that assumptions based on physical form can be easily mistaken.

# T H R E E

EXERCISE

## Choices and Possibilities

Take a close look at the two examples of avatar creation programs (from Second Life and from Yahoo!) on pages 154 and 155. Notice that both programs offer a wide array of choices for creating and modifying an onscreen identity. Notice as well, though, that the choices are not literally unlimited. While Yahoo! allows you to choose the skin color of your character, they offer only five choices. Why do you think Yahoo! might have chosen these particular colors? What different choices could they have offered, both in terms of quantity and hue? Being given the choice of skin color inevitably leads us to reflect on the fraught history of the meanings that have been attached to and the categories created for skin color throughout history, especially American history. If you were creating an avatar, what are some of the decision-making choices you might go through in deciding on skin color? What message would you be sending to other players?

## Working with the Text

1. Starting with the questions about skin color already discussed, compile your own list of what you think might be the most complicated, controversial, or tricky identity choices. What makes these categories so potentially significant, in your opinion? If you were a consultant on designing an avatar creation program, what kinds of choices would you recommend offering to players?

2. If you have created an avatar before for use in a video game or online environment, write about what your character looks like and the decision-making process you went through in creating this identity. Who did you see as your potential audiences? What meanings did you want to create with this identity? What attitude did you want to represent?

   If you have not created an avatar before, speculate on what kind of character you would like to create for yourself. As with those writing about the avatars they have experience with, think about the rhetorical impact of your creation. Who do you see as your audiences? What kinds of reactions would you be interested in exploring in your onscreen identity?

   Working individually, or in teams, explore an avatar creation program, whether on the Sims, Second Life, or a video-game system such as the Nintendo Wii. Make notes about the different kinds of options that the different programs offer. Based on your analysis, what assumptions about the importance of various aspects of physical appearance can you find in these different programs? In what ways do these assumptions and choices defy or reinforce stereotypes about physical identity?

# CREATING CULTURE

## SOCIAL NETWORKING

In 2003 a website called MySpace appeared on the Internet. Initially aimed at musicians who wanted to make information about themselves and samples of their music available online, MySpace exploded in popularity to become a favorite destination for thousands of Web surfers, mostly young people. Along with similar sites such as Facebook, Xanga, and Friendster, MySpace has become part of what is called the social-networking phenomenon. These sites allow anyone to create his or her own webpage and make links with their friends' pages, including friends met exclusively online. Users with a social-networking account will spend hours online chatting with people, posting messages on their blogs, uploading pictures, and downloading music and videos. Members of these websites include the famous and not-so-famous, but in the world of social networking, all sites are in one

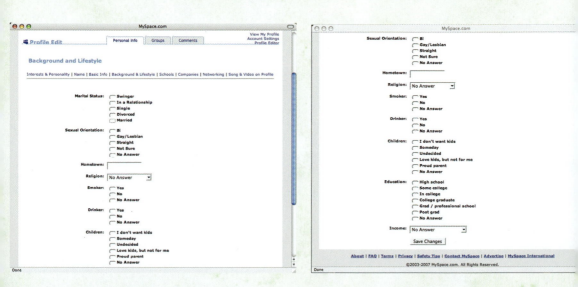

Part of the Profile Section from MySpace.com. As you look at the options listed, discuss which categories you would feel most and least comfortable using. How do the choice of categories and the way the options are worded create assumptions about who the average MySpace user is likely to be and how he or she wants to interact with other social networkers?

sense created equal: the basic format of the webpage of a world-famous musician and that of one of his or her fans are the same. One thing is certain about these websites: you do not just visit these sites, you participate in them. Just like online chat rooms and role-playing games, social-networking sites allow you to craft the identity you wish to present to the online world in relation to the preexisting profile and formatting options each site offers.

In essence, social-networking sites allow you to write your online identity, combining written texts, images, sound files, even video clips, to create an online presence that may be visited by almost anyone, depending on how available you make your page (and most social-networking sites also feature availability restrictions for posters under 17, although verifying the age of subscribers is still largely based on the honor system). Thus, a social-networking page not only allows a person to communicate with his or her real-life friends online but also to acquire a vast number of new virtual friends who know each other only through their cyber identities.

## "Meet My 5,000 New Best Pals"

## Janet Kornblum

*In "Meet My 5,000 New Best Pals,"* USA Today *reporter Janet Kornblum focuses her attention on the virtual aspect of social-networking sites. She asks questions about how an online social life may be changing our understanding of what it means to be a friend and how social interactions on a social-networking site both mimic and change the dynamics of face-to-face relationships.*

## Before You Read

1. Take an inventory of how many people in class participate in one or more social-networking sites. Discuss as a class what people see as the biggest advantages and disadvantages of interacting with others online. What new problems do they encounter? What problems do they see social-networking sites as helping with? What advice would experienced users give to first-timers?

2. How do social networkers define what *friend* means in the online environment? What similarities and differences do online friends have with real-world friends? Given that many online friends are also face-to-face friends, are there any differences between online and in-person interactions?

3. A key component of most social-networking sites is the ability to include a picture of one's self (as indicated, for example, by the very

name Facebook). What considerations come into play when deciding on whether to include a picture and what picture to include? What role does gender, race, or ethnicity play in the decision?

**B**rittnie Sarnes has 5,000 MySpace friends. Actually, make that 5,036. At last count, anyhow. About ten people a day ask to "friend" her.

Usually she says yes.

She knows they're total strangers, but it doesn't matter. Each time she's asked, it feels "kinda cool—like 'Oh, this person thinks I'm cool enough to befriend me,'" says Brittnie, 17, of Columbus, Ohio.

From there, anything can happen. The person might "comment" her page. She might send her email or an instant message, and they could start a conversation. They might even become real-life friends.

But probably, she'll just sit on Brittnie's list, joining the 90 percent of her friends with whom she has virtually no contact.

Call it a hobby. Call it an obsession. Call it the new way of socializing in the networked world.

Call it "friending," the way millions of teens and young adults obsessed with social-networking sites such as MySpace and Facebook are making connections.

Friendship always has been a tricky game, especially for teens. But in the past it was played out in school hallways, on playgrounds, and in late-night phone calls.

These days it is happening in full color on the computer screen—often in front of the world. And it can be confusing, especially for teens trying to fit in.

How many friends should one have? What kind of friends should they be? Are online friends "real"?

Does it help boost self-esteem, or might it be harmful?

### THERE ARE NO RULES

"They're evolving," says Peter Post of Emily Post Institute, the etiquette and manners clearinghouse.

For Valerie Smithers, 17, of Sonoma, Calif., "it's kind of like entertainment." But she adds, "My family members and all my friends make fun of me. I'm so, like, into it."

But Amanda Peters, 17, of Pinole, Calif., worries that friending teaches teens bad social skills. "All these friendships aren't real," says Amanda, who recently wrote a story for a teen literary journal about how friending is getting out of control. "If anything happens where you get annoyed with them, you can just delete them from your list and never have to worry about them again.

"If I get mad at my friend that I go to school with, I can't just erase her from my life. She's still a person. She still exists. I'm going to have to interact with her."

But friends lists are filled with all sorts of friends—from best friends to virtual strangers.

"The idea of actually meeting all your friends on your MySpace page is just strange," says Danah Boyd, a social media researcher for Yahoo!. "You wouldn't do that. These are just people you're connected to. And you connect to them for a ton of different reasons."

Michael Bugeja, director of the Greenlee School of Journalism and Communication at Iowa State University and author of *Interpersonal Divide: The Search for Community in a Technological Age,* says real friends can never be replaced by online ones. "Friending really appeals to the ego, where friendships appeal to the conscience," he says.

When people friend others online, "they're making social contacts." But those friends could develop into "more substantive" relationships, he adds.

For some, friending is not just a pastime, it's also an indication of social success or failure, says Susan Lipkins, an adolescent psychologist in Port Washington, N.Y.

"If you go to college and you don't have a full bunch of people on your MySpace or Facebook, then it's implying that there's something wrong with you," Lipkins says. "Listing your buddies and your friends is a way of establishing yourself, of feeling connected and feeling like you're accepted."

And for younger teens, especially, "friending is a way of finding status and is the definition of who you are online," says Parry Aftab, an expert on teen safety and the Internet. "You're judged by your friends list."

Just in case you were wondering: size matters. For some, such as Brittnie, status comes with having extremely long lists of friends, although most MySpace and Facebook users have a few hundred.

"Some people used to collect pet rocks or trinkets or stamps," says Amanda Lenhart, a senior researcher and specialist in teens and technology at the Pew Internet & American Life Project. "And some people collect friends—to see how many people you can put onto your network. Some of it is seen as a proxy for popularity."

## LISTS CAN BE FAKED

Competition for friends can be so fierce that ad-supported websites are cropping up. They plug you into a system where you can start automatically generating friends—or where you can generate fake friends—to make lists look fat.

And last October, a 19-year-old calling himself "Samy" took credit for writing a computer worm that automatically generated friends on his MySpace page.

Some say overly long lists can smack of desperation.

When Georgia Bobley, 18, a student at George Washington University in Washington, D.C., sees a page with more than 500 friends, she thinks "it's a little creepy."

But having too few friends might mean you're not very popular. "When I go onto somebody's Facebook profile, and they have four friends, I'm like, 'Oh, my God. What? They only have four friends?'" She has 329.

Brittnie won't friend anyone with fewer than 150 friends; it means "nobody likes them."

But Valerie, who has 1,327 friends, says she will sometimes ignore list length for the right reasons. If she encounters someone with "only twelve or twenty friends, but they seem like a cool person, I'll start a conversation with them, and I will still treat them like someone who had a thousand friends or something. They could've just started their site, too."

Then there's the issue of the kinds of friends you keep. Make friends with too many losers, and you might find yourself on the other side of a virtual closed door.

If, for instance, a person friends bands (on MySpace you can friend actors, bands, movies, and even commercial characters) that "suck," Brittnie says, "then that person probably does, too, and you probably don't want to add them."

She has other standards: "The other day I got a friend request, and it was a picture of like this dude's (genitals). I didn't add him."

But mostly, for Brittnie and a lot of others, friending is a kind of game. She'll ask to friend someone "like if you come by somebody's page, and you're like, 'They seem cool; I like their hair.' Or, 'Oh, he's hot,' then, you know, you just add them in hopes of maybe they'll talk to me, and we can become best friends. Or maybe they won't."

For others, though, especially younger teens, it's not a game.

"There are lots of kids who go there looking for friends because they don't have them elsewhere," Aftab says. "And they'll find different ways of getting them. The standards may not be so high."

At its root, competing for friends and fighting for status is hardly new behavior, Aftab says. Kids have always judged each other by the friends they keep.

"If you're snubbed by somebody walking down the hall at school, it's not as obvious as if no one wants to be your friend on your profile. If the other kids think one of your friends is lame, and they start commenting to your site, a lot of kids will drop friends because they're seen as not cool by other kids."

It isn't just kids who are learning the rules or making them up as they go along. Take the perilous issue of the Top 8, which seems to trip up everyone at some point.

That's the top eight friends displayed by default on a MySpace page. The rule is, you put your most important friends on your Top 8. Except if you don't know the rule.

That happened with Bob Christianson, 40, of Hudson, Fla. Christianson originally got on MySpace to keep tabs on his 14-year-old daughter and quickly got hooked on the site, which he uses to date and meet people.

But recently, he had to post an explanation of his Top 8.

"Just so I don't offend anybody," he wrote, "I don't rank my friends, so if you're not in my Top 8 it doesn't mean that you are any more or less of a friend to me."

That kind of explanation may calm adults. But the Top 8 issue constantly causes teen angst, says Amanda Peters. "Some people get really anal about it. They're like, 'I'm on your Top 8, but why am I the eighth person? Like how come I'm not No. 2?'

"I think it's just really stupid. I'm not the only friend people have, so why should I have any say on who they have in their top whatever?"

Nevertheless, she understands what happens when Top 8 status isn't reciprocated.

"You could think you're misjudging the relationship. Which sounds really funny because it's such a small trivial thing. You could feel kind of sad, like 'Oh, I thought we were hecka close.'"

## REJECTION STILL HURTS

Those kinds of feelings are natural, Lenhart says. The online world "is a proxy for our off-line experience. It's not surprising that we get hurt when you see things that in the off-line world would be pretty hurtful. When you're rejected, it's being rejected."

Earlier this month, the issue came to light when Facebook, with 9.3 million members, added a feature that turned people's personal information into head-lines that were displayed on friends' pages.

People always could search their friends' profiles; it's part of the privilege of friendship.

But Facebook members suddenly found routine information, such as when they made a new friend or posted a new picture, being broadcast to their entire network of friends, including casual acquaintances and virtual strangers.

The community rebelled. Tens of thousands of members (mostly college students) signed petitions and sent out emails saying they hated the feature because they didn't want their personal information spoon-fed to all their friends.

Facebook responded, adding privacy controls that let people select what kind of information they will allow to be broadcast.

The flap showed that many people don't necessarily consider online friends to be genuine friends. Bugeja says, "They weren't interested in everything everyone else was doing on a subsurface level."

In the end, the move may cause people to reconsider whom they friend, Lenhart says.

Friending is a work in progress, says Paul Saffo, a Silicon Valley futurist and technology consultant.

"Its a good social experiment. Every generation finds its excuse for people to meet people. This is just this generation's thing. It will die back a little bit, and they will keep the part that works."

---

## Working with the Text

1. At the beginning of her article, Kornblum frames her discussion by suggesting some different ways of referring to social networking—"Call it a hobby. Call it an obsession. Call it the new way of socializing in the networked world"—and poses a set of questions for the reader to consider: "How many friends should one have? What kinds of friends should they be? Are online friends 'real'? Does it help boost self-esteem, or might it be harmful?" After reading the article, what answers do you think Kornblum is suggesting to these questions? Do you think parents would find her article worrying or reassuring? How would you answer her questions? What other questions could we consider about social-networking sites such as MySpace or Facebook that Kornblum's article doesn't directly address?

2. One of the main purposes of Kornblum's article is to introduce social networking to readers who are unfamiliar with it. In particular, she contrasts the views of teenage participants in social-networking sites with those of older experts. Write a response to Kornblum's article from the perspective of a regular user of social-networking sites, based either on your own experiences or on those of a friend or classmate. What would you or they agree with about the observations made in the article? What opinions would you question? What insight or idea about social networking did you or they find most interesting and helpful in thinking about the impact of this new form of social interaction?

3. One of the experts cited in the article, Michael Bugeja from Iowa State University, draws a distinction between "friendships" and "friending": "Friending really appeals to the ego, where friendships appeal to the conscience." How do you understand the distinction he is making? For example, how would you explain the distinction to someone else? In what ways do you agree or disagree with the point he is making?

4. Kornblum offers some examples of "Top 8" experiences among MySpace users that involve hurt feelings and tension between online friends. Interview a variety of MySpace users to test Kornblum's findings. How seriously do people regard the Top 8 list? What variety of perspectives do you find? Do some groups of people take the list more seriously than do others?

# THE FUTURE OF SOCIAL NETWORKING/ THE FUTURE OF SOCIAL NETWORKERS

## "When a Risqué Online Persona Undermines a Chance for a Job"

### Alan Finder

*While digging in a closet at home looking for a lost pair of shoes, you come across a large book with a school crest embossed on the front cover. Glancing through the pages, you realize you've found a parent's high school yearbook. Soon everyone in the family is chuckling over the pictures from your parent's past. "Did you really think you looked good like that?" you might ask in wonder over a particularly outlandish picture. "Why do you think I hid the book in the closet?" is the reply.*

*It's a truism that styles of dress, hair, and makeup change quickly among young people, and a look that seemed cool one day can look ridiculous only a short time later. (As someone with a high school yearbook from 1977, I speak from hard experience.) In the predigital world, the textual evidence of these former identities were available only in material form, in yearbooks and photo albums, school papers and family holiday letters. Occasionally, an intrepid journalist would dig up youthful pictures of celebrities and political figures, but for most people, the past could be as open or remain as hidden as they wanted.*

*The rise of digital technology, where text and images can easily be transmitted and stored, poses new challenges to the reality of our changing identities. A Facebook page created by a college student meant primarily for his or her immediate friends, or for other young people online from the same school or with similar interests, can potentially be accessed by anyone on the Web, and the information accessed can include whatever pictures or self-descriptions are added to the page. Because digital information can be downloaded and stored easily just about everywhere, that same Facebook page can remain available in cyberspace for years to come. Ironically, even though one of the most distinctive features of websites are how changeable and impermanent they are (the reason that citations for webpages in academic writing include the specific day the page was accessed, in case it should change or disappear), the very ease by which websites can be created and altered also means they can potentially last forever, stored on various hard drives around the world.*

*What does all this mean for social-networking sites as new spaces for writing in the text-messaging age? In the modern world, and certainly for the last century, adolescence and young adulthood have been seen as times for testing and experimentation, a chance for people to try out different identities and attitudes as part of figuring out one's place in the world. It's a time of life when change can be pretty rapid; probably many people in your class can look back at themselves only four or five years ago and marvel at the differences between those stages of what psychologists call identity formation.*

In "When a Risqué Online Persona Undermines a Chance for a Job," New York Times *reporter Alan Finder writes about a current example of how the play and experimentation with identity common to young people may be interfering with the attempt to create a professional workplace identity when prospective employers resort to Google searches and investigating social-networking sites. The article suggests that the open and shifting audiences for social-networking sites, part of the attraction of "friending," can also raise new questions about self-presentation and identity creation online.*

## Before You Read

1. Write about what you think has been a significant (that is, significant to you) change in your self-presentation, personal style, or sense of personal identity over the course of your life, one that you would be comfortable sharing and discussing with classmates. What prompted the change? Looking back, what is your current attitude toward your earlier identity? How did your earlier experiences help contribute to your current sense of self?

2. Working with your own experiences or those of a friend or classmate, who do you or they see as the primary audiences for your social-networking page? What new people do you or they most hope to attract to the site? Who would you or they least like to visit the site and why?

3. Again, using your own experiences or those of another, come up with the set of rules, whether spoken or unspoken, that you use in deciding what to put or not put on your social-networking site. Where do you or they draw the line? Where are your own or their boundaries for what is appropriate or what you consider acceptable? What advice would you or they give to a newcomer to social networking?

**W**hen a small consulting company in Chicago was looking to hire a summer intern [in June 2006], the company's president went online to check on a promising candidate who had just graduated from the University of Illinois. At Facebook, a popular social-networking site, the executive found the candidate's webpage with this description of his interests: "smokin' blunts" (cigars hollowed out and stuffed with marijuana), shooting people, and obsessive sex, all described in vivid slang.

It did not matter that the student was clearly posturing. He was done.

"A lot of it makes me think, what kind of judgment does this person have?" said the company's president, Brad Karsh. "Why are you allowing this to be viewed publicly, effectively, or semipublicly?"

Many companies that recruit on college campuses have been using search engines like Google and Yahoo! to conduct background checks on seniors looking for their first job. But now, college career counselors and other experts say, some recruiters are looking up applicants on social-networking sites like Facebook, MySpace, Xanga, and Friendster, where college students often post risqué or teasing photographs and provocative comments about drinking, recreational drug use, and sexual exploits in what some mistakenly believe is relative privacy.

When viewed by corporate recruiters or admissions officials at graduate and professional schools, such pages can make students look immature and unprofessional, at best.

"It's a growing phenomenon," said Michael Sciola, director of the career resource center at Wesleyan University in Middletown, Conn. "There are lots of employers that Google. Now they've taken the next step."

At New York University, recruiters from about thirty companies told career counselors that they were looking at the sites, said Trudy G. Steinfeld, executive director of the center for career development.

"The term they've used over and over is red flags," Ms. Steinfeld said. "Is there something about their lifestyle that we might find questionable or that we might find goes against the core values of our corporation?"

Facebook and MySpace [...] have attracted millions of avid young participants, who mingle online by sharing biographical and other information, often intended to show how funny, cool, or outrageous they are.

On MySpace and similar sites, personal pages are generally available to anyone who registers, with few restrictions on who can register. Facebook, though, has separate requirements for different categories of users; college students must have a college email address to register. Personal pages on Facebook are restricted to friends and others on the user's campus, leading many students to assume that they are relatively private.

But companies can gain access to the information in several ways. Employees who are recent graduates often retain their college email addresses, which enables them to see pages. Sometimes, too, companies ask college students working as interns to perform online background checks, said Patricia Rose, the director of career services at the University of Pennsylvania.

Concerns have already been raised about these and other Internet sites, including their potential misuse by stalkers and students exposing their own misbehavior, for example by posting photographs of hazing by college sports teams. Add to the list of unintended consequences the new hurdles for the job search.

Ana Homayoun runs Green Ivy Educational Consulting, a small firm that tutors and teaches organizational skills to high school students in the San Francisco area. Ms. Homayoun visited Duke University this spring for an alumni weekend and while there planned to interview a promising job applicant.

Curious about the candidate, Ms. Homayoun went to her page on Facebook. She found explicit photographs and commentary about the student's sexual escapades, drinking, and pot smoking, including testimonials from friends. Among the pictures were shots of the young woman passed out after drinking.

"I was just shocked by the amount of stuff that she was willing to publicly display," Ms. Homayoun said. "When I saw that, I thought, 'O.K., so much for that.'"

Ms. Rose said a recruiter had told her he rejected an applicant after searching the name of the student, a chemical engineering major, on Google. Among the things the recruiter found, she said, was this remark: "I like to blow things up."

Occasionally students find evidence online that may explain why a job search is foundering. Tien Nguyen, a senior at the University of California, Los Angeles, signed up for interviews on campus with corporate recruiters, beginning last fall, but he was seldom invited.

A friend suggested in February that Mr. Nguyen research himself on Google. He found a link to a satirical essay, titled "Lying Your Way to the Top," that he had published last summer on a website for college students. He asked that the essay be removed. Soon, he began to be invited to job interviews, and he has now received several offers.

"I never really considered that employers would do something like that," he said. "I thought they would just look at your résumé and grades."

Jennifer Floren is chief executive of Experience Inc., which provides online information about jobs and employers to students at 3,800 universities. "This is really the first time that we've seen that stage of life captured in a kind of time capsule and in a public way," Ms. Floren said. "It has its place, but it's moving from a fraternity or sorority living room. It's now in a public arena."

Some companies, including Enterprise Rent-a-Car, Ernst & Young, and Osram Sylvania, said they did not use the Internet to check on college job applicants.

"I'd rather not see that part of them," said Maureen Crawford Hentz, manager of talent acquisition at Osram Sylvania. "I don't think it's related to their bona fide occupational qualifications."

More than a half-dozen major corporations, including Morgan Stanley, Dell, Pfizer, L'Oréal, and Goldman Sachs, turned down or did not respond to requests for interviews.

But other companies, particularly those involved in the digital world like

Microsoft and Métier, a small software company in Washington, D.C., said researching students through social-networking sites was now fairly typical. "It's becoming very much a common tool," said Warren Ashton, group marketing manager at Microsoft. "For the first time ever, you suddenly have very public information about almost any candidate."

At Microsoft, Mr. Ashton said, recruiters are given broad latitude over how to work, and there is no formal policy about using the Internet to research applicants. "There are certain recruiters and certain companies that are probably more in tune with the new technologies than others are," he said.

Microsoft and Osram Sylvania have also begun to use networking sites in a different way, participating openly in online communities to get out their company's messages and to identify talented job candidates.

Students may not know when they have been passed up for an interview or a job offer because of something a recruiter saw on the Internet. But more than a dozen college career counselors said recruiters had been telling them since last fall about incidents in which students' online writing or photographs had raised serious questions about their judgment, eliminating them as job candidates.

Some college career executives are skeptical that many employers routinely check applicants online. "My observation is that it's more fiction than fact," said Tom Devlin, director of the career center at the University of California, Berkeley.

At a conference in late May, Mr. Devlin said, he asked forty employers if they researched students online and everyone said no.

Many career counselors have been urging students to review their pages on Facebook and other sites with fresh eyes, removing photographs or text that may be inappropriate to show to their grandmother or potential employers. Counselors are also encouraging students to apply settings on Facebook that can significantly limit access to their pages.

Melanie Deitch, director of marketing at Facebook, said students should take advantage of the site's privacy settings and be smart about what they post. But students may not be following the advice.

"I think students have the view that Facebook is their space and that the adult world doesn't know about it," said Mark W. Smith, assistant vice chancellor and director of the career center at Washington University in St. Louis. "But the adult world is starting to come in."

---

## Working with the Text

1. Brad Karsh, the president of a consulting company, says that he uses information about job candidates from sites such as Facebook to ask "what kind of judgment does this person have? . . . Why are you allowing

this to be viewed publicly, effectively, or semipublicly?" How fair do you think it is that some employers use social-networking sites to make evaluations about the judgment and character of job candidates? What kind of answer do you think the job candidate in the example cited in the article (a recent graduate of the University of Illinois) might give to the question that Karsh asks?

2. Finder reports that some companies do not think that checking out the social-networking sites of job candidates is useful or appropriate: " 'I'd rather not see that part of them,' said Maureen Crawford Hentz, manager of talent acquisition at Osram Sylvania. 'I don't think it's related to their bona fide occupational qualifications.' " What do you think Hentz means when she refers to "that part of them" in relation to job candidates? Compare Hentz's response to that of Brad Karsh in question 1. What do their two opinions tell us about the range of attitudes that employers have toward assessing job applicants? What arguments, pro and con, can be made for each point of view?

3. Jennifer Floren, the chief executive of a company that provides job-seeking information to college students, suggests that "[t]his is really the first time that we've seen that stage of life captured in a kind of time capsule and in a public way....It has its place, but it's moving from a fraternity or sorority living room. It's now in a public arena." How might Floren's observations make a young social-networking user reexamine how he or she writes his or her personal profile and online identity? What new questions does the potential "time-capsule" quality of social networking raise for the process of trying out new identities and attitudes?

# F O U R

EXERCISE

## Social Networking for the Future

Alan Finder's article raises concerns for social-networking users thinking about starting their postgraduate careers. In one sense, these concerns stem from the newness of online social networking. MySpace, for example, was founded in 2003, so it's no wonder that we are still figuring out the kinds of effects, both positive and negative, that social networking as a form of communication and identity formation will have. No one really is an expert yet. Add to this newness the fact that Internet-based communication changes rapidly, so how we use social-networking sites now may transform dramatically in as little as six months.

In another sense, though, the questions that Finder examines are really very old ones in terms of rhetoric and writing. In essence, we are looking at issues of audience: who may be reading your social-networking site, and for how long? Given the openness of the Internet, even with the different privacy protections offered and being developed by different networking sites, these questions of audience and readership can never be answered precisely. However, because all writers have implicit audiences in mind, whether they are aware of them or not, we can focus on some potential target readers and design spaces accordingly.

For this project, begin by working in groups to generate a list of potential audiences that you think the typical college-age social-network user might not be considering but that could have a dramatic impact on that user's life. Here are some possibilities:

- Potential employers, now and in the future.
- Parents and family members of a new significant other.
- Future voters.
- Business clients.

You can generate additional possibilities. Keep in mind that career plans change and that our working lives often turn out to be much less predictable than we might think. Some in class, for example, might think that "future voters" would never apply to them. But just as it might have been difficult at age six to predict the kind of person you are now, the person you become in ten, twenty, or thirty years may be equally mysterious. In any case, you might want to keep your options open.

After creating the list, work individually or in groups to come up with guidelines for creating a social-networking site geared toward that potential audience. As you do so, remember that the nature of online relationships is that the audiences remain multiple. How do you balance the needs, for example, of creating an online identity that appeals to friends and reflects who you are with what will also work in conveying the image you want to this new audience? Depending on the technological resources available, you can expand this project to include redesigning existing social-networking sites of your own or of others in the class, or in creating mock sites that illustrate the guidelines you develop.

We understand logos in an almost intuitive way, as thi[s]
of a dual image: both a symbol of a product or compan[y]
a[t] the same [tim]e a kind of argument for the produ[ct]
[c]ompany. How[ever,] when we try to explain exactly how

# FOUR

kind of a [d]
[s]ame time a ki[nd]
[s] to explain e[x]
[f]orm of argumen[t]
[us]ed. After all
[t]hat has an o[b]
[i]on between a
[a]utomobile? Wh[y]
[y] images, imag[e]
[is] simple after
[n]d of a dual
[s] a kind of ar[gument]
[e]xplain exactl[y]
[f]orm of argumen[t]
[us]ed. After all
[t]hat has an o[b]
[i]on between a
[a]utomobile? Wh[y]
[y] images, imag[e]
[is] simple after
[s] a dual image:
[gu]ment for the p[roduct]
[and] work, the me[ans]

**CHAPTER**

# Pop (Up) Advertising

We understand logos in an [almost]
intuitive way, as this kind of
[dual] image: both a symbol of a p[roduct]
or company, and at the same [time a]
kind of argument for the p[roduct]
and company. However, when we [try to]
explain exactly how logos wor[k, the]
means by which a picture can

Look at the images below. In a way, it is almost confusing to call them "images" because we instantly recognize and read them in terms of the companies and products they represent. Our responses are so automatic, we have to make a conscious effort to see these symbols simply as pictures, as a check mark design or a piece of fruit. For many of us, the word that immediately comes to mind when describing these images is *logo,* short for "logotype," a specific kind of symbol with a specific meaning.

Here are two more images that we instantly recognize as symbols, although we might only describe one as a logo:

Similar though not identical in shape and design, these two images produce very different meanings for us. It's not just that one makes us think of a car company and the other of the idea of peace in a nostalgic, 1960s kind of way. We know that the first symbol, the "logo," doesn't just stand for a particular kind of car; it also acts as a kind of advertisement for the car, a form of persuasion and rhetoric.

We understand logos in an almost intuitive way, as this kind of a dual image: both a symbol of a product or company, and at the same time a kind of argument for the product and company. However, when we try to explain exactly how logos work, the means by which a picture can become a form of argument and persuasion, the situation becomes significantly more complicated. After all, it's not as if these logos, or even most logos, use an image that has an obvious resemblance to the company or product. What is the connection between a swoosh and a shoe, an apple and a computer, or a star and an automobile? When we stop to think about them, these simple, common, everyday images, images we read and react to without conscious effort, may not be so simple after all.

# O N E

EXERCISE

## Exploring Logos

Put together a collection of familiar logos that you encounter on a regular basis, whether in the media, on your computer, on products around the home, even on the clothing you and others wear. Choose one or two as case studies of how logos work as forms of communication and persuasion. Some ideas you might consider:
- Do the images represent real objects (like an apple) or are they more abstract (like a swoosh)? What different kinds of associations do you and others in the class have to each kind of image?
- Where do you encounter these logos most often? Why do you think the creators of the logos deploy them where they do?
- How have people adopted and adapted these logos as part of their own wardrobe, décor, or other aspects of their identity? What are the attractions of logos as fashion statements or markers of status? Who is using whom in these transactions, in your opinion?

# T W O

EXERCISE

## Creating Logos

Working in groups, develop your own logo for an organization you are involved with. You could even work on coming up with a logo for your writing class or discussion group. As you work up a design, keep the following issues in mind:
- What ideas and attitudes about your group do you want to communicate with your logo?
- To be eye-catching and memorable, logos are often simple and basic in design. At the same time, they need to be unique and distinct from other logos. What are the challenges involved in designing such a symbol?
- Which logos do class members as a group find most effective? Why do you think the results turned out as they did?

# THE UNIVERSE OF ADVERTISING

**Leela:** Didn't you have ads in the 20th century?

**Fry:** Well sure, but not in our dreams. Only on TV and radio. And in magazines. And movies. And at ball games and on buses and milk cartons and T-shirts and written on the sky. But not in dreams. No siree!—*A conversation from the 30th century, as imagined on the animated television show* Futurama

The example of the logo applies to all advertising in general. We are all so used to seeing, hearing, and reading advertising everywhere we go, we can assume it is as natural as the sun, sky, and clouds. It could also be argued that advertising is our most common form of rhetoric, of the art and craft of using language and images to persuade others to feel, believe, and (most important) to act in certain ways. Although the disciplined study of rhetoric is far older than modern advertising, dating back to the great ancient Greek rhetoricians and philosophers such as Aristotle and Quintilian, we tend to use metaphors drawn from commerce and advertising to describe just about every form of persuasion and argument we use or come into contact with. We will talk about "selling someone" on an idea, for example, whether it's being hired for a job, agreeing to go on a date, or even being elected president of the United States.

On the one hand, the purpose of persuasion in general and advertising in particular seems obvious: to get others to do what you want. In the case of advertising, the desired action is exchanging money for a product or service. On the other hand, while the ultimate goals of advertising and persuasion seem simple, our individual relationships and reactions to advertising are anything but; as a result, the culture of advertising and persuasion raises important questions about ethics, influence, and resistance.

## ADVERTISING AND YOU

Here's a curious aspect about advertising. Ask someone about the purpose of advertising, and he or she will most likely say, "To try and sell you something." Ask them for examples of effective advertising campaigns, and the same person might talk about how the fashion industry can convince people they need to buy a whole new wardrobe every year to remain in style, or how soft-drink manufacturers try to make us think of ourselves as "Coke people" or "Pepsi people." When it comes to his or her personal situation, however, he or she is just as likely to add, "But it doesn't really affect me."

Our relationship to advertising forms a paradox. Every year, over $200 billion is spent on advertising in the United States alone (another way to look at it: almost $700 a year for every man, woman, and child). Clearly, someone must think that advertising is effective. However, many of us believe that we are individually immune to the effects of advertising. Sure, other people might fall for slick commercials and promotional come-ons, but we're in on the game. But how "immune" are we?

Consider advertising as a form of education, for example. Every term, at finals time, students stay up all night poring over notes, trying to cram information into their brains. In spite of their best efforts, however, much of that information may still disappear when the exam is placed in front of them. Try this test, however. Take out a blank sheet of paper and list as many fast-food restaurants as you can in a minute. Chances are, you and your classmates are still writing down names of restaurants when time is up, even though you may have eaten at only a small number of them personally. What's more, you can probably describe their logos, several of their television commercials, and even sing their theme songs. (Here's an interesting survey: ask people around campus to recite the entire first verse of "The Star Spangled Banner." Then ask them to complete this lyric: "Two all-beef patties, special sauce...." Which song proves more familiar?)

Whether you eat at a particular fast-food restaurant or even eat fast food at all is a personal decision, but clearly a lot of time and money has been spent to make sure each of us knows what our options are. Take another look at the picture that opens this chapter. It's from *Supersize Me,* the 2004 documentary about the fast-food industry. In this scene, filmmaker Morgan Spurlock demonstrated that while preschool children couldn't recognize pictures of George W. Bush, George Washington, and other famous Americans, they were already familiar with advertising figures such as Ronald McDonald. Spurlock's point is that advertising provides us with this information even before our formal education begins, so that children still mastering their ABCs will already know where to get a Whopper or where to get a toy with their hamburger. Once you start to think about how much advertising has taught us about the consumer world, whether we wanted to learn it or not, we might rethink the question of how immune to advertising we really are.

## INTERACTING WITH ADVERTISING

In this chapter, we will explore advertising as the most familiar form of rhetoric in popular culture. In particular, this chapter will ask you to consider the relationship among *persuasion, coercion,* and *resistance.* Obviously, nobody forces us to notice advertising, but as the satirical observation from *Futurama* suggests, it's almost impossible to escape it.

## Advertising Inventory

How pervasive is advertising in our culture? Try this experiment in data collection. Choose three or four locations where you typically spend a significant amount of time each day: a classroom, a workplace, a cafeteria, even your room or apartment. Now, make a list of how much advertising is visible or audible in that location. Keep in mind that logos are a form of advertising, so a brand name or logo conspicuously visible on a T-shirt or pair of sneakers are examples of advertising. Compile your lists and share them with others in the class. Use this data to write a personal reflection on how widespread advertising is in your personal environment and in what ways you think this environment might affect and influence you.

To add a visual component to the assignment, take photographs of these locales and use them to illustrate your essay. If you have experience with digital photography and photo software programs, you can incorporate the visuals into the body of your text as well as include language in the photographic images.

The readings in this chapter ask you to explore your relationship to advertising by considering the resources and strategies used by advertisers to influence your decision making as well as looking at how the audiences for advertising (or, to use the more ominous metaphor employed by many advertisers, the target markets) can respond to and even resist these powerful messages. Among the topics to think about:

- When does persuasion become coercion? What is the relative power relationship between advertisers and consumers?
- How have the practices of advertising become part of our everyday language and communication? In what ways do we imitate advertising in our own efforts at persuasion and argument?
- What are the rules of the game, the ethics of advertising? Does anything go, or are there limits, either legal or cultural, to the tactics used in advertising?
- How do the ethical issues raised by advertising as a form of persuasion apply to your own writing?

This chapter also focuses on the interactive nature of popular culture in the digital age by recognizing that advertising is not simply a one-way street. When advertising campaigns involve providing consumers with free decals, stickers, and clothing displaying the corporate logo, the audience is invited not just to buy a product or service but also to identify with and become part of the campaign. This approach suggests that advertising is as much about appealing to people's most deeply held spiritual beliefs and desires as it is about touting the practical features of a particular product. In the section on buzz marketing, for example, contemporary advertisers seek to erase the line between advertiser and audience by enlisting everyone in the process of selling.

When a couple of college students propose licensing themselves as advertising space to raise money for tuition and books, they force us to consider the question of who is using whom in the advertising relationship. Digital software also allows almost anyone to participate in the critique of advertising through parody, satire, and even sabotage. From *Mad* magazine to *Saturday Night Live* and *The Simpsons,* satirists have made fun of advertising and commercials, but in the age of the Internet, such forms of resistance are not just for professional writers and performers—just about anyone with a home computer and basic software package can take part.

More and more, the distinctions between advertising and argument, persuasion and marketing, and information and propaganda have become fuzzy. The infomercial, for example, essentially an extended commercial masquerading as a news or entertainment program, has moved from selling kitchen appliances and cleaning products to promoting political campaigns and government policies. As a result, many of us have become increasingly suspicious of the motives behind every media message we see or hear. Such suspicion can take the form of a healthy skepticism and critical thinking, but skepticism can also turn into a cynicism that can make any kind of communication impossible. In this chapter, we will take stock of how each of us negotiates the complicated relationship between persuasion and resistance in popular culture.

## THE EVOLUTION OF ADVERTISING

### "The Hard Sell: Advertising in America"

#### Bill Bryson

*Advertising is so pervasive in the world around us that it seems as natural as leaves on the trees and the sun in the sky. Yet as Bill Bryson points out in the following essay, modern advertising as we know it dates back only a little over a century. In the time since George Eastman developed a series of marketing strategies to sell his new Kodak cameras (strategies that included the creation of the name "Kodak" itself), advertising has grown into a multibillion-dollar industry; become part of every form of mass media; and influenced our language use, sense of identity, and even how we relate to one another.*

*In "The Hard Sell: Advertising in America," Bill Bryson describes the development of the central practices, theories, and techniques that have informed the creation of advertising and advertising campaigns. His essay ranges from the psychological effects that advertisers hope to create in consumers to the complex and expensive process of developing brand names. Along the way, his style suggests someone who is fascinated, often amused, but always a bit wary of the claims and tactics of advertising.*

*Bill Bryson is a popular writer who has specialized in essays and books recounting his travels around the world as well as explanations of important ideas, trends, and social customs. Among his books are* A Short History of Nearly Everything, A Walk in the Woods, *and* The Mother Tongue.

### Before You Read

Brainstorm a list of the most common strategies that advertisers use to convince you to buy products and services. Work together in small groups and as a class to combine your findings into a master list of common advertising strategies. Then, as a class, rank these strategies from most to least effective. Use your preliminary findings as you read to see how they connect with Bryson's arguments.

In 1885, a young man named George Eastman formed the Eastman Dry Plate and Film Company in Rochester, New York. It was rather a bold thing to do. Aged just 31, Eastman was a junior clerk in a bank on a comfortable but modest salary of $15 a week. He had no background in business. But he was passionately devoted to photography and had become increasingly gripped with the conviction that anyone who could develop a simple, untechnical camera, as opposed to the cumbersome, outsized, fussily complex contrivances then on the market, stood to make a fortune.

Eastman worked tirelessly for three years to perfect his invention, supporting himself in the meantime by making dry plates for commercial photographers, and in June 1888 produced a camera that was positively dazzling in its simplicity: a plain black box just six and a half inches long by three and a quarter inches wide, with a button on the side and a key for advancing the film. Eastman called his device the *Detective Camera*. Detectives were all the thing— Sherlock Holmes was just taking off with American readers—and the name implied that it was so small and simple that it could be used unnoticed, as a detective might.

The camera had no viewfinder and no way of focusing. The *photographer* or *photographist* (it took a while for the first word to become the established one) simply held the camera in front of him, pressed a button on the side, and hoped for the best. Each roll held a hundred pictures. When a roll was fully exposed, the anxious owner sent the entire camera to Rochester for developing. Eventually he received the camera back, freshly loaded with film, and— assuming all had gone well—one hundred small circular pictures, two and a half inches in diameter. [...]

In September 1888, Eastman changed the name of the camera to *Kodak*—an odd choice, since it was meaningless, and in 1888 no one gave meaningless names to products, especially successful products. Since British patent applications at the time demanded full explanation of trade and brand names, we know how Eastman arrived at his inspired name. He crisply summarized his reasoning in his patent application: "First. It is short. Second. It is not capable of mispronunciation. Third. It does not resemble anything in the art and cannot be associated with anything in the art except the Kodak." Four years later the whole enterprise was renamed the Eastman Kodak Company.

Despite the considerable expense involved—a Kodak camera sold for $25, and each roll of film cost $10, including developing—by 1895, over 100,000 Kodaks had been sold and Eastman was a seriously wealthy man. A lifelong bachelor, he lived with his mother in a thirty-seven-room mansion with twelve bathrooms. Soon people everywhere were talking about snapshots, originally a British shooting term for a hastily executed shot. Its photographic sense was coined by the English astronomer Sir John Herschel, who also gave the world the terms *positive* and *negative* in their photographic senses.

From the outset, Eastman developed three crucial strategies that have been the hallmarks of virtually every successful consumer goods company since. First, he went for the mass market, reasoning that it was better to make a little money each from a lot of people rather than a lot of money from a few. He also showed a tireless, obsessive dedication to

## The Kodak Camera

"*You press the button, we do the rest.*"

OR YOU CAN DO IT YOURSELF.

The only camera that anybody can use without instructions. As convenient to carry as an ordinary field glass World-wide success.

*The Kodak is for sale by all Photo stock dealers.*
*Send for the Primer, free.*

**The Eastman Dry Plate & Film Co.**

Price, $25.00 — Loaded for 100 Pictures.  ROCHESTER, N. Y.
Re-loading, $2.00.

making his products better and cheaper. In the 1890s, such an approach was widely perceived as insane. If you had a successful product you milked it for all it was worth. If competitors came along with something better, you bought them out or tried to squash them with lengthy patent fights or other bullying tactics. What you certainly did not do was create new products that made your existing lines obsolescent. Eastman did. Throughout the late 1890s, Kodak introduced a series of increasingly cheaper, niftier cameras—the Bull's Eye model of 1896, which cost just $12, and the famous slimline Folding Pocket Kodak of 1898, before finally in 1900 producing his eureka model: the little box Brownie, priced at just $1 and with film at 15 cents a reel (though with only six exposures per reel).

Above all, what set Eastman apart was the breathtaking lavishness of his advertising. In 1899 alone, he spent $750,000, an unheard-of sum, on advertising. Moreover, it was *good* advertising: crisp, catchy, reassuringly trustworthy. "You press a button—we do the rest" ran the company's first slogan, thus making a virtue of its shortcomings. Never mind that you couldn't load or unload the film yourself. Kodak would do it for you. In 1905, it followed with another classic slogan: "If It Isn't an Eastman, It Isn't a Kodak."

Kodak's success did not escape other businessmen, who also began to see virtue in the idea of steady product refinement and improvement. AT&T and Westinghouse, among others, set up research laboratories with the idea of creating a stream of new products, even at the risk of displacing old ones. Above all, everyone everywhere began to advertise.

Advertising was already a well-established phenomenon by the turn of the twentieth century. Newspapers had begun carrying ads as far back as the early 1700s, and magazines soon followed. (Benjamin Franklin has the distinction of having run the first magazine ad seeking the whereabouts of a runaway slave, in 1741.) By 1850, the country had its first *advertising agency,* the American Newspaper Advertising Agency, though its function was to buy advertising space rather than come up with creative campaigns. The first advertising agency in the modern sense was N. W. Ayer & Sons of Philadelphia, established in 1869. To *advertise* originally carried the sense of to broadcast or disseminate news. Thus a nineteenth-century newspaper that called itself the *Advertiser* meant that it had lots of news, not lots of ads. By the early 1800s the term had been stretched to accommodate the idea of spreading the news of the availability of certain goods or services. A newspaper notice that read "Jos. Parker, Hatter" was essentially announcing that if anyone was in the market for hats, Jos. Parker had them. In the sense of persuading members of the public to acquire items they might not otherwise think of buying—items they didn't know they needed—advertising is a phenomenon of the modern age.

By the 1890s, advertising was appearing everywhere—in newspapers and magazines, on *billboards* (an Americanism dating from 1850), on the sides of buildings, on passing streetcars, on paper bags, even on matchbooks, which were invented in 1892 and were being extensively used as an advertising medium within three years.

Very early on, advertisers discovered the importance of a good slogan. Many of our more venerable slogans are older than you might think. Ivory Soap's "99 44/100 percent pure" dates from 1879. Schlitz has been calling itself "the beer that made Milwaukee famous" since 1895, and Heinz's "57 varieties" followed a year later. Morton Salt's "When it rains, it pours" dates from 1911, the American Florist Association's "Say it with flowers" was first used in 1912, and the "good to the last drop" of Maxwell House coffee, named for the Maxwell House Hotel in Nashville, where it was first served, has been with us since 1907. (The slogan is said to have originated with Teddy Roosevelt, who pronounced the coffee "good to the last drop," prompting one wit to ask, "So what's wrong with the last drop?")

Sometimes slogans took a little working on. Coca-Cola described itself as "the drink that makes a pause refreshing" before realizing, in 1929, that "the pause that refreshes" was rather more succinct and memorable. A slogan could make all the difference to a product's success. After advertising its soap as an efficacious way of dealing with "conspicuous nose pores," Woodbury's Facial Soap came up with the slogan "The skin you love to touch" and won the hearts of millions. The great thing about a slogan was that it didn't have to be accurate to be effective. Heinz never actually had exactly "57 varieties" of anything. The catchphrase arose simply because H. J. Heinz, the company's founder, decided he liked the sound of the number. Undeterred by considerations of verity, he had the slogan slapped on every one of the products he produced, already in 1896 far more than fifty-seven. For a time the company tried to arrange its products into fifty-seven arbitrary clusters, but in 1969 it gave up the ruse altogether and abandoned the slogan.

Early in the 1900s, advertisers discovered another perennial feature of marketing—the *giveaway,* as it was called almost from the start. Consumers soon became acquainted with the irresistibly tempting notion that if they bought a particular product they could expect a reward—the chance to receive a prize, a free book (almost always ostensibly dedicated to the general improvement of one's well-being but invariably a thinly disguised plug for the manufacturer's range of products), a free sample, or a rebate in the form of a shiny dime, or be otherwise endowed with some gratifying bagatelle. Typical of the genre was a turn-of-the-century tome called *The Vital Question Cook Book,* which was promoted as an aid to livelier meals, but which proved upon receipt to contain 112 pages of recipes all involving the use of Shredded Wheat. Many of these had a certain air of desperation about them, notably the "Shredded Wheat Biscuit Jellied Apple Sandwich" and the "Creamed Spinach on Shredded Wheat Biscuit Toast." Almost all involved nothing more than spooning some everyday food on a piece of shredded wheat and giving it an inflated name. Nonetheless the company distributed no fewer than four million copies of *The Vital Question Cook Book* to eager consumers.

The great breakthrough in twentieth-century advertising, however, came with the identification and exploitation of the American consumer's Achilles' heel: anxiety. One of the first to master the form was King Gillette, inventor of the first safety razor and one of the most relentless advertisers of the early 1900s. Most of the early ads featured Gillette himself, who with his fussy toothbrush mustache and well-oiled hair looked more like a caricature of a Parisian waiter than a captain of industry. After starting with a few jaunty words about the ease and convenience of the safety razor—"Compact? Rather!"—he plunged the reader into the heart of the matter: "When you use my razor you are exempt from the dangers that men often encounter who allow their faces to come in contact with brush, soap, and barbershop accessories used on other people."

Here was an entirely new approach to selling goods. Gillette's ads were in effect telling you that not only did there exist a product that you never previously suspected you needed, but if you *didn't* use it you would very possibly attract a crop of facial diseases you never knew existed. The combination proved irresistible. Though the Gillette razor retailed for a hefty $5—half the average workingman's weekly pay—it sold by the millions, and King Gillette became a very wealthy man. (Though only for a time, alas. Like many others of his era, he grew obsessed with the idea of the perfectibility of mankind and expended so much of his energies writing books of convoluted philosophy with titles like *The Human Drift* that he eventually lost control of his company and most of his fortune.)

By the 1920s, advertisers had so refined the art that a consumer could scarcely pick up a magazine without being bombarded with unsettling questions: "Do You Make These Mistakes in English?"; "Will Your Hair Stand Close Inspection?"; "When Your Guests Are Gone—Are You Sorry You Ever Invited Them?" (because, that is, you lack social polish); "Did Nature fail to put roses in your cheeks?"; "Will There be a Victrola in Your Home This Christmas?"[1] The 1920s truly were the Age of Anxiety. One ad pictured a former golf champion, "now only a wistful onlooker," whose career had gone sour because he had neglected his teeth. Scott Tissues mounted a campaign showing a forlorn-looking businessman sitting on a park bench beneath the bold caption "A Serious Business Handicap—These Troubles That Come from Harsh Toilet Tissue." Below the picture the text explained: "65% of all men and women over 40 are suffering from some form of rectal trouble, estimates a prominent specialist connected with one of New York's largest hospitals. 'And one of the contributing causes,' he states, 'is inferior toilet tissue.'" There was almost nothing that one couldn't become uneasy about. One ad even asked: "Can You Buy a Radio Safely?" Distressed bowels were the most frequent target. The makers of Sal Hepatica warned: "We rush to meetings, we dash to parties. We are on the go all day long. We exercise too little, and we eat too much. And, in consequence, we impair our bodily functions—often we retain food within us too long. And when that occurs, poisons are set up—*Auto-Intoxication begins.*"

In addition to the dread of auto-intoxication, the American consumer faced a gauntlet of other newly minted maladies—*pyorrhea, halitosis* (coined as a medical term in 1874, but popularized by Listerine beginning in 1922 with the slogan "Even your best friend won't tell you"), *athlete's foot* (a term invented by the makers of Absorbine Jr. in 1928), *dead cuticles, scabby toes, iron-poor blood, vitamin deficiency* (*vitamins* had been coined in 1912, but the word didn't enter the general vocabulary until the 1920s, when advertisers realized

---

1 The most famous 1920s ad of them all didn't pose a question, but it did play on the reader's anxiety: "They Laughed When I Sat Down, but When I Started to Play…." It was originated by the U.S. School of Music in 1925.

it sounded worryingly scientific), *fallen stomach, tobacco breath,* and *psoriasis,* though Americans would have to wait until the next decade for the scientific identification of the gravest of personal disorders—*body odor,* a term invented in 1933 by the makers of Lifebuoy soap and so terrifying in its social consequences that it was soon abbreviated to a whispered *B.O.*

The white-coated technicians of American laboratories had not only identified these new conditions, but—miraculously, it seemed—simultaneously come up with cures for them. Among the products that were invented or rose to greatness in this busy, neurotic decade were *Cutex* (for those deceased cuticles), *Vick's VapoRub, Geritol, Serutan* ("Natures spelled backwards," as the voiceover always said with somewhat bewildering reassurance, as if spelling a product's name backward conferred some medicinal benefit), *Noxema* (for which read: "knocks eczema"), *Preparation H, Murine* eyedrops, and *Dr. Scholl's Foot Aids.*[2] It truly was an age of miracles—one in which you could even cure a smoker's cough by smoking, so long as it was Old Golds you smoked, because, as the slogan proudly if somewhat untruthfully boasted, they contained "Not a cough in a carload." (As late as 1953, L&M cigarettes were advertised as "just what the doctor ordered!")

By 1927, advertising was a $1.5-billion-a-year industry in the United States, and advertising people were held in such awe that they were asked not only to mastermind campaigns but even to name products. An ad man named Henry N. McKinney, for instance, named *Keds* shoes, *Karo* syrup, *Meadow Gold* butter, and *Uneeda Biscuits.*

Product names tended to cluster around certain sounds. Breakfast cereals often ended in *ies (Wheaties, Rice Krispies, Frosties)*; washing powders and detergents tended to be gravely monosyllabic *(Lux, Fab, Tide, Duz).* It is often possible to tell the era of a product's development by its termination. Thus products dating from the 1920s and early 1930s often ended in *-ex (Pyrex, Cutex, Kleenex, Windex),* while those ending in *-master (Mixmaster, Toastmaster)* generally betray a late-1930s or early-1940s genesis. The development of *Glo-Coat* floor wax in 1932 also heralded the beginning of American business's strange and long-standing infatuation with illiterate spellings, a trend that continued with *ReaLemon* juice in 1935, *Reddi-Wip* whipped cream in 1947, and many hundreds of others since, from *Tastee-Freez* drive-ins to *Toys 'Я' Us,* along with countless others with a *Kwik, E-Z* or *U* (as in *While-U-Wait*) embedded in their titles. The late 1940s saw the birth of a brief vogue for endings in *-matic,* so that car manufacturers offered vehicles with *Seat-O-Matic* levers and *Cruise-O-Matic* transmissions, and even fitted sheets came with *Ezy-Matic* corners. Some companies became associated with certain types of names. Du

2 And yes, there really was a Dr. Scholl. His name was William Scholl, he was a real doctor, genuinely dedicated to the well-being of feet, and they are still very proud of him in his hometown of LaPorte, Indiana.

Pont, for instance, had a special fondness for words ending in -*on*. The practice began with *nylon*—a name that was concocted out of thin air and owes nothing to its chemical properties—and was followed with *Rayon, Dacron, Orlon,* and *Teflon,* among many others. In recent years the company has moved on to what might be called its *Star Trek* phase with such compounds as *Tyvek, Kevlar, Sontara, Cordura, Nomex,* and *Zemorain.*

Such names have more than passing importance to their owners. If American business has given us a large dose of anxiety in its ceaseless quest for a healthier *bottom line* (a term dating from the 1930s, though not part of mainstream English until the 1970s), we may draw some comfort from the thought that business has suffered a great deal of collective anxiety over protecting the names of its products.

A valuable brand name or a cruel stereotype?

A certain cruel paradox prevails in the matter of preserving brand names. Every business naturally wants to create a product that will dominate its market. But if that product so dominates the market that the brand name becomes indistinguishable in the public mind from the product itself—when people begin to ask for a *thermos* rather than a "Thermos brand vacuum flask"—then the term has become generic and the owner faces loss of its trademark protection. That is why advertisements and labels so often carry faintly paranoid-sounding lines like "Tabasco is the registered trademark for the brand of pepper sauce made by McIlhenny Co." and why companies like Coca-Cola suffer palpitations when they see a passage like this (from John Steinbeck's *The Wayward Bus*):

"Got any coke?" another character asked.

"No," said the proprietor. "Few bottles of Pepsi-Cola. Haven't had any coke for a month. . . . It's the same stuff. You can't tell them apart."

An understandable measure of confusion exists concerning the distinction between patents and trademarks and between trademarks and trade names. A *patent* protects the name of the product and its method of manufacture for seventeen years. Thus from 1895 to 1912, no one but the Shredded Wheat Company could make shredded wheat. But because patents require manufacturers to divulge the secrets of their products—and thus make them available to rivals to copy when the patent runs out—companies sometimes choose not to seek their protection. *Coca-Cola,* for one, has never been patented. A *trademark* is effectively the name of a product, its *brand name.* A *trade name* is the name of the manufacturer. So *Ford* is a trade name, *Taurus* a trademark. Trademarks apply not just to names, but also to logos, drawings, and other symbols and depictions. The MGM lion, for instance, is a trademark. Unlike patents, trademark protection goes on forever, or at least as long as the manufacturer can protect it.

For a long time, it was felt that this permanence gave the holder an unfair advantage. In consequence, America did not enact its first trademark law until 1870, almost a century after Britain, and then it was declared unconstitutional by the Supreme Court. Lasting trademark protection did not begin for American companies until 1881. Today, more than a million trademarks have been issued in the United States and the number is rising by about thirty thousand a year.

A good trademark is almost incalculably valuable. Invincible-seeming brand names do occasionally falter and fade. *Pepsodent, Rinso, Chase & Sanborn, Sal Hepatica, Vitalis, Brylcreem,* and *Burma-Shave* all once stood on the commanding heights of consumer recognition but are now defunct or have sunk to the status of what the trade calls "ghost brands"—products that are still produced but little promoted and largely forgotten. For the most part, however, once a product establishes a dominant position in a market, it is exceedingly difficult to depose it. In nineteen of twenty-two product categories, the company that owned the leading American brand in 1925 still has it today—*Nabisco* in cookies, *Kellogg's* in breakfast cereals, *Kodak* in film, *Sherwin Williams* in paint, *Del Monte* in canned fruit, *Wrigley's* in chewing gum, *Singer* in sewing machines, *Ivory* in soap, *Campbell's* in soup, *Gillette* in razors. Few really successful brand names of today were not just as familiar to your grandparents or even great-grandparents, and a well-established brand name has a sort of self-perpetuating power. As *The Economist* has noted: "In the category of food blenders, consumers were still ranking General Electric second twenty years after the company had stopped making them."

An established brand name is so valuable that only about 5 percent of the sixteen thousand or so new products introduced in America each year bear all-new brand names. The others are variants on an existing product—*Tide with Bleach, Tropicana Twister Light Fruit Juices,* and so on. Among some types of product a certain glut is evident. At last count there were 220 types of branded breakfast cereal in America. In 1993, according to an international business survey, the world's most valuable brand was *Marlboro,* with a value estimated at $40 billion, slightly ahead of *Coca-Cola.* Among the other top ten brands were *Intel, Kellogg's, Budweiser, Pepsi, Gillette,* and *Pampers. Nescafé* and *Bacardi* were the only foreign brands to make the top ten, underlining American dominance.

Huge amounts of effort go into choosing brand names. General Foods reviewed 2,800 names before deciding on *Dreamwhip.* (To put this in proportion, try to think of just ten names for an artificial whipped cream.) Ford considered more than twenty thousand possible car names before finally settling on *Edsel* (which proves that such care doesn't always pay), and Standard Oil a similar number of names before it opted for *Exxon.* Sometimes, however, the most successful names are the result of a moment's whimsy. *Betty Crocker* came in a flash to an executive of the Washburn Crosby Company (later absorbed by General Mills), who chose *Betty* because he thought it sounded wholesome and sincere and *Crocker* in memory of a beloved fellow executive who had recently died. At first the name was used only to sign letters responding to customers' requests for advice or information, but by the 1950s, Betty Crocker's smiling, confident face was appearing on more than fifty types of food product, and her loyal followers could buy her recipe books and even visit her "kitchen" at the General Foods headquarters.

Great efforts also go into finding out why people buy the brands they do. Advertisers and market researchers bandy about terms like *conjoint analysis technique, personal drive patterns, Gaussian distributions, fractals,* and other such arcana in their quest to winnow out every subliminal quirk in our buying habits. They know, for instance, that 40 percent of all people who move to a new address will also change their brand of toothpaste, that the average supermarket shopper makes fourteen impulse decisions in each visit, that 62 percent of shoppers will pay a premium for mayonnaise even when they think a cheaper brand is just as good, but that only 24 percent will show the same largely irrational loyalty to frozen vegetables.

To preserve a brand name involves a certain fussy attention to linguistic and orthographic details. To begin with, the name is normally expected to be treated not as a noun but as a proper adjective—that is, the names should be followed by an explanation of what it does: *Kleenex facial tissues, Q-Tip cotton swabs, Jell-O brand gelatin dessert, Sanka brand decaffeinated coffee.* Some types of products—notably cars—are granted an exemption, which explains why General Motors does not have to advertise *Cadillac self-propelled automobiles* or the like. In all cases, the name may not explicitly describe the product's function though it may hint at what it does. Thus *Coppertone* is acceptable; *Coppertan* would not be.

The situation is more than a little bizarre. Having done all they can to make their products household words, manufacturers must then in their advertisements do all in their power to imply that they aren't. Before trademark law was clarified, advertisers positively encouraged the public to treat their products as generics. Kodak invited consumers to "Kodak as you go," turning the brand name into a dangerously ambiguous verb. It would never do that now. The American Thermos Product Company went so far as to boast, "Thermos is a household word," to its considerable cost. Donald F. Duncan, Inc., the original manufacturer of the *Yo-Yo,* lost its trademark protection partly because it was amazingly casual about capitalization in its own promotional literature. "In case you don't know what a yo-yo is..." one of its advertisements went, suggesting that in commercial terms Duncan didn't. Duncan also made the elemental error of declaring, "If It Isn't a Duncan, It Isn't a Yo-Yo," which on the face of it would seem a reasonable claim, but was in fact held by the courts to be inviting the reader to consider the product generic. Kodak had long since stopped saying "If it isn't an Eastman, it isn't a Kodak."

Because of the confusion, and occasional lack of fastidiousness on the part of their owners, many dozens of products have lost their trademark protection, among them *aspirin, linoleum, yo-yo, thermos, cellophane, milk of magnesia, mimeograph, lanolin, celluloid, dry ice, escalator, shredded wheat, kerosene,* and *zipper.* All were once proudly capitalized and worth a fortune.

On July 1, 1941, the New York television station WNBT-TV interrupted its normal viewing to show, without comment, a Bulova watch ticking. For sixty seconds the watch ticked away mysteriously, then the picture faded and the normal programming resumed. It wasn't much, but it was the first television *commercial.*

Both the word and the idea were already well established. The first commercial—the term was used from the very beginning—had been broadcast by radio station WEAF in New York on August 28, 1922. It lasted for either ten or fifteen minutes, depending on which source you credit. Commercial radio was not an immediate hit. In its first two months, WEAF sold only $550 worth of airtime. But by the mid-1920s, sponsors were not only flocking to buy airtime but naming their programs after their products—*The Lucky Strike Hour, The A&P Gypsies, The Lux Radio Theater,* and so on. Such was the obsequiousness of the radio networks that by the early 1930s, many were allowing the sponsors to take complete artistic and production control for the programs. Many of the most popular shows were actually written by the advertising agencies, and the agencies naturally seldom missed an opportunity to work a favorable mention of the sponsor's products into the scripts.

With the rise of television in the 1950s, the practices of the radio era were effortlessly transferred to the new medium. Advertisers inserted their names into the program title—*Texaco Star Theater, Gillette Cavalcade of Sports, Chesterfield Sound-Off Time, The U.S. Steel Hour, Kraft Television Theater, The Chevy Show, The Alcoa Hour, The Ford Star Revue, Dick Clark's Beechnut Show,* and the arresting hybrid *The Lux-Schlitz Playhouse,* which seemed to suggest a cozy symbiosis between soapflakes and beer. The commercial dominance of program titles reached a kind of hysterical peak with a program officially called *Your Kaiser Dealer Presents Kaiser-Frazer "Adventures in Mystery" Starring Betty Furness in "Byline."* Sponsors didn't write the programs any longer, but they did impose a firm control on the contents, most notoriously during a 1959 *Playhouse 90* broadcast of *Judgment at Nuremberg,* when the sponsor, the American Gas Association, managed to have all references to gas ovens and the gassing of Jews removed from the script.

Where commercial products of the late 1940s had scientific-sounding names, those of the 1950s relied increasingly on secret ingredients. Gleem toothpaste contained a mysterious piece of alchemy called *GL-70.*[3] There was never the slightest hint of what GL-70 was, but it would, according to the advertising, not only rout odor-causing bacteria but "wipe out their enzymes!"

A kind of creeping illiteracy invaded advertising, too, to the dismay of many. When Winston began advertising its cigarettes with the slogan "Winston tastes good like a cigarette should," nationally syndicated columnists like Sydney J. Harris wrote anguished essays on what the world was coming to—every educated person knew it should be "as a cigarette should"—but the die was cast. By 1958, Ford was advertising that you could "travel smooth" in a Thunderbird Sunliner and the maker of Ace Combs was urging buyers to "comb it handsome"—a trend that continues today with "pantihose that fits you real comfortable" and other grammatical manglings too numerous and dispiriting to dwell on.

We may smile at the advertising ruses of the 1920s—frightening people with the threat of "fallen stomach" and "scabby toes"—but in fact such creative manipulation still goes on, albeit at a slightly more sophisticated level. *The New York Times Magazine* reported in 1990 how an advertising copywriter had been told to come up with some impressive labels for a putative hand cream. She invented the arresting and healthful-sounding term *oxygenating moisturizers* and wrote accompanying copy with reference to "tiny bubbles of oxygen that release moisture into your skin." This done, the advertising was turned over to the company's research and development department, which was instructed to come up with a product that matched the copy.

If we fall for such commercial manipulation, we have no one to blame but ourselves. When Kentucky Fried Chicken introduced "Extra Crispy" chicken

---

[3] For purposes of research, I wrote to Procter & Gamble, Gleem's manufacturer, asking what GL-70 was, but the public relations department evidently thought it eccentric of me to wonder what I had been putting in my mouth all through childhood and declined to reply.

to sell alongside its "Original" chicken, and sold it at the same price, sales were disappointing. But when its advertising agency persuaded it to promote "Extra Crispy" as a premium brand and to put the price up, sales soared. Much of the same sort of verbal hypnosis was put to work for the benefit of the fur industry. Dyed muskrat makes a perfectly good fur, for those who enjoy cladding themselves in dead animals, but the name clearly lacks stylishness. The solution was to change the name to *Hudson seal.* Never mind that the material contained not a strand of seal fur. It sounded good, and sales skyrocketed.

Truth has seldom been a particularly visible feature of American advertising. In the early 1970s, Chevrolet ran a series of ads for the Chevelle boasting that the car had "109 advantages to keep it from becoming old before its time." When looked into, it turned out that these 109 vaunted features included such items as rearview mirrors, backup lights, balanced wheels, and many other components that were considered pretty well basic to any car. Never mind; sales soared. At about the same time, Ford, not to be outdone, introduced a "limited edition" Mercury Monarch at $250 below the normal list price. It achieved this, it turned out, by taking $250 worth of equipment off the standard Monarch.

And has all this deviousness led to a tightening of the rules concerning what is allowable in advertising? Hardly. In 1986, as William Lutz relates in *Doublespeak,* the insurance company John Hancock launched an ad campaign in which "real people in real situations" discussed their financial predicaments with remarkable candor. When a journalist asked to speak to these real people, a company spokesman conceded that they were actors and "in that sense they are not real people."

During the 1984 presidential campaign, the Republican National Committee ran a television advertisement praising President Reagan for providing cost-of-living pay increases to federal workers "in spite of those sticks-in-the-mud who tried to keep him from doing what we elected him to do." When it was pointed out that the increases had in fact been mandated by law since 1975 and that Reagan had in any case three times tried to block them, a Republican official responded: "Since when is a commercial supposed to be accurate?" Quite.

In linguistic terms, perhaps the most interesting challenge facing advertisers today is that of selling products in an increasingly multicultural society. Spanish is a particular problem, not just because it is spoken over such a widely scattered area but also because it is spoken in so many different forms. Brown sugar is *azucar negra* in New York, *azucar prieta* in Miami, *azucar morena* in much of Texas, and *azucar pardo* pretty much everywhere else—and that's just one word. Much the same bewildering multiplicity applies to many others. In consequence, embarrassments are all but inevitable.

In mainstream Spanish, *bichos* means *insects,* but in Puerto Rico it means *testicles,* so when a pesticide maker promised to bring death to the *bichos,* Puerto Rican consumers were at least bemused, if not alarmed. Much the same happened when a maker of bread referred to its product as *un bollo de pan* and discovered that to Spanish-speaking Miamians of Cuban extraction that means a woman's private parts. And when Perdue Chickens translated its slogan "It takes a tough man to make a tender chicken" into Spanish, it came out as the slightly less macho "It takes a sexually excited man to make a chick sensual."

Never mind. Sales soared.

---

## Working with the Text

1. What does Bryson identify as the "three central strategies" developed by George Eastman to sell Kodak cameras? Of these strategies, which does Bryson think is the most important and why? What evidence does he offer to support his claim that these strategies have "been the hallmarks of virtually every successful consumer goods company since"?

2. Bryson writes that the "great thing about a slogan was that it didn't have to be accurate to be effective." Why not, according to Bryson? If slogans do not have to be accurate, what do they have to be? What are the keys to a successful slogan? What contemporary examples can you find to illustrate Bryson's point?

3. "The greatest breakthrough in twentieth-century advertising," Bryson writes, "came with the identification and exploitation of the American consumer's Achilles' heel: anxiety." What examples of these anxieties does Bryson provide? Which were preexisting anxieties, and which did advertising create? What more recent forms of advertising-created anxiety can you add to his list?

4. Bryson describes the care and trouble that goes into developing brand names for products, as well as trends and fads in product-name design, such as adding *-ex* and *-matic* to words or using strange spellings. Which of these trends do you see continuing today? What new trends can you identify, such as the use of the letters *i* and *e* for Internet and computer goods and services?

5. One implication of Bryson's essay is that advertising campaigns are more important than the actual product or service being advertised. Based on the principles articulated by Bryson, work in groups to develop an ad campaign for an imaginary product or service. Start by coming up with a product and a catchy brand name; expand the project to include designs for ads, logos, and websites, even a script for a commercial. When you finish, write a reflective description and analysis of the strategies you developed for your campaign. Who was your target audience? What emotions and anxieties did you appeal to or try to create in that audience? How did the group feel about the ethics of what you were doing? Bryson quotes a political campaign strategist who asked rhetorically, "Since when is a commercial supposed to be accurate?" How is or isn't this attitude reflected in the campaign you designed? When did you think you were being most honest? When did you think you were being most deceptive? Were there ethical lines you were reluctant to cross? Why?

6. The advertisements included here with Bryson's essay show examples of the development of advertising from 1905 to the turn of the twenty-first century. Analyze these ads in terms of the concepts articulated by Bryson. How well do they illustrate the "three central strategies" described by Bryson? What elements of design and layout have remained the same, and what have changed? How has the relationship between words and images developed over the century, from the first ad to the most recent?

# "Salespeak"

## Roy F. Fox

*When we attend a high school or college sporting event, we are probably not surprised to see advertising for consumer goods on the walls of the stadium or arena. We are probably also not surprised if the sports facility itself is named after a corporate sponsor. Other buildings on your campus may also be named after companies and sponsors, and your college food court might feature national fast-food chains. More and more, the presence of advertising in schools is becoming business as usual.*

*From one perspective, this link makes sense. It's possible to think of advertising as a form of education; in fact, many people involved in advertising describe what they do in this way. Advertising provides consumers with information about products and services they may find useful. Like any good teacher (as well as any good writer), advertisers search for the most effective and efficient means to communicate this information to their audience. Viewed in this way, advertising becomes as vital and necessary a part of contemporary living as schools themselves.*

*Obviously, advertisers will also acknowledge that the goal of advertising is not just the transmission of information. The ultimate purpose of advertising is to persuade us to buy those products and services about which advertising informs us. Issues of objectivity, neutrality, and fairness in presenting multiple points of view, all matters that classroom teachers must deal with in preparing lesson plans and that many students expect from their educational experience, do not apply to advertising. We are not surprised that Coca-Cola does not give equal time to discussing the virtues of Pepsi, or that car companies do not go into detail about the environmental damage that is a definite downside of our reliance on gasoline-powered automobiles.*

*Roy F. Fox, a professor of education at the University of Missouri, argues that the line between advertising and education has become too blurred, that advertisers and advertising are not just becoming a common presence in our schools, but that the methods and goals of advertising are beginning to shape the curriculum in ways he finds both pervasive and disturbing. In "Salespeak," a chapter from his book* Mediaspeak, *Fox describes a future world in which advertising and consumerism dictate all aspects of our lives, especially in school, a world he argues is less far-fetched than it might at first seem.*

## Before You Read

1. Write a list describing the presence of advertising in your various school experiences. Where do you remember encountering advertising at different stages in your career as a student? Were there messages on the walls? Educational programs sponsored by companies? Learning supplies or materials? Vending machines? Instructional videos? Did your school subscribe to the Channel One news service?

2. Once you have written about your own experiences, work together to brainstorm a list of pros and cons related to these various appearances of advertising on campus. How does your class list help explain why the presence of advertising in school has become such a controversial issue?

## A DAY IN THE LIFE

At 6:03 A.M., Mrs. Anderson's voice comes over the intercom into her teenaged daughter's bedroom. Mrs. Anderson asks, "Pepsi? It's time to wake up, dear. Pehhhp-si...are you up and moving?"

Pepsi answers groggily, "Yeah...I'm up. Morning, Mom." As Pepsi sits up in bed, she reaches over and hits the button on her old pink Barbie alarm clock, which rests on her old American Girl traditional oak jewelry box. As both cherished items catch her eye, she pauses and wistfully recalls those days of girlhood, rubbing her hand over the *Little Mermaid* bedsheet. If only she hadn't given away her favorite purple My Little Pony to her best childhood friend, Microsoft McKenzie, who lives next door.

Just then her mother's voice calls her back to reality, "Good deal, sweetie. Let me know when you finish your shower. I just got your Gap sweatshirt out of the dryer, but I couldn't get the Gatorade stain out of your Tommy Hilfiger pants, so I'm washing them again."

Once upstairs, Pepsi sits down for a bowl of Cap'n Crunch cereal. She peels a banana, carefully pulling off a bright yellow sticker, which states, "ABC. Zero calories." She places the used sticker onto her McDonald's book cover. Pepsi's younger brother, Nike, dressed in his Babylon Five T-shirt, places a Star Trek notebook into his Star Wars book bag as he intently watches the Amoco morning newscast on the video wall. The network anchor tells about the latest corporate merger as he reads from his perch within the "N" of the giant MSNBC logo. Then Mrs. Anderson walks into the nutrition pod.

**Mrs. Anderson:** *Hey, Peps, what's going on at school today?*

**Pepsi:** *Nothing much. Just gotta finish that dumb science experiment.*

**Mrs. Anderson:** *Which one is that?*

**Pepsi:** *That one called "Digging for Data." We learned about scientific inquiry stuff and how to deduce conclusions. We learned that American settlers were short because they didn't eat enough meat and stuff like that.*

**Mrs. Anderson:** *Oh, yes! That was one of my favorites when I was in school. Those National Livestock and Meat Board teaching kits are wonderful! I liked it even better than Campbell Soup's "Prego Thickness Experiment." How 'bout you?*

**Pepsi:** *I dunno. Everyone already knows that Prego spaghetti sauce is three times thicker and richer than Ragu's sauce.*

**Mrs. Anderson:** *Well, yes, of course they do. But that's not the only point. There are larger goals here, namely, your becoming the best high-volume consumer possible. Isn't that right, dear?*

**Pepsi:** *Yeah, I guess so.*

Pepsi's school bus, equipped with the latest electronic wraparound billboard, mentions that the price of Chocolate Cheetah Crunch "is being sliced as you read this—down to $48.95 per ten-pounder!" Pepsi takes her seat and discusses this price reduction with her locker partner, Reebok Robinson. They engage in a lively conversation about which of them loves Cheetah Crunch more. Next, the screen on the back of the seat in front of them catches their attention: a large dancing lamb sings, "Be there! Tonight only! At the IBM Mall! All remaining Rickon collectibles must go! Pledge bidding only! Be there!" Even Reebok cannot contain a squeal.

At school, Pepsi watches Channel One, the National Truth Channel, during her first three classes. The first news story documents the precise steps in which Zestra, the new star of the Z-5 Lectradisk corporate communication spots, went about purchasing her new video wall unit. Afterward, Pepsi and her peers receive biofeedback printouts of their responses registered during this program via the reaction console on their desks. Next, the students use voice-print technology to describe what they were feeling during the broadcast.

Then their teacher, Ms. Qualcomm, tells them to take a twenty-minute recess at the Commoditarium before they return for Tech Lab, where they will begin the unit "Product Scanning: Art or Science?" At the Commoditarium, Pepsi purchases one bag of Kwizzee sticks, one can of Channel One soda, and a Oneder Bar, in addition to a pair of Golden Arch earrings she can't live without. The accessories for the earrings, which she also longs for, will have to wait.

Back at the Tech Lab, Pepsi and her peers receive a half hour of AT&T ("Allotted Time & Testing," sponsored by AT&T, in which students are free to explore their own interests on the GodNet). In the upper-left corner of her computer screen, Pepsi watches what appears to be an enlarged part of human anatomy, alternately shrinking and enlarging, as one of her favorite new songs beats in sync. The olfactory port of her computer emits a musky odor. In the background of this pulsating image, sticks of lightning flare randomly against a deep blue sky. Pepsi looks at them more closely and detects that each one contains three small letters: A, T, and T. She smiles, points, and clicks on the window.

Immediately, this message forms on screen in large, puffy blue letters: "A, T, & T Loves You." Then the message begins dissolving and enlarging simultaneously, so that the background is now the same blue as the message. Huge lips fill the screen. Pepsi is unsure whether they are the lips of a man or woman. The lips slowly murmur, "You, Pepsi . . . You're the one . . . Oh, yes . . . Nobody else. Just you."

Pepsi, mesmerized, half whispers to herself, "Me?" as the lips fade at the same time that the blue background re-forms into the previous message, "A, T, & T Loves You." Pepsi clicks again. Three golden books appear on screen. One is titled "A, T, & T's Pledge to You, Pepsi Anderson." Another one is titled, "Making Love Rich," and the third is titled, "Us...Forever." The lights of the Tech Lab dim, signaling students that it's time to begin their new unit. The lights slowly fade out until the lab is nearly dark. Pepsi hears muffled patriotic music from the opposite side of the room—a flute and drum, playing the tune of "Yankee Doodle Dandy." From the far end of the ceiling, an image of the traditional "fyfe and drum corps"—the three ragged soldiers in Revolutionary Army garb—come marching across the screen; above the U.S. flag flies a larger one, with a golden arch on it.

As the tattered trio exit via a slow dissolve on the opposite end of the ceiling screen, the room goes completely dark. Pepsi twists her head and limbers up, as her classmates do, almost in unison. Then, on instinct, Pepsi and her peers look upward to the neon green and pink Laser Note swirling above them: "To thine own self, be blue. And rakest thou joy into thine own taste sphere! Tru-Blu Vervo Dots: now half price at Commoditarium!" A laser image of Shakespeare forms from the dissolving lights. Next, the bard's face dissolves into the blue Vervo Dots. Pepsi, feeling vaguely tired and hungry, saves her place on screen so she can return later to find out what's in the three golden books. Before she exits, she is automatically transferred to another screen so that she can input her biofeedback prints from the past half hour.

At home that night, Pepsi and her family gather in the Recipient Well. To activate the video wall, Mrs. Anderson submits a forehead print on the ConsumaScan. Before any audio can be heard, a Nike logo appears on the screen for two minutes. Mrs. Anderson turns to her daughter.

**Mrs. Anderson:** *So, Peps, you were awfully quiet at dinner. Are you okay? Everything all right at school?*

**Pepsi:** *Fine. I just get tired of learning all the time.*

**Mrs. Anderson (sighing):** *Well, sweetie, I know. Things are so much different nowadays than when I was your age. You kids have to work harder in school because there are so many more products and services to keep up with.*

**Pepsi:** *Yeah, I guess so....*

**Mrs. Anderson:** *But you've also got many luxuries we never had. Why, when I was born, parents were completely ignorant about giving their children beautiful names. My family just called me "Jennifer." Ugh. Can you believe it?*

**Pepsi:** *Oh, gag me, Mom! "Jennifer"?! You're kidding! How did you and Dad name me?*

**Mrs. Anderson:** *Well, let's see.... We first fell in love with your name when Pepsico offered us a lifetime membership at the Nova Health Spa if we'd name you "Pepsi." I* thought it was so refreshing—not to mention thirst quenching and tasty. Besides—it's your generation!

**Pepsi:** *And I'll always love you and Dad for bestowing me with eternal brandness . . .*

**Mrs. Anderson:** *It's just because we love you, that's all. Growing up branded is a lot easier these days—especially after the Renaissance of 2008, just after you were born.*

**Pepsi:** *What was that?*

**Mrs. Anderson:** *You know—life cells! We got them a few years after the Second Great Brand Cleansing War.*

**Pepsi:** *But I thought we always had life cells, that we were just born with 'em. . . .*

**Mrs. Anderson:** *My gosh, no, girl! When I was your age we had to stay glued to National Public Radio to keep up with the latest fluctuations of the NASDAQ and high tech markets.*

**Pepsi:** *Jeez . . . I can't imagine life without life cells.*

**Mrs. Anderson:** *Me either—now! Back then, it all started with Moletronics and the first conversions of Wall Street datastreams into what they used to call "subcutaneous pseudoneurons." But that's ancient history for you!*

**Pepsi:** *Mom?*

**Mrs. Anderson:** *Yes, dear?*

**Pepsi:** *Can we set aside some special family time, so we can talk about that relationship portfolio with AT&T?*

**Mrs. Anderson:** *Well, of course! Maybe during spring break at the cabin? That's not the kind of thing we ever want to slight.*

At this moment, the video wall's audio activates. The Nike swoosh logo forms into a running cheetah as a male voice-over states, "Nike Leopard-Tech Laser Runners. Be the Cheetah you were born free to be." Mrs. Anderson turns back to her daughter and asks, "Would you mind running to the Pantry Pod and seeing if there's any more of that Chocolate Cheetah Crunch left?" "Sure," says Pepsi, turning as she leaves the room, "*If* we can talk about those new shoes I need." . . .

## IS PEPSI'S WORLD ALREADY HERE?

Yes. Most of what happens to Pepsi in this scenario is based on fact. A few other parts are extensions or exaggerations of what already occurs in everyday life. Let's begin with a girl named Pepsi. In Pepsi's world of Salespeak, nearly every facet of life is somehow linked to sales. Pepsi, the girl, lives in a Pepsi world, where person, product, and hype have merged with everyday life.

Salespeak is all-powerful. As small children, as soon as we become aware that a world exists outside of ourselves, we become a "targeted audience." From then on, we think in the voices of Salespeak. We hear them, we see them. We smell them, taste them, touch them, dream them, become them. Salespeak is often targeted at young people, the group marketers most prize because first, they spend "disposable" income, as well as influence how their parents spend money (see the following section, "Notes from the World of Salespeak"); second, people tend to establish loyalties to certain brands early in life; and third, young people are more likely to buy items on impulse. For these reasons and more, Salespeak is most prevalent and vivid for children and young adults. Hence, most of [this essay] focuses on the layers of Salespeak that surround these groups. The core issue is targeting kids in the first place, regardless of the product being sold.

## What's in a Name?

At this writing, I've neither read nor heard of a human being legally named after a product or service (though I feel certain that he or she is out there). I have, though, heard that school administrators in Plymouth, Michigan, are considering auctioning off school names to the highest bidder. It's only a matter of time before kids attend "Taco Bell Middle School" or "Gap Kids Elementary School." Appropriating names—and hence identities—is essentially an act of aggression, of control over others' personal identity. Our practice of naming things for commercial purposes is not new. Consider San Diego's Qualcomm Stadium. Unlike St. Louis's Busch Stadium or Denver's Coors Field, the name Qualcomm has no connections to people or things already traditionally linked with baseball. In Pepsi's world, "AT&T" stood for "Allotted Time for Testing." To my knowledge commercial or corporate names have yet to be used for identifying processes. However, they have been used to identify specific places where education processes occur.

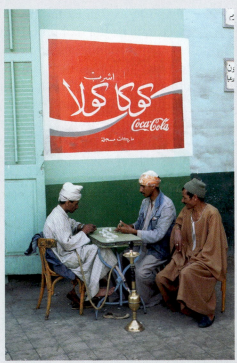

For example, the Derby, Kansas, school district named its elementary school resource center the GenerationNext Center. The district agreed to use the Pepsi slogan to name their new facility, as well as to serve only Pepsi products, in exchange for one million dollars. Even ice cream is now named so that it can advertise something else: the name of Ben and Jerry's butter almond ice cream is called "Dilbert's World: Totally Nuts."

Every time we see or read or hear a commercial name, an "impression" registers. Advertising profits depend on the type and number of impressions made by each ad message. Therefore, Pepsi Anderson and her friend, Microsoft McKenzie, are walking, breathing, random ad messages. (Similar important names) are now devised solely for purposes of advertising. Nothing more. Such names become ads. In earlier times and in other cultures, as well as our own, names were sacred: they communicated the essence of our identity, not just to others but to ourselves as well. To rob someone of her name was to appropriate her identity, to deny her existence. In *I Know Why the Caged Bird Sings,* Maya Angelou speaks of how demoralizing it was for African Americans to be "called out of name" by white people, who would refer to any African American male as "boy," "Tom," or "Uncle."

Similarly, several years ago, the rock musician and composer known as Prince changed his name to a purely graphic symbol. The result, of course, was that nobody could even pronounce it! By default he became known as "The Artist Formerly Known as Prince." In an interview on MTV, this musician-composer explained that the public believed he was crazy because print and electronic media had proclaimed him so, over and over. He therefore changed his name to something unpronounceable to halt this labeling. It worked. In effect, this man regained control of his own life because he found a way to stop others from controlling it for him, as they were doing by writing about him in the media. This man understands the general semantics principle that the word is not the thing symbolized—that the map is not the territory....

The long-term effects of replacing real names with commercial labels (of important spaces, processes, and possibly even people) can benefit nobody except those doing the appropriating—those reaping revenue from increased sales. At the very least, this practice demonstrates, in concrete, definitive ways, that we value materialism and the act of selling above all else.

## Celebrating Coke Day at the Carbonated Beverage Company

At century's end, the question is not "Where and when does Salespeak appear?" Rather, the real question is, "Where and when does Salespeak *not* appear?" Only in churches and other places of worship? (Not counting, of course, the church that advertised itself by proclaiming on its outside message board: "Come in for a faith lift.") Salespeak is more than a voice we hear and see: we also wear it, smell it, touch it, play with it. Ads on book covers, notebooks, backpacks, pencils, and pens are common. So are the girl Pepsi's Gap sweatshirt, Tommy Hilfiger pants, Barbie alarm clock, and *Little Mermaid* bedsheets. The bulletins that Pepsi and her classmates received about current sales are also authentic: PepsiCo has offered free beepers to teens, who are periodically contacted with updated ad messages.

Salespeak is seeping into the smallest crevices of American life. As you fill your car with gas, you can now watch commercials on the small screen on the gas pump. As you wait for your transaction at the ATM machine, you can view commercials. As you wait in the switchback line at an amusement park, you can watch commercials on several screens. As you wait in your doctor's office, you can read about medicines to buy, as well as watch commercials for them. As you stand in line at Wal-Mart's customer service desk, you can watch ads for Wal-Mart on a huge screen before you. As you wait for the phone to ring when making a long-distance call, you'll hear a soft, musical tinkle, followed by a velvety voice that intones, "AT&T."

As your children board their school bus, you'll see ads wrapped around it. When you pick up a bunch of bananas in the grocery store, like our friend Pepsi in the earlier scenario, you may have to peel off yellow stickers that state, "ABC. Zero calories." When you call a certain school in Texas and don't get an answer, you'll hear this recorded message: "Welcome to the Grapevine-Colleyville Independent School District, where we are proudly sponsored by the Dr. Pepper Bottling Company of Texas."

Salespeak also commonly appears under the guise of school "curriculum"— from formal business-education partnerships, to free teacher workshops provided to introduce new textbooks. Corporate-produced "instructional materials" are sometimes thinly veiled sales pitches that can distort the truth. The curriculum unit "Digging for Data" mentioned earlier as part of Pepsi's school day, is actual material used in schools.

For another "learning experience," students were assigned to be "quality control technicians" as they completed "The Carbonated Beverage Company" unit, provided free to schools by PepsiCo. Students taste-tested colas, analyzed cola samples, took video tours of the St. Louis Pepsi plant, and visited a local Pepsi plant. Ads have even appeared in math textbooks. *Mathematics: Applications and Connections,* published by McGraw-Hill, and used in middle schools, includes problems that are just as much about advertising as they are arithmetic—salespeak masquerading as education. Here's a sample decimal division problem: "Will is saving his allowance to buy a pair of Nike shoes that cost $68.25. If Will earns $3.25 per week, how many weeks will Will need to save?" Directly next to this problem is a full-color picture of a pair of Nike shoes. The 1999 edition of this book contains the following problem: "The best-selling packaged cookie in the world is the Oreo cookie. The diameter of the Oreo cookie is 1.75 inches. Express the diameter of an Oreo cookie as a fraction in simplest form." It seems no accident that "Oreo" is repeated three times in this brief message; repetition is an ancient device used in propaganda and advertising. More insidious is the fact that such textbooks present the act of saving money for Nike shoes as a *natural* state of affairs, a given in life. Requiring captive audiences of kids to interact with brand names in such mentally active ways helps ensure product-identification and brand-name loyalty during kids' future years as consumers.

Some schools slavishly serve their corporate sponsors. After sealing a deal with Coca-Cola, a school in Georgia implemented an official "Coke Day" devoted to celebrating Coca-Cola products. On that day, Mike Cameron, a senior at the school, chose to exercise his right to think by wearing a T-shirt bearing the Pepsi logo. He was promptly suspended.

This intense focus on selling products to a captive audience of students is illustrated by the following letter sent to District 11's school principals in Colorado Springs, Colorado. The letter was written by the district's executive director of "school leadership." In September 1997, the district had signed an $8 million contract with Coca-Cola.

> Dear Principal:
>
> Here we are in year two of the great Coke contract....
>
> First, the good news: This year's installment from Coke is "in the house," and checks will be cut for you to pick up in my office this week. Your share will be the same as last year.
>
> | | |
> |---|---|
> | Elementary School | $ 3,000 |
> | Middle School | $15,000 |
> | High School | $25,000 |
>
> Now the not-so-good news: we must sell 70,000 cases of product (including juices, sodas, waters, etc.) at least once during the first three years of the contract. If we reach this goal, your school allotments will be guaranteed for the next seven years.
>
> The math on how to achieve this is really quite simple. Last year we had 32,439 students, 3,000 employees, and 176 days in the school year. If 35,439 staff and students buy one Coke product every other day for a school year, we will double the required quota.
>
> Here is how we can do it:
>
> 1. Allow students to purchase and consume vended products throughout the day. If sodas are not allowed in classes, consider allowing juices, teas, and waters.
> 2. Locate machines where they are accessible to the students all day. Research shows that vender purchases are closely linked to availability. Location, location, location is the key. You may have as many machines as you can handle.

Pueblo Central High tripled its volume of sales by placing vending machines on all three levels of the school. The Coke people surveyed the middle and high schools this summer and have suggestions on where to place additional machines.

3. A list of Coke products is enclosed to allow you to select from the entire menu of beverages. Let me know which products you want, and we will get them in. Please let me know if you need electrical outlets.

4. A calendar of promotional events is enclosed to help you advertise Coke products.

I know this is "just one more thing from downtown," but the long-term benefits are worth it.

Thanks for your help.

John Bushey
The Coke Dude

With visionary leaders such as "The Coke Dude" to inspire them, students will be well prepared to perpetuate a world ruled by Salespeak. Of course, Pepsi (the girl), Mike (the actual student expelled for wearing a Pepsi T-shirt), and their fellow students did not begin encountering ads in high school. It begins much earlier. . . .

## The National Truth Channel

Many other details of Pepsi's day are anchored in fact, not fiction. In Pepsi's not-too-distant world, Channel One television has become the "National Truth Channel." Today Channel One, owned by a private corporation, beams daily commercials to more than 8 million American kids attending middle schools and high schools. It therefore imposes more uniformity on public school kids and their curriculum than the federal government ever has. For all practical purposes, it has indeed been our "national" channel for several years.

Although I made up the "Truth" part of "The National Truth Channel," I want to note that it serves as Doublespeak nested within Salespeak—a common occurrence in real life. For example, the term "corporate communication" (used in Pepsi's world, above, to refer to commercials) is a euphemism that the Benetton company actually used to refer to its ads. And although laser ads have yet to appear on the ceilings of classrooms, as they do in Pepsi's world, it is true that a few years ago, a company wanted to launch into geosynchronous orbit a massive panel that could be emblazoned with a gigantic corporate logo, visible for periods of time, over certain cities. Here, the promise of reality far exceeds what happened in Pepsi's fictional classroom.

Also, remember that "news story" about Zestra, a star of "corporate communication" spots that Pepsi watched on Channel One? More truth than fiction here, too. Since 1989, Channel One has sometimes blurred the lines between news, commercials, and public service announcements. In one study, many students mistook commercials for news programs or public service announcements, such as those that warn viewers about drunk driving. The result was that students knew the product being advertised and regarded it warmly because, as one student told me, "They [the manufacturers and advertisers] are trying to do good. They care about us."

In the worst case of such blurring that I observed during the two-year period of this study, the students could hardly be faulted. Instead, the Salespeak was highly deceptive (merging with Doublespeak). That is, PepsiCo's series of ads called "It's Like This" were designed to look very much like documentary news footage and public service announcements. The actors spoke directly into the swinging, handheld camera, as if they were being interviewed; the ads were filmed in black and white, and the product's name was never spoken by any of the people in the commercial, although the rapid-fire editing included brief shots of the Pepsi logo, in color, on signs and on merchandise.

Just as in Pepsi's world, described earlier in this chapter, real-life ads are often embedded within programs, as well as other commercials, products, instructions, and even "transitional spaces" between one media message and another. For example, when the girl Pepsi took a break from her "learning," she went to the school's Commoditarium, or mini-mall, to shop for items that had been advertised at school. Again, there is truth here. Although schools do not yet contain mini-malls, they do contain stores and increasing numbers of strategically placed vending machines. A ninth-grade girl told me that after students viewed Channel One in the morning and watched commercials for M&Ms candies, her teacher allowed them to take a break. The student said she'd often walk down the hall and purchase M&Ms from the vending machine. In such schools, operant conditioning is alive and well. This is not the only way in which many schools are emulating shopping malls. My daughter's high school cafeteria is a "food court," complete with McDonald's and Pizza Hut.

By establishing itself in public schools, Channel One automatically "delivers" a captive, well-defined audience to its advertisers, more than was ever possible before. "Know thy audience"—as specifically as possible—is the name of the advertising game. Marketers have become increasingly effective at obtaining all kinds of demographic and psychographic information on consumers. Channel One increasingly hones its messages based on the constant flow of demographic information it extracts from viewers, often under the guise of "clubs" and contests, which seek information on individuals, teams, classes, and entire schools. Channel One's printed viewing and "curriculum" guides for teachers, as well as its website for students, also constantly solicit marketing information.[...]

## NOTES FROM THE WORLD OF SALESPEAK

More than anything else, dominant voices may be shaped by their environment. Consider the following facts about the environment that generates Salespeak:

- *$150 billion:* Amount spent by American advertisers each year, a cost that is passed on to consumers in higher prices. Landay summarizes our relationship with advertisers: "We pay their ad bills, we provide their profits, and we pay for their total tax write-off on the ads they place."
- *12 billion and 3 million:* The number of display ads and broadcast ads that Americans are collectively exposed to each day.
- 2: The number of times that we pay for advertising. First, advertising costs are built into the product. We pay again in terms of time, money, and attention spent when processing an ad message.
- *1,000:* The number of chocolate chips in each bag of Chips Ahoy! cookies. The cookie company sponsored a "contest" in which students tried to confirm this claim.
- *$11 billion:* The amount of money dedicated to market research throughout the world.
- *"Gosh, I don't understand—there are so many brands":* This is what one marketing firm has its researchers say, after they go into stores and place themselves next to real shoppers, in an effort to elicit what consumers are thinking in an authentic context (from the May 30, 1997, issue of the *Wall Street Journal*).
- *$66 billion:* The amount of money spent by kids and young adults (ages 4–19) in 1992.
- *16 million:* Approximate number of American children who use the Internet.
- *115.95:* The number of banner ads viewed per week by the average Web user.
- *"Save water. It's precious":* Message on a Coca-Cola billboard in Zimbabwe, where, according to the August 25, 1997, issue of the *Wall Street Journal,* the soft drink has become the drink of choice (necessity?) because of a water shortage.
- *$204 billion:* The estimated amount of Web-based transactions in 2001, up from $10.4 billion in 1997.
- *89:* Percentage of children's websites that collect users' personal information.
- *23:* Percentage of children's websites that tell kids to ask their parents for permission before sending personal information.
- *$29 million:* Net income for Nielsen Media Research during the first six months of 1998.
- *$36 billion:* The amount of money spent by kids and young adults in 1992 (ages 4–19) that belonged to their parents.

- *$3.4 million:* The amount of money received by the Grapevine-Colleyville Texas School District for displaying a huge Dr. Pepper logo atop the school roof. This school is in the flight path of Dallas-Fort Worth International Airport.
- *$8 million:* The amount of money received by the Colorado Springs School District in Colorado from Coca-Cola for an exclusive ten-year service agreement.
- *"A tight, enduring connection to teens":* What Larry Jabbonsky, a spokesman at Pepsi headquarters, said his company seeks.
- *9,000:* The number of items stocked in grocery stores in the 1970s.
- *30,000:* The number of items now stocked in grocery stores.
- *99:* The percentage of teens surveyed ($n = 534$ in four cities) who correctly identified the croaking frogs from a Budweiser television commercial.
- *93:* The percentage of teens who repeated that they liked the Budweiser frogs "very much" or "somewhat."
- *95 and 94:* The percentages of teens who know the Marlboro man and Joe Camel.
- *Great Britain's white cliffs of Dover:* The backdrop for a laser-projected Adidas ad.
- *$200 million:* The amount of money Miller Beer spends on advertising each year.
- *Time Warner:* A corporate empire that controls news and information in America. (There are fewer than twelve.) Time Warner owns large book publishers, cable TV franchises, home video firms, CNN and other large cable channels, and magazines such as *Time, Life, People, Sports Illustrated, Money, Fortune,* and *Entertainment Weekly.*
- *$650 billion:* Annual sales of approximately 1,000 telemarketing companies, which employ 4 million Americans.
- *350,000:* The number of classrooms that view two minutes of television commercials every day on Channel One.
- *154:* The number of Coca-Cola cans that students must find on a book cover and then color in, to reveal a hidden message.
- *50:* The percentage of increase in advertising expenditures during the past fifteen years.
- *560:* The daily number of ads targeted at the average American in 1971.
- *3,000:* The daily number of ads targeted at the average American in 1991.
- *Business Update:* An hourly segment broadcast on National Public Radio. Even though NPR is supposed to focus on "public broadcasting," it does not offer a *Labor Update.*
- *3.4 trillion:* The number of email messages that crossed the Internet in the United States in 1998.

- *80 percent:* The percentage of America's email messages in 1998 that were mass-produced emailings, "most from corporations with something to sell."

It's hardly unusual for a free enterprise system to employ Salespeak. Advertising is a necessary ingredient for informing consumers about the goods and services they need. This is true for much of America's history. A sign hung in a trading post at the beginning of the Oregon Trail, 150 years ago, stating, "Sugar, 2 cents per lb.," contains necessary information for specific readers who had definite goals. Today, though, America is quite different.

First, unlike even forty years ago, most of today's advertising carries scant information about the product or service. Second, the more affluent America becomes, the fewer true "needs" we have. To make up for it, advertisers now focus not so much on what we truly need, but on what we may desire. Third, very few limits are placed upon advertising: we have little control over where it appears, who can see it (note how many of the previous items focus on young people), how often it appears, how messages are constructed, or how much money is budgeted for them (at the expense of, say, improving the product). The field of advertising itself is now a major industry. The Bureau of Labor Statistics reports that in 1995, more people died on the job in advertising than in car factories, electrical repair companies, and petroleum refining operations. Because advertising has such free rein in America, it's become one of our most dominating voices, if not the most dominating voice.

## Working with the Text

1. Define what Roy F. Fox means by "salespeak." What do you find the most effective examples he uses to illustrate this idea? Explore your understanding of the idea by providing examples of your own. How would you describe the main differences between salespeak and non-salespeak?

2. In Fox's description of a future where school and family life are shaped by the needs of advertising, what key differences do you see between the world he describes and our present situation? Which of these developments do you think may happen or already be happening? List these differences in order, ranging from the predictions you see as most possible to those you see as least possible. Compare your list with those of others and discuss why you ordered them in the way that you did. Could you draw a line between what you see as more and less possible?

3. What does Fox see as most disturbing about the use of Channel One in schools? Explore what you find most persuasive about his arguments by

writing a personal response to a proposal to allow Channel One into a local school. Would you be in favor of or opposed to such a move and why?

4. Fox ends his essay with a list of facts about advertising and education. Which items in the list did you find most personally interesting and why? Speculate about why you think he chose to end his essay with this list. What information is he trying to convey to his readers? Just as important, how does the list affect the relationship he has constructed with his readers?

5. How prevalent has salespeak been in your educational experience? What examples of sales-related curriculum activities might Fox identify in the schools you have attended? If you went to a school that subscribed to Channel One or ZapMe.com, compare your experiences with the analysis that Fox offers of the role of Channel One and ZapMe.com in the classroom.

6. Fox describes the Salespeak high school of the future; extend his story by describing the adventures of "Pepsi" in college. What would the Salespeak university look like?

## "They Say"

### Douglas Rushkoff

*Many of us feel that we are pretty savvy about the tactics and strategies that advertisers, politicians, and even teachers, parents, and other authority figures use to try and persuade us to act and believe in ways beneficial to them. After all, we have all grown up surrounded by advertising and other persuasive messages, and the motives (money, power, influence) of those trying to persuade us seem obvious.*

*On the other hand, the fact that hundreds of billions of dollars are put into advertising each year means that somebody thinks it must be effective, and looked at from the perspective of the number, variety, and wealth of the organizations trying to influence our behavior, it's just possible to feel intimidated and overwhelmed by the flood of persuasive messages and images.*

*In his book* Coercion: Why We Listen to What "They" Say, *from which this essay is taken, Douglas Rushkoff examines the increasing sophistication of what he calls the "hidden persuaders" in our society, those devoting impressive amounts of time and resources toward affecting our behavior. He describes a cycle in which, as soon as a consumer or citizen becomes wise to a particular advertising or other persuasive strategy, those involved in the persuasion industry quickly develop new strategies, sometimes built on our awareness of previous strategies. In so doing, he raises questions about the relationship between persuasion and coercion, as well as whether there are any ethical or other constraints on the tactics that can be used to influence our beliefs and behaviors, or whether anything goes. In the end, Rushkoff asks us to think about how prepared and knowledgeable each of us is in confronting the forces of persuasion.*

*Douglas Rushkoff is a journalist, novelist, and critic of contemporary cyberculture. His books include* MediaVirus! *and* Exit Strategy.

## Before You Read

1. Write about a distinct time when you either successfully talked someone into doing something or you were successfully talked into doing something. As you write about the experience, pay particular attention to describing in detail the specific process you followed or that was used with you.

2. Use your narratives to construct a how-to list of strategies and tactics to use in successfully persuading someone. You may even think of this list in terms of dos and don'ts.

3. Now discuss your lists in terms of ethics: where do you see the lines drawn between legitimate persuasion and coercion or deception? What parts of the process present the most gray areas or seem most open to abuse?

They say human beings use only 10 percent of their brains. They say poly-unsaturated fat is better for you than saturated fat. They say that tiny squiggles in a rock prove there once was life on Mars. They say our children's test scores are declining. They say Jesus was a direct descendant of King David. They say you can earn $15,000 a week in your spare time. They say marijuana leads to LSD, and LSD can lead to suicide. They say the corner office is a position of power. They say the elderly should get flu shots this season. They say homosexuality is an environmentally learned trait. They say there's a gene for homosexuality. They say people can be hypnotized to do anything. They say people won't do anything under hypnosis that they wouldn't do when conscious. They say Prozac alleviates depression. They say mutual funds are the best long-term investment. They say computers can predict the weather. They say you haven't met your deductible.

Who, exactly, are "they," and why do they say so much? More amazing, why do we listen to them?

We each have our own "theys"—the bosses, experts, and authorities (both real and imaginary) who seem to dictate our lives, decide our fates, and create our futures. In the best of circumstances they can make us feel safe, the way parents do. They make our decisions for us. They do our thinking for us. We don't have to worry about our next move—it has already been decided on our behalf, and in our best interests. Or so we hope.

For not everyone to whom we surrender ourselves is deserving of our trust. The pretty young "sales associate" at the Gap may not be the best judge of how that pair of blue jeans looks on us, or of which belt we should wear to a job interview. Even though she seems genuinely concerned with our well-being, we must not forget that she's been trained in the art of the "upsell" and is herself under the influence of a barrage of incentives conceived at corporate headquarters. One scheme leads her to compete with her colleagues on the sales floor for daily prizes, while another threatens penalties or termination if she does not meet a certain quota of multiple-item sales by the end of the week. The coercive techniques inflicted on her, and the ones she in turn inflicts on us, are the products of years of painstaking research into methods of influencing human behavior.

The justifiably cynical among us have come to expect this sort of treatment from the professional people in our lives. When we walk into a shopping mall, we understand that we will be subjected to certain forms of influence. We recognize that retail sales are about the bottom line, and that to stay in business, shop owners depend upon our behaving in a predictable and somewhat malleable fashion. If instructing a salesgirl to unfasten the second button of her blouse may garner a larger volume of sales, the store manager owes it to himself and his superiors and their shareholders to do so. And, chances are, it will work.

But these techniques are rapidly spreading from the sales floor and the television screen to almost every other aspect of our daily experience. Whether we are strolling through Times Square, exploring the Internet, or even just trying to make friends at the local bar, we are under constant scrutiny and constant assault by a professional class of hidden persuaders. In most cases, if the coercion works according to plan, we don't even realize it has been used.

It's not always easy to determine when we have surrendered our judgment to someone else. The better and more sophisticated the manipulation, the less aware of it we are. For example, have you ever attended a sporting event, rock concert, or political convention in one frame of mind, but found yourself inexplicably swept away by the emotion of the crowd? How many times have you walked into a mall to buy a single pair of shoes, only to find yourself purchasing an entire outfit, several books, and a few CDs before you made your way back to the parking lot?

Have you ever picked up the phone, realized the caller was from an organization you'd never considered supporting, and gone ahead and pledged a sum of money or bought a magazine subscription? How did that automobile salesman get you to pay more than you'd planned to for a car, and add more features than you wanted, even though you came armed with your *Consumer Reports*?

Why do the advertisements in fashion magazines make us feel inadequate, and after they do, why do we feel compelled to buy the products advertised anyway? How can we feel we're so aware of the effects of advertising and marketing, yet still succumb to them?

Why are our kids tattooing themselves with the Nike "swoosh" icon? Are they part of a corporate cult? If young people today are supposed to be beyond the reach of old-fashioned marketing, then why do they feel the need to find their identity in a brand of sneakers?

No matter how many coercive techniques we come to recognize, new ones are always being developed that we don't. Once we've become immune to the forceful "hard sell" techniques of the traditional car dealer, a high-paid influence consultant develops a new brand with an entirely new image—like the Saturn, whose dealers use friendly "soft sell" techniques to accomplish the same thing, more subtly. Media-savvy young people have learned to reject advertising that tries too hard to make its product look "cool." In response, companies now produce decidedly "uncool" advertisements, which appeal to the cynical viewer who thinks he can remain unswayed. "Image is nothing. Thirst is everything," Sprite advertisers confess to their hype-weary target market. Our attempts to stay one step ahead of coercers merely provokes them to develop even more advanced, less visible, and, arguably, more pernicious methods of persuasion.

Corporations and consumers are in a coercive arms race. Every effort we make to regain authority over our actions is met by an even greater effort to usurp it.

If we stop to think about this invisible hand working on our perceptions and behavior, we can easily become paranoid. Although we cannot always point to the evidence, when we become aware that our actions are being influenced by forces beyond our control—we shop in malls that have been designed by psychologists, and experience the effects of their architecture and color schemes on our purchasing behaviors—we can't help but feel a little edgy. No matter how discreetly camouflaged the coercion, we sense that it's leading us to move and act ever so slightly against our wills. We may not want to admit consciously to ourselves that the floor plan of the shopping center has made us lose our bearings, but we are disoriented all the same. We don't know exactly how to get back to the car, and we will have to walk past twenty more stores before we find an exit.

In order to maintain the illusion of our own authority, we repress the urge to panic. Unfortunately, the more we stifle that little voice telling us we are in danger, the more we repress our ability to resist. We deny what we are feeling, and we disconnect further from what remains of our free will. As a result, we become even better targets for those who would direct our actions.

I was not always predisposed to think this way. On the contrary, for years I believed that we were winning the war against those who would shape our wills. Through the eighties and early nineties, I cheered as cable television, video games, the personal computer, and the Internet seemed to offer the promise of a new relationship to the mainstream media and a chance to undermine its coercive nature. Home-video cameras demystified for us the process by which news is reported, and public-access channels gave everyone an opportunity to broadcast his version of what was going on in the world. C-SPAN revealed to us the pompous rhetoric of our elected representatives, as well as the embarrassing fact that they usually address an empty chamber.

The low cost of video production and the increase in available channels gave rise to countless tabloid television shows. Like their print counterparts, these programs broadcast stories that more established news agencies would have held back—which in turn gave rise to a whole new set of journalistic standards and an unleashing of alternative news sources and outlets. Tabloid and Internet journalists were the first to publish everything from Clinton's trysts with Gennifer Flowers and Monica Lewinsky to Prince Charles's dirty phone calls with Camilla Parker Bowles. *Time* and *Newsweek* have simply struggled to keep up with the rising tide.

Internet discussion groups and bulletin boards gave us a new forum in which to discuss the information that was important to us. Online, we could access the latest word on new AIDS or cancer treatments, and then question our doctors (or our stingy HMOs) about a course of treatment. Even if all we intended to do was shop, the Internet gave us the ability to conduct instant price and feature comparisons, and to talk to others about a product before we bought it.

Meanwhile, young computer hackers had gotten their hands on the control panel of our electronic society. Bank records and other personal data that formerly were accessible only to credit bureaus and loan officers were now within the reach of any skilled 14-year-old. As a result, our privacy finally became an issue to be discussed publicly. We became aware of how information about us was being gathered, bought, and sold without our consent, and we supported activists, organizations, and candidates who promised to enact policies to prevent this invasion.

The Internet made us more aware of the process by which news and public relations are created and disseminated. As we gained access to press releases and corporate data, we have witnessed firsthand how public relations experts are allowed to write the evening news. In the early nineties, there was a participant of an electronic bulletin board who would post the transcripts of local news shows and then compare them, word for word, with the prepared press releases of the companies or individuals concerned. The results were embarrassingly similar, with whole paragraphs lifted directly from press release to newscaster's script.

As the coercive effects of mainstream media became more self-evident, media awareness led to a revival of cultural literacy. Our ability to see through the shameless greed of televangelists changed the way we related to the ritual surrounding the collection plate. Our ability to deconstruct the political process as it took place on TV gave rise to independent, homespun candidates like Ross Perot and Jerry Brown, whose campaigns promised direct access and accountability.

In the meantime, television programs like *Beavis and Butt-head* and *The Simpsons* were deconstructing the rest of the mediaspace for our children. With Bart as their role model, the generation growing up in the last decade has maintained a guarded relationship to the media and marketing techniques that have fooled their parents. While his dad, Homer, was suckered by every beer promotion, Bart struggled to maintain his skate-boarder's aloofness and dexterity. Through Bart, our kids learned to remain moving targets.

As a happy witness to what was taking place in our culture, I began to write books celebrating our liberation through the tools of new media. *Cyberia* applauded the scientists, hackers, and spiritualists who were determined to design a better society with these new tools. The technological revolution seemed to me a populist renaissance through which real people would wake from centuries of heartless manipulation. Hierarchy and social control soon would be things of the past as every individual came to realize his or her role in the unfolding of civilization. I saw my vision confirmed as the Internet rose in popularity, and as the once-ridiculed nerds of Silicon Valley began to engineer the communications infrastructure for the world's business community. The Internet would not fade into obscurity like CB radio. It was here to stay. Our culture was hardwiring itself together.

I became fascinated and inspired by the organic and responsive qualities of this new mediaspace. Just as our chaos mathematicians and quantum physicists had suggested, we were venturing into uncharted cultural turf, where huge systemwide changes could be provoked by the tiniest actions. In a system as dynamic as the weather, we learned, a single butterfly flapping its wings in Brazil could lead to a hurricane in New York. So, too, was the awesome power that "feedback and iteration" offered every member of a networked whole. Now that the media had become such a system, the beating of a black man by white policemen in Los Angeles, amplified throughout our mediated culture via a single, replicated, and endlessly broadcast camcorder tape, could lead to rioting in a dozen American cities.

Spurred on by these developments, in the early nineties I wrote an optimistic treatise on the new possibilities of an organic media space. I proposed that provocative ideas could be launched in the form of mutant media packages—or "viruses"—by anyone who had a video camera or Internet connection. Thanks to the spread of commercial broadcasting, almost everyone in the world had been given access to the media in one form or another. What the people who put all those wires and TV satellites in place didn't realize was that electrons travel in both directions. Home media like camcorders, faxes, and Internet connections were empowering all of us to launch our ideas into the mediaspace.

Huge, well-funded, mainstream publicity campaigns were becoming obsolete. Now, anyone could launch an idea that would spread by itself if it were packaged in a new, unrecognizable form of media. Mutant media got attention because it was strange. And there's nothing the media likes more than to cover new forms of itself. The Rodney King tape proliferated as much because it demonstrated the power of a new technology—the camcorder—as for the image contained within it. One of the reasons why the O. J. Simpson story became the biggest trial in history was because it began with a mutant media event: the nationally televised spectacle of the Bronco chase, during which Los Angeles TV viewers ran outside and literally onto their own TV screens as the motorcade drove by. Similarly, the media stunts of ACT UP activists, Earth First "eco-terrorists," Greenpeace, and even unorthodox political candidates received worldwide attention simply by launching their campaigns through media viruses.

The hegemony of Hearst and Murdoch were over. We had entered an age where the only limiting factor was an idea's ability to provoke us through its novel dissemination. An idea no longer depended on the authority of its originator—it would spread and replicate if it challenged our faulty assumptions. In an almost Darwinian battle for survival, only the fittest ideas would win out. These new, mutated forms of media were promoting our cultural evolution, empowering real people, and giving a voice to those who never before had access to the global stage.

Best of all, young people were the ones leading the charge. Adults were immigrants to the new realm of interactive media, but kids raised with joysticks in their hands were natives. They spoke the language of new media and public relations better than the adults who were attempting to coerce them. What media can you use to manipulate a kid when he is already more media literate than you are? He will see through any clunky attempt to persuade him with meaningless associations and hired role models. By the time this generation came into adulthood, I believed, the age of manipulation would be over.

Once I'd published a book announcing that we'd entered the final days of the marketing wars, I began to get phone calls from politicians, media companies, advertisers, and even the United Nations, anxious for me to explain the new rules of the interactive age. I saw little harm in taking their money just to tell them that the genie was out of the bottle. I felt like an evangelist, spreading the news that the public had grown too media savvy to be fleeced any further. The only alternative left for public-relations people and advertisers was to tell the truth. Those promoting good ideas or making useful products would succeed; the rest would perish.

At first I found it easy to dismiss the writings of naysayer cyber critics like Jerry Manders, Paul Virilio, and Neil Postman, who attacked the notion that the new media had made a positive shift in the balance of power—culturally, economically, or otherwise. There was just too much evidence to the contrary. Although I had some sense that there were people out there attempting to deploy these same innovations coercively, I believed that acknowledging their efforts would only feed their power. If we ignored them, they would go away.

My optimism—and my willingness to consort with the enemy—was met with a number of personal attacks as well. One morning in November 1996, I woke up to a *New York Times* article describing me as a Gen-X guru who sold youth culture's secrets to media companies for upward of $7,500 per hour. Many of my friends and readers wondered how I could have betrayed the "movement," and wrote me to voice their disapproval. Alternative newspapers who had supported me in the past now called me a sellout. Mentors like virtual-community maker Howard Rheingold and Electronic Frontiers Foundation chairman Mitch Kapor warned me that my uncritical enthusiasm might be blinding me to very real threats to the civic revival we were all working for.

"Vigilance is a dangerous thing," I wrote at the time. I was convinced that a guarded approach to the development of new media would only slow things down, giving our would-be oppressors and manipulators a chance to catch up. And even if I was no better than the scores of "cool hunters" who hoped to cash in on corporate confusion about the changing priorities and sentiments of youth culture, since the ideas I promoted were empowering ones, I couldn't see the harm. I told executives at Sony to design a video game console that allowed kids to create their own video games. I told the people developing content for TCI's new interactive television network to make programs that gave viewers the chance to broadcast their own news stories. I told phone companies that the way to please their customers was to stop treating them like criminals whenever they were late with a payment.

I went to conferences and sat on panels alongside my media-hacking heroes like Michael Moore, the director of the GM-bashing documentary *Roger and Me,* and Stewart Brand, one of the original band of Ken Kesey's Merry Pranksters. I delivered keynote addresses to thousands of advertising executives and television programmers, telling them to admit to themselves that their monopoly over the public will was over. The older executives threw up their arms in disgust, while the younger ones transcribed my every word. I couldn't have been more pleased. I felt at least partly responsible for dismantling the engines of propaganda and demilitarizing the coercive arms race. Better yet, I was making good money for doing so. My books were hitting bestseller lists, and my speaking and consulting fees were going through the roof—even if they never quite reached the fabled $7,500 per hour.

I guess it was too good to be true.

In the summer of 1997, I was invited to speak about my book *Media Virus* at a convention of "account planners" (advertising's version of anthropologist-researchers) sponsored by the American Association of Advertising Agencies. I packed up my laptop and headed for Sheraton Bal Harbour in Miami to spread the good news. The conference theme was "Mutant Media/Mutant Ideas," itself a play on the ideas in my book. Had the advertisers come to recognize that their power was dwindling?

Hardly. These friendly, well-dressed, and articulate people had bought and read my book—but for a reason very different from the one I'd had for writing it. They were eager to learn all about the mutant mediaspace, but only in order to figure out ways of creating advertisements that were themselves media viruses! *Media Virus* had become a bestseller not because so many activists, public-access producers, or computer hackers were reading it, but because it was now a standard text in the science of public relations. My work was being taught in advertising school.

Before I had the chance to put on my name tag, a young creative executive asked me what it was like working on the Calvin Klein jeans campaign—the one in which teenagers were photographed in a setting made to look like a porn-movie audition.

"It was a media virus," he congratulated me. "The campaign got more publicity because of the protests! It made Calvin look cool because his ads were taken off the air!" True enough, the campaign became the lead story on the evening news once "family advocates" targeted the ads for their exploitation of young people. They never could have bought as much airtime as they received for free. But I had nothing to do with the scheme's conception.

I assured him that I had never met with the Calvin Klein people, but it was no use. He was convinced they had based their work on my book, and there was no changing his mind. Had they? I certainly hoped not.

The succession of featured speakers soon proved my worst fears. With titles like "Mutants Produce Bounty" and "Giving Birth to Mutant Ideas in a Commercial Context," each presenter sought to regain the ground lost to the chaos-thriving hackers who had taken over the mediaspace. The conference's purpose was to upgrade the advertising industry's weapons systems to the new style of war.

I was flattered—and flabbergasted. I felt honored to be appreciated, but horrified by the application of my work. No sooner had I proclaimed the revolution than it was co-opted by the enemy. And I had aided and abetted them.

It was at that moment, in the Bal Harbour hotel ballroom, that I decided to write [*Coercion: Why We Listen to What "They" Say*]. With my newfound access to the corridors of Madison Avenue and beyond, I would become a double agent—attending meetings, taking notes, analyzing tactics, and then reporting my findings.

For the past two years, I have been studying the ways marketers, politicians, religious leaders, and coercive forces of all kinds influence everyday decisions. I have sat in on strategy sessions with television, advertising, and marketing executives, and read countless documents by professionals in government, law enforcement, the military, and business. I've cozied up to automobile salesmen and multilevel marketers to pry from them their secrets.

What I've learned in my two-year odyssey is that however advanced the tools being used to sway us, the fundamental principles responsible for their effectiveness remain the same. Coercers are like hunters: they can don better camouflage, learn better ways to scent their prey, develop longer-range bullets and more accurate sights, but they still need to find their quarry and then figure out which way it's moving so they can "lead" with the gun barrel and hit it. Sonar, radar, and night-vision specs will only increase their efficiency and compensate for their prey's own increasing skill in evasion.

The prey's only true advantages are its instinct and its familiarity with its environment. Just as a deer "knows" when it is in the hunter's sights, we know on some level when we are being targeted and coerced. The more complex, technological, and invisible coercion gets, the harder it is for us to rely on this instinct. We are lured away from our natural environment and are more likely to depend on directions from our shepherds or the motions of the herd to gain our bearings. As soon as we become familiar with the new terrain—be it in the mall, the television dial, or the Internet—it is the goal of the coercion strategists to make it unfamiliar again, or to lure us somewhere else.

The rapid change we have experienced in the past several decades as we have moved from the postwar boom through the space age and into the computer age has provided ample opportunity for our coercers to retool and rearm themselves. Even when a new technology, like the Internet, appears to offer us a chance to reclaim our mediaspace in the name of community or civic responsibility, it fast becomes a new resource for the direct marketer, the demographics researcher, and the traditional advertiser.

Worst of all, the acceleration of the arms race between us and our coercers deteriorates the foundations of civil society. Telemarketers make us afraid to answer the phone in the evening. Salesmen bearing free gifts (with strings attached) make us reluctant to accept presents from our neighbors. Greedy televangelists twisting Bible passages into sales pitches, and church charity drives employing state-of-the-art fund-raising techniques make us wary of religion. Our president's foreign policy is channeled through spin doctors before it reaches Congress or the people, leading to widespread cynicism about the political process. Our sporting events are so crowded with product promotions that we can't root for a team without cheering a corporate logo. Our movements through department stores are videotaped and analyzed so that shelves and displays can be rearranged to steer us toward an optimum volume of more expensive purchases. Scientists study the influence of colors, sounds, and smells on our likelihood of buying.

It's not a conspiracy against us, exactly; it is simply a science that has gotten out of control.

In a desperate attempt to use any tool available to keep up with our rapidly growing arsenal of filters, marketing professionals turned to high technology. They invented the personalized discount card at the local supermarket, which is used to create a database of our purchasing decisions. This information is bought and sold without our knowledge to direct marketers, who customize the offers filling our mailboxes to match our individual psychological profiles. Home-shopping channels adjust the pacing of sales pitches, the graphics on the screen, and prices of products based on computer analyses of our moment-to-moment responses to their offers, in real time, automatically. The automation of coercive practices is a threat more menacing than any sort of human manipulators. For unlike with real human interaction, the coercer himself is nowhere to be found. There is no man behind the curtain. He has become invisible.

And yet, even when the coercer has vanished into the machinery, we still have the ability to recognize when we are being influenced and to lessen the effect of these techniques, however they originate. There are ways to deconstruct the subtle messages and cues coming at us from every direction. No matter how advanced and convoluted these styles of coercion get, they still rely on the same fundamental techniques of tracking, disorientation, redirection, and capture. Restoring our instinctual capacity to sense what we want, regardless of what we're told, is within our reach.

For instance, as you read the words on this page, consider what is being done to you. Picture yourself reading this book, and consider your relationship to the author. Should the fact that my words have been bound in a book give them more authority than if you had heard them on the bus from a stranger?

Already you have been exposed to a battery of coercive techniques. In fact, everything you have read so far has been concocted to demonstrate the main techniques [exposed in *Coercion*].

The opening paragraph, mixing humor with terror, combined a rhythmic assault with the fear-inducing creation of a powerful "they" that means to shape our destiny. The humor disarmed you just enough for the next barb.

Then came a list of rhetorical questions. Of course the answers were already built-in, but they gave you the illusion of interactivity. Like the responsive readings in a church service, they made you feel like you were actively participating in a deductive process, even though the script had already been written and you had no power to change it.

I asked you to personalize the dilemma I had been describing. I asked you to consider the authorities in your life that act upon you in unwanted ways so that you would personally identify with the threats to your well-being. You were no longer just reading about a problem; you were now in the middle of it.

Once roped in, you could be subjected to standard fearmongering. I personified the enemy as teams of psychologists, working late into the night to devise plans for shopping malls that thwart your natural cognitive processes. These devils hope to disconnect you from your own soul, I implied.

Then came simple presupposition. I suggested what would happen if you read on. "As we'll see," I claimed, presupposing that you will soon see things as I do. I stated it as an inevitability.

What better time to establish my own expertise? I enumerated my qualifications—how I have spent years studying the coercive techniques of leading industry experts, and how I have written books on the effect of media on human consciousness.

After the tone had been set, I was free to engage you in one of the oldest coercive techniques of them all: the story. You were meant to identify with my plight—how my optimistic naïveté about media and culture led me into the clutches of the advertising industry, turning my own work against its purpose. Like a spin doctor relating the tale of a downed jet or sexually deviant politician, I confessed my sins—exaggerated them, even—to turn a disaster into an opportunity for redemption. The comeback kid.

Sadly, my story is true; the point is that I've used the saga to gain your trust and engage you in my fight. The technique is simple. Create or present a character with whom someone can identify, then put that character into jeopardy. If the reader has followed the character into danger, he will look for the storyteller for a rescue, however preposterous. The storyteller alone has the ability to relieve the reader's anxiety, if he chooses to. And the relief I offered was to go to war against our new enemy: the coercers, who, like hunters, mean to track us down and kill us.

Then, just to avoid appearing too forceful, I briefly backed in the other direction. "It's not a conspiracy," I retreated, "just a science that has gotten out of control." I encouraged you to relax by telling you there was no conspiracy, but then I implicated the entire scientific and hi-tech community in the automated conspiracy against humanity.

Once you were reduced by my story to the role of a passive spectator in a state of mild captivation, I could lead you down to the next level of vulnerability: trance. I asked you to envision yourself reading the book in your hands right now. Like a hypnotist asking you to watch your breath, I employed a standard trance-induction technique called "disassociation": You are no longer simply reading this book, but picturing yourself reading the book. By separating your awareness from your actions, you become the observer of your own story. Your experience of volition is reduced to what a New Age psychotherapist would call a "guided visualization." From the perspective of coercion technicians who call themselves "neuro-linguistic programmers" (hypnotists who use the habits of the nervous system to reprogram our thought processes), this state of consciousness renders you quite vulnerable. The moment you frame your own awareness within a second level of self-consciousness is the moment your mind is most up for grabs.

Then I set upon the establishment of an elusive goal—what can be called the "pyramid" technique—in which I promised you that there are ways to escape from the tyranny of our social programmers, if only you follow the course I am about to lay out in this text. Like a cult leader, I presented myself and my text as the key to your awakening and freedom.

Finally came the section we are up to now. I appear to disarm myself by revealing all the tactics I have used so far. I am your friend because I'm disclosing what I am doing to you. I am pulling back the curtain, showing you how the trick is done. You're in on it now. In fact, we're in this together. *Wink wink, nudge nudge.* You're safe because you have an ironic distance from the coercive techniques I'm employing. All of them, that is, except *this* one.

Are you on your guard yet? Does it feel good? Of course not. The point is not to make you paranoid. My purpose is to help us get free of coercion, not simply live in reaction to it—especially if that reaction is to succumb to a constant state of suspicion. It wouldn't be a fun way to go through life. Believe me— researching and writing this [...] has brought me there more than once. Besides, suspicious people are some of the most easily manipulated. Ironically, perhaps, the more fun you're having in life, the more satisfied you are with yourself, the harder a target you are to reach.

The fact is, *everything* is coercive. Even something as minute as the way I put the word "everything" in italics is meant to influence you. There's nothing wrong with attempting to sway others to our own way of thinking, especially if we truly believe we are right. It's how relationships, families, businesses, and societies improve themselves. If someone has a better idea for how to dig a hole, elect a leader, or raise happy children, it's up to that person to convince us why he's right.

Using what influence we have is not in itself a destructive thing. The problem arises when the style and force of a person's or institution's influence outweighs the merits of whatever it is they're trying to get us to do. For example, through carefully managed public relations, a chemical company can convince voters that a proposition is intended to protect the environment, even though it loosens regulations on toxic-waste disposal. A crafty car salesman can make us think he is our friend, that he's conspiring with us against his dealership's manager, even though all he is really doing is working to pad his own commission. A fund-raiser can appeal to our religious inclinations while actually persuading us to donate to a political cause with which we might not agree.

The techniques of coercion have advanced so far over the past several decades that we no longer live in a world where the best man wins. It's a world where the person who has made us *believe* he is the best man wins. Advertisers have dispensed with the idea of promoting a product's attributes in favor of marketing the product's image. This image is conceived by marketing psychologists quite independently of the product itself, and usually has more to do with a target market than the item being sold.

All too often, the decisions we make as individuals and as a society are directed by people who may not have our best interests at heart. To influence us, they disable our capacity to make reasoned judgments and appeal to deeper, perhaps unresolved, and certainly unrelated issues. By understanding the unconscious processes we use to make our choices of what to buy, where to eat, whom to respect, and how to feel, clever influence professionals can sidestep our critical faculties and compel us to act however they please. We are disconnected from our own rational, moral, or emotional decision-making abilities. We respond automatically, unconsciously, and often toward our own further disempowerment. The less we are satisfied by our decisions, the more easily manipulated we become.

To restore our own ability to act willfully, we must accept that we are the ones actively submitting to the influence of others. We are influenced because, on some level, we want to be.

Almost all the techniques of coercion I have studied take advantage of one or more of our healthy psychological or social behaviors. For example, parents are the first real authorities in our lives. Mom and Dad are the first "they." In most cases, they are highly deserving of our respect. Our survival depends on it. By admiring and imitating our parents' behaviors, we learn basic life skills. By trusting in their authority, we are free to explore the world around us without fear. We surrender authority to our parents, and they protect us from harm.

We instinctually long for our parents' approval, and they instinctually reward us with praise when we make progress. Learning to stand, walk, speak, or ride a bicycle is not so much a quest for independence as it is an effort to earn our parents' praise. The authority they exercise over our lives is absolute, and absolutely essential.

Growing up, we transfer this authority to our teachers and ministers. Again, this process is altogether healthy. A wider array of role models allows the developing child to learn a variety of coping skills and behaviors. In this manner, we are socialized and eventually initiated into our parents' world. We become adults, capable of making our own decisions.

But sometimes, even as adults, we find ourselves feeling like children again: helpless and desperate for approval from above. Certain people can make us feel like children simply through the intonations of their voices, the styles of their clothing, the manners in which they regard us, or the ways they position their desks at work. A voice on a loudspeaker or over an intercom can command instant authority. A man in a police uniform can lead us to speak an octave higher than we normally do.

Textbooks on employee management, salesmanship, and interrogation all detail precise methods for eliciting childhood emotional states. The technique is called "induced regression," and it exploits the remnants of our natural childhood urges so that the subject "transfers" parental authority onto the practitioner. Or, to say it another way, it's a technique to create a new "they." Our built-in instinct to respect authority is exploited by people who, for one reason or another, need us to revert to our obedient and praise-seeking childhood state of mind.

There are hundreds of natural and healthy cognitive processes that can be exploited by those who understand them. As individuals hoping to regain a sense of authority over our own lives, we need not purge ourselves of our psychological traits so that they cannot be tapped. We liberate ourselves from coercion not by denying our underlying social and emotional needs—we do so by reclaiming them.

For instance, fund-raisers and salespeople commonly give the prospective donor or customer a free gift. Many charities send us sets of greeting cards along with their pleas for financial assistance, while insurance salespeople give away calendars or appointment books. Are they giving us these things out of the goodness of their hearts? Of course not. They are trying to provoke a sense of obligation in us. Once we accept the gift, a transaction has been initiated. We owe the giver something. If we use the gift without paying anything, we feel a little guilty. Accepting a gift or favor obligates us to return one. Why? Because the development of a set of social and financial obligations is part of what allowed us to form communities in the first place. I help you build your barn today, and you help me swat locusts off my crop next summer. This relationship isn't as mercenary as it sounds. Mutual need, obligation, and reciprocity over time are the bases of any community. Survival depends on them.

Today, we still give gifts as a way of establishing social rapport. When someone moves into our neighborhood, we may bring them food or something to make their adjustment easier. Unless the new neighbors are deeply neurotic about accumulating social obligations, they are thankful to be welcomed. The fact that we have permitted them to owe us something is itself a gift. We have initiated them into the fabric of community relationships.

Enclosing a free gift in a solicitation for donations is meant to capitalize on this evolved set of behaviors. The technique has become so overused by now that it rarely works. We might feel guilty about it. We might throw out the free greeting cards rather than use them, just so we don't have to be reminded about the animals that are suffering without our financial support every time we send a greeting. But most of us won't be swayed enough by the offering to open our checkbooks. We just resent it.

This resentment actually erodes the community spirit on which the manipulative technique is based. We are now suspicious of people who offer us gifts. A stranger who gives us something must want something in return. We are reluctant to perform acts of goodwill ourselves lest we provoke paranoia in the recipients.

The most destructive side effect of coercive techniques is that they prey upon our best instincts and compromise our ability to employ them when we want to. Some of us are simply suckered. Others are made uncomfortable. The most sophisticated and wary of us are made increasingly paranoid and antisocial.

Today, P. T. Barnum's famous insight on suckers can be extended: Currently there are three levels of response to coercion, which exist simultaneously in our culture. Some of us are readily fooled by the simplest of manipulative techniques. These people, who I call the "Traditionalists," are the sort of folks who are emotionally moved by politicians' speeches, dedicated to their local sports teams, and ready to believe that government agencies would prevent us from being duped by misleading advertisements.

The next group—who marketers like to call "sophisticated" audiences—feels they understand how the media hope to manipulate them. These "Cool Kids" respond to coercive techniques that acknowledge their ironic detachment. Their television remote controls and video game controllers have changed their relationship to the television tube. They like to deconstruct every image that is piped into their homes. But they fall for the *wink wink, nudge nudge* plea of the modern advertiser or salesperson who appeals to their media-savvy wit. As long as the coercer admits with a sideways glance that he's coercing, the Cool Kid is likely to take the bait. He is being rewarded for his ironic attitude.

The last group has graduated from the culture of cool and is just plain fed up with everything that has a trace of manipulation. The "New Simpletons" want straightforward, no-nonsense explanations for what they're supposed to buy or do. They like salespeople that dispense with jargon and just tell it how it is. They buy Saturns so they won't have to negotiate, and they like plain-speaking pain-reliever commercials that simply say "This drug works." They go to the Price Club and Home Depot and order computers over the World Wide Web, basing their decisions on RAM, megahertz, and price.

The existence of these three very different reactions to coercion in one culture at the same time is making life hard for advertisers, marketers, and public-relations experts. To appeal to one sensibility is to alienate both the others. (On the other hand, a homespun message meant for New Simpletons may at first attract but ultimately confuse Traditionalists.) No matter how well the advertisers define the "target market," the rest of us are still exposed to the same message. Two-thirds of us are unaffected. And the people who have made a profession of manipulating us are scared.

That's why we have a unique opportunity to disarm our manipulators and to restore the social interactions that their efforts—and our complicity—have eroded over time. More important, we can put an end to the coercive arms race that is fast absorbing so much of our time and resources.

These realizations are just as valuable to advertisers and public-relations experts as they are to us. None of the influence professionals I spoke and worked with while writing this [...] actually likes the direction that the compliance industry has taken. Many of them suffer from migraines or insomnia and pay high bills for psychotherapy and prescription drugs. They would like nothing better than to exchange the guilt-inspiring drudgery of manipulation for the joy of real communication. Many of them want the race to end.[...]

The United States is the only developed nation in the world that does not mandate media literacy as part of its public-school curriculum. There are reasons why. Media literacy is dangerous—not to the individuals who gain it, but to the people and institutions that depend on our *not* having it. Once we master the tools of media literacy, we cannot apply them selectively. If we learn the techniques that an advertiser uses to fool us, we have also learned the techniques that a government uses. If we demystify the role of our hi-tech pundits, we may demystify the role of our priests as well.

We also run the risk of succumbing to full-blown paranoia. Once we gain the ability to perceive the coercive forces acting on us every day from seemingly innocent sources, it will be difficult not to see the work of an influence professional behind every magazine cover. (It's probably there, but that's beside the point.) Once coercive techniques are put into practice, they have a tendency to sustain themselves and multiply. Although someone may have intentionally concocted the technique at some point in the past, chances are it has been on automatic pilot ever since. And once we've programmed these techniques into our computerized marketplace, there's no turning back. On whichever side of the electric fence we find ourselves as the coercer or the coercee—we are equally victimized, and equally to blame.

That's why it would be foolish for us to personify the forces behind our culture's rampant coercive efforts. The chairman of the board is just as victimized by his shareholders and the quarterly bottom line as we are by his public-relations specialists. The art of manipulation has become so prevalent that it drives our culture forward more than any of its best agents do. It is more constructive to think of the coercive forces in our society as part of a big machine that has gotten out of control. As we become more conscious of how it works, we can begin to dismantle it.

We are living through end-stage propaganda, a culture which has been subjected to so much assertion of authority—so much programming—that it exhibits pathological symptoms. Those of us who have been coerced into submission find ourselves feeling powerless, passive, or depressed, and we may even resort to medication. Those of us compelled to resist these authorities tend to become suspicious and cynical. We believe "they" are real and allied against us. "They" have become the enemy.

They're not. As one of the people who has been paid to come up with new strategies for manipulation, I can assure you: they're just us.

---

## Working with the Text

1. Near the beginning of his essay, Rushkoff asks, "How can we feel we're so aware of the effects of advertising and marketing, yet still succumb to them?" What does Rushkoff initially describe as the main strategies of the "hidden persuaders"?

2. Why was Rushkoff initially so optimistic that the computer revolution and the rise of the Internet would make all of us, especially young people, less vulnerable to the persuasive strategies of advertisers, political figures, and others trying to influence opinion and behavior? What caused him to change his mind?

3. In the course of the essay, Rushkoff moves from the idea of *persuasion* to the idea of *coercion*. How do you understand the difference between the two terms? How differently do you view a particular advertising or other rhetorical strategy if you consider it coercive rather than persuasive?

4. Rushkoff uses the metaphor of hunting to describe the relationship between "coercers" and those they are trying to "target." What do you see as the strengths and weaknesses of looking at our relationship to advertising and persuasion in this way? What does it help us understand about the situation? What value judgments does it contain? How does the metaphor itself work as a persuasive strategy?

5. What are the "three levels of response to coercion" that Rushkoff describes at the end of his essay? Which level best describes your own response and why? Which best describe your friends and family members?

6. In the second half of his essay, Rushkoff turns the spotlight on his own work and analyzes the persuasive strategies that he himself uses in the beginning of the essay to win your confidence and trust. First, make your own list of these strategies. Next, analyze the opening of another reading in this textbook in terms of these strategies. Finally, use an example of your own persuasive writing (a previous school-based assignment, an email message to a friend, a letter of application, etc.) to test the strategies that Rushkoff describes.

7. Define what Rushkoff means by "media literacy" and why he thinks it is so important. Working either individually or in groups, develop a model for a media literacy program or single assignment based on Rushkoff's essay aimed at a particular age group. What specific skill and concepts should be developed? What might be the different age-appropriate strategies for younger children? For teenagers and adolescents? For adults?

## BUZZ MARKETING

- You are at a park with friends and someone has brought a cooler filled with a new kind of soft drink you've never heard of. You ask the person who brought the cooler about the drink, and he tells you it's a great new soda that he really likes and thinks you might, too. Before long, you and all your friends have tried one, and some of you decide to look for the brand next time you are shopping.

- You're in the parking lot at school when someone pulls up in a car you've never seen before. She notices that you are looking at her car and tells you that it's a new model that is not even being advertised yet. While you both walk to campus, she tells you more about it and why she likes it so much.

- You notice while out at the movies that many people are wearing an interesting new shirt. You're unfamiliar with the design and the brand, so you are surprised to see so many people wearing it. Finally, you just have to ask someone where he or she got it, and the person directs you to a new store in the mall.

All of these scenarios might be similar to encounters that you have had. Even before we see official advertising or marketing for a new product, we sometimes find out about it from friends or acquaintances or just by noticing it around town. Probably nothing strikes us as particularly unusual or surprising about any of this. But what if the situations described above weren't just chance encounters or random events? What if instead each of these incidents were deliberately designed marketing strategies?

The advertising technique known as *buzz marketing* consists precisely of these types of situations. Rather than relying solely or even at all on a traditional advertising campaign involving television commercials, ads in magazines, or ads on billboards, buzz marketing focuses on using one-on-one encounters to create buzz about a new product or service. A group of professional actors, for example, might be hired to go to clubs around town and order a hot new drink that they talk about in loud and excited voices so that other people in the club assume they are overhearing other customers who have discovered something new. Teenagers might be given free clothes to wear to popular events or shopping areas, or someone might show up in an Internet chat room to promote a new movie or CD, all the while posing as just another fan.

The idea of buzz builds on the unsurprising fact that we trust the word of our friends more than that of advertisers, and that we will also tend to trust people we see as regular consumers just like ourselves more than professional marketers. Buzz builds on the old advertising idea of word of mouth, that some of the most effective advertising comes from friends making recommendations to friends. Just think of how naturally we might see an ad for a new product and then ask our friends if they know anything about it as a way of checking out the validity of the advertising. What if, however, your friends were working for a marketing company? Conversely, what would you do if a marketing company asked you to help sell a new service to your friends?

In a way, we can view buzz marketing not just as a new advertising strategy but also as a new type of media or means of communication. By

Two buzz marketers were arrested after authorities mistook promotional LED boxes for bombs.

*media,* we mean the physical processes used to transmit information, from printing ink on paper to broadcasting electromagnetic waves that can be turned into sound and light waves using special receivers (i.e., radio and television), to transmitting digital code electronically to construct images on a computer screen (the World Wide Web). In the case of buzz marketing, however, the medium is not something outside ourselves, like a newspaper or a television; the medium is actually all of us. Individual human beings become the media used to transmit advertising messages. Unlike other kinds of media, however, we are not passive machines responding to a pre-set program, but active, thinking agents whose own motives, beliefs, and principles can either interfere with or amplify these messages.

In this section, you will read about and discuss buzz marketing and the issues surrounding it. The first reading is from a marketing company that specializes in advertising to young people describing and recommending buzz marketing. The second is a newspaper story about two friends who came up with the idea of financing their college educations by selling them-selves as advertising space. At the end of the section, you will be asked to construct your own argument about buzz marketing.

## Before You Read: Buzz Marketing

1. Brainstorm a list of products and services you think that you learned about primarily through friends and word of mouth rather than through traditional advertising. What were the circumstances involved? How did these circumstances affect how you felt about the product or service?

2. As a class, share your brainstorming results and try to identify some products or services that almost everyone in class first heard about through word of mouth. How popular did these products become? Can you compare your experiences with these products with others that you mainly learned about through traditional advertising?

## "How Buzz Marketing Works for Teens"

### Amy Henry

*It will come as no surprise to any college student that young people in adolescence and early adulthood are a particular target for advertisers. They are seen as a group with disposable income that likes to shop, making them a ready market. At the same time, many adults regard teenagers as almost a separate tribe, with mysterious rituals and an ever-changing language designed to resist adult comprehension. The idea of the teenager as a separate* sphere of human development between childhood and adulthood, complete with its own complex subcultures, developed roughly in parallel with the growth of the modern consumer society and the advertising industry, and some would argue that the similar history is no coincidence. After all, one of the features of the development of marketing and advertising has to do with dividing society into more and more highly defined consumer subgroups, and the teenager has proven to be a valuable marketing idea as well as a useful way of understanding the transition to adulthood.

In "How Buzz Marketing Works for Teens," Amy Henry, an advertising professional who works for a company that specializes in marketing to children and teens, gives us an inside view of how advertisers discuss the teen market among themselves. Specifically, she offers her own insights and research into the nature of teen culture to suggest how buzz marketing can be used to enlist teens themselves in the enterprise of youth advertising.

O ver the past few years the marketing industry has been buzzing about the very concept of buzz. Agencies have begun to specialize in generating word of mouth, and media experts have turned the most mundane occurrences into experiments in nontraditional marketing. In Chicago, clubs and stores paid actors and comics to stand in line, just to beg the question "What are they waiting for?" and in London makers of Red Bull filled rubbish bins in the hippest parts of town with empties to give the illusion of an addictive product—and a potential shortage. Defying convention, Serena Williams became a buzz-causing billboard for Puma when she donned a far-from-tennis-whites black cat suit (a Puma suit, in fact) at the U.S. Open. While these brands may be mavericks in their industries, many mainstream marketers have begun to take note of their tactics.

As many marketers take their fledgling steps into the world of buzz marketing, buzz experts have emerged to provide advice. Malcolm Gladwell's book, *The Tipping Point,* which describes how ideas spread like epidemics (discussed by Procter and Richards in *IJAMC* April–June 2002), has itself been passed around like a virus within the advertising industry—marketers at every rank have challenged their teams to leverage buzz in their marketing plans. But while buzz has been written about in a social context and in a broad marketing context, few writers have discussed more than a one-size-fits-all approach to buzz marketing. This article examines teens' connection to buzz, and provides a point of view on how messages can create a stir among this target.

## DEFINING BUZZ

Defining buzz is more than semantics. How we think about the concept of buzz is critical to our ability to create it as marketers. Many marketers have begun to regard buzz as a new discipline within the marketing and media worlds. Like TV advertising, buzz has become a line item on marketing plans. If objectives for reach and frequency are met through traditional vehicles such as TV and print, and there is money left over, marketers may challenge their agencies to experiment with a buzz-creating idea. This challenge provides the first dilemma for marketers who are attempting to create buzz around their brands for the first time: who "owns" the development of buzz ideas? Is it an advertising agency specializing in creating high-profile brands for the masses? An interactive agency that understands the power of marketing that necessitates consumer involvement? A PR firm who has mastered the development of powerful messages and sound bites? The answer is: all of the above.

Rather than a single discipline, buzz is interdisciplinary. Rather than a new discipline, buzz is a new way of thinking about existing disciplines. In fact, when we think about buzz as a separate discipline, we sacrifice many opportunities to use buzz effectively to build brands.

- *We ignore the potential of mass marketing vehicles to create buzz.* In fact, TV and print can be extremely effective conveyors of buzz, if a buzzable message is infused in copy.
- *We undervalue the power of buzz to build a brand, and relegate it to second-class citizen status.* Simply put, if buzz is undertaken only once all other objectives are fulfilled, it is clearly not a brand priority, and thus can expect to bring only limited success.
- *We place too much emphasis on the media and we disregard the impact of a powerful message.* If we think about buzz as tactics, we get only half of the equation right. As in TV advertising, it is not enough to be advertised during the Super Bowl—you have to develop messages that are compelling, innovative, relevant, and clear.

Buzz requires a different way of thinking about brands. The tactics that generate buzz are sometimes similar to the tactics used in traditional marketing, but we believe that buzz is actually grounded in the disciplines most marketers already know. To understand whether or not buzz can come from traditional media, we reviewed the intention and the objectives regularly met by the most common marketing tactics.

As an example, consider the following disciplines through the lens of buzz.

- PR, especially consumer PR, aims to deliver your message through an expert—who can provide credibility and support for your brand.
- Event marketing relies on creating an event that you invite consumers to attend.
- Sports marketing is about connecting your brand or company with athletes—who are larger than life.
- Alternative media usually provide supplemental awareness to your mainstream media.

- And finally, online marketing has in many cases become an everyday presence—a message in your in-box reminding you of a marketer's brand.

Considering these objectives and aims, it is clear that there is an opportunity to examine the benefits of these disciplines from another perspective—one that better fits today's complex and multidisciplinary culture. In a day and age in which companies are not always trustworthy, does your average consumer value or trust the information given to them by the establishment? In the age of endorsed everything, does the Nike logo on an athlete—or on every athlete—mean as much as it used to, or does it fade into the background? Does online marketing work best when it serves as an everyday reminder, or should it be held in higher regard?

In fact, these marketing disciplines could meet traditional objectives—but when used in innovative ways, grounded in a true understanding of their consumer, they become buzz vehicles. Below are two examples of this.

- When the source of credibility for PR is broadened, and we think of endorsers not only as celebrities and experts but as neighbors and friends, we can begin to see how buzz is related to PR.
- When the principles of event marketing are used to build underground events, we see that events can be discovered, not advertised. It is these subversive events that become worthy of buzz.

Unlike the traditional approach, in which strategy comes first and then media and then content, we think you have to consider your brand's character first. To be a buzzable brand, you have to be:

- invasive but invited
- individualized
- experiential
- provocative
- conspiratorial
- connective
- creative.

Buzz is not concrete and tangible. We think buzz is a way of being that your brand must embrace before teens will talk about it.

## BUZZ FOR OLD PEOPLE

So how do we know buzz when we see it? The beauty of buzz is that if it is done well, and targeted at teens, you as an adult may not have seen it. But buzz lives not only in a teen's world, but also flourishes in the adult world. To give you a few examples that you might recognize:

- a Mojito
- a PDA
- *Sex and the City*
- Viagra.

The alcohol industry functions through buzz. What made Cosmos a hot new drink? No one advertises these concoctions (although a few marketers have begun taking this kind of buzz mass, with subway ads all over New York for drinks like Remy Red). Hard alcohol brands know that the best way to get consumers to buy their brands is to introduce them to a cocktail that they can order and that then becomes a status symbol. No one began advertising Caipirinhas and Mojitos, but suddenly they are all over menus and bars...

The technology category is also fueled by buzz. PDAs are more likely to be purchased based on a friend's recommendation or a glimpse of a coworker's gadgets than on seeing an advertisement.

Our next example is also a hugely effective way of intentionally influencing people. When Sarah Jessica Parker sports a new bag or a new pair of shoes on *Sex and the City,* Barney's displays it in the window the next day. Product placement is a strategy that has leveraged the philosophy of buzz.

And finally, Viagra is a great example of a product with inherent buzz—it's relevant and provocative. Viagra gave people the chance to talk about a very taboo subject in a very public way. You might be surprised to find pharmaceutical companies included in a list of examples of cutting-edge marketing, but they've been doing this for a long time through professional marketing efforts and sampling.

## THE TEEN–BUZZ CONNECTION

To understand the teen–buzz connection, we first cataloged the benefits that buzz has for a consumer. Then we looked for ways in which this connected with teen psychology and culture. We found that many of the benefits of buzz directly answer the needs of teens.

- Teens feel disenfranchised. They feel they have all the responsibility of adults but they don't have the right to make their own choices; they can't vote; and in the USA they can't drink! Buzz puts the power in their own hands—whether they have the information that they can pass along to friends, or they hear brand messages from other teens.
- Teens are a subculture. They have a distinct language, values, and cultural mores. Buzz inherently belongs to the "rebelling against" subculture because it lives beneath the radar of mass marketing.
- Teens are a subculture with their own language, values, and mores. They are iconoclastic by nature—and so is buzz: it counters commercial culture and lives beneath the radar of mass marketing.
- Teens are inherently stimulation-seeking. We know their brains actually have underdeveloped brain functioning when it comes to making sound, reasoned decisions. Buzz is and must be provocative in order to succeed.

Buzz marketing: the body as billboard

- Teens are engaged in a process of selective identity formation—and buzz is anti-ubiquity. Teens can choose which parts to believe and pass on instead of being overpowered by the loud voice of mass media.
- Finally, teens aspire to be passionate people. To them, this is the most admirable character trait they see in themselves and other teens—and it is the attribute that adults often lack. Buzz depends on passion. It isn't spread (and therefore it isn't buzz) unless one person is passionate enough about it to pass it along.

In teen culture, buzz becomes more than just a communication vehicle. Brands that are surrounded by buzz gain a certain mystique that would be difficult for a brand to enforce through advertising.

This should not be surprising: in a culture in which the withholding and the selective leveraging of information is routine, it is not surprising that rumors hold a great deal of influence. Whether it's sneaking out past curfew—a very active form of information suppression—or spreading a lie to gain peer approval, teens often equate survival within their culture with being on the "right side" of rumor. But to understand how to create messages that create buzz among teens, it is critical to understand what motivates and compels teens—negatively and positively. Buzz not only leverages existing behavior within teen culture, but it also fulfills many of the fundamental psychological, social, and cultural needs of that segment of society (see Figure 1).

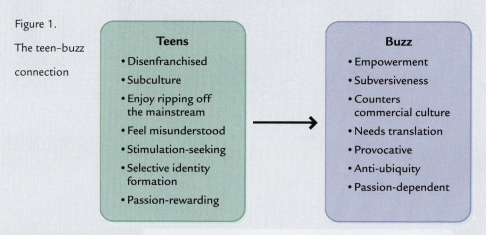

Figure 1.

The teen–buzz connection

**Teens**
- Disenfranchised
- Subculture
- Enjoy ripping off the mainstream
- Feel misunderstood
- Stimulation-seeking
- Selective identity formation
- Passion-rewarding

**Buzz**
- Empowerment
- Subversiveness
- Counters commercial culture
- Needs translation
- Provocative
- Anti-ubiquity
- Passion-dependent

Buzz is part communication strategy, part cache.

## CATALYSTS OF BUZZ

There are three major drivers that can make messages "stick" among teens:
(1) truth distorted
(2) bad behavior
(3) reality romanticized.

The first driver, truth distorted, is a fundamental premise of all buzz. Psychologists talk about distortion theory as the way the brain molds a message to relate to its own needs or the conditions of its specific environment. Anthropologist Richard Dawkins discussed how ideas (or memes) are as vulnerable to the evolutionary game (the survival of the fittest) as species. In his estimation, only the "useful" memes survive.

Urban legends are a cultural phenomenon that seems to be driven by distortion theory. Urban legends are stories without a known source that are widely spread. As the story spreads, the source is often distorted as much as the story itself. Rather than saying "I heard it somewhere," a person spreading an urban legend begins to unknowingly distort the truth, and accredit the story to an expert of some sort. It becomes what one doctor has called "a collective memory of something that never happened."

Often these stories have an element of truth hidden deep within them. When they spread, they are up for the interpretation of the listener and the speaker. This interpretation passes through a filter of appropriation: to continue to spread a message, something about it must resonate with the listener. Often this involves appropriating the story to the listener's own cultural norms or conditions. And often the appropriation is provocative.

The result is usually a message that sounds very different than it originally did. One example of this is the film, *The Blair Witch Project.* This low-budget film became a buzz phenomenon when it began to outstrip its highly marketed competitors through the use of rumor. The legend behind the movie, namely, the Blair Witch, became the subject of a fabricated documentary on the Sci-Fi Channel, and shortly afterward became a true urban legend. Convinced that they would find the real Blair Witch, teens in three suburban areas began scouring the woods near their homes.

Pop Rocks is another great example of how a marketer took advantage of a distorted truth about their brand. General Foods stumbled across an idea that appealed to the marketers who tried it, and to the kids of these marketers, but the product didn't quite fit cleanly within the brand's portfolio. They wanted to test the brand before they launched it to ensure that the brand would be profitable, but would also not compromise their corporate identity.

They chose three markets that would have very little contact with other markets: Laredo, Wyoming; Billings, Montana; and Flagstaff, Arizona. The marketing was kept intentionally secretive, not because of conspiracy or danger, but because marketers don't like their competitors to know what new products they're launching. The "rumor" spread when residents of these towns started talking about the product to "outsiders" and described its unique in-mouth feel (it explodes in the mouth). The interpretation and appropriation: that this was clearly a new government discovered drug that was being hidden from everyday citizens. Knowing that this product was developed in the late

1970s helps to explain this appropriation—government conspiracies and secrets and drugs were the subjects of much of the provocateurs of U.S. culture. A black market for Pop Rocks began—mystifying the marketers who were afraid their pricing—at 25 cents a pack—was too high.

Behaving badly is also a key driver of buzz. We could look at a prominent aspect of teen culture—gossip—to test our theory. The gossip that spreads inevitably oozes of sex, fear, mystery, risk, and danger. The messages are provocative and conspiratorial to say the least. We analyzed some marketing examples of buzz among teens in order to validate our theory.

*South Park,* the Comedy Central show that personifies "politically incorrect," also works as a teen buzz case study. Before the show began airing, an irreverent holiday card, featuring some of the characters of the show, was passed along through email. The subject matter—Jesus versus Santa Claus—was certainly edgy and controversial. The shock value of *South Park* has made it the subject of conversation, and thus, a catalyst for buzz.

The third driver, reality romanticized, may seem unusual in pairing with our other themes. While we know teens do experience the "angst" that we hear so much about, we also know that the teen years are filled with practical idealism—they want to change the world and challenge the assumptions of adults, although, to be clear, they don't want to sacrifice too much to do it.

We looked at two marketers who are creating ways to make teens smile—which is something they're willing to share with their friends. Nike introduced its Presto running shoe in unusually creative ways. For example, it displayed the colorful shoes in an art gallery in Soho, creating a fashionable underside of a brand known for power and achievement. Their product also built-in buzz through something as mundane as its sizing—they come in small, medium, and large.

Phillip Starck's new line at Target was also introduced in an unusual way. Target created buzz among teens when the company changed the face of street signs in New York. In keeping with Starck's design philosophy, these signs made everyday sidewalk commands endearing and rose-colored.

## YOUR BRAND'S ALTER EGO

When we looked at the potential ways in which a marketer could develop these drivers for a brand, we realized that each of these required a risky proposition for marketers: developing an alter ego for your brand.

What is an alter ego? While your public persona is an undisputed truth, the most important attribute, and the equity of your brand, your alter ego is the edge of the acceptable. While this identification of multiple messages may belie marketing wisdom, we think it's an essential risk to take—or to evaluate—if you are committed to creating buzz around your teen brand.

By developing an alter ego for your brand, you can allow yourself and your agencies to take off the handcuffs—buzz requires that you take your brand to the edges of its identity. It may require turning your brand message inside-out—like Nike did when launching the Presto.

For brand managers launching a teen brand, we think you should become intimate with the "dark side" of your brand. You may find power in these messages beyond their ability to be buzzable. For teens, brands that take risks feel like kindred spirits.

Puma really needed to infuse some life into their brand a few years ago, as competing with the Nikes and Adidases of this world wasn't building their business. They still wanted to stand for performance, but they also wanted to create a bold new statement—and show that they understand teens. Instead of joining the mainstream culture of sport, Puma decided to invade it. They rethought the category conventions, and decided to play in an area of white space—fashion over function. They also found new distribution channels to sell their products—underground retailers that teens love, like Urban Outfitters. Finally, Serena Williams's outfit spoke a thousand words at the U.S. Open. Her cat suit not only embodied Puma, but also showed teens and other Puma fans that this brand was willing to take risks.

Mountain Dew Code Red also became a brand surrounded by buzz. This brand's reputation spread like wildfire based on its "bad" beginnings. Mountain Dew Code Red was the inspiration for a group of virus creators in Silicon Valley.

The brand also developed a more intentional alter ego. Unlike the high-energy, yet edgy, parent brand, Code Red was wrapped in grittiness and mystery from the beginning. The very name—Code Red—created talk value. They also sample in the exclusive enclaves of teen culture—like the lounges of the X Games. And finally, their advertising campaign had the feel of hidden cameras catching celebrities like Macy Gray on the authentic city streets where they first began breaking the rules—or redefining their games.

## GETTING BUZZ FOR YOUR BRAND

First, we believe that you need to know exactly who you are before you begin to buzz. And know who you're not—if you can't imagine how your brand could ever adopt an alter ego, maybe your brand should not attempt to buzz.

Next, define your alter ego. Begin by thinking about how teens really see your brand—the good and the bad. Understand the flipside of your public persona and stretch your brand to its outer limits. Identify the influencers—the subgroup of your consumer set who are most likely to buzz about your brand.

Then create innovative ways of reaching them. Don't rely on existing buzz tactics to carry your message. Then send your message, and most important, observe and analyze. Often we're not sure which messages will work. By "reading" your target you can not only begin the buzz but build on it. Finally, extend your buzz campaign and integrate it with the other elements of your media mix. Buzz can only last for so long—then you need to find new ways to stay connected to your consumer.

## BEFORE YOU BUZZ

Before you buzz, heed the following advice. First, develop clear expectations. Buzz does not build in a day and, by its nature, will not directly reach as many consumers as your traditional media buys. Buzz can be a great way to build a brand image and create a connection with your teen consumer, but it is not instantaneous. Second, know your target. Because buzz is a distinctive marketing method, and because it must fit into teens' culture, it requires a deep understanding of your target. Finally, make sure you're looking at your brand through the eyes of your target, and not through the lens of adulthood. You may discover new opportunities that you never would have found—and you may avoid some big mistakes.

### How to buzz

- Know who you are; know who you're not
- Define your brand's alter ego
- Identify the influencers
- Innovate
- Seed the idea (and often the product)
- Observe and analyze
- Extend the campaign
- Integrate with awareness-generating media

## Working with the Text

1. In the section on "The Teen-Buzz Connection," Henry presents a bulleted list describing features of "teen psychology and culture." What are these features? Do her assertions ring true for you and others in the class? Why or why not? How could we test or confirm these ideas (for example, that teens "are inherently stimulation-seeking" and "have underdeveloped brain functioning when it comes to making sound, reasoned, decisions")?

2. According to Henry, there are "three major drivers that can make messages 'stick' among teens." She provides several examples of each; for example, under "truth distorted," she points to the influence of urban legends and how they can be used for marketing campaigns. Can you add to her list of examples? What urban legends are you familiar with? Can you think of any rumors or gossip you have heard connected to decisions about purchasing and consumption?

3. Why does Henry say that bad behavior is appealing to teens? In what ways do you agree or disagree? According to Henry, how can marketers use the appeal of bad behavior to create a buzz campaign?

4. Henry states that the teen years are "filled with practical idealism—they want to change the world and challenge the assumptions of adults, although, to be clear, they don't want to sacrifice too much to do it." Would you agree with Henry's claim? How do the examples of buzz marketing she provides illustrate this desire for "practical idealism"?

5. What does Henry mean by an "alter ego" for a brand? Can you add any examples to hers that you think might be instances of just such an alter ego? How does Henry define "the edge of the acceptable" in creating an alter ego through buzz marketing? Do you think she means her reference to the "dark side" of the brand to be positive or negative? Can you think of other examples of brands that you think have a "dark side"?

6. Henry's article is meant to provide advice and guidance to other advertising professionals. Explore her ideas about marketing to teens by creating a buzz campaign for your college. How could you take advantage of the descriptions of teen psychology and the three major drivers of teen behavior she describes? What would your school's alter ego be? Remember, the idea is to create a buzz campaign; not just a series of ads or webpages, but a strategy that would get teens to advertise the college through word of mouth. As you plan your strategy, how could you take advantage of the various communications media used by young people (conversation, instant messaging, email, cell phones, etc.) as part of your campaign strategy?

   Once you've created a campaign, either individually or as group projects, take a step back to do an ethical analysis of your campaign. How do you define "the edge of the acceptable"? How do your campaigns relate to this edge? Where did you find yourself confronting the difference between "effective" and "ethical"? Use this analysis to begin a discussion of how you understand the ethics of buzz marketing in general.

# "And Now a Word from Their Cool College Sponsor"

## Kate Zernike

*To some, buzz marketing creates a fear that advertising is becoming so sophisticated and pervasive in the age of instant communication, consumers don't stand a chance anymore of resisting or even responding critically to the advertising messages they receive (something like the world Roy F. Fox warns us about in "Salespeak"). Others, however, might agree more with Douglas Rushkoff in "They Say" that, just as advertisers develop new methods of "hunting their prey," that same prey (i.e., you and me) can use similar techniques and digital technologies to become more elusive—and perhaps, in some cases, to turn the tables on advertisers.*

*In "And Now a Word from Their Cool College Sponsor,"* New York Times *reporter Kate Zernike tells the story of two young men from New Jersey who used the Internet and their familiarity with advertising to create their own version of buzz advertising, except in this case the products they were selling were themselves. In exchange for payment of their college expenses, Chris Barrett and Luke McCabe offered themselves as living, breathing advertising spaces, turning their day-to-day lives into opportunities for companies to market their products and services to everyone the two young men came into contact with. When the credit card company First USA took them up on the offer, the story received national attention, and an argument developed over who was using whom in this relationship. As you read, see where you stand on the issue: have Chris Barrett and Luke McCabe sold themselves to the highest bidder, or have they turned the tables on the marketers who spend billions to persuade young people to buy their products and services?*

Chris Barrett and Luke McCabe emerge from the surf, studded with the logos of a credit card company, and begin to work their way across the beach toward a coterie of publicists and a photographer there to capture the moment.

Two bikini-clad young women step in their path and ask about all the attention. The young men, 18 and freshly graduated from high school, lean with tanned arms slung around their surfboards and chat for a few minutes before continuing their saunter across the sand.

"They thought it was really cool," Mr. Barrett says, eyes bright. Mr. McCabe pumps a thumbs-up in the air.

A publicity representative beams. Another hit in the media whirl of Chris and Luke.

Last year, the two men, seniors at Haddonfield Memorial High School, offered corporate America a deal: you pay our way to college, and we'll be your "spokesguys." After entertaining offers from more than a dozen companies, they chose First USA, one of the nation's largest credit card companies, which agreed to pay each $40,000 in tuition, room, board, and books for the academic year when they enter college in Southern California next month. In return, Mr. Barrett and Mr. McCabe will spread the First USA–sponsored message of smart budgeting and financial responsibility. Among other things, they will make campus appearances, serve on a student advisory board, and publicize financial tips for students on their website. In the meantime, of course, they are also attracting millions of dollars in free publicity with an image that is cool, blond, and young.

In a world where kindergartners learn to count with books created by Cheerios, where Channel One beams commercials into classrooms, and where Coke and Pepsi compete for turf alongside hall lockers, this is the last frontier, a perfect synergy between media- and marketing-savvy teenagers and companies desperate to capture the lucrative, yet elusive, youth market.

Critics bemoan creeping commercialism in education, but Mr. Barrett and Mr. McCabe show how far it has already encroached. Students are not just surrounded by marketing tactics; they are adopting them. Among their peers, and First USA's competitors, there is neither shock nor accusations of selling out, but only, "Why didn't I think of that first?"

"They are smart, smart kids," said Doug Filak, the vice president for marketing at First USA, a division of Bank One. He often accompanies the young men on interviews, watching with a smile that is half envy, half cat that ate the canary.

Mr. Barrett and Mr. McCabe have the First USA logo on their surfboards, surf shorts, camp shirts, indeed, an entire wardrobe's worth of clothing, blurring the line between their life as average college students and their role as pitchmen. And that is just how the company wants it.

"We thought we had a powerful message, and we were looking for the best way to spread it," Mr. Filak said. "What better way than to have two cool students, two normal guys, spread it for us?"

When the First USA people refer to Chris and Luke, it comes out Chrisnluke, and in some ways, the two have become one.

"They complement each other well," Mr. Filak said, "and they know it."

Mr. Barrett, who will attend Pepperdine University in Malibu, Calif., is the chattier and more clean cut of the two. He was a former class president and winner of the prize for the highest grade point average in the business courses. Mr. McCabe, who will attend the University of Southern California, plays in a band called Big Fat Huge, wears sideburns tracing the curve of his face, and started a student group to fight racism. They have been friends since sixth grade and started a road hockey team at Haddonfield Memorial High. Both, according to their website, "enjoy golf, surfing, tennis, concerts, and dating."

They thought of the idea on a tour of campuses in California, as they became more and more anxious about how much it would cost to attend. They retreated to a hotel room, where the television clicker happened on Tiger Woods, sporting his usual Nike swoosh gear. Wouldn't it be cool, Mr. Barrett asked, if we could get someone to sponsor us?

They put up a website, posting pictures of themselves toting surfboards: "Your logo here!" Smiling and blond, they offered their services pitching anything from sneakers to cell phone service. "We will drink your soda and eat your chips! Where we go, you go!"

After Yahoo! made it "site of the day," the offers started coming in, a few to pitch cell phone service, another to sell caffeinated mints. Mr. Barrett and Mr. McCabe chose First USA, they said, because the company did not want them to sell a product.

"We wanted a message, one that we thought kids could relate to," Mr. McCabe said. "Everyone can relate to money."

Now, the two men's website is a mix of teenspeak ("We have been getting emails from girls all over the country!") and financial tips ("Start saving that change from those late-night pizza deliveries and see how fast your $2 turns into $100 when you deposit it in a savings account!")

In exchange for the $40,000 for the first academic year, they are expected to wear their First USA clothing whenever they make public appearances on their campus or others for the company. Each has to maintain at least a C average (Mr. McCabe was a straight-A student in high school; Mr. Barrett got As and Bs) and live up to the terms of a moral clause—if they misbehave, the deal is off. But Mr. Filak said he fully expected to "re-sign" them for the full four years of college.

The deal, marketing experts say, represents the evolution of The Sell, with companies analyzing how best to reach their target audiences.

"If you want to talk to college students about financial issues, it's better than some guy in a suit to have kids you see every day saying, 'Make sure you manage your beer money,'" said Barbara Coulon, vice president for trends at Youth Intelligence, a youth marketing company in New York. "With credit card companies in general, college students have this view that they just want you to spend, spend, spend; they're all over the place on campuses, just to make money off you. First USA seems like the credit card that students can trust if it's coming from college students themselves."

Not everyone, though, sees this as a good thing.

"We've gotten to the point where students don't mind being used," said Andrew Hagelshaw, executive director of the Center for Commercial Free Public Education, a nonprofit organization that was founded in 1993 amid complaints about Channel One. "They don't see anything wrong with using themselves to advertise for their sponsors."

He does not necessarily blame Mr. Barrett and Mr. McCabe.

"There's advertising in the hallways, in lunchrooms, in the curriculum," Mr. Hagelshaw said. "After a while, it becomes invisible: you don't understand how it's happening or how they're using you."

## Working with the Text

1. Imagine you are part of a committee at First USA deciding whether to sponsor the two young men. What would the arguments for and against the arrangement be? Then pretend that you are friends of Barrett and McCabe. What would you advise them to be most cautious about in making this arrangement?

2. Zernike suggests that "students are not just surrounded by marketing tactics; they are adopting them," and goes on to assert that most of Barrett and McCabe's peers probably envy rather than criticize them. In what ways would you agree and disagree with Zernike's claim? Would you consider entering a similar arrangement? Can you think of other examples of college students adopting marketing tactics in their day-to-day lives?

3. One professional marketer suggests, "First USA seems like the credit card that students can trust if it's coming from college students themselves." Do you agree? What is the nature of the trust that other students might have in Barrett and McCabe? How would the claim that students are also becoming more sophisticated about how advertising works complicate their reactions to Barrett and McCabe?

4. "We've gotten to the point where students don't mind being used," claims Andrew Hagelshaw in Zernike's essay. "They don't see anything wrong with using themselves to advertise for their sponsors." How do you understand the question of who is using whom in the relationship between the students, Barrett and McCabe, and First USA? What

different resources and advantages do the two students and the corporation bring to their relationship, and how do you think they affect the question Hagelshaw raises?

5. Revisit Amy Henry's description of the major drivers for youth marketing and the key motivators for teens in "How Buzz Marketing Works for Teens." How do you think Henry would judge the First USA advertising campaign as an example of buzz marketing to teens? What suggestions do you think she might make?

6. Many of the readings in this chapter grapple with the question of whether the values and tactics of marketing and advertising are taking over our lives. The term *buzz marketing* suggests that, for young people immersed in marketing and advertising, the lines between ads and non-ads are blurring (a situation also suggested by the following cartoon):

More specifically, we can describe this concern in terms of writing and rhetoric: how have models based on advertising influenced how we communicate and interact with each other, and what do you think about that? What do you see as legitimate causes for concern?

## FAKE ADS

Examine the following webpage:

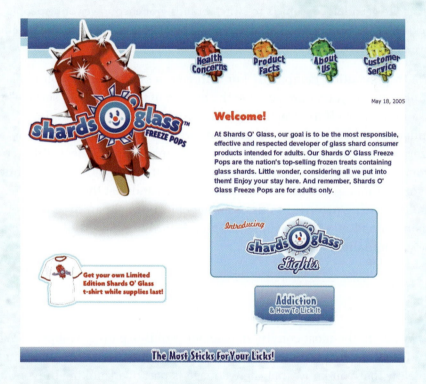

At first glance it appears to be a generic website for a frozen treat, but the longer you look and read, the more things may be other than as they first appear. That name—Shards O' Glass—contrasts the corny use of the contraction "O'" and the bright, cartoony graphics with the ominous and painful idea of a freezer pop embedded with broken glass. The "Welcome!" message is written in the typically upbeat and somewhat anonymous corporate style of many commercial websites, but again the tone seems oblivious to the potential menace of the product. In fact, the product's slogan—"The Most Sticks For Your Licks"—even implies that running your tongue over sharp glass shards could be a desirable experience!

What is going on here? Was this actual website simply a floating piece of twisted humor on the Internet? Is it the result of a Web designer who had a bad experience with a frozen treat? Or is something more going on here? If you surfed the website (which is no longer active), you might have noticed a pattern of references that reminded you of a product other than freezer pops, such as a Shards O' Glass pop in menthol flavor, or the following statement on the About Us page:

> We pride ourselves on our responsible marketing. Our advertising efforts are designed to get adult consumers to switch brands, not encourage young people to lick. In fact, we're proud of our youth prevention campaign with the highly effective slogan "Licking Glass Pops as a teen? Then you're missing the point!"

Youth prevention campaign? For a frozen dessert treat? If you clicked on the link consideryoursource.com at the bottom of the "customer service" page, you found yourself redirected to something called the American Legacy Foundation, whose mission is very different from that of Shards O' Glass freezer pops: "Building a World Where Young People Reject Tobacco and Anyone Can Quit." You would have realized that Shards O' Glass is connected to a youth-smoking prevention campaign, truth®, and that the site was meant to be an advertising parody. In this case, the object of the parody is cigarette advertising aimed at young people, judging from the mission of the American Legacy Foundation.

---

## Working with the Text

1. What are the most convincing elements of this parody webpage? What do the creators imitate most effectively in other forms of advertising?

2. Now that you know that the webpage is part of a smoking prevention campaign aimed at young people, discuss and describe what you think the rhetorical strategy is behind this parody ad. How is it supposed to work in persuading young people not to smoke? How effective do you think it might be, and why? You might share this webpage with others to gauge their reactions.

3. What aspects about the rhetoric of advertising does this webpage draw your attention to? How might this webpage be trying to make you a more critical reader of advertising?

## ADVERTISING PARODIES AND CULTURE JAMMING

Parodies of advertising are as old as advertising itself, and that shouldn't surprise us. Parody involves imitating and often exaggerating features and attributes of an original text to make the reader and viewer more aware of the rhetorical strategy of the original—how the original is trying to persuade, entertain, or affect you. Any form of public speech or writing that is associated with social power, influence, and authority usually becomes a target of parody before too long, and part of the function of the humor in parody is to deflate or defuse some of that social power. No wonder advertising, a multibillion-dollar business aimed at influencing our thoughts, feelings, and behaviors, has been such a prominent target, whether in print or on *Mad TV.*

The age of digital media and the World Wide Web has greatly expanded the potential for and participation in this kind of parody. Before, a person would need access to professional printing facilities or expensive television equipment to produce parodies that still seemed little more than crude imitations of the originals. Now, a regular home computer, some standard word processing and visual editing software, and a digital camera can allow almost anyone to produce parody texts that are nearly indistinguishable from "real" ads, at least on the level of style, design, and visual presentation. Rather than just responding in our heads to the advertising we experience every day, we can now interact with the world of advertising through our own online counter-ads.

A phrase has been coined to refer to this kind of talking back to advertising: *culture jamming.* Culture jamming suggests more than just a silly form of playing with advertising, but an active attempt to interfere with the normal process of advertising and marketing. As Douglas Rushkoff argues in "They Say," the people who have grown up in the digital age take this kind of interactivity for granted, and as a result, they are savvy about the different tactics that advertisers use to persuade them. This is one reason for the rise of buzz marketing as a form of advertising; it is designed for just such a sophisticated audience.

We could say that culture jamming, or using parody as a form of alternative media discourse, has moved from the realm of entertainment to become a regular part of how all kinds of information is delivered. Research shows that many people get much of their regular news from late-night comedy shows and parody programs such as *The Daily Show.*

## THE TRUTH SMOKING PREVENTION CAMPAIGN

Public health campaigns combine elements of both advertising and teaching. Like teaching, the goal of such a campaign is education—providing the public with information they need to make informed decisions about staying healthy and avoiding disease. Like advertising, however, another goal is also to influence behavior, not in terms of buying something but in terms of changing personal habits. Over the last forty years, no public health campaign has been more visible, more controversial, and certainly more involved with the world of advertising than the antismoking campaign.

Smoking rates have dropped dramatically in the decades since the first public health campaigns against smoking began in the late 1950s and early 1960s. In terms of providing information to the public, it would be hard to find anyone who hasn't heard that smoking poses very specific health hazards. At the same time, smoking is a legal activity, as is the sale of tobacco products, and cigarette companies are responsible for some of the most famous advertising campaigns in history. While tobacco advertising has become more strictly regulated than most other forms of advertising, millions of dollars are still devoted to promoting the sale of cigarettes and other tobacco products.

Antismoking campaigns not only have to contend with habit and custom, but they must also create advertising that must compete with tobacco company advertising. This challenge has been especially complex and controversial in relation to young people. Young people are an important target audience for both consumer goods companies and public health campaigns. From the point of view of antismoking advocates, persuading people not to smoke in the first place is a critical goal, and much attention is paid (as you undoubtedly know) to education and persuasion programs in schools and in the media.

As we have been discussing, however, young people can also be a difficult audience for advertisers. Increasingly sophisticated about advertising strategies and the media, young people can also be resistant to lectures from authority figures on how to live their lives. As Amy Henry argues in her article about buzz marketing, teens are "iconoclastic by nature" and want to feel like they are making their own decisions, not simply following rules created by others. Young people, according to Henry, also crave excitement and stimulation from their media, qualities that can seem at odds with a public health campaign.

The Truth represents a smoking prevention ad campaign created by the American Legacy Foundation aimed specifically at teens and preteens, the same campaign that created the Shards O' Glass website. In creating this campaign, the American Legacy Foundation did research to figure out what kinds of strategies would most likely appeal to young people. For example, they found that young people would be more receptive to their message if they used graphic, frank images and language that some older people might find shocking. Other research suggested that young people also enjoyed dark humor and satire, as well as the chance to interact with and respond to the campaign.

As the Shards O' Glass website suggests, one important part of this campaign has been the creation of culture-jamming print ads meant to catch both the attention and, more important, the trust of young people. Visit the current version of The Truth campaign website (www.thetruth.com) and then respond to the following questions.

## Working with the Text

1. What were your immediate reactions—emotional, physical, and intellectual—to the website? Compare your reactions with those of others in the class and come up with a consensus of typical first reactions to the site. Test your findings by asking various people outside the class to visit the site and share their reactions, paying particular attention to how different age groups react. What differences do you notice based on age? Use the reactions you discover to speculate about the strategy behind creating this website.

2. How would you define the message (or thesis) of this website in one sentence? If you didn't know that this website was part of a smoking prevention effort, how would that affect your understanding of its message?

3. As with Shards O' Glass, this website was created for an audience whose members are already very familiar with a wide range of advertising tactics and strategies. As with all parody or culture-jamming, this website is making a comment about advertising itself. What is its message about advertising? What aspects of advertising does it make you more aware of?

4. Synthesize your analysis and discussion of this website by writing an evaluation of how effective you feel it is as part of a public health campaign aimed specifically at young people. You might choose to frame your discussion in the form of Amy Henry's essay on buzz marketing, as advice to other public health organizations about how to best reach young people with their message, using The Truth as your test case.

# CREATING CULTURE

## CREATING YOUR OWN ADVERTISING PARODY

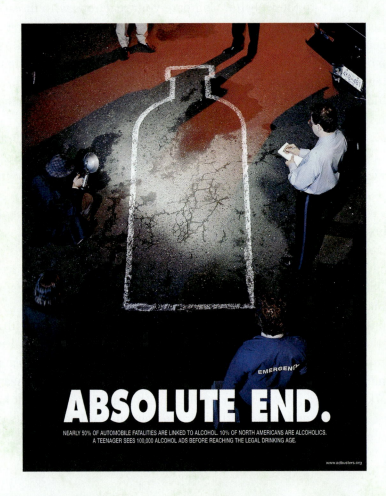

Adbusters is an activist organization critical of the role of advertising in American culture, and they are pioneers in the creation of parody ads as a form of culture jam, as with this one. Part of the philosophy of Adbusters is that anyone can participate in culture jamming, or creating your own response to mass media, in this case, advertising. To encourage such participation, they include the following advice on how to create spoof ads on their website.

## Create Your Own Print Ad

## 1. Decide on your communication objective

The communications objective is the essence of your message. If you want to tell people not to eat rutabagas because it's cruel, then that's your communications objective. A word of caution: though perhaps the most important of your 8 steps, this is also the one that beginners tend most to neglect. A precise and well-defined objective is crucial to a good ad. If your objective isn't right on, then everything that follows will be off as well.

## 2. Decide on your target audience

Who is your message intended for? If you're speaking to kids, then your language and arguments will have to be understandable to kids. On the other hand, if you're speaking to high income earners (for example, if you're writing an ad to dissuade people from wearing fur coats), then your language will have to be more sophisticated. So define who your target audience is, because that will decide how your message is conveyed.

## 3. Decide on your format

Is it going to be a poster, a half-page magazine ad, or a tiny box in the corner of a newspaper? Make this decision based on the target audience you're trying to reach, and the amount of money you can afford to spend. If you're talking to kids, a poster in one high school will not only cost less, it will actually reach more of your target audience than a full-page ad in the biggest paper in town. When it comes to deciding on the size of your ad, the larger the ad, the more expensive it will be to produce and run. Don't let that discourage you. You can do a lot with a small ad so long as it's strong, clear, and properly targeted.

## 4. Develop your concept

The concept is the underlying creative idea that drives your message. Even in a big ad campaign, the concept will typically remain the same from one ad to another, and from one medium to another. Only the execution of that concept will change. So by developing a concept that is effective and powerful, you open the door to a number of very compelling ads. So take your time developing a concept that's strong.

Typically, an ad is made up of a photograph or a drawing (the "visual"), a headline, and writing (the "copy"). Whether you think of your visual or your headline first makes little difference. However, here are a few guidelines worth following.

## 5. The visual

Though you don't absolutely require a visual, it will help draw attention to your ad. Research indicates that 70% of people will only look at the visual in an ad, whereas only 30% will read the headline. So if you use a visual, then you're already talking to twice as many people as you otherwise might. Another suggestion is to use photographs instead of illustrations whenever possible. People tend to relate to realistic photographs more easily than unrealistic ones. But whether you choose a photograph or an illustration, the most important criteria is that that image be the most interesting one possible and at least half your ad whenever possible.

## 6. The headline

The most important thing to remember here is that your headline must be short and snappy and must touch the people that read it. Your headline must affect the reader emotionally, either by making them laugh, making them angry, making them curious, or making them think. If you can't think of a headline that does one of these four things, then keep thinking.

*continued*

Here's a little tip that might help: try to find an insight or inner truth to the message that you're trying to convey, something that readers will easily relate to and be touched by. Taking the rutabagas example once again, it might be tempting to write a headline like: "Stop Exploiting These Migrant Workers." However, with a little thought, a more underlying truth might be revealed—that Migrant Workers are as human as we are, and that our actions do hurt them. From that inner truth, you might arrive at the headline: "Do unto others as you would have them do unto you." Of course, the headline doesn't have to be biblical, though that in itself will add meaning and power for many people. Finally, whenever possible, avoid a headline longer than fifteen words. People just don't read as much as they used to.

## 7. The copy

Here's where you make the case. If you have compelling arguments, make them. If you have persuasive facts, state them. But don't overwhelm with information. Two strong arguments will make more of an impression than a dozen weaker ones. Finally, be clear, be precise, and be honest. Any hint of deception will instantly detract from your entire message. Position your copy beneath the headline, laid out in two blocks two or three inches in length. Only about 5% of people will read your copy, whereas 30% will read your headline. By positioning your copy near your heading, you create a visual continuity which will draw more people to the information you want to convey. Use a serif typeface for your copy whenever possible. Those little lines and squiggles on the letters make the reading easier and more pleasing to the eye.

**Subheads:** If you have lots of copy, break it up with interesting subheads.... This will make your ad more inviting, more organized, and easier to read.

**The signature:** This is where the name of the organization belongs, along with the address and phone number. If you don't have an organization, then think of a name that will help reinforce the message you're trying to convey. Perhaps "Citizens for Fairness to Migrant Rutabagas Pickers" would work for the example we've been using. This isn't dishonest. Your organization doesn't have to be incorporated or registered for it to be real.

## 8. Some mistakes to avoid

The single most common mistake is visual clutter. Less is always better than more. So if you're not certain whether something is worth including, then leave it out. If your ad is chaotic, people will simply turn the page, and your message will never be read. The second most common mistake is to have an ad that's unclear or not easily understood (haven't you ever looked at an ad and wondered what it was for?). The best way to safeguard against this is to do some rough sketches of your visual with the headline and show it around. If people aren't clear about your message, then it's probably because your message is unclear. And however tempting, don't argue with them or assume that they're wrong and that your ad is fine. You'll be in for an unpleasant surprise. Proofread your ad, then give it to others to proofread, then proofread it yet again. Typographical errors diminish your credibility and have an uncanny habit of creeping into ads when you least expect it.

Use the advice from their website to create your own advertising parody. As the guidelines recommend, first choose the issue you want to address, and determine as specifically as possible what your message is going to be. Depending on your access to and familiarity with computer technology and different kinds of software, your project could range from detailed plans for creating a hypothetical ad to the production of a real parody ad. As a capstone to your project, write a critical reflection/analysis of your ad in which you answer the following questions:

_____

## Working with the Text

1. Explain what your message is and the rationale behind the strategy you chose to create your ad. Why did you think this particular design would be effective? What problems or questions arose as you moved from concept to design?

2. What did you learn about advertising as a form of public communication from working on your parody ad? What did you learn about the ethics of advertising?

3. If you were able to produce a finished parody ad, figure out ways of testing the effectiveness of your ad in communicating your central message. Consider different methods of distribution: handouts, posting them in public places, creating a website, etc. You might even work as a class to create a focus group: locate a group of students to act as your trial audience, and then have them look at several of the ads produced by members of the class. Designate someone not involved in the production of a particular ad to lead the discussion of that ad. Did the audience get the message? What suggestions did they have for revising the message?

No area of popular culture inspires more passion than

For many people, their favorite music reveals more tha
.ta..e or person preference; it can signal a lifestyle c
a g oup identi .cation, or a political affiliation. Snea

# FIVE

**CHAPTER**

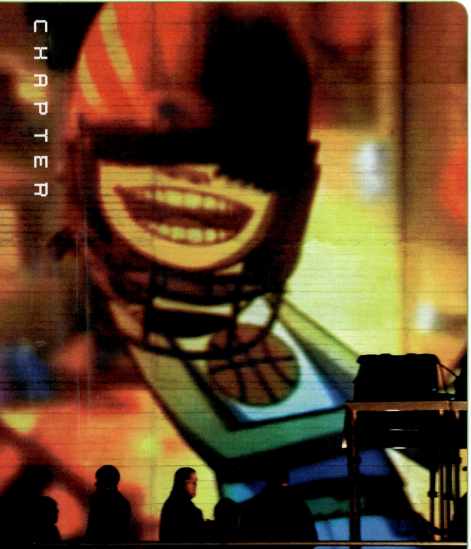

For many peop
preference; i
ffiliation. Sne
y to judge per
one's MP3 play
y social-netwo
te music as a v
ong for their s
r many people,
ence; it can s
liation. Sneal
y to judge per
one's MP3 play
y social-netwo
te music as a v
ong for their s
r many people,
ence; it can s
liation. Sneal
y to judge per
one's MP3 playe
y social-netwo
te music as a v

No area of popular culture in
more passion than music. Fo
people, their favorite
reveals more than just
personal preference; i
signal a lifestyle choice, a
identification, or a pol
affiliation. Sneaking a look

# Pop Music:
# Revolutions You
# Can Dance To

No area of popular culture inspires more passion than music. For many people, their favorite music reveals more than just taste or personal preference; it can signal a lifestyle choice, a group identification, or a political affiliation. Sneaking a look at a new friend's record collection has long been a way to judge personal compatibility, and in recent years, seeing what's loaded on someone's MP3 player has become the latest version of this kind of informal research. Many social-networking sites such as MySpace not only ask members to list their favorite music as a way of identifying themselves but also allow them to include a theme song for their sites.

It's not surprising that we have such strong feelings about music. The non-verbal dimensions of music—melody, harmony, rhythm, and tone—bypass our conscious minds and evoke powerful physical and emotional reactions. When music is combined with lyrics that are poignant or angry, poetic or playful, sincere or irreverent, the meaning of the words is enhanced by the impact of the sounds and beats, and vice versa. Our responses to music are immediate and involuntary, and our likes and dislikes can be visceral and intense.

Music demands an interactive response. A catchy song can stick in your head against your will, and you may find yourself humming or singing it without being aware you're doing so, regardless of whether you even like the song. And it's hard to resist a powerful beat: our bodies want to move, even if it's only a toe tap or a head nod.

People use music not just as a source of entertainment but as a way of defining themselves. Look around your campus: how many people are wearing clothes bearing the name of a musician or group? How many students sport headphones or earbuds as they walk from class to class, carrying their own soundtrack with them as they move through their day? The ability of music to produce powerful emotions in us, to connect our heads and hearts, is key to understanding the rhetorical power of popular music. Music can create strong feelings of loyalty and commitment to a cause or a country and express passionately held ideals and attitudes. It's no wonder, then, that music has been used as an effective political motivator. Many people react strongly when they hear their own national anthem, and every branch of the military includes many kinds of musical groups, from marching bands to choirs, as part of their morale-building arsenal.

While music can strengthen ties to existing political institutions and ways of life, music has also served as an arena of political debate and protest. In the United States, ballads and songs supported both sides in the Revolutionary War, African American spirituals and work songs expressed the commitment of the enslaved to be free, and *corridos* have chronicled the exploits of folk heroes in the Latino communities of the Southwest. In the 1930s, popular music ranging from Tin Pan Alley songs such as "Brother, Can You Spare a Dime?"

and "The Gold Diggers' Song (We're in the Money)" to folk songs like Woody Guthrie's "This Land Is Your Land" expressed the emotions of millions of people struggling with severe economic hardship and dislocation.

# O N E

## A Political Pop Chronicle

Popular music has the ability to generate powerful feelings and emotions associated with particular times and events in our lives, even after years or decades. Explore how music connects with people's historical memories by interviewing your parents, grandparents, or other relatives and acquaintances from previous generations about political music they remember. Allow your interviewees to interpret the word *political* in any ways they want, and discuss with them how they are using the term. See if you can help your interviewee recall at least one or two specific songs or pieces of music. Some questions to ask:

- How old were you when you first heard this song? What did it mean to you at the time? How familiar were you with the issues or social situation it was describing?
- Did you like the song? If so, what aspects of the song did you enjoy the most? The music? The beat? The vocal style? Did the political associations of the song or the content of the lyrics add or detract from your enjoyment of the song?
- Do you associate hearing the song first with a particular event or time? If so, how did the situation in which you first encountered the song affect your emotional reaction to it?
- How has your perception and enjoyment of the song changed over the years? Have you grown more or less fond of the song? If your perception of the song has changed, why do you think that is so?
- What effect, if any, did the song have on either reinforcing or changing your own political perspective? Using this song as an example, do you think music can have a political impact or influence opinion? What do you think the songwriter was trying to accomplish with the song, and how successful was he or she?

Share your research with other members of the class and write about what you found most interesting and surprising. You can present your findings in the form of a report on the particular song and begin your presentation by playing the song.

This assignment can also work by having the class choose a well-known political song of the more recent past, such as John Lennon's "Imagine" or Bob Dylan's "Blowin' in the Wind" and interviewing people about their memories of the time the song came out.

# DIY: POP MUSIC GOES INTERACTIVE

Why has music remained a popular vehicle for political commentary and expression? Many people, for example, have questioned the impact that music (or any art form, for that matter) can have on politics. Rather than writing and singing a song to protest a war, support workers' rights, or criticize prejudice and bigotry, wouldn't that energy be better spent organizing political movements, writing books and articles, running for public office, or engaging in some other more direct form of political action? This is a way of asking, "Is the pen really mightier than the sword?" or the reverse, "Isn't action more effective than talking, writing, or singing?"

These are important questions, and they should be part of any critical analysis of the social power of popular music. But maybe we can reframe these questions. First, one of the central ideas of *Text Messaging* is that writing in all its forms, whether essays, blogs, posters, or lyrics, *is* a form of action, a way of participating in and influencing the world, even if it's just the world immediately around us: our family, friends, classmates, and communities. Second, different means of expression and action are not mutually exclusive. A song can serve multiple roles for different people, from a call to arms to a way to pass a boring afternoon to an excuse to dance.

Perhaps most important, popular music of all kinds, from folk to rock, to rap, has long been an avenue for those who felt they had few other options to express their ideas, opinions, and beliefs and (literally) find a voice. The brutal system of slavery, for example, made formal protest in print almost impossible for most enslaved Americans; important political activists such as Frederick Douglass and Sojourner Truth had to escape slavery and risk their lives in order to raise their voices in print and in speeches. Music, however, served as a powerful means by which the most exploited and oppressed members of American society could speak to each other and to the world. The songs created and sung by enslaved Americans are still part of our musical heritage today. "We Shall Overcome," a song that is still a part of freedom movements around the world, has its origins deep in the musical protest tradition of African American culture.

The punk rock movement of the 1970s adopted a term from commercial speech that expressed the social and political importance of maintaining popular music as a cultural space available to everyone: "Do It Yourself," or "DIY" for short. Punk embraced this spirit through an ethos that valued the passion and commitment of what a person had to express more than musical ability. The rise of hip hop and rap over the last thirty years also adopted a DIY attitude, drawing on the African American cultural traditions of ingenuity and versatility to create an art form that combines technological savvy with artistic imagination but

Punk rock embodied the DIY spirit.

that doesn't require a lot of money or access to expensive recording studios. Using regular turntables, inexpensive mixers, shared sound systems, cheap drum machines, and previously recorded music, hip hop and rap artists created not just new songs but a whole new style of music, one with deep roots in the idea of music as cultural and political self-expression. Perhaps most relevant to a writing course, rap may be the most verbal popular music ever invented. The creative use of language in all of its dimensions—funny, thoughtful, obscene, playful, angry, hopeful—can be found in hip hop and rap.

## DIY IN THE DIGITAL AGE

With the development of digital technology and the Internet, the DIY tradition in pop music has become more interactive than ever. Any musician with access to a computer can post files to the Web and make them available to listeners around the world; blog venues like MySpace feature websites for hundreds of bands and musicians. The hip hop tradition of sampling sounds from different records has morphed into the mash-up, where artists use computer programs to take songs apart digitally and put them back together in new ways, sometimes just to entertain and sometimes to make a political point.

The growing participation of people all over the world in creating and responding to political pop music raises the following question: how can people prevent any one song or message from becoming lost in the shuffle? After all, just because more and more people are expressing themselves musically doesn't necessarily mean people are listening. On the other hand, just the basic action of self-expression itself, whether through music, words, or a combination of both, can foster a sense of agency and action and provide a counterpoint to the feelings of powerlessness or disconnection that conventional politics can sometimes create.

In the world of popular music, as in other areas of popular culture, the digital age has blurred boundaries between artist and audience, creator and consumer, even the definition of the very word *song* itself. In this chapter, we will explore several aspects of our increasingly interactive relationship with popular music. First, we will look at how the phenomenon of the portable MP3 player—most famously the Apple iPod—is creating not just a new way to share and listen to music but a whole new musical culture as well, a culture tied to the ways we create different social identities and personas, a process intimately connected to the writing process. As we create and share playlists, we can also create different versions based on who and what we are to different audiences.

Next, we will explore how our identities connect with our musical tastes from another point of view. Specifically, we will focus on how Web technology allows users to create individual online "radio stations" customized to our personal tastes and preferences, all based on the knowledge of just one of our favorite artists. Such software programs raise interesting questions about just how predictable we might really be when it comes to something we classify as personal and unique: our musical likes and dislikes.

We will then turn to the world of hip hop—one of the most interactive and participatory forms of popular music—by focusing on the appearance of rap CDs made by U.S. soldiers serving in Iraq about their experiences during wartime. These recordings include not only reflections on life in the armed forces but songs written and recorded by soldiers in Iraq, in between going on patrols and carrying out missions. The portability of inexpensive digital music technology has created the conditions for soldiers to communicate their thoughts and feelings through popular music with an immediacy never seen before.

Finally, we'll read and write about the use of digital technology to create mash-ups, new songs and recordings made by combining and recycling parts of other songs, sometimes just for fun and sometimes to make a satirical point. You will be asked to propose or even create your own mash-ups, forms of musical essays that allow you to interact with the world of popular music.

### from *High Fidelity*

### Nick Hornby

*What is your favorite song of all time? It's a simple question, and you might have heard it asked in any number of situations: talking with friends at lunch, hanging out in a dorm room, visiting a friend's website, chatting with a significant other. Depending on the situation, a person might think a lot about the question or just answer off the top of his or her head. For a lot of people, the whole idea of a single favorite song just doesn't work for them; they might ask for more information, such as, "Favorite for what? To dance to? When I'm feeling sad?" Or they may say that their favorite changes from week to week, month to month. A song that you loved when you were 13, for instance, may still be one of your favorites or now a source of embarrassment.*

*From a writing point of view, the way we approach this question has to do with the rhetorical situation. Is the person asking just looking to kill time, or do we suspect that more is at stake? Answering the question is equally a rhetorical act, a way of communicating our thoughts, feelings, and values, or identifying others of like mind and preferences. One form of this musical communication that has found a niche in popular culture is the mix tape. Originally a product of the introduction of easy-to-record cassettes, the mix tape consists of a collection of songs and music created specifically for a given person or social situation. Even though cassette technology has largely been replaced by CDs and MP3 players, the idea and even the name* mix tape *survives.*

*In his novel* High Fidelity, *the English writer Nick Hornby created characters for whom a taste in popular music is everything. The novel tells the story of a thirty-something record-store owner named Rob whose entire life has been devoted to his love of popular music, so much so that he begins to suspect he has allowed his love of music to interfere with his life, especially his romantic relationships. The novel is set in London, although the popular movie version of the novel starring John Cusack moved the location to Chicago.*

*In this excerpt, Nick is telling the story of how he first met his girlfriend Laura. His breakup and subsequent reunion with Laura form the backbone of the plot in the novel. As you will read, their meeting took place at the disco where Rob was a DJ. At the beginning of their relationship, Rob discusses how he approached making her a mix tape.*

## Before You Read

1. Write a list of your ten favorite songs just for yourself (that is, a list you aren't planning to share with anyone else). Next, make versions of this list that you would be willing to share with different audiences: your classmates, your best friends, as part of an online identity or Facebook/MySpace page. What changes did you make from one list to the next? How did your consideration of audience change how you thought about your choices?

2. Does anyone in your class regularly make mix tapes or burn custom CDs? Ask people to bring in examples of their mix tapes (either the actual tapes or CDs or lists of the songs) and discuss how they created the mixes.

3. Working in groups, try creating mix tapes to evoke different impressions in different situations. Each group should create specific scenarios for each other: the beginning of a relationship, joining a new sports team, making a friend online, etc.

For a couple of years, at the end of the eighties, I was a DJ at a club in Kentish Town, and it was there I met Laura. It wasn't much of a club, just a room above a pub, really, but for a six-month period it was popular with a certain London crowd—the almost fashionable, right-on, black 501s-and-DMs-crowd that used to move in herds from the market to the Town and Country to Dingwalls to the Electric Ballroom to the Camden Plaza. I was a good DJ, I think. At any rate, people seemed happy; they danced, stayed late, asked me where they could buy some of the records I played, and came back week after week. We called it the Groucho Club, because of Groucho Marx's thing about not wanting to join any club that would have him as a member; later on we found out that there was another Groucho Club somewhere in the West End, but nobody seemed to get confused about which was which. (Top five floor-fillers at the Groucho, in-cidentally: "It's a Good Feeling" by Smokey Robinson and the Miracles; "No

Blow No Show" by Bobby Bland; "Mr. Big Stuff" by Jean Knight; "The Love You Save" by the Jackson Five; "The Ghetto" by Donny Hathaway.)

And I loved, loved doing it. To look down on a roomful of heads all bobbing away to the music you have chosen is an uplifting thing, and for that six-month period when the club was popular, I was as happy as I have ever been. It was the only time I have ever really had a sense of momentum, although later I could see that it was a false momentum, because it didn't belong to me at all, but to the music: anyone playing his favorite dance records very loud in a crowded place, to people who had paid to hear them, would have felt exactly the same thing. Dance music, after all, is supposed to have momentum—I just got confused.

Anyway, I met Laura right in the middle of that period, in the summer of '87. She reckons she had been to the club three or four times before I noticed her, and that could well be right—she's small, and skinny, and pretty, in a sort of Sheena Easton pre-Hollywood makeover way (although she looked tougher than Sheena Easton with her radical lawyer spiky hair and her boots and her scary pale blue eyes), but there were prettier women there, and when you're looking on in that idle kind of way, it's the prettiest ones you look at. So, on this third or fourth time, she came up to my little rostrum thing and spoke to me, and I liked her straightaway: she asked me to play a record that I really loved ("Got to Get You off My Mind" by Solomon Burke, if anyone cares), but which had cleared the floor whenever I'd tried it.

"Were you here when I played it before?"

"Yeah."

"Well, you saw what happened. They were all about to go home."

It's a three-minute single, and I'd had to take it off after about a minute and a half. I played "Holiday" by Madonna instead; I used modern stuff every now and again, at times of crisis, just like people who believe in homeopathy have to use conventional medicine sometimes, even though they disapprove of it.

"They won't this time."

"How do you know that?"

"Because I brought half of this lot here, and I'll make sure they dance."

So I played it, and sure enough Laura and her mates flooded the dance floor, but one by one they all drifted off again, shaking their heads and laughing. It is a hard song to dance to; it's a mid-tempo R&B thing, and the intro sort of stops and starts. Laura stuck with it, and though I wanted to see whether she'd struggle gamely through to the end, I got nervous when people weren't dancing, so I put "The Love You Save" on quick.

She wouldn't dance to the Jackson Five, and she marched over to me, but she was grinning and said she wouldn't ask again. She just wanted to know where she could buy the record. I said if she came next week I'd have a tape for her, and she looked really pleased.

I spent hours putting that cassette together. To me, making a tape is like writing a letter—there's a lot of erasing and rethinking and starting again, and I wanted it to be a good one, because...to be honest, because I hadn't met anyone as promising as Laura since I'd started the DJ-ing, and meeting promising women was partly what the DJ-ing was supposed to be about. A good compilation tape, like breaking up, is hard to do. You've got to kick off with a corker, to hold the attention (I started with "Got to Get You off My Mind," but then realized that she might not get any further than track one, side one if I delivered what she wanted straightaway, so I buried it in the middle of side two) and then you've got to up it a notch, or cool it a notch, and you can't have white music and black music together, unless the white music sounds like black music, and you can't have two tracks by the same artist side by side, unless you've done the whole thing in pairs, and...oh, there are loads of rules.

Anyway, I worked and worked at this one, and I've still got a couple of early demons knocking around the flat, prototype tapes I changed my mind about when I was checking them through. And on Friday night, club night, I produced it from my jacket pocket when she came over to me, and we went on from there. It was a good beginning. [...]

*[After this promising start, Rob and Laura develop a serious relationship. Just when they begin to consider making a more permanent commitment to each other, Rob panics and engages in behaviors that lead to their breakup. Later, they meet again under difficult circumstances—the funeral for Laura's father—and Laura shocks Rob by revealing that she has a very different attitude to pop music than he does and explaining what his mix tape meant to her. The artists referred to in this section are Solomon Burke, a famous rhythm and blues singer, and Art Garfunkel, half of the popular 1960s folk-pop duo Simon and Garfunkel.]*

[...] "....I can see why you prefer Solomon to Art. I understand, really I do. And if I was asked to say which of the two was better, I'd go for Solomon every time. He's authentic, and black, and legendary, and all that sort of thing. But I like 'Bright Eyes.' I think it's got a pretty tune, and beyond that, I don't really care. There are so many other things to worry about. I know I sound like your mum, but they're only pop records, and if one's better than the other, well, who cares, really, apart from you and Barry and Dick? To me, it's like arguing the difference between McDonald's and Burger King. I'm sure there must be one, but who can be bothered to find out what it is?"

The terrible thing is, of course, that I already know the difference, that I have complicated and informed views on the subject. But if I start going on about Whoppers versus Quarter Pounders with Cheese, we will both feel that I have somehow proved her point, so I don't bother.

But the argument carries on, goes around corners, crosses the road, turns back on itself, and eventually ends up somewhere neither of us has ever been before—at least, not sober, and not during daylight hours.

"You used to care more about things like Solomon Burke than you do now," I tell her. "When I first met you, and I made you the tape, you were really enthused. You said—and I quote—'It was so good that it made you ashamed of your record collection.'"

"Shameless, wasn't I?"

"What does that mean?"

"Well, I fancied you. You were a DJ, and I thought you were groovy, and I didn't have a boyfriend, and I wanted one."

"So you weren't interested in the music at all?"

"Well, yes. A bit. And more so then than I am now. That's life, though, isn't it?"

"But you see . . . *That's all there is of me.* There isn't anything else. If you've lost interest in that, you've lost interest in everything. What's the point of us?"

"You really believe that?"

"Yes. Look at me. Look at the flat. What else has it got, apart from records and CDs and tapes?"

"And do you like it that way?"

I shrug. "Not really."

"*That's* the point of us. You have potential. I'm here to bring it out."

"Potential as what?"

"As a human being. You have all the basic ingredients. You're really very likable, when you put your mind to it. You make people laugh, when you can be bothered, and you're kind, and when you decide you like someone then that person feels as though she's the center of the whole world, and that's a very sexy feeling. It's just that most of the time you can't be bothered."

"No," is all I can think of to say.

"You just . . . you just don't *do* anything. You get lost in your head, and you sit around thinking instead of getting on with something, and most of the time you think rubbish. You always seem to miss what's really happening." [ . . . ]

*[Because the novel is a comedy, the lovers are reunited at the end. Rob has developed a new understanding about relationships and how to communicate with people he cares about. The novel ends with Rob once again playing DJ at a party and thinking about making another mix tape for Laura.]*

[ . . . ] I play "Got to Get You off My Mind" by Solomon Burke, and everyone has a go, just out of duty, even though only the best dancers would be able to make something of it, and nobody in the room could claim to be among the best dancers, or even among the most average. When Laura hears the opening bars she spins round and grins and makes several thumbs-up signs, and I start to compile in my head a compilation tape for her, something that's full of stuff she's heard of, and full of stuff she'd play. Tonight, for the first time ever, I can sort of see how it's done.

## Working with the Text

1. Describe what pop music means to Rob based on these short excerpts from the novel. How does he connect his taste in pop music with his identity as a person? Why do you think he feels this way? How similar or different are his attitudes to your own or to those of people you know?

2. Rob compares making a mix tape to "writing a letter—there's a lot of erasing and rethinking and starting again." Continue Rob's analogy by discussing other similarities between writing and creating a mix tape.

3. Rob begins to describe all that goes into creating a mix tape, but breaks off by saying, "oh, there are loads of rules." Based on the examples that Rob gives of some of these rules, speculate about what you think Rob's other rules might be. Find people who create mix tapes and CDs and ask them for suggestions. As you come up with these rules, include explanations for why these rules exist, examples of when these rules could be violated, and the possible consequences for violating these rules.

4. What surprises Rob the most about Laura's confessions concerning her own attitudes toward popular music? Compare and contrast their different approaches to music and how they relate to it. How did Laura interpret and respond to the original mix tape that Rob made her? How do you think Rob had wanted her to react to it?

5. What is different about Rob's approach to making a mix tape for Laura at the end of the novel? What is different about the kind of impression he hopes to make? Connect the changes in Rob's attitude about mix tapes to his earlier comment comparing mix tapes to writing. What different motives do various writers bring to letter writing? Emailing? IMing?

# "Listening In: Practices Surrounding iTunes Music Sharing"

## Amy Voida, Rebecca E. Grinter, Nicolas Ducheneaut, W. Keith Edwards, and Mark W. Newman

*The excerpt from the novel* High Fidelity *discussed not only how we sometimes judge others by their musical taste, but also how we can use our musical taste to communicate with others, creating specific impressions and possibly even conveying specific emotional messages through the medium of the mix tape. Mix tapes offered a carefully constructed peek into the musical preferences of a person. Before the age of MP3s and digital recording, it was easy to maintain the privacy of a music collection, letting only a chosen few have access to your records and tapes. The popularity of MP3 players such as the iPod and the ease with which music can be shared over the computer, however, have made our musical tastes more visible to others, sometimes whether we know it or not.*

*Many writers in popular magazines, newspapers, and online sites have commented on the rise of playlistism, or snap judgments made about people on the basis of what's on their MP3 players. Music sharing has become so pervasive, however, and our musical likes and dislikes have such strong personal meanings for us that the activity of judging people by their music is attracting serious and scholarly study. Recently, researchers working at the Palo Alto Research Center in California, a think tank run by the Xerox Corporation, and the Graphics, Visualization, and Usability Center at the Georgia Institute of Technology teamed up to investigate what happens when coworkers are able to share their music collections with one another via the iTunes music program over the local company network. The researchers carefully chose their study participants, described in detail how the programs worked and how they collected data, and the conclusions they drew from their study. The excerpt below deals with the judgments coworkers made about each other based on their musical tastes and how they tried to control those judgments about themselves.*

## Before You Read

1. How well do you know the musical tastes of your friends, classmates, family members, or coworkers? Write down your impressions of what these tastes might be for a representative sample of your acquaintances, ranging from people about whom you are fairly certain to some you can only guess about. On what are you basing your judgments? If you feel comfortable doing so, you might share your guesses with some of the people on the list to see how close you came (be careful, though; people can be very sensitive about their musical preferences).

2. Do you have any musical guilty pleasures; that is, songs you secretly like but wouldn't admit to your friends? Would those who know you be surprised that you listen to certain musical groups or singers? How

important is it to you to keep these guilty pleasures under wraps? As a class exercise, ask for musical confessions (instructor included) on a voluntary basis. Why do you think we attach such importance or, conversely, have such a potentially nervous reaction to the idea of others learning about our guilty musical pleasures?

3. Making snap judgments about the musical tastes of others is a form of stereotyping based on generalizations about what preferences for certain types of music mean. Working as a class, create a list of musical genres and styles and then describe the stereotypes attached to each one. For example, what kinds of generalizations might people make about fans of gangster rap? Techno? Boy bands? Country and western? Classical? Are there stereotypes about race, ethnicity, social class, gender, and sexuality connected to these generalizations? Discuss and write about where you think these stereotypes come from as well as experiences you have had that challenge these stereotypes.

## IMPRESSION MANAGEMENT AND ACCESS CONTROL

By turning on iTunes' music sharing, people made their music libraries available to others on their subnet. This act also brought with it varying amounts of additional work—the work of determining what identity to portray through one's own music library, something sociologist Erving Goffman termed "impression management."

The most intentional account of impression management came from a participant who already had a small iTunes library when the version of iTunes with sharing functionality was released.

I just went through it and said, "Eh, I wonder what kind of image this is, you know, giving me," right? I just went through it to see if there was not like stuff that would be like, I don't know, annoying; that I would not like people to know that I had (P11).

For this participant, music sharing led to the additional work of ripping more CDs to create a more "balanced" portrayal of himself.

When the sharing happened . . . I had not ripped everything from my CD collection. . . . It was fairly heavily skewed toward the classical and soundtrack part of my collection...the order in which I'd popped the CDs in. And I remember thinking about this and was like, "Gee, that's not very cool...." So when we started sharing, I started reripping things, adding stuff to my collection.... I added more to kind of rebalance it and cover a wider breadth of genres that I had in my collection (P11).

Another participant had not given the contents of his music library the same degree of scrutiny. With respect to constructing an identity, the contents of his library were complicated by the fact that he occasionally purchased music on-line for his wife. These songs were by artists that he did not listen to or like, and he was disturbed by the impression that these songs could give others.

I mean if people are looking at my playlist to get a picture of the kind of music I like and don't like, you know. Or to get a little insight into what I'm about, it'd be kind of inaccurate 'cuz there's, you know, there's Justin Timberlake and there's another couple of artists on here that...Michael McDonald, you know. Some of this stuff I would not, you know, want to be like kind of associated with it.... I guess part of it is it wouldn't be bad if, you know, people thought I was kind of hip and current with my music instead of like an old fuddy duddy with music. I mean I sort of like to experiment a little bit with stuff. I mean I'm not like totally wild but I like to experiment with, you know, some newer stuff. So I guess it would be okay if people thought that I had good taste. It wouldn't be so good if they said "God! He likes Justin Timberlake? That sucks!" (P1).

Expertise played an interesting and differentiating role in the ways that our participants crafted their identities. Some of the participants felt their libraries should foreground the kind of music in which they had expertise, creating a definitive repository of Jimmy Buffett music, for example. Another participant used his own national identity to give his library...

...a particular focus on all of the German bands actually that I have, because...if I have something to offer on the network, I'd like to be able to give, you know, albums and artists that other people don't have (P11).

However, expertise not only caused users to augment and foreground music in a library, it also caused users to hide and not share music in their library. These participants described their expertise as being in an area they felt that, at best, others would not "relate to" and, at worst, would be a "horrible experience."

I have a lot of Hindi music that is stuff that I listen and I don't expect other people to relate to. So that is not there (P4).

I don't want to bother sharing all of my stupid band clips 'cuz that would probably be a pretty horrible experience (P12).

Sometimes it was not sufficient for users to craft a static identity. As more and more coworkers joined the iTunes community, sometimes the identities were actively managed. Most notable were the changes that one participant attributed to the arrival of some managers to the community.

Some people have expressed some concerns especially when the managers started sharing, started browsing other people's collections, about being exposed to other people and like the contents of their playlists, like how much they like Abba or whatever. . . . I'm trying to remember if [employee] changed her name when [manager] showed up (P12).

The name change referred to by P12 is supported by the ability within iTunes to label one's collection. By default, when a user turns sharing on, the name given is "[OS user name]'s music," but this name can be changed. Making the name of a music library more appropriate for a manager to see was one factor in naming a music library. Other names referred to the hobbies or interests of the library's owner (e.g., "Cat's Meow"), while others commented on the contents of the library (e.g., "Doghouse Blues").

## Design Implications: Supporting Users' Ability to Manage the Presentation of Self

Participants utilized several of iTunes' mechanisms for managing identity. First, people changed the name of their music library in response to the audience of potential music listeners. Second, iTunes allowed users to share either their entire library or to specify which playlists to share. People who wanted to remove certain types of music used playlists as a means of controlling what was shared.

Based on our findings, particularly regarding the role of expertise, we believe other types of sharing control (including share by genre, country of origin, album, and artist) would have been well received. Further, as libraries get large, managing the sharing gets complicated, so offering individuals the choice to make new music part of the shared collection at the time it enters the system may also help.

Several of our participants reported problems with their workplace iTunes music libraries resulting from additionally using iTunes at home. One participant (P1) had music in his library that he had downloaded at work only to take home for his wife. Another participant (P2) had to construct a completely separate music library for work because his music library at home contained so much of his son's music. The overloading of multiple identities in a single library raises other design questions and suggests that providing some mechanism to share based on "which user you are" would be of value.

More generally, the lengths to which people managed their shared music highlights the relationship between identity and access control. Today, many access control solutions are designed by security engineers with secure systems in mind. But this study suggests that access control is more complex than simply restricting who can see what. Access control is a tool through which users manage others' impressions of them. It is a technology that has been appropriated to support the careful crafting of identity.

## CREATING MUSICAL IMPRESSIONS OF COWORKERS

For the potential listening audience, these carefully crafted views into others' music libraries constituted "little windows into what they are about" (P1). Frequently, participants would browse through the list of genres represented in others' libraries to come to the conclusion that someone is "eclectic" or "easy because he has only one genre" (P11). One participant (P1) drew his impressions, not so much from the musical content of others' libraries, as much as from characteristics of the custom playlists others generated from their content.

However, the ability to determine whose collection was whose was made more difficult by some of the features people used to manage their identity. For example, the ability to customize the name of a music library confused potential listeners.

> People can give names to their collections that are not necessarily obvious. So the first few times that SmallieBiggs here appeared on my list, I was really curious who the heck is SmallieBiggs?...So the first time SmallieBiggs appeared on my collection, I spent, I don't know, maybe fifteen to twenty minutes navigating the collection, and thinking who at [this company] in [this department] could possibly be listening to this particular music collection. So that was, you know, enjoyable detective work (P11).

Although P11 enjoyed guessing whose collection it was, others found the same confusion more frustrating. In addition to being confused by the name, users were also puzzled by the intent behind obscuring the owner's name.

> I wish I could find out who these people are. That's one thing that would be cool. I mean its kind of a small group. There's only like five or six things shared here. But like I have no idea who SmallieBiggs is. And I don't know maybe it's because they don't want me to know or because they think it's more fun to have like an interesting name or what (P10).

Many people could make educated guesses about some of the anonymous collections by examining the music itself. Some people figured out whose collection was whose by asking colleagues. Most participants felt certain they knew who owned most of the music libraries. Often, if there were libraries that a user had not mapped to an individual, it was a library that user rarely, if ever, listened to; not knowing whose library it was, in this case, did not seem to concern our participants.

Beyond providing simultaneous customizability and ambiguity in naming music libraries, the iTunes interface was perceived as more directly affecting the impressions that were created. For example, when a person clicked on another person's library, the interface displayed each file (usually this equated to one track of a CD) in the entire library in ascending alphabetical order by artist name.

> [That] people's impressions of what your collection is are probably very heavily influenced by the things that happened to be the first thing in sort order is sort

of a weird thing....If Pete[1] was here...one of the first things that comes up for him...so I think 10,000 Maniacs is in there and then the second thing I think is he listens to this Jewish humor rap group called 2 Live Jews....If you didn't scroll down that would be like your whole impression of [him] (P12).

Another source for judging others' musical libraries came from an individual's own tastes and expertise. By browsing through their music libraries, one participant was hoping to learn something surprising about his coworkers. In the end, he found he didn't know enough about the types of music to which others listened to know if he even should have been surprised: "I don't really know the first thing about music; it's either classical or not" (P7). This same lack of distinguishability was articulated by another participant, also a classical-only listener. "Their collections are pretty much the same as each other's, so you don't need more than one of them" (P13).

These two classical-only participants were better able to distinguish the distinctions and articulate their impressions of each other's music.

He's got quite an eclectic taste and for me, like, I can try out, especially from more difficult, you know, more modern...music (P13).

To contrast, the user that is being referred to in the quote above as being "eclectic" is the same user that another participant had decided was "easy because he has only one genre" (P11).

Despite the close examination of others' libraries, participants seldom felt that these musical impressions significantly changed their view of a coworker. Rather, they felt it mostly "serves to reinforce impressions I've already got" (P12). Occasionally, however, a participant admitted that knowledge of another's musical tastes impacted his opinion of someone else: "[P6] I have learned is a big fan of whatever current pop is which I suppose to some degree lowers my estimation of him but not by too much" (P12).

The more significant and longer-lasting impact of these musical impressions seems to be the binary judgment that frequently gets made.

So when there is someone new, I spend a fair amount of time listening to what they have and then...binary process, either I just decide well there is nothing in there for me or I really like it and will come back to it (P11).

In other words, the first examination of another person's library seems to have a strong influence on whether the visitor will ever return to that library....

## REVISITING THE MUSIC—SHARING DESIGN SPACE
### Intimacy and Anonymity

The workplace, we felt, was a particularly fruitful context for exploring the design space between intimacy and anonymity in music sharing. In fact, the

[1] Pseudonym for an iTunes user who was not a participant in this study.

context of the workplace challenged our implicit assumption that the axis of intimacy and anonymity was a single, straight continuum. Over the course of this study, it became clear that there were many facets to an individual's identity and that interactions and relationships may have a different degree of intimacy depending on which facet of identity was being foregrounded. There were many individuals in our study who worked closely with each other on a daily basis. Many of their workplace interests overlapped to a very high degree. From this perspective, we would probably be inclined to characterize their relationships as being more intimate than anonymous. But until their adoption of iTunes, most of our participants had no idea what kind of music their coworkers listened to. The adoption of iTunes, then, meant that communities that were relatively intimate in some facets of their identities were able to become intimate in previously anonymous facets of their identity.

This study also foregrounded the importance of context in impression management and the ways in which the grey area between intimacy and anonymity in the design space, the space occupied by iTunes, may be the most critical area with respect to impression management. In anonymous music sharing, the only impressions one has of a music sharer are those from the music library. In intimate music sharing, the particulars of a music library may be a small fraction of all of the outside context or prior experience used to form an impression. As one participant pointed out, however, it is the grey area in between that can be most problematic in impression management.

> Music ... says something about your identity, you know, in some ways, right; it says something about who you are. I would talk about music with perfect strangers, like someone that I would never see ever again ... and someone that I know really well I can do this also because I know they'll be able to sort of interpret my taste with enough background information to know where it is coming from. But there is a sort of in-between state where people can form misguided perceptions and you'll have to interact with them again so this can be a problem but they won't have the context and the background to reframe whatever impression they made of you according to the proper information (P11).

It is the grey area represented by iTunes in which these "misguided perceptions" are mostly likely to form, perceptions created from not quite having enough outside context to balance the impressions given off in iTunes.

---

## Working with the Text

1. One of the first respondents quoted above reports how aware he became of the impression he might be making when his coworkers were able to access his iTunes library. He describes how he subsequently worked "to

create a more 'balanced' portrayal of himself." What would you consider to be a "balanced" portrayal of your musical tastes? What concerns would or do you have about others looking through your computer library of music? List several different audiences, both real and imagined, now and in the future, who might have access to your musical library—members of your writing class, coworkers, your professors, future employers, voters, etc.—and describe how you might construct different versions of yourself based on what you include in your library.

2. In the section "Creating Musical Impressions of Coworkers," the study lists several different methods that participants used to make judgments about their coworkers based on their iTunes libraries. What are some of these methods? How would you analyze each method in terms of their strengths and weaknesses? That is, what kinds of information derived from each method would you see as potentially valid and useful, and what kinds as more likely to be mistaken or unfair?

3. Many of the respondents had stronger emotional reactions to the process of sharing music with their coworkers than they might have guessed before they began using iTunes. As the writers put it, "it became clear that there were many facets to an individual's identity and that interactions and relationships may have a different degree of intimacy depending on which facet of identity was being foregrounded." Describe what you see as some of these different facets, and discuss how you manage what you share with or keep private from others in different social situations, whether the classroom, the workplace, or the home. How do your musical tastes fit into this equation?

## "The New Tastemakers"

### Jeff Leeds

*Everyone has his or her favorite styles of music, but how do you find out about new music and artists? The recommendations of friends? Hearing music on the radio? A link on a social-networking site? The history of popular music is also the history of changing ways that people have learned about, shared, and consumed music. At the turn of the twentieth century, sheet music and player piano rolls were the main avenues for distributing and raising awareness of new songs. With the development of recording technologies, music fans began buying specific performances of songs by specific artists, and throughout most of the twentieth century, commercial radio was the dominant way fans kept up with new styles and artists.*

Television played a part as well in introducing new music to the public, from shows like American Bandstand *through the advent of video cable channels such as MTV and VH1.*

From the commercial beginning of popular music, fans have also expressed dissatisfaction with how music was distributed. The system tended to be top-down, driven by the marketing guesses of music and record companies as well as radio stations. Over the years, this process became more and more homogenous as local music programming disappeared from the airwaves and most commercial stations featured musical playlists created at corporate headquarters. Many musicians and music fans were frustrated at how increasingly difficult it was for new and different voices to reach the airwaves.

The rise of digital technology and the Internet has changed and challenged conventional ways of distributing and finding out about music. From file-sharing programs like Napster that allowed fans to easily swap songs to online music stores, to MySpace musician pages, new experiments in how people can find out about, listen to, and obtain popular music emerge almost on a daily basis. Some seem to hold the promise of revolutionizing the way we listen to music; others flame out quickly and disappear from cyberspace.

In "The New Tastemakers," New York Times *reporter Jeff Leeds describes a music Web service based on a new way of asking fans to think about music, one that claims to put more power into their hands. Called Pandora.com, the website hires musicians to listen to and break down individual songs into basic component parts and styles. This information is then put into a database. When visitors to the site enter the name of a favorite song or artist, a virtual station is created for them that showcases music with similar stylistic features. The website calls itself the "music genome project," based on the human genome project, a scientific effort to map the genetic structure of human beings. Leeds explores how sites such as Pandora.com might signal a dramatic new way in how fans relate to music.*

## Before You Read

1. Write the story of how you found out about a specific musician or group who have become particular favorites of yours. Think back to before you were aware of them, and describe in as much detail as you can how you became familiar with them. What was the first song you heard? Did you like the music right away, or did it grow on you? Who introduced you to the music? What were the circumstances? What did you do to find out more about the artist or artists? Compare your story with others in the class. What similarities and differences can you see in how people learn about new music?

2. Conduct an informal poll among friends and family about the main ways that they learn about new music and new musicians. Pay particular attention to the demographic facts about your respondents: gender, age, frequent or infrequent online use, etc. Write an essay about your findings. What seem to be the most popular ways that people find

out about new music? What are the strengths and limitations of the various strategies people use to learn about music? Is there an age when people seem to become less curious about new music and trends? Why do you think this is?

3. What role does commercial radio play in your life? How often do you listen to the radio? When and where? What stations do you listen to and why? Ask these same questions of your parents and grandparents. Write about the generational differences and continuities that you observe. What about radio listening and our relationship to radio has endured over the generations? What are the major changes?

An example of a Pandora.com personalized Web station.

A description of this song by the group stellastarr* features a list of its "musical genome," including "electric rock instrumentation," "demanding instrumental part writing," and "minor key tonality."

**S**eth Ford-Young is a professional bass player who performs up to five nights a week with local jazz and rock bands and occasionally lends his talents to recording sessions for artists like Tom Waits. But these days he has an unusual second gig.

As a senior music analyst at Pandora Media, he spends roughly twenty-five hours a week wearing headphones in an office suite here, listening to songs by artists like Sonny Boy Williamson and Memphis Slim and dicing them into data points. Is the singer's voice gravelly or silky? Is the scope of the song modest or epic? Does the electric guitar sound clean or distorted?

As he listens, in a room not far from an elevated stage with drums, guitars, and amps for employee jam sessions, Mr. Ford-Young fills out a scorecard on which he can rate hundreds of traits in each song on a five-point scale. Bit by bit, Pandora's music analysts have built a massive archive of data, cataloging the minute characteristics of more than 500,000 songs, from alt-country to bossa nova to metal to gospel, for what is known as the Music Genome Project.

At pandora.com visitors are invited to enter the name of their favorite artist or song and to get in return a stream of music with similar "DNA," in effect a private Internet radio station microtailored to each user's tastes. Since the service made its debut [in] November [2005], more than 3 million people have signed up.

But they are tuning in to more than a musicologist's online toy: services like Pandora have become the latest example of how technology is shaking up the hierarchy of tastemakers across popular culture. In music the shift began when unauthorized file-sharing networks like the original Napster allowed fans to snatch up the songs they wanted, instantly and free.

But the field is also full of new guideposts: music blogs and review sites like the hipster darling Pitchfork have gained influence without major corporate backing. And customizable Internet radio services like Pandora, Last.fm, Yahoo's Launchcast, and RealNetworks' Rhapsody are pointing users to music far beyond the playlists that confine most FM radio broadcasts.

All told, music consumers are increasingly turning away from the traditional gatekeepers and looking instead to one another—to fellow fans, even those they've never met—to guide their choices. Before long, wireless Internet connections will let them chatter not only on desktops, but in cars and coffee shops, too. And radio conglomerates and MTV, used to being the most influential voices around, are beginning to wonder how to keep themselves heard.

"The tools for programming are in the hands of consumers," said Courtney Holt, executive vice president for digital music at MTV Networks' Music and Logo Group, who formerly ran the new-media department for Interscope Records. "Right now it almost feels like a fanzine culture, but it's going to turn into mainstream culture. The consumer is looking for it."

If Pandora and other customizable services take off (and so far that's a big if), they could shift the balance of power not just in how music is consumed, but in how it is made. "You now have music fans that are completely enabled as editorial voices," said Michael Nash, senior vice president for digital strategy and business development at Warner Music Group, one of the four major music conglomerates. "You can't fool these people. You can't put out an album with one good single on it. Those days are over."

But if fans become their own gatekeepers, the emerging question is, What sort they will be? Will they use services like Pandora to refine their choices so narrowly that they close themselves off to new surprises? Or will they use the services to seek out mass shared experiences in an increasingly atomized music world?

The idea behind a recommendation engine is essentially to create an online version of a knowledgeable retail salesman, someone to help consumers navigate the dizzingly vast digital marketplace. The most familiar form uses so-called collaborative filtering, software that makes recommendations based on the buying patterns of like-minded consumers. Think of the "customers who bought items like this also bought..." function on Amazon.com.

Pandora's innovation is to focus on the formal elements of songs, rather than their popular appeal. Say your favorite song is Aretha Franklin's recording of "Respect." Pandora will make you a personalized soundtrack that could include Gladys Knight and the Pips' "I've Got to Use My Imagination" and Solomon Burke's "Everybody Needs Somebody to Love." (Why? Click twice and learn that Pandora thinks the Gladys Knight tune resembles "Respect" because it includes "classic soul qualities, blues influences, acoustic rhythm piano, call and answer vocal harmony, and extensive vamping.")

It may not take twenty-first-century technology to deduce a link between Ms. Franklin and Ms. Knight. But the more you tell Pandora about your tastes, the more creative it can get.

For some devotees the core of the experience is being led in directions they did not know they wanted to go. Tara Smith, 43, is a fan of the relaxed rock of Jack Johnson and Jimmy Buffett. After she started toying with Pandora about a month ago, she learned her taste was more diverse than she knew.

"I would never really listen to a country music radio station," said Ms. Smith, who runs a rescue-equipment sales business with her husband in Santa Barbara, Calif. "But because Jimmy Buffett's music has kind of a country bent, it's just played Tim McGraw and Randy Travis. It really goes into some serious country, and I'm surprised I like it as much as I do."

Mrs. Smith said she no longer listened to old-style terrestrial radio, not least because she prefers the Internet's "nonpartisan approach to finding good music."

"Myself, I've always been of the ilk that it's much better to take the broader approach and use my own judgment on what I like and what I don't like," she said. "I'd much rather have five strangers rather than one expert"—like a professional radio programmer—"because you get a much better variety."

Even Mr. Ford-Young, the jazz bassist who is one of Pandora's more than forty music analysts, has discovered some new favorites, like the indie-rock band the Shins. The appeal of the service's computer-generated stations is that "popularity has nothing to do with it," he said. "A song that hasn't ever gotten played on terrestrial radio is going to get played as soon as a No. 1 hit song."

And unlike the stuff that comes across terrestrial radio, Pandora's suggestions are just that: users get to rate new songs with a "thumbs up" or "thumbs down," so if they don't like what they're hearing, they won't hear it again. That has a big effect.

"It's interactive so you feel like it's more yours," said Michael Dory, 26, who until recently worked as a public relations executive in the technology industry and is now entering graduate school in New York. "If a faceless corporation is telling me I should like this music, even if it's the best band in the world, I'll probably be skeptical."

Mr. Dory said he shared suggestions of new bands with his friends via instant messaging and by sharing Web links. But Pandora and similar services, he said, are "creating this atmosphere like you're talking to the clerk at your favorite record shop."

That is exactly the role envisioned by Tim Westergren, who was a founder of Pandora, originally known as Savage Beast, in 1999. The first step was creating the genome, as he calls the musical database, and licensing it to Best Buy and America Online. It wasn't until last year that the company decided to offer a radio service aimed squarely at fans themselves. Now the site is adding about 15,000 new songs a month to the database.

Mr. Westergren, a former rock keyboardist and film composer, says he is particularly proud of the obscure artists in Pandora's library. "I don't have any bone to pick with the hits, but I think what's missing," he said, referring to the music market, "is that a huge wealth of artists never get a crack at it. In any given year there are maybe 100 records that really do big sales. I think there's room for 10,000 artists" to reach a broader audience.

He sees the thumbs-up-or-thumbs-down voting as a concession to human subjectivity, an exception to the algorithms on which the genome is primarily based. But that human element—along with the chance for users of some music services to publicize their own taste, by posting their playlists for other fans to see—may be the most powerful part of the new technology.

It's the same story across the spectrum of these new Internet services. At iTunes, Apple's digital music store, fans have posted more than 898,000 individual playlists. And eMusic, a service specializing in independent-label releases, identifies users' "neighbors"—people who have downloaded tracks from the same artists—and allows them to view a list of everything their neighbors have been listening to.

Pandora has its own take on the trend, allowing fans to create stations and then email them to a friend; other sharing features are in development. As a tool for discovery, it seems to show promise: Mr. Westergren said that 10 percent of the time people tune in to a Pandora station, they end up clicking through to buy a song or album from iTunes or Amazon. That's a much better rate than standard online retailers can claim.

Pandora receives a commission on such sales, and charges for advertising on its website. But so far it has not been enough to turn a profit. [ . . . ]

Mike McGuire, a Gartner analyst and coauthor of the report, said the emergence of the empowered fan represented "the slow death of programmed content." He added, "Unless and until the DJs and programmers can start realizing that, they're going to find themselves inexorably pulled further and further apart from their audiences."

They've started realizing. In Seattle for example the modern-rock station KNDD has offered visitors to its website the chance to submit a list of ten songs. A few of the lists are selected and played on a weekend segment. As a result of these suggestions, says Lazlo, the program director, at least two bands, Band of Horses and the Long Winters, have been added to the station's regular rotation.

"It's about listening to someone else's thoughts on music, and having the input and ability to then share your thoughts on music," he said. [ . . . ]

Personalized recommendation services like MyStrands are already building a presence on handheld mobile devices. Microsoft plans to make fan recommendations a key feature in the device it is designing in hopes of unseating Apple Computer's iPod. According to regulatory filings, its [ . . . ] Zune portable music player will enable fans to play DJ, letting users stream music to others with devices nearby.

MyStrands, based in Corvallis, Ore., plans to allow fans to influence the music played at nightclubs equipped with its new application. The system, currently being tested at a handful of outlets like DoHwa, a Korean restaurant in the West Village, lets patrons send a text message to a screen, identifying their favorite artist. The screen displays album artwork from the selected artist and the name of the fan who entered it. As conversational icebreakers go, most bars have seen a lot worse.

"Instead of trying to personalize a stream of music to one person, what we're trying to do is create a sequence of music that a group of people can be liking," said Francisco Martin, MyStrands' chief executive. Then, turning philosophical, he added: "The human being is very social. Music is not only for yourself. What people really want is to share their tastes."

---

## Working with the Text

1. What were your first impressions as you read about how Pandora.com analyzes songs and creates its database? Were you intrigued? Skeptical? What about the process most changes the way you think about music? What about the process gives you the greatest doubts? Explain Pandora .com to friends who haven't heard about it. What questions do they ask? What do they find most confusing? Most exciting?

2. In the article, two music industry executives, Courtney Holt and Michael Nash, both think that this new approach to learning about music will "turn into mainstream culture" and that today "music fans...are completely enabled as editorial voices." Leeds takes their enthusiasm one step further and asks two critical questions: "Will they [music fans] use services like Pandora to refine their choices so narrowly that they close themselves off to new surprises? Or will they use the services to seek out mass shared experiences in an increasingly atomized musical world?" What do you think about the choices Leeds presents? Will music fans move more and more into their own small, separate worlds, sticking with familiar music, or will an approach like the Music Genome Project encourage music fans to try out new and different sounds?

3. Go to Pandora.com or another similar site and try it out. How well did the "DNA" approach to selecting music for you to listen to work? Did you find yourself learning about new music and musicians? Would you recommend the experience to a friend? Express your thoughts in an essay about the experience of using the website.

## "You Are What's on Your Playlist"

### Benny Evangelista

*"Listening In: Practices Surrounding iTunes Music Sharing" presented the results of a careful study of how a group of office coworkers made judgments about each other and changed their behaviors as the result of how they reacted to the kinds of music each displayed on their iTunes music libraries. Such formal academic studies are mainly read by other scholars and by students in school. Members of the general public might be interested in learning about these findings, but they may not have ready access to social science journals. That's where*

journalists play an important role in spreading awareness about new research findings and in translating those findings to a wider audience.

In "You Are What's on Your Playlist," Benny Evangelista, a reporter for the San Francisco Chronicle, collects information from a number of studies examining the connections between musical taste and personal identity (including "Listening In: Practices Surrounding iTunes Music Sharing"), speaks on the phone with some of the researchers involved, and talks to members of the community in order to interest his newspaper readership in the subject. In doing so, he faces several challenges that are a fact of life for newspapers writers: a limited amount of space to work with, readers browsing through the paper who are not necessarily looking for a story on this subject, the responsibility to be both accurate and entertaining.

As you read his story, think about how Evangelista tries to attract your curiosity about the research he is reporting. Where does he concentrate mainly on explaining the work of others, where is he adding the results of his own research, and where is he drawing his own conclusions about the subject?

## Before You Read

1.  If you were to write a newspaper version of "Listening In: Practices Surrounding iTunes Music Sharing," what would your "lede" or opening paragraph be? You might approach this exercise by first thinking about how you might tell a friend or family member about the research. What hook would you use in casual conversation to turn the topic to the subject of playlists and personality?

2.  In many ways, the headline is really the first sentence of a newspaper story. Using extremely limited space, an editor has to create a headline that will grab a reader's attention and also accurately reflect the focus of the story. First, write about your initial reactions to the headline, "You Are What's on Your Playlist." What assumptions do you make about the essay? What ideas might you anticipate agreeing with, and what ideas might you be skeptical about? After you finish the story, try coming up with some alternative headlines, all using the same number of characters as the original.

Karen Reichstein thought she had a coworker's buttoned-down personality pegged. Then she used her computer to peek into his iTunes digital music library and found some surprises.

"He had a huge collection of the Jam and the Kinks," said Reichstein, an associate editor for a Berkeley book publisher. "Here was a person next to me who even had the whole Carter family collection" of country music.

The old adage used to be "you are what you eat." But with the advent of digital music and the popularity of gadgets like the iPod, now it's "you are what's on your playlist."

Playlists are groups of songs a person can tailor to his or her own tastes or moods for playback on an MP3 player or computer. Those tunes are picked from the larger library of music that a person can store on a portable player or computer.

Last week, musicologists and media pundits around the world had a great time trying to divine what makes President Bush tick by analyzing the songs loaded on his iPod.

The presidential playlist included John Fogerty's "Centerfield" and "Swinging from the Chains of Love" by Blackie & the Rodeo Kings.

But playlist watching has also become a parlor game played by college students and office workers hoping for insight into the lives of people around them. They use a feature in Apple Computer Inc.'s iTunes digital music management program that allows a limited number of people to surf and hear songs in someone else's library.

Playlist peeking isn't limited to your neighbors. A number of famous iTunes consumers have published their lists of favorite songs on the iTunes Music Store site, including San Mateo's Tom Brady, quarterback for the New England Patriots, and Broadway composer Andrew Lloyd Webber. (Brady's list ranged from Aerosmith's "Dream On" to "If I Can't" by 50 Cent. Meanwhile, Lloyd Webber's tastes ran from Elvis to Eminem.)

Experts say these playlists and digital music libraries may even become a new way for people to size up potential mates or political candidates.

"We do find that people are able to make fairly accurate assessments solely on the basis of a person's top ten songs," said Jason Rentfrow, a psychology consultant who coauthored a 2003 University of Texas study of more than 3,500 people that showed musical taste can provide a road map to a person's personality.

Throughout history, music has always been a shared human experience. But what's different now is that technology is allowing people to aggregate their entire musical collections in one place, whether it's on a portable digital music player or in a music management program—like iTunes—on a computer.

So while it used to take hours to browse through a person's CD collection one album at a time, technology now makes that possible with a few clicks of a mouse or the twirl of a scroll wheel.

"It's one of the most intimate things you can create," said Reichstein. "It's like a small diary made up of your songs. You feel like you know them more than you actually do."

Reichstein was one of thirty-four contributors to *The iPod Playlist Book,* published by her company, Peachpit Press [...]

In a report released [in April 2005], researchers from the Palo Alto Research Center, known as PARC, and the Georgia Institute of Technology studied thirteen workers at one small company and found they were forming judgments about coworkers based on the songs they found in each others' iTunes music libraries.

The iTunes program, which works with Windows and Macintosh computers, has a built-in feature designed for users inside one household to stream music from one computer to another as long as they are hooked up to a closed home network.

Researchers Amy Voida, Beki Grinter, and Keith Edwards began tracking stories about how college students were using the same iTunes-sharing feature to form musical communities on campus networks and found a company in which employees were doing the same.

At the company, the employees became aware that their music was projecting an image of themselves to coworkers, Grinter said in an interview.

That caused some playlist anxiety. One worker said he was worried others would get the wrong impression because he downloaded songs by Justin Timberlake and Michael McDonald for his wife. Another worker reported sensing his library was not very cool, so he added artists and genres to make himself appear more balanced.

Some libraries had only the default iTunes name, so its owner remained anonymous, but that only fueled a new game in which the workers tried to match the type of songs listed with coworkers.

"People spent a lot of time trying to figure out who (owned) these anonymous collections," Grinter said.

Christopher Breen, editor in chief of *Playlist,* a San Francisco magazine covering the digital music scene, said he did some eaves-sharing at a recent music industry conference in Texas, using his laptop to scan a dozen iTunes libraries of other conventioneers.

He was surprised to find one acquaintance had a library filled with schmaltzy country, while another had Celtic bagpipe music.

Breen said he keeps his own library in pristine condition.

It's similar to when "your mother tells you always to wear clean underwear because you never know if you're going to end up in the emergency room," he said. "Now you have to worry if someone sees you have 'Me and You and a Dog Named Boo' in your music collection."

Rentfrow, who with Samuel Gosling authored the study on music and personality that was published in the *Journal of Personality and Social Psychology,* said the research showed people have an intuitive feel for matching musical tastes with someone's personality.

"People who were more extroverted tended to have songs in their music collection that had lots of singing," said Rentfrow, who is now an online dating services consultant but is set to become a professor at the University of Cambridge in the fall. People who leaned toward instrumental music, meanwhile, were more introverted.

The *New York Times* reported Bush's iPod is loaded with country artists like George Jones and Alan Jackson, but he does have rock 'n' roller Van Morrison and folk-pop singer Joni Mitchell.

"This suggests he's predominantly someone who is extroverted and a bit relaxed, but not necessarily open to new experiences or who is unconventional by any means," Rentfrow said. "These are more conventional styles of music."

His preferences for rock and country "are related to his athletic ability . . . but also goes negative toward political liberalism," he said.

Sharing playlists and musical libraries has even become a new method for men and women to flirt.

"She was sitting across the coffee shop, and I didn't know who she was," said Alexander Payne, 21, recalling a brief but memorable virtual encounter he had one evening [ . . . ] in his favorite Arlington, Va., java house.

Payne had fired up iTunes when a library titled "Maria's music" appeared from another laptop using the same network. "She had excellent taste, music I hadn't seen in too many other people's libraries, stuff I had been looking for a long time," said Payne, an information security contractor.

Not knowing who she was, Payne changed the name of his own iTunes library to read, "Maria I sweat your music collection." Soon, "Maria's music" changed to "trythenew_dalek." The two carried on a two-hour conversation by changing library titles.

Payne, however, said he never talked to Maria. He saw her at the coffeehouse one other night, but said she "looked like she didn't want to be disturbed."

"It's almost a better experiment unfinished," Payne said last week. "A modern love story, only without a happy ending."

---

## Working with the Text

1. In explaining the appeal of looking at someone else's playlist or iPod library, Karen Reichstein is quoted in Evangelista's article as saying, "It's one of the most intimate things you can create. It's like a small diary made up of your songs. You feel like you know them more than you actually do." Write about what specifically you think Reichstein means when she says, "You feel like you know them more than you actually do." In what ways do you think people might make serious mistakes or incorrect assumptions while analyzing a person's playlist? In what ways is a playlist "like a small diary"? In what ways is it not?

2. Evangelista uses as a topical connection for his story the release of information about some of the music that President George W. Bush had on his new iPod in the spring of 2005. As the story indicates, other

playlists of well-known people can be found in different publications and online. Some, such as those found at the iTunes website, were deliberately created for public consumption; others, such as the "Random Rules" feature at the website of the satirical newspaper *The Onion,* ask celebrities to put their MP3 players on Shuffle and discuss whatever songs come up. Working alone or in groups, examine President Bush's playlist and any other playlists you are able to locate. What do you find most and least surprising about them?

3. [Peter] Jason Rentfrow, the psychologist mentioned in the story who has published research connecting people's musical tastes to their personality types, has created an online quiz, "The Do Re Mi's of Personality," which you can find at http://www.outofservice.com/music-personality-test/. At the site, you can test yourself in relation to his categories of music and personality. Try the test for yourself and write about how well you think it does or doesn't reflect your personality type. In what ways did the test make you think in new ways about your own and others' taste in music? To expand your investigation further, look at the formal research on which the survey is based, "The Do Re Mi's of Everyday Life: The Structure and Personality Correlates of Music Preferences," by Peter J. Rentfrow and Samuel D. Gosling, published in *The Journal of Personality and Social Psychology,* 2003, Vol. 84, No. 6, 1236–1256.

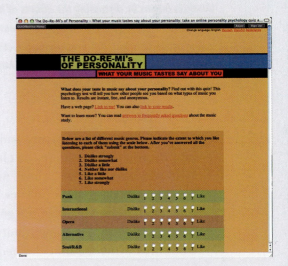

# "Bigger Than Hip Hop"

## S. Craig Watkins

*If the mid-1950s through the early 1980s are thought of as the rock era in popular music, then the last quarter-century might be thought of as the hip hop era. Electric guitar–based rock music has continued to develop and diversify over that same time period. But the various kinds of urban-based rap and dance music known collectively as hip hop have not only changed the basic sounds of the American musical landscape, they have also created a whole subculture, including styles of language use, clothing, and attitude, and new subject matter.*

*While the basic structure and stringed instruments of the classic rock band resemble an electrified version of blues, country, and folk groups from the first half of the twentieth century, hip hop draws on the musical technologies of the electronic age, incorporating turntables, mixing boards, microphone effects, and speaker systems. Built by the imagination and creativity of (mainly but not only African American) urban youth, hip hop takes the discards of an ever-changing music technology to fashion a sophisticated musical form available to people without extensive financial resources. Of special interest to writing teachers and students, hip hop has also been a musical form in love with language. The rise of rap music, with its roots in the West African tradition of the* griot, *a kind of cultural oral historian, has placed a premium value on the rhetorical skills of invention, voice, style, tone, and persuasion.*

*In his book,* Hip Hop Matters: Politics, Pop Culture, and the Struggle for the Soul of a Movement, *popular-culture scholar S. Craig Watkins explores the complex role hip hop plays in contemporary American society, focusing especially on the relationship between hip hop and politics. In his epilogue, "Bigger Than Hip Hop," Watkins begins by discussing the efforts of hip hop artists, most notably the artist known as "Diddy" (Sean Combs), to encourage greater voter participation among young people in the 2004 presidential election. From there, he speculates about the challenges and opportunities in using hip hop and rap as forces for positive social and political change.*

## Before You Read

1. Have you thought of hip hop and rap music as political before? In what ways do you and others in the class think that hip hop and rap do or could address political issues? Are there particular hip hop artists that you associate more with politics than others?

2. How familiar are you with the genres of rap known as conscious rap and political rap? Do some library and Web research to explore these two genres. How are they defined? In what ways do they refer to the same kinds of music, and how do some people differentiate between them?

3. Do you remember hearing about the "Rock the Vote" and "Vote or Die!" campaigns aimed at young voters in 2004? What was your own reaction to them? Locate people who were between the ages of 18 and 24 in 2004 and ask them how aware they were of these campaigns and how seriously they took them.

### Vote or Die!—Sean "P. Diddy" Combs

November 2, 2004, was hip hop's first day of real political reckoning. For more than a year efforts to energize the "hip hop vote" had been in full swing. Russell Simmons's Hip Hop Summit Action Network (HSAN) had called on some of the movement's biggest stars to attract huge crowds to rallies with the intention of registering young voters. In June of 2004 the National Hip-Hop Political Convention gathered in New Jersey. Organizers, aware that hip hop lacks a formal political agenda, tried unsuccessfully to craft a party platform. That same summer Sean "P. Diddy" Combs's Citizen Change, a hip hop inspired initiative, tossed its hat in the national political arena. Combs even attended the Democratic and Republican political conventions, drumming up support for his initiative and the quest to make young people's voices heard on election day.

Two weeks before election Tuesday, Combs took his act to Ohio, Michigan, and Florida, three crucial battleground states. Citizen Change, like the HSAN, relied on a number of well-known faces, including Leonardo DiCaprio, Ben Affleck, and Mary J. Blige, to capture young people's attention. The T-shirt sporting Combs's political slogan "Vote or Die!" was a huge hit. In Detroit he told an enthusiastic crowd of about six thousand that "This year we're not going to sit on the sidelines and complain, we're going to decide the next president of the United States." It was a bold claim and an even bolder goal for a segment of the voting population—urban youth—that had shown little interest in electoral politics. Uninspired by a political process they believe is irrelevant and unresponsive, black and Latino youth are less likely to vote than their white counterparts.

Hip hop was not alone in the effort to energize young voters. MTV launched its "Choose or Lose" project and produced a number of specials focusing on the candidates, the issues, and the importance of young people exercising their right to vote. Filmmaker Michael Moore, fresh off the success of *Fahrenheit 9/11,* a punishing critique of the Bush administration's policy of preemptive war, took his Slacker's Tour to more than sixty cities, determined to heighten young people's interest in the election. College Republicans, too, made a pitch to rally young supporters to their cause.

Amid all of the pre-election hype young voters and their potential impact on the election became a constant source of speculation. Election officials around the country reported that efforts to increase voter registration had led to an impressive increase in young and first-time voters registering. Bitterly contested issues like the war in Iraq, terrorism, and gay marriage were driving a deeper wedge between an already heavily polarized electorate. In this climate, many political gurus argued that a record turnout was not only possible but likely. In the weeks leading up to the election political pundits and reporters found very little to agree on. They did agree, however, that young voters were an unknown factor. If they turned out in record numbers, their votes could be crucial in what was a long and bruising campaign that remained too close to call.

The image of young and first-time voters swinging the election made for an intriguing storyline. In 2000 only 34 percent of voters age 18 to 29 voted. Over the course of the last two national elections the youth vote declined steadily. But in a world made uncertain by terrorism, a soaring deficit, the future of Social Security, and growing prospects for a military draft, young people understood that the stakes were unusually high.

Two days after the election, the data profiling who voted and why began slowly to emerge. According to Peter Levine, the deputy director of the Center for Information and Research on Civic Learning and Engagement (CIRCLE), the election was a watershed moment in terms of the youth vote. In 2000 young adult voters made up 16.4 percent of the vote. Despite a much more aggressive effort to increase the youth vote, the 2004 data indicates that youth made up 18.4 percent of the vote. But those numbers are misleading. In reality 4.6 million more young people voted in 2004 than in 2000. For the first time since 1972—the year 18-year-olds were first allowed to vote—a majority 51 percent of young people voted. In 2000, 42.3 percent of people that age voted. The early data indicates that this age group was the only one that Massachusetts senator John Kerry won, 54 to 44 percent. Some news editorials and commentators noted that the youth vote in states like Michigan and Pennsylvania helped provide Kerry his margin of victory.

It is difficult to determine from the early data what, if any, discernible impact the intense political churn and electioneering in hip hop had on young voter turnout. Still, there are many lessons for hip hop to learn from an election that produced a few surprises at the end.

Shortly after the election, the hip hop movement, like other interested factions, began to assess its political future and ponder its next move. Something had been tapped in the hip hop movement and there was widespread recognition that the momentum needed to be sustained. "I think it's obvious that the youth voter turnout increased," said Combs. "You gotta understand, this community was going backward; it wasn't going forward. This was a community that was going the other way, getting disinterested. We were effective enough to turn them around." To his credit Combs acknowledged that the efforts of groups like Citizen Change were merely the beginning of an uphill struggle to make hip hop matter in the world of electoral politics. Combs told reporters, "We just finished step one—getting people engaged. Step two is to build an infrastructure around the people we've engaged that will help us continue in our mission to educate people about the power they have."

If the hip hop movement learns anything from the 2004 election it should be that the business of politics is serious. Whereas most of the political activity in hip hop was devoted to rallies, celebrity appearances, and voter registration drives, the two major parties invested enormous resources into what political professionals call the "ground game." Both parties understood that despite the millions of dollars spent on TV ads the difference between winning and losing hinged on the ability to enlist an army of paid and unpaid activists to do the real work of politics, identifying and then connecting with real people. Using tactics ranging from knocking on doors to making phone calls to specific voters, the ground game is based on the science and principles of market research. The goal is precision—identifying a base of voters and then targeting them relentlessly with a message tailored just for them.

According to Republican Party consultant Frank Lutz, winning and losing in electoral politics is driven by emotion, the idea that knowing how voters *feel* is more important than knowing how they *think*. Lutz believes, "How you feel is something deeper and stronger, and it's something that's inside you." It is this kind of thinking, many believe, that has enabled Republicans to surge past their Democratic opponents. Republicans, simply put, do a better job than Democrats of exploiting voters' emotions—particularly anger and fear. Targeting evangelical Christians with a precise message and vision of America was a major element in Karl Rove's strategy for getting George W. Bush reelected. By making cultural issues like gay rights (gay marriage) and stem cell research (abortion) crucial in the election Republicans managed to tap into a bed of anger and fear that motivated the evangelical community to vote in large numbers, thus providing a crucial bloc of voters in a tightly contested race.

Before the hip hop movement can have any real impact in electoral politics it will have to develop a more sophisticated appreciation of high-stakes gamesmanship in political electioneering. That includes understanding the importance of a finely orchestrated ground game and the power of emotions in motivating a bloc of constituents to actually vote.

The challenges facing hip hop's entry into politics are immense. First and foremost, the movement will have to define and identify its constituency—who it proposes to speak for. Doing so leads to the second and equally important challenge, defining its political mission and vision. That is, what will hip hop stand up for? If politics are driven by the science of marketing (identifying voters) and the power of emotions (knowing what they feel) hip hop has some serious catching up to do.

The challenges facing hip hop are easy to identify but there is nothing simple about resolving them. Hip hop has always been a community of different voices, experiences, and perspectives. In a hip hop world divided by race and region, pop culture and political aspirations, age and perspective, the challenges are deep. Reconciling these tensions, however, is crucial, especially now that a number of different initiatives are struggling to control hip hop's political destiny.

Despite all of the challenges it faces hip hop is poised to seize the political moment. It has access to the financial, political, and intellectual capital necessary to make a difference in electoral politics. No one understands the art and science of marketing better than hip hop's entrepreneurial elite. Hip hop has a grassroots constituency that is passionate about the movement and what it potentially represents. And yet applying these resources and skills to the world of politics, especially on a national level, demands a level of focus, intensity, and organization that has not been forthcoming.

But even as hip hop develops a finer appreciation of its political future and possibilities it will also have to develop a more astute understanding of a steadily changing world. The key issue that has always permeated hip hop—providing young people real-life chances and choices—is and always has been bigger than hip hop.

Like so many others my relationship with hip hop as well as my thoughts about the movement continue to evolve. Before writing [*Hip Hop Matters: Politics, Pop Culture, and the Struggle for the Soul of a Movement*] I was aware of hip hop's impact in America and beyond. I also knew that I wanted to talk with a wide range of people who have experienced and defined the many different dimensions of hip hop. Still, after writing this book I came away amazed to see just how far hip hop's influence reaches. No matter whether it is the sexual and mental health of young people, the shifting theater of racial and urban politics, the global spread and influence of America's media and pop culture economy, or the untapped power of digital media, hip hop is in the mix.

As I reflect on these pages and the various people and ideas that figure into my account of the struggle for hip hop, I mined my own experiences with the movement and discovered a rich and revealing place in which to ponder. Like many thirty-somethings, I have watched and participated in hip hop as it grew into a full-fledged industry, cultural force, and global phenomenon. The passage of time offers perspective. Though I can recall a world without hip hop, I find it impossible to imagine the world without it today. I was fortunate enough to be among the earliest waves of Ph.D.-trained scholars who grew up with hip hop as part of their cultural experience. Many of us sensed early on in our graduate studies that hip hop was writing a new chapter in America's racial and cultural history. We knew that hip hop had to be reckoned with. We also understood that hip hop was more than a fad and that, like it or not, it embodied some of the period-defining changes of its era. Hip hop produces its own distinct sensibilities and ways of seeing the world that have implications far beyond pop culture.

As a result of my own professional interests regarding issues related to race, youth, politics, media, and pop culture I have had the opportunity to meet, consult, and work with public school teachers and administrators, parole officers, media planners and producers, community activists, state officials, scholars, and students. That such a varied community makes up the sprawling world of hip hop is testament to the movement's resonance in American life. Not surprisingly, each of those communities develops a unique and, for some observers, curious interest in hip hop. It is easy, for example, to dismiss advertising agencies interested in hip hop as simply maneuvering to exploit the culture's appeal with young consumers. Likewise, it would be easy to dismiss a state-run campaign designed to motivate young people to enroll in postsecondary education as a misguided and ill-formed attempt to rob hip hop of some of its charm with young people. But my own experience with these and other efforts tells me that something else is occurring.

Namely, there is considerable and even widespread recognition that hip hop has changed the very nature and disposition of the world we all inhabit. The widespread interest underscores hip hop's undeniable influence in the lives of the young people who live and breathe the culture. But more than young people recognize that hip hop matters.

For the educators I work with it is the recognition that hip hop's influence cuts like a double-edged sword. On one hand, they hear hip hop's impact in the language young people use. They also see it in the dress and behavior of young students. But while those aspects of hip hop may cause some teachers and administrators to panic, they also comprehend hip hop's poetic presence and vivid imagination. They realize that at its best, hip hop can spark the creative mind and the will to learn. For the media professionals I work with it is acknowledgment, after years of denial, of hip hop's power to cultivate new identities, markets, cultures, and lifestyles. No matter whether they are selling soft drinks or messages of empowerment, makers of media messages understand that hip hop forges a path into the hearts, minds, and habits of many young people.

Hip hop's true significance for the community activists and leaders I have worked with resides in its ability to encourage young people to believe that they have the power to make a difference in their lives and communities. Even in the midst of all the temptations—the money, celebrity, and pop prestige—hip hop continues to inspire young people to believe they matter and can change the world.

My most revealing experiences have come from my encounters with hip hop's youngest constituency, students in middle and high school. It is uplifting to see young hip hop heads reading voraciously and thinking quite seriously about the movement they claim as their own. Despite concerns that hip hop's youth are materialistic, apolitical, and self-indulgent, many are socially conscious, engaged in politics, and concerned about the plight of others. Occasionally, the emails that I receive from students include questions that reflect a maturity and vitality that are light-years beyond their actual age. Many young students are making a distinction between what is oftentimes marketed as hip hop and what defines a more optimistic vision for hip hop. Young people, in their own way, understand and even animate the struggle for hip hop.

The purists in the movement believe that in the midst of a commercial explosion hip hop has lost its edge, its spirit of innovation, and its capacity for inspiration. But this view assumes that hip hop has only one destiny, only one true historic course. As the voices, people, and places that define hip hop grow more diverse, the movement continues to develop many different identities and interests. Despite a fascinating history and undeniable influence in America's pop cultural, political, and intellectual life, the struggle for hip hop, amazingly, has only just begun.

Peace.

---

## Working with the Text

1. How did reading Watkins's account of the 2004 youth voter campaigns such as "Vote or Die!" along with comments from campaign organizers like Sean "Diddy" Combs affect your thinking about the purpose and effectiveness of these campaigns? In what ways might they have played a role in the increase in voter participation among young people? In shaping attitudes toward issues and candidates among young people?

2. Watkins refers to the opinions of Republican Party consultant Frank Lutz about how "winning and losing in electoral politics is driven by emotion, the idea that knowing how voters *feel* is more important than

knowing how they *think*." What is your general response to this idea? In writing and rhetoric, the ancient Greek rhetoricians referred to the distinction between *logos,* or the use of logical arguments, to persuade a reader or listener, and *pathos,* or appealing to a person's emotions, as a way of changing someone's opinion. With this distinction in mind, how might popular music in general, and rap and hip hop music in particular, use both logos and pathos to encourage, persuade, and motivate listeners?

3. Watkins writes that for educators, the influence of hip hop is a "double-edged sword." While some of the impact that hip hop has had on the language use, dress, and behavior of young people "may cause some teachers and administrators to panic," others recognize that drawing on "hip hop's poetic presence and vivid imagination...can spark the creative mind and the will to learn." Using information from Watkins's essay, your own experience, and other research, write a recommendation to teachers about how they can constructively use hip hop in their classrooms and schools to improve student learning.

4. One way to test the influence of a popular music culture such as hip hop is to measure how it affects people, whether they are fans of the music or not. Working in teams, devise a series of questions for use in a field research project exploring the effects of hip hop culture. In developing your survey, avoid yes-or-no questions and instead try to encourage your respondents to engage with and think about the influence of hip hop. For example, avoid asking, "Do you think you are influenced by hip hop or rap music?" A more helpful prompt might be, "Describe one or two ways that you think hip hop or rap has affected you in some way." You might even specify types of behavior or attitudes, such as speech or dress.

   Try your questions first on yourself or other members of your team in order to revise and fine-tune them. As you might discover, people are often initially reluctant to admit to being influenced by popular culture. That's why it can help to focus on specific behaviors and examples, such as a particular expression a person might use (e.g., "old school") that they might not immediately recognize as an influence.

   Determine how many people to include in your survey and whether you want to ask these questions in person, online, or some combination of the two. Your project will involve more of a *qualitative* than a *quantitative* approach; that is, you're more interested in exploring a small number of responses in depth than in gathering a statistically significant sample. When you have your results, write an essay (either individually or as a team) detailing what they are and what you find most significant about them. Use your results as a way of evaluating the claims that Watkins makes in his epilogue.

5. Imagine that you are a political adviser offering suggestions to a candidate on how best to use hip hop culture to appeal to young voters. First, create a specific scenario to help you decide what advice you will give. What office is the candidate seeking? What are the demographic characteristics of the candidate (gender? ethnicity? age? income level? etc.)? What party does he or she represent? What are the demographics of the young people in the constituency (ethnicity? rural or urban? etc.)? Use suggestions from Watkins's epilogue, your own research, and your own experience to devise a plan for the candidate.

## SOLDIERS RAP FROM IRAQ

One of the key characteristics of rap and hip hop music is its accessibility. As the title of the old song by Beck had it, all you need is "two turntables and a microphone," although a talent for making drum noises and a gift for rhyme will do just as well. This potential immediacy of rap—the ability to turn day-to-day experiences into on-the-spot artistic expression—has been one of its key attractions for its performers and fans alike. When combined with digital technology and the Internet, rap has become its own kind of global communications network, equal to webpages, email, and text messaging.

The wars in Afghanistan and Iraq have highlighted the immediacy and topicality of rap and hip hop in dramatic ways. For the first time, digital technology, from webcams to cell phones, has allowed soldiers to remain in daily contact with family members at home. Websites let soldiers post messages, images, and videos from the war instantaneously. Now the compactness and portability of digital-recording devices and instruments have helped turn the war zone into a recording studio.

Music has a long association with war, from battle songs and patriotic anthems to protest music and soldiers' ballads. Usually this music about war has been originally written and performed away from the conflict. Recording technology allowed soldiers to carry taped music with them beginning with the war in Vietnam. In the twenty-first century, soldiers and others caught in war can now create and distribute their own original recordings, and rap is proving to be the musical style of choice for these soldier artists.

The following articles, one a newspaper story and the other a transcript of a radio interview, describe two different CDs of original rap music created by soldiers serving in Iraq. One, *Voices from the Frontline,* is a charity project begun by the president of a small punk rock label that features vocals and music recorded in Iraq and the United States. The other, *Live from Iraq,* was created by six soldiers in the First Cavalry Division who call themselves 4th25 ("Fourth Quarter"), and was recorded and mixed entirely in Iraq. Taken together, the two CDs feature a variety of soldiers, both men and women, rapping about their lives and experiences as soldiers.

## Before You Read: Soldiers Rap from Iraq

1. Based on what you have heard or read about the war in Iraq, what do you expect some of the opinions of the soldiers/rappers might be? What attitudes would you anticipate?

2. Some in your class may have served or have friends or relatives who have served in the war. If you or someone you know feels comfortable talking about his or her experiences, what would you or this other person say is most difficult for someone who has not been in a war to understand about the experience?

3. Like all musical and artistic genres—indeed, like writing itself—rap has its own traditions and conventions: common kinds of subject matter, typical personas or attitudes, expected ways of introducing material and addressing the audience. Work in groups to describe the rap conventions with which you are most familiar. In what ways might or might not these conventions be suited to expressing the attitudes and experiences of soldiers?

## "Straight Outta Baghdad"

### Brooke Gladstone with Sergeant Neal Saunders

Soldiers of the 4th25

*The following interview with Sergeant Neal Saunders, the leader of 4th25, was conducted on the public radio program* On the Media *and first aired on August 19, 2005. The interviewer is reporter Brooke Gladstone.*

**August 19, 2005** Soldiers send for those mixtapes, just as in earlier wars they imported music from home when they could, and often they were honored with songs inspired by the very wars they were fighting. One of the biggest hits of 1917 was written by George M. Cohan as the Yanks headed across the Atlantic to fight the Bosch. During the Vietnam War, Staff Sergeant Barry Sadler famously took control over his own musical destiny. He cowrote "Ballad of the Green Berets" while recuperating from a wound incurred in action. It was a number-one hit for five weeks in 1966. But Sadler was stateside. You'd need a technical revolution before yet another sergeant, Neal Saunders, would be able to produce *Live from Iraq,* a rap album recorded and produced in a makeshift studio, while on deployment in Baghdad, while fighting in Iraq. Fifteen tracks of music chronicled the inner life of Sergeant Saunders and five fellow soldier musicians with the 1st Calvary Division deployed from Fort Hood in March of 2004. The group called itself 4th25 (pronounced "4th Quarter") because it seemed that's where they were at in the game of life.

**Neal Saunders:** *The whole album in a sense is chronological from, you know, you have "The Deployment" and that's we're on our way there. Then you have "Life from Iraq." That's as soon as we've experienced, you know, what this war thing in Iraq is truly about. And then from there it goes into "The Mentality." We'd all been doing music for a while but when it came time for us to deploy, we thought like the music thing was going to be put off for a whole year. And, [LAUGHS] you know, that changed as soon as we pulled into Iraq. You know, so much started happening, so much was going on, and we were just like, you know, if we ever considered ourselves artists, how could we not write about the most influential moment in our life? And that's pretty much how the whole album came about.*

**Brooke Gladstone:** *Would you say that* Live from Iraq *is in any way a message album? Does it come down on one side of the debate or the other on whether we should be there fighting to begin with?*

**Neal Saunders:** *No. It really doesn't. You know, we didn't take sides. The fact is that we're there and now it's a matter of life or death to us. What it does say and the side that it does take is on that side of the soldiers. It seems like a lot of people don't understand that, you know, just like a surgeon does surgery, soldiers fight. So I guess [LAUGHS] the one issue that I'm really taking up is the fact that you have soldiers out there and you're not letting them do what they've been trained to do.*

**Brooke Gladstone:** *What weren't they trained for that they're asked to do over there?*

**Neal Saunders:** *I don't think I was ever trained for any type of a peacekeeping operation. You know, I've never trained one time to walk down range and shake some guy's hand or just talk to him. I never walked down to a target during any gunnery and like gave it a chicken or—*

**Brooke Gladstone:** *[LAUGHS]*

**Neal Saunders:** *—you know, pulled a lamb off the back of a truck, then say hey, here you go. What we train to do is we take ammunition and we put holes through things. That's just what soldiers do. And that's where you get the songs like "Behind the Screens" and "24 Hours," you know, where we're talking about we feel like our hands have been tied.*

**Brooke Gladstone:** *Let's talk about "24 Hours." It's an incredibly powerful track. It's basically an explosion of frustration that seems to be directed at the Iraqis, all the Iraqis; everyone who lives there is guilty.*

**Neal Saunders:** *You know, what they're used to is an iron fist. Whoever tells them and stands by what they said is the person that they're going to listen to. So it makes it hard for us to go out there and accomplish anything because we simply can't be out there 24/7. So when they plant an IED [improvised explosive device] in the street and it's right in front of somebody's shop, you know, they're not going to tell us who put it there, even though more than likely they saw who put it there, because they have to live the remainder of that day, you know, scared that this guy's going to come back if they tell us anything. So it's like we, we give them money, we feed them and then we still get shot at. And the rest of the country there is like, wow, you mean these people can like be engaged in fire fights all the time and we're still getting food and being taken care of as if nothing's happening, these people have to be the stupidest people in the world.*

**Brooke Gladstone:** *But it's not the same people necessarily who are firing at you who you're feeding. They're different people.*

**Neal Saunders:** *You know, it's—you probably get a good feeling when you think that, but that's not the truth. We've dropped off aid before, right? And then you'll see the insurgent males, they'll come around and they'll tell everybody to back off of the food. They'll take all of it, they'll go leave, and then twenty minutes later, [MAKING SOUNDS] brrrr, zhew—RPGs, AK 47s going off, ambush right there. After they got what they want, they're going to ambush you.*

**Brooke Gladstone:** *You said that you don't take a side, in the album, and it certainly is democratic in that, with the exception of your fellow soldiers, everyone is a target of your anger—your commanding officers, peaceniks back home, your girlfriends, and especially the Iraqis that you're fighting. There's one song called "Behind the Screens"; it seems to be about the war planners, the ones who make the decisions.*

**Neal Saunders:** *Yeah. That song touches about every bad decision [LAUGHS] that was ever made. You probably remember when the one soldier brought up the question about the 1114s, which is the "up armored" Humvee that they have over there. Correct?*

**Brooke Gladstone:** *Right. He asked Donald Rumsfeld at a town meeting with the soldiers why they had to reinforce their own vehicles with scrap metal from local landfills. And it later came out that a reporter had actually planted that question with the soldier.*

**Neal Saunders:** *Yeah, exactly. But that was a very good question though. You know, the simple fact of the matter is you can go to any base in the Green Zone and there'll be one 2004 Tahoe for every American contractor that's there, you know, all with leather all, you know, with alloy rims. And you're wondering wow, you know, there's money to attract these people to the effort here in Iraq but there's not money to get a soldier an 1114?*

**Brooke Gladstone:** *Did your commanding officers know about this project?*

**Neal Saunders:** *[LAUGHS] That's a good question. I think they knew we were recording something.*

**Brooke Gladstone:** *But they looked the other way?*

**Neal Saunders:** *I don't even think they looked the other way. I think that they misunderstand the seriousness of the album. I think they thought it was going to be just a traditional rap album, you know, where we're talking about going to the club and women. And the stereotypical role of a rapper I guess is what they thought we were going to play. But they just didn't understand the seriousness that we were taking.*

**Brooke Gladstone:** *In "Reality Check" you seem to have some pretty strong words for rappers back home. You basically accuse them of being fakers, of claiming to know what it's like to be a soldier but really having no idea.*

**Neal Saunders:** *Yeah, they don't have an idea. It's—I mean, I understand that, you know, America's probably not the safest place in the world. You know, you can't go out all times of the night. But [LAUGHS] in comparison it's just Americans have it so good. Seeing the difference between what these guys that call them "soldiers" on their albums, you know, go through compared to what your average soldier is going through on a daily basis over there, it's just not the same. And you have not reserved the right to call yourself a soldier, by any stretch of the imagination.*

**Brooke Gladstone:** *Rap always sounds kind of angry to me, or most of the time. This record sounds absolutely enraged. And it seems that much of it is spent in trying to justify the decisions that you make and the choices you feel you don't have.*

**Neal Saunders:** *Well, you obviously feel like you have a loss of any amount of control that a normal person should have on their life. The simple fact that, you know, the ROE stand (ROE is the Rules of Engagement) is so that if I am engaging an enemy that's returning fire on me, when he drops his weapon I have to stop shooting at him. And that's ridiculous!*

**Brooke Gladstone:** *And so basically you're saying—you're asking us to do your dirty work, to follow the rules that will have us killed—and you aren't going to feel guilty about killing civilians.*

**Neal Saunders:** *Well as a soldier I'm not going to feel guilty about killing anybody because, like I said, it's a matter of life or death for every soldier that's out there in the dirt. And people back home may not understand that. You know, we're over there and our weapons are on safety. And we can tell where we're being fired at from but until we see somebody with a weapon, we can't shoot in that direction? And that's a lot of the anger that, that we have.*

**Brooke Gladstone:** *Who are you hoping hears this record?*

**Neal Saunders:** *I think this is something that everybody needs to listen to. A lot of soldiers have told me that before they listened to the album they couldn't open up, because they didn't know what to say. They thought maybe they were the only people that felt the way that they felt.*

**Brooke Gladstone:** *Just one last question, and this may be a weird question, given that the album is so dark. But do you have a favorite song?*

**Neal Saunders:** *I love all of 'em, all fifteen. And I also like—you know, the album isn't dark. The album is what it takes to make it out of there. The album was our light.*

**Brooke Gladstone:** *All right. Thank you very much.*

**Neal Saunders:** *Well, thank you for having me.*

**Brooke Gladstone:** *Sergeant Neal Saunders served with the 1st Cavalry Division in Iraq. While there, he produced the hip hop album* Live from Iraq. *And you can find out more about it on our website, onthemedia.org.*

# "Rapping Straight Outta Iraq"

## Tony Perry

Live from Iraq *by 4th25 is a rap CD recorded in Iraq by a single group of soldiers, all from the 1ˢᵗ Cavalry Division. While this album was being created, a record producer in the United States, Joel Spielman, also came up with the idea of a rap record featuring men and women serving overseas. He used military rapper chat rooms to ask for submissions, and he picked the ones he liked best to rerecord in a stateside studio. Entitled* Voices from the Frontline, *proceeds from the project go to the rappers involved and to a nonprofit group that provides items from home to soldiers in Iraq.*

*While* Live from Iraq *testifies to how digital musical and recording equipment enable artists to create powerful music even in the middle of a war zone,* Voices from the Frontline *demonstrates the power of the Internet to allow instant communication between soldiers in Iraq and civilians back home. Rather than only wonder what fighting men and women were thinking about the war and how they were processing their experiences, Spielman was able to contact them directly and facilitate their musical expression to anyone with a CD player or an Internet connection.*

Camp Pendleton—War and poetry have long been comrades, and for the war in Iraq, much of the verse is rap.

For Marine Cpl. Michael Watts Jr., whose rapper name is Pyro, the creative muse struck while he was riding an assault vehicle back to a base camp after an exhausting seventy-two-hour combat operation in Najaf.

For the 21-year-old from Benham, Texas, it was an experience unlike any other—one that cried out to be captured in a rap.

"There's a big difference between staying up for three days making music and being in Iraq for three days straight getting shot at," said Watts.

From those kinds of experiences in Iraq, Watts and eight other Marines and soldiers have created *Voices from the Frontline,* a rap CD released this week in which troops use the lyrical word to explain the death, boredom, joy, fear, and brotherhood of the war in Iraq.

The compilation is the brainchild of Joel Spielman, 33, president of the punk label Crosscheck Records. He put out a call on Internet chat rooms frequented by military rappers and picked the best submissions for re-recording in a Hollywood studio. The performers—some of whom have already returned to Iraq—will share in the royalties, and 5 percent will go to Operation AC, a nonprofit group supporting troops in Iraq with CARE-style packages.

Spielman calls the CD "an audio documentary" containing real, uncensored voices. "It was important for them to share their experiences and important for the public to hear what it's really like there," he said.

The language is direct but, by rap standards, not particularly shocking. The f-word, the patois of both rap and military life, is present but not in overabundance. The media take a beating for misunderstanding the war, but the songs are not antimilitary.

Sometimes poignant, sometimes laced with bravado, the lyrics capture the apprehension and tension of the ongoing violence directed at American troops and Iraqis alike.

In "First Time," Watts and Navy corpsman Quentin Givens (called Q as a rapper) explain the stomach-tightening uncertainty of deployment to Iraq.

Well we going to Iraq for the first time
I can't explain exactly what's on my mind
So many thoughts runnin' all through my head
Will I come back alive
Or will I come back dead.

The apprehension begins with the convoy from Kuwait:

I see a lot of muzzles of these M16s
While we're in a convoy with a 100-plus Marines
Iraqis lookin' at us with that fear in their eyes
Cause they know in the palm of my hands
Is their lives

So please realize I don't really want to die

And you need to hear the voices

Coming from the front lines.

For Cpl. Kisha Pollard (Miss Flame), rapping about her experiences in Fallouja was only natural. Iraq is the perfect place to rap, said the 21-year-old Nashville resident.

"The reason people freestyle in Iraq or a war zone is to take their mind off a lot of things," she said. "Any chance I got, on patrol, or with other Marines, or by myself, I'm freestyling, I'm hooking and jabbing."

In "Girl at War," she raps about the daily dread of convoys through streets infested with improvised explosive devices, called IEDs, and insurgents armed with rocket-propelled grenades, called RPGs:

Step one, set up for the convoy

Get the brief

Float up in the Humvee now

We're rolling on the streets

And now hopefully it won't end in a beef

Cause if we do, it could possible be a IED

Things are getting hasty, my body feeling nervous

Iraq is shooting at us

RPGs is what they serve us

Stay cool and confident, air support is right above us.

And now we're shooting back

that what you get for... with us.

If there is anger and fear in many of the songs, there is also sorrow, at the injuries inflicted on innocent Iraqis in fighting between insurgents and U.S. forces.

Witness Cpl. Anthony Alvin Hodge (Amp) in "Condolence":

*I see* the light in this war

nobody wins...

I've committed many sins

And I'm far from perfect.

I can't word it any better

But *to tell you this*

*If it was up to me*

*It never would have come to this*

*But it ain't so I gotta keep my*

*Feet in the paint. If I had*

*A wish I wish I had never seen*

*Those tanks.*

*And they say a bullet don't got a name on it.*

*When the bullets hit the kids, who*

*They gonna blame for it?*

There is a kind of desperation among the rappers that unless they tell their story the truth will never be known.

"I just want the message out, not the way TV has it, the real way," said Watts.

"People need to know what it's like when you live with mortars going off and your friends dying," said Pollard.

Music is a way out of the drudgery and danger of a war seemingly without end.

In "Don't Understand," Pyro, Amp, and Q tell of the divide between the civilian and military communities. Like several other songs, it explains that troops fight to protect their buddies, not necessarily out of support for U.S. foreign policy.

*Don't try to play us down*
Cause you don't know what we're about
So alpha company open your eyes, never despise
And realize
It's not only the training
But it's the brotherhood
That keeps us alive,
So we need to stay together and
Combined as one
And you need to keep trying till your enlistment is done.

The song titles speak of the intensity of the Iraqi experience: "Do the Damn Thing," "Some Make It, Some Don't," "Ain't the Same." Army Staff Sgt. Devon Perrymon, a.k.a. Deacon, who's been writing poetry since his teen years, wants the public to know the reality of Iraq from the perspective of the individual soldiers, not the generals in Washington or the reporters. In Iraq, he turned to rap, in the company of other rappers in uniform.

"We're putting it out there for everyone in a way they can relate to," said Perrymon, 25, who grew up in the Crenshaw district and will soon return to Reseda as a recruiter. "When it's in rhyme, they remember it."

In "Five Days in the Wakeup!" Perrymon sings of the anxiety of the short-timer, ready to go home, changed forever.

*I see* the storm over the horizon in Iraq
Mad people dying
Family getting a folded flag and they're crying
I'm not denying the fact I've changed
I just don't think people are ready for the change
I'm seeing faces in the rain . . .
I'm tired of seeing comrades getting slain.

## Working with the Text

1. Corporal Michael Watts, Jr., a contributor to *Voices from the Frontline,* expresses a goal for his music shared by many of the artists on both CDs: "I just want the message out, not the way TV has it, the real way." Based on the interviews in the articles, the excerpts from the songs in "Rapping Straight Outta Iraq," and any listening you may be able to do of either CD, how would you define what Watts and others mean by "the real way"? Do you see a consistent message in these songs, or do you see different points of view? What might the spectrum of opinion be? What further questions are raised by these songs? Can you find online discussions of listener reactions to the CDs?

2. Both articles have headlines that refer to *Straight Outta Compton,* the 1989 CD by the group NWA that helped define the subgenre of gangsta rap. Why do you think the editors of these pieces made the connection between these CDs by soldiers serving in Iraq and gangsta rap in particular? How valid do you find this association? What attitudes and ideas about rap music and culture do the interviewer and reporter seem to have based on these titles and their questions? In what ways do these CDs reinforce or challenge stereotypes about rap music and culture?

3. What do you find most significant about the ability of contemporary soldiers to communicate their thoughts and feelings in such an immediate way to their friends and family and the general public as well? How do you think that CDs such as *Live from Iraq* and *Voices from the Frontline* could influence the debate and discussion about the war?

4. Who do you think Brooke Gladstone and Tony Perry see as the audiences for their stories about these CDs? How familiar do they seem to think their audiences are with rap music and culture? Compare their coverage and description of these CDs with other sources, such as the 4th25 website or the MySpace page for *Voices from the Frontline.* You can also find an interview with Sergeant Neal Saunders conducted by a recent college graduate on the Current TV website. Current is a cable television channel dedicated to airing news reports created by its target audience of young people. This interview, conducted by Jose Flores, can be found at http://www.current.tv/video?id=5582.

## THE IPOD

iPopMyPhoto.com turns an everyday snapshot into an iconic iPod ad.

The transformation of popular culture in the digital age is linked to the development and popularity of key new pieces of technology: the personal computer, the cell phone, and now the portable MP3 player, the most well-known of which is the Apple iPod. Since its introduction in 2001, the iPod has become so ubiquitous that for many people, the terms *iPod* and *MP3 player* are interchangeable, even if not all MP3 players are iPods.

iRaq

**10,000 Iraqis killed. 773 US soldiers dead.**

The political activists at Forkscrew Graphics combine a notorious image from the Abu Ghraib prison scandal with the familiarity of iPod imagery to create protest art.

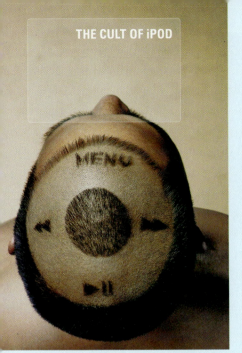

Part of the iPod's popularity has to do with its visual design: the thin, sleek size and shape of the various iPods, the wheel control pad, even the earbud headphones. The series of iPod ads featuring iPod users in silhouette with the iPod and earbud headphones outlined in white has become so familiar that artists have begun to use this imagery for purposes ranging from holiday cards to political protest.

## "The Joy of iPod: iCandy for the Ears"

### Leander Kahney

*The iPod is only the latest development in a chain of technological innovations that began with the transistor radio in the 1960s and continued with portable boom boxes and the Walkman tape player. These inventions radically transformed the relation of music fans to popular music by allowing them to carry music with them wherever they go. Because of the large amount of*

The cover of Leander Kahney's book *The Cult of iPod* suggests just how familiar the design features of the iPod have become.

*memory available on the iPod and other MP3 players, however, these newest devices now not only make music portable—they allow anyone to carry their entire collections of recorded music with them at all times. This development is so dramatic that Leander Kahney argues, in the following essay from his book* The Cult of iPod, *that the iPod has forever changed how we think about popular music.*

## Before You Read

1. Just how widespread are MP3 players? Do a quick survey of the class to see how many people own an iPod or similar device. If you do own and use an MP3 player, write about the impact it has made on your life as a music fan. What recommendation would you give, positive or negative, to someone considering the purchase of an MP3 player? If you do not own one, write instead about your impressions of iPods and other players. How important is it for you to either own or not own one and why?

2. Before you read Kahney's essay, engage in your own speculation on how you think MP3 players will change the music and entertainment industries (especially now that most such players also carry video files of movies and TV shows). What evidence can you provide to support your speculations?

Fire, the wheel, and the iPod. In the history of invention, gadgets don't come more iconic than Apple's digital music player. The iPod is to the twenty-first century what the big band was to the '20s, the radio to the '40s, or the juke box to the '50s—the signature technology that defines the musical culture of the era. And what a marvelous technology the iPod is. Inside Apple's little white box is magic, pure magic, in the guise of music.

Like a cell phone or a laptop, the iPod is kept close and carried everywhere. It's used every day, but not for work or to enslave you by persistent contact. The iPod is used to invoke euphoria. People are in love with music. The sparkling genius of the iPod is that it gives it to you in huge doses. The iPod can store an entire lifetime's worth of music. And so it becomes the most personal of personal devices. More than a computer, a car, or a fancy pair of shoes, it's part of your makeup, your personality. What's on it—the music—tells who you are. Music is deep in your heart and soul.

I'm a music junkie from England, a nation of music junkies. Since late childhood, music has been a passion, sometimes an obsession, that often took precedence over all other interests—food, love, even cigarettes. Like a lot of people, I had a giant collection of vinyl LPs and CDs that grew over the years into an unmanageable archive weighing hundreds of pounds. Too heavy for shelves, the records sat on the floor, spilling into the room. But for the most part the collection was merely for other people to gawk at. I didn't play most of the records, and except for a few disks at the front of the pile, I forgot and neglected most of them.

Fast forward, and now the entire collection can fit inside a small white box the size and weight of a pack of cards. This is to me a miracle. A crowning achievement of technology. That unwieldy pile of vinyl and cardboard has been freed from the living room and is available anywhere and everywhere I go: from the earliest, regrettable singles to my latest obsession.

Inside the iPod, a music collection comes alive. There's delight in loading up a ton of stuff from all genres, eras, and styles and seeing what the machine comes up with. Select Random Shuffle, and the iPod dredges up tunes you might never consciously choose to play. But chosen for you, they're a delight. This mode of play also allows you to discover gems in a collection that previously sat unplayed on a shelf of CDs. Songs previously neglected can become top fa-vorites. And then there are all those tunes you never knew you had. Random shuffle can create great surprises, selecting just the right song at just the right time. Or it can throw together unexpected combinations: Burning Spear fol-lowed by Ludacris. It doesn't always work, but when it does, you're in pop heaven.

The iPod has changed forever my listening habits. No longer do I want to hear an album all the way through (with rare exceptions). What I want is a playlist of my favorites. Listening to the iPod makes a cinematic adventure of a trip to the supermarket or a boring car drive. It adds a sense of otherworldliness to walking down the most familiar street. There's nothing better for exercise—pounding beats and breaks to get you energized to mount the summit of a hill. I like listening to the iPod while riding my bike (yeah, I know it's dangerous and probably illegal). High as a kite off the exercise, the music transports me to nirvana. Sometimes, when the right tune pops up, I'm truly in heaven.

---

## Working with the Text

1. As Kahney recognizes, part of the appeal of the iPod is that it allows him to carry his entire record collection with him and that it does so "inside a small white box the size and weight of a pack of cards." As the examples of iPod-inspired art illustrate, the visual design of the iPod has quickly become iconic; that is, like a Coke bottle or the McDonald's golden arches, the image of the iPod is now a widely recognized cultural symbol, just as the product's name is rapidly used in the same way as words like *Xerox* and *Kleenex:* product names that have transformed into the generic terms for photocopying and facial tissues, respectively.

   What is it about the design of the iPod that has so quickly established it in our visual vocabulary? In what ways has Apple's advertising campaign created an attitude and value for the look of the iPod? For example, why do you think so much emphasis has been placed on the earbud cord?

2. Kahney's essay portrays the iPod as an almost completely positive development in both technology and society. The various examples of art on pages 304–306, however, can be seen as both tributes to the universality of the iPod (obviously, the artists expect their audiences to quickly recognize the reference) and also critiques of that influence and perhaps of iPod culture itself. The Forkscrew Graphics picture, for example, takes as its primary target the war in Iraq, but the artist who

created the image might also be using the iPod reference to criticize aspects of contemporary American culture in general and iPod culture in particular; for instance, the potential insularity and desire to be cut off from the rest of the world suggested by walking around with earphones on all day.

Choose one or more of the illustrations or find other visual examples of iPod references (Kahney's book contains many) and write about the different possible meanings you can derive from how the iPod is used in each. Think about the potential rhetorical goals of each image and how these goals suggest the meanings we find in the images. You might start by making a list of positive and negative images of the iPod in each example.

3. Write an essay in response to Kahney's in which you express your own opinions and attitudes about the value and influence of the iPod, whether positive or negative. Then use your essay to come up with plans for your own visual response to the iPod. Depending on how comfortable you are with creating images, your response could range from a detailed written description of what your image would look like and why, to your own iPod-inspired art, accompanied by a written artist's statement.

# CREATING CULTURE

## MUSICAL MASH-UPS

In 2004, the American hip hop artist Danger Mouse created a musical album for friends called *The Grey Album*. Eventually made available over the Internet, the album became both a sensation among music fans and also the center of a debate over how older ideas of copyright and owning ideas rub up against hip hop's newer models of open-source appropriation and sharing. The album is based on two others: *The Black Album* by rapper and now record company executive Jay-Z, which came out in 2004, and the self-titled *The Beatles* (more famously known as "The White Album"), which originally appeared as a vinyl LP in 1968, long before digital recording and sampling. After releasing his album, Jay-Z (real name Shawn Carter) made the vocal tracks available to any other artists who wanted to add their own music and create new versions of *The Black Album*. Picking up on the allusion to the classic Beatles' record in the name of Jay-Z's CD, Danger Mouse (also known as half of the musical group Gnarls Barkley) sampled and combined different songs on *The Beatles* to create new backing tracks for Jay-Z's vocals. The resulting mix of gangster rap and 1960s British pop music became an Internet hit.

The media corporation EMI, which owned the copyrights to the recorded Beatles' music, took a different point of view than Jay-Z and demanded that Danger Mouse remove *The Grey Album* from the Web because he had not paid for the rights to sample the music. The ensuing controversy involved arguments about the nature and purpose of copyright, the similarities and differences between theft and creativity, as well as a Web-based protest called "Grey Tuesday" on February 24, 2004, in which dozens of websites participated in an act of digital civic disobedience and made the album available for free downloading.

*The Grey Album* is a perfect example of a new digital-age creation called the mash-up, or music made from combining two or more songs into a wholly new creation. Sometimes a mash-up takes the vocals from one song and puts them over the instrumentals from another: one famous example, "A Stroke of Genie-us," by the DJ Freelance Hellraiser, puts the voice of pop singer Christina Aguilera over the guitar-driven rock of The Strokes. Others combine bits and pieces of several different records, none of which becomes the main part of the song, even if the various pieces remain recognizable.

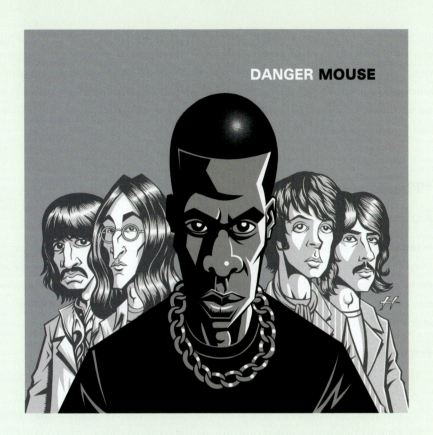

DANGER MOUSE

Mash-ups have also been used as a form of social commentary and political satire. Two pioneering groups of mash-up artists—Negativland and the Evolution Control Committee—specialize in combining musical fragments with samples taken from political speeches, network newscasts, advertising, television programs, etc., to make humorous records that take satirical aim at corporate culture and the media. The Evolution Control Committee's "Rocked by Rape," for example, places excerpts from the *CBS Evening News with Dan Rather* over a hard rock background from the group AC/DC to suggest that newscasts promote fear and anxiety in their viewers through language that emphasizes violence and mayhem (the title of the song, a direct quote from one of Rather's newscasts, being one example).

Many mash-ups, though, are created simply for fun, and they often combine artists, such as Madonna and the Sex Pistols, whom most people would think of as musical opposites. Even when they are all in fun, however, or when the goal seems just to come up with great new dance music, mash-ups represent a radical new approach to how we listen to and interact with popular music. Rather than following settled categories and musical genres, mash-ups challenge listeners to question their assumptions about what we mean by a type of music and who might listen to it. Just as significant, mash-ups invite listeners to join in the creative process by blurring the lines between artist and performer, producer and consumer. As you will see in the next reading, anyone with access to a computer and a basic sound-mixing program can quickly start trying to make a mash-up, whether or not that person has thought of him- or herself as a musician before.

## "The Mash-Up Revolution"

### Roberta Cruger

*In this essay written for the online magazine* Slate, *Roberta Cruger, a long-time music journalist who has also worked in the music industry, introduces her readers to the concept of the mash-up and the artists who make them. Along the way, she explores how the mash-up may be part of a larger trend toward redefining the popular music industry in a more interactive direction.*

### Before You Read

1. How familiar are you with mash-ups? Poll the members of your class: Are they resident experts or do they know of any? Are they fans of mash-ups? Ask them to talk about the genre with you. They may even be able to bring in some examples to listen to in class; otherwise, try to sample several different kinds of mash-ups. Based on your experience listening to or discussing mash-ups, what do you see as most appealing or fun about them?

2. Mash-ups raise questions about who is the actual or primary creator or author of the song. Before reading Cruger's essay, write about how you interpret the creative process involved in making a mash-up. What are the ethics involved? That is, should mash-up makers consult the creators of the recordings they are mixing, or does that seem counter to the spirit of a mash-up? How do you think artists and others might feel about their work appearing in mash-ups?

In the 1993 club hit "Rebel Without a Pause," Chuck D. raps over Herb Alpert's chirpy trumpet: "A rebel in his own mind/ Supporter of a rhyme/ Designed to scatter a line/ of suckers who claim I do crime." That incongruous hybrid of hip-hop and bouncy pop, created by the group Evolution Control Committee, sounds as startling and amusing today as it did a decade ago, and is still ripe with meaning.

The wacky juxtaposition spawned its own kind of revolution, inspiring legions of the club remixes now called mash-ups—with one classic example being "Smells Like Booty," in which Destiny's Child wails over Nirvana's classic dirge and drone, Also referred to as "bastard pop," mash-ups involve blending samples from two songs—generally, one song's vocals atop another's instrumental or rhythm track. The sum of the parts often surpasses the originals. The more disparate the genre-blending is, the better; the best mash-ups blend punk with funk or Top 40 with heavy metal, boosting the tension between slick and raw. Part of the fun is identifying the source of two familiar sounds now made strange—and then giggling over how perfect Whitney sounds singing with Kraftwerk.

Exploding onto Britain's dance club scene [starting in 2001], mash-ups are cut 'n' pasted by superstar DJs whose aliases sound like email monikers: Ultra 396, Kid606, Anon, Mc Sleazy. Distributed free on the Internet, on bootleg CDs, and on twelve-inch "white labels" in U.K. shops, mash-up recordings may be becoming yesterday's news overseas, just as they're beginning to attract a significant audience on this side of the pond. Mash-ups are easy to create on home computers with software any competent downloader can find for free. But because the necessary artistic clearances are tough to obtain at best, mash-up devotées are bootleggers almost by definition.

As in a wrestling match or a courtroom battle, the two "mashed" acts are presented as opposing each other: "Kylie Minogue vs. New Order," "Tag Team vs. Marilyn Manson," or "The Ramones vs. Abba." Mashing the titles of the two tracks adds another layer of wit: Soundgarden matched with Joni Mitchell is "Like Woodstock." Splice the Bee-Gees with Michael Jackson and you get "Billie's Alive"; Chris Isaak vs. Eminem yields "Wicked Superman," and Christina Aguilera vs. the Strokes turns out to be "A Stroke of Genie-us" (which it is).

Mash-ups might be the ultimate expression of remix culture, which has grown out of a confluence of influences: widespread sampling, DJs as performers, and the proliferation of digital technology, as well as a tangle of diverse musical styles from jungle to house to garage and techno. To lapse into postmodern jargon for a sec, mash-ups are the highest form of recontextualization, recycling toasty tunes by fusing pop hooks with grunge riffs, disco divas with hardcore licks. The groove and crunch combination melds black music back into rock, or pulls out a song's surprising inner essence. Toss in something vintage, obscure, silly, or unexpected and the duet totally transcends all musical formats and canons of taste.

"The Remix," a Friday-night show on London's XFM radio ("where dance rocks") has proudly championed mash-ups, providing their primary on-air outlet, says James Hyman, the show's cohost for three years. Though mash-ups are a side dish in the show's diet of remixes, the listeners devour them, and

"The Remix" has launched such hot DJs as Freelance Hellraiser, Jacknife Lee, and Audio Bullys, whose work can be found on the album *The Best Bootlegs in the World Ever,* a critical fave (and a bootleg itself).

Belgian brothers Stephen and David Dewaele, aka Soulwax and/or 2 Many DJs, assembled and released the nonstop, album-length mash-up *As Heard on Radio Soulwax, Part 2* (there was no Part 1, although there have been several subsequent installments), morphing Prince into Sly and the Family Stone slipping into the Velvet Underground's "Waiting for My Man" over the throbbing "Peter Gunn" TV show theme. All forty-five samples were exhaustively cleared—for the Benelux countries only. So buying the album as an import is legal (you can easily find a copy on the Web right now), even if owning and playing it in the United States is a legal gray area at best.

From Vanilla Ice to the Verve, the controversy over sampling rights and the prohibitive costs of clearance payments, potentially due to publisher, label, and artist, keep mash-up bootlegs underground, perhaps contributing to their allure. Ironically, artists who sampled aplenty in the '90s, such as the Beastie Boys and the Chemical Brothers, aren't necessarily eager to grant permissions. Touting the "buy it don't burn it" philosophy, Missy Elliot, whose "Get UR Freak On" has been mashed fifty-plus times, tells consumers to turn their backs on bootleggers.

After radio stations received cease-and-desist letters for playing mash-ups, "Freak Like Me," mashed by Girls on Top (aka Richard X) with Adina Howard backed by a Gary Numan track, was re-recorded with The Sugarbabes' vocals to circumvent legal difficulties—and hit No. 1 on the U.K. charts.

Labels should love mash-ups, insists Jon McDaniels, program director of C89.5, a Seattle high school radio station whose teen DJs constantly play bootleg imports on the daily mix show. "They breathe new life into old stuff," he says. (A current favorite is Dannii Minogue vs. Dead or Alive: "I Begin to Spin.") Admittedly, mash-ups may not inspire the purchase of Celine Dion's CDs, but they may rekindle interest in a forgotten career. Consider the example of the proto-mash-up, Run-D.M.C.'s mid-'80s collaboration with Aerosmith on "Walk This Way."

It wasn't until a landmark case in 1991 that casual sampling or borrowed material was deemed illegal, when Gilbert O'Sullivan sued Biz Markie for unauthorized use of "Alone Again (Naturally)." The judge quoted the Seventh Commandment, "Thou shalt not steal." Would hip hop have survived that long without widespread pilfering—and where would the already crippled music business be without the rap "fad" many thought would fade?

Though credited as the grandfathers of mash-ups, Ohio's Evolution Control Committee is more into satirical audio collage ("plunderphonics") than reinventing pop songs. When threatened with a lawsuit by CBS for sampling news anchor Dan Rather over AC/DC for a track on their latest compilation,

"Plagiarhythm Nation, Vol 2.0," ECC responded that copyright law allows "fair use" of materials for parody purposes.

With Madonna and the Sex Pistols giving permission to Go Home Productions for its "Ray of Gob," mash-ups may yet go mainstream. "If it's official, things could get interesting," suggests XFM's Hyman. On the other hand, says Osymyso (aka Mark Nicholson), whose "Intro Inspection" crams 100 songs into a twelve-minute tour de force, "Legitimizing these tracks will remove the spontaneity that made them work in the first place."

Though there are gazillions of club DJs in the United States, it's tough to find mash-ups on American airwaves outside a handful of free-form stations. WFMU, the legendary indie station in Jersey City, N.J., features turntable artists during the show "Re: Mixology." Program director Ken Freedman (aka DJ Jesuspants) has scheduled such renowned mashers as Go Home Productions and the Australian DJ known as Dsico, "that No-Talent Hack" (sic).

"What does it matter if the remix of Justin Timberlake's 'Cry Me a River' with 'Let It Whip' as the track came from the label or not?" asks Sean Ross of *Airplay Monitor,* a radio trade publication. As long as fifteen different mixes are provided for every song by labels and radio, he adds, "There's no reason listeners won't keep doing their own."

While a growing core of fans adores mash-ups, some consider them one-gag novelties. Some don't get them and others—those who aren't willing to spelunk in the darker corners of pop culture's gray market—literally *can't* get them. Disclaimers on mash-up sites generally state that music copyright is held by the artist, that remixes will be deleted on request, and that listeners are downloading songs for "evaluation purposes only" and agree to erase all material within forty-eight hours.

After the Recording Industry Association of America succeeded in suing three students for file sharing, launching a new front in its battle against piracy, president Cary Sherman proclaimed: "When individuals 'share' copyrighted music, without permission of the copyright holder, they are liable." The RIAA is now gathering evidence to prepare a new round of lawsuits in mid-August [2003], potentially targeting anyone who downloads copyrighted music. To say the least, mash-up entrepreneurs are in the crosshairs.

"Record companies use the Web as too much of a scapegoat," says Hyman, of London's XFM. He notes that Apple's iTunes Music Store sold millions of songs in its first few weeks, clearly indicating that people will pay for music—they just don't want to pay $20 for a crap album. Late to jump on the Internet bandwagon, the music industry is scrambling to recoup revenues it believes it has lost to bootleggers and file-sharers. (The industry's own numbers suggest a catastrophic 26 percent sales drop since 1999.)

The RIAA's refusal to accept downloading is like its fight against blank cassettes in the '80s, says E. Michael Harrington, a music professor at Belmont

University in Nashville who specializes in intellectual property issues and has served as an expert witness in copyright lawsuits. Harrington compares the industry's effort to criminalize customers to the Titanic's captain ignoring the iceberg: "Oh, we're sinking. Let's sue the passengers. Creativity is being stifled by copyright laws that are outdated, unrealistic, and misinterpreted."

There are potential violations galore in the world of sampling, Harrington explains, but the law is tricky. In some cases the lack of qualitative similarity between different songs has led judges to conclude that sampling is not copyright infringement, as the U.S. Supreme Court's 1994 decision that 2 Live Crew's parody of Roy Orbison's "Oh, Pretty Woman" was acceptable under the fair-use doctrine. "At its best, the law reflects our values," says Harrington. "When it's not, it just regulates them."

As far back as Mozart, he adds, "There's an age-old tradition of fooling around with music everyone knows and casting it in a new light, giving it new meaning." It's a murky business when ideas of authorship and artistic control come into question. When is it filching, when is it flattery, and when is it just funny?

Mash-ups may further muddy the legal waters because they can transform their original sources so dramatically. Organizations like the Electronic Frontier Foundation and Musicians Against Copyrighting of Samples say they are seeking "reasonable copyright" reforms that would permit sampling. Members of Negativland, the California experimental band sued by Island Records for its 1991 parody and remix of U2's "I Still Haven't Found What I'm Looking For," support a "sampling license" for remixers' use. BoomSelection, the now-defunct online clearinghouse for bootlegs, referred to the "plundering nature of pop music" in its last-ever Web posting, crediting mash-ups with pushing the boundaries of cool. "There's no longer any shame in loving Hall & Oates," read the site—when mixed with Daft Punk, something new and improved is created.

Mash-ups might be better understood as part of a continuum rather than a new trend. They will likely mutate further and encourage more bands like Detroit's Electric Six, described as "White Stripes gone Studio 54." Anyone who wants to can download the vocal track to their song "Gay Bar," create their own remix, and submit the new version to XFM for possible airplay on "The Remix." So far, Hyman says, the submissions have ranged from "the diabolical to the hilarious to the surreal." He has played "brave, cheeky, and genius" versions backed by the "Batman" theme, reggae classics, the Village People's "YMCA," 50 Cent, and Motorhead.

In DIY culture, consumers are the producers, owning the tools of production—a laptop instead of guitar, bass, and drums. The bedroom is the studio and factory machinery moves out of the nightclub onto the Internet for millions to access. The media monopolies are fighting back, but with the airwaves gobbled up by conglomerates, homespun mash-ups may be the people's digital antidote.

Hot Aussie remix DJ Dsico—"that No-Talent Hack," who mashed Britney Spears vs. Chic to create "Goodtime Girl"—guides the budding mash-up maker with how-to lessons. Select compatible melodies (mix an a cappella vocal with a different music track—say, Snoop vs. Foo Fighters, or maybe J.Lo vs. Ben Folds). The possibilities are endless. Tweak tempos, mix and fix pitch, time loops with cheap or free software (audio apps such as Sonic Foundry, Pro-Tools Free, Cool Edit Pro, Acid, Wavelab, or Peak). Arrange, adjust, upload. "You gunna be da next Freelance Hellraiser," Dsico declares. "The future is now."

---

## Working with the Text

1. In describing mash-up culture, Cruger says, "The more disparate the genre-blending is, the better." That is, the more the artists being combined seem to come from very different parts of the pop music universe, the more interesting the resulting combination. Cruger goes on to theorize about the larger cultural effects of mash-ups:

   > [M]ash-ups are the highest form of recontextualization, recycling toasty tunes by fusing pop hooks with grunge riffs, disco divas with hardcore licks. The groove and crunch combination melds black music back into rock, or pulls out a song's surprising inner essence. Toss in something vintage, obscure, silly, or unexpected and the duet totally transcends all musical formats and canons of taste.

   Write your own explanation of what Cruger might mean by saying that the mash-up "totally transcends all musical formats and canons of taste." How could mash-ups affect or even transform our understanding of musical categories? In what specific ways could mash-ups redefine how we look at popular music?

2. Cruger writes, "In DIY [do-it-yourself] culture, consumers are the producers, owning the tools of production—a laptop instead of guitar, bass, and drums. The bedroom is the studio and factory machinery moves out of the nightclub and onto the Internet for millions to access." Cruger is not the first writer to suggest that the digital age is changing the old models of artist and audience, producer and consumer. In the age of mash-ups, many pop music fans no longer rely on large record companies producing CDs made by professional artists. Instead, they create their own music to swap with other fans, sometimes playing the instruments themselves, but just as often by the mash-up method.

   As Cruger points out, some record companies are upset by the idea of mash-ups, both because of copyright concerns and because they fear do-it-yourself music could hurt their sales. The idea of mash-ups and do-it-yourself music does raise the question of what popular music might be like without a large record industry (after all, music existed before there were record companies). Speculate about what attitude changes would need to occur for more consumers and fans to think of themselves as creators and producers of music. What different expectations might people have for popular music?

3. If you haven't done so, listen to several different mash-ups, from the serious to the silly, from dance records to political satire, to mash-ups that combine a little bit of both. As you listen, write down your observations and reactions. What patterns and trends do you see?

   Then, working alone or in groups, propose your own mash-ups. Think of songs that you would want to combine, or different collages you might create using music and other forms of recorded sounds, from news reports to commercials. Write a detailed description of what the record would sound like and why you would want to create this mash-up.

...ere you on 9/11? For most young people, the events of
...ber 11, 2001, have divided their lives into "before" and
..." similar to the impact of the assassination of ...hn F.
...y or the attack on Pearl Harbor on earlier gener...ns.

# SIX

CHAPTER

...re were you ...
...001, have div...
... of the assa...
...rlier generat...
...ther explana...
... remember wh...
...sly or assum...
...r (being los...
... were you on ...
... have divided...
... of the assa...
...rlier generat...
...ther explana...
... remember wh...
...sly or assum...
...r (being los...
... were you on 9...
...divided their...
...assassination ...
...tions. The t...
...ation. In fact...
...ber where I was...
...sly or assume...

...were you on 9/11? For most young
..., the events ... September 1...
...have divided the...l...s into
...e" and "after," similar to the
... of the assa...nation o...John
...nnedy or the attack on Pearl
... on earlier generations. The
.../11 is instantly recognizable,
...ing no further explanation

## Pop Goes the News:
## Whom Do You Trust?

Where were you on 9/11? For most young people, the events of September 11, 2001, have divided their lives into "before" and "after," similar to the impact of the assassination of John F. Kennedy or the attack on Pearl Harbor on earlier generations. The term *9/11* is instantly recognizable, requiring no further explanation. In fact, if someone asks, "What's 9/11?" or "I don't really remember where I was on that day," we either don't take that person seriously or assume that something extraordinary must have happened to him or her (being lost on a desert island, having just emerged from a coma).

The events of 9/11, in other words, became a news story that almost everyone has heard and remembers. Looking back, it seems as if we have known about it all of our lives. It's hard to remember a time when 9/11 was just another date to us, no more remarkable than 4/23 or 11/17. That we have such vivid memories of that day, however, reminds us of the process we all went through of first learning about 9/11, a process that continues as we discover new information about the events and consider new interpretations and arguments about the meaning of that day. The date 9/11, then, provides us with a good example of how news operates in the contemporary world.

# O N E

## EXERCISE

### Reviewing 9/11

Ask most people what happened on September 11, 2001, and you will hear a reply based not just on personal memories of that day but on a synthesis of everything people have learned about 9/11 since then. References, for example, to al-Qaeda or Osama bin Laden represent aspects of the story that emerged gradually in the days and months following 9/11. What most people probably heard first, however, was that a plane had crashed into the World Trade Center (or maybe simply a building in New York City). Because 9/11 is so widely known, we can use it to trace the different ways we access and evaluate news information in the contemporary world. This exercise asks you to recall how you learned what you learned on September 11, 2001.

- First impressions: Write about the immediate ways you first heard of something unusual happening on 9/11. Use specific details to be as accurate as possible. For example, you might originally say that you heard about it on television, but maybe what actually happened was that a friend or family member told you to turn on the television, which makes that person your first news source. Record as well your initial reactions to the news. Were you shocked? Surprised? Skeptical? Scared? Did you believe the first reports?

- Timeline of sources: Describe as completely as you can the different sources of information you accessed that day to find out more about what was happening. Remember that you may have used multiple sources, some that you deliberately sought out and some that others might have directed you to or were part of the general environment. For example, many current college students were in grade school at the time. Did your teacher turn on a television station? Which one? Who was on the television: news reporters, government officials, designated "experts," etc.? Did your teacher also act as an additional source of information? How were you assessing the reliability of these different sources? What made a source seem more reliable to you? How did your teacher's emotional reaction affect the information you were hearing?
- The days that followed: During the days and weeks after 9/11, what were your most common sources of news information? Why did you choose those sources? Again, how did you assess the accuracy and trustworthiness of these sources? Did you encounter any disagreements among people you knew about what the facts were, what was happening, or who could be trusted to have accurate information?
- Summary: Based on your memories of how you learned about 9/11, draw some conclusions about what kinds of news sources you most trust and find most reliable, and which you are most skeptical of. Write about why you have these opinions and attitudes about different news sources.

The events of September 11, 2001, occurred at a time when the social organization of the news—how information about current events is gathered, analyzed, written, and disseminated—was in a period of revolutionary transition comparable to the introduction of radio and television in the twentieth century, the telegraph and railroad in the nineteenth century, and the first "modern" newspapers and magazines in the eighteenth century. The development of hundreds of cable and satellite TV channels and the rapid growth of the Internet are changing not only the ways we receive news, but also our attitudes, expectations, and relationships toward news.

While human societies have always shared information about recent events via various informal and formal means, from oral gossip to town criers to official proclamations, the idea of the news as we think of it dates back about three hundred years. Indeed, the idea of the news as a collection of factual information about goings-on in our local, regional, and national communities, updated daily by professional newsgatherers, has grown along with modern democratic societies. The concept that citizens who take an active role in the decision-making processes of their societies need reliable information to make those decisions has become a cornerstone of what we think of as democracy, and most of the arguments made in favor of representative forms of government at the beginning of the United States included the free flow of information and ideas as crucial to a free society.

The first newspapers were local affairs, mixing various kinds of statistical and official information (for example, the arrival of ships in the harbor, various government edicts) with gossip and speculation about the affairs of prominent citizens, a function often expressed in newspaper titles such as the *Tatler*. These early newspapers, along with the first magazines and cheaply printed pamphlets that made up the nation's first mass media, were highly opinionated and partisan affairs, often making passionate arguments in favor of various political causes and political leaders and hurling equally passionate slurs against political opponents.

Over the course of the next two hundred years, the idea and structure of the press (a name that derives from the fact that the earliest newspapers were written and published by printers looking for a way to earn a living from operating their printing presses) became more professionalized and a more integral part of the social and political process. By the twentieth century, distinctions arose between the legitimate press and other supposedly less trustworthy (if often more exciting and spectacular) publications. Major city newspapers, and later network-television news broadcasts, acquired reputations for reliability and objectivity of information, and the public's trust in them as news sources provided a measure of the stability of the news as a social institution.

This stability has always been relative, however. Along with a trust in major news providers and what we now call the media have always been questions about whether even the most prestigious and respected newspapers or television journalists might not betray their own biases and limited perspectives, whether deliberately or not. Economic pressures have also caused strains in the news industry because the constant demand to show a profit provides incentives for commercial news sources to tailor the news to what is popular or to avoid subjects that might invite controversy. Indeed, many question whether nonprofit news agencies, either independent or subsidized by the government, might not be more accurate and trustworthy than the commercial press.

## NEWS IN THE DIGITAL AGE

The dramatic increase in the number and kinds of news sources in the digital age has only intensified arguments about the best sources of news. The ability of the Internet and twenty-four-hour cable news services to continuously update information, along with the greater interactivity of Internet sources compared with print news, suggests that we may be undergoing a fundamental reorientation in the way we look at and respond to the news. As we will explore in this chapter, for example, the rise of websites and personal blogs have not only provided alternative news sources to newspapers and television, they have also led to a combination of informal and formal, official and unofficial streams of information. Newspapers have long reported on "the word in the street" and other forms of oral news transmission, but the Internet allows for the direct mix of information from professional journalists and the news you would hear from a coworker, friend, or neighbor.

## GETTING THE NEWS: WHOM DO YOU TRUST?

As citizens, writers, and consumers in the twenty-first century, we now face an unprecedented explosion in the number and variety of news sources available to us. These same new information media allow us equally unprecedented opportunities to participate in the process of newsgathering, news writing, and dissemination of news: we forward stories on the Web via email to friends, respond to a discussion in a chat room, or create our own websites and blogs. With these new levels of participation and sources of news, we are facing equally new challenges in terms of determining the accuracy, reliability, and trustworthiness of the information we encounter. We can less and less rely on the idea that professionals and experts have sorted through and judged the accuracy of what we read and hear. More and more, we need to rely on developing our own judgment and critical thinking abilities when it comes to sorting through the news.

The earlier example of 9/11 illustrates the contemporary news environment. A quick check of my local city library's holdings, one of the largest in the country for a public library, brought up 332 titles under "September 11 Terrorist Attacks, 2001," a fairly intimidating number for the average college student writing a research paper. Google, on the other hand, registered 222,000,000 hits for the topic "9/11," and Yahoo! located "about" 2,180,000,000 sources, more than there are websites that exist on the Internet. The online search engines provide a rough organization of this material by listing the responses in order of popularity, but *popular* and *best* are not necessarily the same thing.

Add to this mix the sheer diversity of sites about 9/11 available, from those created by broadcasters and newspapers to government sites, to sites posted by scholars, to those that accuse the U.S. government of being secretly behind the 9/11 attacks. The explosion of information and opinion that the digital age has brought to our fingertips makes us rethink the definition of news itself. When we say, "the news," just what do we mean? The following exercise asks you to explore your own ideas about this term.

## Defining the News

"What's the latest news about your brother?" "Have you heard the news about the new student housing policies?" "Let's check to see what the news is saying about it." The concept of *the news* is so familiar that we rarely stop to think about just what we mean by that term. The digital age, however, with its increased quantity of information and its greater interactivity, is making us rethink what exactly *the news* refers to.

Begin exploring this issue by brainstorming all the different kinds of information you and your classmates can think of that might be included in the idea of *the news*. For example, what about facts and statistics? Interpretations? Different points of view and opinions? Next, approach the question from a different angle by compiling a list of what we use the news for. What are some of the reasons you and others turn to the news: To get "the facts"? To help form opinions? To settle arguments?

Finally, list your own criteria for what you consider good or reliable news. What makes you trust a news source? What makes you suspicious? After these various idea-generating activities, summarize and synthesize your thoughts and ideas into an essay in which you offer your own personal definition of *the news*. As your class works on drafts of this essay, compare your definitions with those of others, looking for points of agreement and disagreement and seeing how the ideas of your classmates can help you develop and clarify your own.

In this chapter, you will encounter readings that ask you to think about how you interact with the news as both consumer and potential producer of news information. You will be asked to consider what your most popular news sources are, including places that others might not necessarily think of as the news. A section on the future of newspapers invites discussion about how you and members of the class feel about traditional sources of news and information, and a section on *The Daily Show* introduces the consideration of how our sources of news are changing along with our definition of the news itself. This chapter will also introduce you to the concept of blogging, a form of Web-based writing that has already begun to change the landscape of political news and discussion. Blogs invite readers not just to absorb the ideas of others but to respond in kind, a form of interactivity reflected in articles on the idea of the citizen journalist. Finally, the focus on blogging will explore how the idea of interactive news has become a global phenomenon. You will read the work of young Iraqi bloggers who offer insight and news about the conflict in the Middle East on a direct, young person–young person basis, across borders and outside official news and information agencies.

# READING CULTURE

## THE NEWS: EVOLUTION OR REVOLUTION?

### "Abandoning the News"

#### Merrill Brown

*"Extra! Extra! Read all about it!" Many of us recognize these words from television or the movies and have perhaps even used them to preface a surprise announcement. How many of us, though, recognize their origins in the newspaper culture of the early twentieth century, when city newspapers (and most cities, even modest ones, had several daily newspapers) would print extra editions to inform the public about late-breaking events? Extra, that is, in addition to the two or three regular editions each paper normally put out every day. When word came of a major news event, whether local, national, or international, people would gather around newsstands and wait for the papers to deliver the information.*

*The idea of waiting for news seems strange to most people today, especially people age thirty and under, who have grown up in a world of instantaneous information available twenty-four hours a day with the click of a mouse or an alert on a cell phone. Will these younger consumers still have use for older forms of news media that ask people to wait for the next edition or the next regularly scheduled newscast?*

*Motivated by data that showed declining subscription rates for newspapers and ratings for television news, the Carnegie Corporation, a nonprofit think tank, commissioned a survey in the election year of 2004 focused on where people ages eighteen to thirty-four were turning for their news. The results of this survey were analyzed in a report for the Carnegie Corporation by Merrill Brown. In this report, with the provocative title "Abandoning the News," Brown outlines the changing ways that young people relate to the news and makes suggestions about how media news services might adapt to the needs of the digital generation.*

Newspapers then and now

*Merrill Brown began his career as a business reporter, but for the last twenty years he has helped found Court TV and been editor of the MSNBC website. He is currently running his own media consulting business.*

## Before You Read

1. Use the list of news sources below to create your own personal news inventory. For each medium listed, write about how often you use this source for news and information, and why. Evaluate each news source in terms of its usefulness to you.

   - Newspapers
   - Radio
   - Internet (list most commonly accessed sites)
   - Television (local, national, and cable)
   - Others

2. Turn your inventory into a survey to see where class members and friends get their news. What trends and patterns do you find? Expand your survey to include members of different generations. What changes can you see in the ways people from different generations relate to the news over time?

3. One of the issues that the Carnegie survey explored was whether young people today are interested in the news at all. Before reading Brown's report, how would you respond to this question? Why do you think some people might be curious about the news habits of younger people?

There's a dramatic revolution taking place in the news business today and it isn't about TV anchor changes, scandals at storied newspapers, or embedded reporters. The future course of the news, including the basic assumptions about how we consume news and information and make decisions in a democratic society, are being altered by technology-savvy young people no longer wedded to traditional news outlets or even accessing news in traditional ways.

In short, the future of the U.S. news industry is seriously threatened by the seemingly irrevocable move by young people away from traditional sources of news.

Through Internet portal sites, handheld devices, blogs, and instant messaging, we are accessing and processing information in ways that challenge the historic function of the news business and raise fundamental questions about the future of the news field. Meanwhile, new forms of newsgathering and distribution, grassroots or citizen journalism, and blogging sites are changing the very nature of who produces news. [...]

For news professionals coming out of the traditions of conventional national and local journalism, fields long influenced by national news organizations and dominant local broadcasting and print media, the revolution in how individuals relate to the news is often viewed as threatening. For digital media professionals, members of the blogging community, and other participants in the new media wave, these trends are, conversely, considered liberating and indications that an "old media" oligopoly is being supplemented, if not necessarily replaced, by new forms of journalism created by freelancers and interested members of the public without conventional training.

## THE INTERNET MIGRATION

At the heart of the assessment of the news-related habits of adults age 18 to 34 are fundamental changes driven by technology and market forces. Data indicate that this segment of the population intends to continue to increase their use of the Internet as a primary news source in the coming years and that it is a medium embraced in meaningful ways. Newspapers and national television broadcast news fare poorly with this critical demographic group.

Surprisingly to some, among 18- to 34-year-olds, local TV is ranked as the most used source of news, with over 70 percent of the age group using it at least once a week and over half of those surveyed using local TV news at least three times a week. The local TV ranking is driven in an overall sense by women and low- and middle-income groups. Meanwhile, the second-most-used weekly news source, the Internet, is number one among men, high-income groups, and broadband users.

With over half of Internet users now connecting via high-speed broadband services, daily use of the Internet among all groups is likely to climb, because broadband access, the way an increasing number of households go online, makes daily usage more likely. Already, Internet portals—widely used, general-interest websites such as Yahoo.com and MSN.com that include news streams all day, every day—have emerged in the survey as the most frequently cited daily news source, with 44 percent of the group using portals at least once a day for news. Measured by *daily* use, local TV comes in second at 37 percent, followed by network or cable TV websites at 19 percent, newspapers at 19 percent, cable networks at 18 percent, and national broadcast networks at 16 percent. [...]

## A REVOLUTION IN NEWS AND IN PUBLIC DISCOURSE

The dramatic shift in how young people access the news raises a question about how democracy and the flow of information will interact in the years ahead. Not only is a large segment of the population moving away from traditional news institutions, but there has also been an explosion of alternative news sources. Some have been assembled by traditional news organizations delivering information in print, on television, and on the radio as well as via the Internet and mobile devices. Others include the thousands of blogs created by journalists, activists, and citizens at large.

Clearly, young people don't want to rely on the morning paper on their doorstep or the dinnertime newscast for up-to-date information; in fact, they— as well as others—want their news on demand, when it works for them. And, say many experts, in this new world of journalism, young people want a personal level of engagement and want those presenting the news to them to be transparent in their assumptions, biases, and history.

While it is premature to definitively judge the impact of this revolution on public affairs, political discourse, or on journalism itself, the writing is on the wall: the course of how the news will be delivered in the future has already been altered and more changes are undoubtedly on the way. How can we expect anything else, when the average age of a print newspaper reader is 53 and the average age of both broadcast and cable news viewers is about the same? Baby boomers read newspapers one-third less than their parents and the Gen Xers read newspapers another one-third less than the boomers.

Whether the industry is reacting fast enough to these dramatic changes is another question altogether. "By and large, the major news companies are still turning a blind eye to what is happening because it's challenging and they need to consider radical change," says researcher Rusty Coats, Director of New Media at Minnesota Opinion Research, Inc. (MORI). "[Change is] way too incremental at this point," he continues. "Major newspaper companies are embracing the Internet but are still using it as a supplement or as a means to sell print subscriptions and not seeing its unique value." Coats points out that there's a "big buzz" within the newspaper industry about developing "loyalty programs," marketing efforts designed to deepen the customer's commitment to a given product. So a subscriber to the *Chicago Tribune,* for example, might receive airline discounts as part of a program. "I'm all for rewarding valuable customers but I wish there was more thought devoted to developing new products. Does a newspaper publishing a youth-oriented website once a month or once a week really think this will cause fundamental change? The real issue is how are we going to [compete with] Yahoo?" In that regard, Coats suggests that maybe big papers "need to own cellular services" or other large distribution vehicles to reach new audiences. What is needed, Coats and others argue, is a substantial commitment to new product development, investments that news companies—even in their triumphant days of dominance and vast profitability—were reluctant to make.

But these issues can no longer be swept aside by the news oligopolies that have dominated the latter part of the twentieth century, as news executives and researchers generally agree. Indeed, those who gather, report, and administer the delivery of news are increasingly focusing on the reality that technology, the enormous variety of media choices, demographics, and to a certain extent the struggles of traditional news

organizations and the journalism community to adjust to change have left mass audience, mass media newsgathering, and dissemination in peril. And that's unlikely to change. As Lewis Dvorkin, AOL's top editorial executive and a longtime news executive warns, "I don't think that with the lifestyles of people today, the demands on people's time, today's family life, and the extended hours of work, people will come back to the old ways of consuming the news."

Until recently, however, managers in the newspaper industry, for example, generally avoided confronting the decades of data about declining use of newspapers among the younger members of society. Instead, they took what is turning out to be false comfort in historic data that generally affirmed the view that older citizens always wind up with the familiar local newspaper because of their interest in world affairs, their pocketbooks, concern with local schools, and the issues of modern life. But there's no denying that the numbers are changing. The deterioration of the newspaper marketplace has been steady among young people and would appear to be accelerating. From 1972 to 1998, the percentage of people age 30-to-39 who read a paper every day dropped from 73 to 30 percent. And in just the years between 1997 and 2000, the percentage of 18-to-24-year-olds who say they read yesterday's newspaper dropped by 14 percent, according to the Newspaper Association of America. The only conclusion to be reached after noting these trends is that no future generation of new consumers will fit earlier profiles since their expectations and their habits have changed forever—and technology is a big part of the reason why.

"Young people are more curious than ever but define news on their own terms," says Jeff Jarvis, who is president of Advance.net, a unit of Advance Publications, and who publishes a widely read blog, Buzzmachine.com. "They get news where they want it, when they want it. Media is about control now. We used to wait for the news to come to us. Now news waits for us to come to it. That's their expectation. We get news on cable and on the Internet any time, any place."

What this means is that American journalism institutions face risks of extraordinary magnitude. To be sure, the news industry is an evolving business, but even within that context, recent changes in the news business must be viewed as a wake-up call for all involved. Consider the fact that broadcast television's evening news programs, for example, are no longer the family hearth that brings people throughout the country together at meal time. Or that television networks, which used to employ dozens of high-profile correspondents around the world, now deploy just a few. (Certainly, in the years leading up to September 11, 2001, international reporting on television was in rapid decline, often almost invisible on national television.) Afternoon newspapers have disappeared from American life and cities that for decades had multiple newspaper choices now often have but one. The *New York Times, USA Today,* and the *Wall Street Journal* are available on street corners throughout the country. The daily audiences of national news websites dwarf those of their print counterparts.

Even the accepted, historic premise of how a free press and the skills of journalism bind together democratic institutions similarly merits a certain reassessment and reality check. There is little evidence that today's politicians accept the notion that it's mandatory to connect to the population via a "national press corps," often choosing to go around the press and communicate through their own Internet sites, through friendly talk shows and blog forums.

## A TIME FOR RADICAL THINKING

In a world where national leaders are turning away from the news media, citizens have an increasing lack of confidence in the press, and young people are moving perhaps permanently away from traditional newsgathering organizations, a radical rethinking of how news is delivered seems necessary—even overdue. Press watchers and public figures have varying, though often critical views on the performance of the national press, and many critics claim that new forms of citizen or Internet media can help fix general media inadequacies and gaping holes in coverage of important issues. Nevertheless, many feel that the country still needs strengthened newsgathering capabilities to help Americans develop a true understanding of an increasingly complex world, and argue that only strong, national media organizations cover wars, elections, news from around the world and in metropolitan communities in ways that help inform large numbers of citizens. [ . . . ]

## THE CHALLENGE: RETAINING AUDIENCES
## WHILE BUILDING NEW ONES

At its essence, the conclusions of the Magid survey support much of what many researchers and careful students of the media have been saying and raises a set of dramatic red flags about newsgathering in the twenty-first century. One such scholar, Betsy Frank, Executive Vice President, Research and Planning, Viacom's Cable Networks, Film and Publishing, is a preeminent researcher and thinker about young people and media use and calls them "media actives." The media revolution, she says, "affects so many aspects of their lives and news just happens to be one of them. Nothing we see in their comfort with technology will go away as they get older. They have no loyalty to media institutions like their parents did."

Similarly, CBS News President Andrew Heyward says that young people are "information impressionists. News is gathered by the impressions they receive from many sources around them." How news executives today deal with the ways news is consumed, in the form of an image here, an instant message there, a cell phone text message headline, a Web portal story, or a newspaper shoved into a passing hand while racing to the bus, will say a great deal about the future of news as we know it.

For Heyward and other media executives interviewed for this report, the challenge is real. Whether it is thinking about the recrafting of the *CBS Evening News* in the post-Dan Rather-era or how to distribute CBS news content on new and evolving platforms, Heyward, for example, says he's constantly thinking about ways to engage younger viewers. "We are going to have to be accessible without just being bite-sized," he says. "We are way behind in translating the strengths of television to the new media. We are nowhere on storytelling for the new media and for these younger audiences. We have to figure out how to use the new technologies in ways that address our strengths—immediacy and personality. There is a broader, new definition of news that we will need to develop for this next generation."

History suggests that news products tailored to meet the emerging needs of different times and different generations is not a far-fetched idea. Business coverage, for example, an afterthought in many newspapers until the 1980s and 1990s, now gets vastly more attention from most news organizations than in previous eras. But perhaps an even more pressing concern, beyond simply beefing up coverage in one category or another or adding younger faces to a network newscast, is whether approaches to stories and prevailing traditions can really change. Can storytelling evolve to add more interactivity, citizen participation, inclusion of younger newsmakers, and the use of music, innovative pacing, and more engaging graphic and presentation elements? These changes—which represent many once widely observed taboos against embellishing straight news in any way—are at the core of what many in the business wrestle with today.

Progress toward these new definitions of news and public affairs may have been accelerated by the unpredictability and unexpected developments that were the media and new technology story underpinning [...] last November's [2004] general election. The 2004 campaign provided any number of examples—both anecdotal and from the research already available—about the impact of the revolution at hand and how it engaged young news consumers. Former Vermont Governor Howard Dean built his campaign on connecting young Internet-savvy activists, and both the ultimate Democratic nominee, Senator John Kerry, and the Republican victor, President George W. Bush, used the Internet as a critical part of their public relations and fundraising efforts, strategies directed largely at young people. Campaign commentary and coverage from bloggers moved from being perceived as idiosyncratic and away from the mainstream to being a critical part of the debate about the CBS News reporting on President Bush's military record and ultimately, the blogging phenomenon reached the level of attention that comes with a cover story in the *New York Times Magazine.* From a more concrete point of view:

- The Pew Internet and American Life Project determined that among 18-to-34-year olds with high-speed Internet access, 40 percent said the Internet was their main campaign news source, twice the percentage that cited newspapers. The Pew Center also reported that 21 percent of all Americans identified the Internet as their main campaign news source, twice the percentage as in the 2000 election.

- A study of 18-to-29-year-olds carried out as part of "Declare Yourself," a national nonpartisan effort to register voters for [the 2004] election, reported that 25 percent of young voters named the Internet as the first or second most important source for news compared to just 15 percent for newspapers. In that same study, Jon Stewart, host of *The Daily Show* on the Comedy Central network, was identified as the most trusted of the TV anchors among the group that chose the Internet as their top news source, while among the entire group, Stewart tied with then-NBC-anchor Tom Brokaw and came in ahead of ABC's Peter Jennings and former CBS anchor Dan Rather when asked about who they "trust the most" to provide "information about politics and politicians."

It is widely believed that this election year data represents, in some ways, a sea change in both consumption patterns and in how news is consumed. Those

Jon Stewart viewers or consumers of popular blogs like Talking Points Memo (talkingpointsmemo.com) on the left side of the political spectrum and Power Line (www.powerlineblog.com) on the right have, it would seem, changed the way they approach and view the news. Active consumers are unlikely any longer to rely on single sources for coverage of issues that matter to them. And they'll never be consuming news without clear chunks of opinion as part of the mix. [ ... ]

## SUMMING UP: THE MESSAGE IS CLEAR

What the survey data commissioned by the Corporation—as well as the message that's coming in loud and clear from bloggers and their readers—are telling us is that there are new forms of participatory or citizen journalism that can engage those who had been outside today's news environments. Last spring, *The Bakersfield Californian* launched *The Northwest Voice* (http://www.north westvoice.com), a community weekly paper and Internet site. Most of the content is produced by members of the community and submitted via the Internet. Similarly, The Command Post (http://www.command-post.org/) is a site created by a worldwide network of bloggers set up to cover stories and package links to other sites that add documentation. Many news executives cringe at the idea of such projects. But these are bold concepts and their premise—that news can actually be generated by readers—may be precisely what many young, dissatisfied news consumers will respond to. Similarly, news organizations need to connect to consumers through email and instant-messaging services, need to join the virtual online conversations that are a central place where news is discussed, and need to not only embrace these approaches but also use new technologies in order to reach out to younger audiences. [ ... ]

While making investments is imperative, the news industry needs to do so while simultaneously inventing new, creative business approaches. Few news organizations think methodically and creatively about product development, and resources allocated to studying and inventing new news products are generally minuscule. Even at universities and think tanks, research on these critical topics is limited. Nevertheless, the time has come to forge new liaisons among the disparate worlds of research, education, and news organizations in order to maximize intellectual capability and limited resources. [ ... ]

# Working with the Text

1. Brown's report includes many key findings from the Carnegie survey about the newsgathering habits of young people. Choose some specific examples from the survey data to explain how typical or atypical these findings are in reference to you and your friends. How might you

modify the interpretation that Brown makes of these findings? What would you agree with, and what alternative explanations might you have?

2. In his report, Brown writes, "Clearly, young people...want their news on demand, when it works for them. And, say many experts, in this new world of journalism, young people want a personal level of engagement and want those presenting the news to them to be transparent in their assumptions, biases, and history." Explore your reaction to Brown's claims by first defining what you think he means by the idea of news providers being "transparent in their assumptions, biases, and history." Can you think of specific examples of what this might look or sound like? How much do you agree with Brown about what young people want from the news?

3. Brown quotes two television executives, Betsy Frank and Andrew Heyward, who each coin new terms for describing younger news consumers. Frank calls them "media actives," and Heyward calls them "information impressionists." What aspects of the way that younger people seem to be relating to the news does each phrase capture? How would you explain these two concepts to those unfamiliar with Brown's report? Would you describe yourself, for example, as an "information impressionist" or a "media active"?

4. Based on your own experiences with the news and on the ideas in Brown's report, write a series of recommendations to a local news provider, whether television, radio, print, or online, about changes it might make to attract younger people. Base your recommendations on specific examples that you choose from the current practices of the news providers. Be sure to explain what your recommendations are, the evidence you are using to make these recommendations, and why you think the news provider will be interested in taking them seriously.

## "*The Daily Show*: Discursive Integration and the Reinvention of Political Journalism"

### Geoffrey Baym

*A survey conducted during the 2004 presidential election revealed that a significant number of young people used late-night comedy shows in general, and Comedy Central's* The Daily Show with Jon Stewart *in particular, as a main source of information about politics and the news. Since then, media analysts and scholars have been taking* The Daily Show *(as well as its spin-off,* The Colbert Report*) more seriously. What many people regarded at* *first as simply an entertainment program that describes itself as "fake news" has found itself competing with the "serious" news programs that it regularly parodies. This new attention has resulted in the show winning Peabody Awards for excellence in broadcasting and becoming a regular stop for political candidates hoping to reach young voters in particular (although the audience for* The Daily Show *spans more than one generation).*

*In "*The Daily Show: Discursive Integration and the Reinvention of Political Journalism,*" Geoffrey Baym analyzes the program to develop theories about why the show strikes a nerve with so many people and how the development of "fake news" sources such as* The Daily Show, The Colbert Report, *and* The Onion *online newspaper represent, in his view, "an experiment in journalism." Baym says* The Daily Show *not only makes fun of how mainstream news programs operate but offers a substitute model of TV news. By the end of his essay, Baym even argues that* The Daily Show *represents how the news media should operate in a democratic society, a new kind of program he feels is more attractive to young viewers skeptical of mainstream media.*

*Geoffrey Baym is an assistant professor of media studies at the University of North Carolina, Greensboro.*

## Before You Read

1. What are the main structural features of most television news programs? Record and watch several examples of television news shows, both national and local, on major networks and cable channels, and describe the main attributes of a typical newscast. For example, what do the sets look like? How are stories previewed and introduced? How long are most stories? How do the anchors and reporters usually act? How is video used? How are graphics used? Compile your results with others in the class to come up with your own recipe for a standard newscast. As you do so, begin discussing your reactions to and evaluations of the ways news is presented. What aspects of the news do you find most effective? Least effective?

2. Watch one or two episodes of *The Daily Show* as a class. If you are a fan of the show, write about why you watch and what features of the show you find most appealing and entertaining. What did you learn from the program? If you are new to *The Daily Show,* write about your reactions to the program. If you have worked on question 1, compare the features of conventional newscasts with *The Daily Show.* What aspects of these news programs does the show follow and in what ways? What point do you think *The Daily Show* is trying to make about traditional news programs?

3. Survey friends, students on campus, faculty and staff members, and family members to see how familiar people are with *The Daily Show*

and to come up with profiles of some typical fans. What do regular viewers most value about the show? If some do not like the program, why don't they like it? Supplement your discussion by visiting online discussion boards about *The Daily Show.*

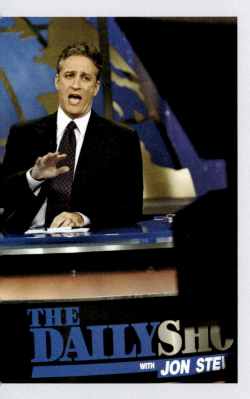

There appears to be a crisis in broadcast journalism. In quantitative terms, there is more of it than ever before, but many would suggest its quality has degraded in recent years. The once-authoritative nightly news has been fractured, replaced by a variety of programming strategies ranging from the latest version of network "news lite" to local news happy talk and 24-hour cable news punditry. In the increasingly competitive battle for market shares, some of the basic principles of good journalism—independence, inquiry, and verification—are often sacrificed to meet the demand for eye-catching content (Kovach & Rosenstiel, 1999). Driven by market pressures, the erosion of journalism-as-public-inquiry has only hastened in the post–September 11 environment, in which most commercial news media outlets aligned themselves soundly with the White House and the apparatus of state security (Hutcheson et al., 2004). [...]

In the midst of this narrative of decline, however, young people are turning to another form of news and campaign information—late-night television and comedy shows. The 2004 Pew survey found that 21 percent of people ages 18–29 say they regularly learn about news and politics from comedy shows such as *Saturday Night Live,* and 13 percent report learning from late-night talk shows such as NBC's *Tonight Show* with Jay Leno and CBS's *Late Show* with David Letterman. Among the programs regularly cited as a rising source of political information is Comedy Central's mock news program *The Daily Show with Jon Stewart.* With the post–September 11 passing of ABC's *Politically Incorrect, The Daily Show* has risen to the cutting edge of the genre. Its unique blending of comedy, late-night entertainment, news, and public affairs discussion has resonated with a substantial audience. For the 2004 calendar year, Comedy Central estimates the nightly audience for the show's first run at 1.2 million people, with another 800,000 tuning in to one of the program's subsequent repeats (S. Albani, personal communication, February 24, 2005). National Annenberg Election Survey (NAES) (2004) research has found that 40 percent of the audience is between the ages of 18 and 29, but perhaps surprisingly, the show also attracts an older audience, with 27 percent above the age of 44. The NAES data further reveal that the audience is more educated, follows the news more regularly, and is more politically knowledgeable than the general population.

The show's host, comedian Jon Stewart, and his co-producers label their work as "fake news," and insist that their agenda simply is "to make people laugh" (S. Albani, personal communication, May 3, 2004). The label of "fake news" has provided the primary frame for conversations about the show, both in popular and academic circles. That moniker, however, is problematic on two levels. For one, it fails to acknowledge the increasingly central role the show is playing in the domain of serious political communication. The program has won a Peabody Award and also was nominated as one of television's best newscasts by the TV Critics Association (CBC, 2004). At the start of the 2004 presidential campaign, *Newsday* named Stewart as the single most important newscaster in the country (Gay, 2004). Further, the show's nightly interview segment regularly features members of the national political, legislative, and journalistic establishment. Senator John Edwards chose *The Daily Show* as the media venue from which to announce his candidacy for the 2004 Democratic presidential nomination. Bill Moyers, the dean of American public service television news, may be correct in his assertion that "you simply can't understand American politics in the new millennium without *The Daily Show*" (PBS, 2003).

The label of "fake news" also has a deeper problem. Any notion of "fake" depends upon an equal conception of "real." Fake news necessitates assumptions about some kind of *authentic* or *legitimate* set of news practices, ideals that one rarely hears articulated or necessarily sees as evident today. In the absence of any codified set of professional guidelines, a standardized entrance examination, or a supervisory guild, news instead is defined and constrained by a set of cultural practices, informal and often implicit agreements about proper conduct, style, and form that today are in flux, increasingly multiple, debatable, and open for reconsideration. Thus, in his interview with Jon Stewart, Bill Moyers asks if *The Daily Show* is "an old form of comedy" or a "new kind of journalism" (PBS, 2003). The suspicion here is that it is both—something of the former and much of the latter. Seen against a backdrop of declining audiences, boundary contestation, and textual exploration (e.g., Bishop, 2004), *The Daily Show* can be understood as an experiment in the journalistic, one that this study will argue has much to teach us about the possibilities of political journalism in the twenty-first century. [...]

This is not simply the move toward "infotainment," although the fundamental blurring of news and entertainment—a conflation that cuts both ways—certainly is a constituent element. Rather, it is a more profound phenomenon of *discursive integration,* a way of speaking about, understanding, and acting within the world defined by the permeability of form and the fluidity of content. Discourses of news, politics, entertainment, and marketing have grown deeply inseparable; the languages and practices of each have lost their distinctiveness and are being melded into previously unimagined combinations. Although some may see this as a dangerous turn in the realm of political communication, it also can be seen as a rethinking of discursive styles and standards that may be opening spaces for significant innovation.

## THE DAILY SHOW

*The Daily Show* is the epitome of such discursively integrated media. Its hybrid nature is evident from its opening moments. The show begins each night with a full-screen graphic of the date, an American flag, and the globe, accompanied by a music track serious in tone and suggestive of a network newscast. An unseen announcer then pronounces the date, followed by "From Comedy Central's world news headquarters in New York, this is *The Daily Show with Jon Stewart.*" The initial emphasis on the date borrows a technique from broadcast journalism that seeks textual authority through a claim to immediacy. The phrase "world news headquarters in New York" similarly contains obvious connotations, invoking the power and prestige of the New York–based national news. The connotation, however, quickly is complicated as the graphic gives way to a live camera shot that swings through the studio, a technique of fast motion more common to entertainment than to news. At the same time, the audio cuts to a decidedly more upbeat, rock-and-roll soundtrack, while the live studio audience cheers in the background.

From the start, then, the program interweaves at least two levels of discourse, borrowing equally from traditions of authoritative nightly news and the entertainment talk show. Although the opening may suggest that discourse of entertainment supersedes a discourse of news, the two are placed not in binary opposition, but in complementary arrangements. The show functions as *both* entertainment *and* news, simultaneously pop culture and public affairs. Its format is built on the familiar structure of late-night talk shows such as Leno's *Tonight Show* and Letterman's *Late Show,* which move from the host's introductory monologue to sketch comedy and conclude with the desk-and-couch interviews with noted personalities (see Timberg, 2002). *The Daily Show* reworks each of these production elements, however, blending humor with a serious concern for current events in ways that render the program difficult to pigeonhole. Its hybrid combinations defy simple generic taxonomies as well as reductionist labels such as "fake news." It undoubtedly is comedy—often entertaining and at times absurd—but it is also an informative examination of politics and media practices, as well as a forum for the discussion of substantive public affairs. This study now turns to an examination of each of these specific elements, arguing that *The Daily Show* invites us to reconsider journalistic conventions in an age of media multiplicity and discursive integration.

## INTERROGATING POWER

The first of the program's three major content elements—the satire news update—represents a significant development in the genre of comedic news, building on the introductory monologue common to the late-night talk show since the 1950s. Still readily apparent on shows such as Letterman and Leno, the host makes brief references to current events to set up a punch line. Although the politically oriented one-liner uses the news for its inspiration, its focus usually falls on the personal foibles and character flaws of the primary political actors (Niven et al., 2003). Thus, the late-night joke appears to contain little relevance to the sphere of policy debate, what Bennett and Entman (2001) refer to as the *political* public sphere. *The Daily Show*'s approach also can be traced to the more complex style of fake news offered by *Saturday Night Live*'s "Weekend Update" segment, a feature on that program from its inception in the mid-1970s. There, one of the cast members plays the role of news anchor, seated at what appears to be a traditional television news set. The segment complicates the late-night monologue with the addition of visual elements, usually suggestive photographs or newspaper headlines placed in an over-the-shoulder graphic. The "anchor" offers a brief explanation of the image and then the punch line. Again, like the one-liners of late-night talk, the focus of the "Weekend Update" joke rarely falls on substantive political issues and often turns to the surreal to find its humor. [...]

The Daily Show, however, while borrowing from these styles of "fake news," offers a considerable advancement over them, more deeply melding approaches of news and comedy. To the standard comedic style, *The Daily Show* adds more elements common to news, including video clips, soundbites, and [...] complete reporter packages. The satire news segment does at times focus on the trivial aspects of the political domain, but it more often tackles national and global issues of unquestioned significance. During the shows examined here, recurrent topics included American foreign policy and the Bush administration's war on terrorism, the occupation of Iraq and the Abu Ghraib torture scandal, the search for weapons of mass destruction and the failure of prewar intelligence, and the presidential election campaigns of both candidates, including the party conventions and debates. In discussing such topics, *The Daily Show* forsakes the "now this" model, often providing single-issue coverage for as long as eight minutes. The segment also places its topics in wider contexts, often providing background information and drawing historical linkages of the sort uncommon to television news.

Soundbites from the primary political actors provide the grist of the segment. Here the format is reminiscent of an earlier style of network news built around soundbites from lawmakers and other political actors (Baym, 2004). President Bush and his administration earn the main focus of the segment, but considerable attention also is paid to Senate hearings, congressional debate, and press conferences with various governmental figures. This material is culled from CSPAN, 24-hour cable news, and other readily available sources. The visuals are complemented with information gained from major newspapers such as the *New York Times, USA Today,* and the *Wall Street Journal.*

The Daily Show thus is enabled by the multiplicity and availability of news and information in a hyper-mediated era. Stewart acknowledges the point during the show's coverage of CIA Director George Tenet's resignation in early June [2004]: "Huge breaking news story," Stewart begins, "we're gonna get right to it, because you know when news breaks . . . we may not be the first people on the scene, but we've got televisions, we know what's going on" (6/3/04). Stewart's line appears on the surface to be self-deprecating humor, a reminder that the show refuses to take itself seriously. It also is significant commentary, however, on the volume of informational resources now publicly available and the decreasing role traditional news sources play in filtering the flow of information. It is possible, *The Daily Show* suggests, to construct a newscast simply by mining the raw material available on the average cable television system.

Drawing on live broadcast coverage of public statements and government proceedings, the content of *The Daily Show* resembles much of the mainstream news media. Empowered by the title of "fake news," however, *The Daily Show* routinely violates journalistic conventions in important ways. For one, while it covers the same raw material as does the mainstream news, its choices of soundbites turn contemporary conventions on their head. The unwritten rules of journalism define a good quote as a coherent statement of policy or attitude, ideally containing emotion or character and completed neatly in about eight or twelve seconds. Professional journalists are trained to ignore long, rambling verbal presentations; quotes with poor grammar or misstatements; and soundbites with long pauses or any significant absence of verbal content. In the effort to package eight seconds of speech, that which does not conform to conventional expectations is left on the proverbial cutting room floor. *The Daily Show,* however, mines those outtakes for a wealth of informative content.

Consider the coverage of Bush's statement following Tenet's resignation. ABC's *World News Tonight* offered the following soundbite from the president: "I told him I'm sorry he's leaving. He's done a superb job on behalf of the American people" (6/3/04). On the CBS *Evening News,* the only soundbite from Bush showed him proclaiming "He's strong, he's resolute, and I will miss him" (6/3/04). Here, however, is part of *The Daily Show*'s selection:

**Bush:** *George Tenet is uh . . . is . . . a . . . the kind of public service, uh, servant, you like to work with. He has been a, a, um . . . a strong and able leader at the agency. He's been a, uh . . . he's been a strong leader in the war on terror. (6/3/04)*

In their coverage of Bush's statement, the network newscasts hold to standard conventions, and in so doing reduce Bush's sloppy, pause-saturated speech to a tightly constructed set of words that suggest clarity of thought and purpose. *The Daily Show,* however, reveals a different aspect of Bush's statement, one that calls into question his focus and perhaps his sincerity. Both versions are "accurate" in the strict sense of the word, but each achieves a markedly different textual effect.

In rejecting the standard conventions of quote selection, *The Daily Show* achieves a critical distance that cannot be said of the networks. Mainstream journalism's reliance on predictable conventions can render it susceptible to manipulation by the professional speech writers and media handlers who seed public information with prescripted soundbites and spin (Jones, 1995; Underwood, 2001). The Bush administration, especially, has been remarkably adept at playing to journalistic conventions in ways that limit inquiry and encourage the news media to amplify the administration's rhetoric without critical challenge (Fritz et al., 2004). As "fake news," however, *The Daily Show* is not beholden to conventions that arguably have outlived their usefulness. *The Daily Show*'s refusal to abide by standard practices may offer a measure of resistance to manipulation, a counterbalance to the mutual embrace between press and politics.

A second convention *The Daily Show* freely rejects is the mainstream news media's insistence, at least in name, on a dispassionate observation that elides the journalist's subjectivity. If the insistence on objectivity too easily can become amplification, *The Daily Show* instead engages in subjective interrogation. Consider the treatment of the Bush statement quoted above. Here is how it appeared on air:

**Bush:** *George Tenet is uh . . . is . . . a . . .*
**Stewart:** *Um, a convenient fall guy . . . um . . . liability to our intelligence operation.*
**Bush:** *the kind of public service, uh, servant, you like to work with.*
**Stewart:** *I was gonna say that, that was on the tip of my tongue.*
**Bush:** *He has been, a, a, um . . . a . . .*
**Stewart:** *Uh, uh, an albatross around the neck of your administration, an albatross.*
**Bush:** *a strong and able leader at the agency. He's been a, uh . . . he's been a . . .*
**Stewart:** *He's been around too long. No, that's not it.*
**Bush:** *been a strong leader in the war on terror.*
**Stewart:** *No, that's not it. It's right here, I don't know what it is . . .*

The humor lies in Stewart's interruptions, in his willingness to read Bush's statement against the grain and confront it with his own reactions and responses. Stewart's presentation is explicitly situated; he speaks with the voice, as Douglas (2003) has noted, of the "outraged individual who, comparing official pronouncements with his own basic common sense, simply cannot believe what he—and all of us—are expected to swallow." This kind of juxtaposition, between official pronouncements and Stewart's version of common sense, is the primary strategy of *The Daily Show*'s news updates. Juxtaposition also is a basic principle of the genre of political satire, which pits the "presumptions and pretensions of the politicians" against the "intuitions and instincts of the commonplace" (Street, 2001, p. 69). Like all satire, *The Daily Show* is *dialogic* in the Bakhtinian sense, the playing of multiple voices against each other in a discursive exchange that forces the original statement into revealing contexts (see Griffin, 1994).

One can see the strategy of dialogic confrontation in a lengthy but revealing example from the July 13 program. The day after the Senate had released its report documenting the breakdown in the prewar intelligence, Bush gave a thirty-two-minute speech addressing the war in Iraq in which, as Stewart notes, he "used a particular phrase eight times." This exchange then follows:

> **Bush:** *Because America and our coalition helped to end the violent regime of Saddam Hussein, and because we're helping to raise a peaceful democracy in its place, the American people are safer.*
>
> **Stewart:** *[surprised and enthusiastic] Oh! Oh good! We're, we're, we're safer! That's why we did this, because America is safer! [changes tone] Granted, some have said that Iraq now is a bigger breeding ground for anti-American groups, and even Tom Ridge has said that Al-Qaida plans on attacking us before the election, uh, so, some might think we're... less safe... but...*
>
> **Bush:** *The American people are safer.*
>
> **Stewart:** *Oh! So, uh, well he said it again! That was his second time. So, you know, the thing is, even Bush's own State Department released a report that, once that report was de-f\*\*\*ed up, it said that there were more terrorist attacks last year than at almost any point since it's been tracked.*

At this point, a clock superimposed on the screen while Bush is talking tracks the time from which his soundbites were drawn.

> **Bush:** *[11:37 a.m.] And the American people are safer.*
>
> **Stewart:** *[hanging head] Oh, oh, OK. But let me ask you this, just for schnicks between the two of us... what criteria are you using to prove that? I mean what evidence is there other than you saying it?*
>
> **Bush:** *[11:39] The American people are safer.*

**Bush:** *[11:43] And the American people are safer.*

**Bush:** *[11:45] The American people are safer.*

**Bush:** *[11:47] And the American people . . . are safer.*

**Stewart:** *[After a moment of silence] So basically, what it comes down to is this, the Bush administration's strategy to fight terrorism is . . . repetition. [pause] You know what, give us one final "America is safer," and this time, give it a flourish that says "stop questioning me about any of this."*

**Bush:** *[11:50, with his finger pointing] And America and the world are safer.*

**Stewart:** *Boom! Nicely done.*

The treatment of Bush's speech functions on multiple levels. By emphasizing his *rhetorical* strategy of repetition, it lays bare Bush's clear attempt to plant the soundbite "the American people are safer" in that day's news. At the same time, Bush's one-sided, singular-voiced presentation is reworked into dialogue ("let me ask you this, just for schnicks between the two of us"), his certainty forced into critical exchange. Stewart speaks as interlocutor, confronting the president with counterargument and suggesting he lacks both the factual evidence and logical criteria to support his claim. Here Stewart engages in *undermining* humor (Paletz, 2002, p. 13), challenging not just the legitimacy of the president's statement but the wider authority upon which it relies. Finally, Stewart shifts to the voice of choreographer ("this time, give it a flourish") to make the point that Bush's speech is more theatrical spectacle than it is reasoned argument, designed ultimately to shut down avenues of inquiry ("stop questioning me") rather than inform the public.

In contrast to *The Daily Show*'s dialogue, conventional news is *monologic,* pretending to "possess a ready-made truth" (Griffin, 1994, p. 42). Satire instead represents a searching for truth through the process of dialogical interaction. Unlike traditional news, which claims an epistemological certainty, satire is a discourse of *inquiry,* a rhetoric of challenge that seeks through the asking of unanswered questions to clarify the underlying morality of a situation. The show's coverage of the Iraqi prisoner abuse scandal is illustrative here. Says Stewart on the May 6 program, the revelation of torture is "difficult for all of us to wrap our heads around. Clearly this is a time for our defense secretary to speak clearly and honestly to the American people about these egregious instances of torture." A soundbite from Donald Rumsfeld follows:

**Rumsfeld:** *Uh, I think that . . . uh [scratches his head] . . . I'm not a lawyer, my impression is that what has been charged thus far is abuse, which I believe, technically, is different from torture [audience groans], and therefore I'm not gonna address the torture word.*

**Stewart:** *I'm also not a lawyer, so I don't know, technically, if you're* human, *but as a fake news person, I can tell you, what we've been reading about in the newspapers, the pictures we've been seeing . . . it's f\*\*\*ing torture.*

Stewart's response is distinctly subjective ("*I* can tell you"), an approach he suggests he is allowed to pursue because he is not a journalist, but a "fake news person." Conventions of objectivity would disallow comment here: Traditional journalists can reiterate Rumsfeld's troubling quote in hopes it will "speak for itself," but they cannot engage with it as does Stewart. He uses satire to challenge it with a statement of morality, suggesting that both the incidences of torture and Rumsfeld's obfuscation, his refusal to speak "honestly and clearly," are fundamental violations of human decency.

In an age of disconnect between words and actions, *The Daily Show* uses satire to hold the leadership accountable to both. The June 21 program covers the 9/11 Commission report that the Bush administration was wrong in its insistence on a connection between Iraq and Al-Qaida, which in the absence of weapons of mass destruction became the primary justification for the invasion of Iraq. We see a recent clip of a CNBC interview with Vice President Cheney, who aggressively insists, much to the interviewer's surprise, that he "absolutely never said" that the alleged meeting between 9/11 hijacker Mohammed Atta and an agent of the Iraqi government had been "pretty well confirmed." From there we return to Stewart, who merely scratches his chin in puzzlement. A replay immediately follows of Cheney on NBC's *Meet the Press* in which he says, word for word, that the meeting had been "pretty well confirmed." With Cheney's blatant lie thus exposed, Stewart follows simply by saying "Mr. Vice President, your pants are on fire."

*The Daily Show*'s satire news can be understood as a discourse of inquiry that seeks to penetrate a political communication system Stewart himself suggests has become "purposefully obtuse" (Schlosser, 2003). In an age in which few power holders are willing to speak clearly and honestly, *The Daily Show* uses humor as the license to confront political dissembling and misinformation and to demand a measure of accountability. In so doing, the program is attempting to revive a spirit of critical inquiry and of the press as an agent of public interrogation that largely has been abdicated by the post–September 11 news media. In the frantic competition for ratings, in the fear of appearing "unpatriotic," and in the professional need to avoid alienation from the halls of power, a journalism of supervision and accountability has been replaced by one of conformity and complicity. As Griffin (1994) argues, it is in such times that satire most readily appears:

> It is the limitation on free inquiry and dissent that provokes one to irony—and to satire. If open challenge to orthodoxy is freely permitted, then writers will take the most direct route and debate the ideas and characters of political leaders openly in newspapers, protected by guarantees of free speech. It is difficult, or unnecessary, to satirize our political leaders when the newspapers are filled with open attacks on their integrity and intelligence. But if open challenge is not permitted, writers will turn to irony, indirection, innuendo, allegory, fable—to the fictions of satire. (p. 139)

With its discourse of inquiry, *The Daily Show* thus may be better understood not as "fake news," but as a new form of critical journalism, one which uses satire to achieve that which the mainstream press is no longer willing to pursue.

## REINVENTING POLITICAL JOURNALISM

*The Daily Show* represents an important experiment in journalism, one that contains much significance for the ongoing redefinition of news. Unquestionably, its primary approach is comedy, and much of the show's content is light and, at times, vacuous. Often, however, the silly is interwoven with the serious, resulting in an innovative and potentially powerful form of public information. The blending of news and satire confronts a system of political communication that largely has degenerated into soundbites and spin with critical inquiry. The use of parody unmasks the artifice in much contemporary news practices, while the interview segment endorses and enacts a deliberative model of democracy based on civility of exchange, complexity of argument, and the goal of mutual understanding. Lying just beneath or perhaps imbricated within the laughter is a quite serious demand for fact, accountability, and reason in political discourse.

Both the increasing commercial success and the political significance of *The Daily Show* may be due to its hybrid form, its willingness to blend once-distinct discourses into previously unimagined combinations. Comedy provides its initial appeal; humor assembles the audience. In an age when young people increasingly are abandoning sources of traditional news, *The Daily Show* attracts many of them with its initial discourse of entertainment. But comedy also provides the method to engage in serious political criticism; the label of "fake news" enables *The Daily Show* to say that which the traditional journalist cannot. So too does categorization as comedy grant it immunity from accusations that it violates journalistic standards. Never claiming to be news, it can hardly be charged with being illegitimate journalism, either by the political structure it interrogates or the news media it threatens.

*The Daily Show* is indeed a threat to the mainstream news media. While the latter have responded to the continual hemorrhaging of audiences with various versions of news lite, happy talk, and political punditry, *The Daily Show* pursues a different path. In a time when most media have turned to shallow infotainment to try to ensure ratings points, *The Daily Show* offers instead a version of *news that entertains.* Entertainment here must be understood as a doubly articulated concept. On one hand, "to entertain" means to interest, to amuse, to give one pleasure. It can also mean, however, to engage with and to consider. *The Daily Show* suggests that that which gives pleasure need not necessarily divert and distract from significant issues. The mainstream news media, however, have been unwilling or unable to learn this lesson. They have tried at times to incorporate the comedy—consider former *Daily Show* comedian Mo Rocca's inane contribution to CNN's convention coverage—but have so far failed to grasp the deeper insight that in an age of discursive integration, it is possible to be entertaining in the sense of both amusement and serious thought, and that each one may have the ability to embrace the other.

It may be possible for a television newscast to be both profitable and substantive, an argument Stewart himself has made. "For some reason, people think that solid, good, in-depth all equals dull, low ratings, low profitability," he argues. "I don't think that's the case. I think you can make really exciting, interesting television news that could become the medium of record for reasonable, moderate people" (Schlosser, 2003). It is indeed possible, and as news audiences increasingly come of age in a discursively integrated world, it may be absolutely necessary. Graber (2001) has argued that political news must begin to meet the needs of "21st-century Americans" who generally find "the abominable quality of the content and presentation of much of the televised news...neither salient nor attractive" (pp. 445–446). The perceived political apathy of younger Americans, she argues, may be due less to their own intellectual shortcomings than to the poor quality and apparent irrelevance of contemporary broadcast news. The increasing success of *The Daily Show* gives weight to that argument.

The suggestion here is not that *The Daily Show* itself should become *the* news of record, the twenty-first-century, discursively integrated version of Walter Cronkite's *CBS Evening News.* The program is a product of a specific historical moment, fueled both by the post–September 11 dissuasion of open inquiry and the particular talents of its current host. Whether its specific approach can withstand the test of time certainly remains to be seen. The greater significance of *The Daily Show,* however, lies in its willingness to experiment, in its opening of a door to a world of discursive possibilities. *The Daily Show* thus offers a lesson in the possible to which all students of journalism, political communication, and public discourse would be wise to pay attention.

## References

Baym, G. (2004). Packaging reality: Structures of form in U.S. network news coverage of Watergate and the Clinton impeachment. *Journalism, 5,* 279–299.

Bennett, W. L., & Entman, R. M. (2001). *Mediated politics: Communication in the future of democracy.* New York: Cambridge University Press.

Bishop, R. (2004). The accidental journalist: Shifting professional boundaries in the wake of Leonardo DiCaprio's interview with former President Clinton. *Journalism Studies, 5,* 31–43.

Bohman, J., & Rehg, W. (1997). *Deliberative democracy: Essays on reason and politics.* Cambridge, MA: MIT Press.

CBC. (2004, February 10). *CBC News: Disclosure.* Retrieved April 8, 2004, from http://www.cbc.ca/disclosure/archives/040210_pop/stewart.html

Douglas, S. (2003, May 5). *Daily Show* does Bush. *The Nation.* Retrieved April 8, 2004, from http://www.thenation.com/doc.mhtml%3Fi=20030505&s=Douglas

Fritz, B., Keefer, B., & Nyhan, B. (2004). *All the president's spin: George W. Bush, the media, and the truth.* New York: Touchstone.

Gay, V. (2004, January 19). Not necessarily the news: Meet the players who will influence coverage of the 2004 campaign. You might be surprised. *Newsday,* p. B6.

Graber, D. (2001). Adapting political news to the needs of twenty-first century Americans. In W. L. Bennett & R. M. Entman (Eds.), *Mediated politics: Communication in the future of democracy* (pp. 433–452). New York: Cambridge University Press.

Griffin, D. (1994). *Satire: A critical reintroduction.* Lexington: The University Press of Kentucky.

Hutcheson, J., Domke, D., Billeaudeaux, A., & Garland, P. (2004). U.S. national identity, political elites, and a patriotic press following September 11. *Political Communication, 21,* 27–51.

Jones, N. (1995). *Soundbites and spin doctors.* London: Cassell.

Kovach, B., & Rosenstiel, T. (1999). *Warp speed: America in the age of mixed media.* New York: Century Foundation Press.

National Annenberg Election Survey. (2004). Daily Show viewers knowledgeable about presidential campaign. Retrieved February 24, 2005, from http://www.annenbergpublicpolicycenter.org/naes/2004_03_late-night-knowledge-2_9-21_pr.pdf

Niven, D. S., Lichter, R., & Amundson, D. (2003). The political content of late night comedy. *Press/Politics, 8,* 118–133.

Paletz, D. (2002). *The media in American politics: Contents and consequences.* New York: Longman.

PBS. (2003, July 11). *NOW with Bill Moyers.* Retrieved April 8, 2004, from http://www.pbs.org/now/transcript/transcript_stewart.html

Schlosser, E. (2003). The kids are alright. *Columbia Journalism Review, 41,* 27–30.

Street, J. (2001). *Mass media, politics, and democracy.* London: Palgrave.

Timberg, B. M. (2002). *Television talk: A history of the TV talk show.* Austin: University of Texas Press.

Underwood, D. (2001). Reporting and the push for market-oriented journalism: Media organizations as business. In W. L. Bennett & R. M. Entman (Eds.), *Mediated politics: Communication in the future of democracy* (pp. 99–116). New York: Cambridge University Press.

## Working with the Text

1. How would you summarize Baym's article for a friend? That is, if someone asked you, "What does he think is significant about *The Daily Show*?" how would you answer?

2. Baym writes, "From the start, then, the program interweaves at least two levels of discourse, borrowing equally from traditions of authoritative nightly news and the entertainment talk show," an example of what he calls "discursive integration" in *The Daily Show.* Work in groups to explore what Baym means by "discursive integration" and test your understanding by locating examples that you think illustrate

the idea of "discursive integration" in *The Daily Show* episodes that you watched. Present your findings to the class and see what examples other groups come up with as a way of understanding and analyzing Baym's point.

3. Baym points out that rather than just showing brief uninterrupted video clips of politicians and other public officials in the way that conventional newscasts do, *The Daily Show* features extended video segments that include pauses and corrections. The host Jon Stewart often engages in a satirical conversation with the clips, adding his own commentary or asking questions that the news clips seem to answer. Baym calls this a "dialogic" presentation of the news, something he opposes to the "monologic" style of conventional newscasts. Why does Baym feel that this dialogic style of *The Daily Show* is more effective in promoting a critical perspective on the news? How does he make you look at *The Daily Show*'s use of video clips in new ways?

4. At the end of his article, Baym argues that *The Daily Show* "represents an important experiment in journalism," but one that he thinks most television news programs are failing to learn. What does Baym see as most valuable or innovative about *The Daily Show* experiment? What aspects of *The Daily Show* approach to news do you think would be effective in reversing the widespread dissatisfaction many younger viewers have with traditional newscasts?

## "Introduction to Participatory Journalism"
### Shayne Bowman and Chris Willis

*On the evening of March 3, 1991, a police chase of a speeding motorist in Southern California ended in a physical confrontation between the driver of the car and several police officers. At the end, the driver, Rodney King, lay on the ground after being repeatedly struck by metal police batons. Across the street, a man named George Holliday was awakened by the noise and looked out his apartment window. Holliday had recently acquired a home video camera, and as the confrontation started, he began taping.*

*The resulting video footage was soon broadcast around the world, and Rodney King became a household name. Four of the officers involved in the beating that night were brought up on charges that they had violated the civil rights of King, an African American. When an all-white jury acquitted the four officers, all of whom were also white, Los Angeles experienced its worst civil disturbance—described as a riot by some, an uprising or rebellion by others—since the summer of 1965.*

MAR. 3 1991

*While the Rodney King incident, as it was eventually known, became a focal point for discussions of race relations and the use of police force, it likewise was seen as a turning point in the history of journalism resulting from easily available home video technology. The work of amateur photographers has always formed part of our chronicle of important news events; the most well-known perhaps is the home movie footage shot by Abraham Zapruder of the assassination of President John F. Kennedy in 1963. The last thirty years, however, has seen an explosion in the number of people who own video and digital cameras. The fact that such cameras require no film to be developed and, in the case of digital technology, produce images that can be easily duplicated and transmitted means that we are almost constantly surrounded by photographers, especially now that many cell phones come with the ability to take digital images. As a result, incidents such as the 9/11 attacks were recorded by dozens of people, portable phones famously relayed images of panic and terror from inside the London subway bombings, and television networks ran cell phone videos recorded by students at Virginia Tech on the scene of the tragic shooting there. It has now become almost a reflex for people to get out their cellphone cameras as soon as something unusual or unexpected seems to be happening.*

*In "Introduction to Participatory Journalism" taken from their longer report,* We Media: How Audiences Are Shaping the Future of News and Information, *former reporters and current media consultants Shayne Bowman and Chris Willis describe what they see as a new era in the history of news reporting. Nonprofessional "citizen journalists" are challenging the authority and monopoly of mainstream news media. In this introduction, they discuss the pros and cons of participatory journalism and how this trend toward a more democratized newsgathering culture will redefine what we think of as news and how we gather information about the world around us.*

## Before You Read

1. What makes you and your friends get out a camera? Locate people you know (including yourself) who regularly carry some sort of camera with them every day, such as a picture-taking cell phone. Discuss how they most typically use their cameras. What kind of pictures do they take most often? You might also ask them to inventory what is on their cell phones currently. Have any of them taken pictures of events that you might consider potentially newsworthy, from a traffic accident to a local arts event to a high school football game? If a major news event were to

occur, how likely would they or you be to think of getting out a camera?

2. Make a list of news events in which amateur or eyewitness video played a significant role and write about what, if any, difference you think it makes to view these eyewitness accounts as opposed to more professional reporting. What makes amateur reporting most compelling to you? What concerns does it raise?

3. Where do you get your news? When you hear about something happening and you want to know more, where are you most likely to turn? Make a list of your typical "newsgathering" behavior. Talk with others about how they get their news, and compare your experiences.

In his 1995 book *Being Digital,* Nicholas Negroponte predicted that in the future, online news would give readers the ability to choose only the topics and sources that interested them.

"The Daily Me," as Negroponte called it, worried many guardians of traditional journalism. To actively allow a reader to narrow the scope of coverage, observed some, could undermine the "philosophical underpinnings of traditional media."

The vision that seemed cutting edge and worrisome eight years ago seems to have come partly true. The *Wall Street Journal,* MSNBC.com, the *Washington Post* and CNN, to name a few, all offer readers some degree of personalization on the front pages of their sites.

Millions of Yahoo! members customize their MyYahoo personal news portal with the same news wire reports that editors use in daily newspapers across the globe. Google's news page uses a computer algorithm to select headlines from thousands of news sites—creating a global newsstand, of sorts.

And media outlets from Fox News and the Drudge Report to individual weblogs offer the kind of opinionated slant to the news that Negroponte envisioned.

But is the future of online news simply a continued extrapolation of this trend—news à la carte? Does greater personalization necessarily mean greater understanding for a democracy?

In the view of futurist and author Watts Wacker, the question is not about greater personalization but about greater perspectives. According to Wacker, the world is moving faster than people can keep up with it. As a result, there are fewer common cultural references that can be agreed upon. Ideas, styles, products, and mores accelerate their way from the fringe to the mainstream with increasing speed.

To combat the confusion, consumers are seeking more perspectives, Wacker says. They research an automobile for purchase by spending time online and reading both professional and amateur reviews alike.

But what are they doing when it comes to news? And what will they be doing in the future?

To understand that, Wacker advises, you must seek out people from the future today and study them. How do you find people from the future? Locate early adopters—people who are using and appropriating technology in new ways.

In South Korea, it looks like one future of online news has arrived a few years early.

OhmyNews.com is the most influential online news site in that country, attracting an estimated 2 million readers a day. What's unusual about OhmyNews .com is that readers not only can pick and choose the news they want to read— they also write it.

With the help of more than 26,000 registered citizen journalists, this collaborative online newspaper has emerged as a direct challenge to established media outlets in just four years.

Unlike its competitors, OhmyNews has embraced the speed, responsiveness, and community-oriented nature of the Web.

Now, it appears, the vision of "The Daily Me" is being replaced by the idea of "The Daily We."

## THE RISE OF "WE MEDIA"

The venerable profession of journalism finds itself at a rare moment in history where, for the first time, its hegemony as gatekeeper of the news is threatened by not just new technology and competitors but, potentially, by the audience it serves. Armed with easy-to-use Web publishing tools, always-on connections, and increasingly powerful mobile devices, the online audience has the means to become an active participant in the creation and dissemination of news and information. And it's doing just that on the Internet.

- According to the Pew Internet Project, the terrorist attacks of Sept. 11, 2001, generated the most traffic to the traditional news sites in the history of the Web. Many large news sites buckled under the immense demand and people turned to email, weblogs, and forums "as conduits for information, commentary, and action related to 9/11 events." The response on the Internet gave rise to a new proliferation of "do-it-yourself journalism." Everything from eyewitness accounts and photo galleries to commentary and personal storytelling emerged to help people collectively grasp the confusion, anger, and loss felt in the wake of the tragedy.
- During the first few days of the war in Iraq, Pew found that 17 percent of online Americans used the Internet as their principal source of

information about the war, a level more than five times greater than those who got their news online immediately after the Sept. 11 terrorist attacks (3 percent). The report also noted that "weblogs (were) gaining a following among a small number of Internet users (4 percent)."

- Immediately after the Columbia shuttle disaster, news and government organizations, in particular the *Dallas Morning News* and NASA, called upon the public to submit eyewitness accounts and photographs that might lead to clues to the cause of the spacecraft's disintegration.

Cell phone pictures of the July 2005 London Underground bombings taken by passengers and relayed to news media represent one dramatic form of participatory journalism.

- ABCNews.com's *The Note* covered 2004 political candidates and [gave] each an individual weblog to comment back on what was reported. In addition, presidential candidate Howard Dean guest-blogged on Larry Lessig's weblog for a week in July 2003. (A future president of the United States might be chosen not only on his or her merits, charisma, experience, or voting record but on the basis of how well he or she blogs.)
- College coaches, players, and sports media outlets keep constant vigil on numerous fan forum sites, which have been credited with everything from breaking and making news to rumor-mongering. "You can't go anywhere or do anything and expect not to be seen, because everyone is a reporter now," says Steve Patterson, who operates ugasports.com a website devoted to University of Georgia sports.
- Before the Iraq war, the BBC knew it couldn't possibly deploy enough photojournalists to cover the millions of people worldwide who marched in anti-war demonstrations. Reaching out to its audience, the BBC News asked readers to send in images taken with digital cameras and cell phones with built-in cameras, and it published the best ones on its website.

## WEBLOGS COME OF AGE

The Internet, as a medium for news, is maturing. With every major news event, online media evolve. And while news sites have become more responsive and better able to handle the growing demands of readers and viewers, online communities and personal news and information sites are participating in an increasingly diverse and important role that, until recently, has operated without significant notice from mainstream media.

While there are many ways that the audience is now participating in the journalistic process, [...] weblogs have received the most attention from mainstream media in the past year.

Weblogs, or blogs as they are commonly known, are the most active and surprising form of this participation. These personal publishing systems have given rise to a phenomenon that shows the markings of a revolution—giving anyone with the right talent and energy the ability to be heard far and wide on the Web.

Weblogs are frequently updated online journals, with reverse-chronological entries and numerous links, that provide up-to-the-minute takes on the writer's life, the news, or on a specific subject of interest. Often riddled with opinionated commentary, they can be personally revealing (such as a college student's ruminations on dorm life) or straightforward and fairly objective. [...]

The growth of weblogs has been largely fueled by greater access to bandwidth and low-cost, often free software. These simple easy-to-use tools have enabled new kinds of collaboration unrestricted by time or geography. The result is an advance of new social patterns and means for self-expression. Blog-like communities like Slashdot.org have allowed a multitude of voices to participate while managing a social order and providing a useful filter on discussion.

Weblogs have expanded their influence by attracting larger circles of readers while at the same time appealing to more targeted audiences. "Blogs are in some ways a new form of journalism, open to anyone who can establish and maintain a website, and they have exploded in the past year," writes Walter Mossberg, technology columnist for the *Wall Street Journal.*

"The good thing about them is that they introduce fresh voices into the national discourse on various topics, and help build communities of interest through their collections of links. For instance, bloggers are credited with helping to get the mainstream news media interested in the racially insensitive remarks by Sen. Trent Lott (R.-Miss.) that led to his resignation as Senate majority leader."

Mossberg's description of weblogs as a new kind of journalism might trouble established, traditionally trained journalists. But it is a journalism of a different sort, one not tightly confined by the traditions and standards adhered to by the traditional profession.

These acts of citizen engaging in journalism are not just limited to weblogs. They can be found in newsgroups, forums, chat rooms, collaborative publishing systems, and peer-to-peer applications like instant messaging. As new forms of participation have emerged through new technologies, many have struggled to name them. As a default, the name is usually borrowed from the enabling technology (i.e., weblogging, forums, and usenets).

The term we use—*participatory journalism*—is meant to describe the content and the intent of online communication that often occurs in collaborative and social media. Here's the working definition that we have adopted:

> **Participatory journalism:** The act of a citizen, or group of citizens, playing an active role in the process of collecting, reporting, analyzing, and disseminating news and information. The intent of this participation is to provide independent, reliable, accurate, wide-ranging, and relevant information that a democracy requires.

Participatory journalism is a bottom-up, emergent phenomenon in which there is little or no editorial oversight or formal journalistic workflow dictating the decisions of a staff. Instead, it is the result of many simultaneous, distributed conversations that either blossom or quickly atrophy in the Web's social network.

While the explosion of weblogs is a recent phenomenon, the idea of tapping into your audience for new perspectives or turning readers into reporters or commentators is not. Many news organizations have a long history of tapping into their communities and experimenting with turning readers into reporters or commentators. In the early 1990s, newspapers experimented with the idea of civic journalism, which sought participation from readers and communities in the form of focus groups, polls, and reaction to daily news stories. Most of these early projects centered around election coverage. Later, newspapers sought to involve communities in major deliberations on public problems such as race, development, and crime.

According to a report from the Pew Center for Civic Journalism, at least 20 percent of the 1,500 daily U.S. newspapers practiced some form of civic journalism between 1994 and 2001. Nearly all said it had a positive effect on the community.

Civic journalism has a somewhat controversial reputation, and not everyone is convinced of its benefits. While civic journalism actively tries to encourage participation, the news organization maintains a high degree of control by setting the agenda, choosing the participants, and moderating the conversation. Some feel that civic journalism is often too broad, focusing on large issues such as crime and politics, and not highly responsive to the day-to-day needs of the audience.

Yet, the seed from which civic journalism grows is dialogue and conversation. Similarly, a defining characteristic of participatory journalism is conversation. However, there is no central news organization controlling the exchange of information. Conversation is the mechanism that turns the tables on the traditional roles of journalism and creates a dynamic, egalitarian give-and-take ethic.

The fluidity of this approach puts more emphasis on the publishing of information rather than the filtering. Conversations happen in the community for all to see. In contrast, traditional news organizations are set up to filter information before they publish it. It might be collaborative among the editors and reporters, but the debates are not open to public scrutiny or involvement.

John Seely Brown, chief scientist of Xerox Corp., further elaborates on participatory journalism in the book *The Elements of Journalism*: "In an era when anyone can be a reporter or commentator on the Web, 'you move to a two-way journalism.' The journalist becomes a 'forum leader,' or a mediator rather than simply a teacher or lecturer. The audience becomes not consumers, but 'prosumers,' a hybrid of consumer and producer."

Seely Brown's description suggests a symbiotic relationship, which we are already seeing. But participatory journalism does not show evidence of needing a classically trained "journalist" to be the mediator or facilitator. Plenty of weblogs, forums, and online communities appear to function effectively without one.

## Broadcast: Top-down news
Model also called transmit, push. Characterized by media organization control. All news is filtered through organization before getting to audience.

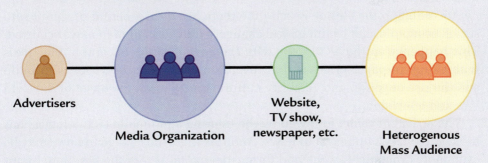

Advertisers

Media Organization

Website, TV show, newspaper, etc.

Heterogenous Mass Audience

## Intercast: Bottom-up news
Model also called peer-to-peer, social network. Participants are peers and have ability to change roles. News is often unfiltered by a mediator before getting to its audience.

Advertisers

Editors

Reporters

Community

Reporters

Audience

Publisher

Community

This raises some important questions: If participatory journalism has risen without the direct help of trained journalists or news industry initiatives, what role will mainstream media play? And are mainstream media willing to relinquish some control and actively collaborate with their audiences? Or will an informed and empowered consumer begin to frame the news agenda from the grassroots? And, will journalism's values endure?

## JOURNALISM AT A CROSSROADS

In his 1996 book *News Values,* former *Chicago Tribune* publisher Jack Fuller summed it up well: "The new interactive medium both threatens the status quo and promises an exciting new way of learning about the world." This deftly describes both camps of opinion concerning participation by the audience in journalism.

It's not just the Internet that threatens the status quo of the news business. In their 2001 book *The Elements of Journalism,* Bill Kovach and Tom Rosenstiel make a compelling argument that the news business is undergoing "a momentous transition."

According to the authors, each time there has been a period of significant, social, economic, and technological change, a transformation in news occurred. This happened in the 1830s–40s with the advent of the telegraph; the 1880s with a drop in paper prices and a wave of immigration; the 1920s with radio and the rise of gossip and celebrity culture; the 1950s at the onset of the Cold War and television.

The arrival of cable, followed by the Internet and mobile technologies, has brought the latest upheaval in news. And this time, the change in news may be even more dramatic. Kovach and Rosenstiel explain, "For the first time in our history, the news increasingly is produced by companies outside journalism, and this new economic organization is important. We are facing the possibility that independent news will be replaced by self-interested commercialism posing as news."

Kovach and Rosenstiel argue that new technology, along with globalization and the conglomeration of media, is causing a shift away from journalism that is connected to citizen building and one that supports a healthy democracy.

Clearly, journalism is in the process of redefining itself, adjusting to the disruptive forces surrounding it. So it's no surprise that discussions about forms of participatory journalism, such as weblogs, are frequently consumed by defensive debates about what is journalism and who can legitimately call themselves a journalist.

While debating what makes for good journalism is worthwhile, and is clearly needed, it prevents the discussion from advancing to any analysis about the greater good that can be gained from audience participation in news. Furthermore, the debate often exacerbates the differences primarily in processes, overlooking obvious similarities. If we take a closer look at the basic tasks and values of traditional journalism, the differences become less striking.

From a task perspective, journalism is seen as "the profession of gathering, editing, and publishing news reports and related articles for newspapers, magazines, television, or radio."

In terms of journalism's key values, there is much debate. After extensive interviews with hundreds of U.S. journalists, Kovach and Rosenstiel say that terms such as fairness, balance and objectivity are too vague to rise to essential elements of this profession. From their research, they distilled this value: "The

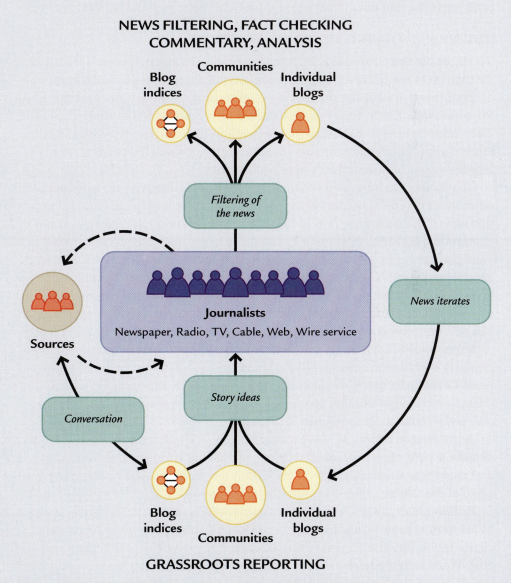

## NEWS FILTERING, FACT CHECKING COMMENTARY, ANALYSIS

Blog indices

Communities

Individual blogs

Filtering of the news

Sources

Journalists
Newspaper, Radio, TV, Cable, Web, Wire service

News iterates

Conversation

Story ideas

Blog indices

Communities

Individual blogs

## GRASSROOTS REPORTING

Based on "Blogosphere: The Emerging Media Ecosystem" by John Hiler, Microcontent News primary purpose of journalism is to provide citizens with the information they need to be free and self-governing."

In the case of the aforementioned South Korean news site, we see that traditional journalism's basic tasks and values are central to its ethos. The difference essentially boils down to a redistribution of control—a democratization of media. "With OhmyNews, we wanted to say goodbye to 20th-century journalism where people only saw things through the eyes of the mainstream, conservative media," said Oh Yeon-ho, editor and founder of South Korea's OhmyNews.com.

"The main concept is that every citizen can be a reporter," Yeon-ho says. "A reporter is the one who has the news and who is trying to inform others."

## THE NEW EVOLVING MEDIA ECOSYSTEM

The most obvious difference between participatory journalism and traditional journalism is the different structure and organization that produce them.

Traditional media are created by hierarchical organizations that are built for commerce. Their business models are broadcast and advertising focused. They value rigorous editorial workflow, profitability, and integrity. Participatory journalism is created by networked communities that value conversation, collaboration, and egalitarianism over profitability.

Clay Shirky, an adjunct professor at New York University who has consulted on the social and economic effects of Internet technologies, sees the difference this way: "The order of things in broadcast is 'filter, then publish.' The order in communities is 'publish, then filter.' If you go to a dinner party, you don't submit your potential comments to the hosts, so that they can tell you which ones are good enough to air before the group, but this is how broadcast works every day. Writers submit their stories in advance, to be edited or rejected before the public ever sees them. Participants in a community, by contrast, say what they have to say, and the good is sorted from the mediocre after the fact."

Many traditional journalists are dismissive of participatory journalism, particularly webloggers, characterizing them as self-interested or unskilled amateurs. Conversely, many webloggers look upon mainstream media as an arrogant, exclusive club that puts its own version of self-interest and economic survival above the societal responsibility of a free press.

According to Shirky, what the mainstream media fail to understand is that despite a participant's lack of skill or journalistic training, the Internet itself acts as editing mechanism, with the difference that "editorial judgment is applied at the edges... after the fact, not in advance."

In *The Elements of Journalism,* Kovach and Rosenstiel take a similar view: "This kind of high-tech interaction is a journalism that resembles conversation again, much like the original journalism occurring in the publick houses and coffeehouses four hundred years ago. Seen in this light, journalism's function is not fundamentally changed by the digital age. The techniques may be different, but the underlying principles are the same."

What is emerging is a new media ecosystem where online communities discuss and extend the stories created by mainstream media. These communities also produce participatory journalism, grassroots reporting, annotative reporting, commentary, and fact-checking, which the mainstream media feed upon, developing them as a pool of tips, sources, and story ideas.

Scott Rosenberg, managing editor of Salon.com, explains, "Weblogs expand the media universe. They are a media life-form that is native to the Web, and they add something new to our mix, something valuable, something that couldn't have existed before the Web.

"It should be obvious that weblogs aren't competing with the work of the professional journalism establishment, but rather complementing it. If the pros are criticized as being cautious, impersonal, corporate, and herdlike, the bloggers are the opposite in, well, *almost* every respect: They're reckless, confessional, funky—and herdlike."

Dan Gillmor, one of weblogging's most vocal defenders and a technology journalist and weblogger for the *San Jose Mercury News,* describes this ecosystem as "journalism's next wave." In a post to his weblog on March 27, 2002, Gillmor described the principles that define the current "we media" movement:

- My readers know more than I do.
- That is not a threat, but rather an opportunity.
- We can use this together to create something between a seminar and a conversation, educating all of us.
- Interactivity and communications technology—in the form of email, weblogs, discussion boards, websites, and more—make it happen.

## Working with the Text

1. In this introduction, Bowman and Willis distinguish between traditional and participatory journalism and offer both verbal and visual representations of how each kind of journalism works. Working alone or in groups, create your own chart or graphic that compares and contrasts what you see as the most significant features of traditional and participatory journalism. As with any kind of writing, your chart or graphic should convey a central point or main idea about the similarities and differences between these two kinds of journalism.
2. Bowman and Willis focus on the role and importance of "filtering" in each kind of journalism. Based on their discussion, write about your own views on the importance of "filtering" news. Should potential

news stories be carefully reviewed by editors before being published or broadcast, or should the public decide which stories emerge as the most useful and credible? Use your own experiences as a consumer and creator of news to analyze the ideas that Bowman and Willis raise.

3. Can you find examples of participatory journalism on your campus? Does your student newspaper, for example, feature blogs or reader feedback pages? In what ways do social networking sites such as Facebook or MySpace operate as alternative news sources? Write about different ways participatory journalism could work at your school.

4. Current TV is an online network featuring news stories created by visitors to the site. Visit the Current TV website at www.current.com and familiarize yourself with some of the stories being submitted by amateur journalists. Working in groups, choose a topic to explore and propose a story. Work with your group to decide on the audience and purpose for your story, do research, and compose potential copy. If resources and time allow, keep developing your story into something you would submit to Current TV or another website.

## "From Cave Painting to Wonkette: A Short History of Blogging"

### Dan Burstein

*One of the fascinating aspects of the digital revolution in popular culture has been the rapid creation of new spaces for writing. It started only ten or fifteen years ago with email, a written hybrid of the letter, memo, and quick note that has become such a regular part of daily life that it seems almost old-fashioned by computer-age standards. The once little-used "@" key is now a regular feature of modern language and even slang. Since the creation of email, we have seen the emergence of both text and instant messaging. (Being able to tell the difference between the two has become a marker of how computer literate a person is or to which generation they belong.) Even cell phones have become writing tools.*

*During the hotly contested 2004 presidential election, yet another new writing space gained national prominence. Called a blog, short for "weblog," this type of Web-based writing had been around for several years but began to attract serious attention when journalists and scholars discovered a vigorous political culture occurring almost completely online, a culture significant enough to produce campaign surprises such as the emergence of Howard Dean as a major candidate. Like other emerging forms of digital writing, blogs are both radically new and a combination of older forms of writing such as the diary, the essay, the newspaper op-ed piece, and the personal journal or log (hence, Web log). Like participants in other aspects of popular culture in the digital age, people who write political* blogs see themselves not just as commenting on the news but also as creating it, acting as both reporters and subjects of the news.

Since then, the term blogosphere has been coined to refer to the thousands of blogs in cyberspace. Most blogs are not overtly political and are more like personal diaries focused on the activities, social lives, and pop culture preferences of individual bloggers. Most social-networking websites like Facebook or MySpace include blogging options, and others such as Xanga allow anyone to set up a quick blog.

"From Cave Painting to Wonkette: A Short History of Blogging" is the introduction to the book Blog! How the Newest Media Revolution Is Changing Politics, Business, and Culture by David Kline and Dan Burstein. The book features essays from scholars about the significance of blogging in modern life as well as pieces written by bloggers themselves about the significance of this new space for writing. In his introduction to the book, Dan Burstein argues that blogging draws on a basic human need to create and share ideas and thus opens up opportunities for more and more people to participate in the cultural life of the world around them.

Dan Burstein is both a journalist and venture capitalist who has written extensively about and invested in new media technologies.

## Before You Read

1. How familiar are you with blogs and blogging, both as terms and as activities you may have participated in? If the word *blog* is a new concept for you, look it up in dictionaries and online. Visit some blogs and write about them. What strikes you as innovative about the blogs? What do you find most and least interesting about them? How much do they inspire you to try your hand at blogging?

2. List the ideas, opinions, topics, and issues that you discuss most often with your friends and family on a day-to-day basis, for example, school, movies, music, work, politics, etc. Which of these topics do you think would be most interesting to a wider audience? How could you attract the attention of readers who might come across your blog on the Internet?

3. In your day-to-day life, how do you make decisions about whether the opinions you encounter are valid or not? For example, if a friend offers an opinion about a television show, a professor makes a comment about a popular news story, or you hear a review of a movie on the radio, what process leads you to take these ideas seriously or not? What are your "markers of authority": Personal relationship? Institutional affiliation? Style of speaking or writing? What makes you trust or distrust a new opinion you encounter?

A four-letter term that came to symbolize the difference between old and new media during this year's presidential campaign tops U.S. dictionary publisher Merriam-Webster's list of the ten words of the year. Merriam-Webster Inc. said on Tuesday that blog, defined as "a website that contains an online personal journal with reflections, comments, and often hyperlinks," was one of the most looked-up words on its Internet sites this year. . . . Americans called up blogs in droves for information and laughs ahead of the presidential election. Freed from the constraints that govern traditional print and broadcast news organizations, blogs spread gossip while also serving as an outlet for people increasingly disenchanted with mainstream media. . . . Blog will be a new entry in the 2005 version of the *Merriam-Webster Collegiate Dictionary,* Eleventh Edition. —**From a Reuters report, " 'Blog' Tops U.S. Dictionary's Words of the Year," November 30, 2004**

Over the years, philosophers, anthropologists, and scientists have tried to define what makes Homo sapiens uniquely Homo sapiens. We are toolmakers, some experts tell us. We possess the capacity for complex language, others point out. We enjoy sex and engage in it for purposes other than procreation. We feel and express emotions. We experience wonder and curiosity, and we have the ability to contemplate why we exist and what the meaning of our lives may be. All of these statements are arguably true. But there is another distinguishing characteristic of human beings that has been unknown or underestimated until recently:

We blog.

I make this observation having just returned from a fascinating set of travel experiences through the Dordogne and adjacent regions of southwest France. There, my family and I wandered through magnificent caves whose walls showed off the brilliant engravings and paintings created fifteen to twenty thousand years ago at the dawn of modern human history. In learning about how these works developed, I discovered that in a number of places, the period of decoration of the cave walls went on for several generations—even, in some cases, for several hundreds or thousands of years. The paintings were often first inspired by the physical forms in the caves and were a kind of commentary on those forms. Then later painters and storytellers made subsequent commentaries about what they saw on the walls and what they had experienced in their lives. Having no written alphabetic language they used the mysterious visual languages of the figurative and abstract—multicolored paintings and carved engravings—to describe their ideas and beliefs about the hunt; the

spirit of bison, mammoths, deer, and various other animals; shamanism; the sacred feminine; initiation rites; sickness; mortality; the afterlife; the earth.

All of this was, of course, a very complex process, which I don't mean to oversimplify or trivialize here. Great thinkers have written hundreds of volumes describing the meaning and role in human development of these prehistoric art forms. But among the many mind-altering, paradigm-shifting ideas I took away from this experience was the observation that much of this art emerged as part and parcel of a long and highly compelling *conversation*: one member of the tribe initiating another, one generation speaking to the next, one group of humans inspired by and reacting to the ideas of those who came before. The conversation continues and is stored and archived for future access. The group memorializes and institutionalizes knowledge—and learns as a result.

Once you start to look for bloglike phenomena in the history of our civilization, you start to find them everywhere. The Talmudic tradition, for another example, is also a form of proto-blogging—scholars and thinkers debating the meaning of text passages from another era and creating commentaries, refinements, additions, and different shades of interpretation. Renaissance artists and thinkers were bloggers of a kind as well, commenting on what they found of interest and beauty from the cultures of Greece and Rome. Leonardo da Vinci probably wrote the greatest unpublished blog of all time in his more than thirty thousand pages of diary entries.

Tom Paine and the great American revolutionary zeal for political pamphleteering in the eighteenth century is another form: passionate political rants, delivered in real time, designed to be read and discussed by groups of people who are then moved to action as a result. (Rereading these in the light of the twenty-first-century day, I marvel at the vocabulary, the cadence, the brilliance of the rhetorical style, and the obvious intellect of the mass audiences that were capable of grasping the new ideas and the complex sentence construction. But if you think today's political bloggers are shrill, uncivil, or unobjective, they look reasoned and responsible by comparison to the Revolutionary War–era pamphleteers!)

The tradition of "commonplace books" provides another kind of example. These handwritten diaries were popular among Europeans, especially from the late Renaissance through the Enlightenment. The tradition continued to flourish into the nineteenth century in England and America. In these commonplace books, diarists collected and wrote down their favorite quotations and passages from a wide range of books, letters, and other sources. Sketches and hand-drawn illustrations were often included. Sometimes these diarists shared their notebooks with others and incorporated the reactions of their friends and colleagues, very much like a slow-moving, handwritten, in-person version of today's blogs.

So, although the word *weblog,* contracted into *blog,* may have first appeared in 1997, and there may have only been a few hundred blogs in 1999 around the time that Pyra Labs launched its Blogger software to make it easy for the rest of us to blog, I believe we are dealing with a phenomenon that has ancient antecedents and deep cultural roots. That is why, in my humble opinion (IMHO, as they say), blogging is not a passing fad, although there are faddish aspects to it that (mercifully) will probably pass quickly out of view with next-generation blogging.

Another reason blogs will embed themselves into our new cultural DNA is that we are living in a unique moment in time when the ancient human urges to converse, communicate, argue publicly, learn collaboratively, share experiences, and archive collective knowledge—urges that are part of the definition of who we are as a species—have suddenly been married with incredibly powerful, fast, ubiquitous technologies. And increasingly, the ordinary mortal doesn't need to know anything about technology to become a blogger or to read blogs or to participate in this new media revolution, because the power of technology is appropriately baked way down in the deepest regions of software infrastructure. The technologists and the engineers have done their job and given the rest of us a new tool that we do not have to understand in order to use, any more than we have to understand auto mechanics to drive a car.

The results of this unusual moment in time may be nothing short of a new paradigm for modern human communication, conversation, argument, and collaborative knowledge creation. Blogging represents one important wave of innovation that is contributing to restoring the lost voice of the ordinary citizen in our culture. The citizen-expert, the citizen-journalist, and the informed amateur in many realms of knowledge and human endeavor are all gaining prominence as a result of the blogging phenomenon. Yes, crazies and irresponsible people are also gaining access to wide audiences, as are people with evil and even criminal intent. And there is, of course, an overabundance of trivial drivel in blogs. But within all the noise, among the billions of words and pixels of new content being generated every day, lies a very important and steadily rising voice: the ordinary citizenry, on a national and global basis, re-engaging in the lost art of the public conversation.

Despite the oft-heard promises over the past century that each leap forward in technology would democratize communications, the fact is that information, knowledge, and policymaking have gravitated increasingly toward a relatively elite class of experts and professionals. The mainstream media grew to power and influence and, by the late twentieth century, these media had emerged as truly the fourth branch of government, absolutely critical to the function of democracy. In era-shaping controversies such as the Vietnam War and the Watergate scandal, the media frequently established their role as mechanism of last resort for checks and balances on governmental power. But as the press gained this new and important role—even becoming in many situations the check and balance mechanism of *first* resort—it also continued to coalesce into a relatively closed loop of professionals who knew the ropes, understood the systems, and had the credentials. They could make *their* voices heard, but not always *everyone's* voice heard. While niche and micro media have been growing for years (in print, on talk radio, on websites, on cable TV), challenging this mainstream media monopoly, blogging represents a significant qualitative change in the equation. The professionals still have control over the biggest, most powerful, most visible mainstream media (and I believe they will continue to play that dominant role for decades to come, with positive and negative effects), but "everyone" now has a meaningful shot at being heard as well.

A. J. Liebling, the great twentieth-century journalist, once famously said: "Freedom of the press is limited to those who own one." This powerful observation, profoundly true in the last century, is less true in the era of blogs. Today, as a result of the blogging phenomenon, it is not just that anyone has the freedom to speak in the abstract. The growing reality is that anyone can actually turn their words and ideas into published form, that anyone can have at least a small audience, and that anyone who desires a broad hearing can at least be armed to fight for one.

Any student of civilization's pageant knows the powerful changes in every aspect of society wrought by the major developments in communications technology: hieroglyphics, alphabets, papyrus, the Gutenberg press, newspapers, telegraphy, telephony, radio, television, the Internet, and the Web. The evolution of blogs and blogging over the last few years—and, more importantly, the next few—may turn out to be a seminal vein in time. It may resemble the period after Gutenberg's printing presses finally started working and churning out print books across Europe. (Incidentally, Gutenberg's influence was felt most strongly a number of years *after* his many years of failures, the big financial losses he incurred for his investors, and several battles between Gutenberg and his backers over who owned the intellectual property of his inventions.)

We have been talking for more than a generation about the "information age" and "the knowledge society." We have heard for at least two decades about the explosion of data that is leading to information overload and overchoice. We have watched the splintering of mass markets, mass institutions, mass media, and mass culture into thousands of customized, specialized, fragmented mini-markets, new institutions, personalized media, and emerging subcultures. I believe that blogs and blogging represent the missing link—or at least the metaphor and paradigm—for the ultimate software on which the knowledge society will operate. In the blogging phenomenon, we can see at least the software kernels that will be essential to creating structure and architecture (real order would be too much to hope for) out of the chaos of today's torrential information flows. Blogs, in their present form, are primitive tools gesturing in the direction of the new kinds of filtering, contextualization, and information-aggregation utilities that are already desperately needed—and will become even more crucial as billions of global citizens try to wrestle with increasingly complex societies fed by increasingly massive oceans of information.

Ice Age cave painters, Talmudic scholars, revolutionary pamphleteers, and commonplace bookmakers didn't have access to any technological tools to speak of. Equally obviously, much more separates DailyKos and Wonkette from Talmudic scholars and Tom Paine than links them. Nevertheless, as we set out on this journey to understand why the word *blog* was the most looked-up word of 2004; why the number of blogs is increasing by up to forty thousand a day; why tens of millions of people in America and around the world are reading, writing, and posting to blogs; why magazine cover stories are telling us that blogs will change our politics, our businesses, and our lives; we would do well to remember that what we know as a blog today is only the latest, most optimized, most evolved expression of one of the most basic human-felt needs.

Blogs, in the broadest sense, derive from the human urge to give voice to our ideas; to have our ideas understood, acted on, and remembered; and to engage in the quest for knowledge and understanding interactively and collaboratively. Our biological and cultural DNA causes us to want to articulate an idea or a vision and "publish" it, thereby taking ownership of it and credit for it. For most of us, it is very hard to keep our ideas inside our minds. Our biocultural DNA contains instructions that cause us to want to announce our ideas and denounce others, that make us want to interact, comment, converse, communicate, react, respond, elaborate, tweak, inform, refine, argue, criticize—and to do all of this with other members of our tribe across the boundaries of time and space. Blogs today, as well as their forerunner forms over thousands of years, are tools that allow us to engage in these processes. If, as scientists tell us, we are toolmakers, we are also idea generators.

Eventually, of course, quantity can turn into quality, essence can redefine existence. Today, in the middle of the first decade of the twenty-first century, the technologies and social changes that underlie the blogging phenomenon have arrived at their proverbial tipping point. For a brief moment, the medium really is the message (and the massage) and blogs deserve attention in their own right as a special kind of global, instantaneous, mass idea–generation farm; a special volcanic eruption of significant proportions and consequences within the history of the human conversation.

The blogging phenomenon is an exemplar of what James F. Moore of Harvard's Berkman Center for Internet & Society has dubbed "the second superpower." Moore's "second superpower" is not a nation-state but the social force of enlightened citizenry all over the globe, their co-created consciousness, and their collective power to invent, act, and change the world. Bloggers, Moore argues, are among the key citizens of this second superpower. "The current enthusiasm for blogging is changing the way that people relate to publication, as it allows real-time dialogue about world events...Metablogging sites crawl across thousands of blogs, identifying popular links, noting emergent topics, and providing an instantaneous summary of the global consciousness of the second superpower." Unlike the traditional democracy of the quadrennial voting booth, "participation in the second superpower movement occurs continuously through participation in a variety of web-enabled initiatives." Second superpower citizens are "alive," constantly "touching and being touched by each other, as the community works to create wisdom and to take action." In Moore's visceral descriptive prose, "Like a mind constituted of millions of inter-networked neurons, the social movement is capable of astonishingly rapid and sometimes subtle community consciousness and action."

The political, social, and cultural effects of blogging (and the many bloglike kinds of interactive tools and technologies now proliferating across the electronic cosmos) have analogous trends within the world of business and economics. Business guru C. K. Prahalad talks regularly about leading-edge companies that are "co-creating" their products with their customers. In new media businesses, "customer-created content" (think of Amazon.com reviews, for example, or the protean and constantly growing user-created encyclopedia that is Wikipedia) is suddenly valuable, despite the obvious fact that it costs nothing to generate in the traditional accounting sense of "cost." Visionary tech publisher Tim O'Reilly speaks of the "architecture of participation" in the creation of valuable databases and open source code; author James Surowiecki refers to the "wisdom of crowds"; Yale Law professor Yochai Benkler terms the phenomenon "peer production"; author Howard Rheingold speaks provocatively about "smart mobs"; *Business Week* reports on a theme it calls "mass collaboration" and "the power of us." Pharmaceutical companies, automobile manufacturers, fashion brands, snack foods, and others are tapping the collective wisdom of online communities, as are online focus groups and hundreds of other enterprises. Major daily newspapers have even invited readers to use blogs to become "citizen journalists" and participate in reporting the news.

Blogging is not by any means synonymous with all of the above-referenced phenomena. But it is highly correlated and almost always related in one way or another to the new and rising social software that is at the heart of the new, new economy, the new global culture, and the new way of doing things in our increasingly complex, interactive, electronic world.

Exactly ten years ago, my coauthor, David Kline, and I published our book *Road Warriors: Dreams and Nightmares Along the Information Highway.* That book was one of the first in-depth forecasts to sort out the hype and make a reasonable assessment of the impact that the Web and digital media were likely to have on business and society. We challenged two extreme poles in the debate back then: the neo-Luddites, who somehow hoped that the rise of the new technology could be stopped, and the far more prevalent (and insidious) neo-utopians, who argued that digital technology changed everything, overturned the business cycle, stood the basic laws of value on their head, educated the uneducated, liberated the poor, and democratized society. We coined a term in *Road Warriors* to describe our standpoint in opposition to these extremes: *real-world futurism.* To us, real-world futurism meant being incredibly excited about the potential of digital technology to change our world, yet recognizing that it would take time to suffuse its way into the deep fabric of business, economics, political life, education, and entertainment. It would not happen all at once as many then-experts, drunk on the elixir of the Internet bubble, then thought. It meant understanding that change would come in fits and starts and amid confusion, chaos, and the fog of business warfare. There would be bubbles and burst bubbles to come, as well as policy debates, ethical arguments, government regulations, and much more.

A critical principle of the real-world futurist viewpoint is the understanding that technology *can* be a force for liberation, democratization, and social cohesion, but is not *inherently* so. People and policymakers have to work at making technology a positive force in our lives. Inevitably, all technological change brings with it huge positives and many negatives as well. And, although technological change happens much quicker these days, it still doesn't happen overnight. Even phenomena like cell phones and iPods have been a surprising number of years in arriving at the juncture of critical mass that we see all around us today. The direction of technological change in the future is determined in large part by the political, social, and economic realities of today. Technology's evolution, moreover, is a constantly self-correcting, self-adapting balancing act in the marketplace, overshooting here and there, sowing the seeds of creative destruction, releasing new engines of ingenuity and innovation. [ . . . ]

[ . . . ] I should probably offer up a few of my own ideas before logging off. So here is my personal list of observations and expectations that come out of the pages of my own "commonplace book," as I have been interviewing bloggers and thinking about the current state and future direction of the blogosphere.

1. **Blogs are the key development at the center of a much wider suite of innovations that, taken together, are beginning to deliver on the promise of the 1990s.** This includes the last decade's promises about the high degrees of interactivity, personalization, and contextualization we would experience on the Web, as well as the promise of ubiquity, centrality, and ease of use of Web-based communications. RSS feeds, wikis, new search tools, new ways to integrate and process images and voice, the movement of music and television content to the Web, podcasting,

and mobile blogging are all part of the same phenomenon: we are now getting the multimedia, always-on, highly interactive, highly personalized next-generation Web we imagined a decade ago.

2. **Blogs are particularly interesting because they marry so much personality and attitude with this complex mix of software technologies.** They are the raw, human face of the brave new technological world, showing that we can have more technology without necessarily becoming more depersonalized and alienated as a society. Blogs point the way toward restoring real voice and personality to the citizenry at large—locally, nationally, globally. In an ever-expanding population, with an ever more sophisticated elite set of knowledge workers setting the public agenda, blogs provide counterweight and ballast to the quality of public discussion. The blogging phenomenon may well represent a revitalization of real citizenship in the political and governmental sense, as well as the door-opening tool giving visibility and voice to diverse individuals with diverse ideas that never could have been seen or heard before.

3. **Blogging, in addition to being a huge phenomenon in its own right, is the key metaphor for interactivity, community-building, and genuine conversation: one to one, one to many, many to one, many to many.** Years from now, the kind of blogs we know today may or may not exist in a big way as a discrete genre, but the

breakthrough principles of community-building and genuine interactivity they represent will be incorporated into the way much of our media functions in the future. Blogging is the "killer app" of the current generation of Web innovation, just as email and instant messaging were at the core of the last version.

4. **Blogs will coexist with other media for a long time to come, and there will be continual interactions and cross-fertilizations.** Some of today's top bloggers will become newspaper and magazine columnists and TV news talent; almost all of today's traditional media will develop blogs of one type or another to extend their reach, connect to the younger

demographic, be able to expand their coverage, and have more advertising product to sell. Many blogs will develop codes of journalistic ethics appropriate to the blogosphere and take other measures to maintain and enhance credibility. These may not be the exact same rules of the road that have guided traditional journalism, but they will be explicit operating precepts just the same. Meanwhile, bloggers will continue to break new ground in covering stories and paying attention to issues the mainstream media tend to ignore, and will continue to gain grudging respect, credibility, and credentials as the creators of one more important type of media.

5. **Blogging is going corporate.** Its repercussions will be felt deep inside the business world, as a number of our interviews [...] point out. Many of the early Web enthusiasts were horrified a decade ago as advertising and ecommerce proliferated in the once pristine Garden of the Internet. If there are any such naïfs left in the age of blogging, they should get ready to see huge impacts on the blogosphere as the impact of the business world is felt in more and more ways. As a May 2005 *Business Week* cover story screamed: "Blogs will change your business...Your customers and rivals are figuring blogs out. Our advice: Catch up... or catch you later." The first conferences I attended on blogging two or three years ago were populated by academics, literary types, and political pundits. The more recent conferences have had significant turnouts from the likes of General Motors, DaimlerChrysler, Microsoft, and Procter & Gamble. The interaction of business and blogging will be many-sided and multidimensional. Business is obviously being changed in a number of superficial ways as a result of these trends. But it is also safe to predict that business will be changed in some profound ways as well, just as politics and other aspects of our culture are morphing as a result both of what is said in the blogosphere and the process of saying it.

6. **Blogging is going global.** It is not just us wild 'n crazy, uninhibited, populist Americans who like to rant. The core elements of blogging, as I pointed out at the beginning of this discussion, are connected to some universal human qualities, urges, and needs. There are numerous examples of how blogs are already changing culture and politics around the globe. One good example was the impact of a blog by Etienne Chouard, a schoolteacher from Marseille, widely credited with inspiring the opposition vote against the European constitution in France in May 2005. The rightist government of Jacques Chirac and most of the

leftist intellectual establishment were united in their support for the European constitution, but Chouard's and other blogs contributed to a sudden public realization that this movement could be stopped. One could certainly question whether the influence of Chouard's blog was positive for France; nevertheless, the influence was undeniable when the votes were counted and the "no" vote won. When one scans down Technorati's list of the most influential blogs, the names of blogs in Hindi, Urdu, Arabic, Farsi, Japanese, Chinese, and Korean immediately show up. A very knowledgeable Chinese friend recently predicted that blogs would have more impact on revolutionizing China and bringing it fully into the modern world than any other influence. A month after he made these comments to me, the Chinese government seemed to concur with his view of blogs as a forum for revolutionary thought by issuing a series of edicts designed to control and constrain their spread. Blogs are having a powerful impact in all the obvious places where freedom of the press has always been a part of the culture. Blogging software now allows more voices to be heard on more subjects in countries like the UK or Australia or Sweden. But blogs are also proving influential in places like Iraq, Iran, and elsewhere in the developing world. Just as many developing countries found in the 1990s that cell phone technology could proliferate even without a strong land-line infrastructure, many of the same cultures are now discovering that a free, diverse blogosphere can exist even without a free traditional media environment.

7. **Blogs are segmenting.** Personal interactive journals are a huge and growing phenomenon—and interesting to think about. But these personal journals don't have all that much in common with the big political and opinion blogs. They share a style, they share an interface, they are indexed by search engines, they may even share underlying software architecture. But they are their own media form. It is also hard to imagine all the one-man and one-woman bands who are today's top bloggers just continuing forever into the future blogging every day. Some will develop their blogs as real businesses, just as many people have become power sellers on eBay or Amazon. Some will burn out and drop by the wayside, pleased they had their voices heard but exhausted and unhappy that they have not been able to make any money at it. At some point many bloggers will choose to further professionalize, hire small staffs, partner with other bloggers, begin to pool resources, and participate in advertising syndicates.

8. **Blogging is not inherently liberal or conservative, Right or Left.** As the events of the American presidential race in 2004 amply demonstrated, blogging can be used by the right as well as the left. Just because some people might assume that liberals would have more affinity for writing personal streams of consciousness late at night in their pajamas, doesn't make it so.

9. **The numbers of bloggers will continue to grow because the numbers of knowledge workers in our societies are continuing to grow.** Our complex, sophisticated, postmodern societies are turning out very large numbers of literate people trained in critical thinking skills and interested in developing new ideas and participating in the discussion of them. Blogs are being used by people in all sorts of professional niches and subcultures to exercise their intellectual muscles and evince their thought leadership. Indeed, blogs are so low-cost to start, they can exist below the minimum threshold for starting a newsletter, a think tank study, or an academic publication. As a result, blogs are becoming the communications centers for many kinds of new ideas and new thinking. Blogs are a bully pulpit for ideas. Rather than seeing the proliferation of specialty blogs as an indicator of the fragmentation of our society, we should see this trend as providing a way for citizen-experts to emerge and to bring together global constituencies in many disparate fields.

10. **Blogs will engender a variety of successful businesses, but may not create the kind of large new investment category that venture capitalists typically look for as technology paradigms change.** Entrepreneurs will build successful blog-oriented software companies; some will build successful small media companies; some will build valuable aggregation, syndication, and measuring tools. Rupert Murdoch's July 2005 purchase of Myspace.com's parent company for more than $500 million demonstrates that there is, indeed, gold in these hills. But the really big money—the billions, not the millions, as well as the big business battles of the future—will lie in the outcome of the clash of the titans for strategic control of the blogosphere. And the names will be familiar: Google, Microsoft, Yahoo, AOL, for example.

11. **Blogs will continue to be important in politics for a long time to come.** They may turn out in retrospect to have been as important as the advent of televised debates and live coverage during the 1960 presidential campaign. Curiously, if the electorate is not polarized, blogs could actually be less important in the 2008 U.S. presidential election than

they were in 2004. They can have their maximum influence in a time of a closely and evenly divided electorate. Like other media, their role is important but actually marginal. It's when marginal matters that blogs can be most influential. If that's the case in 2008, then blogs may make the difference in who is elected. But if a clear majority opinion develops, blogs will still be an interesting part of the campaign coverage, but less strategically significant.

12. **Blogs (in many cases) may lose their association with a single individual and become aggregation platforms for like-minded or complementary bloggers.** While certain changes are implied in moving from one-person blogs to aggregation platforms, I believe it is possible to retain much of the appeal of today's blogs and, at the same time, leverage the resources of larger platforms.

We can't know in advance all the new forms that will be created, but it is a given that there will be a long period of constant change ahead in how blogs are created and how we experience them. They will change not only our language, but the actual architecture of human knowledge, conversation, and interaction. As today's teenagers and college students grow older, they will remake the form and the genre of blogging they have grown up with. My own view is that the blogs of the future will appear quite different from today's. The word *blog* itself may disappear, along with many of the faddish elements of today's blogging world.

Yet I believe that the global always-on, always-linked, always-archived, always-immediate public conversation of the rest of the twenty-first century will continue to draw on the fundamental ideas and principles that emerged in this decade in what we called the blogosphere. For it was in this decade that we first married the ancient human impulse to publish ideas and converse about them with the powerful new technologies now available to us.

---

# Working with the Text

1. Throughout his essay, Burstein argues that the very modern phenomenon of blogging stems from some very ancient and fundamental human impulses: the need to communicate and the need to share ideas, the same needs that motivate all writing and reading. Given your experiences as a writer, both in and out of school, speculate about why blogging has become such a popular form of writing. For example, when does writing seem most vital and interesting to you? What most powerfully motivates your own writing?

2. Burstein refers to several historical examples of what he calls "bloglike phenomena," ranging from ancient cave paintings to the Talmudic tradition to political broadsides from the Revolutionary War. Explore this idea that "bloglike phenomena" are common features of human cultures by listing some activities from your life and from the contemporary world that also seem bloglike (for example, graffiti artists). What about these examples makes them bloglike? In what ways do they differ from blogs?

3. Burstein suggests that blogs represent a movement away from "a relatively elite class of experts and professionals" dominating most political and cultural discussion to a more open and democratic arena where anyone with access to a computer can participate, debate, and offer his or her opinions. If Burstein is right, what do you think would be the most difficult parts of this transition? What habits or attitudes toward the way politics or culture works would we have to change or adapt? How far-reaching an effect do you think blogs and the trends that blogs represent have on how ideas are created, argued about, and shared?

4. Work alone or as part of a group to create your own blog. Choose a subject or topic of interest to you and write several postings. (This activity can either be done online via free blog software and sites, using discussion boards on Blackboard or other classroom software, or even via paper on a bulletin board.) In addition to your own postings, visit the other blogs produced by your class members and respond to their postings.

## "Blogging in the Early Republic"

### W. Caleb McDaniel

Everything old is new again. *This familiar cliché suggests that even the most cutting-edge and innovative new ideas, fashions, art forms, and ways of communicating often represent the return of older and even ancient kinds of cultural practices. This idea has been applied from the very beginning to the changes brought about by the Internet age. Consider how the terminology of the World Wide Web combines language from both the high-tech world and the traditional world of print culture: URLs and webpages, RSS and bookmarks.[1] The ubiquitous habit of adding an e- to familiar words to indicate a new development in*

---

[1] RSS stands for Rich Site Summary, a Web feed format that automatically sends you daily summaries of updates from your favorite websites.

*cyberspace (email, etrade, etail, emagazine) likewise suggests that for everything about the digital age that seems radically new, there's also an aspect that is equally traditional.*

*In "Blogging in the Early Republic," W. Caleb McDaniel considers the many comparisons made in the popular press between blogging and older methods of participating in popular debate and discussion, such as pamphlets, newspapers, and broadsheets. In their focus on famous political writers of the past such as Tom Paine or George Orwell, however, McDaniel feels that analysts of blogging pay too much attention to only one particular kind of blog writing—political blogging, meant to have a wide readership and make a significant impact on public debate—at the expense of the blogs that constitute the majority of the blogosphere: personal blogs devoted to highly selective areas of interest, written mainly for a small reading community of fellow bloggers. Whether the focus is knitting, playing a particular video game, or raising show dogs, McDaniel argues that these more common kinds of blogs share qualities with the then radically new forms of reading and writing that developed from the explosion of print culture in the early nineteenth century. By understanding how ordinary Americans adjusted to the rapid growth of newspapers, magazines, and books in that earlier time, he suggests that we can learn more about what blogging means for our own.*

*W. Caleb Daniel is a professor of American history at the University of Denver. He is also an experienced blogger.*

## Before You Read

1. Write a detailed description of your readings habits, excluding the reading specifically assigned in your classes. If you think of yourself as a reader, write about what you enjoy about reading, the kinds of reading you most like to do, and whether you discuss your reading with friends and family. If you don't consider yourself as someone who enjoys reading as a leisure activity, write about when you do most often find yourself reading as part of your day-to-day activities. (And remember: all webpages involve reading of some kind.)

2. Given the overwhelming number of cultural choices we face every day, from magazines, newspapers, and books, to websites, music, television, and movies, how do you decide what to read, watch, listen to, and interact with? You might start with the waiting-room decision: while waiting for your name to be called at the doctor's office, which magazine are you most likely to pick up? If you go channel surfing on television, where do you usually start and why? What are your second and third choices? What websites do you go to first? What kinds of links are most likely to grab your attention?

3. Interview a friend, classmate, family member, or teacher and write a profile of that person's reading, viewing, and listening habits. Compare

your findings with those of others in the class, especially across demographic categories such as age and gender. What do you find most and least surprising about what you learn?

Henry Clarke Wright was an antebellum American reformer whose eclectic interests ranged from antislavery to radical pacifism to health reform and beyond. Born in 1797 and educated as a minister, he later abandoned institutional religion and became a prolific writer and speaker. In countless lectures delivered across the American North and the British Isles—where he spent most of the 1840s—Wright inveighed against war, corporal punishment in the home, slavery, loveless marriage, church and state, traditional medicine, and much else.

Above all, Wright wrote. According to the count of his only biographer, he authored eleven books, numerous articles in reform newspapers like William Lloyd Garrison's *Liberator,* and over two dozen tracts and pamphlets. The Irish abolitionist Richard D. Webb, who hosted Wright in his Dublin home in 1844, reported to a mutual friend in Boston that Henry was lately spending "the greater part of the day writing in his room. I suppose he thinks he is shaking the world, but I can perceive very little of the motion so far."

As a writer with grand aspirations for shaking the world, Wright was also an inveterate journal keeper. For most of his adult life, he filled a steady stream of over one hundred diaries. In these, comments on world events and social reform jostle with reflections on the diarist's loveless marriage and his struggle for faith. While private, the journals were also public. Wright mailed pages and even whole volumes to his friends or read them excerpts from the diaries, and many pages were later published in his numerous books. Thus, as his biographer Lewis Perry notes, in the case of Wright, "distinctions between private and public, between diaries and published writings, meant little."

In *Human Life: Illustrated in My Individual Experience as a Child, a Youth, and a Man* (1845), one of his published writings in which diary entries were frequently excerpted, Wright confessed that "writing a journal does me good. I can let off my indignation at the wrongs I see and hear. I am far happier when I write a little every day. I take more note too, of passing events, and see more of what is going on around me. I live less in the past and future, and more in the present, when I journalize...It saves me from many dark hours to write down what I see and hear and feel daily. My soul would turn in upon and consume itself, if I did not thus let it out into my journal."

Wright died in 1870, already a relatively forgotten reformer. Yet—and I speak from my own experience in 2005—his reflections on writing are eerily evocative of what it is like to blog. Wright shared several traits with the prototypical blogger—his eccentric range of interests, his resolution "to write down what I see and hear and feel daily," his use of journals to "let off" rants of "indignation," his utopian conviction that writing might change the world, and (not least) his practice of spending the "greater part of the day writing in his room." Was Wright a blogger? Are not his journals the fossilized originals of a species?

If you scoff at this suggestion, this is probably because you hold this truth to be self-evident: in the course of human events, blogging is the newest of newcomers.

After all, blogs—short for "Web logs"—are webpages, which means that they cannot be older than the World Wide Web. Moreover, a blog refers to a kind of webpage that has only become widespread in the past five or six years. Blogs are frequently updated pages that list brief, time-stamped posts. These can contain text, links, images, or all of the above. Though seemingly ubiquitous today, the form itself is relatively new, even in the abbreviated history of cyberspace. The term *Web log* was never used until circa 1997, when it was coined to refer to a few dozen journals that were being published online by early Internet users, mainly as annotated lists of links to interesting webpages.

As these early bloggers began to link extensively to other blogs, the "blogosphere" was born—about fourscore and seven months ago. That makes the career of the blogosphere only slightly older than that of Britney Spears—hardly a hoary age, and certainly not old enough for Henry Clarke Wright to be a blogger.

Yet as blogging has quickly become a cultural—and now political—phenomenon, speculations about the historical precursors to blogging have become matters of course. Tens of thousands of new blogs are now created every day, on subjects ranging from the highly personal to the political, from careers to crochet, from academia to art, from movies to "moblogs"—collections of photographs taken using mobile phones. Technorati, a special search engine that tracks links between blogs, now follows over ten million blogs. In the last few years, the dynamic growth and diversification of blogging has attracted attention from journalists, political pundits, and scholars, and many pixels are now being spilled about the political influence of blogs—as bellwethers of opinion, as sources of trenchant social criticism, as innovative forms of citizen journalism, or as tools for political organization.

For every writer who says that blogging is beginning to shake the world, there is another who confesses that it is difficult to feel the motion. But it is worth noting that both the true believers in blogging and the skeptics are leavening their debates with allusions to history—along with suggestions that blogging is not as new as you think. Three years ago, in the *New York Times,* Emily Eakin called the blogger a "new breed of pamphleteer," who would have pleased George Orwell, "if he had lived to surf the Internet." The headline declared that the "ancient art of haranguing"—practiced so well by pamphleteers like Orwell and "master rhetoricians" like Daniel Defoe and Thomas Paine—"has moved to the Internet, belligerent as ever."

For Eakin, blogs were both "new" and "ancient"—the same old whining in new wineskins. Yet on the whole, writers about blogging cannot seem to decide whether blogging is more continuous or discontinuous with the past. Bits of historical flotsam float, willy-nilly, through many discussions about blogs, available for use by boosters and critics alike. In 2002, for example, blogger Andrew Sullivan compared the invention of group blogs to the way that "reviews and magazines started out decades and centuries ago: a few like-minded souls collaborating on a literary-political project." Sullivan mused that "perhaps blogs—and the technology that enables them—will take us back to the eighteenth century. I sure hope so." Similarly, on his blog PressThink, media critic Jay Rosen has argued that if bloggers are the faces of journalism's future, their faces are also turned toward the past. "The people who will invent the next press in America—and who are doing it now online—continue an experiment at least 250 years old." Rosen admires TomPaine.com, a progressive website for news and commentary, because it "leaves the arrow pointing backward to Paine the troublemaking democrat and political journalist, reviving his name for symbolic purpose in the present." Fittingly enough, TomPaine.com has a blog.

Yet if some writers use history to compare blogging to some halcyon yesteryear, other writers use history to put a damper on the hype. A recent *USA Today* headline advised "blogophiles" to "chill," admonishing them that "you're not the first to do what you're doing." "Thomas Paine was basically a blogger—in 1776," wrote technology columnist Kevin Maney, who also identified the works of Orwell and Martin Luther as "historical antecedents" for blogs. "The printing press gave Luther a way to distribute his thesis— an early version of blogging.

Next thing, we had Protestants." Blogs, said Maney, are just "another turn of history's wheel, not a radical departure."

Are blogs really just another turn of history's wheel? Yes and no. Bloggers do have some historical antecedents in the eighteenth and nineteenth century. But the usual suspects in the examples above—Paine, Luther, Orwell—are in various ways misleading. Treating these highly influential writers as analogues for bloggers serves a particular understanding of blogging as primarily political. Moreover, it perpetuates a picture of the blogosphere that is skewed toward elite and highly visible blogs. The better analogues for bloggers may not be towering literary figures like Paine, but more forgotten writers like Wright. The arrow for blogging should be left pointing backwards, as Rosen suggests, but where it points is another question.

Just five years ago, blogs were still a rarity, but since September 11, 2001, their numbers have skyrocketed. The growth has been especially staggering among "poliblogs" and "warblogs," many of which model themselves on the punditry of sites like Glenn Reynold's Instapundit. By the 2004 election, prominent bloggers like Ana Marie Cox of Wonkette were being invited to the presidential nominating conventions of both parties, and mainstream news organizations have proclaimed polibloggers a force to be reckoned with. In 2002, Joshua Marshall, who blogs at Talking Points Memo, helped to discredit former Senate majority leader Trent Lott for his statements on racial segregation, which led to Lott's eventual resignation. More recently, bloggers exposed forged memos used by CBS News for a story on President Bush's military service during the Vietnam War.

This, at least, is the conventional history of blogging. But the story is a skewed one. Although famous poliblogs receive the lion's share of attention from bloggers and journalists alike, most blogs go largely unnoticed by the mainstream media. Of the millions of blogs tracked by Technorati, the vast majority are not concerned primarily with political influence or alternative journalism. There are knitting blogs, book blogs, poetry blogs, academic blogs, cooking blogs, photo blogs, religion blogs, gossip blogs, teaching blogs, parenting blogs, and more.

The full history of blogging, then, cannot be told simply as a story of how the poliblogs rose into mainstream consciousness or acquired political influence, because the story fails to account for the size and heterogeneity of the blogosphere as a whole. Yet when historical analogies to blogging are offered, they usually reinforce the idea that blogging is mainly a political enterprise, dominated by a few leading figures. Consider the historical figures mentioned above as the progenitors of blogging—Paine, Luther, Orwell. Organizing a genealogy of blogging around such monumental writers only underlies the sense that prominent poliblogs are the endpoints in a teleological progression of popular political writing. Blogging analysts who focus on the elite poliblogs are likely to see their aspirations for influence as defining features of blogging itself, as if most blogs exist primarily to act as molders of public opinion.

Instead, I would like to suggest some analogues to blogging from antebellum America that contradict a history of blogging built on a long list of great writers. Those analogues can be found not primarily in the history of writing, but rather in the history of American reading.

Most historians agree that major transformations in printing and reading took place in the United States between 1750 and 1850—changes that seemed as phenomenal to contemporaries as blogging seems to many in our own time. At the beginning of this roughly hundred-year period, printed material was scarce, and the diffusion of information was severely limited in terms of time and space. In the seventeenth and early eighteenth centuries, colonial printers used their presses mainly to publish official proclamations, almanacs, commercial newsletters for merchants, and occasional sermons. But these materials were not produced in large quantities, and print was even scarcer in rural areas than in port cities.

Yet by 1850, this scarcity of print had given way to a bewildering abundance— a rapid growth no less impressive in its own time than the exponential proliferation of blogs in the last few years. Newspapers began to crop up not just in major urban areas but in smaller towns, and as print became more abundant, it was also diffused more widely and rapidly, thanks to a transportation revolution fueled by steam, railroads, and internal improvements like roads, canals, and an expanding postal service. These changes were, of course, not unique to the United States, but even foreign travelers to the young nation were awed by its burgeoning print culture. Alexis de Tocqueville, after touring the United States in 1831, wrote. "[W]hen I compare the Greek and Roman republics to these republics of America, the manuscript libraries of the first…to the thousand newspapers that crisscross the second…I am tempted to burn my books so as to apply only new ideas to a social state so new."

Tocqueville's references to republicanism and a new social state were not coincidental, because social and political democratization was both a cause and effect of the print revolution. In the colonial period, print remained scarce partly because information was thought to be a privilege of the few. As historian Richard Brown has argued, those with power—political and religious elites, wealthy planters and merchants, white men all—controlled the flow of knowledge, and access to print and public information required deference to their power. The shift from a scarcity of print to abundance was therefore accompanied necessarily by a measure of increased democratization. Such, at least, was what Tocqueville concluded. In answer to Europeans who thought that reducing taxes on print would "increase newspapers indefinitely," he argued that "newspapers multiply not only relative to their cheapness." In addition, "the empire of newspapers" would grow "as men became equal."

The growth of the empire of newspapers had two related effects on the practices of American readers. First, the new surplus of print meant that there was more to read. Whereas readers in the colonial period had been intensive readers of selected texts like the Bible and devotional literature, by 1850 they were extensive readers, who could browse and choose from a staggering array of reading choices. Second, the shift from deference to democratization encouraged individual readers to indulge their own preferences for particular kinds of reading preferences that were exploited and targeted by antebellum publishers. In short, readers had more printed materials to choose from, more freedom to choose, and more printed materials that were tailored to their choices.

These were prime conditions for the emergence of reading practices similar to blogging. For nineteenth-century Americans, unprecedented access to reading material "bred the feeling of independence," argues Brown. "Instead of being obviously and directly dependent on public officials and social superiors for information," readers could now "acquire information on their own in the marketplace, more or less on an equal basis." But as readers became more extensive in their reading, they also had to develop principles for selection. What should one read, when there was so much to choose from? And now that information was not always mediated by the interpretations of colonial elites, how should one deal with the glut of information available? As Brown continues, "Selecting what information to acquire replaced access itself so as to emerge as a central challenge for people in varied social circumstances."

One of the ways that readers met these challenges was to "journalize," to borrow the word used by Henry Clarke Wright. Surrounded by ephemeral print, many began to make references in their journals to what they had been reading—the rough equivalent of what bloggers do by linking to a webpage. During the Revolution, for instance, Christopher Marshall, a Philadelphian radical and friend of Thomas Paine, peppered his journal with references to the papers, often with brief comments on the news. "Sundry pieces of news last night in the *Evening Post,* Numb. 147," he jotted in December 1775. Earlier in the year, after recording the casualties at Bunker Hill, Marshall tipped his hat to "*Evening Post,* No. 74, and J. Humphrey's *Ledger,* No. 25" for the information. With more news available, diarists like Marshall began to construct their own networks of information, annotating the news to create a record of their reading.

Wright's journals, written decades after Marshall's in a period of even greater print abundance, similarly recorded his reading and punctuated that record with commentary. One typical Wright entry must have been written while reading the latest paper brought by the Atlantic packets that ran from Liverpool to Boston: "*News from England.* Queen Victoria has a daughter. Millions of dollars are being expended to celebrate the babe's birth. This money comes from the mouths of the children of the poor who cry for bread…The British Army in India has been defeated by the Natives. What right has that robber Nation to hold Dominion over India? Only the Robber's right. England is a Robber and a Pirate. Great excitement in England on the Woman Question." Wright's selection of news—mixed with his views—demonstrated the freedom with which antebellum readers interacted with printed news.

Other readers skipped over copying from their papers and simply cut out articles to paste directly into scrapbooks, scribbling commentary in the margins around the clippings. In his book *City Reading,* historian David M. Henkin describes a multivolume journal by New Yorker Edward Neufville Tailer, Jr., entitled "Journal of Some of the Events Which Have Occurred in My Life Time." In the 1840s and 1850s, says Henkin, clippings from newspapers began to "dominate Tailer's diary," which became a "record of his daily reading habits."

As individual readers freely made choices about what information to acquire, they also freely came together as groups of like-minded readers. In the more heavily urban Northern states, Americans began to join voluntary associations at remarkable rates—library clubs, lyceums for hearing speeches and discussing ideas, political parties, and religious and reform organizations. Each of these associations was also a reading community, which connected members by official publications and common reading habits. Within these groups, readers also found new opportunities to become writers, as many amateur writers now produced articles for reform papers or poems for religious magazines. Whereas private reading choices in the colonial period had governed vertical relationships between elites (who possessed information) and non-elites (who did not), reading choices in the early nineteenth century became public matters, defining horizontal relationships among individuals who met on a more equal footing. Tocqueville also noted this aspect of the print revolution when he observed in the United States "a necessary relation between [voluntary] associations and newspapers: newspapers make associations, and associations make newspapers."

Perhaps there is a similar relationship between blogging and the print culture of the twenty-first century, a culture that now includes not only an abundance of printed pages, but also an abundance of webpages. American readers at the turn of the nineteenth century found themselves afloat on a sea of print, whose tide had risen along with democratic ideas about the diffusion of information. They responded to these liberating circumstances by selecting what to read and interpreting the news according to the individual preference. Privately, records of reading—and the writing they inspired—could be kept in journals and scrapbooks. But those private records also pushed readers outward into communities of like-minded readers. In these communities, readers also became writers.

The blogosphere as a whole represents a similar pattern in a different medium: confronted by an ever-growing number of webpages and a massive amount of online information, bloggers use their blogs to mix quotidian reflections about life together with records of their reading. Like Christopher Marshall and Edward Tailer, they link these reflections back to the source—"clipping" sites that interest them. But their interests and choices about what to read also connect them to small communities within the blogosphere, much as a reader-writer like Henry Clarke Wright was drawn into the circle of abolitionist and pacifist reformers by their common pathways through the abundant print culture of the antebellum North. The typical blog links not only to pages outside of the blogosphere, but also to other blogs, and these links often create small networks of like-minded bloggers. In addition, most blogs are equipped with technology that allows readers to leave comments on posts or to alert authors that they have replied to a post on their own blog. Through these interactive practices, associations of a certain kind are formed. To paraphrase Tocqueville, webpages make blogging networks, and blogging networks in turn make their own webpages.

This historical analogy, of course, represents my own highly individualized selection of readings from a huge abundance of writing both on the blogosphere and on early American print culture. But the fact that I can make a selective reading is a testament to the phenomenon of democratization and information growth that I am describing. Moreover, there are virtues to my selective reading. By comparing the rise of blogging to events in the history of reading rather than to epochal events in the history of political dissent, we can take into account a larger number and a wider range of blogs. Not all bloggers are would-be Thomas Paines. But almost all bloggers make their own small worlds by offering highly individualized collections of reading choices. Through these choices as readers, they also join virtual associations of other readers. The basic practice that underlies most blogging is therefore not unprecedented. Historically, when an abundance of public information is conjoined with democratized ideas about the flow of information, something like blogging usually results.

Of course, for all the similarities I have outlined between bloggers and antebellum diarists like Henry Clarke Wright, there are probably as many differences between the two periods. You might point out, for instance, that if Wright had possessed access to a computer and a broadband Internet connection, he could have written even more than he did and reached even larger audiences. He could have. But the vast majority of bloggers, despite their considerable technological advantages over Wright's paper and ink, have regular audiences and communities that may be even smaller than Wright's circle of friends. And despite our differences from antebellum readers, the central challenge for us, as it was for them, is not how to gain access to an abundance of information, but how to decide what information to acquire and which associations to make. In real terms, bloggers do have access to more information than nineteenth-century readers did, but there is only so much information that any one reader can digest, so the problem for both still becomes what to read and how to read it.

Indeed, blogging demonstrates the persistence of a key truth in the history of reading, an insight as obvious to Tocqueville as it should be to most bloggers today. The insight is that readers, in a culture of abundant reading material, regularly seek out other readers, either by becoming writers themselves or by sharing their records of reading with others. That process, of course, requires cultural conditions that value democratic rather than deferential ideals of authority. But to explain how new habits of reading and writing develop, those cultural conditions matter as much—perhaps more—than economic or technological innovations. As Tocqueville knew, the explosion of newspapers in America was not just a result of their cheapness or their means of production, any more than the explosion of blogging is just a result of the fact that free and user-friendly software like Blogger is available. Perhaps, instead, blogging is the literate person's new outlet for an old need. In Wright's words, it is the need "to see more of what is going on around me." And in print cultures where there is more to see, it takes reading, writing, and association in order to see more.

---

## Working with the Text

1. McDaniel notes that many writers who want to argue that blogs are just the newest version of a very old cultural practice point to the example of well-known political writers such as Thomas Paine or George Orwell. The result, according to McDaniel, is to "reinforce the idea that blogging is mainly a political enterprise, dominated by a few leading figures" and to see "aspirations for influence as the defining features of blogging itself, as if most blogs exist primarily to act as molders of public opinion." What does McDaniel see as the main problems with this way of looking at blogs and blogging? What aspects of blogging does he argue that this approach overlooks?

2. In describing the impact of the print revolution between 1750 and 1850, McDaniel contrasts the "intensive readers" before the print revolution and the "extensive readers" who developed as a result of the explosion of print materials in the first fifty years of the United States (a growth he writes is "no less impressive in its own time than the exponential proliferation of blogs in the last few years"). Explain how you understand the distinction he is making between "intensive" and "extensive" readers by using examples from your own reading

experiences. At what times have you acted more as an intensive reader? At what times as an extensive reader? How well does the concept of the extensive reader help make sense of the way most of us approach reading in the digital age?

3. McDaniel refers to the way that readers in the nineteenth century formed voluntary associations and reading communities based on shared interests and attitudes. Provide contemporary examples of such voluntary associations and reading communities. What groups to which you belong could be described in this way? Connect this discussion to blogging and the Web by finding people who like to spend time on the Web in a cyberspace version of a reading community. You might also consider the ways in which social-networking sites such as Facebook and MySpace constitute modern versions of voluntary associations and reading communities.

# VIEWING CULTURE

## THE ETHICS OF PHOTOJOURNALISM

It became one of the most famous images of World War II. In February 1945, as American and Japanese soldiers fought a fierce battle for control of the tiny Pacific island of Iwo Jima, news photographer Joe Rosenthal snapped the following picture of a group of GIs erecting a flag on Mount Suribachi:

The photograph appeared in newspapers across the United States and around the world, and the U.S. government was quick to capitalize on its emotional power. The three surviving soldiers involved in the flag raising, John Bradley, Rene Gagnon, and Ira Hayes, were brought home and sent on a national tour to promote the sale of war bonds.

The photograph has proved so enduring that the story of how the photograph was taken and its impact on American culture has itself become an object of discussion, most notably in the book and movie *Flags of Our Fathers*. The photo uses the language of images to invite viewers to supply their own meanings and reactions to the picture. Yet the cultural history of the photo has not been without controversy. Some wondered if the photograph had been staged; that is, had the photographer deliberately posed the soldiers to emphasize a sense of heroic struggle and teamwork? While further research indicated that the soldiers were not posed and that Rosenthal did capture the picture spontaneously, other details emerged that suggested a more complex understanding of the picture. For example, the picture does not represent the first but the second flag raised on Mount Suribachi. "Raising the Flag on Iwo Jima," the title that the photograph acquired, could just as well be called "Replacing the Flag on Iwo Jima."

While the difference may seem slight from one perspective, some of the soldiers involved in raising the first flag wondered if they received so little attention because the photograph of that event proved less popular. Here is that photo:

## Working with the Text

1. Compare and contrast the photographs of the two flag raisings on Iwo Jima. Why do you think the photograph of the second flag raising became so much more popular? What if only the photograph of the first flag raising had existed? What are the strengths and weaknesses of that photograph? What difference, if any, does it make to know that the more famous photograph was not the first of the day?

2. Why do you think people wanted to know if the more famous photograph had been staged or posed? After all, everyone has posed for a photograph many times. What difference might it make in how people respond to "Raising the Flag on Iwo Jima" if it had been staged?

## SEEING IS BELIEVING? THE ETHICS OF PHOTOJOURNALISM IN THE DIGITAL AGE

As the questions raised over half a century ago about the famous photograph from Iwo Jima indicate, the same powerful emotional pull of images that leads us to seek them out when trying to understand a news event also makes us suspicious of them, and if anything, that suspicion has only increased in the digital age. Here are three more recent examples of photos that have raised questions about the ethics of using pictures to convey the news. The first comes from April 2003, soon after U.S. and other forces had captured the city of Baghdad in the Iraq war. An event in the center of Baghdad produced several photographs that appeared everywhere in the world media, in newspapers, on television, and on websites. Like "Raising the Flag on Iwo Jima," these photos produced feelings of pride and patriotism in many Americans. Here is an example of one of these photos that appeared on CNN:

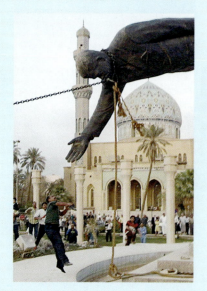

The story that accompanied the photo on the CNN website began: "Iraqis danced and waved the country's pre-1991 flag in central Baghdad's Firdos Square after a U.S. Marine armored recovery vehicle helped topple the square's huge statue of Iraqi President Saddam Hussein." Take a close look at the image and discuss what messages it conveys about the incident in the square, the progress of the war, and how American citizens might respond to this image. Expand your discussion by showing the image to others and getting their opinions.

Not long after these images appeared, another photograph of the same event began to appear online and in the media. Taken from a greater distance, this photo shows the entire square and the area in Baghdad around it:

## Working with the Text

1. Compare and contrast these two photographs of the statue toppling in Firdos Square. How well does the CNN description fit the second photograph?
2. Locate viewers who have seen only the first image of the statue toppling and show them the second photograph. What reactions do they have? What effect does the second picture have on their impressions of the first?

To some of the people who began to distribute the second, longer-range photograph of the events in the square, the widescreen image suggested not just a different perspective but also a different meaning for what happened that day. Instead of a spontaneous celebration by a large crowd of Iraqi citizens, the effort to topple the statue seemed limited to a small group in an otherwise deserted square. The fact that the square also seems surrounded by military vehicles made some suspect that the entire event might have been organized by the U.S. military and had more to do with public relations among the American public than the attitude of the Iraqi public. Referring to the iconic photograph from World War II that you examined, one British journalist suggested the events in Firdos Square were "the most staged photo opportunity since Iwo Jima."

Which interpretation is correct? Does the second Iraq photograph really refute the first, or does it only complicate our interpretations? While arguments continue over just what we are seeing in these photographs of Firdos Square, the controversy itself points to some critical issues involved in interpreting photos of news events:

- "Seeing is believing" is not as simple as it seems.
- How a photograph is taken, processed and presented—whether wide angle or close up, the focal point of the composition, what is included

in the frame and what isn't—can dramatically affect our understanding of that photograph.

- Perhaps most important, photographs themselves are rhetorical texts; that is, photographers think about purpose and audience just as writers do. Photographs can be thought of as visual arguments, nonverbal texts that nevertheless can be used to persuade, convince, or confront an audience.

## Working with the Text

1. Locate a news photograph in a newspaper, magazine, or on the Web. How does that photograph function as part of the rhetorical purpose of the story? Is it meant to illustrate an idea? Prove a point? Stir the reader's emotions? In what ways does the photograph make an argument? Come up with alternative arguments or interpretations that could be made about the same photograph.
2. Assume the role of a photo editor and think about what other pictures might help to tell the story, based on information in it. If you were working with a photographer, what kinds of shots would you suggest the photographer look for? What would be the composition of an ideal shot for your story and why?

### DIGITAL MANIPULATION

The kinds of questions raised by the two images of Firdos Square have been with us since the beginning of photography. Where the camera is pointed, how much is included in the frame, and how close the photographer is to the action are factors that have always been part of the ethics of photojournalism. But what about altering the nature of the image itself? What if what we see isn't just a matter of a close-up or a long shot, but of whether what we're seeing was exactly what was there? Take retouching: since photography began, photographers have been altering their work to add or eliminate colors, features, shadows, and lines. If you had a high school yearbook picture taken by a professional, chances are the final version of that photograph featured a face with smooth, even skin tones, free of blemishes or other marks. Rather than objecting, most of us are happy to go along with this kind of deception.

Digital photography and software have made altering photographs so easy that it is no longer something only the pros can do. Most basic digital photograph programs on home computers allow us to crop images, lighten and darken skin tones, change colors, even eliminate the scary red eye from portraits. If you have more advanced programs such as Adobe Photoshop, you can transform almost every aspect of the pictures you take. The Internet game of

Photoshop Tennis invites anyone to explore how digital technology allows us to transform photographic images in creative and fun ways.

The ease with which anyone can alter a digital photograph has had a profound impact on news photography. In 2006, for example, a photojournalist named Brian Walski admitted that a photo of his showing a British soldier coming under fire as he was helping civilians in Iraq was actually a composite of two different photographs that Walski had digitally combined. The picture had run in the *Los Angeles Times* and been picked up by other newspapers across the country before some sharp-eyed readers noticed small discrepancies that suggested the photo had been altered.

Walski resigned from his position after being confronted by his editors at the *LA Times.* The incident, however, added to an ongoing debate about the ethics of photojournalism in the digital age. Most journalists condemned what Walski had done as dishonest and deceitful. A few defended Walski, however, arguing that his combined picture did not really alter the basic facts of the situation but instead produced a more concise, effective summary of what was going on. Others pointed out that, even if most people agreed this example crossed the line of what was ethically acceptable, the line itself was not necessarily that clear. Think again, for example, of that retouched yearbook photo. Deceptive? Acceptable? How does our judgment differ depending on what we feel are the stakes involved?

The reality is that in the digital age images are just as flexible—and just as ambiguous and slippery—as words. In fact, some defenders of Walski argued that what he did was no different than a writer revising her text to make her points more vivid and effective. Others countered that the correct analogy would be to a writer who deliberately changed a direct quotation. What do you think the new rules are? Where can the line be drawn between acceptable and unacceptable manipulation of news images?

When Katie Couric was introduced as the first woman to anchor a network news broadcast alone, CBS released a publicity photo. Soon after, another photograph surfaced which suggested that CBS had altered the photo to make Couric appear slimmer. Acceptable or unacceptable?

## Working with the Text

1. You and your classmates are news editors, whether print, online, or on the air. In response to the Firdos Square and Walski examples, develop a set of guidelines for photographers and editors to follow in manipulating digital images. (Keep in mind that the issue is *not* whether but *how* to manipulate images. By framing a shot in the camera lens, adjusting focus, and pointing the camera in a specific direction, manipulation has already begun.) As you develop your guidelines, come up with test cases. If a photograph comes out overexposed, for example, would it be acceptable to use a software program to lighten the picture so that the image is clearer? Do you draw distinctions between the different kinds of news photos, say, war photography versus pictures of celebrities at an award show?

2. Explore the analogies between writing and photography in the digital age. As any computer scientist can tell you, anyone who uses a digital camera or writes on a computer produces the same kind of information: strings of binary code. How do the ethics of writing and photography compare and contrast with each other? When does writing become deceptive? When does photography become deceptive?

# CREATING CULTURE

## IRAQI WAR BLOGS

The development of blogs has allowed anyone around the world with Internet access to publish online his or her thoughts, feelings, and opinions on any subject, whether significant or trivial, on a daily basis. When the wars in Afghanistan and Iraq began in early 2003, the instant communication available through the World Wide Web meant that soldiers and civilians alike could share their experiences of the war with readers across national borders and lines of conflict. For the first time in history, Internet users could read direct, daily updates from people involved in war, unfiltered by official news media and government sources.

### from *Baghdad Burning: Girl Blog from Iraq*

### Riverbend

*Most war blogging occurs among small networks of family and friends, unnoticed by newspaper and television reporters and difficult to track by academics and scholars. A few blogs, however, achieve wider popularity through word of net: users recommend a blog site to other users until eventually more prominent websites and publications begin to take notice. One such site is Baghdad Burning (at http://riverbendblog.blogspot.com/), written by a young Iraqi woman who goes by the pseudonym of Riverbend to protect her identity. Her blog first appeared in August 2003, the month and year that the United States invaded Iraq. Hers is one of a number of blogs written by Iraqis about the war, including one she refers to often in her blog by a young Iraqi man who uses the name Salam Pax (a combination of the Arabic and Latin words for "peace"). In 2007, Riverbend fled Iraq and now lives with her family as a refugee in Syria.*

*What distinguishes both the blogs by Riverbend and Salam Pax is that they are written in English and meant to be read by an English-speaking audience. This linguistic border crossing defines one of the most significant aspects of blogging during the Iraq war: relatively speaking, there are many more Arabic- and Kurdish-speaking Iraqis who are also fluent in*

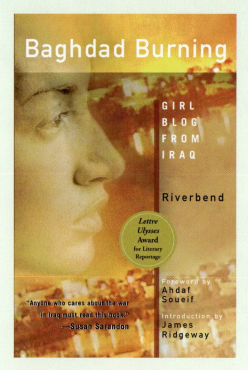

Baghdad Burning

GIRL
BLOG
FROM
IRAQ

Riverbend

*Lettre Ulysses Award for Literary Reportage*

"Anyone who cares about the war in Iraq must read this book."
—Susan Sarandon

Foreword by
Ahdaf Soueif

Introduction by
James Ridgeway

English than there are native English-speaking Americans who can speak and write fluent Arabic. As a result, many Iraqis (and others in the Arabic-speaking world) are able to read and listen to American media sources and websites in English, but most Americans have to rely on multilingual writers such as Riverbend to gain an Iraqi perspective on world events.

Riverbend's blog has attained such international interest that her postings have now been compiled into two books, Baghdad Burning: Girl Blog from Iraq *and* Baghdad Burning II: More Girl Blog from Iraq. *In the following samples, Riverbend introduces herself and her blog, writes about life in Baghdad during wartime, expresses her opinions about the war and her encounters with the U.S. military, and reacts to American media accounts of the war and of Iraqi and Islamic culture.*

## Before You Read

1. What are your impressions of Iraq in general and Baghdad in particular? What are your expectations about what you might read in Riverbend's blogs, and on what do you base your expectations—news accounts? Discussions with friends and family members? Talking with someone who has served in Iraq, or your own military service?

2. As a class, organize your impressions and expectations into three categories: "Information About Life in Iraq That We Are Certain Of," "Information About Life in Iraq We Think Is Probably True," and "Information About Life in Iraq That We Have Heard of But Have Doubts About." What information or impressions are easiest to categorize? Which are most difficult?

**Sunday, August 17, 2003**

**THE BEGINNING...**

So this is the beginning for me, I guess. I never thought I'd start my own weblog...All I could think, every time I wanted to start one was "but who will read it?" I guess I've got nothing to lose...but I'm warning you—expect a lot of complaining and ranting. I looked for a "rantlog" but this is the best Google came up with.

A little bit about myself: I'm female, Iraqi, and 24. I survived the war. That's all you need to know. It's all that matters these days anyway. Riverbend **posted by river @ 7:36 P.M.**

**WAKING UP**

Waking up anywhere in Iraq these days is a trial. It happens in one of two ways: either slowly, or with a jolt. The slow process works like this: you're hanging in a place on the edge of consciousness, mentally grabbing at the fading fragments of a dream...something creeps up around, all over you—like a fog. A warm heavy fog. It's the heat...120 F on the cooler nights. Your eyes flutter open and they search the dark in dismay—the electricity has gone off. The ceiling fan is slowing down and you are now fully awake. Trying to sleep in the stifling heat is about as productive as trying to wish the ceiling fan into motion with your brain. Impossible.

The other way to wake up is to be jolted into reality with the sound of a gunshot, explosion, or yelling. You sit up, horrified and panicked, any dream or nightmare shattered to oblivion. What can it be? A burglar? A gang of looters? An attack? A bomb? Or maybe it's just an American midnight raid? **posted by river @ 8:02 P.M.**

**Monday, August 18, 2003**

**ANOTHER DAY...**

Normal day today. We were up at early morning, did the usual "around the house things," you know—check if the water tank is full, try to determine when the electricity will be off, checked if there was enough cooking gas...

You know what really bugs me about posting on the Internet, chat rooms, or message boards? The first reaction (usually from Americans) is "You're lying, you're not Iraqi." Why am I not Iraqi, well because, a. I have Internet access (Iraqis have no Internet), b. I know how to use the Internet (Iraqis don't know what computers are), and c. Iraqis don't know how to speak English (I must be a Liberal). All that shouldn't bother me, but it does. I see the troops in the streets and think, "So that's what they thought of us before they occupied us...that may be what they think of us now. How is it that we're seen as another Afghanistan?"

**Tuesday, August 19, 2003**

**TIRED**

How is it possible to wake up tired? It feels like I've been struggling in my sleep...struggling with nightmares, struggling with fears...struggling to listen for gunshots or tanks. I'm just so tired today. It's not the sort of "tired" where I want to sleep—it's the sort of tired where I just want to completely shut down...put myself on standby, if you will. I think everyone feels that way lately.

Today a child was killed in Anbar, a governorate northwest of Baghdad. His name was Omar Jassim and he was no more than 10 years old, maybe 11. Does anyone hear of that? Does it matter anymore? Do they show that on Fox News or CNN? He was killed during an American raid—no one knows why. His family is devastated—nothing was taken from the house because nothing was found in the house. It was just one of those raids. People are terrified of the raids. You never know what will happen—who might be shot, who might react wrong—what exactly the wrong reaction might be...Things are getting stolen too—gold, watches, money (dollars)...That's not to say ALL the troops steal—that's unfair. It's like saying all of Iraq was out there looting. But it really is difficult having to worry about looters, murderers, gangs, militias, and now American troops. I know, I know—someone is saying, "You ungrateful Iraqis! They are doing this for YOU...the raids are for YOU!" But the truth is, the raids only accomplish one thing: they act as a constant reminder that we are under occupation, we are not independent, we are not free, we are not liberated. We are no longer safe in our own homes—everything now belongs to someone else.

I can't see the future at this point, or maybe I don't choose to see it. Maybe we're just blocking it out like a bad memory or premonition. Eventually it will creep up on you, though. We're living, this moment, the future we were afraid to contemplate 6 months ago. It's like trying to find your way out of a nightmare. I just wish they would take the oil and go...

### Thursday, August 21, 2003

#### EMAILS

Wow. Dozens of emails were the result of being on Salam's blog. I was astounded. I guess I never thought so many people would end up reading the blog. It has made me appreciative and nervous all at the same time.

Most of the emails moved me to...gratitude. Thank you for understanding...no, thank you for even *trying* to understand. Other emails, on the other hand, were full of criticism, cynicism, and anger. You really don't have to read my blog if you don't want to and you certainly don't have to email me telling me how much you hate it. It's great to get questions and differing opinions—but please be intelligent about it, and above all, creative—if I want to hear what Fox News has to say, I'll watch it.

And keep one thing in mind—tanks and guns can break my bones, but emails can be deleted.    **posted by river @ 3:13 P.M.**

#### MY NEW TALENT

Suffering from a bout of insomnia last night, I found myself in front of the television, channel-surfing. I was looking for the usual—an interesting interview with one of the council, some fresh news, a miracle...Promptly at 2 A.M., the electricity went off and I was plunged into the pitch black hell better-known as "an August night with no electricity in Iraq." So I sat there, in the dark, trying to remember where I had left the candle and matches. After 5 minutes of chagrined meditation, I decided I would "feel" my way up the stairs and out onto the roof. Step by hesitant step, I stumbled out into the corridor and up the stairs, stubbing a toe on the last step (which wasn't supposed to be there).

(For those of you who don't know, people sleep up on the roof in some of the safer areas because when the electricity goes off, the houses get so hot, it feels like you are cooking gently inside of an oven. The roof isn't much better, but at least there's a semblance of wind.)

Out on the roof, the heat was palpitating off of everything in waves. The strange thing is that if you stand in the center, you can feel it emanating from the walls and ground toward you from all directions. I stood there trying to determine whether it was only our area, or the whole city, that had sunk into darkness.

A few moments later, my younger brother (we'll call him E.) joined me— disheveled, disgruntled, and half-asleep. We stood leaning on the low wall enclosing the roof watching the street below. I could see the tip of Abu Maan's cigarette glowing in the yard next door. I pointed to it with the words, "Abu Maan can't sleep either..." E. grunted with the words, "It's probably Maan." I stood staring at him like he was half—wild—or maybe talking in his sleep. Maan is only 13...how is he smoking? How can he be smoking?

"He's only 13." I stated.

"Is anyone only 13 anymore?" he asked.

I mulled the reality of this remark over. No, no one is 13 anymore. No one is 24 anymore...everyone is 85 and I think I might be 105. I was too tired to speak and, in spite of his open eyes, I suspected E. was asleep. The silence was shattered a few moments later by the sound of bullets in the distance. It was just loud enough to get your attention, but too far away to be the source of any real anxiety. I tried to determine where they were coming from...

> **E:** *How far do you think that is?*
>
> **Me:** *I don't know... 'bout a kilometer?*
>
> **E:** *Yeah, about.*
>
> **Me:** *Not American bullets—*
>
> **E:** *No, it's probably from a...*
>
> **Me:** *Klashnikov [Kalishnikov].*
>
> **E (impressed):** *You're getting good at this.*

No—I'm getting great at it. I can tell you if it's "them" or "us." I can tell you how far away it is. I can tell you if it's a pistol or machine-gun, tank or armored vehicle, Apache or Chinook...I can determine the distance and maybe even the target. That's my new talent. It's something I've gotten so good at, I frighten myself. What's worse is that almost everyone seems to have acquired this new talent...young and old. And it's not something that anyone will appreciate on a résumé...

I keep wondering...will an airplane ever sound the same again?  **posted by river @ 3:15 P.M.**

**Friday, August 22, 2003**

**SETTING THE RECORD STRAIGHT**

I'm going to set the record straight, once and for all.

I don't hate Americans, contrary to what many people seem to believe. Not because I love Americans, but simply because I don't hate Americans, like I don't hate the French, Canadians, Brits, Saudis, Jordanians, Micronesians, etc. It's that simple. I was brought up, like millions of Iraqis, to have pride in my own culture and nationality. At the same time, like millions of Iraqis, I was also brought up to respect other cultures, nations, and religions. Iraqi people are inquisitive, by nature, and accepting of different values—as long as you do not try to impose those values and beliefs upon them.

Although I hate the American military presence in Iraq in its current form, I don't even hate the American troops...or wait, sometimes I do:

—I hated them all through the bombing. Every single day and night we had to sit in terror of the next bomb, the next plane, the next explosion. I hated them when I saw the expression of terror, and remembrance, on the faces of my family and friends, as we sat in the dark, praying for our lives, the lives of our loved ones, and the survival of Iraq.

—I hated them on April 11—a cool, gray day: the day our family friend lost her husband, her son, and a toddler daughter when a tank hit the family car as they were trying to evacuate the house in Al-A'adhamiya district—an area that saw heavy fighting.

—I hated them on June 3 when our car was pulled over for some strange reason in the middle of Baghdad, and we (3 women, a man, and a child) were made to get out and stand in a row, while our handbags were rummaged, the men were frisked, and the car was thoroughly checked by angry, brisk soldiers. I don't think I'll ever be able to put into words the humiliation of being searched.

—I hated them for two hours on July 13. As we were leaving Baghdad, we were detained with dozens of other cars at a checkpoint in the sweltering, dizzying heat.

—I hated them the night my cousin's house was raided—a man with a wife, daughter, and two young girls. He was pushed out of the house with his hands behind his head while his wife and screaming daughters were made to wait in the kitchen as around 20 troops systematically searched the house, emptying closets, rummaging underwear drawers, and overturning toy boxes.

—I hated them on April 28 when they shot and killed over a dozen kids and teenagers in Falloojeh [Falluja]—a place west of Baghdad. The American troops had taken over a local school (one of the only schools) and the kids and parents went to stand in front of the school in a peaceful demonstration. Some kids started throwing rocks at the troops, and the troops opened fire on the crowd. That incident was the beginning of bloodshed in Falloojeh.

On the other hand...

—I feel terrible seeing the troops standing in this merciless sun—wearing heavy clothes...looking longingly into the air-conditioned interiors of our cars. After all, in the end this is Baghdad, we're Iraqi—we've seen this heat before.

—I feel bad seeing them stand around, drinking what can only be lukewarm water after hours in the sun—too afraid to accept any proffered ice water from "strange Iraqis."

—I feel pity watching their confused, frightened expressions as some outraged, jobless, father of five shouts at them in a language they can't even begin to understand.

—I get hopeless, seeing them pointing their guns and tanks at everyone because, in their eyes, anyone could be a "terrorist" and almost everyone is an angry, frustrated Iraqi.

—I feel sympathy seeing them sitting bored and listless on top of their tanks and in their cars—wishing they were somewhere else.

So now you know. Mixed feelings in a messed up world.

I talk about "American troops" because those are the only ones I've come into contact with—no British soldiers, no Italians, no Spaniards...I don't know—maybe they feel the same towards the British in the south.

Someone wrote that I was naïve and probably spoiled, etc., and that "not one single American soldier deserves to die for you." I completely agree. No one deserves to die for me or for anyone else.

This war started out a war on WMD [weapons of mass destruction]. When those were not found, and proof was flimsy at best, it turned suddenly into a "War Against Terrorism." When links couldn't be made to al-Qaeda or Osama bin Laden (besides on Fox and in Bush's head), it turned into a "Liberation." Call it whatever you want—to me it's an occupation.

My suggestion? Bring in UN peace-keeping forces and pull out the American troops. Let the people decide who they want to represent them. Let the governing council be composed of Iraqis who were suffering the blockade and wars *inside* of Iraq. People are angry and frustrated and the American troops are the ones who are going to have to bear the brunt of that anger simply because the American administration is running the show, and making the mistakes.

It always saddens me to see that the majority of them are so young. Just as it isn't fair that I have to spend my 24th year suffering this whole situation, it doesn't seem fair that they have to spend their 19th, 20th, etc., suffering it either. In the end, we have something in common—we're all the victims of decisions made by the Bush administration.

On the other hand...they'll be back home, safe, in a month, or two or three or six...and we'll be here having to cope with the mess of a homeland we have now.   **posted by river @ 7:51 P.M.**

## ABOUT RIVERBEND

A lot of you have been asking about my background and the reason why my English is good. I am Iraqi—born in Iraq to Iraqi parents, but was raised abroad for several years as a child. I came back in my early teens and continued studying in English in Baghdad—reading any book I could get my hands on. Most of my friends are of different ethnicities, religions, and nationalities. I am bilingual. There are thousands in Iraq like me—kids of diplomats, students, expatriates, etc.

As to my connection with Western culture...you wouldn't believe how many young Iraqi people know so much about American/British/French pop culture. They know all about Arnold Schwarzenegger, Brad Pitt, Whitney Houston, McDonalds, and M.I.B.s...Iraqi TV stations were constantly showing bad copies of the latest Hollywood movies. (If it's any consolation, the Marines lived up to the Rambo/Terminator reputation which preceded them.)

But no matter what—I shall remain anonymous. I wouldn't feel free to write otherwise. I think Salam and Gee are incredibly brave...who knows, maybe one day I will be too. You know me as Riverbend, you share a very small part of my daily reality—I hope that will suffice.   **posted by river @ 11:33 P.M.**

## COUSINS AND VEILS...

This is some further commentary on John Tierney's article "Iraq Family Ties Complicate American Efforts for Change," printed in the *New York Times.*

> "A key purpose of veiling is to prevent outsiders from competing with a
> woman's cousins for marriage," Dr. Kurtz said. "Attack veiling, and you
> are attacking the core of the Middle Eastern social system." ("Iraqi Family
> Ties Complicate American Efforts for Change," *NY Times,* September 28, 2003,
> http://query.nytimes.com/)

Thank you Stanley Kurtz, anthropologist at the Hoover Institution.

He took hundreds of years of wearing the veil for religious reasons and relegated it all to the oppression of females by their male cousins. Wow—human nature is that simple.

I can see the image now—my cousins roaming the opening of our cave, holding clubs and keeping a wary eye on the female members of their clan... and us cowed, frightened females all gathered in groups, murmuring behind our veils...

I have a question: why is Dr. Kurtz using the word "veil" in relation to Iraq? Very, very few females wore veils or burqas prior to the occupation. Note that I say "veil" or "burqa." If Dr. Kurtz meant the general "hijab" or headscarf worn on the hair by millions of Muslim females instead of an actual "veil," then he should have been more specific. While a "veil" in Saudi Arabia or Afghanistan is quite common, in Iraq it speaks of extremism. It is uncommon because the majority of moderate Muslim clerics believe it is unnecessary.

A "veil" is a piece of cloth that covers the whole face and head. It is called a "veil" in English and called a [burqa], "khimar," or "pushi" in Iraq. The khimar or burqa covers the whole face, or it covers it all with the exception of the eyes.

The standard "hijab" or "rabta" is a simple headscarf that covers the hair and neck, and can be worn in a variety of ways. The majority of "covered" females in Iraq wear a simple hijab. Some fashionable females wear a turban-like head cover and something with a high collar that generally serves the same purpose. The hijab can be any color. Some women prefer white, others black, and I have friends who own every color and design imaginable and look so good, it almost seems more like a fashion statement than a religious one.

The "abaya," on the other hand, is a long, cloak-like garment and is more traditional than it is religious. Although designs vary, the abaya is similar in style to the standard graduation robe—long, wide, and flowing. Some abayas are designed to cover the head, and others are made only to wear on the shoulders. Men, as well as women, wear abayas. The feminine abayas are often black and may have some sort of design on them. Male abayas are plain, with perhaps some simple embroidery along the edges, and are brown, black, gray, beige, or khaki. Abayas are often worn in Iraq, although the younger generations don't like them—I haven't worn one yet.

The hijab can be worn with ordinary clothing—skirts, shirts, and pants as long as they are "appropriate." The skirt should be somewhat long, the shirt a little bit loose, and the sleeves should be below the elbows and, if worn with pants, a bit long. The purpose of the hijab is to protect females from sexual harassment. It acts as a sort of safeguard against ogling and uninvited attention.

Muslim females do not wear a hijab or veil because their male cousins *make* them wear it. They wear it for religious reasons. I personally don't wear a hijab or headscarf, but I know many females who do—in Baghdad, in Mosul, in Najaf, in Kerbela, in Falloojeh…in Jordan, in Syria, in Lebanon, in Saudi Arabia—and *none* of these females wear a headscarf because their *cousins* make them wear it. They wear the headscarf out of a conviction that it is the correct thing to do and out of the comfort and security it gives them. Cousins have nothing to do with it and Dr. Kurtz's very simplistic explanation is an insult.

Dr. Kurtz would have better said, "Attack the headscarf or the hijab and you are attacking the core of the Middle Eastern social system because the majority of the Middle East is Muslim and the headscarf is considered a required part of Islam by a huge number of Muslims." Attacking the hijab would be the equivalent of attacking a Christian's right to wear a cross, or a Jew's right to wear a yarmulke...   **posted by river @ 11:04 P.M.**

**CHRISTMAS IN BAGHDAD...**

Explosions and bombing almost all day yesterday and deep into the night. At some points it gets hard to tell who is bombing who. Resistance or Americans? Tanks or mortars? Cluster bombs or IEDs [improvised explosive devices]? Nothing on the news...to see the reports on CNN, Abu Dhabi, and Al-Arabia you'd think there was nothing going on in Baghdad beyond the usual thumps and thuds. Yesterday was *very* unusual. Embassies, mines, residential areas, and the Green Zone...and the sirens. I hate the sirens. I can stand the explosions, the rattling windows, the slamming doors, the planes, the helicopters...but I feel like my heart is wailing when I hear the sirens.

The explosions haven't really put anyone in a very festive spirit. The highlight of the last few days, for me, was when we went to our Christian friends' home to keep them company on Christmas Eve. We live in a neighborhood with a number of Christian families and, under normal circumstances, the area would be quite festive this time of year—little plastic Santas on green lawns, an occasional plastic wreath on a door, and some colored, blinking lights on trees.

Our particular friends (Abu Josef's family) specialized in the lights. Every year, a week before Christmas, they would not only decorate their own plastic tree (evergreens are hard to come by in Iraq), but they would decorate 4 different olive trees in the little garden in front of their home with long strings of red lights. Passing by their house, the scene of the green olive trees with branches tangled in little red lights always brought a smile...you couldn't help but feel the "Christmas spirit"—Christians and Muslims alike.

This year the trees weren't decorated because, as their father put it, "We don't want to attract too much attention...and it wouldn't be right with the electricity shortage." The tree inside of their house *was* decorated, however, and it was almost sagging with ornaments. The traditional tree ornaments were hanging, but the side of the tree was covered with not-so-traditional Pokemon toys. Their 8-year-old is an avid collector of those little Pokemon finger puppets and the bottom section of the tree was drooping with the weight of the little plastic figures which took Iraq by storm a couple of years ago.

Kids in Iraq also believe in Santa Claus, but people here call him "Baba Noel" which means "Father Noel." I asked the children what he looked like and they generally agreed that he was fat, cheerful, decked in red, and had white hair. (Their impertinent 11-year-old explains that he's fat because of the dates, cheerful because of the alcohol, and wears red because he's a communist!) He doesn't drop into Iraqi homes through the chimney, though, because very few Iraqi homes actually have chimneys. He also doesn't drop in unexpectedly in the middle of the night because that's just rude. He acts as more of an inspiration to parents when they are out buying Christmas gifts for the kids; a holiday muse, if you will. The reindeer are a foreign concept here.

The annual ritual around Christmas for many Christians in Baghdad used to be generally hanging out with family and friends on Christmas Eve, exchanging gifts and food (always food—if you're Iraqi, it's going to be food) and receiving guests and well-wishers. At 12 A.M., many would attend a Christmas service at their local church and light candles to greet the Christmas spirit. Christmas day would be like our first day of Eid—eating and drinking, receiving family, friends, and neighbors, and preparing for the inevitable Christmas party in the evening at either a friend's house or in one of the various recreational clubs in Baghdad. The most famous for their Christmas parties were the Hindiya club and the Armenian club.

This year, the Christmas service was early and many people didn't go because they either didn't have gasoline, or just didn't feel safe driving around Baghdad in the evening. Many of them also couldn't join their families because of the security situation. Abu Josef's family have aunts and uncles in a little village north of Mosul. Every year, the extended relatives come down and stay in their house for a week to celebrate Christmas and New Year. This year they've decided to stay in their village because it just isn't safe to leave their home and head for Baghdad.

At one point during the evening, the house was dark and there was no electricity. We sat, gathered around on the ground, eating date-balls and watching Abu Josef's dog chew on the lowest branch of the tree. The living room was lit by the warm light radiating from the kerosene heater and a few Christmas candles set on the coffee table. Abu Josef's phone suddenly rang shrilly and Abu Josef ran to pick it up. It was his brother in Toronto and it was the perfect Christmas gift because it was the first time Abu Josef got an overseas call since the war— we were all amazed. An Iraqi phone conversation goes like this these days:

*III = Iraqi Inside Iraq*

*IOI = Iraqi Outside Iraq*

*Ring, ring*

**II:** *Alloo?*

**OI:** *ALLOO?!*

**II:** *ALLOOOO? MINNOOO? (Hello? Who is it?)*

**IOI:** *ABU (fill in the blank)??! Shlonkum? (How are you?)*

**III:** *Aaaagh! Is it really you?!*

*(Chorus of family in the background, "Who is it?! Who is it?!")*

**IOI:** *How are... (the voice cracks here with emotion) you?*

**III:** *We're... (the line crackles)... and is doing well.*

**IOI:** *I CAN'T HEAR YOU! Doing well? Thank God...*

**III:** *Alloo? Alloo...? (speaker turns to speak to someone in the background, "Sshhh... I can't hear anything!" The family go silent and hold their breaths.)*

**III:** *Alloo? Alloo?!*

**IOI:** *Alloo? Yes, yes, your voice is back—are you ok?*

**III:** *Fine, fine.*

**IOI:** *Is my mother ok? My brothers and sisters?*

**III:** *All fine... we're fine, thank God.*

**IOI:** *Thank God (the voice cracks again)*

**III:** *How are you? (a vague echo with "you... you... you...")*

**IOI:** *We're fine but terribly worried about all of YOU...*

**III:** *Don't worry—we're alright—we're doing alright... no electricity or fuel, but we'll be alright...*

**IOI:** *(crackling line... fading voices)... tried and tried to call but... (more crackling line)... and we heard horrible... (static)*

**III:** *Alloo? Alloooooooo? Are you there? (silence on the other end)*

**III:** *Alloo? If you can hear me, I can't hear you... (the hovering relatives all hold their breath)*

**III:** *... I still can't hear you... if you can hear me just know that we're fine. We're ok. We're alive and wondering about your health. Don't worry... yallah, ma'a al salama... don't worry. Alloo... Alloo...?*

And everyone exhales feeling a bit more relieved and a little bit empty as the phone is returned to the cradle and the momentous event passes.

Although it's late—Merry Christmas.   **posted by river @ 5:25 P.M.**

### January 12, 2006

**THANK YOU FOR THE MUSIC...**

When I first heard about the abduction of *Christian Science Monitor* journalist Jill Carroll a week ago, I remember feeling regret. It was the same heavy feeling I get every time I hear of another journalist killed or abducted. The same heavy feeling that settles upon most Iraqis, I imagine, when they hear of acquaintances suffering under the current situation.

I read the news as a subtitle on TV. We haven't had an Internet connection for several days so I couldn't really read about the details. All I knew was that a journalist had been abducted and that her Iraqi interpreter had been killed. He was shot in cold blood in Al-Adil district earlier this month, when they took Jill Carroll...They say he didn't die immediately. It is said he lived long enough to talk to police and then he died.

I found out very recently that the interpreter killed was a good friend—Alan, of Alan's Melody, and I've spent the last two days crying.

Everyone knew him as simply "Alan," or "Elin" as it is pronounced in Iraqi Arabic. Prior to the war, he owned a music shop in the best area in Baghdad, A'arasat. He sold some Arabic music and instrumental music, but he had his regular customers—those Westernized Iraqis who craved foreign music. For those of us who listened to rock, adult alternative, jazz, etc., he had very few rivals.

He sold bootleg CDs, tapes, and DVDs. His shop wasn't just a music shop—it was a haven. Some of my happiest moments were while I was walking out of that shop carrying CDs and tapes, full of anticipation for the escape the music provided. He had just about everything from Abba to Marilyn Manson. He could provide anything. All you had to do was go to him with the words, "Alan—I heard a great song on the radio...you have to find it!" And he'd sit there, patiently, asking who sang it? You don't know? Ok—was it a man or a woman? Fine. Do you remember any of the words? Chances were that he'd already heard it and even knew some of the lyrics.

During the sanctions, Iraq was virtually cut off from the outside world. We had maybe four or five local TV stations and it was only during the later years that the Internet became more popular. Alan was one of those links with the outside world. Walking into Alan's shop was like walking into a sort of transitional other world. Whenever you walked into the store, great music would be blaring from his speakers and he and Mohammed, the guy who worked in his shop, would be arguing over who was better, Joe Satriani or Steve Vai.

He would have the latest Billboard hits posted on a sheet of paper near the door and he'd have compiled a few of his own favorites on a "collection" CD. He also went out of his way to get recordings of the latest award shows—Grammys, AMAs, Oscars, etc. You could visit him twice and know that by the third time, he'd have memorized your favorites and found music you might be interested in.

He was an electrical engineer—but his passion was music. His dream was to be a music producer. He was always full of scorn for the usual boy bands—N'Sync, Backstreet Boys, etc.—but he was always trying to promote an Iraqi boy band he claimed he'd discovered, "Unknown to No One." "They're great—wallah they have potential," he'd say. E. would answer, "Alan, they're terrible." And Alan, with his usual Iraqi pride would lecture about how they were great, simply because they were Iraqi.

He was a Christian from Basrah and he had a lovely wife who adored him—F. We would tease him about how once he was married and had a family, he'd lose interest in music. It didn't happen. Conversations with Alan continued to revolve around Pink Floyd, Jimmy Hendrix, but they began to include F. his wife, M. his daughter, and his little boy. My heart aches for his family—his wife and children...

You could walk into the shop and find no one behind the counter—everyone was in the other room, playing one version or another of FIFA soccer on the Play Station. He collected those old records, or "vinyls." The older they were, the better. While he promoted new musical technology, he always said that nothing could beat the sound of a vintage vinyl.

We went to Alan not just to buy music. It always turned into a social visit. He'd make you sit down, listen to his latest favorite CD, and drink something. Then he'd tell you the latest gossip—he knew it all. He knew where all the parties were, who the best DJs were, and who was getting married or divorced. He knew the local gossip and the international gossip, but it was never malicious with Alan. It was always the funny sort.

The most important thing about Alan was that he never let you down. Never. Whatever it was that you wanted, he'd try his hardest to get it. If you became his friend, that didn't just include music—he was ready to lend a helping hand to those in need, whether it was just to give advice, or listen after a complicated, difficult week.

After the war, the area he had his shop in deteriorated. There were car bombs and shootings and the Badir people took over some of the houses there. People went to A'arasat less and less because it was too dangerous. His shop was closed up more than it was open. He shut it up permanently after getting death threats and a hand grenade through his shop window. His car was carjacked at some point and he was shot at so he started driving around in his father's beaten-up old Toyota Cressida with a picture of Sistani on his back window. "To ward off the fanatics..." He winked and grinned.

E. and I would stop by his shop sometimes after the war, before he shut it down. We went in once and found that there was no electricity, and no generator. The shop was dimly lit with some sort of fuel lamp and Alan was sitting behind the counter, sorting through CDs. He was ecstatic to see us. There was no way we could listen to music so he and E. sang through some of their favorite songs, stumbling upon the lyrics and making things up along the way. Then we started listening to various ring tones and swapping the latest jokes of the day. Before we knew it, two hours had slipped by and the world outside was forgotten, an occasional explosion bringing us back to reality.

It hit me then that it wasn't the music that made Alan's shop a haven—somewhere to forget problems and worries—it was Alan himself.

He loved Pink Floyd:

Did you see the frightened ones?

Did you hear the falling bombs?... —"Goodbye Blue Sky," Pink Floyd

Goodbye, Alan... **posted by river @ 10:05 P.M.**

# Working with the Text

1. In her first blog entries, how does Riverbend introduce herself? What impression do you think she is trying to make and why? What about this initial persona do you find most surprising? Most interesting? Most and least inviting?

2. In particular, what kinds of relationships do you think she is trying to establish with American readers and why? What assumptions does she appear to be making about readers in the United States? What common values, interests, and experiences does she use to connect with her readers?

3. Choose one of the entries and write a response to it in the form of an email or blog posting. Try approaching your response from the perspective of a conversation or dialogue. For example, in what ways might her entry be either openly or by suggestion asking a question or questions of her American readers? What sorts of opinions or responses do you think she would be interested in hearing? How can you craft your response to invite a response in turn? What more information would you like to read from her to understand her position more clearly?

4. Riverbend uses her blog to comment on an important world event—the war in Iraq—that has a direct and immediate impact on her day-to-day life. Choose a significant political, social, or cultural issue about which you feel strongly and have a personal connection to, and design your own blog as a way of chronicling your day-to-day thinking about this issue. Keep in mind that blogs work best when the writer selects a subject that he or she thinks about or has to deal with on a regular basis, that is, an issue that produces more than just a one-time response or statement of opinion. Write about why you think this issue will continue to inspire you to produce blog entries on a regular basis.

   As you continue to design your blog, consider the following criteria:
   - **Persona:** Even if you are writing a first-person blog using your real name, you still need to think about what aspects of your personality to portray in your blog persona. For example, in *Baghdad Burning*, Riverbend writes about her own experiences, but she does so in a way that suggests she realizes that many readers will see her as a spokesperson for many Iraqis in general, a persona that she probably doesn't assume when chatting or emailing her friends. One way to think about persona is to ask yourself, If a stranger visited my blog, how would I like him or her to describe me to a friend?

- **Target audience:** In your opinion, who would be most likely to visit your blog? How can you design your blog to attract readers you would most like to be in a conversation with? As you write postings to your blog, how do you imagine your readers?
- **Purpose:** Does your blog have some long-term or enduring goals? We might say that all bloggers share the common goal of self-expression, but since writing is a social activity, all writing either implicitly or explicitly connects with social goals as well. For example, we might assume that one of Riverbend's larger goals is to open a dialogue with American and other English-speaking readers in order to influence perceptions of Iraq in U.S. society.

on TV? This question, a staple of the American home
the early 1950s, has gotten a lot harder to answer
ent years. People of a certain age (including the
of this textbook) can remember when the range of

# SEVEN

CHAPTER

's on TV? This
ten a lot hard
ter of this
uestion was p
uction of tel
television-co
d over the ai
al broadcaste
k (hence their
on TV? This q
a lot harder
ter of this
uestion was p
uction of tel
television-co
d over the ai
al broadcaste
k (hence their
on TV? This q
a lot harder
iter of this
uestion was p
uction of tel

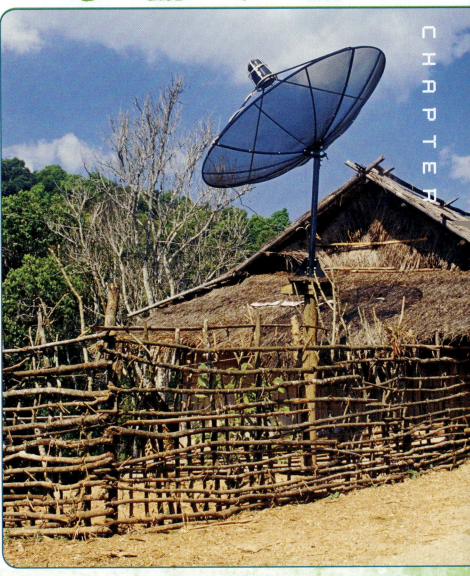

on TV? This question, a staple
American home since the early
has gotten a lot harder to
in recent years. People of a
n age (including the writer
s textbook) can remember when
ange of possible answers to
question was pretty simple.

## Video Pop:
# Television in the
# Digital Age

What's on TV? This question, a staple of the American home since the early 1950s, has gotten a lot harder to answer in recent years. People of a certain age (including the writer of this textbook) can remember when the range of possible answers to this question was pretty simple. For almost thirty years following the wide-scale introduction of television after World War II, all of the programming we thought of as television—comedy, action, and drama shows; sports events; commercials—was carried over the airwaves from a limited number of sources. There were three main national broadcasters—NBC, CBS, and ABC—and they broadcast their programs via a network (hence their label) of local affiliate stations in cities across the country.

These local stations filled in the time when there wasn't network programming to show by airing old movies, reruns of cancelled shows, and some locally produced programming. Depending on the size of a city, there might be anywhere from one to five independent local stations that broadcast the same basic combination of programs and network shows. With the advent of UHF programming and public broadcasting, the number of options increased slightly, but their programming proved to be limited as well. In fact, just about every broadcast station signed off sometime after midnight and showed test patterns until the morning!

What's on TV? In this earlier world of television, a quick glance at a printed guide could give you the four or five choices available at any given time. Starting in the late 1970s and early 1980s, however, new technological developments and distribution methods began to permanently change the way we watch television, both here and around the world. Cable television suddenly expanded the amount of programming that could be delivered to individual television sets. At the same time, the production of mass market video-recording equipment, from videocassette recorders to the more contemporary digital video recorders, meant viewers were no longer required to adjust their daily lives around the television schedule. Videocassettes and later DVDs created new competition for television because consumers could now choose to watch recorded programming such as movies available for rent at local video stores or for free at public libraries.

The changes were both profound and swift. There has never been a greater number or variety of programs available to most television viewers, but now no single program or network can match the number of viewers that a popular show from the 1960s or 1970s could command. Special television events such as the moon landing or the mini-series *Roots* would draw huge ratings and viewer shares (the percentage of all television viewers watching that program). In 1982, an amazing 77 percent of everyone watching television in America tuned into the final episode of the comedy/drama *M\*A\*S\*H*. Today, popular shows such as *American Idol* create headlines if less than half of that percentage of viewers watches, and not even most Super Bowl broadcasts today can capture the attention of so many people at the same time.

# O N E

## Television Then and Now

Locate several television viewers whose experience with the medium goes back before the advent of cable television, or if you are such a person, you can write about your own experience. Choosing people born before 1970 might be a good rule of thumb. Interview them to find out how their relationship to television has changed over the years. Do they find themselves watching more or less television? Are there changes in how they locate programs or when they watch? Which changes would they describe as most positive and negative? Do they feel that the influence and importance of television has grown or diminished, or perhaps changed in crucial ways?

## WHAT IS TV IN THE DIGITAL AGE?

The development of cable television has changed the medium in radical ways. The addition of satellite television has only added to the availability of channels and globalized television viewing; people around the world can now access an international array of programming. Across the globe, the computer dish affixed to the outside of even the most humble dwelling has become as ubiquitous as the television set itself.

And speaking of the television set, even that staple of late twentieth-century American home décor has been transformed. As the total number of sets per household has grown, so too have the kinds of sets, from mini-TVs that fit in the back of car headrests to big screen and plasma TVs that dominate what are now called home theaters. And television programming has moved away from the television set as well: programs can be watched on computer terminals or downloaded to digital music players such as the iPod.

Given all of this diversity, we may be led to ask the question, Just what do we mean by the term *television* anyway? Are cooking shows, reality television programs, sporting events, animated sitcoms, the proceedings of Congress, and video of live courtroom trials really all the same kind of experience? When people talk about television, what are they really talking about?

This question is important to writers because people have been discussing, arguing about, and analyzing television from the day it was invented. Indeed, if there is one factor that has remained the same as television has been radically transformed in the digital age, it is that people have been worried about its influence on society. If we are honest, most of us have probably been raised to think of television viewing as not exactly beneficial, an experience more like eating candy than a nutritious meal. The more popular television has become, the more concerns have been raised about it as a source of information and entertainment, and (in the view of many) as part of the education and upbringing of contemporary children.

# T W O

EXERCISE

## TV Concerns

What are the main concerns people have about the influence of television? Begin by describing the rules governing television viewing in your own home growing up. Was television seen as harmful or just annoying? A pleasant diversion or an educational resource? How have your family's attitudes toward television shaped your own?

Write down your own thoughts about what you think people worry about in relation to television, and then test your ideas by discussing this issue with a variety of people. As you talk with people, you might classify them according to various demographic categories such as age, gender, level of education, level of television consumption, or any other factor you think might be significant. Look for interesting correlations and connections. For example, do frequent television viewers have different concerns than those who watch little or no television? Do people believe their concerns about television have changed over the years, and if so, how and why?

In this chapter, you will find readings that discuss both the historic and more contemporary versions of the debate over television. Recently, arguments about television have grown beyond the individual TV set and have come to include other forms of entertainment deemed comparable, such as computers and video games.

## TELEVISION IN THE INTERACTIVE AGE

Television has grown more diverse and television programming has become more competitive, but just as with other aspects of popular culture in the digital age, the relation between television producers and consumers is changing. Video recorders such as VHS machines and digital video recorders such as TiVO mean that viewers can watch their favorite programs when and how often they want. Most disturbing to many television executives, the audience can now fast-forward through commercials, thereby increasing enjoyment while challenging the basic economic structure of for-profit television.

The smaller profit margins created by the new television environment have also led to efforts to lower production costs for programming, and one effect has been the rise in so-called reality television, where nonprofessionals perform and take part in various game-show-like contests. The dream of making it big in show business has long been part of the mythology of the entertainment industry, but never before have so many made the rapid transition from audience member to performer. The diversity of reality programming has become bewildering as contestants vie for everything from romancing European royalty to being a fashion designer to even becoming a superhero.

The availability of inexpensive digital cameras means that, as in other areas of popular culture, television fans can more easily make the transition to television producer and creator, especially via the Internet. Indeed, the World Wide Web has become its own new television network, where for the cost of Internet service, just about anyone can begin posting his or her own shows. As we shall see, this practice has grown so popular that traditional television networks are now looking to the Web for new talent. In Creating Culture, you will be asked to imagine yourself as a homegrown television producer.

## FANTASY AND REALITY ON TV

### "How Reality TV Fakes It"

#### James Poniewozik and Jeanne McDowell

*To many, the phrase* reality TV *seems like an oxymoron, a contradictory pairing of logical opposites. Television, after all, is a mass medium, meaning that what the camera records and what is reproduced on various screens is* mediated: *between any actual event and the television viewers who see the event, there exists a large and complex chain of production, involving technology and technicians, camera people and producers, and multinational corporations. The word* reality, *on the other hand, suggests just the opposite:* unmediated *experience, the world as it really is, seen with our own eyes and without interference.*

*Philosophers, psychologists, and neuroscientists might challenge the idea that any of us experience the world as it really is, free from any preconceptions, biases, or our shifting moods and attitudes, but almost everyone would agree that if we could achieve reality, television would not seem the likely means of doing so. Yet as we know from our experiences as media consumers and participants, television can exert a powerful reality effect on us. But just how real is reality TV? Or maybe another way to put it: what are the rules for reality TV? When does a program cross the line between reality and fiction? How do viewers of reality TV understand the genre? What are their expectations?*

*In "How Reality TV Fakes It,"* Time *magazine reporters James Poniewozik and Jeanne McDowell explore how the creators of reality television turn the raw footage of contestants participating in these shows into programs that viewers will find compelling enough to watch. Their point of departure is a dispute between the story editors and the producers of* America's Next Top Model *over whether these editors should be classified as writers (and therefore eligible for the benefits of membership in the Writer's Guild). Poniewozik and McDowell describe five key techniques that reality television creators use to increase the drama and interest on their programs.*

### Before You Read

1. What assumptions do you have about what constitutes a reality television show? How do you understand what the rules are governing reality TV? How do you see reality television as differing from non-reality television? What might lead you to view a reality program as cheating?

2. The term *reality television* covers a wide variety of programming, from pioneering shows such as *The Real World* to contest-based programs, makeover shows, and lifestyle programs. Compile a list of the different programs watched by members of the class that you would classify as reality television. What do these shows have in common? How do you define the reality component in each?

Phony quotes, bogus crushes, enhanced villains: the makers of "unscripted" TV spill its secrets.

The heart, Woody Allen said, wants what it wants. For the producers of the ABC reality show *The Dating Experiment,* that was a problem. The heart of one of their female participants did not want what they needed it to want. She disliked one of her suitors, but it would make a better story if she liked him. So they sat her down for an interview. Who's your favorite celebrity? they asked. She replied that she really loved Adam Sandler. Later, in the editing room, they spliced out Sandler's name and dropped in audio of her saying the male contestant's name.

That's love, reality-style. This trick, says Todd Sharp, who was a program consultant on the series, is called Frankenbiting. And it happens more often than you may suspect. Frankenbites, he says, are the work of "desperate people who had to deliver a story in a few days"—producers under pressure to deliver a tidy story that's zippier than real reality.

Granted, in the pantheon of shocking headlines, "Reality Shows Manipulated" ranks with "Pork Rinds Fattening, Researchers Suspect." But even savvy viewers who realize that their favorite reality shows are cast, contrived, and edited to be dramatic may have no idea how brazen the fudging can be. Quotes are manufactured, crushes and feuds constructed out of whole cloth, episodes planned in multiact "storyboards" before taping, scenes stitched together out of footage shot days apart.

And while we may have long suspected that a cast of camera-smitten future trivia answers can't really be that interesting without professional help, details of how these shows manipulate reality have begun leaking out—because of a dispute with the employees hired to do the jiggering. Those staff members—who create story lines, coach interview answers, and cobble together video—say their work amounts to writing, and they are suing their networks and production companies, arguing that they deserve to be covered by the Writers Guild of America.

Their employers call them story editors, segment producers, and so forth, and don't recognize them as union employees. Those designations save money—guild members have better pay, benefits, and protections. But they also preserve an illusion: that the shows are authentic and true to life, free of anything close to "writing."

It's not that the shows have line-for-line scripts (although reality writers have charged that Paris Hilton was fed lines on *The Simple Life*). But Jeff Bartsch, a freelance reality-show editor, says there are many ways of using footage to shape a story. Bartsch worked on *Blind Date*, a syndicated dating show that features hookups gone right—and comically wrong. If a date was dull or lukewarm, the editors would juice the footage by running scenes out of order or out of context. To make it seem like a man was bored, they would cut from his date talking to a shot of him looking around and unresponsive—even though it was taken while she was in the restroom and he was alone. "You can really take something black and make it white," Bartsch says. (NBC Universal Television, the studio that makes *Blind Date*, had no comment.)

Those devices, producers emphasize, can be used not just to deceive but also to tell a story clearly, entertainingly, and quickly. News producers, documentarians—and, yes, magazine writers—selectively edit raw material and get accused of cherry-picking facts and quotes. But on an entertainment show the pressure to deliver drama is high, and the standards of acceptable fudging are shadier. The first season of *Laguna Beach*, MTV's reality series about rich teens in Orange County, Calif., centered on a love triangle among two girls (LC and Kristin) and a boy (Stephen). The problem, says a story editor who asked not to be named, was that the triangle didn't exist. LC and Stephen, he says, were platonic friends, so the producers played Cupid through a montage. LC "would say things about [Stephen] as a friend," says the editor. "[LC] said, 'I just love this guy.' All you have to do is cut to a shot of the girl, and suddenly she's jealous and grimacing."

Tony DiSanto, executive producer of *Laguna Beach*, says the show's story was "enhanced" but genuine. "Stephen and LC were friends, but in the raw footage, you could see an attraction," he says. "Anytime you take anything into the editing room, you are enhancing it and editorializing. But we never make up something that hasn't happened."

If reality participants think the enhancement amounts to a lie, they have little recourse, since they usually sign a thick stack of waivers. On *The Amazing Race* [...], Jonathan Baker savagely berated his wife Victoria Fuller and alienated fellow contestants and service workers around the globe. But Baker says his villainy was trumped up in the editing room. One episode showed him appearing to be kicked out of a cab after browbeating the driver. Really, Baker says, the driver had an accident and couldn't continue. "I got the worst rap of anyone in reality television ever," Baker says. CBS spokesman Chris Ender replies that the fender bender was not bad enough to disable the cab. "Although

*America's Next Top Model:* real or written?

Jonathan may have had softer moments," he says, "what was captured on film during the broadcasts accurately represents his behavior."

That's a nice way of saying Baker did plenty of obnoxious things that couldn't be made up—pushing his wife on camera, for instance, during a tense moment. Which raises the question, is dramatic editing wrong if it captures the essence of the moment? Reality producers say they often have to shuffle footage to tell a story concisely or make a babbling interviewee coherent. "We're using things said at different times, put together to imply a statement or observation that may not have been succinctly demonstrated," says J. Ryan Stradel, who was a story editor on *The Bachelorette.* "That's where Frankenbiting may come in." Or producers may withhold information—such as downplaying a budding romance—to create suspense.

Cheating? Sure. But viewers want suspense. The problem is that makers of reality TV have the power to imply or outright fabricate things about real people who have to carry their fake reputations into their real lives. Sarah Kozer, a contestant on the Fox dating show *Joe Millionaire,* says producers doctored a scene in which she went for a walk behind some trees with the show's bachelor, Evan Marriott, to make it seem as if they had oral sex. The producers added sound effects and captions, she says, and dubbed in a line—"It's better if we're lying down"—that she had said earlier in the day in a different context. "It couldn't have been more misrepresented and fictional if it had been completely scripted," she says. (Fox declined to respond.)

It's a harder case to make, though, that taking liberties is a crime against viewers, who widely accept that the shows use the term *reality* loosely. True, the shows sell themselves as more authentic than scripted programming. But in a recent *Time* poll, only 30 percent of respondents believed that the shows largely reflect what really happened, and 25 percent of them believed that the programs are almost totally fabricated. More than half said accuracy was not a factor in their enjoyment of reality TV. Fans watch *Laguna Beach,* for instance, not for facts about LC, Kristin, and Stephen's lives but for a gorgeously shot, engrossing story of the envy, entanglements, and casual cruelties of rich, hot teenagers. That view of reality TV may veer close to the James Frey "essential truth" defense, but let's face it, *Blind Date* does not have quite the same literary aspirations.

And what about contestants? Once Frankenbitten, twice shy? Kozer feels badly used by Fox, but Baker says he would do *Amazing Race* again, albeit more self-consciously. Likewise, says perhaps the biggest reality villain ever, Omarosa Manigault-Stallworth of *The Apprentice,* who says the show demonized her. "When I was a good girl, there were no cameras on," she says. "The minute I started arguing, there was a camera shooting me from every angle." She was vilified by viewers across the country. But she has since gone on to do *Fear Factor* and to play host to Style Network's Oscar coverage. "I was on track to become the biggest bore in history," she says. "Being on the show changed my path." Reality TV's Dr. Frankensteins have tremendous power indeed. And sometimes it pays to be the monster.

## Five Tricks of Reality TV

### 1. Frankenbiting

Sometimes used to clarify an incoherent interview, sometimes to flat-out put words in subjects' mouths, this technique stitches together clips from different scenes to make participants say what the makers of the show wish they had said.

### 2. Fake Settings

On *The Apprentice,* according to some insiders, Donald Trump's "boardroom" is actually a stage set, while the "apartment" the contestants stay in is a set built on extra space in Trump Tower. (NBC declined to respond.)

### 3. Misleading Montage

Looks can deceive, literally. Cutting to a contestant looking unhappy—for whatever reason—can make him or her seem jealous, angry, or outraged if the cut is inserted after the right scene, even if the clips were shot days apart.

### 4. The Leading Interview

Reality-show makers rely on "confessional" Q&As to fill in when an actual event didn't provide enough drama. Questioned the right way, contestants can make a conflict sound more dramatic than it looked on camera.

### 5. The Overdub

On Fox's 2003 hit *Joe Millionaire,* lead hunk Evan Marriott disappeared into the bushes with date Sarah Kozer. Kozer says the producers added lusty noises and captions to suggest they were doing more than kissing.

## Working with the Text

1. The writers suggest that most of us suspect reality television programs are manipulated to heighten drama and tension, and they cite a survey reporting that 25 percent of viewers assume the programs are completely fabricated. Conduct your own survey of reality television fans on your campus and in your community. How do your results compare with the conclusions reached by the writers and by the survey they refer to? In creating and administering your survey, consider whether you wish to obtain quantifiable results (by asking people to agree or disagree with a series of prewritten statements), qualitative data (by asking for opinions in short interviews), or a combination of both.

2. Poniewozik and McDowell argue that the producers of reality television not only save money by not officially listing any writers for a program (thus avoiding paying union salaries) but also "preserve an illusion: that the shows are authentic and true to life, free of anything close to 'writing.'" How important do you think this illusion is to viewers of reality television, and how disturbing do you think viewers would find the listing of writers for a given program? If viewers saw such credits, speculate on what you think viewers would assume about how these writers contributed to the show.

3. At the end of the article, Poniewozik and McDowell list five tricks of reality TV. Rearrange their list in order of which tricks you find most to least deceptive, and why. Which seem to violate the implicit rules of reality television, which seem to be pushing the boundaries, and which seem to be acceptable forms of enhancing the presentation of the

program? Also consider the different types of reality programming. Is it more disturbing, for example, to use these tricks as part of a contest-based program such as *The Amazing Race?* How about a lifestyle-based show such as *Laguna Beach,* which seems more like a melodrama than a game show?

4. Choose a key scene from a reality television program that you are familiar with and analyze it in terms of the tricks that Poniewozik and McDowell write about in their article. Explain the significance of the scene in terms of the overall plot of the program (a key conflict between two contestants, for example, or an important revelation about a relationship), and then examine in detail how the kinds of scripting and manipulation discussed in the article may have been used to heighten the impact of the scene or even to create a plot development that may not have really happened. What are the potential implications in terms of a viewer's relationship to the program if these possible manipulations would prove true?

## "*The Amazing 'Race'*: Discovering a True American"

### Jordan Harvey

*As communication technologies grow more and more powerful, the world is becoming smaller and smaller. The very name* World Wide Web *conveys this mix of the global and the local: websites from across the globe are only a mouse click away on anyone's desktop computer. Sending an email to Thailand is as simple and quick as instant messaging a friend at school. Never before has it seemed so easy to learn about countries and cultures around the world.*

*Satisfying our curiosity about faraway places and people has long been a staple of literature and the arts, and as mass media have grown over the last two centuries, there has been a steady market for stories about and images from unfamiliar lands. Looking back at the many ways the mass media of previous decades depicted global cultures and people, it seems easy to see how these representations of unfamiliar customs and societies were marked by stereotypes, prejudice, and bias. Stories written by explorers who traveled to "exotic" places often worked as much to confirm preexisting ideas about what the world was like as to challenge the audience's sense of its own superiority. "Natives" were depicted as primitive, childlike, devious, or mysterious, and the storytellers and entertainers assured their listeners and readers that "our" way of life was the best and most enlightened.*

*It is equally easy to feel that in the age of the Internet and satellite television, we are much more sophisticated and better informed about the world than those in the past, and that popular culture reflects this greater awareness of the world. In "The Amazing 'Race':*

Discovering a True American," Jordan Harvey challenges us to think about what has changed and what has stayed the same in our understanding of the world, especially in relation to those countries in what is sometimes called the Third World, by looking at how the world is represented on the television reality show The Amazing Race. On the program, teams of "typically American" contestants from the United States are sent to locations around the world to complete different tasks and reach certain destinations before their competitors. Harkening back to the adventure stories of the late nineteenth century but equally a product of the modern era of high-speed transportation and communication, The Amazing Race presents us with a particular example of how American media sees the rest of the world.

## Before You Read

1. What comes to mind when you hear the phrase *typical American?* What are the main difficulties involved in defining this concept? When you think about the contestants and participants who appear on different reality television programs, what principles of selection do the producers of these programs seem to be following? What seems to be a typical mix of participants on various shows, and how do shows differ from one another?

2. How familiar are you and your classmates with different countries around the world? Work with the list below (you may add to the list) and respond to three questions for each country: What am I sure I know about this country? What do I feel somewhat confident I know about this country? What do I think I know but am not confident about at all? Compare the findings from across the class. Where do your various sources of knowledge about other countries come from: Personal experience (living in, having family in, or coming from that country)? Information from a class you took? Something you heard or read in the news? Something you saw in a movie or other story?

   - India
   - Venezuela
   - France
   - Egypt
   - Nigeria
   - Afghanistan
   - China

Teetering on the edge of cancellation, CBS's *The Amazing Race* finally emerged in its fifth season, assisted by an Emmy award. CBS relegated earlier seasons to the menial sections of TV's schedule, namely, summer and winter. Now, after back-to-back Emmy awards, *The Amazing Race* has solidified its spot in CBS' primetime fall and spring lineups. Its unique concept of sending American teams of two on a race around the world conjures up images of a Jules Verne escapade. Millions of viewers regard the show's picturesque locations as incomparable and its grueling system of travel and challenges as strenuous and burdensome to even the firmest of relationships.

The idea of "nation" is a hallmark of the series. During each leg of the race, contestants must traverse from continent to continent and accomplish "detours" and "roadblocks" in which they perform a task symbolic of the culture/nation they currently inhabit. For example, in season seven the contestants performed a "detour" in Cuzco, Peru, in which they chose either to rope two llamas into a pen or carry alfalfa in a basket on their backs to a nearby store while wearing a colorful Indian poncho. The next episode found the contestants performing a "roadblock" in Santiago, Chile, in which one member had to shine shoes supervised by a shoe shine tradesman for one Peruvian sole per client (about $0.30 USD).[1] At each "pit stop" host Phil Keoghan along with a representative from each country (usually dressed in symbolic garb) eagerly await the arrival of each team. The last team to arrive at each "pit stop" receives the unfortunate news that they have been eliminated from the race and a chance for one million dollars. Eventually, the team "that best blends speed with brains, tenacity, and a decent sense of direction" is deemed the winner of *The Amazing Race* (Bianco 1D). Along the way, viewers vicariously encounter many different nations and cultures.

How does the show treat these other nations? Quite often, race sites trivialize foreign cultures by focusing on their food, alcohol of choice, or methods of labor, thus forcing an ideal of otherness upon them. This paper will primarily focus on the most recent seasons (four through seven) of *The Amazing Race.*[2] Transitioning from the placement of other cultures into workable categories of otherness, we will then discuss the creation of a national American identity.

I believe that *The Amazing Race* offers audience members a template with which to formulate and reinforce a dominant ideal of true Americanism, while simultaneously discounting African Americans, gays, and women as prototypical Americans. [ . . . ]

## THE CREATION OF OTHERNESS: ORIENTALISM AND *THE AMAZING RACE* ABROAD

Placing Americans in other nations revitalizes old power relations. Who has the power to control the representations of other nations on *The Amazing Race*? Ultimately, the producers on the show as well as the contestants control how a foreign nation is represented through actions, words, and editing choices. Contestants are often put into Third World countries markedly different from America's "land of opportunity." As a result, contestants frequently remark on the impoverished people with a tone of superiority and disgust. The foreigners are characterized as sexually perverse and culturally unstable. Through casting choices, producers are able to secure the personalities needed to propagate and maintain the slanted power relationships. Assisted by contestant actions and words, producers edit the show in order to impart the notion of America's western ideals as culturally and economically superior.

By providing contestants with "the real universal language...a flash of some cash," producers are able to maintain economic control through the use of the American dollar, which is predominately worth a considerable amount more than the currency in most nations *The Amazing Race* visits (Behr 15). Equipped with monetary power, contestants are often susceptible to the deceitfulness of foreigners, as we will see later. As a result, producers garner additional footage to help shape a nation's representation through the contestant's constructed power relationships. [...]

Producers on *The Amazing Race* claim to be docile and objective towards other cultures, but contrasting their words are the visuals from India and other places.[3] For example, India's industry is depicted as archaic and its cities as filthy and chaotic. Contestants on season five must make mud bricks one by one at a brick factory. Unlike America's assembly-line style of making colorful and long-lasting bricks, India still relies on a tedious, 6,000-year-old method to produce a structurally and aesthetically disappointing product. The time commitment put into making just a small batch of bricks is unbelievable to the contestants. The show also criticizes the lack of basic hygiene in the locales visited. Each team comments on what they see, most likely prompted by questions from the cameramen, and their responses typify the results of a construction of otherness. Phrases such as "these people" are often uttered upon gazing at pigs scrounging through the dirty "residential" streets of India. Tirades at incompetent cab drivers in Egypt and China are much more commonplace than European criticism. [...]

## AMERICA'S CONSTRUCTION OF A HOMOGENIZED CULTURE

America's history as the great melting pot, however, does not translate here into equal respect for the diverse gathering of American contestants, reflecting our history of exclusion. Our process of cultural consolidation involved the inclusion and exclusion of certain racial groups. European whiteness served as the foundation for our cultural existence, while other groups were cast out into the cultural borderlands. The vast number of non-European races and ethnicities that helped push this nation into prominence never reaped the benefits. America still functions under the veil of equality; in reality and on reality TV, however, white males are the great benefactors of wealth and privilege. It seems our melting pot served only to homogenize whiteness, while ridiculing and oppressing others. The characterizations of *The Amazing Race*'s participants portray America's true *raison d'être.* Highly competitive teams predominately consist of young, strong, heterosexual whites. The producers of the show also provide several token teams: the older couple, gays, females, and black team. However, these teams generally do not make it into the final groups vying for the million dollar prize. Before delving into the portrayal of these teams on *The Amazing Race,* we must first look at the reality genre in itself and its inherent meanings to our society.

Rick Altman theorizes that genres function like nations in their comparable abilities to tie social groups together through certain textual choices. The reality TV genre unifies our factions into a "single social fabric." Regardless of our race, gender, or sexual preference, we all read reality TV's texts and are bound together invisibly by them. However, genres, like nations, emanate from a symbolic center and do not allow the periphery to contribute. The creators of reality TV shows constitute the center and broadcast out to the periphery certain messages about how we should think of different races, genders, and sexual preferences. Similarly, the construction of a nation through the influence of its genres does not allow the collective minorities (blacks, women, and gays) a culturally nationalistic representation. Thus, America through texts such as *The Amazing Race* produces a template for nation building and the construction of an ideal cultural identity. [ ... ]

*The Amazing Race* also constructs troubling representations of African Americans and their place in America. On the surface, *The Amazing Race* welcomes the inclusion of African American teams, which have appeared, sometimes multiple teams, on each season. However, blacks are unable to choose their preferred mode of representation within the framework of American culture; they merely fall into the dominant characterizations forced upon them.[4] Our texts on black history tend to portray a "mass black constituency" as the only source of African culture (Baker, Jr. 9–10). Lumped all together, blacks are presented in this manner so as not to offend the largely white audience. For example, the diversity amongst the black experience in Africa is neglected in order to show Africa as the great homeland. Over the last few seasons, *The Amazing Race* has become extremely formulaic in its treatment of blacks in Africa. Only the black teams receive extended airtime to reflect on what they experience in Africa. Filled with emotion, the black teams are proud of their heritage and the African heartland. Interestingly, only once have we learned where the black teams genealogy originates from within Africa. Amazingly, in a continent that spans over eleven million square miles, everyone is from the same place. Yet, in America (one-quarter as large), we would never think of bringing a Seminole Indian home to Washington State.

We do not see white participants commenting on their homelands; we merely assume that their respective homeland is America. Black contestants, however, all become "African." On season five, the teams travel to Tanzania where Kim, teamed with her husband Chip as a black duo, states, "I've always wanted to come to Africa, ever since I was a little girl learning about my history, my heritage." The producers of the show provide the audience with a virtual wonderland for the black duo. During one of the "detours," the couple must deliver rocking chairs to an address in town. After delivering the chairs to an older black couple, Chip and Kim receive an amazing amount of respect, almost familial. They are asked to take a rest in the chairs and offered food. Chip declares, "Everywhere we look people look like we do, we are not used to this." Clearly, Africa is a homecoming of sorts for Chip and Kim.

Capitulating to expectations, black teams refuse to acknowledge their diversity. Instead, they opt to accept their "Africanization." This practice may occur for a number of reasons. For one, America's recognition of multiple cultures within Africa is nonexistent. Therefore, most African American teams may not know where their family derived from, due to a lack of historical sources. They may simply consider Africa as the all-encompassing homeland. Also, we cannot forget the possibility that the producers do not present footage of African diversity to the largely white audience. Host Phil Keoghan's summary of one African episode reinforced the restriction of African diversity with the line, "Chip and Kim felt right at home [in Africa]."

Unfortunately, the white teams do not have the same jovial experience in Africa. The white teams in Africa are frightened by black bodies and frustrated with the deceitfulness of the African people. While Chip and Kim return to their homeland, Christian models Brandon and Nicole and twins Kami and Karli pay $100 per team for a bus trip that others receive for a considerable amount less. Brandon called one of the money collectors "shady," and Nicole, quite frustrated after being confronted by the collector, eventually threw the money on the ground upon arrival at the destination.[5] In another encounter, Colin says "very bad" to the cab driver who drove with a donut as a tire and then proceeded to get a flat. Shaking his finger from side to side as if scolding a child, Colin fits right into the role of master. An irate Colin refused to pay the driver the $100 cab ride fee upon arrival, sparking an incident with the local police and possible jail time. Brandon and Nicole also were angered about the $100 cab ride and felt they were getting ripped off because they were American; meanwhile, Chip gave his cab driver a $20 tip on top of the $100 fare.[6]

Season six presents similar circumstances as the groups arrive in Senegal. Driving through town, white model Kendra comments, "We're in ghetto Africa." In addition, Kendra and her boyfriend Freddy fight with the cab driver who wanted more money for the cab trip. Kendra states, "Ten dollars here, five dollars here. They want to rip us off all the time." But not to be out done by her previous statements, Kendra also says when riding through town, "This country is wretched and disgusting. And they just keep breeding and breeding in this poverty. I just can't take it." The "they" is a powerful statement in terms of its negative connotations and placement of Africans in the category of otherness, but using the word "breeding" equates the African people to animals.

Although Africa is depicted as very dangerous for the whites, once again the black team gets emotional. The teams begin the next leg of the race with a trip to the Slave House, a place where slaves boarded ships through the "Door of No Return" to voyage to the New World. Each team placed a rose on the archway in remembrance. Yet, it is the black father and daughter team of Gus and Hera who steal the scene. Gus begins to cry and states that he did not cry at either of his parent's funerals, but when he "went through those doors, [he] saw himself" and then felt the connection between his inner self and his historical slave beginnings.[7] [...]

However, if African American teams are not part of America's cultural fabric, how do we explain the winners of season five, black married couple Chip and Kim? Despite their achievement, Chip and Kim were often characterized as sneaky and untrustworthy as the race neared its conclusion. Before the final episodes, it seemed as if Chip strove to be liked by the white teams. He helped Brandon with a difficult task in Egypt, one that required brute strength. However, as the contest neared its conclusion, there came a sudden reversal of respect from the other teams. In Manila, Chip and Kim "yielded" Colin and Christie (this is where a team must wait one hour before continuing with the task). This was the only time the "yield" was used on the entire race by any team. Once Colin and Christie did wait out the clock and finished their task, Christie distraughtly pleaded with her driver to hurry to the next destination because Chip and Kim "played unfair." Also on this leg of the race, Chip and Kim betrayed the Christian couple Brandon and Nicole. While searching for the correct clue box on one of three islands, Chip lies to Brandon when both teams arrive at one of the islands. Brandon waited in the boat while Chip went to the clue box, which contained the next clue, but Chip told him it was the wrong island. Earlier Brandon claimed to trust Chip, but now the "true" side of Chip and Kim's Compton roots emerges. The very next challenge forced the players to scuba dive for a large clamshell holding the subsequent clue. When it appeared that

Nicole was in danger of drowning, Chip comes to offer help, but Brandon says, "Beat it," fearing Chip will steal the clue from the helpless Nicole.[8]

If black teams are depicted as untrustworthy and un-American, all female teams do not fare much better. Thus far, the best an all-female duo has placed is fourth, a feat accomplished twice. The physical toll of the race's travel schedule is enough to handicap women physically without the addition of multiple tasks. Ultimately, the message portrayed is that women are in need of a man both for protection and to complete physical tasks in life and on *The Amazing Race.* Males on the show are physically and mentally superior to their female counterparts. In a race where sleep deprivation, unusual eating schedules, constant physical and mental stress, and emotional struggles persist, someone needs to be the rock on which the team can count. Unfortunately, the women in the most recent seasons are depicted as emotionally unstable under pressure and continually suffer breakdowns. The competitiveness to win pushes men to compete harder, but the women often end up crying in the face of adversity.

In season six, in particular, the representations of women include numerous moments of emotional stress, instability, and physical weakness. Season six is the first season in which no group member could complete more than six "roadblocks" on the entire race. Clearly, the producers changed the rules of the game in response to the males on the previous five seasons completing most of the demanding challenges. Now, the women were forced to complete tasks that previously fell under the man's domain. Tears and hysteria seem to be the reaction of choice for the women on this race. Victoria, always pushed by her demanding husband Jonathon, has frequent struggles that result in a total loss of control. She gets hay fever and complains of her inability to breathe while rolling out hay bales. Jonathon states, "That's why women don't rule the world" in response to her weaknesses.[9] In addition, she sobs hysterically when Jonathon pushes and yells at her for picking up his bag when he purposely dropped it during a frantic sprint to the "pit stop." Victoria's obstreperous reaction to Jonathon caused host Phil Keoghan to intervene in an attempt to calm the situation. Aaron's partner Hayden is also a troublesome female. Her incessant panic about completing tasks as soon as possible culminates with her breaking a key while searching for the right padlock amongst over a thousand possibilities during a "roadblock." Eventually, the team quits the challenge and is eliminated. When women do complete difficult tasks, they are applauded and congratulated for doing something out of the ordinary. For example, most viewers were surprised to see the bowling moms of season five make it to the final four. Most of the confessional time concerning the two women dealt with their own surprise that two homemakers were getting along in the world.

Regardless of inherent weaknesses or strengths, women generally are portrayed as helpless during the race without the aid of a strong man. On *The*

*Amazing Race,* female displacement from American culture centers on the inability of "women" to remain calm under pressure. From the audience's perspective, the best combination for success begins with two white heterosexual males, followed closely by a team combining a strong male and a subservient female. Usually characterized as strong, fast, and smart, these two combinations appear to be racing against themselves, as there are usually multiple teams fitting into these categories as the race nears its conclusion.

Homosexuals appearing on *The Amazing Race,* on the other hand, are also discounted because of social stereotypes. Generally, homosexual characters are depicted as moody, vitriolic, un-athletic, and vain. In an issue of the *Advocate,* the seven gay contestants from the first three seasons of the show were asked to provide some gay travel advice. The most common responses were to carry hair clippers (not just for the head), hair dyes, moisturizers, lotions, hand sanitizers, and face wipes on any trip (Allen 32). This sort of representation continues with the later seasons. Season seven brings us three gay participants, two males partnered together (Alex and Lynn) and Patrick, who is teamed with his mother Susan. Patrick is physically weak and has a very poor attitude throughout his quick stint on the race. Susan gets frustrated with her son's pessimistic attitude and poutiness when things are not running smoothly. He does not take advice from his mother very well, even though she has accepted his homosexuality and wishes he could find a partner. Instead of a positive portrayal of a homosexual, the audience sees Patrick as a whiny quitter who is angry at a culture that does not accept him.

Lynn and Alex are quite different from Patrick, although they also fulfill a common stereotype about gays. One might describe Lynn and Alex as the "flaming" homosexual types. At a market in Santiago, they are given a fish that is slightly less than the required three pounds. After discovering their error, the irascible couple confronts the fishmonger they purchased the fish from, demanding they get their money back for his faulty scale. As they cause a scene, other natives surround the pair and start to voice their disapproval for the ill treatment of one of their own. The only thing Lynn and Alex can say in response is, "Bitches." This phrase is uttered numerous times by the competitive duo. At another point during the race, the pair is in last when Lynn playfully states, "We're good at pulling up the rear." Everything from the high-pitched tone of their voices to their "girly" jogging style to Lynn's desire for eye cream reinforces common perceptions about homosexuality.

In spite of the stereotyped depiction of homosexuals on this show, in season four the gay married couple, Reichen and Chip, wins *The Amazing Race,* assumingly disproving the hegemonic rules about homosexuality. Unlike previous and subsequent gay participants, Reichen and Chip possess attributes that are seemingly heterosexual. Neither of the two well-built men is depicted as "feminine" in any way. Instead, these young and athletic homosexuals are incredibly analytical and full of magnanimity when it comes to running the race. In essence, Reichen and Chip embody the characteristics of the prototypical heterosexual teams while distancing themselves from the hegemonic perceptions of homosexuality. Unlike other gay teams, these two figures are not shown in petty squabbles with other participants or complaining about their need for revitalizing moisturizers. Both are determined to win the million-dollar prize, which they achieve. One team calls Reichen and Chip, "Chip and Dale," in reference to their good looks and well-toned bodies. If one were catching the show for the first time, the viewer might assume the two were friends instead of married to each other. The show downplays the relationship between the two men, instead choosing to portray the participants as methodical and physically superior. These two men exemplify what the American culture attempts to be, except for the fact that they are gay, so their homosexuality is simply downplayed.

## CONCLUSION

Premiering just days before September 11th, the first season of *The Amazing Race* almost never aired. Low-ratings and the fear of presenting an adventure show largely reliant on international air travel seemed insensitive and dangerous after the terrorist attacks. The fast-paced nature of the show involves buying one-way tickets and sprinting through terminals to get outside of airports and into cabs, activities that are considered threatening in America's post-9/11 mindset. In a time when America was redefining its heroes, *The Amazing Race* served as a form of escapism to many. Yet, buried within the show's premise lay the foundations for strengthening the ideals of American culture and the ability to displace many entities from within our cultural framework.

*The Amazing Race* is the quintessential 9/11 series: it uses the world as a stage to define who counts as an American. By traveling from country to country, the show is able to showcase the "backwardness" of several other cultures. Magnifying the oddities of these respective cultures allows America to set itself apart from the non-western world, a practice also implemented within the discourses of the Bush presidency. Thus, by reenacting the popular dress styles, labor methods, gender roles, and cuisines from these countries, *The Amazing Race* is able to place foreign cultures into the realm of otherness. Some cultures are not even visited due to safety concerns and are placed into a deeper category of otherness simply through their invisibility (Keveney 4). This method of Orientalism ushers America into the role of hegemonic power.

Not only does the cultural work of this show place foreign cultures in the role of others, but it prevents many American contestants from assimilating into the national culture, particularly African Americans, women, and homosexuals. Chip and Kim were not supposed to win season five, but their late-night finish on the second-to-last leg allowed them to gain information the other two "all-American" groups were not privy to.[10] Nevertheless, the perceptions of Chip and Kim were unfavorable from the standpoint of the white teams. Uchenna and Joyce's victory on season seven only solidifies the negative characterizations of black contestants. Instead of portraying the black participants as winners, the producers showcased their begging for money in Jamaica. With Rob and Amber headed toward an anticlimactic finale, the airlines re-opened the doors to the plane (a regular occurrence for all of us travelers) and allowed Uchenna and Joyce to catch and pass Rob and Amber. Cheating, lying, and luck seem to be the only way black teams can defeat the powerful white couples. Instead, *The Amazing Race* provides the black teams with a homecoming to their native Africa. Filled with emotion, all of the black teams rejoice in the chance to walk on their native soil, even if their lineage traces back to a site tens of thousands of miles away.

By concentrating on the perceptions of race and gender roles displayed on the show, we begin to see the ideal definition of an American. Women and gays are not admired for their physical and emotional abilities. Instead, these two groups are discounted because of their inferiority to young, white males. No female team is strong enough to win the race, and no gay team or gay member of a team can win because of their femininity. The ideal winners of *The Amazing Race* should always be a white couple or two white friends; any other winning couple is an aberration (Reichen and Chip from season four, Chip and Kim from season five, and Uchenna and Joyce from season seven). Ultimately, with its ability to promote hegemonic ideals of America's culture, *The Amazing Race* continues with the long-standing western tradition of assimilating white culture while pirating and rejecting the others. In the end, we learn who the amazing race truly is, white American males.

## Works Cited

Allen, Dan. "Amazing Travel Tips." *Advocate* 884 (2003): 32.

Baker Jr., Houston A. *Black British Cultural Studies: A Reader.* Chicago: Chicago UP, 1996.

Behr, Zachary G. "Around the World in 30 Days." *New York Times* 22 Aug. 2004, Travel 15.

Bianco, Robert. "And the 'Race' Is on—for a Fifth, Fun-Filled Season." *USA Today* 6 July 2004, ID.

Keveney, Bill. "New Travel Realities Add Tension to *Amazing Race.*" *USA Today* 11 March 2002, Life 4.

Rhodes, Joe. "An Audience Finally Catches Up to *Amazing Race.*" *New York Times* 16 Nov. 2004, Arts 1.

Tucker, Lauren and Hemant Shah. "Race and the Transformation of Culture: The Making of the Television Miniseries *Roots.*" *Critical Approaches to Television.* Ed. Leah R. Vande Berg et al. Boston: Houghton Mifflin Co., 1998.

## Notes

1. *The Amazing Race* (season seven) episodes aired March 1 and 8, 2005, respectively.
2. Choosing these four seasons has more to do with their availability than a discrepancy in content from the first three seasons. As of yet, there are no DVDs of the series on sale. Instead,

I have relied on my own tape recordings, which allows me to cite specific descriptions of content and idea similar to those found on the first three seasons.

3. See Joe Rhodes, "An Audience Finally Catches Up to *Amazing Race*," *New York Times* 16 Nov. 2004, The Arts, p. 1. Co-creator and Executive Producer Bertram Van Munster of *The Amazing Race* (former producer for *COPS*) claimed in the article when talking to leaders in international locations, "I'm not here to criticize your country or your culture. I'm here to bring Americans to learn from you and have a good time."

4. For a good example on turning black cultural diversity into a white-friendly text see Lauren Tucker and Hemant Shah's "Race and the Transformation of Culture: The Making of the Television Miniseries *Roots*," *Critical Approaches to Television,* ed. Leah R. Vande Berg et al. (Boston: Houghton Mifflin Company, 1998) 405–416.

5. *The Amazing Race* (season 5), episode aired August 17, 2004.

6. Ibid., episode aired August 24, 2004.

7. Ibid. (Season 6), episodes aired on December 7 and 14, 2004.

8. Ibid. (Season 5), finale episode aired on September 21, 2004.

9. Ibid. (Season 6), episode aired January 4, 2005.

10. By arriving later than the other teams to the hotel, Chip and Kim learned that the flight everyone else was on would be delayed due to fog. By the time the teams learned of the delay the next morning, it was too late to make up the head start Chip and Kim attained by changing their flight.

## Working with the Text

1. According to Harvey, what are the dominant characteristics of an American as portrayed on *The Amazing Race*? What do you find most influential about his argument? What questions about or arguments with his description do you have, and how do you think Harvey would answer your questions or objections?

2. What patterns does Harvey find in the way that many of the contestants on *The Amazing Race* react to the countries they visit, particularly countries in South America, Africa, and Asia? What does he find most disturbing in these reactions? Test his thesis by watching an episode of the program or viewing video clips online. What kinds of comments do the contestants make about the countries they visit? Why do you think the producers wanted to include these clips in the program?

3. Harvey writes, "*The Amazing Race* has become extremely formulaic in its treatment of blacks in Africa," expecting all African American contestants to have an instant connection to African culture, even though Africa is a massive continent with many different countries and cultures: "Amazingly, in a continent that spans over eleven million square miles, everyone is from the same place." Why does Harvey feel it is important to critique this aspect of *The Amazing Race*? What new ways of looking at the issue did Harvey raise for you? Now put yourself

in the position of the producers of *The Amazing Race.* What are some of the responses they might make to Harvey's analysis? How might they justify their representation of the contestants in Africa?

4. Harvey argues that the real impact of *The Amazing Race* is not just to offer stereotypical views of other countries, but to "formulate and reinforce a dominant ideal of true Americanism, while simultaneously discounting African Americans, gays, and women as prototypical Americans." Visit message boards and websites devoted to *The Amazing Race* and analyze how avid viewers of the program react to the various teams of contestants. Find reactions that both affirm and challenge Harvey's thesis.

## "Cartoons from Another Planet: Japanese Animation as Cross-Cultural Communication"

### Shinobu Price

*In the midst of watching cartoons such as* The Jetsons, The Flintstones, *and* Looney Tunes, *with stars like Bugs Bunny and Daffy Duck, American children in the 1960s were introduced to a new character who seemed both familiar and exotic, a cartoon like any other but with a difference that was hard to define. Called* Speed Racer, *the program centered on the title character, a race-car driver actually named Speed Racer, and his family, as he encountered adventures with each new race he entered. While many of the plot lines seemed like standard Saturday morning cartoon fare, something about the graphic style of the cartoon, its use of still pictures to suggest motion, and the presence of the mysterious Racer X, who turned out to be Speed Racer's long-lost older brother and who lent an air of tragic destiny to the show, set* Speed Racer *apart.*

*Few young viewers at the time suspected that one feature setting* Speed Racer *apart was its country of origin.* Speed Racer, *along with a few other imports such as* Kimba, the White Lion, *was one of the first examples of Japanese anime to reach a broad American audience. Originally entitled* Mach Go Go Go *when it aired in Japan,* Speed Racer *underwent considerable alteration before it was deemed suitable for American tastes: changes in plot lines, and episodes mixed together. It was obviously dubbed into English, often featuring characters speaking lines that had no connection to the original scripts. Still, many American children were fascinated by what they saw (I speak from experience), and the American interest in the art of Japanese animation had begun.*

*Since the 1980s, there has been a steadily growing interest in Japanese popular culture among young people in the United States, from adaptations such as the* Mighty Morphin Power Rangers *to the popularity of manga graphic novels. The style of Japanese animation*

*Speed Racer,* a 1960s anime import.

has had a profound affect on American animation as well, especially on Cartoon Network, which has featured both anime from Japan and American-made programs drawn and told in the style of anime.

As Shinobu Price explains in her essay, "Cartoons from Another Planet: Japanese Animation as Cross-Cultural Communication," anime *is a term that in Japan refers to all kinds of animation. In the United States and Europe, the term has come to suggest a very particular style of Japanese cartoon. Unlike animated storytelling in America, where cartoons are still largely associated with children's programming, anime is used in Japan to tell all kinds of stories to all kinds of audiences. Every genre of program you can think of on television and any genre of movie you see in a theater can be found in animated form in Japan.*

*Why have American audiences, especially young people, been so taken with anime? And what happens when culturally specific kinds of storytelling and animation travel across borders to be interpreted by new audiences? For decades, American movies and television programs have been sent around the world, delivering images and representations of life in the United States and influencing local cultural traditions in complex ways. In her essay, Price defines anime and explains the cultural differences and cultural attractions that come into play when anime is marketed to American audiences. Price's article appeared in* The Journal of American and Comparative Cultures, *but it is based on the senior thesis she wrote as an undergraduate studying world arts and culture at the University of California, Berkeley.*

# Before You Read

1. You or members of your class may already be fans of anime, and many college campuses feature student anime clubs. Locate some anime fans (known as *otaku*) at your school and interview them about what they enjoy most about anime. Ask specifically if the fact that anime comes from Japan might make any difference in their enjoyment and interest in the art form. Does Japan represent an unfamiliar or very different culture compared to U.S. culture, or is it seen as a part of a person's cultural heritage or of the multicultural heritage of the United States?

2. Locate examples of anime art on the Web and look at some Japanese *manga*. What strikes you as characteristic or distinctive about the drawing styles you encounter? What seems most new to you? Most interesting? Most unusual?

Geisha, samurai, kimono, sushi, sumo…eccentric mind-boggling animation? For years, Japanese animation has been heralded as an exciting, albeit bizarre, artistic phenomenon from the same country that introduced us to the tranquil Zen garden and the shockingly hard-working businessman. Despite often being stereotyped as nothing more than senseless cartoons featuring cutie-pie romping pocket critters, anime, as it is commonly called, is a delightfully inventive reference manual into the world of Japanese symbols, folklore, religion, history, social musings, and aesthetic traditions. When audience members are no longer exclusively Japanese, anime unexpectedly becomes a vehicle for cross-cultural communication. Examining the history of anime distribution and fan appreciation in America is a free-for-all revelation into the effects of cultural appropriation, as well as a reflection of western mores and artistic preferences. It also serves as an example of how art forms can cross national boundaries, uniting audiences from all over the globe under the guise of pure unadulterated entertainment. Disney fans beware; the following just might have dear Uncle Walt spinning in his cryogenic freezer!

## DON'T CALL ME A CARTOON

Once upon a time, in a far away land, there lived a beautiful princess trapped in a shining castle. One moonlit night, a handsome prince rode up on his brilliant white horse and rescued her to live happily ever after. Unfortunately, being the cyberpunk flesh-craving gamine cyborg that she was, the princess had to neuromancer his brain, then decapitate and eat him. Naturally the prince, a genetically engineered resistance fighter, willingly sacrifices himself to her vampire-like appetite in accordance to his people's code of honor. But I digress…

This is not your father's animation. Nor is it really yours. Or is it? Welcome to the world of Japanese animation, a world where any imaginable subject, setting, or theme can pretty much find itself represented in the likeness of entertainment. *Anime* (a term borrowed from the French by the Japanese to refer to the entire medium of animation, but adopted by the West to refer solely to animation from Japan; go figure) is an art form used to tell stories in ways barely even alluded to in western animation. In America especially, with the Disney name brand practically inseparable from the word *animation,* this particular art form unfortunately suffers a restricted and limited fate. Animation here is predominantly kiddy fare (or at least stereotyped as such), stuck in the overly exhausted realm of fairy tales with manufactured happy endings and token animal sidekicks voiced by television comedians who were annoying enough before they were animated. American animation that veers away from the so-called harmless Disney model (Bambi is excluded; I still find it traumatizing!) always seems to be forced into subcultural, limited exposure film festivals labeled with such names as "Sick and Twisted."

This is not to say that anime (also called Japanimation) is only intended for older viewing generations. Much of it is highly geared to appeal to youngsters of a variety of ages. Japanese animation, however, does have a much freer palette from which to choose its audience and subject matter. It is hard to think of any cinematic or literary genre that is not represented in anime. Within the medium of Japanese animation, you can find: wrenching dramas, cheesy romances, storybook adventures, spooky thrillers, historical fantasies, robot shows, gothic fairy tales, slapstick parodies, futuristic dystopias, sports dramas, sci-fi series, gimmicky sci-fi series, sexy cyberpunk technomythologies, misogynistic violent pornography, sword and sorcery stories, spoofs of sword and sorcery stories, epic environmental cautionary tales, Norse Goddess romantic comedies, not to mention your normal, everyday-life family soap operas. All of this is achieved with nowhere near the stratospheric budgets allotted to big Disney productions, which tend to reach skyward of $100 million. The most expensive animated film in Japanese history was [...] *Princess Mononoke,* which cost an unprecedented $20 million; it made $130 million at the box office, by the way. In other words, Japanese animation studios are getting extraordinarily powerful effects with creative storytelling and handmade artistic achievements on only a fraction of the monetary and technological expenditure of Disney films.

So what exactly is anime? The most common mistake that people make is in categorizing it as a style of animation—the kind with big eyes, big boobs, big guns, sailor outfits, and little critters with names like Pikachu and Jigglybug. A characteristic *USA Today* article wrote that anime is "that fast-paced style of animation rarely seen on TV in the USA." TV stations "don't air the graphic Japanese cartoons known as 'anime.' Anime is so different from what airs here. It's far edgier—and violent…driven by intense moments" (Fujii 14). The paradox of this statement is that U.S. television stations have been airing anime since the 1960s, usually disguised and edited so well that the only way you could tell it was from Japan was by looking at the Japanese names during the credits. Actually, the only thing that really classifies anime as, well, anime, is the fact that it is made in Japan by Japanese artists within a Japanese context. Stylistic experimentation within the medium is expected—rewarded if it's good and critically pissed on if it's bad. The creative realm of anime is vast, the possibilities endless. The product ends up as varied as *Pokemon,* a ridiculously popular child-oriented adventure romp of cute and furry battling pocket monsters, to *Grave of the Fireflies,* a devastating World War II aftermath tragedy where two cute little kids watch their mother disintegrate from the firebombing of their city, go live in a cave by a river, and then eventually watch each other die from starvation.

Now, about the whole cartoon thing. Americans often call anything that is animated a "cartoon." I did in the very title of this paper. *USA Today* did in the article quoted above. The problem is that there really is not another word in the English language to describe animation. *Merriam-Webster's Dictionary* defines a cartoon as one of four things,

> a preparatory design, drawing, or painting…a drawing intended as satire, caricature, or humor…a ludicrously simplistic, unrealistic, or one-dimensional portrayal or version…[or] an animated cartoon. (176)

It's no wonder westerners often treat animation, or "cartoons," with such hierarchical disdain that forces it to be labeled as an inferior art form, whether "preparatory" for some greater art to follow, or "unrealistic" in its portrayal of the human condition. That would explain why animation in the West is generally a medium for telling simplified stories in a funny and pretty (read: safe) manner, perfect for the inexperienced and yet-to-be-educated youths of America. But when the term *cartoon* is applied to the world of Japanese animation, a great injustice is made. Partaking in this mindset is just another form of ethnocentrism, looking at a different culture through your own culturally specific set of values and definitions. There are, of course, many Japanese animated films and series that meet this "cartoon" mentality (the most popular of these being the phenomenon that is *Pokemon*). But when you really look at the versatile creative arena of anime; such children-only animated fare makes up only a small portion of the greater art form as a whole. [ … ]

## GUESS WHAT? I AM JAPANESE!

A funny thing about anime: no matter how popular it is in the West and how universal it just might be, there is no way to disguise its very "Japaneseness." Anime is deeply imbedded in all aspects of Japanese society: folklore, legends, history, religion, moral assumptions, and aesthetic standards, to name a few. Fans around the world might be surprised to know that anime is created with only the Japanese audience in mind. The intention to create a boundary-defying art form is not a preconceived goal. The fact that anime has become so popular outside of Japan is quite a mystery to many Japanese animators. As Hayao Miyazaki states,

> I discovered that my work was a product of Japanese historical perspective and sense of nature...So I have no plans to start making films with a global market in mind... Japan will always remain very much the foundation of my work. (Ledoux 31–32)

Many references to Japanese culture in anime are quite blatant. It's hard to ignore that it is Japanese when people are walking around in kimonos, eating with chopsticks, praying to the Buddha at the local temple, and other such stereotypical actions ingrained as "Japanese" to the western conscience. Surface Japaneseness can range from the obvious to the not so obvious. A good example of the former would be the long running TV show *Sazae-san,* a very "normal" depiction of a family living in suburban Tokyo. The people in the show always do the usual Japanese things at the right Japanese moments. They attend Shinto festivals, eat Japanese food, and sleep on futons on tatami floors. One writer goes so far to say that *Sazae-san* is basically "a manual for proper Japanese social behavior" (Schilling 224). Other surface Japaneseness can be less obvious, and certainly puzzling to western viewers. For instance, Japanese can often be seen wearing surgical masks while going about their daily lives. This is a common custom for someone who is sick; the mask is worn to avoid spreading their colds to other people. In a particularly funny episode of *Urusei Yatsura,* a whole classroom of sick students is seen wearing surgical masks—a sight that would undoubtedly make uninitiated westerners think it is a classroom filled with young medical surgeons.

More difficult to decipher is the use of symbols which have specific cultural meanings in their Japanese context. Many foreigners look at Japan and see a level of artificiality in their artistic endeavors. They see a society that places the importance of exterior beauty over taste (in the preparation of food) and unreality over the real (what exactly is going on in Noh theater!?). The problem with this train of thought is that it is not this pretension that Japanese prefer, but the symbolism imbued in it. In Japan, the Zen garden is symbolic of boundless islands scattered in the sea, the tea ceremony is symbolic of the entire social order inside an enclosed space, flower arrangements are symbolic of the relationship between heaven and earth, and scene-capturing woodblock prints are symbolic of the larger world that surrounds each image (Levi 23). So it is rather natural for anime to also incorporate such insights into Japanese culture. For example, whenever you see a cherry blossom tree in anime you can pretty much make two conclusions: (1) that it is spring, and (2) that someone is going to die. The latter of these two may seem like an odd conclusion, but it is the symbolism contained in the cherry blossom that leads us to it. The cherry blossom only blooms for about three days out of the year. It is this impermanence that makes it so highly regarded and symbolic in Japanese culture. So when you're watching anime and you see cherry blossoms falling, it most likely means that someone of great beauty (inside or out) is not going to live on this earth for much longer. Another often-used symbolic image in Japanese anime is that of the bleeding nose. Sometimes in comedies, when a male character sees a beautiful girl his nose starts to bleed erratically. This references the old Japanese belief that staring at a pretty girl will make your nose bleed. This symbolic connotation makes a particularly funny appearance in *Patlabor OAV (Original Animation Video) 6,* when a rather trigger-happy character gets a nosebleed when he looks at a really big gun (Poitras 141).

A scene from *Princess Mononoke*

One of the most exciting traits of anime is how animators can constantly incorporate ancient Japanese legend, myth, and history into their animation with a contemporary twist. Shinto, the native religion of Japan (it's not really a religion actually, but more a way of life) is a natural resource for anime artists. Shinto basically provides thousands of stories and ancient myths which Japanese become familiar with from an early age. The *manga* and anime artist Rumiko Takahashi often uses Japanese folklore in her works because of the simplicity in creatively manipulating stories that everybody already knows (Ledoux 20). In a typical Takahashi anime episode of *Urusei Yatsura,* the character Ataru comes across what he thinks are *tennyo,* mythological nymphs, bathing in the sea. He steals one of their robes and perversely clutches it to his face only to find out that it's a loincloth. This scene is actually a parody of the ancient story of a farmer who comes across one of these bathing heavenly maidens and steals her robe. When she asks for it back, the man agrees but only if she dances for him (Poitras 135). The character of Lum, also in *Urusei Yatsura,* is a variation of an ancient demon called an *oni. Oni* are horned, tiger skin–clad, mythological creatures with wildly colored hair who are known for lusting after humans. Lum is a beautiful flying creature with two cute little horns, green hair, and a wild temper. She dresses in a tiger-striped bikini and has a frighteningly intense crush on a neighborhood schoolboy.

Shinto mythology could also be the reason for so many wild, strong female characters in anime. Unlike much of western folklore and heroics, many of the ancient Japanese tales of gods and demons are composed of female deities and spirits. Japanese history is also dominated by powerful empresses, priestesses, writers, and artisans. As a result, anime is chock-full of female protagonists and villains. Contrary to the subservient "geisha" stereotype of Japanese women, Japanese society is actually quite tolerant of strong women in the family and in the workplace, quite possibly because ancient history and Shinto belief are filled with powerful heroines that played prominent roles in the shaping of Japan.

If you dig even deeper into the so-called Japaneseness of anime you begin to uncover certain themes that reflect the very nature of what it is to be Japanese. A casual viewer of anime could make the conclusion that Japanese artists have sado-masochistic tendencies because they really like to kill off their heroes and make bad things happen to good people. However, similar to the cherry blossom example above, Japanese have a time-honored appreciation for short-lasting beauty. According to Donald Richie,

> Unhappy events are simply accepted because they exist. Japanese art observes *mono no aware*, the transience of all earthly things . . . It implies not only an acceptance of evanescence but also a mild celebration of that very quality. (170–71)

The Japanese attitude towards death gets to the very nature of the definition of heroics. In the West, a hero is someone who accomplishes his goal and triumphs in the results even if he dies because of it. *Braveheart,* John Wayne movies, *The Odyssey,* and [. . .] *Gladiator* are all examples of this archetype. In Japan, heroics are all about motivation and duty, the intent to do right and good. Japanese heroes often never achieve their goal and die prematurely, but this is what makes them heroes. Winning and justice are not important because the world is in no position to care. It happens all the time in real life, so why not deal with it in anime. In the very first episode of *Space Cruiser Yamato,* two heroic people die for no apparent reason. And why did those two innocent kids have to die from starvation in *Grave of the Fireflies*? There is tragic beauty in these deaths that dig deep into the history of Japanese aesthetics. (This might also explain the extreme popularity of *Titanic* with the Japanese audience.) Such portrayals force the viewer to actually deal with the consequences of death, an issue almost completely missing in Disney animation because no one dies and everyone lives happily ever after (except poor Bambi's mother!). Many of the endings in anime are unconcluded, and quite frankly, unfair. The popular movie *Akira* ends with a warning against future applications of rampant scientific technology, ending basically with a big fat question mark on the future of mankind. Such plot lines also give anime a heightened level of excitement and tension since you never know what's going to happen or who's going to die next.

Anime often disguises contemporary struggles and themes in its entertaining medium. The fact that so many anime shows and movies take place in futuristic or ancient worlds of social upheaval and political unrest says a lot about the current state of mind of Japanese animators. Anime such as these deal with issues of how to reconcile ancient tradition and nature with the advent of new technology. This dichotomy of the ancient and the new is a theme dealt with on a daily basis in Japan, where tourists are often delighted to see geisha running around the streets of Kyoto in kimonos and wooden geta while talking giddily on their minuscule high-tech cell phones. In *Princess Mononoke*, the ancient Japanese world of forest gods and demons is threatened by an encroaching civilization of humans and their polluting industries. The resulting conflict that ensues is about how to reconcile new advances in technology and humanity with the natural order of the world. Another Miyazaki work, *Nausicaa of the Valley of the Wind*, which takes place in another world and another time so seemingly unrelated to Japan, has a strong ecological theme while romanticizing ancient feudalistic society. This is a strong manifestation of Miyazaki's criticism to rapid modernization and the industrial excesses of current Japanese society (Schodt 279). *Galaxy Express 999* is about people who give up their human bodies in exchange for robotic ones, raising the question of how to retain humanity in a mechanical futuristic world. In *Galaxy Express,* people travel on a train that takes them away from their industrial homelands through the endless possibilities of space and into any galaxy they wish to choose. Interesting enough, the train is not modeled after the high-speed technological achievement that is the *shinkansen* bullet train, but an old man-run steam engine locomotive.

Another such theme dealt with in Japanese anime is the subtextual confrontation of women's issues and feminism, especially by female animators. Rumiko Takahashi's ever-popular comedy series *Ranma 1/2* is about a cursed boy who changes into a girl whenever he's splashed with water. As a woman, he constantly encounters sexual discrimination and unwanted advances from horny schoolboys. When he takes his martial arts classes as a woman, he learns agility, speed, and intelligence—traits other than the sheer strength he deemed so important when he was a man (Levi 131). Takahashi slyly asserts her feminist position through her character's gender-bending experiences and the revelations that he makes because of it. Similar issues are dealt with in manga and anime by the four-women team CLAMP, who often delight at objectifying men in their work by exploiting them as pretty male versions of their ample-breasted female counterparts. Female animation artists often manage to remain somewhat anonymous (in terms of gender) behind their creations. After all, who would have thought that the artists responsible for the new renaissance of gothic horror anime such as *Ogre Slayer* and *X* would be women? [...]

Japan's almost factory-like educational system, strict orderly way of life, and close urban living quarters could naturally lead to some very unhappy campers if it were not for an external refuge of entertainment. That's where anime comes in. In fact, Frederik Schodt reveals that despite Japan's already low violent and sexual crime rate, both rates have gone down significantly in the periods when *magna* and anime were thriving in popularity (50). Plus, in Japan there is no universal idea of morality that everyone must adhere to. Native Japanese religion has no moral code contained within it. Issues of right and wrong are imbedded within social relationships, not universally upheld religious doctrines (Levi 99). Violent and erotic fantasies are not even considered immoral like they are in the West. There is no sense of universal moralistic judgment from higher powers of existence. This might explain much of the dichotomy in villain and hero characterization throughout many Japanese theatrical forms. The lines between what is defined as good and bad are often unclear. Anime villains tend to wrestle with their sympathetic sides. They are complex characters with desires, reasons, and principles. They are rarely pure evil for evil's sake like the ugly witches and stepmothers and all-around bad guys in Disney animation. Likewise, heroes are often depicted as fallible characters that make mistakes and often fall to the dark side.

Japanese know full well that what they are watching and reading is not real. A healthy imagination is seldom the sign of an immanent psychotic breakdown. The main reason for this can be traced to the fact that Japan is a shame-based culture rather than a guilt-based one. Japanese rarely cross the line between fantasy and reality because of the shame their embarrassing or harmful actions would bring to their families. Although this is a rather sweeping generalization (and often an unfair stereotype), it does help to explain Japan's low crime rate. And besides, Japan has a long tradition of honest aesthetic appreciation of the unreal and of the widespread desire to break away from everyday reality through art.

This leads to another, almost contradictory reason for portraying violence in anime, one that chooses to directly confront those unpleasant subjects that disturb modern civilization. Because Japanese animation is not considered an inferior artistic medium for telling stories, it often tackles the same issues that are dealt with in novels and contemporary films. Along with its realistic portrayal of death, anime also depicts graphic brutality and sensuality. As animator and comic artist Kosuke Fujishima reveals, "It happens often enough in real life and besides, sex isn't evil. I think pretending sex and violence doesn't exist only breeds ignorance" (Ledoux 75). This is not to say that violent and erotic anime goes wholly uncriticized by the Japanese public. Many of the more conservative types are more than willing to voice their displeasure at the lurid and brutal content. Yet violence and erotica alone do not compose the majority of anime entertainment. In most cases, sex and violence make up only parts of the story. There are, of course, some very offensive and disturbing anime (like the *Overfiend* series, to which I wouldn't subject my worst enemy), but they compose only a slight percentage of the entire animation market. Unfortunately they are disproportionately popular in the western world, which leads us into the next portion of this paper: What happens when the popularity of anime crosses over into other countries? How did it all begin, what happens to its "Japaneseness," and why on earth is it so popular?

## MICKEY MOUSE EATS SUSHI...OR WHEN GOOD NINJAS GO BAD AND OTHER MISUNDERSTOOD TV SHOWS

So how exactly did anime jump ship and find its way to an appreciative western audience? For starters, anime has been appearing on major U.S. television networks since the 1960s with such series as *Speed Racer, Astro Boy,* and *Kimba, the White Lion.* But the true crossover boom came in the early 1980s when a new generation of Americans began to acknowledge the artistry and entertainment value of anime. Japanese historian Antonia Levi found that these were often students who participated in the growing number of foreign exchange programs, created by a Reagan-era curiosity of Japan's newfound wealth and prosperity (8). Japan's economic bubble in the 1980s, stimulated by a boom in real estate, banking, and the stock market, was certainly a curiosity to the American government. All of a sudden, exchange programs began popping up that encouraged eager American youths to learn the Japanese "secret of success." These students quickly acquired an interest in what they saw on Japanese television. Helped along with the advent of VCRs and a new market for videos, these kids brought back tapes upon tapes of anime. They showed and traded these tapes with their friends who intently watched them even if no one had the slightest clue what the characters were talking about. Military personnel stationed in Japan also brought these intriguingly different "cartoons" back with them to the states. This coincided with the newfound popularity of anime shows like *Star Blazers* on U.S. television. Videotapes also helped to expose fans all across America to non-edited anime with not-so-Disney-like content, anime that could never hope to be shown on mainstream U.S. television.

This marked the beginning of a rather ambitious cultural exchange. American fans started to learn Japanese, or find some new Japanese friends who could translate the videos for them. Anime soon began to show on local television channels in cities with large populations of Japanese immigrants. These programs started to attract even non-Japanese speakers who belonged to an almost cult following of fans now utterly devoted to this "exotic" new art form from the East. Soon conventions began to spring up about where anime and manga fanatics could trade videos and comics, meet some of their favorite artists, and show off their spiffy handmade Captain Harlock costumes. In the 1990s, movies like *Akira* and *Ghost in the Shell* had limited theatrical releases stateside, which won over even more fans who were previously unaware of this new genre-defying approach towards animation. (*Ghost in the Shell* later became the first anime feature film to hit number one on the U.S. video sales chart.) College campuses quickly jumped on the bandwagon, forming anime clubs which meet in anywhere from dirty, laundry-littered dorm rooms to the 300-seat lecture halls. With the advent of the Internet, exposure to anime became even easier. Thousands of websites are currently devoted to anything from video distributor catalogs to cute short-lived anime characters who appeared for only five seconds in the forty-seventh episode of *Urusei Yatsura.* Computer technology also allows fans to subtitle previously untranslated (or really badly translated) versions of anime. Strangely enough, anime basically owes much of its popularity in the U.S. to "illegal" transactions such as bootlegging, pirating, and unauthorized distribution. [ . . . ]

Film critics and various other non-fans have had an interesting opinion of anime throughout the years. When anime was first being stocked in U.S. video rental stores, many of them ended up in the children's section despite being quite mature and/or graphic in nature. A vast majority of the American public still stereotypes anime as being either infantile cartoons of the *Pokemon* variety, or perversely violent films for nut cases. Critics and journalists who were only recently becoming acquainted with the anime explosion were often not cognizant of its wide variety of subject matter and historical evolution. What they saw as "low grade" animation was actually older material that was just beginning to be released in the West (McCarthy, *The Anime!* 214).

Other film critics also tend to misunderstand the Japanese cultural perspective of anime. Despite the almost unanimous praise for [ . . . ] *Princess Mononoke* (many critics, including Roger Ebert, placed it on their top ten lists [in 2001]) some critics complained about Miyazaki's inability to master the art of facial expressions and fluid movement as well as Disney films could. These critics were filtering their artistic evaluation of the film through their own culturally accepted ideas of what animation should be. Not only did they not understand the historical and artistic development behind anime's purposeful use of a low cel count, but they also overlooked the reason behind the lack of variety in facial expression. Japanese are not as openly willing to wear their hearts on their sleeves as Americans are. Emotions tend to be withheld and are not readily revealed to the everyday passerby. Therefore, anime characters tend not to come equipped with the symphony of facial expressions that are so prevalent in American animation. Deep resounding emotion is found instead in a slight twinkle of a character's eye or in an intensely furrowed brow. After all, symbolic resonance is more important than stoic realism in Japanese artistic traditions. [ . . . ]

## STRANGER IN A STRANGE LAND

Quite possibly the weirdest thing about anime, weirder than all guts, guns, and green-haired sexy aliens combined, is the fact that it is so popular in the West. What is it that inspires thousands of foreigners to glue themselves with zealous abnormality to marathon anime showings on those TV sets of theirs? The fact is, people all over the globe like anime. France and Italy, strangely enough, have huge populations of *otaku.* But why do they metaphorically travel to the other end of the earth to find an art form that they can lovingly appreciate? What does it say about their own artistic traditions that they choose to go as far as Japan to find their entertainment? In some countries, anime and *manga* are so popular that they cause considerable backlash. In nations that were once former colonies of Japan (like Korea, for example) many conservatives even view anime as another attempt at cultural takeover (Schodt 307). Anime there is strictly edited and, in some cases, utterly banned. But not all anime series and movies make it out to the rest of the world. And when they do, not all of them find a home. What's popular in America does not necessarily mirror what's popular in Japan. There is a reason why anime is often stereotyped as being gruesomely vile and pornographic. This type of anime is disproportionately popular in America, whereas in Japan, it constitutes just another tiny segment of the various genres of Japanese animation. There are a variety of reasons why American *otaku* love anime: It allows the viewer to be able to see the world through a stranger's eyes, entitles them to find a voice within an exciting realm of fantasy, and lets them relate to real life human emotions.

The uniquely odd world of Japanese animation may be the very reason why it appeals to so many outsiders. The way anime uses its medium of animation is so fundamentally different from the artistic tradition of Walt Disney, that it creates a freshly intriguing aroma that lures foreigners into its mist. The unfamiliarity of all those cultural references can be an attractive selling point. The fact that death can strike at any time to any character may indeed be a culturally significant characteristic, but it also makes for one hell of a plot twist. There's an element of vicarious pleasure in looking out at the world from another person's perspective. This gives anime a rather exotic charm. From an Orientalist perspective, Japanese animation provides the foreigner with a sensuous gaze into an alien eastern land. The fact that sci-fi/fantasy worlds make up such a large percentage of anime just makes the thrill even better. So in a sense, Americans are seeing an inventive worldview filtered through a Japanese perspective. This creates a realm that is doubly removed from western reality, and therefore, doubly mysterious and enticing. As several students in the anime club of the University of California, Los Angeles, state, "Anime expands my imagination." "It's like an escape from the mundane." "Our imagination runs wild and free."

Another reason why American fans find anime so attractive is that it provides them with appealing alter ego–like characters to relate to. For the men, anime provides what Antonia Levi calls "nerd heroes," archetypal characters who can be extraordinarily, well, ordinary, and yet surrounded by beautiful and adoring women (130). Two extremely popular shows, *Oh, My Goddess!* and *Urusei Yatsura,* are both about ordinary and passive schoolboys who become the cherished love objects of a Scandinavian goddess and a cute alien demon, respectively. Also popular among male *otaku* are the superhero types of anime where ordinary males are given superhuman powers. Stereotypically (this is an enormous generalization), male anime fans tend to be somewhat dorkier than their beer-guzzling, football-playing frat boy counterparts. But I mean this with the deepest admiration. Anime fans have resources of imagination and creative impulses that more socially integrated people tend to underutilize because their worlds are so...acceptable. The same goes for those constantly maligned sci-fi convention-attending "freaks" out there. You may laugh at those Spock ears, but their wearers have more spectacular fantasy lives than you could ever imagine. Anime provides characters who are mirror images of the audience, and yet, who are dearly adored or unexpectedly powerful. This gives those spectating males in the audience a sense of visceral, empathetical power to the otherwise passive act of sitting in the dark watching images go by.

Female *otaku* also enjoy a sense of role-play when watching anime. Tough, sexy femme fatales abound. In this case, the attraction to strong heroines can be seen as a reflection of the lack of such characters in American entertainment. Traditional Hollywood films have always been dominated by warrior men and their eye candy serving, scantily clad, female sidekick love interests. When they do include heroic woman it's seen as almost revolutionary (think Sigourney Weaver in *Alien*). Anime provides the female audience with sexy characters who have the extraordinary talent...to kick ass. And who wouldn't want to relate to that?

But perhaps the most intriguing aspect of Japanese animation to American viewers is its realistic approach to mature, relatable topics and its sincere depiction of human emotion. Fans often comment on how anime's creative storylines are treated with genuine, non-glossed-over honesty. Characters don't live happily ever after, bad things happen to good people, and villains go unpunished. The Japanese aesthetic tradition of morbidity through art just so happens to mirror real-life situations. The emotions that arise from such storylines—sorrow, regret, shame, anger, love—are easy to relate to no matter what nationality you are. And Americans appreciate this. But why do they like these stories to be portrayed in such a colorful entertaining medium? The fact that anime is such a visually striking creative arena just makes this appreciation more profound. Animators are telling such stories through their art. Western animation has never really chosen to tackle serious and mature themes. One diehard anime fan once said to me, "I am interested in the telling of stories. Anime is the most beautiful way to do so." Perhaps the global appeal of Japanese animation is indeed based on these understandable themes and emotions. But can anime really be universal?

## WHY NOBODY LIKES KABUKI, AND OTHER TALES OF ARTISTIC FAVORITISM

What is it about anime that makes it quite possibly the most popular export from Japan since the Walkman? And why are there not any Noh and Kabuki college fan clubs where kids can partake in marathon viewing sessions of their favorite plays by Chikamatsu Monzaemon? Besides all the reasons previously stated, there is one more theory left. One anime fan told me that he liked the "western" look of the characters. The people in anime could be any race, any kind of human, or alien being, for that matter. The places depicted in anime could be anywhere. All those culturally specific artistic choices made by the animators have somehow miraculously developed their own subtext. The wide range in hair color to differentiate between character, the big eyes to show emotion, the foreign lands to promote fantasy—these can all be interpreted as being independent of the Japanese perspective. In essence, these characteristics give a western sense of appeal to the animation. What were once stylistic choices made by the animators, are now interpreted as a means for universal relativity. When asked about the capability of anime to serve as a universal art form, one fan remarked that it was possible, but "only if the setting and language do not refer to Japanese culture." What does this say about the importance of contextual realization in art appreciation? Or is Japanese animation just unadulterated entertainment and not a potential learning experience?

To be perfectly honest, there are a lot of anime fans who could care less about Japan. Anime might as well be from Siberia, Timbuktu, or from another planet for that matter. In fact, a lot of fans begin their appreciation of Japanese animation with just this type of attitude. After all, they're just cool cartoons, right? But soon enough for most fans, anime begins to take on new meaning. It begins to have a strange effect on their identities as passive viewers from another country. They no longer love anime only for its absoluteness, its independence from cultural reality, and its function as pure entertainment. Sooner or later, fans actually begin to like the cultural baggage that comes naturally ingrained within anime. True *otaku* proudly relish in the ambitious cultural exchange that is involved in its appreciation. Sooner or later, fans become fluent in Japanese from watching so much anime and taking language classes to better understand what they're watching. An overwhelming majority of the fans read the inserts and watch the extra video segments that explain cultural references. Furthermore, most American fans are adamant that the true appreciation of anime lies in its challenging nature. Real *otaku* rise to accept this task.

Japanese animation is basically, as Antonia Levi puts it, "escapism raised to a high art" (30). When fans lose themselves to the visual and impressionable feast of anime, they are unconsciously learning about new modes of aesthetic creation that are inherently different from their own. One of the most exciting aspects about art is that it allows for constant interpretation and insight beyond its initial time and space of creation. All forms of appreciation then, from casual enjoyment to in-depth introspective cultural understanding, should be validated. Japanese animation is a vast communicative vehicle that has been transcending language barriers and national boundaries for years. This may be one of the subliminal intentions behind anime's creation, even if it is purposefully steeped in Japanese tradition. As Hayao Miyazaki says,

> The most important thing that Japanese animation should not do is to categorize the fans as a certain kind of people and then make movies only for them....We need to get nearer to that universal appeal of animation when making a movie, or all our efforts will have been for nothing. (Ledoux 26)

Those who love to watch anime, whether they know it or not, are participating in a widespread global exchange that may just have greater implications than they could ever have thought.

## WE COME IN PEACE

The answer concerning whether or not anime can have a universal audience is open to interpretation. Some fans say it can because of its pure entertainment value. Some say it cannot because of those deeply imbedded references that are impossible for uninformed foreigners to decipher. But the fact that anime is being zealously watched, hoarded, traded, and discussed in hundreds of areas all over the world already classifies it as a globe-trotting art form. The world is steadily shrinking. Anthropologists have exhausted their descriptive catalogues of far away cultures. Explorers have hunted down every nook and cranny of the earth's surface. Scientists and inventors have created universally available tools, machines, and medicines. The Internet lets people from all over the world share their information in a matter of seconds. Frederik Schodt describes this environment as a "postwar mind-meld" between industrialized societies that share such common levels of experience and emotion that it makes it easier than ever to truly understand one another (339). Anime's popularity across barriers of language and nationality is an extension of such unity in diversity. Many animators feel the same way. Leiji Matsumoto says to his American fans, "I'll be very happy if doing this will help to reduce the distance between you and I, little by little" (Ledoux 157). Anime, for all its weirdness, eccentricity, poignancy, hilarity, and Japaneseness, is a learning experience no matter how you value it. Hayao Miyazaki hopes that western fans can view anime and say, "There's something other than the place where I live, things that I'm familiar with, there is something else out there that has value to it" (McCarthy, *Miyazaki* 191).

So if you have a neighbor, a roommate, a student, a father, or a best friend who sits religiously in front of their TVs watching marathon sessions of those bizarre cartoons from Japan, don't call them couch potatoes. Call them diligent intercultural diplomats who are bridging the gaps between East and West, all for the sake of entertainment.

## Works Cited

"Cartoon." *Merriam Webster's Collegiate Dictionary.* 10th ed. 1999.

Fujii, Satoru, ed. *Japan Edge: The Insider's Guide to Japanese Pop Subculture.* Markham: Cadence, 1999.

Ledoux, Trish, ed. *Anime Interviews: The First Five Years of* Animerica, Anime *and* Manga Monthly (1992–97). San Francisco: Viz Communications, 1997.

Levi, Antonia. *Samurai from Outer Space: Understanding Japanese Animation.* Chicago: Open Court, 1996.

McCarthy, Helen. *The Anime! Movie Guide: Movie-by-Movie Guide to Japanese Animation.* Woodstock: Overlook P, 1997.

———. *Hayao Miyazaki: Master of Japanese Animation: Films, Themes, Artistry.* Berkeley: Stone Bridge P, 1999.

Poitras, Gilles. *The Anime Companion: What's Japanese in Japanese Animation?* Berkeley: Stone Bridge P, 1999.

Richie, Donald. *A Lateral View: Essays on Culture and Style in Contemporary Japan.* Berkeley: Stone Bridge P, 1992.

Schilling, Mark. *The Encyclopedia of Japanese Pop Culture.* New York: Weatherhill, 1997.

Schodt, Frederik L. *Dreamland Japan: Writings on Modern Manga.* Berkeley: Stone Bridge P, 1996.

## Working with the Text

1. At the beginning of her essay, Price says that in America, animation is "predominantly kiddie fare," and that the pervasiveness of Disney cartoons has greatly influenced American perceptions and attitudes about animation. How valid do you find her suggestions about how animation is understood in America? Starting from this initial assertion, create a chart showing the differences she describes between American and Japanese attitudes toward animation. How do these differences cause you to look and think about American animation in new ways?

2. In the section, "Guess What? I Am Japanese!" Price describes several examples of what she sees as the "Japaneseness" of anime, from specific cultural symbols and references to larger ideas about heroism, the relationship between life and death, the influence of Shinto traditions, and understandings of gender identity. Choose one specific instance of "Japaneseness" that Price defines and summarize it in your own words. Then, working alone or in a group, find examples of American

storytelling that both support and complicate her argument about the differences between anime and U.S. animation. Look for examples of American storytelling that you think may have been influenced by some of the Japanese qualities that Price describes.

3. Price provides her own explanation and theories about a phenomenon that many cultural observers have noticed: in the United States, debate is ongoing and intense about the possible relationship between fictional depictions of violence and actual violence, particularly in cultural products aimed at young people; in Japan, anime and *manga* featuring scenes of explicit violence and sex that would be controversial in the United States coexist with far lower rates of actual social violence than in America. How does Price explain the potentially different effects of violent animation on American and Japanese youth? What do you find most persuasive about her argument? How might her discussion inform U.S. arguments about violence in the media?

4. Summarize the various reasons Price thinks that anime appeals to American audiences. Which reasons does she see as most and least positive? Test her hypotheses with American fans of anime. Which explanations do they most agree with? Which do they seem to resist the most?

## "The Many Tribes of YouTube"

### Virginia Heffernan

*"He just loves to stare at the screen all day." A parent complaining about a son's TV viewing habits? A student commenting on a Web-addicted roommate? As the ease and popularity of watching videos on the Internet grows, the line separating TV and the computer becomes hazier. The growing popularity of digital video recorders only adds to this trend, as more and more TV viewers watch their favorite programs on their own time, zipping by the commercials with their remote controls. Already, many people can surf the Web on their home television sets, and the ability to download movies and other programming directly from the Internet to new kinds of home entertainment devices that combine the home computer with traditional TV is quickly becoming a reality.*

*Perhaps no phenomenon exemplifies this convergence of TV and the Web more than YouTube, a site that first appeared in early 2005 and quickly became an Internet hit. The idea behind YouTube was simple enough: anyone could easily upload a favorite video of almost any kind to the site for viewing. Wedding videos, clips from popular TV shows, news stories, pet tricks, music tutorials, video diaries from soldiers in Iraq—the variety and number of videos available on YouTube and similar sites such as Google Video continue to grow exponentially. Just as channel surfing has become a popular form of television viewing, YouTube surfing has become a deceptively addictive way to kill time online. In fact, the name of the site itself along with its distinctive logo reinforce the idea that YouTube can be seen as a new kind of television.*

*In "The Many Tribes of YouTube," New York Times television reporter Virginia Heffernan comments on the popularity of YouTube and its distinctly interactive and participatory nature. Unlike TV, videos on YouTube invite not only written comments, but also video responses that match the form and genre of the original, leading to the development of online video communities where members use video the way previous generations used pen and paper.*

## Before You Read

1. How familiar are you and others in your class with YouTube? If you are a regular visitor, write about the types of videos you watch most frequently. How do you and other YouTube viewers in the class search for clips to watch? Are there any types or genres of videos that especially interest you? If you haven't been before, visit the site and keep track of how you explore YouTube. What on the site attracts you? What search strategies do you use?

2. If you or someone in class has uploaded videos to YouTube, discuss why you wanted to post to the site. Who was your intended audience: Friends and family? People at school? What kinds of reaction and feedback did you or the poster receive? Did any of the reactions surprise you?

3. Both Web surfing on a computer and channel surfing on your television involve watching screens. Compare and contrast television viewing and Internet browsing as forms of leisure and recreational activity. What overlaps do you see between the two different media?

W hat do you think of the latest video on YouTube? Wait. Don't answer that, or at least don't answer with words. Because almost the instant you start to talk about one of the beautiful, puzzling videos that pervade the site that Google acquired last fall for $1.65 billion, you reveal that you're missing the point. Really the only authentic response to a YouTube video is another YouTube video—the so-called "video response."

YouTube appeared in February 2005, when it was modestly billed as a site on which people could swap personal videos. Since then, however, its video-response feature, which essentially allows users to converse through video, has managed to convene partisans of almost every field of human endeavor, creating video clusters that begin with an opening video, and snowball as fans and detractors are moved to respond with videos of their own. In answer to a lousy stammering video, say, a real YouTuber doesn't just comment, "You idiot—I could do that blindfolded!" He blindfolds himself, gets out his video-capable Canon PowerShot, and uploads the results.

There are music-making videos about music, dance videos about dance, and architecture videos about architecture. Music people respond to musical performances by filming a musical performance of their own. The same principle holds for dancers, athletes, pundits, pedants, comedians, film editors, poets, stunt people, propagandists, and showoffs of every stripe.

What's more, YouTube's interface allows users to track the history of anything they watch, as well as to peruse video responses to it. As a further inducement to stay on the site, YouTube proposes a half-dozen works that might interest you whenever you're streaming a video.

When you enter the site, then, be warned: before you know it, you've entered one of YouTube's great unmarked communities—the shred guitarists, the torch singers, the Christopher Walken impersonators. Each community is filled with so many small obsessive pursuits colliding and colluding with one another that it's awfully tempting to skip your lunch break—or take the day off—and watch them all.

What follows, then, is not a list of the top videos on YouTube. That would be too simple, too old-Web. Instead, here are five of the most fascinating worlds to get lost in on YouTube. Every single one of them is worth a detour.

## 1. PETER OAKLEY, AKA GERIATRIC1927

Last August [2006] Peter Oakley, a British pensioner, posted a video that he promised would contain grumbling and griping under the screen name geriatric1927. In fact, it was a love letter to YouTube, and an expression of hope that the video blogs he was planning to post regularly would interest users of the site. In record time the entries, which tell the story of a widower, blues fanatic, and former radar technician in the British Army, inspired a tribute video from a hipster admirer, who dubbed Mr. Oakley "The OG of Blogging"—that's original gangsta.

A grandpa who knows about radar? What techie kid doesn't dream of that? Then came the imitators: Right, I'll have a go myself, resolved jimsan1, another YouTuber who appeared close to Mr. Oakley's own age. (Mr. Oakley turns 80 in August.) Before long, Mr. Oakley's videos were attracting a million views and more, and his series of videos are among YouTube's ten most heavily subscribed to. Now the senior-citizenry of YouTube regularly posts video oral histories in serial form, talking straight into the camera without pyrotechnics or theatricality in tribute to the understated style of the master.

Mr. Oakley can now be heard singing with the Zimmers, a vast rock group formed of elderly retirees and overseen by Mike Hedges, the U2 producer. The band released its first album, "My Generation," [in May 2007], but its first music video—a performance of the Who's "My Generation" with Pete Townshend—was uploaded to YouTube [in April 2007].

## 2. TIME-LAPSE PAINTING

Just as YouTube has made room for producers and consumers like Mr. Oakley who have been shut out of earlier pop-culture revolutions, it also accommodates art forms that other media have threatened for years to make obsolete; witness the many origami how-to videos on the site, as well as lute and gamelan recitals, polka dancing, and happenings of the Dada–Yoko Ono kind.

It should come as no surprise, then, that the august art of portrait painting has made modest inroads into the consciousnesses of the MySpace generation. Of course, painting is typically appreciated face-to-face, but painters on YouTube have added drama by creating time-lapse films of themselves at their easels. The videos, which move too fast to be instructive, nonetheless address both the most childlike questions we have for realist painters (How did you do that?) and the most suspicious (Did you do it yourself?). They also exude infectious bravado, as the painter accomplishes a day's work in three or four minutes, without anxiety or second thoughts.

Laura Karetzky, a figurative painter in New York, was drawn to the time-lapse portraits because she thought they might provide a window into the private agonies and ecstasies of other painters. They did. In one video, titled "Heather Paints Melissa," a hobbyist paints and repaints a child's face, each time unintentionally deepening the portrait's flaws. "I find myself hanging on the edge of my seat clasping my hand to my forehead," said Ms. Karetzky. "I'm actually rooting for her in the end not to make the same mistakes she just painted out three or four times earlier."

## 3. PARKOUR

Speaking of performance art and mysterious spectacles, parkour—a form of extreme gymnastics invented in France—thrives on YouTube. What good, after all, is scaling buildings, leaping down staircases, and jogging over cars if no one is around to see you pull it off? That's where videos, and their international dissemination, come in.

Some parkour videos are professionally made programs about the art of movement, in which the whole world is an obstacle course and no structure is insurmountable. These gorgeous minifilms feature muscled figures, often shirt-less, looking like jewel thieves or Spiderman, atop buildings where they skip and leap with such death-defiance and frank grace that it's hard to keep from calling their sport dance.

But no: parkour is meant to be martial, efficient, and tough. Amateurs from all over the world have also shared their stunts on YouTube. The homemade spinoffs mimic professional ones in that they strew together scenes from dis-parate places and times, cherry-picking only the players' best stunts and sup-plying no clear course trajectories. But many of the participants in the amateur videos look like teenagers, their jangly movements plainly influenced by hip hop and skateboarding as much as by dance, circus art, and gymnastics. And unlike the pros—who really appear to risk their lives—the copycats wisely use jungle gyms and rubber surfaces for soft landings. After a pileup of decidedly self-serious parkour offerings, a comedy team called the Suggestibles posted a parody response, "Pour Quoi," in which two Englishman (naturally) talk in phony French accents and struggle to get through a revolving door.

## 4. BLASPHEMY

Individual religious testimony abounds on YouTube, as do sermons from mis-cellaneous (and sometimes extinct) religious institutions, but these are posted to fire up discussion, not to lay down any laws. Versions of the last sermon of the prophet Mohammed are posted—one runs *Star Wars*–style with the words receding into outer space—as are Christian sermons on sexual purity and Palestinian sermons that contain anti-Semitic slurs.

Viewers are urged to discuss them, and they do. Curiously, the religious group that makes the most imaginative and despotic use of YouTube are athe-ists. The Rational Response Squad, a furtive organization devoted to curing theism, has challenged YouTubers to post videos of themselves denying the existence of the Holy Spirit and thereby—in the group's reading of Mark 3:29—damn themselves for eternity.

More than 1,200 people have posted blasphemy videos as of this writing. In each one, a single person speaks the line, "I deny the Holy Spirit." Sometimes he or she adds more: a name, a speech, a further denial of Easter Bunny–like entities.

Some blasphemers are jaunty, some are insolent, some are scary, some are nervous. But all of them (young and old, mostly English-speakers, but with a range of accents, and ethnicities) seem to believe they are making a statement of some gravitas—issuing a reproof to doctrine, possibly risking their salvation. On the face of each participant is both a wonderful purity of purpose—the mandate is so simple, the one-line script so unforgettable—and a clear vulnerability.

Will anyone regret taking the so-called Blasphemy Challenge? If so, can they retract their videos?

## 5. FAT RANTS

Joy Nash became this spring's latest YouTube star for her Fat Rant, in which she flaunted her plus size, bashed retail chains for not stocking XXL, and ran down her fellow Americans for their hypocrisy about weight. Ms. Nash performed much of this rant in various costumes with a high-spirited stage manner that suggested self-confidence, humor, and a refined sense of glamour.

Ms. Nash, who gave her weight at 224 pounds, said that she ate what she wanted, watched her health, and had stopped considering her weight the prime mover of every event in her life. YouTubers loved it.

Watch "A Fat Rant" these days and thumbnail images from response videos run down the middle of the page. A typical one is called YES!!!!!!!!!!!! Unlike the glossily produced original, the responses to "A Fat Rant" are ad-libbed solo soundoffs with minimal stagecraft.

They are new fat rants, then, delivered by Ms. Nash's fans and semi-fans, people with equally piquant opinions about obesity, appearance, and American doublespeak about weight. Though each video pretends to particular clarity on the subject, many run into versions of the same conundrum: being fat is O.K., except when it's unhealthy. But when is that, again? And should fat people try to be skinny? Or be happy with how they are?

The video responders are less ideologically resolute than Ms. Nash, with some resolving to diet; still others manage to outdo Ms. Nash in fat-power-speak. In general, the video responders are profoundly moved by "A Fat Rant," and take Ms. Nash's video as an occasion, paradoxically, to expose their bodies, as if inviting comment. This being YouTube, with its emphasis on responses, both taunts and catcalls arrive, ready for worldwide consumption, right on cue.

---

## Working with the Text

1. Although each YouTube video allows for written comments (and the most popular videos can generate literally thousands of them), Heffernan writes, "the only authentic response to a YouTube video is another YouTube video—the so-called 'video response.'" Why do you think she sees the video response as more authentic? What definitions of the term *authentic* does she mean to emphasize? How does her statement reflect what she sees as the most interesting and significant aspects of the YouTube phenomenon?

2. In introducing newcomers to YouTube, Heffernan does not offer a list of top videos, something she says would be "too simple, too old-Web." Instead, she discusses five different YouTube worlds (or, as the title of the article refers to them, "tribes"). What do you think Heffernan means

by "old Web"? Define your understanding of the distinction between "old Web" and "new Web."

3. Write your own definition of what constitutes a YouTube world. In what ways can we compare these worlds to the concept of a channel on television? To the idea of television genres (e.g., sitcoms, soap operas, reality shows, sporting events, etc.)?

4. Explore one of the worlds that Heffernan describes, or find one of your own, on YouTube and write a description of the membership rules that seem to govern this world. What are the customs of this video "tribe"? What values do the participants share? What rituals or disagreements?

5. Choose a YouTube video that you have a strong response to and try scripting and describing a response video. If you or your school has the resources (and this can be as simple as finding a computer in a campus lab that has a built-in camera), record your response. In either case, consider the combination of images and language that you want to include in your response, and write a description and justification of the video response that you create. If you wish, you can post the video and see if you generate any further responses. (*Note:* Be careful when posting online about how much of your identity and location you wish to reveal.)

# VIEWING CULTURE

## PRIMETIME ANIMATION

Many people think of cartoons and animation as primarily children's entertainment, a connection that television networks reinforced in the 1960s and 1970s with the Saturday morning block of cartoon series for children. There were occasional exceptions: in the 1960s, programs such as *The Rocky and Bullwinkle Show, The Flintstones,* and *The Jetsons* appeared as primetime sitcoms aimed at adults as well as children, with story lines that referred to popular celebrities and pop culture fads of the time. But even these series found their way to Saturday mornings and weekday afternoons after school when the programs went into syndication, their appeal to children proving more enduring than their appeal to adults.

The automatic association between children and cartoons on television began to change in 1989, however, when a primetime cartoon debuted on the then-new Fox network. *The Simpsons* was created by Matt Groening, an underground cartoonist whose work had been popular for a decade in alternative newspapers around the country. Edgy, irreverent, willing to tackle the most sensitive and controversial social issues with sometimes dark humor and irony, *The Simpsons* became a hit for Fox and a national sensation. Critics praised the show, political figures argued over its effect on children, and some schools banned the wearing of T-shirts bearing the face of Bart Simpson and the caption, "Underachiever and Proud of It!" *The Simpsons* has since become the longest-running cartoon series and longest-running sitcom in television history, and Homer, Marge, Bart, Lisa, and Maggie Simpson have become household names. In fact, many of you reading this may have grown up watching (or perhaps being forbidden to watch) *The Simpsons*.

*The Simpsons* also started a new era in primetime animation. From *Beavis and Butt-Head* to *South Park,* cartoons for grown-ups have become a television staple in the age of cable television. *The Critic, The Family Guy, Daria, King of the Hill, Futurama, American Dad, Space Ghost Coast to Coast, Aqua Teen Hunger Force*—these cartoon shows may differ considerably in format (from parodies of the conventional suburban sitcom family to a talk show in outer space, to the adventures of animated fast food), but they all share a certain sensibility and outlook. All of them take on subjects often considered taboo on other television series, such as religion, death, sexuality, and politics, and most pride themselves on how much they push the envelope in terms of humor and satire. In other words, cartoons—with such a long history as children's entertainment—are among the least child-centered programs currently on television.

This Viewing Culture section asks you to explore, analyze, and write about why these primetime cartoon programs can tackle subjects that other programs are reluctant to address. What is it about cartoons that make them such an effective medium for social satire and commentary?

---

## Working with the Text

1. What do fans of these shows most value about them? Work with your own experiences and perspectives if you are a fan of one or more primetime animated programs, or interview someone who is a fan. How do you see them as different from live-action programs? What difference do you think it makes that these shows are cartoons? Similarly, locate television viewers who especially do not like these programs and write about their points of view. Compare and contrast these different attitudes toward primetime animation to come up with your own theory about how primetime animation functions on television.

2. Choose a particular primetime animated program and focus on an episode that you think deals with a particularly controversial subject. Watch the episode carefully, then write about how the episode might be received differently were it done with live actors. What if all of the actual dialogue was kept the same?

3. Consider these familiar faces from primetime animation:

These three drawings demonstrate various degrees of realism in relation to human faces. First, write about what is most and least realistic about each drawing. Then discuss how you think the difference in drawing styles and representation might lead viewers to think of and relate to these characters differently. How do these different drawing styles in turn relate to the natures and reputations of the three programs—*The Simpsons, South Park, King of the Hill*—that they represent?

# from *Understanding Comics*

## Scott McCloud

*Just as with animated cartoons, many Americans consider comic strips and comic books as child's play, not really worthy of adult consideration, despite the fact that comics have flourished in the United States since the late nineteenth century. More recently, many comic artists, along with literary and art critics, have been insisting on the expressiveness and complexity of comics as a method of storytelling that combines the verbal and the visual. In* Understanding Comics, *artist Scott McCloud offers theories about why we are attracted to comics and why we respond to them so strongly. His ideas are relevant to television animation as well.*

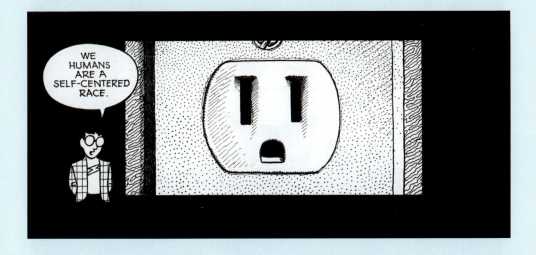

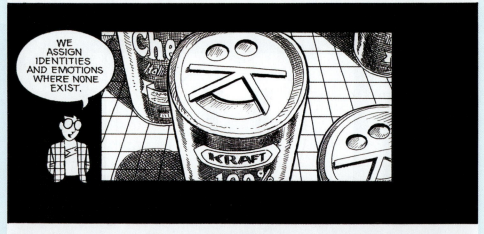

ALL SET?

GOOD.

NOW, *SMILE*.

C'MON, NOBODY'S LOOKING.

GOOD. NOW, WHAT *CHANGED* WHEN YOU SMILED? WHAT DID YOU SEE?

*NOTHING*, RIGHT.

YET, YOU *KNOW* YOU SMILED! NOT JUST BECAUSE YOU FELT YOUR CHEEKS COMPRESS OR THE CRINKLING AROUND YOUR EYES!

YOU *KNOW* YOU SMILED BECAUSE YOU TRUSTED THIS MASK CALLED YOUR FACE TO *RESPOND!*

BUT THE FACE YOU SEE IN YOUR *MIND* IS NOT THE SAME AS *OTHERS'* SEE!

WHEN TWO PEOPLE INTERACT, THEY USUALLY LOOK DIRECTLY *AT* ONE ANOTHER, SEEING THEIR PARTNER'S FEATURES IN *VIVID DETAIL*.

EACH ONE *ALSO* SUSTAINS A CONSTANT AWARENESS OF HIS OR HER *OWN* FACE, BUT *THIS* MIND-PICTURE IS NOT NEARLY SO VIVID; JUST A SKETCHY ARRANGEMENT...A SENSE OF SHAPE..., A SENSE OF *GENERAL PLACEMENT*.

SOMETHING AS *SIMPLE* AND AS *BASIC*--

--AS A *CARTOON*.

THUS, WHEN YOU LOOK AT A PHOTO OR REALISTIC DRAWING OF A FACE--

--YOU SEE IT AS THE FACE OF *ANOTHER*.

BUT WHEN YOU ENTER THE WORLD OF THE *CARTOON*--

--YOU SEE *YOURSELF*.

I BELIEVE THIS IS THE *PRIMARY CAUSE* OF OUR CHILDHOOD FASCINATION WITH *CARTOONS*, THOUGH OTHER FACTORS SUCH AS *UNIVERSAL IDENTIFICATION, SIMPLICITY* AND THE *CHILDLIKE FEATURES* OF MANY CARTOON CHARACTERS ALSO PLAY A PART.

THE CARTOON IS A *VACUUM* INTO WHICH OUR *IDENTITY* AND *AWARENESS* ARE PULLED...

...AN *EMPTY SHELL* THAT WE INHABIT WHICH *ENABLES* US TO TRAVEL IN *ANOTHER REALM*.

WE DON'T JUST *OBSERVE* THE CARTOON, WE *BECOME* IT!

THAT'S WHY I DECIDED TO *DRAW* MYSELF IN SUCH A SIMPLE *STYLE*.

WOULD YOU HAVE *LISTENED* TO ME IF I LOOKED LIKE *THIS*??

## Working with the Text

1. In *Understanding Comics,* McCloud offers, in cartoon form, his theory of why we respond to and identify with cartoons differently than to other kinds of visual representation, including live action. Choose a particular character from an animated television program and apply McCloud's theory to explain why we respond to drawings of a human face differently than we respond to photographs of a human face. How do McCloud's ideas help explain our different expectations for cartoon characters as opposed to live-action actors?

2. Use McCloud's ideas to return to the question of the different reactions we might have to the visual portrayals of Lisa Simpson, Cartman, and Hank Hill. How would McCloud analyze each of the faces?

3. McCloud makes his serious theoretical argument in comic book form. Discuss the advantages of using comics and animation to write a serious essay or argument. How might the association between comic books and comedy (as suggested in the very phrase "comic book") enhance or complicate the ability to connect with and persuade a reader? Extend this discussion to a consideration of a particular animated television program as a form of social commentary.

# CREATING CULTURE

## DO-IT-YOURSELF TV

Over the course of its history, the idea of television has changed dramatically. From consisting solely of electronic programming beamed to TV sets centrally located in living rooms, television has seen the massive proliferation of channel options made available by cable systems and satellite dishes, the sale of television programs via DVD, and the custom downloading of content onto desktop computers and portable electronic devices.

The creation of the World Wide Web as perhaps the ultimate broadcast network has not only opened up new ways of connecting with television programs via fan sites and discussion groups, it is also changing the ways we think and talk about television. Originally, the term *television* referred to both the technology used to watch various kinds of programs as well as the programs themselves. "I'm watching television" meant both watching TV programs and watching the TV set because that was the only way to interact with television. Now, however, we can watch television on a TV set, an iPod, or even a mobile phone. How does that change what we mean by the word *television*?

In Los Angeles and New York, two new kinds of TV "networks" have developed to bring TV fans and TV creators together without the aid of major broadcasters. Both Channel 101 in Los Angeles and later Channel 102 in New York started as a way for producers of new TV shows who were frustrated with the difficulty of getting new shows on conventional television to hold regular viewing parties at local night spots where they could screen their new shows. Anyone could come and vote on which shows they liked best on any given night. The winning shows were then made available on websites that mimic regular television channels. Programs can stay on the air, or on the Internet, based on ratings (number of hits and downloads) and on the willingness of the creators to make more shows.

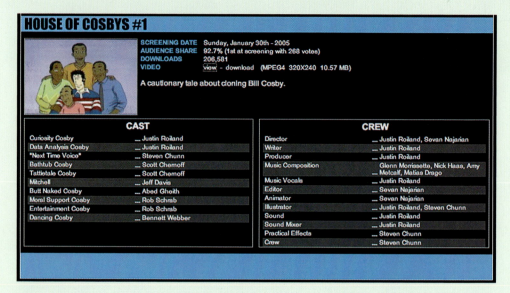

HOUSE OF COSBYS #1

SCREENING DATE   Sunday, January 30th - 2005
AUDIENCE SHARE   92.7% (1st at screening with 268 votes)
DOWNLOADS        206,581
VIDEO            view - download  (MPEG4 320X240 10.57 MB)

A cautionary tale about cloning Bill Cosby.

| CAST | | | CREW | |
|---|---|---|---|---|
| Curiosity Cosby | ... Justin Roiland | | Director | ... Justin Roiland, Sevan Najarian |
| Data Analysis Cosby | ... Justin Roiland | | Writer | ... Justin Roiland |
| "Next Time Voice" | ... Steven Chunn | | Producer | ... Justin Roiland |
| Bathtub Cosby | ... Scott Chernoff | | Music Composition | Glenn Morrissette, Nick Haas, Amy Metcalf, Matias Drago |
| Tattletale Cosby | ... Scott Chernoff | | Music Vocals | ... Justin Roiland |
| Mitchell | ... Jeff Davis | | Editor | ... Sevan Najarian |
| Butt Naked Cosby | ... Abed Gheith | | Animator | ... Sevan Najarian |
| Moral Support Cosby | ... Rob Schrab | | Illustrator | ... Justin Roiland, Steven Chunn |
| Entertainment Cosby | ... Rob Schrab | | Sound | ... Justin Roiland |
| Dancing Cosby | ... Bennett Webber | | Sound Mixer | ... Justin Roiland |
| | | | Practical Effects | ... Steven Chunn |
| | | | Crew | ... Steven Chunn |

*House of Cosbys* was one of the most popular shows on the original Channel 101.

Almost all of the shows are comedies, parodies of different genres of television programming, from sitcoms to crime shows to the news. In a strict sense, none of these programs is officially "on television"; they are television shows mostly on the basis of how they imitate and make fun of the conventions of typical television fare. In other words, to get the most appreciation of these new Web-based channels, you need to be familiar with a wide variety of types of television programming.

# THREE

E X E R C I S E

## Television Conventions

Working as a class, come up with a list of typical television shows. What are the kinds of programming you most associate with television? Then, in smaller groups, work on describing the defining characteristics of these different genres of television. Consider both the typical content of such shows and how they are structured, including stylistic details, modes of presentation, use of video or film, etc. For example, in thinking about local news broadcasts, you might notice that the content of most shows focuses on three general categories: news, weather, and sports. Within those categories, you may notice subcategories such as consumer reports, crime stories, or human interest stories. Local newscasts also share some common structural and stylistic features, such as the use of teasers before commercials (e.g., "when we come back..."); the placement of two anchors behind a desk, each holding a sheaf of papers, the use of the news crawl across the bottom of the screen, etc.

As you share and compare the information each group produces, come up with some definitions and characteristics of what makes any kind of programming or cultural text remind us of television. To put it another way, if you were asked to write in the style of television, how would you approach that assignment?

# "A Can-Do Little Website, on the Hunt for Homegrown Stars"

## Richard Morgan

*In this article from the* New York Times *on the emergence of Channel 101 and Channel 102, reporter Richard Morgan interviews participants who describe what they find most liberating and inspiring about these new channels.*

Early this month, about 100 people gathered in a drab room with mismatched chairs at the Anthology Film Archives on the Lower East Side to watch a group of five-minute films, and to choose their favorites. Among the films that were cheered were one that was a lecture on neuroscience and another on a street fight in Williamsburg.

The winning videos, quirky as they may have been, have a future. New episodes of those shows will be shown on Channel 102, a [...] website based in New York that selects much of its programming through democratic devices like these public screenings, where viewers vote on their favorites.

The approach, whose offerings can be found at www.channel102.net, has yielded shows like *Cat News,* whose anchor is a cat called Smiley Muffin; *Going Up,* set entirely in an elevator; and *Locked in a Closet,* a riff on cramped urban life.

The formula seems to work for people both on screen and off. "102 gives all the New York artists out there the ability to make whatever they want without standards, practices, censors, or the need for advertisers and production value," said Tony Carnevale, 28, a founder of 102 and a writer for VH1.

Not only artists like the result. Comedy Central has optioned two of 102's shows for an online channel it launched this month. Even more auspicious is the success of www.channel101.com in Los Angeles, which started in 2003 and was the inspiration for Channel 102. Channel 101 turned a major corner [...] when its three biggest stars—Andy Samberg, Akiva Schaffer, and Jorma Taccone, all in their late 20s—joined *Saturday Night Live.* Mr. Samberg is an actor; Mr. Schaffer and Mr. Taccone are writers.

"I'm very proud of the fact that we're basically the first people to be hired out of the Internet, on the strength of our own product as opposed to improv troupes or stand-up acts," Mr. Samberg said. "We did it ourselves."

At public screenings of both channels, talent agents and network representatives are already on the prowl for the next Andy Samberg, according to Dan Harmon, a founder of 101. The two channels also attract comedians who have already arrived, with Jack Black and Sarah Silverman appearing on 101, and Rob Corddry on 102.

"Its greatest success is its total lack of capitalism," Mr. Harmon said. "The currencies of ego, creativity, Samaritanism, and talent are worth much more as legal tender."

Indeed, performers say the big lure for them is the forum's creative freedom. "It's the opportunity to work with something you know is cool, whether or not other people have picked up on it," said Rob Huebel, known best (if at all) as the Inconsiderate Cellphone Man whose skits run during movie previews. Mr. Huebel, 35, is a star in a 102 show called *Shutterbugs,* about ruthless talent scouts who handle child actors with brutally adult professionalism.

*Cat News* was an early hit on Channel 102.

On Channel 102, Mr. Huebel said, "You can do anything. And it can be anyone doing it—some N.Y.U. kid or some married dude on the Upper West Side. It's so open, as long as the material is good."

## Working with the Text

1. Tony Carnevale, one of the creators of Channel 102, praises the format for allowing "artists out there the ability to make whatever they want without standards, practices, censors, or the need for advertisers and production value." Define what these standards and practices seem to be for conventional television programs. For example, what topics or themes are most popular? Which are taboo? What are the freedoms and constraints affecting different television programming? How does broadcast television differ from cable and satellite TV? Explore as well what you think Carnevale means by "production value." What are the assumptions viewers make about the production values of most television shows, and in what ways do these values enable or limit what the creators of the programs can do?

2. Dan Harmon, who helped start Channel 101 in Los Angeles, also points to the "total lack of capitalism" as responsible for the initial success of the "network." What do you think Harmon means by "lack of capitalism"? What kind of relationship is he implying between the need for commercial television stations to make a profit and the creative process?

3. Why do you think some well-known performers (such as Jack Black and Drew Carey) have been attracted to working on Channel 101 and Channel 102? In what ways does their presence on some of these programs change or not change the idea of openness and accessibility? What do you see as presenting the greatest potential problems for these ventures?

4. The success of Channel 101 and Channel 102 has been followed by the development of Web sitcoms, situation comedies produced solely for viewing online or downloading onto a video player. Programs like *Duder* (on dudershow.com) are not parodies of sitcoms but are new, DIY-type of sitcoms for the digital age. Locate and watch some of these Web sitcoms, and write about how they mirror traditional television programming and the chief ways you see them as exploring new possibilities for the form.

## Do-It-Yourself TV

Explore some of the offerings found on both Channel 101 and Channel 102 (and be prepared: there is little censorship on either site). Choose one or two programs that you particularly enjoy or find interesting, and write about why you chose them and what you think they say about the nature of television and television programming. What specific aspects of television form and content do these programs most often parody or imitate?

*Duder* is an example of a Web sitcom. Like a television program, fans can follow sequential episodes that chart the evolving relationships among a group of 20-something friends living in the city.

Work in groups to propose your own "television" program. Choose a genre or type of programming and define a central concept for your project. Think about what specific aspects of television form and content you want to highlight or parody with your show. Once you have created a proposal, write a sample scene. Explore and reflect on your experience by writing about how creating your own program affects the way you watch and think about other television programming.

# EIGHT

CHAPTER

From Bollywood to
Hollywood: Movies at Home
and Around the World

# MOVIES FROM PAST TO PRESENT

Of all the major forms of mass media, none seems to embody the mix of the new and the old, the past and the future, the traditional and the innovative the way that the movies do. Born in the nineteenth century out of developments in photography, movies quickly evolved from short novelty films depicting famous landmarks and brief action sequences, such as a train pulling into a station, into one of the most powerful forms of storytelling ever invented. Movies helped introduce the very concept of mass media, created the entertainment industry with the development of Hollywood, and produced the modern idea of the celebrity in the form of the movie star.

Yet for all the newness of the movies, they still retain aspects of the older world of popular culture from which they derived. From the beginning, movies adapted storytelling techniques from the novel and the theater, and many of the most enduring types, or genres, of movies had their origins in printed fiction and on the stage, from the western to the detective story, the historical epic to the romantic comedy. To this day, close ties remain among novels, plays, and movies, and now the influence goes in both directions. Not only do movies continue to be based on popular novels and plays, but movies and moviemaking techniques now influence the way novels are written and the way plays are staged.

In spite of movies' enduring popularity and influence, their disappearance and demise have also been the subject of much speculation. As far back as the first movies with sound, in the late 1920s, people both in and out of the movie business have fretted about whether the heyday of the movies has passed. With the introduction of each new form of communications technology, from radio and television (which many were certain would destroy Hollywood), to home videos and the Internet, concerns have been raised about whether movies would remain relevant in the new era.

To be sure, there have been significant changes in the ways we watch movies over the years. The advents of radio and television did result in a huge drop in average movie attendance from the highs reached in the 1930s and 1940s, when many people went to the movies two or three times a week. How and where we see movies has also changed considerably, as ornate movie palaces and theaters featuring two different movies a night, plus cartoons and newsreels, have given way to a smaller number of multiplex theaters, some of which feature twenty screens. More and more, of course, we watch movies in the comfort of our homes, whether on cable television or on DVD.

## My First Movie

While most of us don't have specific memories of the first television show we ever watched or the first time we heard radio, our first excursions to an actual movie theater often leave strong and lasting impressions. Write about your first memories of going to the movies, trying to recall as much detail as you can. What was the name of the movie? What images from that movie have stuck with you? What sounds and smells can you remember? Who did you go with?

After recalling your own experiences, gather the experiences of others about their first movies. If possible, try to ask people across a range of ages to get a sense of how the movie-going experience may have changed over the years. As you compare and contrast your experiences with those of others, reflect on how you think those early experiences have shaped your current attitudes toward and taste in movies.

Movies and, in particular, the rituals of going to the movies have persisted in spite of all these social and technological changes. Movies remain as much a part of the pop culture landscape as the projection equipment and the popcorn poppers (which are as necessary as the projection equipment!) in any movie theater. Digital technology has not eliminated the movies, but the technology is creating new ways for us to interact with them, just as with television. One symbol of these new developments on many college campuses are course and program names changing from "Introduction to Film" or "Film Studies" to "Media Studies" or "Introduction to Cinema," all in recognition that the use of celluloid film is no longer synonymous with moviemaking in the age of digital cameras and computer-generated images.

## MOVIES AROUND THE WORLD

As we have seen throughout this book, the digital revolution has gone hand in hand with the globalization of pop culture, and the movies are no exception. Google the name of almost any country in the world followed by the word *movies,* and you will find dozens of websites devoted to providing information about that country's cinema and to selling DVDs featuring movies from that country. Once again, however, this internationalization of movie culture is an example of "back to the future," because in reality, the movies have always been a global art form. Although the name *Hollywood* is synonymous with the movies for many, Los Angeles, California, was actually a bit of a latecomer to the movie industry. By the time movie production began in earnest on the West Coast of the United States, there were already thriving film industries in Europe, Asia, South America, and Africa. Many Americans are surprised to learn, for example, that the largest movie industry in the world is not found in the United States but in India, headquartered in Mumbai (formerly Bombay), with an output that dwarfs the American film industry.

From the beginning, moviemakers around the world have shared with and influenced one another. The history of the American film industry is bound up with the history of immigration and global conflict. For example, when hundreds of German and French writers, directors, actors, and others fled the Nazi regime in the 1930s and moved to Hollywood, they brought with them styles, techniques, and storytelling traditions from European cinema. Gritty hard-boiled crime thrillers, for example, may seem all-American, but their mysterious and suspenseful use of shadow and light, a staple of movies and television from *The Maltese Falcon* to *CSI,* owes much to the techniques brought by the abstract-expressionist German filmmakers who found safe haven in the United States during World War II. Likewise, as American pop culture began to dominate world markets in the twentieth century, American movies had major influence on the movies in other countries, sometimes in welcome ways and sometimes in the form of local resistance by moviemakers to the Hollywood style.

The trade in international movies has become more intense than ever in the digital age, from the black market in bootleg DVDs of popular Hollywood blockbusters to the desire of immigrants everywhere for movies from their homelands. More and more, movie producers think globally when they make a new movie, considering not just box-office sales in the home country but ticket and DVD sales around the world. A movie that might be considered a box-office disappointment in the United States, for example, could still prove to be a global hit.

This international orientation also affects the kinds of stories that movies tell and how they tell them. Movies that rely more on action and visual spectacle than on complicated dialogue and character development, for example, tend to travel more easily across boundaries of language and culture. A verbal joke, after all, might suffer in translation or when read in subtitles, but a car chase is exciting to watch regardless of language. However, this preference for marketing American-style action-adventure movies around the world can also present a skewed view in different cultures. For example, many movie fans in other countries assume that shootouts and explosions are a common feature of day-to-day life in America based on what they see in movies and television programs from the United States.

## T W O

### EXERCISE

### Exploring World Cinema

How aware are you of movies around the world? Can you list any movies from other countries that you have seen or that are favorites of yours? Do you or does anyone in class have an interest in movies from another country or culture? As a way of exploring world cinema, work individually or in groups to select a particular country to investigate. You might choose the country on the basis of a quick Internet search, talking with teachers on your campus, or recommendations from fellow students. Based on your research, choose and locate one or two movies to watch and write about your viewing experience. Discuss what most interested you in researching the movies of the country and why you chose these particular movies. Pay special attention to what you found most familiar and what you found new. As a final project, write a viewer's guide for college students interested in learning more about the movies of the country you studied.

## INTERACTIVE MOVIES

Throughout *Text Messaging,* we have been considering how digital technology has been making the field of popular culture more interactive by shrinking the distance between producers and consumers. The effect of digital cameras and computer editing programs on moviemaking has been especially dramatic. Movies have long been the most expensive of popular culture art forms, involving not only significant amounts of money to make but also requiring the skills of a team of artists and crew members to create even a modest project. The biggest Hollywood blockbusters now cost about $200 million to make (almost twice the yearly budget of the university where I work and about equal to the gross domestic product of the entire nation of Tonga), and even small independent features can reach the $1 million level.

The development of relatively inexpensive digital moviemaking equipment has opened up this costly art form to thousands of people who otherwise would never have had access to any kind of moviemaking technology. The last ten to fifteen years has seen an explosion in small, independent moviemaking, with many films distributed via the Web and through a circuit of local film festivals that are homegrown in spirit but international in perspective. Now more than ever before, the experience of watching movies can serve as the inspiration for taking part in the creative process of moviemaking, an activity that will change the way a person thinks of and responds to movies. In this chapter, you will be given the opportunity to consider movies from these multiple perspectives: as a popular form of mass entertainment, as a global phenomenon, and as an arena for your own creative participation.

## MOVING BEYOND STEREOTYPES

### "Taking Stupid Seriously"

### Mark Olsen and John Horn

*How seriously should we take funny movies? From the Keystone Kops in silent film to the latest Will Ferrell picture, comedies have always been among the most popular movies. At the same time, comedies have proven notoriously difficult to evaluate. After all, what one person finds hilarious might leave another cold. And while some creators of movie comedy such as Charlie Chaplin and the Marx Brothers have been called geniuses by many critics, other viewers find it difficult to see as much significance in jokes and pratfalls as in supposedly more serious movies that don't try to tickle our funny bones. In fact, out of the almost eighty movies that have won the Academy Award for Best Picture, only about four could be considered comedies.*

To be sure, the link between laughter and social commentary has a long and important cultural history. Satires that target the excesses and faults of human behavior and society are a staple of classical Greek and Roman drama, and the literary tradition of using humor to make a serious point stretches from those ancient playwrights through Chaucer, Shakespeare, Mark Twain, and Oscar Wilde, to Kurt Vonnegut and Chuck Palahniuk. In an effort to make the case for the seriousness of comedy, some people make a distinction between smart and silly comedies, between stories that use language and ideas to make us laugh and those that use slapstick and body noises. Even that distinction has proved difficult to maintain, however. Even the "smartest" examples of movie comedy are not above the occasional fart joke, and it's rare to find a movie comedy that doesn't mix the verbal and the physical, the witty remark and the tumble down the stairs.

In "Taking Stupid Seriously," written in the fall of 2006, Los Angeles Times reporters Mark Olsen and John Horn look at some examples of movie comedies that get their laughs from main characters distinguishable not by their cleverness or verbal agility but by their stupidity and foolishness. In spite of or even because of how silly these comedies appear, however, Olsen and Horn argue that they may also be offering pointed social, cultural, and political commentary about contemporary American life.

## Before You Read

1. Compile a class list of favorite comedies from the past few years. Invent a classification system for these movies. For example, you might try out the idea of *smart* versus *silly, subtle* versus *obvious,* or some other set of adjectives. Write about why you chose the classification system you did and how the terms you decided on help explain what you find most characteristic and most (or least) appealing about these movies.

2. Continue the discussion started in the introduction to this reading by exploring the question of why we have such mixed attitudes about movie comedies. Why, for example, are so few comedies named Best Picture or are included on Ten Best lists, in spite of their enduring popularity?

Stupid has never looked so smart.

Dimwitted comedies have been making a killing at the ticket counter. *Talladega Nights* has grossed $147.9 million. *Jackass: Number Two* was a No. 1 box-office hit and has grossed $64.1 million. And there's a frenzy building for the [movie] *Borat,* a travelogue by the titular Kazakh journalist.

But the reward isn't merely financial. A number of these seemingly low-brow movies are surprisingly high-minded and have more on their agendas than just fart jokes: it's the difference between the Marx Brothers and the Three

Stooges. *Borat* is ultimately a story about ignorance and racism, while *Talladega Nights* offers a sly sendup of NASCAR culture. Even though it received a stumblebum release, Mike Judge's *Idiocracy* scores more political points than a week's worth of *The Colbert Report.*

These movies still try to satisfy the mass audience's appetite for physical, visceral comedy—*Borat*'s signature scene is an extended wrestling match between two naked men. But the films still manage to turn foolishness into pointed social commentary.

"I don't want to speak for my movies; you could say my movies are just completely silly and dumb, but in the case of *Idiocracy* and *Borat,* without a doubt there is a really subversive and sophisticated assault on American culture," says Adam McKay, director and co-writer of *Talladega Nights: The Ballad of Ricky Bobby.* "It's one thing to mess stuff up and break stuff, but [*Borat*] is really pointing out the ideology of America. It's one thing to break stuff and damage people's possessions, but when you start aiming at the ideology of America, that's dangerous comedy."

*Talladega Nights,* written by McKay and Will Ferrell, finds the heart of contemporary America in the world of stock-car racing: the movie's champion driver is a fun-loving, hard-charging, star-spangled "doer" played by Ferrell with more than a touch of George W. Bush, who meets his nemesis in the guise of Sacha Baron Cohen (who also plays Borat) as a gay, espresso-sipping, jazz-loving, Camus-reading racer.

"As soon as we talked about doing a NASCAR movie and came up with the Ricky Bobby character, we realized the tension of it. We'd mention it to people and they'd have two responses, either 'I hate NASCAR' or 'NASCAR is awesome.' It was so polarizing right off the bat...we were very aware we were going into this cultural hot zone, that this was the epicenter of red state culture," says McKay. "The living nightmare for a red state NASCAR driver would be a gay French driver."

*Borat: Cultural Learnings of America for Make Benefit Glorious Nation of Kazakhstan* follows a hopelessly unsophisticated television host as he makes his way across America. Shot in a run-and-gun style, the film shows Borat in a number of scenes where he encounters ordinary Americans.

As a consequence of Borat's naive but nonetheless leading questioning (the movie lists five screenwriters), these seemingly average citizens quickly and casually expose their own racism, homophobia, misogyny, and anti-Semitism. At one point, Borat asks a gun store salesman which weapon is best for killing Jews. Without missing a beat, the guy behind the counter reaches for a suitable hand gun.

"I think it's part of the genius of Sacha, his ability to bring that out in people through the innocence of the character. He created a character who is so naive and lovable that people want to teach him, want to show him things and help, and in doing so reveal themselves," says Todd Phillips, the director and co-writer of [...] *School for Scoundrels*. (Phillips was the original director of *Borat* before exiting the project and receives a co-story credit on the final film, which was directed by Larry Charles.)

Meanwhile, writer-director Mike Judge's *Idiocracy*—a comedy starring Luke Wilson as an average American who participates in the government's top-secret hibernation program only to wake up 500 years later—attracted critical attention for its satirical portrayal of a distant future in which dumbing down has bottomed out. The film is an angry and disillusioned portrait of a world where nuance, subtlety, and discourse have been swallowed by a lowest-common-denominator hegemony. (The era's most popular—and Oscar-winning—movie is called simply *Ass*.)

Its studio, 20th Century Fox, didn't have a clue what to do with *Idiocracy* (Fox didn't preview the long-delayed movie for critics before releasing it with hardly any publicity or marketing support) and Judge, who co-wrote the script with Etan Cohen, declined interview requests. But critics and a small handful of moviegoers—ticket sales totaled just $444,000—took notice.

"Judge has a gift for delivering brutal satire in the trappings of low comedy and for making heroes out of ordinary people whose humanity makes them suspect in a world where every inch of space, including mental, is mediated," *Times* critic Carina Chocano wrote in her *Idiocracy* review. "The plot, naturally, is silly and not exactly bound by logic. But it's Judge's gimlet-eyed knack for nightmarish extrapolation that makes *Idiocracy* a cathartic delight."

## DO AUDIENCES GET THE JOKE?

In some ways, these new movies are following in the footsteps of seemingly lowbrow, secretly smart comedy, from Buster Keaton to Bugs Bunny to *Blazing Saddles, The Simpsons,* and *South Park*.

There is likely no real, empirical way to determine how much of what's going on in the new group of films will register with audiences. *Borat, Idiocracy,* and *Talladega Nights* were made for mainstream moviegoers, after all, and none of their filmmakers wants to be seen as a detached elitist, a navel-gazing solipsist, or a seltzer-in-the-pants vaudevillian.

By directly addressing contemporary culture through a sleight of hand referential joke telling, these projects exploit the pop vocabulary, illustrating more esoteric points while keeping audiences happy. The marionettes in 2004's *Team America: World Police*, for example, spoofed action-movie conventions, but the film's story focused on the perils of patriotic fever.

David Zucker, who directed the last two entries in the *Scary Movie* franchise as well as such revered classics as *Airplane!* and two of the three *Naked Gun* pictures, says that in any comedy, regardless of one's position on the sliding scale of smart versus dumb, "the audience is the boss."

"We definitely write with the audience in mind," Zucker says, referring to the team of writers who create the cavalcade style of his films. "We think everything is funny until we put it in front of an audience, and if they don't get it we can't leave it in there. We don't say the audience is dumb or wrong; we respect what the audience gets."

But sometimes audiences will go wherever filmmakers take them, as long as they are guided along the way.

"The director of any movie is a purveyor of tone," says Phillips, whose credits include *Old School* and *Starsky & Hutch*. So for me it's about the humor falling within the world you've set up. I think an audience, even subconsciously, recognizes when you break out of the world of a movie. So it's not that you're 'going too far,' it's a matter of watching the tone of the movie."

Not every dumb comedy engages in the strategy of the secretly smart to make satirical points. Perhaps nothing manages to obliterate the line between stupid and smart quite like the wildly successful *Jackass* movies.

In the recently released sequel, *Jackass: Number Two,* star Johnny Knoxville and his band of daffy stuntmen create another nonnarrative series of excruciating physical, yet somehow gut-wrenchingly funny, stunts. In one, a man puts his penis inside a sock puppet, and then allows a snake to chomp down on it. Other pranks are even more crudely homoerotic.

Jeff Tremaine, the director of both *Jackass* films, will admit to no higher intentions than laughter in making his movies, nor is he particularly bothered by those who don't find his brand of humor amusing.

"We know what we think is funny, so if someone doesn't think it's funny we're just different from that person," he says.

But Hollywood has always been a political town, and other directors see their works engaging moviegoers on issues. Ed Zwick can let his [...] drama

*Blood Diamond* bring attention to exploitive mining practices; Michael Moore's documentaries touch on guns, war, and healthcare; and Judge can use *Idiocracy* as a wake-up call against apathy.

For a filmmaker such as McKay, an occasional contributor to political blog the Huffington Post, the resurgence of mixing smart and stupid is also a way to navigate the concerns of corporate ownership and globalized initiatives that are such a part of the current world of mainstream Hollywood filmmaking.

"I think the reason it came back is because of the way entertainment is now structured, whether it's the movies or TV or radio, you have to entertain to get on the stage," he says. "You have to, to play the game at all. If you're making comedies, they have to have fun and a rhythm to them. It's much harder now to make a movie like Albert Brooks' *Real Life.* Look what happened to *Idiocracy.* It's a real harsh environment. You need to entertain on this visceral level to really captivate people."

Ruminating further, McKay alights upon another, perhaps purer, reason for the reemergence of this roughhouse mix of high and low, what truly makes stupid the new smart.

"We're in this era of so many talking heads and pundits and so much discourse about the direction of our country—two dimensional talk—the idea of just laughter is a great, powerful thing, and there's something to be said for it," he says. "What better way to couch ideas than in a big, silly comedy."

---

## Working with the Text

1. Referring to the movie *Borat: Cultural Learnings of America for Make Benefit Glorious Nation of Kazakhstan,* Adam McKay, the director and cowriter of *Talladega Nights: The Ballad of Ricky Bobby,* says that the movie "is a really subversive and sophisticated assault on American culture," and that a target of its humor is "the ideology of America." What do you think McKay means by the phrases *American culture* and *the ideology of America*? How would you define "American culture"? What do you see as the ideology (or primary belief system) of America?

2. Olsen and Horn ask the question, "Do audiences get the joke?" That is, if we can consider either *Borat* or *Talladega Nights* as political commentary as well as "stupid" comedies, how many members of the audiences for these movies also see them this way? While Olsen and Horn contend "There is likely no real, empirical way to determine how much of what's going on in the new group of films will register with audiences," we can still explore the question by interviewing movie viewers and by surveying how audience members are discussing these

movies. Choose a particular movie mentioned in the article, or one that you feel also fits the topic, and locate people who have seen the movie and would be willing to discuss it with you. You can also investigate online discussion boards and blogs to read how a variety of viewers are talking about the film. Use your findings to write a reaction to the question, "Do audiences get the joke?"

3. One significant aspect of the movies referred to in the article that Olsen and Horn don't address directly is gender. In the typical kind of "new" comedy they are describing, the main characters are men who participate in traditionally male-identified activities (a trend continued in the string of movies associated with writer/director Judd Apatow, *The 40-Year-Old Virgin, Knocked Up,* and *Superbad*). How significant is the fact that these movies feature male actors? What might be some examples of women in movie comedies that Olsen and Horn might include in an expanded version of their discussion? Working in groups, come up with a proposal for a seriously stupid movie that would feature a woman comic actor in the lead. How did the process of writing the proposal cause you to think differently about the issues that Olsen and Horn discuss?

## from *G Movies Give Boys a D: Portraying Males as Dominant, Disconnected, and Dangerous*

### Joe Kelly and Stacy L. Smith

*How do the movies we see affect the ways we understand and relate to the world around us? This question is always certain to start a lively discussion or heated debate, and it has motivated a wide variety of studies and other research projects. The subject takes on a special urgency, however, when it comes to the viewing habits of children. Even many adults who are skeptical of the argument that they are powerfully changed by the movies they watch react differently when the conversation turns to the impact of mass media on children, particularly very young children. What guidelines, for example, should parents follow in selecting programming for their children to watch? What kinds of movies are appropriate for them?*

*Since the modern movie-rating system began in the 1960s, parents and caregivers have struggled with those categories that recommend "parental guidance." Why do PG-13 movies choose that age as a cutoff? When, if ever, could a young child watch an R-rated movie, and are all R-rated movies the same? One category that has seemed much less fraught with uncertainty has been the G rating. After all, these movies have been screened and rated as appropriate for a general audience of any age. Surely any parent can feel safe with a G-rated movie.*

*But what effect might even G-rated movies have on how children learn about themselves and the world? In the age of videocassettes and DVDs, watching a particular movie is often not a once-a-month or once-a-year occurrence for children. A child may watch a favorite video dozens of times, practically memorizing whole parts of it. "G Movies Give Boys a D: Portraying Males as Dominant, Disconnected, and Dangerous" is a report for the See Jane Foundation, a group dedicated to improving gender portrayals in children's media. In the report, Stacy L. Smith, a communications professor at the University of Southern California, and Joe Kelly, a journalist and president of the Dads & Daughters organization, argue that the images of gender portrayed in popular G-rated children's movies can have a serious impact on the ideas and attitudes children develop about gender and gender roles. They report on a study they conducted that shows how movies for children focus disproportionately on male characters, especially white male characters, and they argue that the image these movies portray of "typical" male behavior may produce a distorted and even unhealthy perception of gender roles for both young boys and girls.*

## Before You Read

1. Take a class survey of your favorite G-rated movies from your own childhoods. What were some of the movies that you and your classmates loved to watch again and again? List some of these titles, and write about what you remember most about the portrayal of gender in these movies. How many of the main characters, for example, were male? How many were female? Did there seem to be more of one kind of character than another?

2. What were your family's rules about watching movies? Did you have videos at your house? What restrictions were there on how often or whether you could watch movies? Compare your experiences with those of others in the class. What seemed to be the most common rules? Write about how you felt about your family's attitudes toward movies at the time and what you think about them now. Do they seem sensible to you? Too restrictive? Not restrictive enough?

3. Recall and write about an early incident from your life when gender roles played an important part or when you first became aware of gender roles. Why do you think this memory has stayed with you? In what ways did this experience affect your understanding and opinions about gender roles?

### INTRODUCTION

*G Movies Give Boys a D* analyzes how male characters in G-rated films outnumber female characters by a lopsided margin, are seldom in significant relationships, and are more likely to be physically aggressive.

This report draws on the most in-depth content analysis of popular G-rated movies ever conducted. Researchers from the Annenberg School for Communication (ASC) at the University of Southern California (USC) studied the 101 top-grossing G-rated films released from 1990 through 2004, analyzing a total of 4,249 speaking characters in both animated and live-action films. *G Movies Give Boys a D* is the second report in a series drawing on the Annenberg/USC research. It analyzes several key dimensions of how males are portrayed.

The research found that G-rated movies, whether animated or live-action, are dominated by white male characters and male stories. These disproportionate numbers offer young children a transparent message that being male and white is not just the norm, but preferable.

Characters of color are most often sidekicks, comic relief, or villains. Non-white male characters are portrayed as more aggressive and isolated. The result is that the majority of children do not see themselves reliably reflected on the screen.

In addition, G-rated films show few examples of male characters as parents or as partners in a marriage or committed relationship. [ . . . ]

## WHAT THE RESEARCH FOUND

The *G Movies Give Boys a D: Portraying Males as Dominant, Disconnected, and Dangerous* report reveals disturbing patterns in the representation of male characters in widely-viewed G-rated films. Male characters dominate casts and stories, are less involved in relationships and parenting, and are more physically aggressive than female characters. In addition, male characters of color appear significantly less often than white male characters, but are portrayed significantly more often as aggressive and disconnected.

> The early exposure of children to less stereotyped gender roles will contribute to less sexism and improved relationships between the sexes, as well as a balanced approach in rearing male and female children.—**Alvin F. Poussaint, M.D., Professor of Psychiatry, Harvard Medical School and Judge Baker Children's Center, Boston, MA**

### Dominant

Male characters dominate children's movies. In the 101 films studied, there are three male characters for every female character (even though slightly less than half of the world's population is male). More than two out of three (72%) of speaking characters (both real and animated) are male. More than four out of five (83%) of the films' narrators and speaking characters in crowd scenes are male.

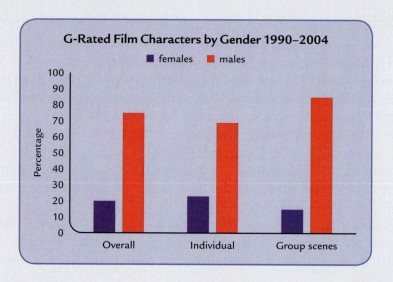

**G-Rated Film Characters by Gender 1990–2004**

■ females　■ males

This lopsided imbalance presents our youngest, most impressionable children with a distorted worldview in which males and male-driven stories overshadow females and their stories. As will be shown, the world of G-rated movies also presents a worldview which overshadows, and sometimes makes invisible, portrayals of and stories about nonwhite males.

## Disconnected

G-rated films show very few examples of male characters as parents or as partners in a marriage or committed relationship. This lack of role models is especially notable given society's struggle with divorce and father absence, and the shortage of initiatives to prepare boys and young men for fatherhood and life-long relationships.

> What do boys learn about the social roles of both males and females when they are raised from an early age on a steady diet of male-centric movies in which male characters are highly stereotyped, and female characters are either highly stereotyped or simply not there?—**David Kleeman, Executive Director, American Center for Children and Media**

Male characters in G-rated films are only half as likely (34.6%) as females (66.3%) to be identifiable as parents. They are about half as likely (31.9%) as females (60.7%) to be identifiable as married or in a committed relationship.

When analyzed by apparent ethnicity, the fathering and relationship picture is even bleaker. Among those characters developed enough to ascertain their parental and/or relationship status, more than half of the white males are parents (53.1%), but only about a third (34.6%) of nonwhite males are. Meanwhile, nearly half of white males (45.3%) are in married or committed relationships, compared to less than a quarter of nonwhite males (22.2%).

## Dangerous

Among primary and secondary characters, 44.1% of males and 36.9% of females are portrayed as physically aggressive or violent. Since there are three times more male than female characters, the actual number of physically aggressive males in G-rated films is much higher than the number of females displaying the same behaviors.

Matt Damon as Jason Bourne: a positive or negative image of masculinity?

Physical aggression is another area where nonwhite males are cast in a much more negative light. Almost twice as many nonwhite males (62%) as white males (37.6%) are portrayed as physically aggressive or violent.

In addition, males of color are hard to find at all in G-rated movies. When compared to census data*, nonwhites are grossly underrepresented at only 14.5% of male characters, while making up 35.5% of the male U.S. population (a 21-point deficit). Whites account for 85.5% of male characters, but only 75.2% of the U.S. population (a 10.3-point overrepresentation).

| Male Race/Ethnicity | G-Rated Films | 2000 U.S. Census | Difference |
|---|---|---|---|
| White | 85.5% | 75.2% | +10.3% |
| Hispanic | 1.9% | 13.2% | −11.3% |
| Black | 4.7% | 11.9% | −7.2% |
| Asian | 3.3% | 3.6% | −0.3% |
| Native American, Alaskan Indian, Pacific Islander | 1.3% | 1% | +0.3% |
| Middle Eastern | 3.3% | n/a | n/a |

*U.S. Census percentages equal more than 100 because the "White" category includes people who reported White as well as one or more other races, and Hispanics who reported their race as White, either alone or in combination with one or more other races.

This study evaluated films released from 1990 through 2004. There was no significant improvement in gender imbalance or change in male role portrayals during the fifteen years.

> It is surprising that in 2006, we still need to be focusing on gender balance.
> —Linda Simensky, Senior Director of Children's Programming, *PBS Kids*

Finally, the gender portrayals and imbalance do not appear to be influenced by which company distributed the films. The 101 movies analyzed were released by twenty different companies.

## DOES THE PORTRAYAL OF MALES MATTER?

Gender portrayals seen in films can have a strong impact on children ages 0–11 because these children are so impressionable. Entertainment images and stories help influence a child's important developmental task of understanding what it means to be male or female.

The portrayals are especially important for preschool children, who are having their ideas of manhood and womanhood shaped and integrated into their own personalities. The images of mainstream media images matter because they are important components (along with family, religion, and other factors) in creating the personalities who become adult women and men.

> Children are influenced by what they see around them, and the repeated viewings of these movies make them a powerful force in shaping children's developing ideas about gender. Research conducted in the 1970s showed that when young children see someone on the screen that looks like them but engages in nonstereotyped activities, they are more likely to try out those activities themselves.
> —Lawrence Cohen, PhD, psychologist and author of *Playful Parenting*

In a 2003 nationwide survey, the Kaiser Family Foundation found that over half (53%) of parents say that their 0 to 6-year olds have at least twenty videos or DVDs in the home. Further, almost half (46%) of the caregivers surveyed reported the children they care for watched at least one video or DVD per day. Content in G-rated movie videos and DVDs may have a particularly strong influence on children's social learning about gender because children tend to watch the same movies over and over.

More research has been conducted on how children's gender attitudes are influenced by television viewing than has been done on how children's gender attitudes are influenced by movies. However, because children repeatedly view popular G-rated films on their TV screens, via DVD and VCR, results of TV research may be relevant.

The TV research suggests that television viewing can have an impact on developing or possibly reinforcing children's stereotypical attitudes and beliefs about gender. In fact, a meta-analysis of thirty surveys and experiments reveals that exposure to television is a significant and positive predictor of sex role acceptance and attitudes among children and adults (Herrett-Skjellum & Allen, 1996, pp. 174–176). With repeated television viewing of characters engaging in traditional sex roles, a child's gender expectations for his/her own sex or the opposite can become simplified, skewed, and stereotypical in nature. These effects are particularly problematic when we consider that females are seen less frequently than males on television (Aubrey & Harrison, 2004; Sternglanz & Serbin, 1974).

It is important to note that children are not impacted exclusively by how characters of their *own* gender are portrayed on the silver screen. Along with expectations for themselves, children's expectations for members of the other gender, now and into the future, can be influenced by repeated viewing of characters and stories that reinforce particular notions about male and female roles.

In the world of G-rated movies, our youngest boy viewers are left with far fewer socially engaged and diverse male role models than they need. And we must remember that young girls also benefit from viewing such male role models.

## WHAT CAN BE DONE?

Families, entertainment industry professionals, educators, and communities all have roles and opportunities in changing narrow portrayals of females and males seen in children's movies. See Jane has specific recommendations for parents, industry professionals, and professionals who work with children.

> Boys need male characters in films who are not laughed at, but seen as heroic when they stand up against sexism and violence. Such characters are too rare in popular culture, even though they are the ones with real strength and courage.
> —Jackson Katz, co-founder of Mentors in Violence Prevention and author of
> *The Macho Paradox*

In the context of this report, See Jane believes it is essential that fathers and stepfathers actively participate in conversations about gender portrayal in movies for children. In our role as "First Men" in the lives of our children, fathers and stepfathers hold immense influence. Through our attitudes, actions, and words, we set our children's standard for what to expect from males. Our example and perspective help shape the possibilities our children see for themselves as boys and girls.

### Parents

- Choose to see, buy, and rent films that feature balanced and diverse female and male characters.
- Purchase a selection of movies which, in the aggregate, show a balance and diversity of female and male characters.
- Watch films with your children and discuss similarities and differences between males and females. In doing so, parents—especially fathers

## See Jane's Tips for discussing male portrayals with children

1. Compare the number of male and female characters and talk about what impact you think that has.

2. What behaviors are most common for the males? How about for the females?

3. Compare the number of nonwhite and white male characters and talk about what impact you think that has.

4. How often do nonwhite characters have white characters in their circle of friends? How often do white characters have nonwhite characters in their circle of friends? Do you think it is okay for film characters to have a circle of friends that doesn't include another ethnicity? Why or why not?

5. Are more of the parent characters male or female? Why do you think the film has this ratio? What impact do you think that has?

6. Are more of the aggressive or violent characters male or female? Nonwhite or white? Why do you think the film has this ratio? What impact do you think that has?

7. How do the kids in the story relate to their parents? What do you like or dislike about that?

8. Who created the story? Was the writer male or female? White or nonwhite? How about the director? If you don't know, what would you guess?

9. What would you do differently if you were making the movie?

and stepfathers—can take a step toward protecting children from the potentially negative effects of imbalanced gender portrayals.

Whoever tells the story defines the culture. This report clearly shows that we have a long way to go before Hollywood gives boys and girls role models that will encourage them to break through limiting and damaging stereotypes.
—David Walsh, Ph.D., Founder, National Institute on Media and the Family

### Industry professionals (including producers, distributors, writers, animators, directors, casting directors, and others)

- Embrace the widened creative possibilities opened up by greater balance and diversity among female and male characters.
- In collaboration with See Jane, engage in new research to assess the commercial potential (for theatrical release and DVD markets) of creating a more diverse and realistic assortment of male and female characters.
- Evaluate project development and production as the first step to support stories and roles that:
  - More accurately reflect the gender ratio of the real world children inhabit.
  - Emulate the diversity of real-world girls, boys, men, and women.

**Professionals who work with children (including child-care workers, educators, clergy, counselors, etc.)**

- Maintain a selection of movies which, in the aggregate, show a balance and diversity of female and male characters.
- Watch films with children and discuss similarities and differences between males and females within the film and in comparison to other films they see.
- Advocate for comprehensive media literacy education for all children.
- Use See Jane's Tips for viewing and discussing films with children.
- Introduce parents to materials like See Jane's Tips for viewing and discussing films with children.
- Provide other information that responds to the gender imbalance and stereotypes depicted in most G-rated films.

The influence of findings and suggestions like those in this report can be wide-ranging. Entertainers, parents, educators, and communities can support films that more accurately reflect the real world our kids live in—a world shared by boys and girls, men and women. The result will be that all of our children are better off.

> Thirty years ago, researchers examined Caldecott and Newberry award-winning children's books and found similar problems: mainly male characters, and boys and girls being introduced to a stereotypic world of restricted roles and emotions. That research inspired new publisher guidelines and today's Newberry and Caldecott winners (along with other children's books) are frequently exemplars of gender equity and multicultural inclusion.—**David Sadker, Ed.D., Professor, American University**

## References

Aubrey, J. S., & Harrison, K. (2004). The gender-role content of children's favorite television programs and its links to their gender-related perceptions. *Media Psychology, 6,* 111–146.

Herrett-Skjellum, J., & Allen, M. (1996). Television programming and sex stereotyping: A meta-analysis. *Communication Yearbook, 19,* 157–185.

Sternglanz, S. H., & Serbin, L. A. (1974). Sex role stereotyping in children's television programming. *Developmental Psychology, 10*(5), 710–715.

## Working with the Text

1. Compare the specific empirical findings of Kelly and Smith's report with your earlier discussion of the movies that people in the class most enjoyed watching as children. Test the authors' research by visiting a

local library or video store and reading summaries of G-rated movies for children. How surprised were you by the wide differences in the number and importance of male versus female characters that the report found?

2. In the section, "Does the Portrayal of Males Matter?" Kelly and Smith write, "Gender portrayals seen in films can have a strong impact on children ages 0–11 because these children are so impressionable. Entertainment images and stories help influence a child's important developmental task of understanding what it means to be male or female." If this is true, what kinds of understandings of gender roles do you think the authors fear a child could develop from the portrayal of males as "dominant, disconnected, and dangerous"? How well do they convince you that this is a problem to be taken seriously? What would you recommend to a parent after reading this report? If you are a parent, what effect has this report had on how you think about movies and their potential impact on your own child or children?

3. Rather than incorporating direct quotes from other writers into their prose, Kelly and Smith use the technique of highlighting ideas from others in set-apart quotes that appear next to their own writing. Why do you think they use quoted material this way? As a reader, what connections do you make between these set-apart quotes and the arguments that Kelly and Smith are making? Which of the quotes do you find most effective or thought provoking and why?

4. In the section, "What Can Be Done?" Kelly and Smith provide a sidebar called "See Jane's Tips for discussing male portrayals with children." Explore the effectiveness of these questions by first answering them yourself in relation to a specific G-rated children's movie with which you are familiar or that you watched for this assignment. What about your own answers did you find most interesting or even surprising? Next, try asking these questions of a young child about his or her favorite G-rated movie. What kinds of conversations and discussions did these questions prompt? Write about your experiences discussing gender roles in movies with a young child. What suggestions can you make for additional questions or discussion?

5. This report and the program See Jane are sponsored by Dads & Daughters. Visit the website at http://www.DadsandDaughters.org to learn more about the group. How does the fact that a fathers' group sponsored this report affect your understanding and reaction to the

arguments made about gender? Would you react differently if the report were sponsored by a women's organization? Why or why not?

# "Where Are the Female Directors?"

## Michelle Goldberg

*The Hollywood movie community has acquired a reputation (even a stereotype) for its supposedly liberal political values, and actors and others in the movie industry have received both praise and criticism for speaking out on social issues and championing various candidates and causes. In spite of this reputation, however, Hollywood remains surprisingly old-fashioned in terms of providing opportunities for women filmmakers, especially when it comes to movie directors, the people most responsible for creating what we see on the big screen or on our DVD players. While women have assumed the top production positions at some major studios, they still number in the minority when it comes to who sits in the director's chair.*

*In "Where Are the Female Directors?" originally written for the online magazine* Salon, *journalist Michelle Goldberg explores the various contributing factors that have prevented women from directing and that still present barriers to women directors in Hollywood, from assumptions about who goes to the movies and why, to cultural attitudes and mythologies that surround the position of director.*

## Before You Read

1. How aware are you and other moviegoers about the directors of the films you see? How important is the director of a movie in determining your movie-going choices? List the movie directors you are most familiar with and write about how important the director is in your decisions as a viewer. Expand the discussion by discussing this question with other movie fans you know. What conclusions can you draw about the importance of directors for moviegoers?

2. Knowing that you are going to read an article about the lack of women directors in Hollywood, write about the assumptions or guesses you would make about this topic. Share your assumptions with others in the class.

3. Before the Academy Awards ceremony in 2002, the feminist arts group known as the Guerrilla Girls created the billboard in Hollywood, shown on page 494, that brought up issues about the role of women and people of color in the mainstream movie industry:

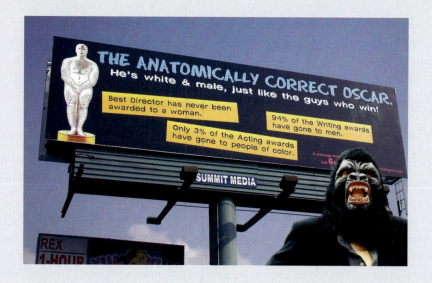

Write about what you imagine would be your immediate reactions if you drove past this billboard. What do you think the Guerrilla Girls would want you to take away from seeing this billboard? Their motto is "Fighting discrimination with facts, humor, and fake fur!" How does their motto affect your perception of the rhetorical purpose of the ad?

Towering over the corner of Highland and Melrose in Hollywood last March [2002] was a billboard featuring the "Anatomically Correct Oscar." Pallid and stocky rather than sleek and golden, he stood covering his crotch next to the tag line, "He's white and male, just like the guys who win!" A project by art-world activists Guerrilla Girls and Alice Locas, a [...] secretive group of female filmmakers, the billboard highlighted the fact that a woman has never won the Oscar for best directing. In fact, only two have ever been nominated—Lina Wertmüller for *Seven Beauties* in 1976 and Jane Campion for *The Piano* in 1993.

After the breakthrough best actor and actress wins by Denzel Washington and Halle Berry, Hollywood reveled in self-congratulation for its ostensible progressiveness. Yet just as black filmmakers remain marginalized and decent black roles remain scarce, the situation for women making movies is grim. As stickers from another Guerrilla Girls campaign proclaimed, "The U.S. Senate is more progressive than Hollywood. Female Senators: 9%, Female directors: 4%." That's according to a study undertaken at San Diego State University, and it suggests the extent to which the dreams that radiate off theater screens and into our culture are still almost exclusively the dreams of men.

At a time when film schools are graduating almost equal numbers of men and women, why is the movie business still such a closed shop? Many women from every stratum of the directing world—established Hollywood types and shoestring independents, celebrated art-house stars and creators of light teen comedies, film school deans and movie historians—tell remarkably similar stories of deep-rooted prejudices, baseless myths and sexual power struggles that litter the path to the director's chair with soul-wearing obstacles. "It is absolutely consistently more difficult for women from the beginning to the end," says Debra Zimmerman, executive director of the nonprofit organization Women Make Movies.

And things might just be getting worse. According to a study by Martha M. Lauzen, a San Diego State professor who studies the role of women in film and TV, women directed 7 percent of the top-grossing 100 films released in 2000. (In a sample of the top 250 films, the percentage was a little higher, at 11 percent.) [In 2001,] that already dismal number plummeted. "We're just putting together preliminary figures for films released in 2001. The percentage [of the top 100 films] has gone way down. It looks like 4 percent, which means it's below 1992 levels."

Adds Martha Coolidge, president of the Directors Guild of America and director of such movies as *Rambling Rose* and *Introducing Dorothy Dandridge,* "I'm not seeing the hiring of women directors improving at all. It's a terrible testament to where the industry is going."

Contrary to expectations, things aren't much better in the indie world than in Hollywood. Using a sample of 250 films, Lauzen compared the top-grossing 50 films with the bottom-grossing 50, which tend to be indie films. "We've never found a significant difference in terms of women behind the scenes" in the bottom category, she says.

These numbers are important in understanding the problem because, as any male director will tell you, moviemaking is a brutal business for all involved. Mary Harron, director of *I Shot Andy Warhol* and *American Psycho,* is married to director John Walsh, who has had a far more difficult time in the business than she has. "It's very difficult for women or men if what you're doing doesn't fit into industry standards of what people expect from a movie," she says.

Famed screenwriter and director Nora Ephron, whose movies include *Sleepless in Seattle* and *You've Got Mail,* adds, "I always think every movie should begin with a logo that says, for example, 'Warner Bros. did everything in its power to keep [us] from making this movie.'"

Nevertheless, Harron says of the situation for women directors, "It is not all OK. It really isn't. It's still much harder for women to get started." The

reasons why are a complex mix of economics, sexism, the tastes of executives, and even self-sabotage.

Often, the hurdles start with discouragement in film school. When Coolidge applied to New York University's film school more than 30 years ago, she says she was told that she couldn't be a director because she was a woman (though she was accepted anyway).

One would like to think things have improved a lot since then, but according to Christina Choy, chair of the graduate division of NYU's film school, the mostly male faculty there still discourages female students in unconscious ways—largely because its members don't relate to their work. [ . . . ]

In the hallways of San Diego State, says Lauzen, "I have heard male professors say to female students, 'Don't even think about directing or being a cinematographer. Get into producing.'"

Those who do stick it out in school face sexual tensions that keep them from penetrating the groups of funders and mentors that help young male filmmakers along. "We can't be in the boys club, and the boys club is how a lot of films get financed," says Tara Veneruso, who made the documentary *Janis Joplin Slept Here* and is now working on her first feature.

She explains, "Let's say you have a short at a film festival and it's doing well. Chances are high you'll be at a party and have an opportunity to pitch your idea over drinks. If your idea is good enough perhaps you'll get it financed." For women, though, chatting up an older man over drinks isn't construed as business—it's seen as flirting. That, Veneruso says, is why women are "always on the outside" of the casual networks where much of the film business gets done. Like many directors, she's quick to say that this isn't only men's fault. "A lot of time these guys have wives and girlfriends who don't like the idea of them talking to you. What happens in this whole conversation is that men think they're being blamed for excluding women, but I don't think it's as simple as that." Going out to dinner with an older financier simply isn't as straightforward for a woman as a man. "They have more reservations because of the implied nature of your conversation," she says.

Once women make contact with backers, received notions about the filmgoing audience make female-centered projects seem less lucrative. Over and over, directors say they've run up against the Hollywood assumption that girls and women aren't a sufficiently lucrative market, despite the overwhelming success of chick flicks such as *The First Wives Club, Waiting to Exhale, Clueless,* and *Bridget Jones's Diary.*

The conventional wisdom, says Coolidge, is that men make movie-going decisions for themselves and for their girlfriends. "The audience that studios have cultivated are young men. Young men, they feel, are easy to please. They seek out action, and then they'll take girls on dates." Similarly, when Sarah Jacobson brought her do-it-yourself sexual awakening triumph *Mary Jane's Not a Virgin Anymore* to Sundance, distributors told her, "Girls don't go to the movies without their boyfriends. It's just not a viable market."

Never mind that pair-dating is virtually obsolete as a social ritual, that teen girls were the ones who turned *Titanic* into a monolith, or that, as Coolidge says, "the adult female audience is the biggest audience in the world." The industry, she says, "is run primarily by young men who understand the audience that runs out on a Friday night and sees movies that have violence or sexual exploitation in them. When you get to making a movie from a girl's point of view, they don't know what to make of it."

This is also true, arguably, of the Motion Picture Association of America's ratings board. *Coming Soon,* Colette Burson's comedy about satisfaction-seeking high-school girls, was initially slapped with the deadly NC-17 rating despite having no nudity or violence whatsoever. At the same time, as Michelle Chihara wrote in the *Boston Phoenix,* Joel Schumacher's *8mm,* a movie about snuff films that took place in the S/M [sadism and masochism] demimonde, had no problem getting an R rating, which allows a film to play in normal multiplex theaters and be advertised in heartland daily newspapers.

Given these prejudices, it's not surprising that a study done by Women Make Movies found, according to Zimmerman, that "women who were trying to make films about women were getting the lowest amount of money" of any prospective filmmakers.

Not every woman wants to make specifically female films. Then they run into other problems. Women don't get to do blockbuster movies, and those rare exceptions, like Mimi Leder, who directed the George Clooney action spectacular *The Peacemaker,* and Kathryn Bigelow, director of *K-19: The Widowmaker,* simply prove the rule.

"Many, many times I've gone to a studio or producer with the idea of doing a movie that I'm passionate about and found that they can't conceive of a woman doing material that is not completely chick-centric," says Coolidge. She badly wanted to make a movie about Johnny Spain, a mixed-race member of the San Quentin Six who was too black for white society and too white for the Black Panthers, but was told it would be un-PC for a white woman to direct a film about a black man. (Few flinched when Michael Mann beat out Spike Lee for *Ali.*)

According to Mira Nair, director of the acclaimed *Salaam Bombay* and the wildly successful *Monsoon Wedding,* no one will come out and tell a director that she's not being considered because she's a woman, but it's easy to sense. "Once I was very keen on a political thriller," she says. "I went out to L.A. to lobby for it and I got the vibe that they were humoring me."

Harron notes that while she's happy with her career, "*American Psycho* made a huge amount of money. It did very, very well in Europe and tremendously well on video, and I think if I was a guy I would have had a lot more offers having made that film. It doesn't bother me so much because I do my own work and I have two small children, but if I was younger and single, it would be very frustrating to wonder why Darren Aronofsky [director of *Pi* and *Requiem for a Dream*] gets offered some huge thing and I don't."

Regardless of what type of film they make, says Lauzen, there's no evidence to suggest films by women earn less in the domestic market than films by men. "In Hollywood there's this perception that films made by women do not earn as much as films made by men, and that actually is not true," she says. "We have done the statistical analysis on box office grosses, comparing films that had women behind the scenes with others. The notion that films made by women don't earn as much just doesn't hold up."

But those analyses don't take the foreign market into account, and Ephron says that market's importance is a crucial reason why action movies—which many women don't want to direct, while those who do are rarely permitted to—dominate studio output. "The movies that make the most money are aimed at a subliterate market. By which I mean not just teenage boys, but the entire Third World. The effect of the foreign market on the movies that are getting made is huge." The movies that do well in those markets, she says, "are very much like video games. They have very little dialogue and a great deal of action and explosions. They do very well, so you're always going to find people more receptive to making movies like that."

The people in Hollywood, says Ephron, "are always looking for the safest thing they can do. The safest thing a studio can do is pay $20 million to a male star who is big in Asia. If you aren't making a high-budget action movie with one of those male stars, everything you are doing gets harder and harder going down the scale, until you get down to independent filmmakers trying to make a $1 million movie about a woman."

If a director battles through and makes these most difficult of movies, often she'll face problems with distribution. Sarah Kernochan, who won her second Oscar [in 2002] for her short documentary *Thoth,* said that "after seven years of tireless hustling to get it done," her cult teen comedy *All I Wanna Do* was sabotaged because Miramax bought the film but had no idea what to do with it.

Starring Kirsten Dunst, Rachael Leigh Cook, and Lynn Redgrave, the movie was set in a New England boarding school whose students were fighting a proposed merger with a nearby boys' academy. Though Miramax paid $3.5 million for it, the company decided to send it straight to video. Kernochan begged for permission to use her own money to open the movie in New York and Los Angeles, and emptied her savings account to pay for weeklong engagements.

"They convinced themselves that there was no way to get an audience, no way to get teenage girls into theaters," says Kernochan, a Hollywood screenwriter who also won a directing Oscar for her 1972 documentary *Marjoe.* The idea was that girls "always went to see the boys' movie."

Miramax executives had a slightly different interpretation of events. "There was a difference of opinion regarding the marketability of the project," says Matthew Hiltzik, Miramax's vice president of corporate communications. Kernochan "declined to make certain changes" that Hiltzik says were needed to make the film more appealing to all audiences, not just to boys. "We respected her passion for the project and offered her the opportunity to distribute it through other means," he says. "Ultimately, the film's performance suggests there was merit to our suggestions." (It also suggests that teen films can't take off without a marketing budget and a wide release.)

Nevertheless, *All I Wanna Do* finally did make money on video. "I know by the size of my residual checks that it's done well, because I'm getting checks bigger than anything I've made off studio movies I've written," Kernochan says. Despite that, and the fact that she's won Oscars for two of the three films she's directed, Kernochan has yet to find backing for the dark comedy she wants to direct next.

In fact, after all the barriers women overcome to make a first film, many times the real struggle doesn't begin until they want to do a second one. According to an analysis by the Guerrilla Girls and Alice Locas, [by 2001] 56 percent of the men who'd had films in the 1996 Sundance festival had made another movie. Only 33 percent of women had.

Even though Rebecca Miller's first film *Angela* won the Filmmakers' Trophy and the cinematography award at the 1995 Sundance, it took her until [2001] to make her second movie, *Personal Velocity,* which won the Dramatic Grand Jury Prize at Sundance [in 2002]. Five years passed between Nicole Holofcener's 1996 indie hit *Walking and Talking* (which the *New York Times* called "a date movie so enjoyably prickly it will seem funniest if you don't have a date") and her latest, *Lovely & Amazing.* There was a seven-year gap between Alison Maclean's first movie, *Crush,* and her fulsomely praised *Jesus' Son.* Maria Maggenti hasn't made another film since her lovely, influential 1995 *The Incredible Adventures of Two Girls in Love.*

Partly, says Allison Anders, whose movies include *Gas Food Lodging, Grace of My Heart,* and *Things Behind the Sun,* this is a result of Hollywood's fetishization of the boy wonder. "There's always going to be some boy who they're going to be five times more excited about" than any woman director, she says. "There's never been a 'girl wonder' mythology."

Thus, no matter how well received a woman's first film is, it rarely generates the kind of frothing excitement with which Hollywood greets a parade of male prodigies such as Quentin Tarantino, Paul Thomas Anderson, and Wes Anderson. "Male executives are looking for fantasy images of their younger selves," says Mary Harron, and this pertains to both the people and the films they celebrate.

At the same time, Anders says women are partly responsible for their failure to get second films done. As soon as a director makes her first movie, she says, "You have to have the next thing ready to go. I've been amazed watching people who are not ready with their scripts when they're getting a lot of attention. Preferably you should already be shooting your second one before the first one's out there. You've got to strike while the iron's hot. *When Gas Food Lodging* was released I had already shot *Mi Vida Loca.*"

For some reason, she says, women get caught unprepared more than men. "I don't know if women have this illusion that suddenly the doors are going to open up, but I think that women really have to be five times more conscientious about what they're going to do next. The doors are only going to open up for a second."

It's here that the issue gets complicated, because as much as some of these stories lend themselves to a straight-up feminist analysis, there are also internal barriers that keep women back. Despite her problems with Miramax, Kernochan also says her obstacles have been largely psychological (she also says that, at 54, ageism is a bigger problem for her than sexism). "In Jungian psychiatry it's called the spoiler, the voice that blames. It says, 'Of course this isn't happening for you, you're a woman, or your project isn't good enough.'"

Similarly, Alex Sichel, director of the sweet, searing 1997 riot-grrl lesbian film *All Over Me,* is still workshopping material for a follow-up. She talks about feeling anxious once her work was out in the world and of struggling with writing. Women, she says, sometimes need "a different process to come out with their ideas."

And then there's that old bugaboo of successful women—balancing work and children, which both Nair and Choy cite as their biggest hurdle. "It's difficult to raise children when you have to be on the set for six weeks," says Choy, noting that after leaving her family for a three-month shoot in Namibia, she had to face her own guilt and her husband's resentment, and she decided that "on my next project I wouldn't go so far away."

But while self-imposed limits enter into the equation, there's still a very real hierarchy of power to contend with, and it puts men on top, nonwhite men and white women somewhere below, and nonwhite women on the bottom. As Anders says about second films, "If you're not white, tack on another couple of years. It's almost like, thank you, black woman lesbian, we've heard that voice. Goodbye."

Thus despite the fact that Leslie Harris' first movie, *Just Another Girl on the IRT,* got positive reviews and made a profit, ten years later she's still trying to put together funding for her follow-up, *Royalties, Rhythm and Blues,* a behind-the-scenes look at a woman working in the hip-hop industry. Though written for a multicultural cast, Harris says, "My passion is to make a three-dimensional black woman who is the lead of the film. That has been a challenge for me. I've been told—a lot—that black women can't carry a film."

Despite such frustrating responses, Harris evinces remarkably little bitterness. "I'm confident that I'll get it done. Hopefully things will change and the industry will be more receptive and I'll be there waiting with this great script and they'll greenlight it."[...]

As the success of TV shows from *Buffy the Vampire Slayer* to *Sex and the City* suggests, there's an enormous audience for stories revolving around interesting heroines. Women buy more novels than men. They've made hits out of the mainstream movies that truly address their concerns.

But the movie industry is a dream factory, and the resistance to women in it seems based, in part, on the subterranean longings of the men who run it. "Whoever is putting up the money—as much as they might want to be eclectic and varied in their thinking, their taste and experience and subconscious desires come into it," says Nancy Savoca, whose films include *Dogfight, Household Saints,* and *The 24 Hour Woman.* "If you look at the movies, they're all the fantasy of a studio executive who's making the decision to greenlight a movie. It's about whether you've caught his imagination. His imagination says a middle-aged man having a problem with his wife, that seems really good. His imagination says a woman should look a certain way, and there's your A-list actresses."

Ephron disputes this idea, noting the ascendance of women studio executives like Columbia head Amy Pascal and Universal chair Stacey Snider. "Ten years ago almost every studio was run by men, and if you were interested in doing a movie about a woman it was very hard to find someone with power who even understood what you were talking about," she says. That's no longer true. "I don't think you can blame the men who run the industry anymore. There are too many women running the industry."

Some in Hollywood, though, say that the women who've scaled the studio hierarchy have done so by adopting retrograde ideas. "One thing we have to remember is they've grown up in the boys' network. They've been acculturated to believe that a commercial film is a male film," says Linda Seger, a script consultant and the author of *When Women Called the Shots: The Developing Power and Influence of Women in Television and Film.* "Some of this is really unconscious. This is a very practical business. These women are working 12, 15, 16 hours a day. They haven't been taking classes on feminist theory."

In fact, many directors say the number of women studio heads only adds to their disappointment with the current situation. After all, in the early 1990s, few anticipated the current stagnation. Back then, as some women were moving into positions of power in Hollywood, others were garnering praise in the burgeoning indie world, a scene that was electric but still obscure enough that the profit motive hadn't occluded all other values.

"Nancy Savoca and I came along at a brilliant time," says Anders. "People weren't expecting to make huge amounts of money, so you could do very personal, character-driven work and you could set up your next project based on the fact that you got into some prestigious festivals. Now it's much harder." [ . . . ]

To address this, Veneruso and Katie Lanegran run "The First Weekenders Group," an email list encouraging its 1,600 members to see women's films as soon as they open. When it comes to independent films, such audience-building measures will likely be more effective than badgering industry bigwigs. Businessmen may never defer to the call for equality, but they can be convinced by the possibility of profits.

The First Weekenders Group is but one encouraging recent development. The very existence of Alice Locas, which aims to do for the film business what the Guerrilla Girls did for the art world, is another. When the Guerrilla Girls formed in 1985, according to pseudonymous member Kathe Kollwitz, the art world looked a lot like the film industry does today, with only a tiny fraction of women showing at major galleries. Today, the proportions are nearly equal. Perhaps the greatest reason for optimism was Sundance [in 2002], where women swept the top prizes. In addition to Rebecca Miller's *Personal Velocity,* there was *Daughter From Danang,* co-directed by Gail Dolgin and Vicente Franco, which won the Documentary Grand Jury Prize, and Patricia Cardoso's *Real Women Have Curves,* which took the Dramatic Audience Award.

So it's obvious, at least, that women can make great movies. What's less clear is just how many more they need to make before their stories stop being dismissed as irrelevant, their talents as narrow, and their audience as nonexistent.

## Working with the Text

1.  Working as a class, list the different reasons suggested by Goldberg and others in her article about why Hollywood has been slow to provide opportunities for women movie directors. Working alone, prioritize this list in terms of which explanations seem most likely or make the most sense to you. Write about why you find these explanations more convincing than the others.

2.  The director Martha Coolidge refers to the "conventional wisdom" about how people make movie-going decisions that she says guides motion picture studio executives in their decision making about what movies to finance and whose movies to make. One such assumption is that "men make movie-going decisions for themselves and for their girlfriends" and that "[g]irls don't go to the movies without their boyfriends. It's just not a viable market." Both Coolidge and Goldberg cast doubts on the validity of this assumption. Test this idea out yourself by conducting interviews with a range of people who go to the movies (the lobby of the local multiplex might be a great place to start). Start with your own observations: How many moviegoers seem to be heterosexual couples? How many are going alone? How many are same-sex couples? How many are going in groups? Next, see if people will share some of their decision-making processes with you. How did they choose the movies they saw or are going to see? Are they satisfied with the typical range of offerings at their local theater? Do they wish certain kinds of movies were represented more often? Use your findings to write recommendations to studio executives about the factors they should consider in choosing which movies to finance and support.

3.  What are the consequences of the lack of representation of women among Hollywood movie directors? What differences might it make if more mainstream movies were directed by women? Write your response to the question, What if half of all movies were made by women? Would the changes be significant, or would movies still seem the same? To what extent would the conventional practices of Hollywood moviemaking change the directors, and to what extent might the directors change Hollywood?

4.  Conduct additional research on the careers of specific women directors, both those mentioned in the article and others. As the result of what you learn, write an essay and/or create a website offering advice to

young women thinking of careers as movie directors. What challenges should they expect? What strategies would you recommend to women trying to break into movie directing? How do the experiences of other women directors provide useful information about the best ways for women to find a place within mainstream moviemaking?

## "Do We Really Need Movie Ratings?"

### The Editors of Cineaste

When director Quentin Tarantino's Kill Bill, Part One premiered in 2003, it received an R rating from the Motion Picture Association of America's (MPAA's) ratings board for "strong bloody violence, language, and some sexual content." The R rating was the result of a careful negotiation between Miramax, the studio that produced the movie, and the MPAA, which originally planned to give the movie an NC-17 rating. Among the concessions made by Tarantino, a long, complicated, over-the-top sword battle between the main character, a female assassin named the Bride, and the members of a Japanese crime gang known as the Crazy 88 that featured simulations of severed limbs and fountains of artificial blood was changed from color to black and white.

The practice of negotiating changes in the content of a movie to receive a favorable rating from the MPAA, a regular part of the moviemaking process, has long drawn criticism from many different people for many different reasons. To free-speech advocates, the ratings system suggests censorship. To those who believe that movies can have a harmful effect on social values and behavior, the ratings system can seem lax. Regardless of your feelings about free speech and the effect of movie violence on human behavior, you might also wonder how much difference a change from color to black and white really makes.

Some think that the system of movie ratings is administered by the government and enforced by law, but actually the Motion Picture Association of America is a private movie-trade organization. Adherence to the movie-rating system by both studios and movie theaters is voluntary, although refusing to take part in the rating system can mean a movie will have great difficulty finding a distributor or a theater. The present ratings system dates back to 1968; before then, Hollywood studios adhered to a self-imposed Production Code that dictated what could and couldn't be shown in any movie (examples of content forbidden by the Production Code included "Dances which emphasize indecent movements" and "sex relationships between the white and black races.")

In "Do We Really Need Movie Ratings?" the editors of the journal Cineaste (the word cineaste means "a movie fan") used the occasion of the 2006 release of a documentary critical of the ratings system called This Film Is Not Yet Rated to take issue with the current ratings system, especially the secrecy surrounding how ratings decisions are made and even the identity of the members of the rating board. In so doing, they raise questions about the purpose of the movie-rating system in particular and our larger attitudes toward free speech in popular culture in general.

## Before You Read

1. Describe your own understanding of what the various movie ratings are and what you take them to mean. How important are they in your decisions about what movies to see or not see? What do you anticipate when you see that a movie has a particular rating?

2. Tell a story about an experience you had as a moviegoer with the ratings system. For example, you might write about when you first became aware of movie ratings and what made you aware of them, particular rules that your family may have had related to movie ratings, a desire to see a particular movie that was thwarted by the film's rating, your first experience seeing a movie with a certain rating, etc. How do you think this experience has shaped your attitudes toward watching movies?

3. How would you explain the U.S. movie-rating system to someone unfamiliar with it? For instance, what would you say to a young child asking what a particular rating meant? To someone your age visiting

from another country? Analyze your response and those of others in the class in terms of whether you find yourself endorsing or criticizing the ratings system.

Ever since the movies began, this hybrid art form has been considered slightly disreputable. After all, it took until 1952 for the Supreme Court to rule that films deserved the freedom of speech guarantees enshrined in the First Amendment. In addition, it took until 1968 for the notoriously hidebound Motion Picture Association of America to scrap the antiquated Production Code and to substitute a controversial, and much-contested, ratings system. Ostensibly designed to inform, and implicitly warn, filmgoers—particularly parents—of violent or salacious "content," the MPAA ratings have been, from their inception, plagued by inconsistencies and contradictions.

A cursory inventory of the last thirty-eight years of arbitrary, and occasionally slightly inane, decisions by the MPAA reveals a string of follies and a trail of de facto censorship. To begin with, the "X" ratings originally awarded to *Midnight Cowboy* and *Medium Cool,* classics that now seem far from sexually explicit (both films were subsequently re-rated as "R"; the "X" category, with an unmistakable pornographic taint, was changed to "NC-17" in 1990) do not merely remind us of the shifting values that inevitably influence what is deemed acceptable as artistic expression. There is little doubt that *Medium Cool* was awarded a "political X" for an ideological orientation that was apparently considered too incendiary for impressionable teenagers and that *Midnight Cowboy* was stigmatized for intimations of a homosexual relationship between the two protagonists portrayed by Dustin Hoffman and Jon Voight.

Kirby Dick's recent documentary exposé, *This Film Is Not Yet Rated* (an interview with Dick is featured in [the Dec. 22, 2006] issue of *Cineaste*) proves that little has changed in the intervening years. Dick's reportage wittily confirms that films highlighting heterosexual sex and full-frontal female nudity are far less likely to receive the dreaded NC-17 rating (studios are loath to release NC-17 films and many theater chains refuse to screen them) than those which foreground gay couplings or male nudity. Furthermore, in sharp contrast to practices in, say, Scandinavian countries, films with hefty amounts of graphic violence are treated with kid gloves and are, in many instances, not even off limit to youngsters.

When all is said and done, the most infuriating aspects of the MPAA ratings remain their obliviousness to the artistic intentions of directors, producers, and screenwriters. While novelists would howl in protest if their books were pruned of offensive material in order to please prudish booksellers, studios think nothing of capitulating to theater owners' demand for more circumspect "product." It is only sufficient to cite a litany of examples that drive home the absurdity of capricious decisions that have undermined various directors' artistic visions. In 1990, a ludicrous "X" rating for Pedro Almodóvar's dark, but distinctly untitillating, S&M tragicomedy, *Tie Me Up! Tie Me Down!* prompted the board to institute the "NC-17" category, a bogus reform if there ever was one. "NC-17" soon became as much of a kiss of death as "X" and, by 1999, Warner Bros. felt compelled to clumsily trim Stanley Kubrick's *Eyes Wide Shut* shortly after the director's sudden death. Even the famous Kubrick imprimatur couldn't prevent studio executives from maximizing profits and cynically eviscerating the work of an acknowledged master—even though the film's artistic importance is obviously subject to debate.

Dick's film zeroes in on a number of equally scandalous MPAA blunders. Kimberly Pierce convincingly argues that the ratings board's squeamishness regarding "female pleasure" required her to tone down a tender lesbian love scene in her Oscar winning *Boy's Don't Cry*; she clearly views the resulting avoidance of the NC-17 rating, the commercial "mark of Cain," a decidedly Pyrrhic victory. Following an all-too-common pattern, a pivotal three-way, bisexual tryst saddled Atom Egoyan's *Where the Truth Lies* with an NC-17. Considering the farcical cuts that John Waters admits he was forced to impose on his characteristically kinky *A Dirty Shame,* is it any wonder that John Cameron Mitchell and his distributor decided to release *Shortbus,* his hymn to polymorphous perversity, without an MPAA rating?

In the light of this sorry track record, is there any hope that the ratings system can be at least seriously improved, if not trashed altogether? Even parents—perhaps especially parents—admit that ratings do little to help them supervise their children's filmgoing choices. When the autocratic Jack Valenti retired as President of the organization in 2004, there was some hope that the hopelessly outmoded ratings would at least be subject to further scrutiny. Dan Glickman's new regime, however, has done little to rectify the ongoing ratings follies.

Given this stalemate, perhaps one might heed Dick's advice that "the most important function a ratings board can perform is to give concise, comprehensive descriptions of a film's content." And most importantly, even if this fatally flawed system cannot be abolished, we can insist that the often perplexing decisions of the secretive members of the ratings board, most of whom are patently unqualified to make sophisticated artistic assessments, can be made more transparent. If the MPAA remains intransigent and refuses to clean up its own house, their imperious judgments will continue to be a national embarrassment.

## Working with the Text

1. The opening sentence of the editorial states, "Ever since the movies began, this hybrid art form has been considered slightly disreputable," without explicitly stating why this is so. The sentence suggests that the writers assume that most readers of *Cineaste* (that is, movie lovers and scholars) will be familiar with this idea. How familiar is this idea to you? Why do you think movies might have always been a source of anxiety and concern? What might be disreputable about them? How does the rest of the argument made in the editorial suggest what this sentence means?

2. According to the point of view of the writers of this editorial, "the MPAA ratings have been, from their inception, plagued by inconsistencies and contradictions." By looking at the examples they give in the editorial, summarize what you think they believe are the main inconsistencies and contradictions. If you were to paraphrase the argument of this editorial in a single sentence, what would it be?

3. Although the editors say that the ratings board is especially critical of movies that simulate sexual activity, "films with hefty amounts of graphic violence are treated with kid gloves and are, in many instances, not even off limits to youngsters." Would you agree that the ratings system seems more concerned with limiting exposure to simulated sex than to simulated violence? Why or why not? If you agree that sex is judged more harshly than violence, speculate about why you think this might be. What cultural values are at play here? What is your own view about the effects on viewers of seeing different kinds of human activity represented in the movies?

4. Read the following descriptions of the MPAA ratings system guidelines. What do you find most or least surprising about the descriptions of the ratings? Then compare and contrast the U.S. system with the ratings system used by the British Board of Film Classification. Where are the main points of similarity? What distinctions does the British system make that the American system doesn't, and vice versa? Which system seems superior to you and why?

## American Movie Ratings

### G: General Audiences

A G-rated movie can be viewed by all ages. It contains no nudity, sex, or violence, or language that goes beyond often-heard expressions. Any depictions of violence are minimal.

### PG: Parental Guidance Suggested

A rating of PG indicates that parents are advised to watch the movie before they let their children view it. There may be "mature" themes, profanity, and limited depictions of violence or brief nudity, but none of drug use.

### PG-13: Parents Strongly Cautioned

A rating of PG-13 indicates that parents need to decide whether their children under age 13 can see the movie. Some material might not be suited for this age group. PG-13 indicates that the movie may go beyond a PG-rated movie in theme and in inclusion of violence, nudity, adult language, and adult activities, including drug use. Since PG-13 movies can include violence and some expletives, parents are strongly advised to view the film before they decide whether their children should see it.

### R: Restricted

An R-rated movie definitely contains "adult" material, such as strong language, intense or persistent violence, sexually oriented nudity, drug abuse, or other adult themes. Children under 17 are not allowed to attend R-rated movies unless accompanied by a parent or adult guardian. Parents are strongly cautioned to determine whether an R-rated film is appropriate for their children.

### NC-17

A rating of NC-17 is intended to denote a motion picture that most parents would not want their children to attend, and no one under 17 will be admitted. The rating is based on the inclusion of "excessive" violence, sex, deviant behavior, drug abuse, or other "adult" themes or behaviors.

## British Movie Ratings

**Universal** – Suitable for all

**Parental Guidance** – General viewing, but some scenes may be unsuitable for young children.

Suitable for 12 years and over. No-one younger than 12 may see a '12A' film in a cinema unless accompanied by an adult.

No-one younger than 12 may rent or buy a '12' rated video or DVD. Responsibility for allowing under-12s to view lies with the accompanying or supervising adult.

Suitable only for 15 years and over. No-one younger than 15 may see a '15' film in a cinema. No-one younger than 15 may rent or buy a '15' rated video or DVD.

Suitable only for adults. No-one younger than 18 may see an '18' film in a cinema. No-one younger than 18 may rent or buy an '18' rated video or DVD.

To be shown only in specially licensed cinemas, or supplied only in licensed sex shops, and to adults of not less than 18 years.

# "Bollywood Cinema: Making Elephants Fly"

## Meenakshi Shedde

*To many moviegoers in the United States, the lavish musical* Moulin Rouge!, *directed by the Australian moviemaker Baz Luhrmann and starring Nicole Kidman and Ewan McGregor, was like nothing they had ever seen before in a Hollywood musical. While the story of a doomed love affair between a poet and a showgirl was firmly in the tradition of both* Romeo and Juliet *and Italian opera, the way that music and dance were incorporated into the story broke with the expectations established by the Broadway and Hollywood musicals of the past. Combining lush operatic music with contemporary pop songs, mixing* The Sound of Music *with the grunge rock of Nirvana,* Moulin Rouge! *created a dreamlike collage of fantasy and reality, slapstick and tragedy. Viewers weren't sure whether the movie was meant to be serious or ridiculous, deeply moving or deeply laughable.* Moulin Rouge! *produced extreme reactions, both positive and negative, but went on to be a box-office hit and earn an Academy Award nomination.*

*For many Americans of Indian descent and fans of Indian cinema,* Moulin Rouge! *seemed anything but unfamiliar and strange. In the movie's everything-and-the-kitchen-sink style, bold use of imagination, and willingness to mix aspects from almost every kind of moviemaking, these viewers recognized the influence of Bollywood, the catch-all name created from the combination of Bombay and Hollywood given to the segment of India's massive movie industry located in Mumbai, the present-day name of Bombay. Dwarfing the American film industry both in terms of the number of movies made and the devotion of movie fans, Indian cinema has long been popular outside India with film enthusiasts and the nonresident Indian (NRI) population. Over the last twenty years, however, the lavish combination of epic storytelling; vast and astonishing music and dance sequences; and the mix of the comic and tragic, melodramatic and serious, that for many defines the classic Bollywood movie has been gaining popularity and influence outside India.*

*From Hollywood movies inspired by Bollywood such as* Moulin Rouge! *to the work of NRI filmmakers like Gurinder Chadha's* Bend It Like Beckham *and* Bride and Prejudice *(a Bollywood-style retelling of Jane Austen), to full-fledged Bollywood productions such as Ashutosh Gowariker's almost four-hour-long* Lagaan *(the genre description on its Internet Movie Database page says it all: "Drama/Musical/Romance/Sport [more]"), Indian cinema is opening the eyes of many Americans to the diversity of world moviemaking and how different cultural traditions bring very different assumptions about how to tell stories on the big screen to the movie-going experience.*

*In "Bollywood Cinema: Making Elephants Fly," Meenakshi Shedde, a reporter for the* Times of India *and a filmmaker herself, gives a concise overview of what Bollywood is and some of the challenges facing the Indian film industry and Indian filmmakers in the new century.*

# Before You Read

1. What do moviegoers anticipate when they go to see a movie described as a musical? What assumptions do they bring with them? For example, what subjects do they see as more or less appropriate for a musical? What kinds of stories do they think work best as musicals, and what kinds of stories do they think should not be told as musicals? Why do they hold these feelings and opinions? Begin by exploring your own history of watching musicals and expand your investigation by discussing the question with friends and family members.

2. How familiar are you with Bollywood films? Do they represent a new subject to you or a type of moviemaking you are already familiar with, either from your cultural heritage, personal interest, or both? If you have seen any Bollywood movies, write a brief introduction to watching this form of Indian cinema that you might give to a friend who is new to the experience. If you are that newcomer, locate people in your class or on your campus who are fans of Bollywood and ask them what to expect when beginning to study Indian cinema.

Watching a Bollywood film in an "ice-cream palace of a theater" in Rajasthan, Western India, Baz Luhrmann, director of *Moulin Rouge!,* said it represented a seminal moment in his understanding of cinema. The audience was singing aloud the songs in the film, chatting, answering mobile phones—the viewers' interaction with the film onscreen was utterly amazing. Respectful silence is not at all integral to the way Indians express their appreciation of cinema. He said he tried to generate Bollywood's interactive quality when making *Moulin Rouge!,* which went on to win an Oscar nomination for "Best Picture."

When I took a friend from Paris to a Bollywood film in Bombay, she was frustrated by distractions from the audience. The French watch films in a theater as if they were in a cathedral—with awe and reverence. In India, attending a movie is more like going on a picnic—the audience chats, sings, wanders out for a smoke. The film is the centerpiece of the evening's entertainment, but by no means the only distraction. The best way to tackle most of Bollywood today is to let your brains go AWOL, put your feet up, and enjoy.

Bollywood's (Bombay + Hollywood, mainstream cinema in Hindi, the national language) *masala* films (a mixture of spices) cheerfully toss in several genres—romance, melodrama, comedy, spectacle, action, adventure, with at least six high-protein songs and dances, all topped off with a happy ending.

They are characterized by a *joie de vivre,* a celebratory attitude towards life, despite all the knocks of destiny. In a country that is still largely poor (and considerably rich, but then India is full of contradictions), and people lead tough, grueling lives, these films are an escapist fantasy. The *masala* attitude in films—let's have it all at once—is deep-rooted in the Indian psyche, and is also reflected in Indian cuisine. Not only do we use *masalas* in our curries, but even the basic *thali* (platter, meal) serves starters, Indian bread, rice, lentils, curry, vegetables, papads, pickles, and dessert, all at one go, in bowls on a single plate.

Though cinema technology came from the West, the esthetic principles of Indian cinema derive from its own theater. These were based on Bharata's classic treatise on theater, the *Natyashastra* (second century B.C.), which called for dramatic action, song, dance, conflict, and a happy ending—all based on the *rasa* (essence/emotion) theory, aiming at "the joyful consciousness that the spectator feels when his conflicts are resolved and he feels in harmony with himself and nature."

The Lumière brothers' film *Arrival of a Train at a Station* was shown in Mumbai (Bombay) in 1896, just six months after it was projected on a screen in France. A year later, Harishchandra Bhatvadekar had made his own film, kickstarting an entire industry, but making the cinema an expression of our own voice.

Many Indian directors find the term *Bollywood* derogatory. This is because, in contrast to the Hollywood musical, a specific genre that essentially evolved as an antidote to the Great Depression of 1929, the Indian musical—and dancical—is generic, predates the Hollywood musical, and grew independently from its own cultural roots. Indian cinema has its origins in Urdu-Parsi theater, as early theater owners such as J. F. Madan of Madan Theatres, Kolkata (Calcutta) became cinema owners. Early cinema was partly filmed theater, and it reflected the theater of those days—with classic epics, mythologicals, and Parsi historicals (the Parsis are immigrants from Persia), with lively folk music and dance traditions. The Bhangwadi theater tradition, in fact, emphasized an interactive relationship with the audience, incorporating encores during the performance, as well as ditties about topical events or in praise of the patron.

It is said that when the Lumière brothers' film *Arrival of a Train at a Station* was shown in Bombay, the audience did not leap out of its seats, thinking the train would run over them, as audiences elsewhere did. They were quite used to extraordinary, otherworldly events in folklore like the *Jataka Tales,* in which lions conducted afternoon conversations with rabbits, and mythological epics like the *Ramayana,* in which flying monkeys bring medical aid to the hero or burn an enemy city to the ground with a flaming tail. For this reason, Indian audiences can feel a genuine kinship with Thai director Apichatpong Weerasethakul's *Tropical Malady,* which features monkeys chattering with human beings and whose climax suggests the metamorphosis of a man into a tiger.

But let's get a few facts straight, just to put Bollywood in proper perspective. First, Indian cinema makes the most films in the world, averaging 1,000 features a year. In 2005, it made 1,041 films (the United States makes about half that number, France barely a quarter). Second, while Hollywood has decimated national cinemas worldwide, dominating 80 to 90 percent of their national markets, India is perhaps the only spot on the planet where Hollywood is barely 3½ percent of the national market—this despite dubbing in Hindi, Tamil, and Telugu, in addition to the English version, and the combined might of the biggest studios and stars with the clout of the Spielbergs and Tom Cruises. The truth is, Indians simply adore their own cinema. In addition, Indian cinema is produced in thirty-nine languages and dialects. That's probably more than all the film languages of the entire European Union—it's a whole continent of cinema. Noted screenwriter-lyricist Javed Akhtar once observed that Hindi cinema is the twenty-second state of the Indian union, with its own particular language, customs, and codes understood by viewers all over the country.

For all that, Bollywood accounts for barely one-fourth of Indian cinema; there are healthy mainstream cinemas in the four southern languages—Tamil, Telugu (each of which make 200–250 films annually, the same as Bollywood), Malayalam, and Kannada. While Bollywood films are distributed all over the country, the southern languages rarely cross beyond one or two states.

Hollywood, long accustomed to counting its success in dollars, may find it hard to appreciate other yardsticks of success and the peculiar nature of movie addiction in India. Nobody bats an eyelid that *Sholay (Flames)* ran for seven years and *Dilwale Dulhaniya Le Jayenge (Braveheart Takes the Bride)* ran for ten years in the theaters. It is perfectly normal for fans to see these films twenty-three times, especially for the pleasure of singing all the songs and reciting the dialog in real time. Which Hollywood film commands such devotion from its audience? Bollywood superstar Amitabh Bachchan's fans have actually built a temple to him in Kolkata. Once, when he was hospitalized, the nation came to a halt. People offered all kinds of penance for his speedy recovery, including a man who walked backwards in the hot sun with bare feet for hundreds of kilometers, unable to think of a more original sacrifice for his hero. It's another matter whether stars in either Bollywood or Hollywood desire, or deserve, such devotion.

India is a movie-mad and music-mad nation. Hollywood dominated 90 percent of the Indian market during the silent era till the twenties (India was a British colony before gaining independence in 1947). But sound came in 1931 and, as soon as we could make movies in our own languages by the mid-thirties, the ratios were reversed and Hollywood slumped to barely 10 percent of the market. So it was the advent of sound that ended Hollywood domination of India. It has been struggling for a toehold ever since. It is a trend unlikely to change drastically in the foreseeable future, simply because Bollywood is not only incorporating Hollywood elements and cheerfully doing Hollywood remakes after its own fashion, it is rapidly adapting to globalization as well. Of course, a great deal of Bollywood, like Hollywood, is mainstream pap, but Indians would rather consume their own pap than Hollywood's. [...]

The fierce competition between A-list film festivals to discover new and original world cinemas has undoubtedly contributed to the burgeoning interest in Bollywood. Berlin was among the earliest to jump on the Bollywood bandwagon, followed by Cannes, Venice, Rotterdam, Locarno, and many others. Suddenly, world audiences were exposed to this bewildering cinema—loud, melodramatic, kitschy, with stars bursting into songs without logic or reason, and wondered if they had missed something.

Western attention is still largely patronizing and amused, and there is shock and awe that these films are celebrated at festivals and the subject of so many Ph.D. dissertations and seminars in the high groves of academe. Other spinoffs include the West End and Broadway hit, *Bombay Dreams,* Bollywood music and *bhangra* rap, as well as the current fad of Bollywood dance classes. There is also the sudden realization that Bollywood composer A. R. Rahman coolly outsells Madonna. For many Indian intellectuals, who would rarely stoop to see a Bollywood movie, there is a reverse snobbery in paying fancy prices for Bollywood posters celebrating low kitsch as high art.

All this attention has thrown Bollywood in a turmoil. "Does the West love our songs or does it laugh at them?" directors ask despairingly. But there's no clear answer. Once, when I was on a FIPRESCI Jury in Berlin in 2000 and Derek Malcolm, former film critic of *The Guardian* was our president, a print of Mani Ratnam's film *Dil Se (From the Heart)* arrived. Ratnam had sent an "international version" without the songs. "What?" Malcolm exploded in mock horror. "Tell him we want *only* the songs!" A "local print," songs intact, was rushed in and saved the day—with the brilliant opening song "Chhaiyan Chhaiyan," distinguished by a comely wench accompanied by an ensemble of dancers cavorting on the roof of a running train. Intoxicatingly shot by Santosh Sivan, it marks a high point in Indian song picturization. The film was selected for the Berlin Film Festival.

The art of song picturization, although common to many film cultures, is a unique specialization in Indian cinema, a generic film staple that has buttressed our films over a century. It stands in contrast to the stylized cheer of Hollywood, as well as many cultures with musical genres from China and Hong Kong to Egypt to Mexico to the nationalistic films of the fifties and sixties in the former East Germany. Usually, in these films, the protagonist is a singer or dancer, allowing songs to flow logically. The Danish Lars von Trier's *Dancer in the Dark* with Bjork was an exception, an antimusical with a tragic ending.

But in India, the song, in the hands of a skilled director, is a means of advancing the story, of articulating unspoken feelings. Traditionally, the art of song picturization fused the talents of great poets, choreographers, musicians, cinematographers, editors, and directors. Great directors who were also skilled song craftsmen include Raj Kapoor (*Awara*), Guru Dutt (*Pyaasa*), Bimal Roy (*Devdas*), Mehboob Khan (*Mother India*), and in recent decades, Sanjay Leela Bhansali (*Devdas, Hum Dil De Chuke Sanam*), Mani Ratnam (*Roja, Dil Se*) and Farah Khan (choreographer-turned-director; *Main Hoon Na*).

Today, films are sold on the basis of the director, stars, and music director; the story and screenplay are secondary. "Item numbers"—songs and dances with no connection to the story—are crammed in so that films themselves are perfunctory. The idea is that music videos are used as promos and music sales recover some money, even if the film flops. Moreover, music companies funding films have insisted on up to twelve songs in a single film. This is hardly new: pre-Independence films such as *Shirin Farhad* had forty-two songs, and *Indrasabha* boasted fifty-nine songs! Since song and dance is considered sacred in Indian cinema, some directors put in horrendously crude sex and vulgarity into song picturization, which the shortsighted censor board would cut if it was merely filmed as part of the spoken narrative. [ . . . ]

The nineties were decidedly a turning point for Bollywood. There were two key events in 1991 that altered our culture and markets forever. India liberalized her economy, and opened her markets to globalization. The same year, former deputy prime minister L. K. Advani spearheaded a 10,000-km *Rath Yatra* (chariot journey, with mythological echoes of the sacred epic *Ramayana*) through several states to consolidate Hindu votes, provocatively communalize the nation, and sway public opinion in order to build a Hindu Ram temple on the site of the disputed *Babri Masjid* (Mosque) in north India. Advani received a rousing reception and his campaign eventually catapulted his right-wing party, the Bharatiya Janata Party (BJP, Indian People's Party) to the forefront of Indian politics.

These two very different and coincidental forces left an enduring imprint on India's culture, especially in cinema. As international tensions increased—globalization and the perceived threat of foreign domination—people instinctively drew closer to their ethnic roots and identities. In India, stirred as well by Hindu fervor and jingoistic nationalism, it led to the revival of conservative Hindu family values onscreen. So while our films became considerably glossier and the stars flaunted hip global brands, leather jackets, and miniskirts, they were invariably Indian in their hearts and likely to break into a Hindu hymn at the drop of a mascaraed eyelash.

Two of the biggest box-office grossers of the nineties were Sooraj Barjatya's *Hum Aapke Hain Koun? (Who Am I to You?)* and Aditya Chopra's *Diwale Dulhaniya Le Jayenge (Braveheart Takes the Bride)*. In *Hum Aapke Hain Koun?*, 'love marriage' is discarded in favor of an arranged marriage; a young woman in love agrees instead to marry her dead sister's husband "so their baby can have a mother." Her sacrifice is rewarded, as true love is discovered and the lovers are reunited, thanks to the antics of a thoughtful Pomeranian named Tuffy. The film, which set off Bollywood's spate of "wedding-video films," in the nineties, was a rank celebration of consumerism and religiosity, most of the story unfolding under the watchful eye of the family deities.

In *Diwale Dulhamya Le Jayenge* (another of those wedding-video films), the moment the father of the London-based NRI (nonresident Indian) girl discovers she's committed the ultimate, unspeakable sin of falling in love with an NRI boy in London, he uproots the entire family and moves to Punjab to safeguard

Mira Nair's *Monsoon Wedding* made clever use of Indian wedding-video conventions.

"Indian values." He quickly fixes an arranged marriage that formalizes a child marriage—he had promised her hand in marriage to a boy twenty years ago. And what does London lover boy do when her Mummy suggests that they elope? He insists he will marry her only after Daddy and Mummy give him their blessings for the marriage!

In an earlier age, people fought an unjust political system, social inequities, and corrupt bureaucrats; as far as their own interests were concerned, they at least risked life and limb for love. And here, at the turn of the millennium, was a well-to-do, educated boy in London, rooting for that peculiarly Indian institution, the arranged-cum-love marriage! While glossy and hip on the surface, they marked an enthusiastic return to feudal patriarchy. That the film ran in theaters for ten years says something about the film—and a lot about Indian society. [...]

The new millennium has ushered in cinematic unpredictability, as all of the old formulas are challenged. New York–based Mira Nair's *Moonsoon Wedding* (2001) cleverly tweaked the Bollywood wedding-video convention, investing a Western sensibility into a story about rich, globalized, urban Indians. She won the Golden Lion in Venice and Golden Globe and BAFTA nominations, and touched a universal chord that no director living and working in India has managed so far. *Lagaan,* made the same year, earned an Oscar nomination as "Best Foreign Language Film." The following year Sanjay Leela Bhansali's heavingly opulent tragedy *Devdas* made it to Cannes—significant for being a Bollywood film in the official selection.

The multiplex boom caters to sophisticated urban audiences that also watch Pedro Almodóvar and Wong Kar-wai on DVD and cable TV. As the stranglehold of the romantic triangle loosens, young directors are exploring new stories, narratives, and urban legends, many without stars, some without song and dance. Last year, twenty films were made in English, and two in Hinglish (Hindi–English). While many are faltering debuts, there are also jewels like Aparna Sen's English film *Mr. and Mrs. Iyer,* a delicate love story set in a time of communal violence. Sudhir Mishra's *Hazaaron Khwaishein Aisi* (*A Thousand Dreams Such as These,* 2003, shown at the Berlin Film Festival) was sophisticated and daring for tackling political issues, if somewhat schematic. So perhaps there is room for optimism about the future.

While in an earlier era, art-house and commercial cinema were not on speaking terms, there is an increasingly middle-of-the-road cinema where mainstream films also try to tackle sensitive issues and art-house cinema tries to incorporate song and dance in an attempt to reach out to mass audiences. Two lavish period Indo-British collaborations—*The Rising* and *Kisna,* specifically aimed at global audiences—didn't quite make the grade, despite being shot in Hindi and English versions.

Certainly, there are good Bollywood films. These include Ashutosh Gowariker's *Lagaan,* Vishal Bhardwaj's *Maqbool,* Madhur Bhandarkar's *Chandni Bar,* Ram

Gopal Varma's *Satya* and *Company,* Sanjay Leela Bhansali's *Khamoshi,* Vidhu Vinod Chopra's *Parinda,* Priyadarshan's *Virasat,* Mani Ratnam's *Roja* and *Bombay,* Ramesh Sippy's *Sholay* and Pradeep Sarkar's *Parineeta.* There are also "offbeat mainstream films" like Aparna Sen's *Mr. and Mrs. Iyer* and Madhur Bhandarkar's *Page 3,* sensitive films made within the mainstream format, but without big stars. There is also Sanjay Leela Bhansali's incredibly daring if melodramatic *Black,* made with the biggest stars, on a blind-mute protagonist inspired by Helen Keller. But these are so few and far between, given that Bollywood churns out 250 every year.

In the hardcore Bollywood tradition, where certain allowances must be made for their maniacal obsession with romantic triangles, somewhat dispensable logic, with people incessantly bursting into song and dance, the better films include *Hum Dil De Chuke Sanam, Dilwale Dulhaniya Le Jayenge, Kuch Kuch Hota Hai,* and *Kal Ho Naa Ho.*

Bollywood is adopting many strategies to adapt to globalization. While it is too early to say if the studio system will return, there is certainly greater corporatization, as senior directors become producers to fledgling directors to feed the multiplex boom. Amazingly, for the most prolific industry in the world, the majority of film finance remains private. There is minimal support from the government, which in fact imposes some of the highest entertainment taxes in the world (as high as 60 percent in some states). Since the film business was conferred "industry status" in the early nineties, about 15 percent of film funds now come from institutionalized sources like banks and equity issues. But the majority remains private, and (a part of it) has been closely associated with the mafia, as in many other nations such as Russia, Japan, and Hong Kong.

In all this globalization back-chat, it is important to remember that while everybody would like a film that does well in India and abroad, the truth is that India, like the U.S., has a large enough domestic market to support a healthy film industry. Not everyone is bending over backwards to go global, and this brings a certain contentment and attitude of laissez faire.

The enduring irony about Indian cinema is that even after a century of existence, it is better known worldwide by its NRI directors—Mira Nair (*Salaam Bombay, Monsoon Wedding*), Deepa Mehta (*Fire, Earth, Water*), Gurinder Chadha (*Bend it Like Beckham, Bride and Prejudice*), or Shekhar Kapur (*Elizabeth, The Four Feathers*) rather than Indian directors living and working in India. When will India make a *Crouching Tiger, Hidden Dragon* that sweeps the world? Taiwanese director Ang Lee took a gritty martial-arts film out of its ghetto in blue-collar Hong Kong, and transformed it with kinetic poetry into a film with universal appeal. He went decidedly "glocal," reaching global markets even with a film in Mandarin, with a multi-Asian cast and crew. When, we wonder, will India make its elephants fly?

# Working with the Text

1. At the beginning of her article, Shedde describes some differences between how people watch movies in India, where "attending a movie is more like going on a picnic," and in France, where the audiences "watch films in a theater as if they were in a cathedral—with awe and reverence." How would you describe expectations for watching a movie in the United States? What metaphor would you use: a picnic, a cathedral, or something else? For example, what are the customs regarding talking in the movie theater, either between patrons or about the movie itself? Focus initially on your own behavior: what do you see as the "rules," and how closely do you follow them, bend them, or disobey them?

2. Define what Shedde means by the "*masala* attitude in [Indian] films." What does she see as the main differences between Indian audiences and European and American audiences in terms of what they expect of a movie? What about the Indian attitudes toward movie storytelling seem most interesting to you and why? Given the popularity of Hollywood-style films inspired by Asian and South Asian moviemaking, from *Moulin Rouge!* to *Kill Bill,* in what ways might American expectations for movies be changing or becoming more flexible?

3. Shedde explains the importance of music, song, and dance in many Bollywood movies, referring to the "art of song picturization" and the sheer number of different songs in a typical movie. How would you describe the meaning and purpose of musical numbers in a traditional Hollywood musical? Based on Shedde's description, compare and contrast how songs and musical numbers seem to operate in Indian cinema and in Hollywood musicals. What assumptions or even stereotypes about the seriousness or purpose of musical sequences in movies might account for the worry that some Indian directors have over whether non-Indian audiences "love our songs or . . . laugh at them?" Shedde speculates about when India will "make a *Crouching Tiger, Hidden Dragon* that sweeps the world," a Bombay movie made by an Indian director that will truly become a worldwide hit. Watch one of the twenty-first-century Indian movies that Shedde mentions and write about your ideas of what such a movie might look like. What recommendations would you make to an Indian filmmaker about creating "a film with universal appeal" that nevertheless stays true to the cultural traditions of Indian cinema?

# VIEWING CULTURE

## COMPUTER-GENERATED IMAGERY

Live action and animation. Real life and cartoons. Each one of us may prefer one form of visual entertainment over the other, but we can all agree that a movie like *The Lion King* or *Howl's Moving Castle* is very different from *Wedding Crashers* or *Casino Royale*. Or can we? What about movies like *The Lord of the Rings* trilogy or the *Spiderman* franchise?

In Chapter Seven, "Video Pop: Television in the Digital Age," the section on Viewing Culture examines how primetime animation on television—programs such as *South Park* and *The Simpsons*—challenges the idea that cartoons are mainly for children. However, before we can think about the different ways a cartoon or a live-action program might handle a sophisticated theme or subject matter, we have to assume that we can easily tell the difference between the two. If we think about it more closely, this distinction may be difficult, especially given the history of what used to be called special effects in movies and what is more often called today computer-generated imagery (CGI).

From the beginning, movies have been about the simultaneous and sometimes contradictory projects of both capturing reality and creating new realities. The first movie audiences were fascinated (and sometimes frightened) by a film of a busy train station, a horse at full gallop, or (more provocatively) two people kissing. They could see the familiar world outside the theater projected in light on a screen inside the theater. At the same time, early moviemakers also began experimenting with images that no one could possibly see in reality, such as a spaceship crashing into the eye of the man in the moon:

or a drawing of a dinosaur come to life, as in the legendary cartoon artist Winsor McCay's *Gertie the Dinosaur* from 1914:

These early experiments with special effects and animation remind us that in a very fundamental way, all movies are special effects, rays of light projected through a piece of film or, increasingly in the digital age, colored pixels excited by electrical impulses stored on a computer disk or drive. In other words, there is really nothing natural about any image we see in a movie, whether we think of what we see as a special effect or not.

# T H R E E

## First Experience with Special Effects

Most of us first encounter movies as children, often as we are still negotiating the tricky distinction between what is real and what is pretend, between what is possible and what is only imaginary. As a result, the powerful and persuasive imagery of those first movies we encounter can leave a lasting impression. Write about an experience you had with a movie that made you think the impossible was possible, or an imaginary effect that you have never forgotten. This experience could be one of wonder, terror, or curiosity—or maybe a combination of all three. As you became more experienced with and sophisticated about movies, how did your understanding of this early experience change, and why?

## THE DIGITAL AGE AND THE RISE OF CGI

With the advent of computer technology and digitally created images, a new way of creating visual reality in the movies began to develop in the 1980s. Called computer-generated imagery (CGI), this new form of moviemaking didn't rely on elaborate models, stop-motion photography, or hidden wires. In fact, it often didn't rely on cameras at all. Just as words on a page can conjure fantastic and even impossible images in the minds of a reader, the digital language of the computer—the strings of 1s and 0s that make up binary code—can be arranged to create an equally amazing and unlimited variety of images. Movies like *The Terminator* series introduced audiences to a blending of live-action and computer-created effects that seemed a quantum leap in terms of realism, scale, and power and raised their expectations about what to expect in a motion picture.

In the world of animation, the appearance of Pixar studio's *Toy Story* in 1995 changed the world of feature-length cartoons forever with its enhanced illusion of 3D depth. Soon computer-created cartoons dominated the marketplace, resulting in Disney studios shutting down their historic and legendary hand-drawn animation division. But as the character of Gollum from *The Lord of the Rings* movies demonstrates, CGI has done more than just create new special effects or ways of making cartoons. The digital revolution in moviemaking has further blurred the lines between the ideas of live-action and animation, between regular scenes and special effects.

Ever since *Gertie the Dinosaur,* movies have long combined real actors with cartoon characters, but *The Lord of the Rings* movies not only mixed human actors and animated figures, they combined the human and the animated into a new kind of hybrid actor. Actor Andy Serkis portrayed the actions and facial expressions, and spoke the dialogue of Gollum wearing a special light-suit in front of computerized cameras that translated his actions into a CGI character.

Andy Serkis wearing his computer-coordinated suit. Note the dots on his face, which were used by the computer program to transfer his facial expressions onto the computer-generated character.

Serkis/Gollum as he/it appeared in the movies.

This seamless combination of the human and the digital was so unprecedented and the resulting performance was so convincing that it caused a new kind of dilemma for the Academy Awards: should Serkis be nominated in the Best Supporting Actor category, or should Gollum be recognized as part of the technical awards for visual effects? Although Serkis was not nominated, many moviemakers and critics agreed that the traditional acting and special effects categories used by the Academy Awards may not fit the digital age.

## "*300* Changes the CGI Game"

### MaryAnn Johanson

The Lord of the Rings *demonstrated some of the exciting possibilities for integrating computer technology and human actors in motion pictures. When the action-adventure movie 300 opened in early 2007, it was a hit at the big box-office but received mixed, and at times confused, reactions from movie critics. Although unsure whether to regard 300 as more like a comic book or as a conventional big-screen epic, reviewers recognized the visual power of a movie that combined live action and CGI effects more completely than any other film before. But they also puzzled over how to regard the main characters, who were portrayed by human actors but seemed like cartoon characters.*

From the film *300*

*In her article for the website film.com, independent movie critic and blogger MaryAnn Johanson argues that 300 represents a new era in moviemaking, an era comparable to the moment when sound was first introduced almost eighty years before. In so doing, she suggests that this new use of CGI will change the way we look at and interpret movies.*

Have you seen *Singin' in the Rain*? It's a fictional story about the very real upheaval that occurred during Hollywood's last great paradigm shift, when films that had been silent suddenly found their voice, and performers who couldn't cope with the combination of emoting and speaking at the same time—or those whose voices were less than melodious—suddenly found themselves unemployable.

That first talkie was [in 1927,] *The Jazz Singer,* and it heralded the almost instantaneous death of silent movies. I think we will look back at *300* in much the same way: as the harbinger of a new era in filmmaking, one that perhaps will not be quite so profound as the end of the silent era, but one that will redefine how we look at film...and might leave some old-school actors behind in the process.

It's like this: CGI has been a tool in the filmmaker's toolbox for more than a decade now, but it's been used, for the most part, to create spaces and elements within those spaces that are meant to be "real." No matter how fantastical the element, whether it's the liquid-metal T-1000 Terminator or the sad, twisted figure of Gollum, it is meant to be taken as it appears: as genuine, authentic, something that really is what it looks like. Even when entire worlds are invented—as in the recent *Star Wars* prequel trilogy—and exist nowhere but in the filmmaker's imagination and then in a computer, they are meant to represent real buildings, real cities, real landscapes.

But *300* uses CGI in a new way, to create a world that is figurative (even more so than *Sin City* a few years ago). It brings a new kind of visual metaphor to film that only CGI could achieve, to generate an environment that is felt as much as, if not more than, seen and heard. The impossibly huge moon rising behind the bluff Leonidas climbs to visit the lecherous old priests and their captive oracle early in the film, for instance, is not a "real" moon—it's a representation of how concepts of changeability and mysterious power hovered over the ancients, especially through their mythology. It's a representation of danger, of the night, of the unknown. We're not meant to believe the moon ever actually appeared so large over Sparta—we're meant to feel the influence of what it represents to the Spartan people.

And under this filmmaking ethos—more impressionistic than we've ever seen in a film that is not entirely animated—what the cast brings is as much a puzzle piece of an element as the visuals. Which doesn't mean the actors only need to look right to fit into the overall tapestry—paradoxically, it requires a different kind of acting…one that some film actors working today may not be able to bring. Acting in front of a green screen leaves actors with few of the visual cues that working on location or on a fully constructed set provides. (Only one shot of *300* was filmed on location, that of the horses approaching Sparta in the beginning of the film; everything else was shot on a soundstage with minimal sets and props.) All that's left are the actors one is playing against, turning this into something more like stage acting…and yet it's still as intimate as film acting, too, with the camera right in one's face and demanding carefully modulated performances even as one knows that what will eventually appear around you on the big screen may be larger than life, or odder than life. And this new kind of acting may also demand, as *300* did of its cast, that actors mold their bodies to fit the visual aesthetic even more so than we're used to hearing about. This wasn't Renee Zellweger gaining thirty pounds to play Bridget Jones—this was a band of actors being turned into a regiment of soldiers, sculpting their bodies into visual metaphors as well. (Oh, and the near nudity of the men? That's a metaphor, too. Of course Spartan soldiers didn't fight in leather Speedos and nothing else; what we have here are those Spartan soldiers reduced to nothing more than their fighting prowess, in a figurative way.)

We're already seeing many film critics unable to get their heads about the impressionism of *300*. There will be many actors who won't be able to make that transition either. They'll be okay—nonimpressionistic movies aren't going away, and plenty of films will continue to be shot on location and with a grounded sense of the real. But as soon as other imaginative filmmakers come to grips with the sudden widening in the range of stories that can be told as *300*'s is told, we're going to see a whole new kind of film being made, ones that are more painterly than we've ever seen before.

---

## Working with the Text

1. How does Johanson describe the key difference between what she sees as the old ways of using CGI in movies dating back to the 1980s and the new use of CGI in a movie such as *300*? How well do you understand the point she is making? Try condensing and summarizing her first three paragraphs into a single paragraph using your own words.

2. Johanson says that *300* "brings a new kind of visual metaphor to film that only CGI could achieve, to generate an environment that is felt as much as, if not more than, seen and heard." In what ways do you understand the idea of "feeling" a movie? Explore her idea by trying to come up with your own examples of visual experiences in the movies

that you would describe as "felt as much as, if not more than, seen and heard."

3. In explaining the difference made by this new, high-tech mode of computer-assisted filmmaking, Johanson refers back to an older visual medium, describing the look of *300* as "impressionistic" and "painterly." If you are unfamiliar with the term, look up the word *impressionistic* as well as the specific artistic movement called impressionism. What particular aspects of artistic impressionism does Johanson draw on in trying to get her readers to look at their movie-going experience in a new way?

4. As mentioned in the introduction to Johansan's article, *300* has drawn a wide and diverse range of critical responses. Go to a website such as Rotten Tomatoes at www.rottentomatoes.com, which collects a large sample of reviews from print sources, websites, and blogs. Explore some of the divergent reactions to *300*. Use them as the basis for writing your own reaction to the controversy.

# CREATING CULTURE

## DO-IT-YOURSELF MOVIES

While movies have long been one of the most popular forms of popular culture, they have also had the distinction of being one of the most expensive art forms in the world. Even the most modest of films traditionally required access to expensive cameras and sound equipment, costly film stock, and a company of actors and crew members who needed to be paid, housed, and fed for weeks and usually months. Once filming was completed, the postproduction process—visual and sound editing, creating multiple copies of the movie—represented additional expenses that rivaled the initial production costs. Add the price of advertising and distributing a movie, and you have a situation where a movie that cost $1 million could be called low budget.

Although the do-it-yourself spirit has made its way into most other forms of creative expression, from writing to music, to art, the sheer cost of movie-making prevented access to all but the most dedicated and fortunate filmmakers. This relative lack of access is one reason that diversity has moved more slowly in the movie industry than in some other areas of popular culture.

*The Blair Witch Project* helped launch the DIY movie-making trend.

# "Here's the Price of Fame: $218.32"

## Jason Silverman

*As in other areas of popular culture, the digital age is even changing the economic playing field in the expensive world of movie production. In "Here's the Price of Fame: $218.32" from the January 20, 2004, version of the online magazine* Wired, *reporter Jason Silverman tells the story of a new documentary that was not only garnering critical acclaim but also making people rethink the question of who can make a movie.*

Before he taught himself about cameras and editing, Jonathan Caouette designed a do-it-yourself method for making movies. He'd record the audio of a Hollywood film and, with crayons, pencils, and looseleaf paper, draw it out.

When Caouette turned 11, he borrowed his first camera and tripod, intending to translate his strange, painful life into movies. His first short film featured Caouette, in makeup and a dress, playing a battered woman.

Now 31, Caouette continues to depend on the most basic filmmaking tools available. Using his boyfriend's iMac and the editing program iMovie, Caouette distilled his VHS home movies, his Super-8 experimental films, and a suitcase full of photos and audio tapes into *Tarnation,* a hybrid documentary that [premiered in 2004] at the Sundance Film Festival.

*Tarnation* may be the first feature-length film edited entirely on iMovie, and it cost $218.32 in videotape and materials. Despite its low budget, the film has already earned a high profile. Both John Cameron Mitchell, the actor and director of *Hedwig and the Angry Inch,* and independent film maverick Gus Van Sant have signed on as executive producers.

*Tarnation* tells the harrowing story of Caouette's dysfunctional family. His mother was a fashion model and a victim of severe abuse who spent most of her adult life bouncing from one mental institution to the next. Caouette's childhood, spent partly in foster homes, included daily doses of violence, drugs, and unpredictability.

Caouette said his survival was due in part to his use of video cameras as a weapon and means of defense. As a teen, he began making violent experimental genre parodies with gaudy titles like *The Spit and Blood Boys* and *The Ankle Slasher.* Now an actor and doorman living in New York City, Caouette has continued to document his personal life, including his complicated relationship with his mother, who suffered brain damage after a lithium overdose.

Caouette's autobiographical footage—160 hours of tape and film—serve as the raw material of *Tarnation.* The film also includes more than 200 photos

culled from Caouette's huge archive. Unable to afford to scan the photos, Caouette tacked the images to a white wall and filmed them.

It's not the typical method of digitizing photos, but editing a feature on iMovie is unusual, too. Caouette was just doing what he could with the tools he had on hand.

"People told me, 'Why don't you throw iMovie away and graduate to Final Cut Pro?' But iMovie is so easy," Caouette said. "I didn't know any editors, didn't know anyone in the film industry. Everything that has happened with this film has been an explosion and happened so quickly."

The self-taught Caouette obviously has a native talent as a filmmaker. *Tarnation* is both haunting and frenetic, with a strong sense of rhythm. Sundance programmer Shari Frilot called Caouette "a natural autobiographer," and cited *Tarnation* as a powerful example of the new possibilities of homemade movies.

"*Tarnation* is a very strong statement for low-budget filmmaking," she said. "It's a testament to what someone can accomplish with simple desktop tools, and it's exciting and encouraging to see how much can be done with so little."

Van Sant described *Tarnation* as "amazingly original," and the kind of film he'd been waiting to see since the 1970s.

"People assumed that one day film would be as accessible and inexpensive as writing, and now it practically is," Van Sant said. "For the price of a typewriter, you can make films with sound and burn them on a DVD.... Filmmakers can afford to work now. No more excuses, or filmmakers' block, or procrastination. Either they start shooting, or they are waiting for the vanity crew, or they aren't filmmakers."

## Working with the Text

1. With the rise of digital moviemaking, dozens of websites have appeared where moviemakers can show off their work. From Atomfilm.com, where the website moderators exercise some editorial control over what movies are shown, to more freewheeling sites like YouTube, thousands and thousands of video movies from around the world are now available to anyone with an Internet connection. These movies range

from extended features to short clips lasting sometimes less than a minute, and the subject matter is equally varied. How does this new diversity in "moviemaking" change how we think about what a movie is? Start by trying to define the term *movie,* then work in groups to come up with examples that lead you to revise and expand your definition. What common elements can you find among these many different examples of "movies"?

2. The movie director Gus Van Sant, who became a producer of *Tarnation,* describes the impact of computer technology on moviemaking in this way: "People assumed that one day film would be as accessible and inexpensive as writing, and now it practically is." Explore the ways that Van Sant's comparison makes us think differently about the movies. For example, list the different uses you make of writing every day, from jotting notes to instant messaging, to writing papers for your composition course. What would the equivalent of informal movie-making be? What different kinds of moviemaking styles would compare with different writing styles?

3. The movie that Jonathan Caouette made, *Tarnation,* is an autobiography, a genre that also lends itself easily to writing. In fact, we could think of his movie as a kind of visual essay. Jason Silverman's article describes the composition process that Caouette followed in making his movie. As a way of exploring moviemaking as a form of writing, try your hand at developing your own visual autobiography. Whether you work on your autobiography solely as a writing project or as an attempt to make your own movie, use the following steps as guidelines:

   a. Assemble the visual materials for your autobiography: snapshots, school photos, home videos, childhood drawings, etc. You can decide whether you want your autobiography to cover your entire life or focus on a specific period. In either case, write an extended caption for each visual component, including both a description of what the picture or video shows and your thoughts about its significance in your life story.

   b. Once you have captioned your pictures, write a preliminary version of your autobiography based on the memories and feelings associated with your visual materials. At this point, you can create an illustrated version of your story by scanning your visuals and incorporating them into the document you are creating in your word-processing program.

   c. Now begin to think of your narrative as a movie by creating a storyboard for your autobiography. A storyboard looks like a series of comic-strip panels and is used by moviemakers to outline the different shots and images that will make up their movie. Here is an example of a storyboard:

Courtesy of Corinna Downing, London Film Festival Education. Camera shots from *Elina* (*Elina — Som on jag inte fanns* / Finland 2002).

In each frame of your storyboard, you can use sketches or simply copies of your visuals to layout each shot in your movie. Remember, in Caouette's case, he couldn't afford to scan images into digital format, so he just used digital photos of them pinned to a wall, creating an artistically interesting effect. Use similar ingenuity in thinking about how to acquire images that could be put onto your storyboard. Below each image, write the narration that accompanies each visual, and then use the language of moviemaking—*long shot, medium shot,* and *close-up*—to describe each shot in detail.

d. If you wish to continue with the project, use a digital video camera and any available digital editing software, such as iMovie, to create your own DVD. If you have never used editing software before, take advantage of this opportunity to develop some basic moviemaking and editing skills. Digital information can be easily erased and re-recorded, so trial and error is not an expensive process, as it is when using traditional film stock.

4. When you have completed your project, write an essay about how the process of developing your own autobiography has changed the way you look at movies in general. What did you learn about telling stories visually? What were the most challenging aspects of the project? How did telling your life story visually make you think about your autobiography differently?

# GLOSSARY

**ADVERTISING** Text and/or images intended to persuade a consumer to buy a product

**ANIME** In Japan, any kind of animation. In the U.S., animation from Japan

**AVATAR** A digital identity or persona created to represent oneself in computer games or online

**AUDIENCE** The intended recipients of a particular message, whatever the medium

**BIAS** The individual perspectives and values you bring to the consideration of any given situation

**BLOG** A journal or log maintained on a website (short for Web log), available for anyone to read

**BOLLYWOOD** A combination of the words "Bombay" and "Hollywood," used to refer to a particular type of Indian movie, generally featuring complex plots, lavish production values, and often involving extensive music and dance

**BUZZ MARKETING** Marketing or advertising a product through one-on-one encounters, or "word of mouth"

**CITATION** Acknowledging words or ideas that are taken from another writer

**CLUSTERING** An invention strategy; creating a visual representation of related words to assist you in developing ideas for a piece of writing

**COMPUTER-GENERATED IMAGERY (CGI)** Digitally created images, often used for special effects in movies and other visual media

**COUNTERCULTURE** A segment of a society with values that are in opposition to the mainstream beliefs and values of the majority

**CRITICAL READING** An analysis of a text, including questions about its authorship, tone, point of view, and intended audience

**CRITICAL THINKING** An organized process of evaluation and analysis that clarifies understanding

**CRITICAL VIEWING** An analysis of a visual medium, such as a photograph, illustration, video, movie, or image from the Internet

**CULTURE** Knowledge, values, attitudes, and behavior of a particular social group or organization

**CYBERCULTURE** Rules and values shared by users of computers on the Internet and the World Wide Web

**DISCOURSE COMMUNITY** An area or arena for communication that is governed by specific rules, whether formal or informal

**DIY** "Do It Yourself," an expression adopted by some contemporary cultural communities, such as punk rockers and rappers, to signify the importance of self-expression not tied to commercial media or outlets

**DRAFTING** In writing, the process of creating an initial version of a text

**EMAIL** A particular form of written communication sent over the Internet

**FONT** A visual aspect of a written text; a character set of one style of type, such as Times New Roman

**FREEWRITING** An invention strategy involving writing without stopping, meant to capture a flow of ideas or associations

**GENDER ROLE** A set of socially reinforced behaviors identified as "male" or "female" within a culture

**HIP HOP** A form of popular music that has also become a subculture, with its own styles of language, clothing, attitude, and more

**ICON** An image or representation, often symbolic of a wider idea or belief; in computing, a small functional image, such as a file folder or clipboard

**IMAGE** Any visual representation of an object or person; includes photographs, drawings, and computerized renderings

**INSTANT MESSAGING/IMing** A form of real-time online written communication

**INVENTION** In writing, the process of developing ideas for a text

**LISTING** An invention strategy that calls for making a list of everything you know or recollect about a particular topic, to aid in developing a piece of writing

**LOGO** Short for "logotype," a visual symbol that represents a company or product

**MANGA** Japanese comics, graphic novels, and print cartoons

**MARKETING** All of the processes, including advertising, used to distribute information about a product or service

**MASS MEDIA** Sources that disseminate information to a broad audience, such as newspapers, television, and the Internet

**MASH-UP** A compilation of two or more existing songs or recordings to create a new work, often one that makes a point through juxtaposition of different styles

**MEDIA** Physical processes used to communicate or transmit information, whether via print (books, newspapers), broadcasting (radio and television), or computer (the World Wide Web)

**MMORPG** Massively Multiplayer Online Role-Playing Games; large and complex forms of MUDs

**MUD** Multi-User Domain; an online environment that is accessed in real time by multiple users or players, often involving role playing

**NETWORKING** The creation or maintenance of online communities

**PARAPHRASE** Restating a text in your own words

**PARODY** An imitation or exaggeration of a work that is intended to be humorous

**PERSONA** From the Greek word for "mask," a character or voice in a literary text; also, the identity an author creates in writing

**PLAGIARISM** Intentionally using and representing another person's words or ideas as your own

**PLAYLIST** An individual's collection of preferred music; a listing of one's digital music "library"

**POPULAR CULTURE** Expressions of a society in mass media such as music, television, film, and print; can also include clothing styles, trends or fads, holidays and celebrations, sports, and more

**PURPOSE** In the context of written communications, the reason that the author has written a particular work; his or her intention or motivation for writing

**RAP** A music style involving rhyming words spoken against a strong percussive beat

**REALITY TV** Television shows that supposedly portray non-actors in unscripted settings and situations

**REVISION** In writing, the process of reviewing, rewriting, and making changes or corrections to a particular piece of text

**RHETORIC** The study of communication strategies, initially developed in ancient Greece

**STORYBOARD** A series of panels that provide a visual "script" for movies or television

**TEXT MESSAGING/TEXTING** Typing out a short message (generally less than 160 characters) that is transmitted over a cell phone or via the Internet

**THESIS** In writing, the central topic or main point of a particular text

**VIRAL VIDEO** A (usually amateur) video that reaches a wide audience through distribution on popular websites and via email

**VISUAL ANALYSIS** See critical viewing

**VISUAL CULTURE** The aspects of culture that are represented by seen (visual) media, such as photographs, films, animations, and images on the Internet

**VISUAL DESIGN** Principles of graphic representation used to incorporate text and images into a usable or artistic form

# CREDITS

## TEXT CREDITS

**ADBUSTERS,** courtesy www.adbusters.org.

**BAYM, GEOFFREY,** excerpt from Geoffrey Baym, "*The Daily Show:* Discursive Integration and the Reinvention of Political Journalism," *Political Communication* 22: 259–276, © 2005 Taylor & Francis, Inc. Reprinted by permission of Taylor & Francis, Ltd. Political Communication website, www.informaworld.com.

**BOWMAN, SHAYNE AND CHRIS WILLIS,** "Introduction to Participatory Journalism," from *We Media: How Audiences Are Shaping the Future of News and Information* by Shayne Bowman and Chris Willis. Copyright © 2003 Shayne Bowman, Chris Willis, and The Media Center at The American Press Institute.

**BROWN, MERRILL,** from Merrill Brown, "Abandoning the News," *Carnegie Reporter,* Vol. 3, No. 21, October 18, 2006. Reprinted by permission.

**BRYSON, BILL,** from MADE IN AMERICA by Bill Bryson. Copyright © 1995 by Bill Bryson. Reprinted by permission of HarperCollins Publishers.

**BURSTEIN, DAN,** reprinted courtesy of the author.

**CINEASTE,** "Do We Really Need Movie Ratings?" The Editors of *Cineaste* magazine, *Cineaste,* December 2006. Reprinted by permission of *Cineaste* Magazine.

**CRUGER, ROBERTA,** "The Mash-Up Revolution," Salon.com, August 8, 2003. This article first appeared at Salon.com. An online version remains in the *Salon* archives. Reprinted by permission.

**EVANGELISTA, BENNY,** "You Are What's on Your Playlist," *San Francisco Chronicle,* April 18, 2005; www.sfgate.com. Reproduced with permission of SAN FRANCISCO CHRONICLE in the format Textbook via Copyright Clearance Center.

**FINDER, ALAN,** copyright © 2006 by The New York Times Co. Reprinted by permission.

**FOX, ROY F.,** from Roy F. Fox, "Salespeak," from MEDIASPEAK (Westport, CT: Praeger, 2001). Reproduced with permission of Greenwood Publishing Group, Inc. Westport, CT.

**GERHARDT, DEBORAH R.,** reprinted by permission of the author.

**GLADSTONE, BROOKE,** "Straight Outta Baghdad," *Voices from the Frontline,* August 19, 2005; www.onthemedia.org. Reprinted by permission.

VOIDA, AMY, REBECCA E. GRINTER, NICOLAS DUCHENEAUT, W. KEITH EDWARDS, AND MARK W. NEWMAN, "Listening In: Practices Surrounding iTunes Music Sharing," *Proceedings of ACM Conference on Human Factors in Computing Systems* (CHI 2005); 2005 April 2–7, Portland, OR: USA: NY: ACM 2005; pp. 191–200. © 2005 Association for Computing Machinery, Inc. Reprinted by permission.

WATKINS, S. CRAIG, from *Hip Hop Matters* by S. Craig Watkins. Copyright © 2005 by S. Craig Watkins. Reprinted by permission of Beacon Press, Boston.

ZERNIKE, KATE, copyright © 2006 by The New York Times Co. Reprinted by permission.

## PHOTO CREDITS

**i, iii:** © Rodolfo Clix

**CHAPTER 1: 1:** © David Young-Wolff/PhotoEdit Inc.; **3:** © A. Ramey/PhotoEdit; **5:** AP Images/Coeur d'Alene Press, Jerome A. Pollos; **10:** © runsilent/Alamy; **11:** © Corbis. All Rights Reserved.; **12:** © Mary Evans Picture Library/Alamy; **16** (*left and right*): Courtesy of Taber Buhl/www.airtoons.com; **19:** Copyright © 20thCentFox/courtesy Everett/Everett Collection; **23:** From JOURNALS by Kurt Cobain, copyright © 2001 by The End of Music, LLC. Used by permission of Riverhead Books, an imprint of Penguin Group (USA) Inc.; **32** (*left*): Lambert/Getty Image; (*right*): © Jim Craigmyle/Corbis; **43** (*left*): © 20thCentFox/Courtesy Everett Collection; (*right*): © 20thCentFox/courtesy Everett/Everett Collection; **44** (*left*): TM & Copyright © 20th Century Fox Film Corp./courtesy Everett Collection; (*right*): © Warner Bros./Topham/The Image Works; **45** (*left*): Courtesy Everett Collection; (*right*): ©Warner Bros/Courtesy Everett Collection

**CHAPTER 2: 48:** AP Images/Gerald Herbert; **52:** © Sarah-Maria Vischer/The Image Works; **54:** © Simon Marcus/Corbis; **64:** © Mike Baldwin/Cornered/Cartoon Stock; **66:** © Najlah Feanny/Corbis; **75:** www.wikipedia.org; **81:** Mario Tama/Getty Images; **86:** CSU Archives/Everett Collection

**CHAPTER 3: 88:** © Keren Su/Corbis; **91:** Robert W. Kelley/Time & Life Pictures/Getty Images; **101:** Courtesy of Myke Armstrong/www.nerdyshirts.com; **102:** AP Images/Eckehard Schulz; **110:** SECOND LIFE is a trademark of Linden Research, Inc. and the Second Life world features copyright materials owned by Linden Lab Copyright © 2003–2007 Linden Research, Inc. All Rights Reserved.; **116:** © jeremy sutton-hibbert/Alamy; **123–131:** Pages 23–40 from AMERICAN BORN CHINESE by Gene Leun Yang. Copyright © 2006 by Gene Yang. Reprinted with permission of Henry Holt and Company, LLC.; **142:** Paul J. Richards/AFP/Getty Images; **148:** TM and Copyright © 20th Century Fox Film Corp. All rights reserved.; **154:** SECOND LIFE is a trademark of Linden Research, Inc. and the Second Life world features copyright materials owned by Linden Lab Copyright © 2003–2007 Linden Research, Inc. All Rights Reserved.;

155: Reproduced with permission of Yahoo! Inc. © 2007 by Yahoo! Inc. YAHOO! and the YAHOO! logo are trademarks of Yahoo! Inc.; 158 (*left and right*): Reprinted by permission of Fox Interactive Media; 166: AP Images/News Sentinel, Jeff Adkins

CHAPTER 4: 172: © Samuel Goldwyn Films/Courtesy Everett Collection. Used with permission of Morgan Spurlock.; 173 (*top left*): © Howard Harrison/Alamy Royalty Free; (*top right*): © Jerzy Dabrowski/dpa/Corbis; (*bottom left*): © Tim Graham/Alamy; 181: © Bettmann/CORBIS; 184: © Mary Evans Picture Library/The Image Works; 186 (*left*): © Bettmann/CORBIS; (*right*): © Arnold Gold/New Haven Register/The Image Works; 191: © Norbert von der Groeben/The Image Works; 199 (*left*): Tim Boyle/Getty Images; (*right*): © Caroline Penn/CORBIS; 227: Darren McCollester/Getty Images; 233: © James Leynse/Corbis; 234: Reprinted by permission; 243: Keith Meyers/The New York Times/Redux; 244: Hugh MacLeod/www.gapingvoid.com; 245: Reprinted courtesy of The American Legacy Foundation; 250: Courtesy of www.adbusters.org

CHAPTER 5: 254: © Felipe Trueba/Alamy; 258: AP Images; 261: © Buena Vista Pictures/Courtesy Everett Collection; 267: © Kevin Dodge/Corbis; 275 (*top and bottom*): Reprinted by permission; 285: Reprinted by permission; 287: Scott Gries/Getty Images; 295: AP Images/LM Otero; 304 (*left and right*): Courtesy of iPopMyPhoto.com; 305: Courtesy of Forkscrew Graphics: iRaq (Series), Screenprint, Los Angeles, CA 2004, www.forkscrew.com; 306: Reprinted with permission of No Starch Press; 311: © Justin Hampton

CHAPTER 6: 319 (*left*): © Reuters/CORBIS; (*right*): Nancy Kaszerman/ZUMA/Corbis; 325: © H. Armstrong Roberts/CORBIS; 326 (*left*): © Bettmann/CORBIS; (*right*): © David Young-Wolff/PhotoEdit Inc.; 329: Peter Cade/Getty Images; 336: Paul Hawthorne/Getty Images; 349: Photo by CNN via Getty Images; 352: AP Images/Alexander Chadwick; 355, 357: Copyright © 2003 Shayne Bowman, Chris Willis, and The Media Center at The American Press Institute; 362: © C. Walker/Topham/The Image Works; 369: © Stephanie Sinclair/Corbis; 378: © Roger-Viollet/The Image Works; 386: © Topham/The Image Works; 387: © Corbis; 388: © Reuters/Corbis; 389: © ReutersTV/Reuters; 391: © Larry Mulvehill/The Image Works; 392: © David Young-Wolff/PhotoEdit Inc.; 394: Courtesy of The Feminist Press. Used with permission.

CHAPTER 7: 409: Diehm/Iconica/Getty Images Rights Ready; 417: © 2007 The CW Network, LLC. All Rights Reserved/Landov LLC; 422: Copyright © CBS/Courtesy Everett Collection/Everett Collection; 433: Courtesy Everett Collection; 438: © Miramax/Courtesy Everett Collection; 457: © 20thCentFox/Courtesy Everett Collection; 458: (*top*): © Comedy Central/Courtesy Everett Collection; (*bottom*): © 20thCentFox/Courtesy Everett Collection; 459–463: 6 pages from UNDERSTANDING COMICS by Scott McCloud. Copyright © 1993, 1994 by Scott McCloud. Reprinted by permission of HarperCollins Publishers; 466: Reprinted by permission of Justin Roiland—creater, head writer, artist; 468: Reprinted courtesy of Julie Klausner; 470: Reprinted courtesy of Matthew Kirsch

**CHAPTER 8: 471:** J. R. Eyerman/Time Life Pictures/Getty Images; **474:** Dana White/ PhotoEdit; **477** (*left*): Courtesy Everett Collection; (*right*): © 20thCentFox/ Courtesy Everett Collection; © Paramount/Courtesy Everett Collection; **487:** © Universal/ Courtesy Everett Collection; **494:** Copyright © by Guerrilla Girls, Inc. and the credit line Courtesy www.guerrillagirls.com; **496:** © Sony Pictures/Courtesy Everett Collection; **505:** © Miramax/Courtesy Everett Collection; **509:** These symbols are the property of The B.B.F.C. and are Trademark and Copyright protected; **512:** © Miramax/ Courtesy Everett Collection; **516:** © USA Films/Courtesy Everett Collection; **521** (*top*): © Corbis. All Rights Reserved.; (*bottom*): Courtesy Everett Collection; **523** (*top*): © Walt Disney Co./Courtesy Everett Collection; (*bottom left*): © New Line Cinema/ Courtesy Everett Collection; (*bottom right*): New Line Pictures/Topham/The Image Works; **524:** Copyright © Warner Bros/courtesy Everett Collection/Everett Collection; **530:** © HBO/Courtesy Everett Collection; **532:** Courtesy of Corinna Downing, London Film Festival Education. Camera shots from *Elina* (*Elina—Som om jag inte fanns*/ Finland 2002); **528:** © Artisan Entertainment/Courtesy Everett Collection

# INDEX